the BOOK of
OBERON

About the Authors

Daniel Harms is the author of *The Cthulhu Mythos Encyclopedia*, *The Necronomicon Files* (co-authored with John Wisdom Gonce III), and *The Long-Lost Friend: A 19th Century American Grimoire*. His articles have appeared in the *Journal for the Academic Study of Magic*, *The Journal of Scholarly Communication*, *Abraxas*, *Fortean Times*, *Paranoia*, and *The Unspeakable Oath*. His work has been translated into four languages. His blog, Papers Falling from an Attic Window, provides commentary on topics including the horror writer H. P. Lovecraft and the history of books of magic. He lives in upstate New York.

James R. Clark has been working in various fields of philosophical and esoteric study for nearly two decades. His primary areas of focus are philosophy of number, Golden Dawn, and alchemy. James is a self-taught artist. He has illustrated *The Essential Enochian Grimoire* (2014) and the seventh edition of Israel Regardie's *Golden Dawn* (2015). He currently resides in Chicago.

Joseph H. Peterson has been studying esoteric texts for decades, intrigued by the Renaissance intellectual and experimental approach to spirituality. After years of collecting and digitizing rare texts for his own research, in 1995 he created the avesta.org and esotericarchives.com websites to share them with a wider audience. He lives near Rochester, Minnesota.

the BOOK of OBERON

A Sourcebook of Elizabethan Magic

Daniel
HARMS

•

James R.
CLARK

•

Joseph H.
PETERSON

Llewellyn Publications
Woodbury, Minnesota

First Edition
First Printing, 2015

Cover art: V.b.21(1) Page 200 from Book of Magic, with Instructions for Invoking Spirits: By permission of the Folger Shakespeare Library; iStockphoto.com/12363556/©ShutterWorx
Cover design: Kevin R. Brown
Interior illustrations: James R. Clark

Llewellyn Publications is a registered trademark of Llewellyn Worldwide Ltd.

Special thanks to the Folger Shakespeare Library for allowing us access and permissions to Folger Shakespeare Library, Washington, DC, MS V.b.26.

Note: The contents in this book are historical references used for teaching purposes only. All herbal formulas are given for historical understanding and reference. Please consult a standard reference source or an expert herbalist to learn more about the possible effects of certain herbs used within spells and charms. Llewellyn Worldwide does not suggest, support, or condone the animal mistreatment or sacrifices detailed in this book. These practices should be viewed as a historical curiosity; the reader may revivify these practices with symbolic substitutions rather than harming live animals.

Library of Congress Cataloging-in-Publication Data
Book of Oberon. English.
    The book of Oberon : a sourcebook of Elizabethan magic / Daniel Harms, James R. Clark, Joseph H. Peterson ; translated and annotated from the Folger Shakespeare Library's 16th Century Manuscript. — First edition.
        pages cm
    Translation of the anonymous 2 volume Latin manuscript, compiled from around 1577 to sometime after 1583, and held at the Folger Shakespeare Library in Washington, D.C, number V.b.26.
    Includes bibliographical references and index.
    ISBN 978-0-7387-4334-9
1. Magic—Early works to 1800. 2. Spirits—Early works to 1800. 3. Evocation—Early works to 1800. 4. Magic—England—History—16th century—Sources. 5. Book of Oberon. 6. Folger Shakespeare Library. I. Harms, Daniel. II. Clark, James R., 1981– III. Peterson, Joseph H. IV. Title.
    BF1601.B6613 2015
    133.4'3094209031—dc23
                        2014028274

Llewellyn Publications
A Division of Llewellyn Worldwide Ltd.
2143 Wooddale Drive
Woodbury, MN 55125-2989
www.llewellyn.com

Printed in the United States of America

Other Books by Daniel Harms

The Long-Lost Friend
The Cthylhu Mythos Encyclopedia
Necronomicon Files: The Truth Behind the Legend

Other Books Illustrated by James R. Clark

The Essential Enochian Grimoire
The Golden Dawn Seventh Edition

CONTENTS

NOTE: The table of contents has been added to give a quick overview of the parts of the text but has been worded differently in some cases for clarity.

Part 2: The Key of Solomon   491

THE BOOK OF OBERON: AN INTRODUCTION

Daniel Harms with Joseph H. Peterson

It was summer in Washington, DC, and I was late to my demon hunt. I walked quickly down Pennsylvania Avenue from Washington Circle, stopping only briefly to pick up a late breakfast sandwich. Tourists were photographing themselves in front of the White House, but I hurried past toward the Capitol. The trees on Capitol Hill provided welcome moments of shade as I skirted the House chambers. Behind the building was a block mostly taken up by the Adams Building of the Library of Congress, its doors bearing reliefs of the gods of writing and scholarship—Nabu, Thoth, and Quetzalcoatl. I hoped they would smile upon me that day.

The remainder of the block was taken up by the world's foremost center for research on William Shakespeare—the Folger Shakespeare Library. Founded by Henry Clay Folger, a nephew of the famous coffee entrepreneur, the library has become a major center for research and cultural events dealing with the Bard and his era. It is host to an amazing collection of books, paintings, photographs, playbills, movies, musical instruments, and manuscripts—and one of them was an unprecedented collection of spells and incantations from the time of Shakespeare, with ghastly illustrations of spirits to be called.

I acquired my gold reader's card and entered the oak-paneled reading room, finding a seat beneath an impressive stained glass window showing the Seven Ages of Man from *As You Like It*. When I went to the desk, however, I found disappointment. My tardiness had taken me into lunchtime, and the manuscript would not be sent up for an hour and a half. But the one I wanted was on microfilm. Would I like to see it?

I certainly did, and I trundled off down the stairs into the concrete labyrinth of the Folger basement. I was happy to find a port for a flash drive, and I was ecstatic when I realized the microfilm was clear, well shot, and highly detailed. I spent the next hour or so happily creating a PDF file of the entire manuscript. The book itself was waiting when I returned upstairs, and I was confronted with page upon page of minuscule text and bright red lettering signifying holy names, along with the spirits and the circles into which the magician must call them. Reading the book was going to be a monumental task, but my initial opinion of it was confirmed. It was an important work for the study of magic, and one which readers with all sorts of interests should be able to view.

After I returned home, I discussed the book with my friend Phil Legard, a scholar and artist who spends much time investigating the psychogeographic landscape of Yorkshire through both folklore and music. Having looked it over, we decided it was certainly worth bringing the book to print. We were anxious for advice on how to proceed, so we consulted with Joseph Peterson, known for the Esoteric Archives website and a series of published editions of various grimoires. Joe suggested that he join us and work on the translations from the Latin. He became a most-welcome addition to our team. His own collection of manuscript reproductions allowed him to find connections between the Folger's manuscript and many others that have yet to see print.

The first step was to conduct a painstaking transcription of the entire text. This was no easy matter. Most of the text was written in secretary hand, a sixteenth- and seventeenth-century script that is quite different from modern letters and calligraphy. Nonetheless, this was easy in comparison with dealing with the book's many variant spellings, abbreviations, and long passages of Latin. My other collaborators worked on the same transcriptions, and Joe took it upon himself to compare our different texts to minimize variant readings.

As we e-mailed back and forth, I realized we would need a better title than the "Folger manuscript" for the book.[1] Two of its operations were intended to summon the king of the fairies Oberion, a variant of Oberon from Shakespeare's *A Midsummer Night's Dream*. As we considered these to be items of great interest to potential readers, we decided to call the manuscript "The Book of Oberon" (henceforth the BoO).

Phil was originally slated for drawing the book's talismans, magic circles, and spirits, but he was called away by the responsibilities of family and a well-earned academic position. Elysia Gallo, our editor at Llewellyn, suggested James Clark for the project. James brought his experience in ceremonial magic, alchemy, and sacred geometry to rendering the numerous figures within, and it was his research that revealed the origins of many of the book's spirit portraits. As such, the three of us have

---

1. The original manuscript title has been lost to us, if there ever was one (See On the Manuscript: Title). Folger Shakespeare Library gave it the descriptive title "Book of Magic, with instructions for invoking spirits, etc." Please see the digital collection (http://luna.folger.edu/luna/servlet/detail/FOL GERCM1~6~6~367711~131311?qvq=q:Call_Number=%22V.b.26+(1)%22;lc:FOLGERCM1~6~6, BINDINGS~1~1&mi=12&trs=292) and Folger articles.

conducted extensive transcribing, research, editing, and discussion of various aspects of the text.

Despite all of the work that we have done, we should not be considered the "discoverers" of the book by any means. Credit goes to the Folger Shakespeare Library and its excellent and helpful staff. Not only did the library acquire both parts of the manuscript, its former director of research, Barbara Mowat, had published an article on the manuscript in *Shakespeare Quarterly*,[2] and the book had appeared in two of the library's exhibitions.

Religion and Magic in Elizabethan England

Many think of the Renaissance as a time in which rationalism and science came to prevail over medieval worldviews. Instead, it is better considered as a period in which various strands of previous thought—whether classical or medieval, approved or heterodox—interwove with explorations of the new frontiers of geography and experimentation. As such, learned individuals often held ideas that are seen as incongruent or irrational by today's standards. Perhaps the shining exemplar of this was John Dee, who made major contributions to mathematics and navigation while holding private conversations with angels.

This diversity of views did not always come with safety, however. England was embroiled in religious turmoil following the decision of King Henry VIII to abolish English Catholicism and set himself up as the head of the country's church. This situation set Catholics and Anglicans against each other, with the situation evolving through the brief reigns of Edward and Mary. The ascension of Queen Elizabeth meant that Catholic sympathizers found themselves dealing with an escalating succession of oaths, restrictions, and propaganda. Protestants portrayed Catholicism as monolithic and subversive, creating an atmosphere rife with paranoia and scapegoating.[3] Many Catholics fled to France, where the seminary at Douai, founded in 1568, served as a training ground for English priests who, it was hoped, would eventually be allowed back into the country. Late in 1577, the first year given in the BoO, Cuthbert Mayne, a Douai-trained priest who had returned to England, became the first to be martyred.

Magic and witchcraft were also ubiquitous parts of the Elizabethan milieu, often tied to Catholicism in the popular imagination. Certainly this reflected the common social tendency to classify disreputable practices together, but magical literature relied

2. Barbara Mowat, "Prospero's Book," *Shakespeare Quarterly* 52, no. 1 (2001), 1–33.

3. Carol Z. Wiener, "The Beleaguered Isle. A Study of Elizabethan and Early Jacobean Anti-Catholicism," *Past & Present,* no. 51 (1971), 27–62.

greatly on Catholic theology and practice as essential parts of its rhetoric and practice. Centuries of usage of Catholic elements—prayers of the Church, names of saints, the privileged place of the clergy when dealing with spirits—could hardly be overcome via a change of national policy, especially when much of the literature was not in open circulation. In addition, a key structural element of such magic was mediation—layman speaking to priest, saints and angels to God, and divine forces to the diabolical. The Protestant ideal of a direct relationship with God left no room for the flexibility that a larger spiritual hierarchy provided to pursue goals, such as those involving wealth, lust, and influence over the powerful, that might not be entirely consistent with the Creator's motivations. As such, magic retained many of the beliefs and trappings of Catholicism, and was thus widely condemned in connection with that faith. The *Confessio Fidei Scoticanae II* of 1580 listed the "conjuring of spreits" alongside more orthodox Roman Catholic practices that were to be abjured.[4]

In 1561, Catholicism and magic were further tied together in the popular imagination due to a plot uncovered among priests and prominent families of Essex to use occult means to predict Queen Elizabeth's date of death. Among the other offenses of which they were accused were the conjuration of demons and the holding of a Mass to consecrate a love spell. The Crown's prosecution was hampered due to the decriminalization of such practices by Edward VI, leading to the passage of laws against sorcery and witchcraft. Thus, performing magic was considered not only heresy, but was associated in the popular imagination with sedition.[5] The queen's 1563 statutes banned all manner of incantations, with treasure hunting, finding stolen goods, and love spells bringing a year in prison for the first offense, and conjuration of evil spirits and spells calling for execution. Nonetheless, the prevalence of jury trials and reluctance to use torture were instrumental in preventing the same excesses that characterized the Continental witch trials. The first glimmers of skepticism regarding the existence of witches were visible, most notably in Reginald Scot's *The Discouerie of Witchcraft* in 1584. Nonetheless, most still believed that magic was a real, vital, and dangerous force.

Despite our emphasis on criminal prosecution, magic and the occult sciences were still an important factor in Elizabethan England. They found their legitimacy in traditional religious methods of seeking help from God or other spiritual beings. This

---

4. P. Schaff, *The Creeds of Christendom: The Evangelical Protestant Creeds, with Translations* vol. 3 (Harper, 1877; Google eBooks, 2006), 483.

5. le Baron Kervyn de Lettenhove, *Relations Politiques Des Pays-Bas et de l'Angleterre*, vol. 2 (Bruxelles: F. Hayez, 1883), 561; Norman Jones, "Defining Superstitions: Treasonous Catholics and the Act Against Witchcraft of 1563" in *State, Sovereigns & Society in Early Modern England* (New York: St. Martin's Press, 1998), 187–203.

and similar texts frequently quote biblical passages illustrating this fact, by way of averring its legitimacy. Traditional authorities are not always in agreement on the matter. When God is seen as too exalted or unknowable to be demeaned with trivial human wants, other spiritual or supernatural beings are frequently petitioned, such as saints and angels.

"Everyday ritual" was perceived as either acceptable or not, depending on which authorities made the discrimination. An illustrative case is the practice of bringing home palm leaves blessed on Palm Sunday as a blessing, often fashioned into crosses. This practice, officially banned in England in the 1540s, continued in folk practice.[6] Another example is the traditional prayer to one's guardian angel, recited daily by many Catholics to this very day, which many Elizabethan Protestants viewed askance but nonetheless tolerated.[7] The very process of banning such practices often lent them power and mystique for those who did not find the conventional religious rites efficacious or satisfying.

Nonetheless, magic was a topic of interest at very high levels of society. Magicians such as John Dee competed for favors at court; Sir Walter Raleigh wrote on magic in his *History of the World*; the explorer Sir Humphrey Gilbert experimented with contacting demons and the dead; and the annals of the time describe numerous cases of magic conducted for one or another of the proscribed purposes.[8] Even the queen herself was fascinated by the concept of alchemy and, according to one recent author, was actively engaged in such experiments herself.[9] British historian Keith Thomas provides numerous examples underlining the prevalence of magical practices among the common people of the era.[10]

The same period saw a flourishing of authors and playwrights, of whom the most famous was William Shakespeare. Shakespeare's works often touch upon supernatural themes, whether the ghost of the former king in *Hamlet* or the three witches who

---

6. Stephen Wilson, *The Magical Universe: Everyday Ritual and Magic in Pre-Modern Europe* (London: Hambledon and London, 2000), 33–34; Palm leaves and palm crosses are used magically in several places in the BoO, for example on p. 110.

7. Peter Marshall, "The Guardian Angel in Protestant England" in *Conversations with Angels: Essays towards a History of Spiritual Communication, 1100–1700*, edited by Joad Raymond (New York: Palgrave Macmillian, 2011), 295–316.

8. Marion Gibson, *Witchcraft and Society in England and America, 1550–1750* (2003), 3–5; Brian P. Levack, *The Witch-hunt in Early Modern Europe* (1987), 182–7; Keith Thomas, *Religion and the Decline of Magic* (1971), 252–300; Frank Klaassen, "Ritual Invocation and Early Modern Science: The Skrying Experiments of Humphrey Gilbert" (2012), 341–366; Walter Raleigh, William Oldys, and Thomas Birch, *The Works of Sir Walter Raleigh, Kt., Now First Collected: To Which Are Prefixed the Lives of the Author* (1965), vol. 2, 378–405.

9. G. J. R. Parry, *The Arch-conjuror of England: John Dee*, 77.

10. Thomas, *Religion and the Decline of Magic*, 252–300.

treat with Hecate and proclaim Macbeth's ascension to the throne. Of particular interest to us are *A Midsummer Night's Dream*, which made the fairy rulers Oberon and Titania into cultural icons, and *The Tempest,* in which Prospero, the Duke of Milan, calls up spirits while exiled on an island. We know little of Shakespeare's attitudes toward the supernatural, but it is clear that he considered them good entertainment.

Less remembered today, but nonetheless influential, are other works by Shakespeare's fellow playwrights and authors. Christopher Marlowe adapted German compilations regarding Faust and his dealings with devils for his play *Doctor Faustus* (c. 1592), mentioning authors of actual works of necromancy such as Petrus de Abano (1257–1315)[11] and Roger Bacon (1214–1292). In Robert Greene's *The Scottish History of James IV* (c. 1590), Oberon intercedes in the action to save the son of a nobleman from the king's wrath. The poet Edmund Spenser took the trappings of fairy, including two mentions of Oberon himself, and used them to frame allegorical depictions of the virtues in his unfinished poem *The Faerie Queene* (1590–1596).[12] Magic, fairies, demons, and the like were not merely subjects of belief, but they were also sources of entertainment to many audiences.

Significance of the Manuscript

The BoO is an unusual work that sits apart from the majority of works on ritual magic familiar to today's readers. The most popular texts—*The Key of Solomon, The Goetia, The Book of the Sacred Magic of Abra-Melin the Mage,* and others—are comprehensive systems of magic, complex rites intended to carry out a number of purposes based upon the particular spirit to be called or talisman to be consecrated. In particular, the idiosyncratic selection of texts and editorial choices of Samuel Liddell MacGregor Mathers (1854–1918) still have immense influence on publishing, reading, spiritual practice, and scholarship. The BoO, on the other hand, is a magical miscellany, a compilation of material gathered by a magician or magicians over time as needs or opportunities presented themselves and with little effort made at overall organization or systematic labeling of the texts.

In many ways, the BoO typifies early modern magic texts. It contains excerpts from a wide number of sources, including psalms and traditional prayers, such as Catholic indulgences (excerpted from the *Raccolta*), along with excerpts from more

---

11. Petrus de Abano has several variant spellings of his name. In this text, he may appear as Petrus de Abano, Pietro d'Abano, or Peter de Abano. The text *Heptameron* is probably falsely attributed to him.

12. W. W. Greg, ed., *Marlowe's Doctor Faustus* (Oxford: Claredon, 1950); Robert Greene, *The Scottish History of James IV* (London: Methuen, 1970); Edmund Spenser, *The Faerie Queene* (New York: Penguin, 1978).

patently magical texts. The latter often included passages from Heinrich Agrippa (1486–1535), Petrus de Abano, *Clavicula*, or (little) *Key of Solomon*,[13] *The Book of Raziel*, *The Book of Consecrations*, *A Book of the Offices of Spirits*, and later *Arbatel*, often abstracted hastily.

In early modern Britain, such miscellanies were the norm for presentations of ritual magic.[14] Even so, such material has rarely been published, as most scholars have concentrated their attention upon either theoretical works (e.g., the *Picatrix* and texts by Agrippa, the philosopher Marsilio Ficino (1433–1499), Paracelsus (1493–1541), and Filippo (Giordano) Bruno (1548–1600), etc.) or more popular books of magic that have undergone editorial selection of content, to the benefit or detriment of the text.[15] None of these can be said to portray the notebook of a working magician, seeking whatever sources came to him to enhance his repertoire. Only a few such texts have been printed: the manual of sorcery kept at the Bayerische Staatsbibliothek (MS. Clm 849) and published by Richard Kieckhefer,[16] the grimoire of the London cunning-man Arthur Gauntlet (Sloane 3851),[17] and a fifteenth-century collection that includes several Middle Dutch magical texts (Wellcome MS. 517).[18] As such, the BoO is an important addition to the literature on this topic, which enhances our understanding of magic as practitioners recorded it.

But what sort of magic might this be considered? In medieval times, magical works were often divided into three categories: natural magic, dealing with the inherent properties of stones, herbs, and other substances; image magic, in which talismans were created based on astrological conjunctions with no assistance from spirits; and ritual magic, calling upon God or spirits to intercede in this world to accomplish a goal set forth by the magician. Despite newfound interest through the works of Ficino and Agrippa, image magic had mostly fallen out of favor by this time, with few manuscripts

---

13. The term *Clavicula* is a diminutive. Thus, the text known to modern readers as *The Greater Key of Solomon* is another "Little Key."

14. Frank F. Klaassen, "Religion, Science, and the Transformations of Magic: Manuscripts of Magic 1300–1600" (PhD thesis, University of Toronto, 1999), 146.

15. Compare to S. L. MacGregor Mathers, ed., *The Key of Solomon the King (Clavicula Salomonis)*; Carleton F. Brown and Johann Georg Hohman, "The Long Hidden Friend," *The Journal of American Folklore* 17, no. 65 (1904), 89–152; J. Scheible, *Das Kloster. Weltlich und Geistlich. Meist aus der Ältern Deutschen Volks-, Wunder-, Curiositäten-, und Vorzugsweise Komischen Literatur* (Stuttgart: J. Scheible, 1845).

16. Richard Kieckhefer, *Forbidden Rites: a Necromancer's Manual of the Fifteenth Century* (University Park, PA: Pennsylvania State University Press, 1998).

17. Arthur Gauntlet and David Rankine, *The Grimoire of Arthur Gauntlet* (London: Avalonia, 2011).

18. Willy Louis Braekman, *Magische experimenten en toverpraktijken uit een middelnederlands handschrift: with an English Summary* (Gent: Seminaire voor Volkskunde, 1966).

being created during this period. Ritual magic, on the other hand, retained its popularity, and it is unsurprising that the BoO consists mostly of such material.[19]

Nonetheless, the BoO is unique in that it has much fuller treatment of some material from the printed tradition. One interesting example is the "Offices of Spirits." Various versions of this "catalogue of demons" are found in manuscripts dating at least as far back as the thirteenth century.[20] A version of this text went on to become very popular in ritual magic to the present day, due to its inclusion in the collection of texts known as *The Lesser Key of Solomon*. The relevant section, book one, is known as *Goetia*. The *Goetia* version can be shown to derive from a version included in Johann Weyer's *Praestigiis Daemonum* (1563), via an English translation included in Scot's *Discouerie of Witchcraft*, with the addition of seals of the spirits. Unfortunately, the Weyer, Scot, and *Lesser Key* versions all suffer from severe editing by Weyer, who admits to omitting many passages from the text "in order to render the whole work unusable … lest anyone who is mildly curious, may dare to rashly imitate this proof of folly."[21] In his detailed comparison of Weyer's version with older versions, professor of medieval history Jean-Patrice Boudet concluded that Weyer's text seems to be missing text from the beginning that would have had information on Lucifer, Beelzebub, Satan, and the four demons of the cardinal points. Moreover, the ritual is much shorter.[22] The publication of the BoO finally reveals the material that Weyer sought to suppress, along with some later additions made by the book's author, showing that these lists were not simply repeated verbatim, but were part of a living tradition.

Another important aspect of the BoO text is the pictures of the spirits. Such pictures only appear occasionally in the literature of magic, and our initial hypothesis was that they represented visions or hallucinations that a practitioner of the techniques might have had during rituals. As James discovered in his research on the illustrations, this was not the case for at least some. Many of these illustrations are copied from woodcuts in Pierre Boaistuau and Edward Fenton's *Certaine secrete wonders of nature* (1569), a translation of Pierre Boaistuau's *Histoires prodigieuses* (1560),

---

19. For more on distinctions among these types of magic, see Frank Klaassen, "Medieval Ritual Magic in the Renaissance," *Aries* 3, no. 2 (2003), 166–199.

20. MS. CLM 849 contains one of the older examples. See Kieckhefer, *Forbidden Rites*, 291–293. Other examples are found in Additional MS. 36674, 65r ff, and MS. Florence BNC II III 214, fols. 26v–29v for which see Jean-Patrice Boudet, "Les who's who démonologiques de la Renaissance et leurs ancêtres médiévaux," *Médiévales* 44 (2003), Web, http://medievals.revues.org/1019.

21. Translation by JHP of *Ne autem curiosulus aliquis, fascino nimis detentus, hoc stultitiæ argumentum temere imitari audeat, voces hinc inde prætermisi studio, ut universa delinquendi occasio præcideretur.* From "Pseudomonarchia daemonum" appended to *Praestigiis Daemonum* in Johann Weyer, *Opera Omnia* (1660), 649.

22. Boudet, "Les who's who démonologiques de la Renaissance et leurs ancêtres médiévaux."

a work describing mysterious animals and horrific birth defects.[23] As such, they most likely represent figures added to the text to impress onlookers—although, as the description of Bilgall in the Offices of Spirits described above indicates, those descriptions managed to seep back into the spiritual lore of the manuscript itself.

Authorship

The BoO contains at least four names or initials that might indicate authorship or ownership of the work. These should be treated with some skepticism, due to the traditional practice of attributing books of magic to various historical or mythical individuals, including King Solomon, Cyprian, the Apostle Paul, Adam, and others. Those within the BoO fall into neither of these categories, but some might have been included in material copied from another source.

What clues does the manuscript give as to the author? The poor quality of the Latin in the book is suggestive of its origins. By the late sixteenth century, a school could be found in almost every town in England, and literacy was certainly available to the upper classes, readily available to the burgeoning middle classes, and sometimes available for the lower classes. Latin grammar was a key component of schooling even at the lowest levels (whence comes the term "grammar school"). The Latin curriculum in schools throughout the sixteenth century was largely consistent across the board, down to the small group of texts used to teach the subject, although the quality of the instruction varied considerably.[24] Thus, we are dealing with an individual who likely had little training in Latin (or, less likely, who had forgotten much of the schooling), and who had certainly not gone on to university or to be employed in a capacity in which knowledge of Latin was a requirement.

The majority of the text in the BoO is written in secretary hand. Given that this was a common script, it does little to narrow down either the potential dates of the latter part's composition or the geography of the author. Perhaps a specialist in early modern paleography could find some clue within.

Part two of the manuscript includes some enciphered text, including charm titles, ingredients, and instructions. The cipher in question is quite simple, with only the vowels being swapped out while the consonants are left in place, and it would have been unsuccessful at either concealing the magical nature of the manuscript or

---

23. Fenton was a soldier who later went on to accompany Frobisher on his explorations of the Northwest Passage and to take up piracy in the South Atlantic while attempting to become king of the island of St. Helena.

24. I. M. Green, *Humanism and Protestantism in Early Modern English Education* (Farnham, England: Ashgate, 2009).

preventing a rival from deciphering the text. A similar cipher can be found in Sloane 3853, and examination of these texts and others from the period suggest that these were part of an aesthetic strategy to add an air of magic and mystery to the text.[25] As such, its inclusion does not indicate any great level of learning by the author.

J. B.

This individual is named within a set of prayers on pages 21–22 of the manuscript as a recipient of their blessings against foes, misfortune, and weapons. These prayers are taken from the classic grimoire, the *Enchiridion*,[26] supposedly given to Charlemagne by Pope Leo III. These initials do not appear in other texts of the *Enchiridion*, but it is unknown whether they are those of an author of the BoO or merely part of material copied from elsewhere.

John Porter

Given that his name was encoded, this is the most likely candidate for an actual owner of the book. A John Porter was appointed as the vicar of Colston Bassett on January 15, 1560, and Cropwell Bishop on April 23, 1562. He was still present at Colston Bassett in 1587, and thus was active during the period in which this manuscript was written.[27] We have no assurances, however, that this is the same individual. Various laymen with the same name also appear in the historical record, but there is no particular reason to select any of them as the author.

John Weston

John Weston's name appears soon after the encoded name of John Porter, implying a transfer of the BoO's ownership from one man to another. Weston, the supposed author of one section of the book, tells us of how he performed a working for the "Prince of Pavoye" and the prince's lieutenant, "Monsieur Brettencourt," along with a canon who taught him how to make a miraculous ointment allowing him to see fairies.[28] The rite supposedly took place in the city of "Dewway," or Douai, now in northern France. It bears noting that Emmanuel Philibert (1528–1580), Duke of Savoy,

---

25. Klaassen, "Religion, Science, and the Transformations of Magic: Manuscripts of Magic 1300–1600," 195–96.

26. There are many editions of this text. Presently, the oldest edition listed in Worldcat is in the Bibliothèque nationale de France: *Enchiridion Leonis Papae; contenant plusieurs oraisons de St Augustin, St. Cyprien et autres: ensemble les sept pseaumes* (Lyon: 1601).

27. Clergy of the Church of England Database; BI, Inst. AB.1; BI, Inst. AB.2; Notts Presentment Bills (Visitation Returns): 1587.

28. One of the "rules and observations" for invoking Oberion in Sloan 3846, 107r, is to anoint the eyes with rose water. Compare BoO pp. 139–140.

governed Douai from 1556–59, though this historical fact might be used to validate an invented tale.[29] Tracking down Monsieur Brettencourt or proving that a John Weston was present in Douai during the period in question might aid in supporting this hypothesis.

We might have a few candidates for this "John Weston" in other sources. One was a John Weston who gained his MA from Oxford in 1575, becoming rector of Wimbotsham, vicar of Stow Bardolph, and rector of Snetterton, who passed away in 1582.[30] Another would be the "clark" John Weston or Wesson, who married Joane Cowper on June 29, 1579, and died May 6, 1582.[31] The latter is especially tempting, given that his widow would quickly marry the con-man, magician, and scryer, Edward Kelley. Both of these identifications are problematic, however, as the section purporting to be written by Mr. Weston appears after the given date of 1583, placing it after both men's deaths. Also, neither individual is known to have been present at Douai or to have expressed an interest in magic.

N. M.

On page 192 of the BoO, the initials N. M. are noted as those of the magician in the conjuration of Oberion. As with J. B. above, it is impossible to determine from the context if these belonged to the owner of this manuscript or another person.

Owners

After the initial authors, the manuscript seems to have passed through a number of hands, the names of whom are lost to us.

The earliest reported owner of the manuscript is Richard Cosway (c. 1740–1821), a noted miniature painter and occultist. The manuscript was likely acquired in the latter part of his life, when the painter became increasingly concerned with occult topics.[32] It might have been among his twenty-five undescribed manuscripts of magic auctioned by Mr. Stanley on June 12, 1821.[33] After his death, the book passed to the

29. Eugène François Joseph Tailliar, *Chroniques de Douai* (vol. 1, Douais: Dechristé), 105.

30. University of Oxford and Joseph Foster, *Alumni Oxonienses: The Members of the University of Oxford, 1500–1714: Their Parentage, Birthplace, and Year of Birth, with a Record of Their Degrees,* vol. 4 (Oxford and London: Parker and Co., 1891), 1604.

31. Susan Bassnett, "Revising a Biography: A New Interpretation of the Life of Elizabeth Jane Weston (Westonia), Based on Her Autobiographical Poem on the Occasion of the Death of Her Mother" (*Cahiers Élisabéthains* 37, 1990), 1–8.

32. George Charles Williamson, *Richard Cosway, R. A.* (London: G. Bell and Sons, 1905), 57–58.

33. George Stanley and Richard Cosway, *A Catalogue of the Very Curious, Extensive, and Valuable Library of Richard Cosway, Esq. R. A.* (London: s.n, 1821), 44.

London bookseller John Denley (1764–1842), who sold it to George W. Graham (1784–1867).

Graham was a noted balloonist, who, with his wife, has been referred to as "the most accident-prone of all the well-known aeronauts."[34] Among his most famous flights were a 1825 crash landing at sea, an 1838 flight at Reading that killed a pedestrian when it knocked loose part of a building, and a near-collision with the Crystal Palace, with thousands of people inside, in 1851. In the latter year, Graham also tried to market a riot shield to the Home Office, claiming it would be useful when tens of thousands of immigrants rose up and attacked London using caltrops and incendiary time bombs shot through blowguns.[35] He was also a likely member of a group of magicians known as the Mercurii, who were reputed to have a large collection of manuscripts on mystical topics.

A key member of the Mercurii was Robert Cross Smith (1795–1832), better known under the moniker of "Raphael." Indeed, the current first page of the manuscript bears the initials "R. C. S., 1822," which raises a question of how quickly Raphael might have taken possession of the book from Graham.[36] Raphael seems to have reproduced part of the manuscript—an abbreviated form of the invocation of the spirit Egin—in his publication *The Astrologer of the Nineteenth Century* (1825). He nearby mentions a publication from Cosway's collection on magic valued at 500 guineas,[37] which Hockley insisted was the same work, though the specific passage the statement is attached to is not in the manuscript.

After Raphael passed on in 1832, the work became part of the collection of the accountant, book collector, and mystic Frederick Hockley (1808–1885). Hockley had worked for Denley and was familiar with his clients, referring to Raphael as "that puffing philosopher." In the same year, John Palmer (1807–1837), known as the astrologer "Zadkiel," made a copy of several pages of the manuscript, including the list of spirits, for himself, to be recopied by Hockley and others.[38] Hockley is known to have possessed Part 1. The presence of charms from Part 2 in one of his notebooks, in the same order as in the manuscript, shows that he also had access to that section.[39]

34. L. T. C. Rolt, *The Aeronauts: a History of Ballooning, 1783–1903* (New York: Walker, 1966), 112.

35. B. Porter, *The Refugee Question in Mid-Victorian Politics* (New York: Cambridge University Press, 2008), 86–87.

36. Colin Campbell, *A Book of the Offices of Spirits* (York Beach, ME: Teitan Press, 2011), xviii.

37. Raphael and Anglicus, *The Astrologer of the Nineteenth Century* (London: Knight & Lacey, 1825), 216.

38. Campbell, *A Book of the Offices of Spirits*, 44.

39. Frederick Hockley and Silens Manus, *Occult Spells: A Nineteenth Century Grimoire* (York Beach, ME: The Teitan Press, 2009), 48–49.

Hockley kept the book for over half a century until his death, after which the manuscript turns up as lot 380 in the Sotheby's sale of Hockley's book collection, conducted on April 6–7, 1887.

The manuscript resurfaces in a sale by Maggs Brothers in 1929, at which the British author Edward Harry William Meyerstein (1889–1952) purchased it. Meyerstein had an interest in occultism since childhood, and he accumulated what one biographer called "one of the most important collections of manuscripts and books [on magic] ever in private hands."[40] He placed the date "July 8, 1929," on the manuscript, and wrote a short poem, "Fairy Lore," at the end of Part 1.

The book was sold with Meyerstein's library at Sotheby's of London on December 15–17, 1952, as lot 474. The Folger Library purchased it from Day's (Booksellers) Ltd. in Highfield in 1958.

The second part of the manuscript comes from the collection of Robert Lenciewicz (1941–2002), the noted artist. It was sold as a "manuscript grimoire" with portions of Lenciewicz's collection at Sotheby's on July 12, 2007, to the B. H. Breslauer Foundation, who donated it to the Folger.

On the Manuscript

The manuscript published herein as the "Book of Oberon" (BoO) is listed as Manuscript V.b.26 at the Folger Shakespeare Library in Washington, DC. The original measures approximately 35 by 23 centimeters (13.8" by 9"), and it is written in black and red ink on vellum. Before the library's acquisition, the work had been split into two parts, one of 191 pages bound in half calf in the nineteenth century, and the other of 30 pages, bound in tan calfskin.

The physical manuscript has undergone several changes over time. In addition to the aforementioned separation, the manuscript has also lost pages and been paginated on two occasions. We have little idea as to the exact dates for these, save that they all were completed after 1583, which is the last date given in the manuscript, and that all, save perhaps for the final separation, occurred before Raphael's acquisition of the book in 1822. The changes are listed below in order of occurrence:

1. Composition of the manuscript, at least some in separate quires

2. Insertion of notes in cursive script in some unfinished quires

3. Compilation and foliation of the same in brown ink

---

40. Edward Harry William Meyerstein, *Of My Early Life, 1889–1918* (London: N. Spearman, 1957), 25.

4. Loss of original leaves 15–17, 26–28, 38, 40, and 111–113 and the combination of the two sections

5. Repagination of the manuscript in blue ink

6. Loss of pages 1–14 and 33–34

7. Separation of the two sections

More recent accretions have appeared in both sections of the manuscript. Part 1 includes a poem, "Fairy Lore," by E. H. W. Meyerstein written on September 8, 1929, and revised on May 30, 1935. Meyerstein was also responsible for the insertion of his horoscope, drawn up by the president of the Poetry Society T. W. Ramsey, which has been removed and catalogued separately as Folger MS. Y.d.70. Part 2 concludes with a brief set of notes on linkages between the text and the classic grimoire the *Lemegeton*,[41] based upon a text published by the de Laurence Company of Chicago in 1916,[42] and including two full-color seals.

Title

Any title that might have appeared at the beginning of the manuscript is now long gone. In fact, many magicians' miscellanies had no title whatsoever.[43] The current binding on the two volumes identifies them as "Theurgia" and "Key of Solomon," respectively, neither of which is the original title. Either would likely lead modern readers to mistaken conclusions about the contents. "Theurgia" has been used in a wide variety of contexts across many different faiths, which tells us little about the text.[44] The "Key of Solomon" genre covers a great number of manuscripts, but none of these seem comparable in content to what appears in this work.[45] The title we have selected, "The Book of Oberon," is in itself slightly misleading, as the king of the fairies named

---

41. Joseph H. Peterson, *The Lesser Key of Solomon: Lemegeton Clavicula Salomonis* (York Beach, ME: Weiser Books, 2001).

42. L. W. de Laurence, *The Lesser Key of Solomon: Goetia, The Book of Evil Spirits* (Chicago, IL: de Laurence, Scott & Co., 1916), 7.

43. Federico Barbierato, "Writing, Reading, Writing: Scribal Culture and Magical Texts in Early Modern Venice" *Italian Studies* 66, no. 2 (2011), 265.

44. Fanger, Claire, "Introduction: Theurgy, Magic, and Mysticism," *Invoking Angels: Theurgic Ideas and Practices, Thirteenth to Sixteenth Centuries* (University Park PA: Pennsylvania State University Press, 2012), 1–33.

45. Robert Mathiesen, "The Key of Solomon: Toward a Typology of Manuscripts," *Societas Magica Newsletter*, no. 17, (2007), 1, 3–9.

herein is actually Oberion, but the title makes clear the book's link to both folklore and literary traditions.

Dating

The book provides us with two dates—May 8, 1577, on page 51, and 1583, on page 105, almost halfway through. We can be relatively certain that the text before page 51 was not composed long before that date, as material in the early pages likely dates to texts published in 1575. We still might ask how long after the 1583 date the text continued to be worked upon.

Organization

Along with the title, the loss of the first pages of the text has also taken with it any possible table of contents that might have accompanied the work. It is difficult to reconstruct what the organizing principles might have followed in the BoO. Although the text is primarily one of ritual magic for summoning spirits, procedures for other purposes also appear alongside them with no clear effort being made to distinguish amongst them. As for the individual items, some are labeled prominently, while others appear with no heading whatsoever. Given the similarity in purpose and the modular nature of some of these operations, where one prayer can be used for multiple spirits, it becomes difficult at times to definitively declare where one item ends and another begins. The BoO appears to be a text assembled with no overall plan, in which particular items were added as they became available or became of interest to the author. Thus there are several repetitions in the text, such as the headache cure from Cardano and the first chapter of the Gospel of John.

The Motivation and Context of the Text

One key question is whether the work was compiled by a collector or collectors fascinated with the topic, or if it was intended for practical use. An excellent indicator is the presence of material copied from the Bible in the work. A collector would have little motivation to spend time and effort transcribing material that was commonly available, while a practitioner would be interested in having relevant passages close at hand during a ritual. The presence of Psalms, the Lord's Prayer, the Athanasian and Apostle's Creeds, Hail Mary, and the first chapter of John indicates that the book was intended for actual use, at least for some of the time of its composition. At the same time, there are places in the text, such as on manuscript page 195, where blank spaces were accidently left in the manuscript, obviously for switching pens; this suggests that at least some portions of the text were not put into practice, as these omissions most likely would have been noticed and corrected.

We might also point to the sheer volume of material collected herein as an indicator of a sincerity of purpose. Ritual magic has, at its center, both belief and doubt. The magician is not only sincere of faith, but must believe that words and actions spoken by humans can bring about communion with spirits of Creation and lead to the accomplishment of great works. At the same time, the magician must express doubt toward the efficacy of any particular operation, whether due to mistranslation, shoddy copying, or other interference. As such, the ritual magician always seeks out as many magical texts as possible, that the failure of one might be only a temporary setback. The BoO represents how both belief and doubt came together to create what is a truly impressive compilation of ritual magic.

Nonetheless, the same thoroughness could also point us toward the collector possibility, especially when it comes to the Latin passages therein. Despite the BoO being a primarily English text, a considerable amount of the text within is Latin, sometimes in the form of brief conjurations, and at others entire rituals, including instructions. The Latin texts are riddled with all manner of basic errors—such as "equa" for "aqua," "trimores" for "timores," "errare" for "esse"—which, even if they had appeared in another text being copied, could have been easily corrected. This hardly precludes the author from practicing magic—indeed, incantations often are seen as powerful due to the presence of words incomprehensible to the reader[46]—but the presence of operations that are entirely in Latin, including the directions, raises questions as to how much our scribe understood and was able to practice the material therein.

It might also be asked whether our author was an individual working in a solitary manner or was part of a broader network of magicians and collectors communicating with each other. The authors (there are at least two, and likely more, different hands) do sometimes state that this work went on among the members of a group, whether as those who carried out a working intended to impress the Prince of "Pavoye" in Douai (on manuscript page 142), or a network of scholars from both Orleans and English universities who worked together on the magical art (on manuscript page 213). At the present, it is difficult to confirm the accuracy of either of these stories, and indeed they contain or are juxtaposed with clearly mythic elements.

A more certain indication can be found on pages 21–24 in the manuscript, in which the ceremonies of conjuration are broken into for a transcription of the "little book," or *Enchiridion*, after which the regular text continues. We can infer that the

---

46. Claudia Rohrbacher-Stickler, "From Sense to Nonsense, from Incantation Prayer to Magic Spell," *Jewish Studies Quarterly* 3 (1996), 24–26.

author had one manuscript of spirit conjuration that he knew he could pick up and transcribe later, and a copy of the "little book" which might have been available for a shorter period of time. This suggests that one author was part of an informal network of others interested in magic, among whom various magical manuscripts traveled, and he copied down items as time permitted.

Some elements of the BoO have implications for the study of magic that have not yet filtered into much writing on the topic. One striking element is the integration of a large number of spiritual beings into the text, most particularly fairies. These appear not only in the two operations to summon Oberion, but those to summon the fairy Sibilia into a candle and a ritual for invisibility on manuscript pages 38–39. The hard-and-fast divisions that we have drawn between the worlds of angels, demons, and fairies break down here, with spells calling upon all three appearing in close textual relation. Indeed, Oberion appears on the list of the Offices of Spirits along with Satan, Lucifer, and other members of the infernal hierarchy, and his wife Mycob is listed immediately after the list ends. On manuscript page 93, we have a list of Greek and Roman deities, given without commentary but possibly for some usage of the magician. Gods, angels, spirits, demons, and fairies are conflated within the text, as the magician seeks knowledge and power through whatever entities are available.

The Offices of Spirits is another section worthy of comment. Another such list, published in the book the *Goetia*, has become a staple of magical practice in the West from the early twentieth century.[47] The list has been generally acknowledged to be comparable to those given in Weyer's "Pseudomonarchia Daemonum" in *De Praestigiis Daemonum* (1583 edition)[48] and Scot's *Discouerie of Witchcraft*. The list in the BoO provides a useful counterpoint to the ones previously published, with major differences in both the spirits listed and the order in which they appear in the other sources. It also shows that magicians were not averse to adding other names they encountered, as those at the very end reflect the spiritual operations elsewhere in the work.

Another striking aspect of this manuscript is the presence of short operations, mostly clustered near the end of Part 1, that are to be used for the conjuration of particular demons. Much of the published literature of spirit summoning has provided a general system for evoking any desired spirit. Ceremonies directed toward a particular spirit are by no means unique here—those for Birto and Oberion have appeared

---

47. Aleister Crowley, *The Book of the Goetia of Solomon the King* (Inverness: Society for the Propagation of Religious Truth, 1904).

48. J. Wier, *De Praestigiis Daemonum, & Incantationibus Ac Veneficiis* (Oporinus, 1583; Google eBook, 909–31).

elsewhere [49]—and the manuscript also includes the modular rites at other points. Nonetheless, the rituals given herein are interesting for the number thereof and the intriguing illustrations with which they are coupled.

As lengthy as the BoO is, many occult fields are passed over. As with other ritual magic texts of the period, it does not display much interest in "astrological literature, alchemy, books of secrets, natural philosophy, and other naturalia." [50] In fact, rituals for summoning, binding, and dismissing spirits often supersede the purpose of other such material, whether indirectly (e.g., calling up a spirit to teach the magical properties of herbs) or directly (e.g., asking a demon to bring a treasure directly to the magician instead of creating gold). We do find a few natural magic recipes, especially near the end of the work, but overall the book deals with ritual magic.

The most crucial point about the BoO is that, despite its other notable qualities, it is by no means a reflection of one particular individual set apart from the milieu of his time. Rather, it is one element in an exploration of an underground Elizabethan world of criminals, dissenters, scholars, and heretics.

Ritual Implements

Page 110 of the manuscript has a summary of the requisite implements. Elsewhere the following are used:

- Amulets, such as paper cure for headaches
- *The* Book: The present book is regarded as the primary ritual implement. Page 141 refers to a "booke of pictures."
- A circle, sometimes accompanied by a triangle or second circle for the spirit to appear in. Usually they are drawn in the soil with a metallic instrument such as sword or knife, but sometimes made with oil, chalk, or palm ashes.
- Fire, sometimes made with special wood such as elder or thorn
- Food offerings for the spirits
- Fumigations or incense to purify and attract spirits, as well as various noxious substances such as sulfur to punish uncooperative spirits

---

49. Gauntlet, *The Grimoire of Arthur Gauntlet*, 260–261; Ebenezer Sibley, Frederick Hockley, and Joseph H. Peterson, *The Clavis or Key to the Magic of Solomon* (Lake Worth, FL: Ibis Press, 2009), 189–194.

50. Klaassen, "Religion, Science, and the Transformations of Magic: Manuscripts of Magic 1300–1600," 151.

- Garments, as in de Abano's *Heptameron*,[51] a priestly garment, or a garment made of white linen
- Ink
- Oil (usually olive oil)
- Parchment
- A pen and a pen stand
- Pentacles, and especially the "pentacle of Solomon," of kidskin parchment, as described by de Abano
- A ring with the name "Tetragramaton" for controlling the spirits. Another ring is described for enclosing a spirit.
- Rose water
- Scepter (with "crowne imperiall" and "misticall scripture") [and?] pentacle
- Scryer, usually a virgin child. The wording of some of the prayers indicate that the virginity of the child is a proxy for the practitioner's own lost virginity.
- Scrying stone, crystal ball, or "glass" (i.e., mirror)
- Sword
- Table
- Wand of hazel
- Water, consecrated or lustral
- Whistle: described in detail in the *Liber Iuratus Honorii*,[52] but mistranslations have obscured it from *Heptameron* and subsequent texts

Other isolated experiments call for special ritual apparatus, such as a nail and silver foil (manuscript page 137), a basin for water or other vessels, and candles.

The ubiquitous hazel wand deserves special attention. It was a symbol of the master's authority and power and an unspoken threat to evil spirits. The original intent was to use new-growth, green hazel—a common tool of the medieval schoolmasters to "correct" or chastise students or subordinates. Like the staff, it is a symbol of power,

---

51. Agrippa von Nettesheim, Heinrich Cornelius, Robert Turner, and Petrus de Abano, *Henry Cornelius Agrippa His Fourth Book of Occult Philosophy. Of Geomancy. Magical Elements of Peter de Abano. Astronomical Geomancy. The Nature of Spirits. Arbatel of Magick. Translated into English by Robert Turner, Philomathes* (London: Printed by J. C. for John Harrison, at the Lamb at the East-end of Pauls, 1655), 69–110.

52. Honorius and Gösta Hedeård, *Liber Iuratus Honorii: a Critical Edition of the Latin Version of the Sworn Book of Honorius* (Stockholm, Sweden: Almqvist & Wiksell International, 2002), for description and details on its preparation see pp. 148–149; for ritual directions see pp. 140, 142.

but less threatening. The essential element is that it is very flexible, like a switch. As the saying goes, *Magister non poenit baculo, sed corrigat virga* ["The master does not punish/beat with the staff, but corrects with the wand/switch"]. Modern practice may differ.

Preparation

As in many other magic texts, preparation for the practice of magic here includes abstinence, fasting, traditional Catholic confession, and charity. The weather should have been clear and calm for three days.

The Spirits

The spirit conjurations within the BoO call upon a wide range of different beings. Some of these are known from other texts, the most prevalent of these being the *Lemegeton*, as well as the largely unplumbed manuscript tradition of the period. Others, including Romulon, Mosacus, Alastiell, and Annabath or Annobathe, are previously unknown to the corpus of ceremonial magic. Those that are featured prominently in the manuscript and known from other sources are below.

For the most part (e.g., manuscript page 121), spirits are expected to be tricky. They might change the treasure to something worthless or mask it; produce fantasies, visions, or illusions; or molest the practitioners in various ways, especially in the days following the operation. Mostly they could be compelled to cooperate, sometimes by calling upon their superiors, and occasionally their advisors, to intercede. Although a particular spirit might be assigned particular powers, the rituals themselves often provide few details on the appearance or capabilities of a particular spirit, simply outlining the procedure for calling them.

Why would spirits do the magician's bidding? From an orthodox perspective, demons could be exorcized via bringing them into contact or proximity with holy words, items, gestures, locations, and individuals. Contact with the same, for the magician, could compel a spirit to appear and render service. The BoO also gives another reason: that the spirits hope to redeem their fallen state by doing good deeds for mortals. This is not in line with the Church's position; Thomas Aquinas, one of the church's greatest authorities, had declared that evil spirits had made their choice for all eternity at the beginning of time.[53] As such, the magical doctrine herein was heretical in the extreme.

---

53. Thomas Aquinas, *The De Malo of Thomas Aquinas* (New York: Oxford University Press, 2001), 876–7.

Oberion / Oberon

Oberon, the king of the fairies, is a figure known to millions from Shakespeare's *A Midsummer Night's Dream*. In that play, Oberon is feuding with Titania, his queen, over an Indian boy he wants to train as a knight. The two monarchs have separated, wreaking havoc in nature, causing pestilence, crop failure, and the confusion of the seasons. He sends his minion Puck to find a flower with love-bestowing juice to sprinkle upon his queen's eyelids so she will love the first creature she sees—in this case, a weaver named Bottom, who Puck adorns with an ass's head. Oberon uses the same power to cause discord and later harmony among the play's human lovers, in the end blessing them with fortunate and healthy offspring. Shakespeare's powerful depiction has been responsible for countless works of literature and art, as well as the naming of one of the moons of Uranus after the king. It is less known that Oberon was also an important figure in both the literature and popular spiritual practices at the time.

Oberon's first appearance is in the fourteenth century epic *Huon de Bordeaux: chanson de geste*. In Huon, he is the offspring of a lady from a secret isle and Julius Caesar. At his birth, he was given many gifts but was also cursed to grow no more after three years of age. Notably, the description here mirrors the stipulation that Oberion appear as a three-year-old spirit in the present work, although this appears in ceremonies for other spirits. Oberon becomes a friend of the knight Huon, helping him to escape obstacles in his adventures with magic.

Yet Oberon has more ancient roots, as his name derives from the Old High German Alberich in which *alp/alb* = elf, and *-rich* = ruler. Alberich appears in the epic *Nibelungenlied*, written circa 1200, as a dwarf defeated by the hero Siegfried, taking away his cloak of invisibility and forcing him to serve as a vassal. The poem *Ortnit*, in which the hero learns that the dwarf king Alberich is his father and calls upon his aid to acquire him a princess for his bride, came a few decades after the *Nibelunglied*. Ortnit's Alberich and Huon's Oberon are both quite similar: diminutive yet mighty kings who provide the hero with all manner of supernatural help against their foes.[54]

Starting with the sixteenth century, we also have a number of ritual magic manuscripts providing operations to summon a spirit called Oberion. Among these is the "Raxhael" from Sloane 3826, bound with a copy of the Sepher Raziel,[55] which calls upon Oberion as an angel perceived in a crystal via a special unguent placed in the

---

54. John Warrack, *Carl Maria Von Weber* (Cambridge; New York: Cambridge University Press, 1976), 321; Burton Raffel, *Nibelungenlied* (New Haven, CT: Yale University Press, 2006), 16; John Wesley Thomas, *Ortnit and Wolfdietrich* (Columbia, SC: Camden House, 1986).

55. Raziel (pseud.), "Liber Salomonis: Cephar Raziel" (2006).

eyes.[56] The ceremony in Sloane 3851 calls upon Oberion to appear in either the air or the circle, either as a beautiful soldier or a seven-year-old boy.[57] Another such call appears in Bodleian Library manuscript e. Mus. 173.[58] Finally, the BoO includes not only two operations to call the spirit, but its Offices of Spirits provides a description of his abilities. According to that entry, Oberion is under the power of the sun and the moon, and the king of the waters. His primary purpose, based upon the emphases given in the manuscript, would seem to be the discovery of treasure, but he might be called upon to assist in operations of invisibility, medicine, and natural magic.

Those who called upon this spirit also came to the attention of the authorities. In 1444, a London man was placed in the pillory for his operations involving a spirit called "Oberycom."[59] More famous is the early-sixteenth-century case reported by the clerk William Stapleton, who tells of Sir John of Leiston and the parson of Lesingham summoning the spirit Oberion via a magical plate with two others, Andrea Malchus and Inchubus. Oberion was supposedly silent upon his appearance, with the other spirit claiming that this was due to being bound to the Lord Cardinal Wolsey! The plate used in the experiment passed to the clerk, and thence to Sir Thomas Moore.[60] The same year, the priest James Richardson was accused of writing mystical names, including those of Oberion and Storax, on a lamin.[61] These cases might not be unique to the British Isles; the infamous witchhunter Pierre de Lancre mentions a case of a man in the French commune of Brigueil who had dealings with a spirit named Abiron.[62]

Even after the fairy king's appearances in new dramas waned, popular belief in Oberion continued. Wellcome MS. 4669, written in 1796, includes an experiment "To Have a Familiar Spirit Called Ebrion at Your Disposal," which is derived from older

56. Don Karr, "Liber Lunae and Other Selections from British Library MS. Sloane 3826" *Esoterica* 3 (2001), 295–318.

57. Gauntlet, *The Grimoire of Arthur Gauntlet*, 261–62.

58. K. M. Briggs, "Some Seventeenth-century Books of Magic," *Folklore* 64, no. 4 (1953), 457.

59. James Gairdner, et al., *The Historical Collections of a Citizen of London in the Fifteenth Century* (Westminster, NY: Camden Society, 1965), 185.

60. Dawson Turner, "Brief Remarks, Accompanied with Documents, Illustrative of Trial by Jury, Treasure-trove, and the Invocation of Spirits for the Discovery of Hidden Treasure in the Sixteenth Century," *Norfolk Archaeology* 1 (1847), 57–64.

61. James Raine, "Proceedings Connected with a Remarkable Charge of Sorcery, Brought Against James Richardson and Others, in the Diocese of York, AD 1510," *The Archaeological Journal* 16 (1859), 71–81. Compare BoO pp. 186, 187.

62. Pierre de Lancre, *L'Incredulité et Mescreance du Sortilege Plainement Convaincue* (Paris, 1622), 771–72.

experiments directed at the fairy king.[63] In the nineteenth century, invocations of Oberion appeared in both *The Astrologer of the Nineteenth Century* edited by Raphael, one of the owners of the BoO, and in the back pages of an elaborately illustrated *Key of Solomon* originating from the shop of London bookseller John Denley.[64]

How much knowledge of the folk traditions surrounding Oberion might Shakespeare have known? *A Midsummer Night's Dream* was first performed around a decade after the BoO was written. Given the character of Oberon in the play (portrayed as a mature man contrasting with the young changeling), his companions (Titania and Puck, as opposed to the queen Micol and the servitor's described in the BoO), and his functions (fertility and marital bless, against the wide range of capabilities listed in the Offices of Spirits), any direct connection between the two seems unlikely. More likely influences for Shakespeare were *Huon of Bordeaux*, first published in English in 1534, or Robert Greene's play *The Scottish History of James IV* (c. 1590).[65]

Yet are the Oberon of plays and poems and Oberion of the magical texts the same? Given the general lack of detail on the spirit in magical writings, even Katherine Briggs was reluctant to do more than note the similarity in names.[66] The BoO provides us with one magician's answer: Oberion is indeed the king of fairies, a powerful figure who appears as a young man and can bestow great riches and even invisibility if brought into a person's service. Although the particulars might differ, his overall appearance and purpose is very close to both the Oberon from *Huon* and the Alberich of the German epics. As such, the BoO provides the long-awaited link between ritual and fiction.

Micob / Mycob / Micoll, Titam, and the Seven Fairies

Micob is depicted as the queen of the fairies. We might expect her to be paired with Oberion in the hierarchy, but the separate references in the text indicate the convergence of two different traditions. She teaches medicine, natural magic, and the Ring of Invisibility, and she commands seven fairies that perform similar functions. The spelling Micoll is also found in the BoO. A similarly named individual, Micol, the queen of the pygmies, appears in Sloane 1727. It seems possible or even likely that Mab, queen of the fairies in Shakespeare's *Romeo and Juliet*, is a variant of Micob in

---

63. Stephen Skinner and David Rankine, eds., *A Collection of Magical Secrets* (London: Avalonia, 2009), 42–46.

64. Raphael, *The Astrologer of the Nineteenth Century*, 220–26; Frederick Hockley, *Experimentum Potens Magna in Occult Philosophy Arcanorum* (Hinckley, England: Society for Esoteric Endeavour, 2012), 24–31.

65. Greene, *The Scottish History of James the Fourth*.

66. Katharine Briggs, *Anatomy of Puck: an Examination of Fairy Beliefs Among Shakespeare's Contemporaries and Successors* (London: Routledge & Paul, 1959), 114.

the BoO. Likewise Shakespeare's fairy Titania is likely a variant of Titam, which also occurs in magic texts as Tytan (Sloane 1727) and Titan (Sloane 3885).

The seven fairies themselves appear first as seven fevers in an eleventh-century charm attributed to Saint Sigismund.[67] Later on, they appear with some variations in the exact names in a few different locations, including another manuscript at the Folger, X. 234, which describes a ritual to summon one of these women for treasure, knowledge, and sex.[68]

Baron

Baron is a spirit mentioned frequently in the unpublished literature of magic; alternate spellings include "Barahan or Baron," elsewhere Barahim or Barachim (in Sloane 3853), also Barachin (Wellcome MS. 110). A spirit with a similar name, Barron, was instrumental in the trial of the infamous noble, companion of Joan of Arc, and mass murderer of children, Gilles de Montmorency-Laval, baron de Rais (1404–1440). In the summer of 1439, de Rais and a priest named Prelati called upon this demon to appear in the lower hall of the castle of Tiffauges. This and subsequent evocations failed to yield any appearance of the demon when de Rais is present, even after it was offered the remains of one of his victims.[69]

In BoO, we have three different operations for Baron, one of which is brief and includes no incantation. The spirit is chiefly employed for operations to find treasure, although according to the second operation, he can also procure maidens or bring about agreement or disagreement. The illustration of Baron provided with the third operation likely derives from a translation of Boaistuau's work on prodigies, in which a virtually identical satyr is shown speaking with Saint Anthony.

Rituals to Baron would appear after the BoO as well. In 1549, William Wycherle or Wicherly confessed that he and four men, ten years before at the town of Pembsam (Pepplesham?) in Sussex, had attempted unsuccessfully to conjure the spirit "Baro" using a crystal, a ring, and a circle of Solomon.[70] Another ritual to Baron appears in Sloane 3851, in the writings of early seventeenth-century cunning-man Arthur Gauntlet.[71] The University of Leipzig possesses two manuscripts, one Italian and one

---

67. Ernest Wickersheimer, *Les manuscrits latins de médecine du haut Moyen Age dans les bibliothèques de France* (Paris: Centre national de la recherché scientifique, 1966), 32–33; Faith Wallis, *Medieval Medicine: a Reader* (Toronto: University of Toronto Press, 2010), 69.

68. Frederika Bain, "The Binding of the Fairies: Four Spells," *Preternature: Critical and Historical Studies of Preternatural* 1, no. 2 (2012), 323–354.

69. Georges Bataille, *The Trial of Gilles de Rais* (Los Angeles, CA: Amok, 1991), 203–10.

70. John Foxe, Thomas Cranmer, and John Gough Nichols, *Narratives of the Days of the Reformation: Chiefly from the Mss. of John Foxe the Martyrologist* (London: Camden Society, 1859), 332–33.

71. Gauntlet, *The Grimoire of Arthur Gauntlet*, 222–24.

German, featuring brief operations for calling the spirit.[72] The most recent mention we have of this spirit in the magical literature appears in 1770, when a spirit named "Baran" is invoked, along with Satan, Beelzebub, and Leviathan, in the "Equinox Working" of the Ordre des Elus Coëns began by Martinez de Pasqually (1727–1774).[73]

Birto

Birto is a spirit best known for the curious image of a dragon that often appears in the illustrations associated with his rite. The BoO includes the earliest known ritual for summoning the spirit. Another appears in Rawlinson D. 253, from the seventeenth century, and later examples can be found in the Clavis tradition and other manuscripts transcribed by Frederick Hockley and possibly others for the London bookseller John Denley.[74]

Ceremonies to evoke Birto might be seen as falling into two categories defined by ritual implements, with the first calling a white-handled knife and the second requiring a portrait of a wyvern (the spirit itself?) drawn on parchment. The ritual in this book is of the first category. Even though Hockley would eventually own the Folger manuscript, the manuscripts he created for John Denley are taken from the second category.

Ascariell

The spirit Ascariell, to be conjured into a crystal, appears in a few contemporary works. One of the most notable is a charge to the spirit in Sloane 3849,[75] with additional material in Sloane 3853. In 1549, William Wycherle was able to call a spirit named Scariot into a crystal a hundred times to help with the recovery of stolen goods.[76]

Named Individuals

"Friar Bacon"

At least two Bacons are mentioned in this book, and more often use is made of his last name, raising the question of which individual is being referred to. The first, the

---

72. Universitätsbibliothek Leipzig Cod. Mag. 12, 96.

73. René Le Forestier, *La Franc-maçonnerie Occultiste Au XVIIIe Siècle : & L'ordre Des Elus Coëns* (Paris: La table d'emeraude, 1987), 81–82.

74. Sibley, Hockley, and Peterson, *The Clavis or Key to the Magic of Solomon.*

75. James Douglas, *Nenia Britannica or, a Sepulchral History of Great Britain; from the Earliest Period to Its General Conversion to Christianity* (London: 1793), 17–18.

76. Foxe, Cranmer, and Nichols, *Narratives of the Days of the Reformation*, 333.

thirteenth-century Franciscan theologian and philosopher Roger Bacon (1214–1294) had a reputation for magic and had texts thereof attributed to him (such as *De nigromancia*[77]), so his appearance here is not unexpected.

A more troubling individual is "William Bacon," referred to as a Franciscan friar who created the "Experiment of Rome" to gain knowledge of all things throughout time with Satan's help, as well as "approving" the experiment of Birto. Some controversy has evolved over his identity, with some postulating that his name as a corruption of that of Roger Bacon,[78] and others drawing parallels with the astrologer William Bacon (1577–1653).[79] Although some ambiguity exists as to the dating of the material mentioning him in the present work, we can say with some confidence that the astrologer was far too young at the time. Thus, either William Bacon is a modification of Roger Bacon, or is in fact another individual who has gone without remark before.

To further muddy the waters, a later section of the book tells the tale of a small group of wizards working together "with the helpe & counsell of Friar Bacon." The author's tone and the presence of one possible historical figure, Thomas Drury, suggest that this "Friar" was a contemporary of the manuscript. This could still be a mythical figure, of course.

Thomas Drury / Drowre

Mr. Drowre or Drury, the "clerk in divinity" is the head of the association of magicians described on page 213 of the manuscript. The tale told there is intended to justify the status of the steward in the rites of a magician, so it is likely that Mr. Drury is a figure whose reputation would have been familiar to potential readers.

Nonetheless, we have few records of any clergyman of this name being present at the time. The closest we might have are a Thomas Druery or Dewrye serving as curate at the parish of Broughton on January 24, 1605, and as curate of Broughton and Bossingdon on September 30, 1607.[80] Another Thomas Drewry served as the curate of Checkendon in 1540.[81] None of these individuals seem to have been particularly well-known.

We might also consider another Thomas Drury, this one without any clerical status. Possibly born at Maids Moreton in Buckinghamshire, this Thomas Drury ma-

---

77. Rogerus Bacon and Michael-Albion Macdonald, *De Nigromancia: Sloane Ms. 3885 & Additional Ms. 36674* (Gillette, NJ: Heptangle Books, 1988).

78. Frank Klaassen, "Three Early Modern Rituals to Spoil Witches," *Opuscula* 1, no. 1 (2011), 9.

79. Gauntlet and Rankine, *The Grimoire of Arthur Gauntlet*, 14–15.

80. Clergy of the Church of England Database; PRO E179/57, HRO 21M65 B1/23.

81. Clergy of the Church of England Database; LA, Visitation Book Vj 11.

triculated as a pensioner at Jesus College, Cambridge, on Michaelmas 1571, and joined the Inner Temple in 1577.[82] Drury later served as the instigator of Baines's report to the queen on Christopher Marlowe's supposed heresies that eventually led to the author's death.

What interests us here is an incident in which this Drury was involved in 1585 with a fellow Temple student named John Meeres. Meeres was arrested for threatening Edetha Beast, a widow who spurned his advances, that he would invoke the devil against her. Drury turned informant against Meeres and only spent a brief time in jail.[83] Thus, Drury would have been connected with the summoning of infernal powers only two years after the latest date in our manuscript. Nonetheless, he does not appear to have been a member of the clergy.

Sources

Although the BoO has many unique aspects, it can be placed squarely within the religious and magical literature of the time. One prominent element is the use of Biblical passages as part of the ceremonies therein. Most of the passages given come either from the Vulgate Latin Bible, or from the "Great Bible" published from 1539–69. Much material was also adapted or taken wholesale from Catholic prayer books or the Mass. Aside from these, we find a number of other passages with ties to various breviaries and other religious texts. Shading into the magical side, various works attributed to Agrippa, Hermes, Cyprian, and other such authors can also be found in the text. Some of the more prominent magical works deserve special mention.

Arbatel

This book of forty-nine aphorisms on the topic of Christian planetary magic was first published in Basel in 1575, two years before the composition of the BoO began. Contemporary accounts indicate that the identity of the author, though lost to us, was known in Basel at the time. A prayer on page 19 of the BoO corresponds to one contained in Aphorism 14 of the *Arbatel*.[84] If this prayer does indeed originate in the *Arbatel*, that would indicate that the writer was a keen student of magic who managed to access this work two years after its original publication. This is more impressive given that the next published edition of the book appeared as part of Agrippa's *Opera*

---

82. Venn, *Alumni cantabrigienses*, part 1, vol. 2, 69.

83. Charles Nicholl, *The Reckoning: the Murder of Christopher Marlowe* (New York: Harcourt Brace, 1992), 302.

84. Joseph H. Peterson, *Arbatel—Concerning the Magic of the Ancients: Original Sourcebook of Angel Magic* (Lake Worth, FL: Ibis Press, 2009), 24–27.

published in the same town in 1579.[85] More material from the *Arbatel* appears later in the book.

Sepher Raziel

This book, attributed to the angel Raziel, or "Secrets of God," is known at least from the sixteenth century, and possibly as far back as the thirteenth. (Note: Another book of the same title appears in an extensive Hebrew tradition, but it bears little correspondence with this book.) It includes seven chapters dealing with such topics as astronomy, natural magic, suffumigations, operations of the hours of the day and night, and other topics.[86] The author takes quite a bit of material from Raziel on topics such as the creation of ink, the virtue of various stones and animals, and the sacred names of God. The coverage is often curious, as the author of the text will stop in the middle of a procedure to refer to Raziel. It is clear that at least one of the authors had a copy of Raziel in his library along with the BoO.

Agrippa, in his highly influential *De occulta philosophia libri tres* (hereafter OP), drew heavily from *Sepher Razielis*,[87] which in turn drew from an older text, the *Cyranides* (or *Kyrranides*). This is especially true for the material on plants, stones, animals, and other natural magic. In modern derivative texts, the associations of various plants, birds, fish, and stones seem haphazard at best, but from studying the older work, the logic becomes clear. They are organized around the theory of sympathy based on the first letters of their names in the Greek *Cyranides*. Thus in the first chapter, Alpha, white vine, eagle, eaglestone, and eagle-ray are associated because their Greek names all start with the letter Alpha.[88]

Enchiridion of Pope Leo

The BoO includes one of the earliest known manuscripts of the *Enchiridion*.[89] According to the book itself, Pope Leo III granted its protective prayers and signs to

85. Carlos Gilly, "The First Book of White Magic in Germany" in *Magia, Alchimia, Scienza Dal '400 al '700* (Firenze: Centro Di, 2002), 209–16.

86. Raziel, "Liber Salomonis: Cephar Raziel."

87. As abundantly illustrated by V. Perrone Compagni in the footnotes to his edition.

88. Maryse Waegeman and Hermes, *Amulet and Alphabet: Magical Amulets in the First Book of Cyranides* (Amsterdam: J. C. Gieben, 1987).

89. For example, Gabriel Grasset's *Enchiridion Leonis Papae*, 1775 French and Latin edition (Anconae: G. Grasset?, 1775) shows errors not in Folger, making the BoO an important early exemplar. In general, we find many errors in the 1775 edition, including transcription errors and omissions. Comparing the editions in Michael Cecchetelli's *Crossed Keys* (Scarlet Imprint, 2011) and the translation in Dumas's *Grimoires et Rituels* (Paris: Belfond, 1972), it is apparent the Dumas translation also adds a lot of new errors. The *Crossed Keys* edition seems to follow the French translation, sometimes missing better readings in the Latin.

Charlemagne circa 800. The actual text is first mentioned in the sixteenth century. As stated above, it appears that the manuscript passed through the hands of the scribe on a short-term basis.

Editorial Principles

One constant struggle we have had as we have proceeded with this project has been deciding upon what we wanted to present. Should we use modernized spelling? What about the passages in cipher? Should we render each figure exactly as it appears? What if the words in a figure had been written inaccurately? What if a mistake appeared in the Latin?

As it happened, the Folger Library solved our difficulties by placing graphic files of its manuscript online. (At this time, it can be found at http://luna.folger.edu, if one searches for "Book of magic.") This has given us the freedom to move to the other end of the spectrum, creating a text that is both accessible to today's reader and ties the manuscript to the broader tradition of Western ceremonial magic. Those who wish to double-check our work, or to ensure its accuracy, may refer to the Folger website and easily track down the page in question.

Note the following changes from the original that can be found in the BoO:

* **Abbreviations:** have been expanded.

* **Capitalization and punctuation:** have been normalized for readability.

* **Catchwords** (words written in the lower margin of a page that repeats the first word on the following page): are rarely used in the manuscript; these are not included in the transcription. (The first few examples occur on pages 36, 41, 67, and 70.)

* **Christ, names of:** The manuscript generally uses the common practice of abbreviating the name Iesus Christus with Greek letters IHS XP (Iης Xρ); these have been expanded. Note particularly the frequent use of Greek "XP" or "χρ" for "Christ." In textual studies this is commonly referred to as "chi rho." Thus "XPus" (abbreviation for "*Christus*") looks like Latin "Xpus," and is frequently misunderstood by nonspecialists. This same abbreviation occurs on the lamin in *Heptameron* and countless derivatives, which almost nobody recognizes as simply a very common abbreviation for "Christ." Similarly the Greek "IHS" or "ιης," standing for the Latin "Iesus" ("Jesus") is found throughout the text and

illustrations. Refer to footnotes for more information on some of the illustrations found herein.

* **Original corrections:** are generally noted, with the exception that text that has been stricken through in the original has not been included.

* **Decorated initials** (Litterae florissae): are not indicated in the transcription.

* **Latin text:** in the original manuscript that is purely descriptive (i.e. not part of prayers or incantations) has been replaced with the English translation. The full transcription however can be found online at esotericarchives.com.

    Longer Latin passages are generally accompanied by our translation in parallel columns. For shorter passages where this is not practical, we indicate Latin text in italics, followed by translation in quotation marks.

    The Book of Oberon, like most other manuscripts of the genre, abbreviates the Latin, which is a great space saver. This poses a problem for modern audiences, who want both understanding as well as authenticity. Additionally, in a tradition going back thousands of years, a great deal of the text and illustrations is alinguistic, i.e., has no discernible linguistic content. In the illustrations in particular they are often mixed, making it impossible to classify them as either linguistic or alinguistic, just as it is the spoken texts cannot readily be classified as either prayer or spell.

* **Line fillers,** or illustrative elements intended to finish lines: are not included.

* **Marginalia:** have been included in the footnotes when legible. Due to the quality of the text and uncertainty as to dating, many instances of these have been omitted.

* **The abbreviation N.:** stands for a place in the original manuscript at which the name of the operator, spirit, or client should be inserted, based upon context.

* **The original page numbers:** have been included in brackets. These are from the second, more complete and legible set of pagination in the manuscript. When page numbers are referred to in footnotes, it is these to which they refer. Those in text translated from the Latin appear in italics, due to changes in the word order between the languages.

* **The term *Pseudo-Agrippa*:** refers to the *Fourth Book of Occult Philosophy*, which most scholars believe was falsely attributed to Henricus Cornelius Agrippa.

* **Red:** Such ink was used to indicate beginnings of passages, important words, and holy names at the times when the scribe possessed ink of the said color. We have included the use of red in this edition.

* **Running titles:** are not included in transcription.

Abbreviations and Typographic Symbols

<>	Errors in the original that should be ignored are indicated in <>, such as erroneous duplication of words.
[]	Original page numbers are shown in []. Damaged or missing text, where it can be reasonably deduced is included in [].
[+]	Text that has been added by us for clarity, or deduced from other sources.
["..."]	Translation of preceding text.
[*]	Corrected reading of previous text, i.e., the reading assumed by the translator.
[* (?)]	Corrected reading, but with more uncertainty.
[???]	Letters illegible and no conjecture. Number of '?' indicate approximately how many letters are missing.
(?)	Reading is uncertain; (?-) Reading of first letter or glyph is uncertain.
ELP =	*Enchiridion Leonis Papae*
Folger =	Original Folger Manuscript V.b.26 that has been transcribed to become the Book of Oberon
Gk. =	Greek
H. =	*Heptameron*, in Agrippa (1967).
JHP –	Joseph H. Peterson
KJV =	King James Version of the Bible
LIH =	*Liber Iuratus Honorii*
marg. =	In margin
M. =	In most cases the manuscript uses "M." to indicate when an appropriate name for a place or object should be inserted, whether that is a location, place, or item to be conjured in.
MS, MSS =	Manuscript, Manuscripts
N. =	In most cases the manuscript uses "N." to indicate when an appropriate name should be inserted, whether that of the operator, spirit, or person for whom the spell is intended.
OP =	Agrippa, *De occulta philosophia libri tres*
r =	*Recto*
RT =	Robert Turner translation of *Heptameron* in Agrippa (1655).
sec. man. =	*Secunda manu*, i.e., written in a different handwriting.
v =	*Verso*

Conclusion

The most compelling reason to publish this manuscript is how much it offers the reader, whether a historian, a spiritual seeker, or a casual reader. By the time you read these words, I will have gone over its text at least half a dozen times, and yet I find something new each time I revisit it—the prayer to Saint George, a fragment of a famous grimoire, or a clue as to the origins of the folklore surrounding the toad-bone. No set of annotations that we can provide can capture all of these, and it is my hope that having thousands of eyes view the same material might tell us much more about the book and the culture of which it was a product.

PART 1: THEURGIA

[15]

[+ Prayers for Purification Before the Rite and Protection]

Prayer

From the throne of thy majesty, O most mighty Jehovah, look down here below upon us, thy unworthy servant and son of thy handmaid. Extend thy favour and pity towards me as thou didst on David, Peter, Mary Magdalene, and diverse other sinners and offenders. Think not, O Lord, on the frailty of my youth and sins past, but in my contrition. Take mercy upon me, cleanse me, and I shall be clean; wash me, O Lord God, and I shall be whiter than snow. Purge me, O Lord, and I shall be purged from all unjust and sinful acts, for thou, O Lord, art pitiful of all pities and merciful of all mercies, god of all gods and king of all kings and lord of all lords, the ruler and power of all powers, dominations, and all creatures in heaven, in earth, in hell, and in the seas, without beginning without ending, Alpha and Omega, the first and the last. Whom thou savest are saved, what thou sayest is done, for none can alter it. Even the same God art thou that madest all things and preservest all things. Thou art the same God which, for their pride, disobedience, and presumption, threwest down the stately angels from their seat of glory to their state of foul devils. Thou, for the sin of man, didst drown the whole world, right only excepted. Thou confoundedst the language of all nations. Thou bindest in the sea and hast set her bonds which she shall not pass, and hast ordained to thine angels that which they shall not go beyond nor break their limits and bond without thy licence. Thou gavest wisdom, gifts, and grace to men, to learned and unlearned, to thy twelve Apostles knowledge of tongues and power to cast out devils, to Solomon wisdom, to Saint Stephen faith, to thy prophets, martyrs, virgins, and confessors constancy, to Moses and Aaron boldness and eloquence in speech. Thou art the only well and fountain of all wisdom, grace, and goodness, thou that hast promised, "Seek and ye shall find; knock and it shall be opened; ask and ye shall receive." Bow down thy ear, O Lord, unto me, thy unworthy servant, for thy dear son's sake, Christ Jesus. Say unto me, O Lord, "Lo, I give thee power over all clean and unclean spirits," for I know, O Lord, that thou hast power to do it. Let not them nor any of them be able to delude, condemn, or in any wise disobey me, but as all spirits were through thy grace obedient to thy Apostles to come forth and obey their commandments, so grant, O sweet Jesu, lamb of God that takest away the sins of the world, unto me, thy unworthy yet true servant, the like grace, virtue, faith, wisdom, power, strength, courage, and boldness that all such spirits which I shall either call or command to come or to avoid out,[1] or remove from any place, may be by thy grace, virtue, and power so constrained and forced to come and to come forth and avoid to fulfill and accomplish my will and commandments to their uttermost power and diligence, even as speedily as the walls of Jericho fell down, after they were compassed of thy people seven times without stroke or force of man, only in obedience of thy will they fell down, so let these N.[2] and all such N. fall down and avoid, and come from all places and coasts,[3] and obey me, and be as obedient unto me as the wind and the sea became calm. O Lord mighty Jehovah, so let them come calm and quietly, and as the foul spirits came out and possessed the swine at thy bidding, so mighty and great Adonay, I do beseech thee, let all N. which I call to come or to avoid from any place may through thy grace, will, and power be obedient to come unto me, and let them be as obedient unto me as the hail, rain, lightning, thunder, grasshoppers, frogs, thick darkness, botches, blains, and sores, were by thy will ready to come and accomplish thy commandments at the lifting up of Moses's hands, to come into the land of Egypt. So my god Eloy, Eloy, Eloy, let all such spirits which I shall call or command to come or avoid from any place be present and ready with all diligence to obey my will and commandments to their uttermost powers, and to be as obedient unto me as the Red Sea that divided itself by thy will and power, and as obedient to obey my will and commandments as the bears and fire were by thy will ready to obey the commandment of Elisha, and let them be as obedient unto me to go, come, and stand still and avoid from all places, as the Sun and Moon that stood still at the commandment of Joshua and Moses. And further, O Lord mighty Jehovah, grant me the assistance of thy holy mighty and blessed angels, Michael, Gabriel, Anael, Raphael, Cassiel, Sachiel,

---

1. Avoid out: to remove.

2. In most cases the manuscript uses "N." to indicate when an appropriate name should be inserted. In this prayer, however, apparently we are to substitute the class of spirit, such as "spirit" or "angel."

3. Compare Agrippa, ed., *Henry Cornelius Agrippa His Fourth Book of Occult Philosophy* (London: Printed by J. C. for John Harrison, at the Lamb at the East-end of Pauls, 1655), 63.

and Samael,[4] or some one of them, to be present with me in this my work and business, which I undertake to do in thy name and power, yea even as thy holy and blessed angel Raphael was guide to young Tobias,[5] in his journey against the monstrous fish and devouring spirit Asmodeus, and as the same Asmodeus was constrained, bound, and avoided by thy will, and the power of thy mighty angel, so my god Eloy, Eloy, Eloy, let all such N. as I shall call or take on me to avoid from any place in thy name and power, through thy good will and might unto me given, may be forced to come and obey me and to fulfill my will and commandments in all things faithfully and truly, to the uttermost of their powers, and if they or any of them delude, despise, refuse, and condemn my will and commandments or disobey me or refuse and neglect to fulfill and accomplish them in any part, then let thy holy and blessed angels be present and ready to be with me in my work and business, and to take, bind, carry, and throw them into the lake which burneth with fire and brimstone which is the second death,[6] there to be grievously punished for their disobedience unto me and for the little regard they have to obey me, being called and commanded to come to me by the virtue and power of thy holy names by me pronounced in calling and binding of them, which, if they refuse to obey unto the virtue of them, then let thy holy angels carry them into the bottomless pit of fire and brimstone after the malediction pronounced upon them by me when as they disobey me. Let them be punished in the lake of fire and brimstone which is the second death, there to be grievously punished and tormented without any ease at all, but let their pains be increased and augmented according to the number of the sands of the sea, until they will fulfill and accomplish my will and commandments in all things speedily, justly, and truly to their uttermost powers in whatsoever I shall command them and let them not, O Lord God mighty Jehovah I do beseech, come from out of that place of torment until that I call them from thence and that they will and do obey my will and commandments with all meekness and humbleness, fulfilling my will and commandments to their uttermost powers, and then Lord hear my prayer and grant my request to release them and give me faith, might, and power to keep them always in awe and let them fear and tremble before me whensoever I shall call them. O send thy holy spirit

---

4. These are the seven planetary archangels. This matches Petrus de Abano *Heptameron* in Agrippa, ed., *Henry Cornelius Agrippa His Fourth Book of Occult Philosophy. Of Geomancy. Magical Elements of Peter de Abano. Astronomical Geomancy. The Nature of Spirits. Arbatel of Magick. Translated into English by Robert Turner, Philomathes* (London: Printed by J. C. for John Harrison, at the Lamb at the East-end of Pauls, 1655). Abraham Avenares (circa 1145) lists them as Michael, Gawriel, Anael, Raphael, Caffiel, Satkiel, and Samael in Peuckert, *Pansophie* I (Berlin: E. Schmidt, 1976), 150.

5. Apocryphal Book of Tobit 3:17. Recounted frequently in magic literature, e.g., *Arbatel* Aph. 13; OP Book 3 chapter 17; *John Dee's Five Books*, 85; Sloane 3825, *Janua Magica Reserata*, part 1 chap. 15.

6. Revelation 21:8 (KJV).

of power and might into my heart and fill me with power, grace, and comfort, [16] which thou didst send to the Apostles after thy ascension up to heaven. Fill me with the power and verity of the Holy Ghost that I may flow and abound with power and might, that the devils and spirits may be made obedient unto me. So shall I rejoice in thee and be glad for evermore. Grant this, O mighty and omnipotent Jehovah, for thy dear and only beloved son's sake Christ Jesus, which liveth and reigneth with thee forever, one god, world without end, to whom with God the Father, God the Son, and God the Holy Ghost be rendered all praise, might, majesty, and dominion both now and forever, world without end. Amen, Amen, Amen.

A prayer before you call

O Lord Jesus Christ, king of glory, God of all celestial virtues, holy Father and marvelous disposer of all things which from God the Father camest human into the world, that thou wouldst loose the world from sin and show unto man true judgment which without beginning and without ending art one God, and true to remain Alpha and Omega, the first and the last, the beginning and the ending, which of the Blessed Virgin Mary hast willed to be born, in whose sight all things visible and invisible are ope n and manifest, in whose presence is all things pure and clean, and from whom no secret is hid, unto whom every heart is open and to whom every soul doth confess itself and every tongue doth praise and speak of thy loving kindness, to whom all things doubtful, unknown, and hid is manifest and open, of whose unspeakable sweetness the heavens and the earth and infernal doth obey, I do beseech thee, O Adonay, to grant me my petition. I require thee, O Saday, to be present with me. O Alpha and Omega, be my coadjutor and helper, thou which hast the keys of hell and of death which bindest and no man looseth, which openeth and no man shutteth, and shutteth and no man openeth, give me leave and power to bind and to loose, to call and compel all such spirits which thou in thy just judgments hast thrown out of heaven for their pride and presumption. O give me might, power, force, and strength to bind them and compel them to come to me and to cause them to avoid from all places, and that they may with all diligence, readiness, and willingness obey me, to their uttermost power. O mighty and merciful Emanuel my saviour, I beseech thee meekly to hear me, help me, and mercifully to preserve me, and keep me in protecting of me in this my work and business, which I undertake to do in thy name. I do require thee, O mild and merciful Saviour, for the tender love that thou barest unto mankind, when thou offeredst thy body to be [7] crucified and sufferedst thy blood to

---

7. In marg.: "w" glyph.

be shed for the washing away of mine iniquities, hear me and help me, and send thy holy angels to be present and ready to succour me, and to bind all those disobedient spirits which shall seem to resist or disobey me, and to make them humble and meek unto me, and to cause them to fulfill my will and commandments in all things faithfully and truly in as ample manner as I do or shall require. If they or any of them refuse this to do, then let thine holy, mighty, and blessed angels take and bind them so surely as thou my saviour and redeemer of the world in thy humanity wast bound to the cross, and as truly as thou wast wrapped in linen clothes and laid in a new sepulcher where never was none laid before thee, so truly, O thou mighty lion of the tribe of Judah, let thine angels bind all those disobedient N. which shall despise or condemn the words of my mouth, and deny to obey me, and as truly as Michael the Archangel threw down Satan out of heaven and overcame him and bound him up for a thousand years, so truly let me bind all such N. which I do or shall call or command to come before me and that they never have power to resist or stay in any place until they have accomplished and fulfilled my will and commandments, and as truly as thou wast bound in linen clothes and laid in a new sepulcher where none was never laid before thee, so truly let thine angels Michael, Gabriel, Anael, Raphael, Samael, Sachiel, Cassiel, or some of thy holy and blessed angels take all such disobedient N. and torment them with new plagues, increasing and adding affliction upon affliction, upon them which offer to disobey me and deny to come when I call them, and as truly as thou didst feel the torments due to sin sustaining the anguish thereof upon the Holy Cross, so truly, O my saviour Christ Jesus, let all N. which seek to delude, deceive, or disobey me feel the tortures and torments of hellfire, and as truly as thou didst cry in the vehemency of thy spirit unto thy Father, "Eloy, Eloy Eloy," so truly do I cry unto thee in the vehemency of my spirit, "Eloy Eloy Eloy," that all such N. do seem to disobey me or condemn and despise me or refuse to come with all diligence and quickness to obey me and show me the truth of all such questions which I shall ask or demand be bound and thrown down into the depth of all pain, horror, and sorrow and never to be released or come from thence until that I do call them and that they will obey me and help me to their uttermost powers and as truly as thou wast comforted by the administration of angels, so truly let me have the comfort, help, aid, and assistance of thy holy and blessed angels to be present with me in all my works and business, and as truly as the voice came from heaven, in saying, "This is my well-beloved Son, in whom I am well pleased, hear ye him," so truly, O lamb of God which takest away the sins of the world, let me see thy holy and blessed angels and have their help and aid in all my work and business which I take in hand to do at this time or at any other time hereafter, and as truly as thou didst raise Lazarus out of his grave from death to life, so truly, O my God and merciful saviour, give unto me leave, power, force, and might through the virtue of thy holy names to raise all such N. which I shall call or command to come before me or to avoid from any place, and as truly as thou, O Christ Jesus, didst rise the third day from death to life and didst show thyself unto thy Apostles after thy resurrection, saying unto Mary, "Go tell my brethren that I ascend unto my father and to your father, to my god and to your god," even so truly as thou didst speak to Mary these words and didst appear to thy twelve Apostles, so truly, O my God, let all such N. which I call or shall call, show unto me the truth of all things which I shall ask or demand, and so truly let them obey my will and commandments even as truly as thou didst obey [17] and ever fulfill the will and commandments of God the Father in all things, and as truly as the graves of the saints did open and the saints did rise and appear to many at thy death, so truly, O my God, let all spirits arise from all places and come unto me and yield unto me their obedience quietly and peaceably, showing me the truth of all my questions and demands and as truly as thou didst breathe on thy disciples and saidest, "Receive ye the Holy Ghost," so truly, O my God, breathe into me the spirit of power and might that all N. be willing and ready to obey me, and as all N. were obedient to come forth by the commandment of thy Apostles, so, O my God Eloy Eloy Eloy, let all such N. which I call to come be obedient unto me and be ready to obey me and fulfill my will and commandments in all things to their uttermost powers. Grant this, O merciful God and father, for thy dear son's sake, Jesus Christ's sake, which liveth and reigneth with thee, ever one God, world without end, to whom with the Father, the Son, and the Holy Ghost be rendered all praise, glory, might, majesty, and dominion, both now and forever. Amen, Amen, Amen.

Let us pray

O Almighty and everlasting, wise, and merciful God and Saviour, redeemer of all mankind, judge of all men, the guider and preserver of all men that trust in thee, O holy, pure, and blessed Trinity, I now do call unto thee seeking and suing for grace, faith, might, and power, and help and assistance from thee, beseeching thee to send thy help unto me with the company of thy holy, powerful, and blessed angels, that by the help of thee I may be able to accomplish all those things which I do now take in hand or shall ever hereafter take in hand to do, that through thy might and power, I may have might and power at this time and all other times to bind, to loose, to call, and to command, to compel, and to constrain all such N. which thou for their pride and presumption didst throw out of heaven, and also over all other N. which I do take in hand at this time that so soon as I shall once begin to name or invocate them by N.

that then they do presently come and appear [8] with all quietness, humility, and diligence, fulfilling my will and commandments, to their uttermost powers, faithfully and truly, and that they never depart until I shall licence them. I do beseech thee, O holy and merciful Father, for thy dear son's sake Christ Jesus, and through the power of these thy holy names, give me power, might, courage, strength, and boldness to overcome and bind and bring to my obedience all those N. which I call or shall call at this time or hereafter at any other time. I do beseech thee, O mighty and merciful + [9] Tetragrammaton [10] + יהוה + Agla + Saday + Haley + Kes + El + Amye + Semy + Hasy + Hayn + Venmissoy Saacodere + Barew + Adabahcw ⊦ Eya + Hey + Hew + Hew + Va + Ha + Eye + Eye + Eye + Ya [11] + Ya + Evef + El + El + Ahey + A + Ha + Ahue + Ahue + Ahne + Va + Va + Va + Vadua + Ylaye + Alenda + Le + Ane + Hy + He + Ha + Ysale + Ne + He + Ha + Araya + Acamine + Leena + Quiloso + Lyeneno + Phealet + Neale + Ye + Ye + Malahe + Huana + Nethe + Heyrete + Hasyonada + Balysany + Methe + Pheniphatol + Comithomon + Sedalay + Thro + Thro + Homos + Zepny + Aglatha + Vyell + Ioell + Sacomith + Paconith + Pyfam + Ytomor + Hygarom + Ynquiron + Cengaron + Myron + Mycon + Dasnot + Cassas + Jatas + Yeton + Eya + Rabba + Raba + Rabarman + Sarus + Eyessaraye + Ala + Yana + Maysay + Sye + Sere + Myge + Mehata + Sare + Maasame + Evanat + Ate + Dacye + Byne + Rahew + Yabe + Astrolye + Lroe + Saye + Gole + Maha + Samoer + Byby [12] + Loey + Ybyyre + Tylay + Raby + Lee + Vel + See + Leace + Cade + Lethe + Lyby + Yre + Tylay + Raby + Lee + Vel + See + Leace + Cade + Lethe + Lyhele + Meamare + Tyrya + Hyse + Saquiel + Mum + Seyme + Yele + Have + L Hele + Amye + Hara + Eyesserye + Agios + Iskiros + Athanatos + Agla + On + Tetragrammaton + Jehovah + by these thy holy, fearful, fearful [sic], honourable, dreadful, and mighty names, being full of all honour, glory, praise, might, and power, by the might and power of them, suffer me and give me leave and power to bind all thine N. which were put out of heaven, for their pride and disobedience against thee, and as thou didst throw them down by thy might and power, so, O thou mighty and powerful + Tetragrammaton + give me leave and power through and by thy mighty power to bind, loose, and compel and command all those which thou threwest out of heaven, and make them obedient and serviceable

---

8. In marg.: "w" glyph.

9. The manuscript frequently sets sacred names or words apart with crosses. These seem to be simply punctuation, not a rubric to make the sign of the cross.

10. Compare Raziel: See Peterson, *The Sixth and Seventh Books of Moses, or, Moses, Magical Spirits-Art: Known As the Wonderful Arts of the Old Wise Hebrews, Taken from the Mosaic Books of the Cabala and the Talmud, for the Good of Mankind* (Lake Worth, FL: Ibis Press, 2008), 264–271. Another version of this prayer can be found below, Folger p. 70.

11. In marg.: "+" glyph.

12. Folger has an "i" (no dot) written above the first "y."

unto me, with all diligence and faithfulness, speed and quietness, in truth and verity, O + Agla + Pater Kirie + Adonay + O thou Creator and Redeemer, saviour and sanctifier of me, and also of all humankind, O thou El + and Eloy Lamabatani +[13], O thou of incomprehensible majesty, now forsake me not, poor sinful wretch that I am, forsake me not, now in this my work, business, and enterprise, although I am not worthy to receive any comfort, aid, and assistance from thee or by thy might and power, O merciful Saviour, which hast ever been benign and bountiful, unto all those that call on thee. Now let me not be without thy aid, help, comfort, and assistance, filling me with all might, power, strength, courage, boldness, faith, and ableness, bringing my desire and work to effect, to my comfort and consolation, and to thy eternal praise and glory, I ask mercy and forgiveness of thee, O Father of mercy, for thy son Jesus Christ's sake, hear me now. I do desire thee to [18] hear me, O my God, which heareth and seeth me totally as well in words, cogitations, and thoughts, O thou God of Abraham, Isaac, and Jacob, which hast promised to those which diligently seek after thee shall find thee, and to those that call on thee, that thou wilt hear them, and those that ask of thee unfeignedly in the name of thy son Jesus Christ they shall receive of thee, O thou my great and mighty redeemer, now hear me and help me now. I call unto thee now, I seek thee now, let me find thee, in giving me might and power. Now I ask of thee for thy dear son's sake Christ Jesus + now let me receive the spirit of grace, might, and power, in helping me in this my enterprise. O you three persons in trinity and one God in unity which didst deliver Daniel out of the lions' den, Shadrach, Meshach, and Abednego out of the fiery furnace, and deliveredst Susanna from her false accusers, which deliveredst Joseph and madest him ruler over Egypt which madest the children of Israel to overcome their enemies, at the lifting up of Moses's hands, as thy sweet son Christ Jesus + overcame hell, death, and damnation by his lifting upon the Cross in shedding his precious blood for the redemption of mankind, so, O my God, give me power, might, faith, and strength, and the help and assistance of thy holy and blessed angels to bring this my desires to effect, that as I lift up my hands, heart, eyes, and soul unto thee, so may I receive from thee, and have power [and] might, by thee, to me given, to bind, constrain, loose, and compel, command, and bring to my obedience all N. which I shall call at any time and at this present do intend to call. Grant this, O Lord God, for Christ Jesus's sake, Alpha and Omega which liveth and reigneth with thee, ever one God, world without end, to whom with God the Father, God the Son, and God the Holy Ghost be rendered all praise, glory, might, majesty, and dominion, both now and forever. Amen, Amen.

---

13. Elsewhere in text, parallel passages read "lamazabathani," "Lamazabathany," "lama Zabacthani," etc. This is apparently derived from "Eloi, Eloi, lama sabachthani" from Mark 15:34, which is often found in magical texts.

Another oration

O magnificent, omnipotent, most merciful, and everlasting God, the great creator of all men, the sweet comforter of thy afflicted servants, I thine unworthy yet true servant do most humbly fall down and prostrate myself before thee, O thou pitiful and merciful Saviour, my sweet and comfortable guider in all my afflictions, my helper and preserver in all my necessities, my aider, and succourer, in all my works and businesses, which I take in hand to do through thy leave and help, beseeching thee as thou art true God and man to give me leave and licence by the virtue of thy holy names, to bring my desire to effect, that thou mayest thereby be glorified and I satisfied to the great comfort of thy poor servants, and to the sweet and ghostly comfort of mine own soul. I do desire and pray thee, O thou powerful Tetragrammaton [14] + to hear this my request and prayers in giving me faith and divine power to constrain and compel all thine angels N. which were cast down from heaven, to draw them, to bind, and to loose them, to command and compel them to come before me and to be meek and obedient unto me presently and speedily, without any delay, defraud, deceit, or guile, and that through the virtue and power of thy mighty names they may be made humble and meek to bow, bend, and obey me, yielding [15] themselves serviceable unto me with all readiness and meekness, and to obey and fulfill my will. With all humility and lowliness I do beseech thee, O mighty Jehovah, the ruler of all the world, thou that orderest the heavens and rulest the earth, which hast dominion over the heavens, earth, hell, and the seas, give me power to bring this my desires to effect, even for thy own name's sake, and for thy son's sake Christ Jesus + which died for the sins of the people. I do now require (?) thee by the tender love which thou barest unto mankind, O which art first and last, Alpha and Omega, per thy humanity, mercy, and grace, that thou give me dominion and power over all thine angels and spirits thrown out of heaven for their pride and presumption and give them into my hands through thy power unto me given thy holy and blessed angels, aiding, assisting, and helping me in all my works and business to tie them and bind them, to loose them, and also to gather them together and to bring them from all places and make them to obey me. O hear me and help me now, I cry to thee meekly from the bottom of my heart with sincerity, O Yana, Yana, Yana, look upon me, my maker, with the eyes of thy mercy in sending thy holy and blessed angels to be my help, even by the virtue of this thy name, Yseraye, Yseraye, Yseraye, let them be with me and be my coadjutor and helper in all my works and businesses, to my comfort and thy glory for evermore, and profit of these which shall need my help and comfort, and by the virtues of these thy mighty

---

14. Folger: Tertragramaton.

15. In marg.: "w" glyph.

holy and sanctified names to be assistant unto me, showing thy mighty power in binding and in gathering together all N. which I would bind and gather together to come before me, even by the virtue of these thy powerful names let the heavens and all therein contained be willing to help me and accomplish my will and desires to bind all spirits and demons which are in the compass of the four parts of the whole circle and globe of heaven, air, earth, hell, and seas, even by the virtue of these thy names + Adona + Sabaath + Adonay + Cados + Addona + Amora + let the virtue and power of these thy wonderful names be assistant unto me, showing thy mighty power in binding and in gathering together all spirits which I do or shall desire to bind and gather together to come before me, to loose and remove all spirits which I would loose and remove from all places, they obeying my will and commandments with all diligence faithfully and truly to their uttermost powers without the hurt of my body, soul, mind, or goods, or any living creatures whatsoever, or wheresoever, and further with thy gracious help I require thee to give me leave and licence to have to my help the company of thy holy and blessed angels eve[?] through the virtue of these thy pure and blessed names Letamynym [16] + Letalogan + Letafyryn + Vabagana + Rytyn + Letarymytnun + Letafatazin + let the winds, air, and all things be my help to bring those spirits before me and to my obedience quietly, peaceably, meekly, and mildly unto me, even as meekly as thou, O merciful redeemer of mankind, did[st] suffer the reviling, rebukes, and strokes of the wicked counsel of the Jews, and as meekly and as willingly as thou didst suffer the pains of the Cross for the redemption of mankind, so meekly, quietly, peaceably, and obediently let them yield their obedience unto me in fulfilling my will and commandments to their uttermost power, faithfully and truly without the hurt [19] of my body, soul, goods, or any living creature. This grant, O thou powerful, omnipotent, and everlasting God, to me which doth ask and require to have my desires accomplished in giving me leave and power to bind and to loose all spirits which I do or shall ever hereafter to bind and loose, bringing to my obedience all those spirits which were thrown out of heaven for their pride and disobedience, that they come and accomplish my will and commandments faithfully, truly, and justly to their uttermost powers presently and speedily, even by the virtue of these thy holy names: Saday [17] + Hayleos + Loez + Elacy + Citonii + Hazyhaya + Yeynimesey + Accida + Vacuc + Hyadonenni + Eya + Hiebu + Ven + Vaha + Oyaha + Eye + Eye + Ha + Hia + Haya + Zihia + Hahya + Yaia + El + Ehehel + Ya + Ya + Va + by the virtue of these thy powerful names do I trust to obtain, and by the virtue of these thy names

---

16. This list of names is found in Sepher Raziel, Semiforas 6: See Peterson, *The Sixth and Seventh Books of Moses*, 268.

17. This list of names is found in Sepher Raziel, chap. 5: See Peterson, *The Sixth and Seventh Books of Moses*, 270.

I do believe my will shall be accomplished: Nicracon [18] + Incly + Xeddam + Peddem + Roexi + Saconits + Patrint + Pyston + Ycymor + Hygaron + Ygnyron + Temgaron + Mycon + Micondasnos + Castas + Laceas + Astas + Yecan + Cina + Tabluist + Tablanao + Zacuss + and I do humbly call unto thee, O my creator, to send thine angels to be my helpers in this my work and business both now at this present and ever hereafter, giving me virtue, courage, boldness, faith, and divine power with the help of thy holy, mighty, and blessed angels assisting me to bring my desires to a good end. Now I earnestly call on thee in the anguish of my soul from the depth and bottom of my heart, crying unto thee to hear me and send me thy help. Even I do beseech thee to hear me even by the might, virtue, and power of these thy sanctified names to help me now, I call, Yana + Yane + Sya + Abibhu + Vanohia + Accenol + Tivgas + Yena + Eloym + Ya + Vehu + Yane + Hayya + Vehu + Ahyaema + that all spirits whatsoever may be brought and come before me quietly and yield me their obedience, showing me justly and truly my questions and demands, fulfilling my will and desires whereunto I shall command them, O mighty, benign, merciful, and everliving God, Saday + Samora + Ebon + Pheneton + Eloy + Eneyobcel + Messias + Iahe + Yana + Oreloyen + *deus vive verax magne fortis potens pie sancte munde omni bonitate, plene, benedicte, domine, benedictum nomen tuum tu completur meam compleas questionem tu factor fac me ad finem mei operis elarg[i]untu[r] sancte et miserationis mei miserere nomen tuum + yseraye + sit per verbum benedictum* ["O God, living, true, great, powerful, mighty, pious, holy, pure, full of all goodness, O blessed-one, O Lord, blessed be your name; you who are fulfilled, fulfill my question; O maker, make me come to the end of my work; O holy and merciful one, have mercy on me; may your name + Yseraye + be blessed through the word"] + that thou fulfill my questions and bring my desires to effect. O thou my maker, make me to come to the end of my work and accomplish it to my comfort and profit. Thou holy and merciful, have mercy on me, and hear me, thy glorious name Yseraye + be it blessed and sanctified by me, both now and evermore, and further I call on thee, O thou my Creator, by these thy mighty names Yaena + Adonay + Cados + Ebreel + Eloy + Ela + Egiel + Ayom + Sath + Adon + Sulela + Eloym + Delyom + Yacy + Elym + Deliis + Yacy + Zazael + Paliel + Man + Myel + Evola + Dylatan + Saday + Alma + Papyn + Saena + Alym + Catmal + Vza + Yarast + Calphi + Calsas + Safna + Nycam + Saday + Aglataon + Fya + Emanuel + Joth + Zalaph + Om + Via + Than + Domyfrael + Muel + Lalialens + Alla + Phenor + Aglata + Tyel + Piel + Patriceion + Cepheron + Baryon + Yael + do I vehemently call on thee that thou wilt vouchsafe to help me and send me aid and comfort to bring my desires to effect. Thou knowest, O Lord, better to give than I am able to ask, and knowest

---

18. This list of names is found in Sepher Raziel, chap. 4: See Peterson, *The Sixth and Seventh Books of Moses*, 270.

before I ask what I would desire, and knowest my thoughts long before they appear or approach. Seeing that thou knowest all my doings and all my ways, I acknowledge thee to be the giver of all goodness. Open thy hand which is full of all blessings and fill me with thy holy power and spirit of grace that I may abound and be full of all blessings to the obtaining of this my desires, which I so willingly would and do seek to accomplish this. Grant, O most merciful God and loving Father for thy dear son's sake, Christ Jesus, which liveth and reigneth with thee ever one God, to whom with God the Father and the Holy Ghost be rendered all glory, power, might, majesty, and dominion both now and for evermore, world without end. Amen. ⊂⊣

Therefore you should pray thus: [19]

Domine Celi ac [*et] terre omnium visibilium et Invisibilium conditor et creator: ego Indignus te Iubente, te Invoco per fillium tuum unigenitum dominum nostrum Iesum Christum ut des mihi spiritum sanctum tuum qui me in veritate<m> tua dirigat ad omne bonum tuum, Amen, quia vero desider[i]o desidero artus [*artes] huius vitae et necessarias, nobis perfecte cognoscere, quae immersa[e] sunt tantis tenebris et conspurcate infinitis humanis opinionibus, ut ego videam me meis viribus nihill in iis assequ[u]turum te non docente: da mihi unum de spiritibus tuis, qui me doceat ea, quæ vis nos discere et cognoscere, [ad laudem & honorem tuum et vtilitatem proximi. Da mihi etiam cor docile, vt] qua[e] me docueres [*docueris] facile percipiam et in mentem	O Lord of Heaven and Earth, maker and creator of all that is visible and invisible; I, though unworthy, call upon you and invoke you, through your only begotten son our Lord Jesus Christ, in order that you give your Holy Ghost to me, which may direct me in your truth, for the good of all. Amen. Because with true longing I desire to learn fully the skills of this life, and those things which are necessary for us, who are immersed in immense darkness and fouled with unending human beliefs, as I see that I can understand nothing through my own power, unless you teach me. Grant to me therefore one of your spirits, who will teach me whatever you wish me to learn and understand, [for your praise and honour, and the usefulness of our neighbors. Grant to me also a heart that

19. From Peterson, *Arbatel* (Lake Worth, FL: Ibis Press, 2009), 24–27, Aph. Xiiii. There is a glyph after the "Amen" that looks like an anchor, which is written in faded brown ink. In marg.: "w" glyph and the anchor glyph is repeated. It also occurs on Folger pp. 48, 56, and 63. It is unclear what it indicates.

| meam recondam inde proferenda, tanquam da [*de] tuis inexhaustis thesauris ad omnes usus necessarios: et da mihi gratiam ut tantis donis tuis humillime cum metu et tremore utar, per do[m]inum nostrum Iesum Christum cum sancto spiritu tuo. Amen. | is easily taught, so] that I may easily retain in my mind what you have taught, and I will secure them there to be brought forth, as from your inexhaustible treasures, for all necessary uses. And grant to me your grace, that I may use these great gifts of yours only with humility, fear, and trembling, through our Lord Jesus Christ with your Holy Ghost. Amen. |

Prayer to Jesus [20]

| O bone Iesu o piissime Iesu, o dulcissime Iesu, o Iesu fili mariae virginis, plena miserecordia, et pietata: o dulcis Iesu secundum magnum miserecordiam tuam miserere mei. o clementissime Iesu, te deprecor per Illum sanguinem pretiosum, quem pro peccatoribus effundere voluisti ut abluas omnes iniquitates meis: et in me resspicias misserum, et indignum humilliter veniam petentem, et hoc nomen sanctum Iesus Invocantem o nomen Iesu nomen confortans: quid est enim Iesus nisi salvator? Ergo Iesu propter nomen sanctum tuum, esto mihi Iesus, et salva me: ne | O good Jesu! O most tender Jesu! O most sweet Jesu! O Jesus, Son of Mary the Virgin, full of mercy and kindness! O sweet Jesu, according to thy great mercy,* have pity on me! O most merciful Jesu, I entreat thee by that precious Blood of thine, which thou didst will to pour forth for sinners, to wash away all my iniquities, and to look upon me, poor and unworthy as I am, asking humbly pardon of thee, and invoking this holy Name of Jesus. O Name of Jesus, sweet Name! Name of Jesus, Name of joy! Name of Jesus, Name of strength! Nay, what meaneth the Name of Jesus but |

---

* This phrase seems to be an adaptation of Psalm 50:3 (KJV 51:3): *Miserere mei, Deus secundum magnam misericordiam tuam; et secundum multitudinem miserationum tuarum, dele iniquitatem meam* ["Have pity on me, O God, according to your great mercy, and according to your many mercies, destroy my iniquities"].

---

20. Translation from Catholic Church and Ambrose St. John, *The Raccolta: Or Collection of Indulgenced Prayers* (1880), 64. Compare *Officium Beatae Mariae Virginis, nuper reformatum, et Pii V. Pont. Max. jussu editum* (Antuerpiae: Christophori Plantini, 1575), 452 ff.

permittas me damnari, quod tu de nihilo creasti: o bone Iesu ne perdat me iniquitas mea, quem fecit omnipotens bonitas tua. o dulcis Iesu recognosce quod tuum est [et] absterge quod alienum est o benignissime Iesu, miser[e]re mei dum tempus est miserendi, ne damnes in tempore Iudicandi "que utillitas in sanguine meo dum descendero in eternum corruptionem" "non mortui laudabunt te domine Iesu neque omnes, qui descendunt in Infernum," o amantissima Iesu: o dessederati Iesu, o mitissime Iesu, o Iesu Iesu Iesu admitte me intrare numerum Electorum tuorum O Iesu salus in te credentium o Iesu solatium ad te confugietium o Iesu dulcis remissio omnium peccatorum. o Iesu fili Mariae virginis, infundae in me gratiam, sapientiam, charitatem, castitatem et humilitatem, ut possim te perffecte deligere, te laudare, te perfrui tibi servire, et in te gloriare, et omnes qui Invocant nomen tuum, quod est Iesus, Amen.

Saviour? Wherefore, O Jesu, by thine own holy Name, be to me Jesus, and save me. Suffer me not to be lost—me, whom thou didst create out of nothing. O good Jesu, let not my iniquity destroy what thy Almighty goodness made. O sweet Jesu, recognise what is thine own, and wipe away from me what is not of thee! O most kind Jesu, have pity on me while it is the time of pity, and condemn me not when it is the time of judgment. "What use is there in my blood, while I descend into eternal corruption?"[†] The dead shall not praise thee, Lord Jesu, nor will those who go down into hell."[‡] O most loving Jesus! O Jesu, most longed for by thine own! O most gentle Jesu! Jesu, Jesu, Jesu, let me enter into the number of thine elect. O Jesu, salvation of those who believe in thee. Jesu, consolation of those who fly to thee. Jesu, Son of Mary the Virgin, pour into me grace, wisdom, charity, chastity, and humility, that I may be able perfectly to love thee, to praise thee, to enjoy thee, to serve thee, and make my boast in thee, and that all those who invoke thy Name, which is Jesus, may join with me in these acts. Amen.

---

† Compare Psalm 29:10 (KJV 30:9).
‡ Compare Psalm 113:25 (KJV 115:17).

[20]

A prayer in affliction [21]

O dulcissime domine Iesu Christe verus Deus, qui de sinu summi patris omnipotentis missus es in mundum peccata relaxare, afflictos redimere, in carcere positos soluere, dispersos congregare, peregrinos in suam patriam reducere, contritis corde misereri, dolentes et lugentes consolari dignare domine Ie[su] Christe absoluere, et liberare me famulum tuum N de afflictione, et tribulatione, in qua positus sum et tu domine qui genus humanum in quantum homo, A deo patre omnipotente in custodiam recepisti; et ex pietat[e] tua, crudeli passione, nobis paradisum pretioso sanguine tuo mirabiliter mercatus es, et inter angelos et homines pacem fecisti. tu domine Iesu Christe digneris inter me et Inimicos meos stabilire, et confirmare concordiam et pacem: et gratiam tuam super me ostendere, et infundere misericordia tuam: et ad omne odium et Iracundiam Inimicorum meorum, quod contra me habent, digneris extinguere, et mitigare, sicut Iracundiam et odium Esau abstulisti, quod habe[ba]t adversus Iacob fratrum suum ita domine Iesu Christe super me famulum tuum brachium tuum extendere, et me liberare digneris ab omnibus me odio habentibus et tu domine Iesu Christe [sicut]

O most sweet Lord Jesus Christ, true God, who, from the bosom of the Almighty Father, wert lent into the world to release sinners, to redeem the afflicted, to deliver the imprisoned, to gather the dispersed, to restore strangers to their country, to have mercy on the contrite in heart, to comfort the sorrowful and mourning; vouchsafe, O Lord Jesus Christ, to absolve and deliver me, thy servant, out of the affliction and tribulation into which I am fallen: and thou, O Lord, who from God the Father Almighty had received mankind, inasmuch as thou art man, into thy protection, and hast of thy pity, by thy cruel passion, after a wonderful manner, purchased paradise for us with thy precious blood, and had made peace between angels and men; thou, O Lord Jesus Christ, vouchsafe to establish and confirm agreement and peace between me and my enemies, and to shew thy grace upon me, and to pour upon me thy mercy; and vouchsafe to extinguish and mitigate all the hatred and anger of my enemies, which they have against me, as thou tookest away the anger and hatred of Esau, which he had against his brother Jacob: even so, O Lord Jesus Christ, vouchsafe to stretch over me, thy servant,

---

21. Also found in *Officium Beatae Mariae Virginis, nuper reformatum, et Pii V. Pont. Max. jussu editum,* 456 ff. Compare *Horae secundum ordinem sancti Benedicti* (Barcelona: Johannes Luschner, [1498?]). Translation from the Catholic Church, *The Primer, or Office of the Blessed Virgin Mary* (London: J. P. Doghlan, 1790), 296–99.

liberasti Abraham de manibus caldeorum et fillium eius Isaac de Immolatione sacrificii cum ariete, et Iacob de manu Esau fratris sui et Ioseph de manu fratrum suorum, Noe per Arcam diluuii, et Loth de civitate sodomor[um,] famulos tuos Moysen et Aaron, et populem Israelem de manibus pharaonis, et de servitute Aegipti, dauid regem, de manu saulis, et goliae gigantes: susannam de falso crimine testimonio: Iudith de manu holiphernis danielem de lacu leonum tres pueros sidrach, Misach, Abdenago de camino ignis ardentis Ionam de ventre ceti, et filium chananeae, que erat tormentata per diabolum, et Adam de profundo puteo inferni, pretiosissimo sanguine tuo, et petrum de Mari, et paulum de vinculis: ita me famulum tuum N dulcissime domine Iesu Christe, fili dei vivi, liberare digneris de omnibus Inimicis meis, et sucurrere in adiutorium meum per sancta beneficie tua: per sanctam Incarnationem tuam quam accepisti ut homo de virgine Maria: per sanctam natiuitatem tuam per famem per sitim per frigus per calores, per labores, et afflictiones, per sputa, per alapis, per fflagella, per clauos, per lanceam, per spineam coronam: per potationem fellis, et aceti per sevissimam mortem crucis, per septam verba, que pendens in cruce dixisti, scillicet, deo patri omnipotenti ignosce illis quia nesciunt, quid faciunt dixisti domine latroni in cruce pendenti: Amen Amen, dico tibi hodie mecum eris

thy arm and thy grace, and deliver me from all that hate me. And thou, O Lord Jesus Christ, as thou didst deliver Abraham from the hands of the Chaldeans, and his son Isaac from being offered in sacrifice with the ram; and Jacob from the hand of Esau his brother; and Joseph from the hands of his brethren; Noah by the ark from the flood; and Lot from the city of Sodom; and thy servants Moses and Aaron, and the people of Israel, from the hand of Pharaoh, and from the bondage of Egypt; King David from the hand of Saul, and of Goliath the giant; Susanna from false crime and accusation; Judith from the hand of Holofernes; Daniel from the den of lions; the three children, Sidrach, Misach, and Abednago, from the furnace of burning fire; Jonah from the whale; and the daughter of the woman of Canaan, who was tormented by the Devil; and Adam from the deep pit of Hell, by thy most precious blood; and Peter from the sea; and Paul from his bonds: even so, O most sweet Lord Jesus Christ, Son of the living God, vouchsafe to deliver me thy servant from all my enemies, and come speedily to my help, by thy holy benefits, by thy holy incarnation of the Virgin Mary, by thy holy nativity, by thy hunger, by thy thirst, by thy cold, by thy heats, by thy labours and afflictions, by the affronts and buffets, by the scourges, by the nails, by the lance, by the thorny crown, by the drinking of gall and by

in paradiso dixisti domine patri tuo heli heli, lama Zabacthani quod est interpretatum: deus meus, deus meus, ut quid dereliquisti me; dixisti domine matre tue: mulier ecce filius tuus, deinde descipulo, Ecce mater tua, ostendas curam habere tuorum amicorum dixisti domine [Sitio: scilicet salutem animaram sanctarum, quae in limbo fuerunt, et nostra cupiendo. Dixisti Domine] patri tuo: In manus tuas commendo spiritum meum, dixisti domine consumatum est: significans labores et dolores, quos pro nobis miseris suscepisti, iam finiri, propter hos etiam rogo te, redemptor domine Iesu Christe ut me famulum tuum N custodias ab hoste maligno, et ab omni periculo hic in presenti, et in futuro, defende me per descentionem tuam ad inferos, per sanctam resurrectionem tuam et frequentem discipulorum tuorum consolationem: per admirabilem assensionem tuam: per adventum spiritus sancti paracliti per diem trimendi Iuditii: per hac omnia exaudi me domine et per sancta [*cuncta] beneficia tua, et etiam pro cunctis beneficiis tuis mihi famulo tuo collatis, quia tu me fecisti ex nihilo, tu produxisti me tu ad fidem sanctam tuam perduxisti me: et contra diaboli tentationem me premunisti, vitam eternam promitendo. Propter ista, et omnia alia, que occulis [*occulus] non vidit, nec auris audivit, nec in cor hominis assendit [*ascenderunt]: Rogo te dulcissime domine Iesu Christe:

the most cruel death on the cross, by the seven words, which, hanging on the cross, thou spakest, to wit, to God the Father Almighty, "forgive them, for they know not what they do." Thou saidst, O Lord, to the thief hanging on the cross, "Amen, Amen, I say to thee, this day thou shalt be with me in paradise." Thou saidst, O Lord, to thy Father, "Eli, Eli, lama sabacthani," which is interpreted, "My God, my God, why hast thou forsaken me?" Thou saidst, O Lord, to thy Mother, "Woman, behold thy Son;" then to thy Disciple, "Behold thy Mother, shewing thyself to have care of thy friends." Thou saidst, O Lord, ["I thirst, to wit, the salvation of holy souls, which were in Limbo, and with desire of ours." Thou saidst, O Lord,] to thy Father, "Into thy hands I commend my spirit." Thou saidst, O Lord, "It is consummate;" signifying thy labours and sorrows now to be ended, which thou tookest upon thee for us sinners. For these therefore, I beseech thee, O Lord Jesus Christ, my redeemer, that thou keep me thy servant from the malignant enemy, and from all danger here in this present world, and in that to come. Defend me by thy descending into Hell, by thy holy resurrection, and the often comforting thy disciples; by thy wonderful ascension; by the coming of the Holy Ghost the Comforter; by the day of dreadful judgment: by all these hear me, O Lord, and by all thy benefits, and also for all thy benefits

ut ab omnibus periculis animae, et corporis pro tuo [*tua] pietate, et misericordia, me famulum tuum N. nunc et semper liberare digneris, et post huius vitae cursum ad te deum vivum et verum me perducere digneris qui [+ viuis et regnas in saecula saeculorum. Amen.]

bestowed on me thy servant, for that thou hast made me of nothing, thou hast produced me, and perfectly guided me unto thy holy faith, and hast defended me against the temptations of the Devil, promising eternal life. For these and all other, which eye has not seen, nor ear heard, nor has ascended into the heart of man, I beseech thee, O sweetest Lord Jesus Christ, that thou vouchsafe to deliver me thy servant N., now and ever, from all perils of body and soul, for thy pity and mercy's sake; and, after the course of this life, vouchsafe to bring me to thee, the living and true God, who [+ lives and reignest, world without end. Amen].

A prayer to God, to be said in the four parts of the world, in the Circle [22]

Amorule, Taneha, Latisten, Rabur, Taneha, Latisten, Escha, Aladia, α et ω, Leyste, Oriston, Adonay, clementissime pater mi celestis, miserere mei, licet peccatoris, clariffica, in me hodierno die, licet Indigno filio tuo tue potentie brachium, contra hos spiritus perticinacissimus: ut ego te volente, factus tuorum divinorum, operum contemplator, possim illustrari omni sapientia, et semper glorificare et adorare nomen tuum, supplicitur exoro te et invoco vt tuo iudicio hi spiritus: N quos invoco, convicti et constricti, veniant vocati et dent vera responsa, de quibus eos Interrogavero:

Amorule, Taneha, Latisten, Rabur, Taneha, Latisten, Escha, Aladia, Alpha & Omega, Leyste, Oriston, Adonay: O my most merciful heavenly Father, have mercy upon me, although a sinner; make appear the arm of thy power in me this day (although thy unworthy child) against these obstinate and pernicious spirits, that I by thy will may be made a contemplator of thy divine works, and may be illustrated with all wisdom, and always worship and glorify thy name. I humbly implore and beseech thee, that these spirits which I call by thy judgement may be bound and constrained to

---

22. Here begins excerpts from *Heptameron*. H., 119–120.

dentque et differant nobis eaque per me vell nos precipietur eis, non [nocentes alicui creaturae, non laedentes, non] firmentes, nec me sociosque meos vell aliam creaturam ledentes, et neminem terrentes: sed petitionibus meis in omnibus que precipiam eis, sint obedientes.	come, and give true and perfect answers to those things which I shall ask them, and that they may declare and show unto us those things which by me or us shall be commanded them, not hurting any creature, neither injuring nor terrifying me or my fellows, nor hurting any other creature, and affrighting no man; but let them be obedient to my requests, in all these things which I command them.

Then standing in the middle of the circle, he should hold his hand near the pentacle and say,

per pentacculum salomonis advocati [*advocavi] dent mihi responsum verum.	Through the pentacle of Solomon I have summoned you; give me a true answer.

Then he should say:

Beralanensis, baldachiensis, Paumachiae et Apologie sedes per Reges potestatesque magnanimas, ac princepes prepotentes, genio liachidae, ministri tartareae sedis: primac hic princeps sedes Apologie, nona cohorte: ego vos Invoco et Invocando vos coniuro, atque supernae maiestatis munitus virtute potenter Impero per eum qui dixit et factum est, et cui obediunt omnes creaturae: et per hoc nomen ineffabile, + Tetragramaton + יהוה Iehovah in quo est plasmatum omne seculum, quo audito Elementa corruunt, Aer concu[t]itur, mare retrogradatur, ignis extinguiter terra tremit, omnesque exercitus	Beralanensis, Baldachiensis, Paumachia, and the seat of Apologia/justification, through the noble kings and powers, and the most powerful princes, with the Genii of Liachida, ministers of the Tartarean seat: Primac,* this prince of the seat of Apologia/justification, in the ninth court: I call upon you, and in calling upon you I conjure you, and protected by the strength of the heavenly majesty, I potently command you, through him who spoke, and it was done, and to whom all creations obey: And through this ineffable name + Tetragrammaton + יהוה Iehovah, by which all the world was formed, which

---

* Francis Barrett, *The Magus, or Celestial Intelligencer; Being a Complete System of Occult Philosophy* (1801), misreads "primae" (first).

celestium, terrestium et infernorum tremment, turbantur et corruunt: quatenus cito et sine mora et omni occasione remota, ab universis mundi partibus veniatis, et rationabilliter de omnibus quecunque interrogavero, respondeatis vos et veniatis pacifice visibiles, et affabiles: [et] nunc <et> sine mora manifestantes, quod cupimus: Coniurati per nomen eterni, vivi et veri dei Helioren [*Heliorem]: et mandata nostra perficientes, persistentes semper usque ad finem et intentionem meam, visibilis nobis et affabilis, clara voce, nobis intelligibili [et] sine omni ambiguitate.

being heard the elements crumble, the air shakes violently, the sea retreats, the fire is extinguished, the earth trembles, and all the celestial, terrestrial, and infernal armies tremble, are disturbed, and crumble: Therefore come quickly, and without delay, from all parts of the universe, setting aside all other matters, and answer reasonably everything that I will ask, and come peacefully, visibly and sympathetic, now without delay, revealing whatever we wish. Being conjured by the eternal name of the true and living God *Heliorem,[†] and fulfilling our orders, persisting always, all the way to the end, visible to us, and sympathetic to my intent, with a voice that is clear and intelligible to us, and without any ambiguity.[‡]

† Heliorem: H. has Helioṙe (with a tilde over the final e), which could be read "Heliorem" or "Helioren." However, since the form "Elyorem" occurs in LIH, JHP considers the former to be more correct (Gösta Hedegård, "97th name of God," *Liber Iuratus Honorii* [Stockholm: Almqvist, 2002], 112). RT (1655) and Francis Barrett (1801) both follow the reading in Agrippa, *Opera* I (Hildensheim: G. Olms, 1970): "Helioren."

‡ This passage from H. was also used in the *Lemegeton, Goetia*: first conjuration as seen in Peterson, *The Lesser Key of Solomon: Lemegeton Clavicula Salomonis: Detailing the Ceremonial Art of Commanding Spirits Both Good and Evil* (York Beach, ME: Weiser Books, 2001), 48.

Visions and apparitions

With these things duly completed, boundless visions will appear, and phantasms beating on devices and all sorts of musical instruments, and it is done by the spirits in order to terrify the associates and force them to flee from the circle, because they are able to face the master himself. After this you will see boundless archers with the boundless multitude of awful beasts, which compose themselves thus, as if they wish to devour the associates: However, they have nothing to fear. Then the priest or master, holding out his hand to the pentacle, should say:

fugiat hinc Iniquitas vestra virtute vexilli dei.	Cease your hostilities at once through the virtue of the banner of God.

And then the spirits will assemble to obey the master, and the associates will see nothing further.

Then the exorcist, holding his hand near the pentacle, should say:

Ecce Ecce pentaculum salomonis, quod ante vestram adduxi presentiam: Ecce personam exorcizatoris, in medio exorcismi, qui est optima a deo munitus, Intrepidus, providus, qui viribus potens vos exorcizando invocavit et vocat, ve[nite] ergo cum festinatione in virtute novum [*nominum] istorum, + Aye + Saraye + Aye + Saraye + ne differatis venire per nomina eterna dei vivi et veri + Eloy + Archima + Rabur + et per hoc presens pentaculum quod super vos potenter Imperat: et per virtutem celestium spirituum, dominorum vestrorum: et per personam Exorcizatoris, [+ coniurati, festinati venire, & obedire præceptori vestro qui vocatur Octinomos.]	Behold, behold the pentacle of Solomon, which I have brought before your presence: Behold the person of the exorcist in the middle of the exorcism, who has been very well fortified by God, unshaken, observant, who with mighty force has called upon you, and calls you with exorcising. Come therefore with haste, by the power of these names, + Aye + Saraye + Aye + Saraye + do not delay coming, through the eternal names of the true and living God + Eloy + Archima + Rabur + And through this present pentacle which rules potently over you: And through the power of the heavenly spirits, of your lords, and through the person of the exorcist, [+ being conjured, hasten to come and obey your master, who is called Octinomos.]*
* The last line of text is cut off, but has been included per H.	

(Look into the second leaf for the rest which followeth this.) [23]

[+ Excerpts from the *Enchiridion*] [24]

    [21]

---

23. Text is in marg. in a different handwriting. The text from H. resumes after the "Little Book" section, i.e., the heading "The Rest as Follows" on Folger p. 24.

24. In the marg. is ⊕ in same brown ink as the anchor glyph on Folger pp. 19, 48, 56, and 63. This section is excerpted from the *Enchiridion* of Pope Leo III, said to have been printed first at Rome (1523), with multiple printings between 1584 and 1633 (Christian, *History* cited by Waite, *The Book of Ceremonial Magic* [Secaucus: Citadel, 1911]). Beneath this, in pencil, is a marginal note "[Here] begins (?) a new book—see bottom of 20."

Here beginneth the little book

Rogo vos omnes sanctos et sanctas martires, confessores [&] virgines dei ut intercedatis pro me miser[o] peccatore a[d] dominum nostrum Iesum Christum qui cum patre + et spiritu sancto vivit et regnat in eternum ut su[u]m mihi dignetur concedere regnum Amen deus Abraham + deus Isaac + deus Iacob + deus Moysis + deus Aaron + deus helia + deus Noe + Iste deus mecum sit Amen Angelus Michaell angelus gabriell, angelus Raphael, Arcangelus cherubin atque seraphion Isti angelei Isti arcangeli et omnes sancti [sint] in adiutorum meum omnibus diebus vite mea [ut] deus meus <ut> omnipoten[s] me producat ad vitam eternam Amen + Amedum + tanstos + tanstazo + berachedio + memor + gedita + Eleyson + maton + egion + erigam + fides + veloy + unit + Regnas + sadan + hagios + otheos + sanctos deus agios + Isquiros + sanctos fortis + agios + Athanatos + Elishon hima[s] + sanctus immortalis miserere mihi + peccatori Amen + Angeli michaell + Raphael + Urie[l] + gabriel + barachel + cherubin + seraphin + intercedite pro me ecce cruce[m] domini fugite[s] partes adversae

I ask all of you saints, both male and female, martyrs, confessors, and virgins of God, to intercede with our Lord Jesus Christ, who with the Father and the Holy Spirit lives and reigns forever, on behalf of me, a wretched sinner, that I may be deemed worthy to enter his kingdom. Amen. O God of Abraham + God of Isaac + God of Jacob + God of Moses + God of Aaron + God of Elijah + God of Noah + may the same God be with me. Amen. May the angel Michael, the angel Gabriel, the angel Raphael, archangels, cherubim and seraphim, these same angels, archangels, and all of the saints aid me all the days of my life, in order that my all-powerful God may lead me to eternal life. Amen. + Amedum + tanstos + tanstazo + berachedio + memor + gedita + Eleyson* + maton + egion + erigam + fides + veloy + unit + Regnas† + sadan + "hagios + otheos + Holy God + agios + Isquiros + Holy Strong + agios + Athanatos + Elishon hima[s] +‡ O Holy Immortal, have pity on me,"§ a sinner. Amen. O you angels Michael, Raphael, Uriel, Gabriel, Barachel, the Cherubim and Seraphim, intercede

---

* *Eleyson*: Gk. "have mercy"

† *Fides … Unit + Regnas:* "Faith … unites, you reign"

‡ In marg. there are the symbols ☽ ☽.

§ *Hagios otheos … himas, have mercy on me:* This is the ancient Greek Trisagion prayer, but it was also used in the Latin liturgy. More properly, *Agios o Theos, Agios ischyros, Agios athanatos, eleison imas*, with Latin translation interspersed: *Sanctus Deus, Sanctus Fortis, Sanctus Immortalis, miserere nobis* ["Holy God, Holy Strong, Holy Immortal, have mercy on us"].

tua Iudica me + qui das salutem regibus qui redemisti david servum tuum de gladio maligno eripe me + Christus vincit + Christus regnat + Christus Imperat + Christus ab omni malo me defendat Amen.

for me. Behold the Cross of the Lord! Flee ye adversaries! The Lion from the Tribe of Judah, the Root of David, has conquered, alleluia!⁋ Deliver me from my enemies,** O God and from the workers of iniquity, and from those who are after my blood. Amen. O God, in your name save me, and in your strength judge me.†† Just as you save kings, just as you redeemed your servant David, so rescue me from the sword of the wicked. Christ conquers, Christ reigns, Christ commands; may Christ defend me from all evil. Amen.

⁋ The short exorcistic poem *ecce cruce … alleluia* ["Behold the Cross of the Lord! Flee ye adversaries! The Lion of the Tribe of Juda, the Root of David has conquered, alleluia!"], known as "St. Anthony's Brief" dates to the thirteenth century. It is based on Apoc. 5:5. It is also found in the "Dismissio jesuitarum" section of *Verus Jesuitarum Libellus* ["The True Petition of the Jesuits"]. Pope Pius VI had these words carved in the Pagan obelisk in St. Peter's Square in 1586.
** Psalm 142:9 (KJV 143:9).
†† Psalm 54:1 (KJV).

Otheos in nomine tuo saluum me fac: Hagios delictum meum cognitum tibi feci, et iniusticias meas non abscondi. Sanctus, sanctus, sanctus, da mihi intellectum et instrue me te adorare, glorificare, et magnificare: Otheos, Elyson, iudica me noce[n]tes domine leo fortis, expugna impugnantes me: Messias, Sother: Emanuell, qui inteprecator [*interpretatis] nobiscum deus, aprehenda [*apprehende] arma et scutum, Iesu salva me et exurge in adiutorum mihi, panis, flos, lux, laus, lancea, mens, ianua, petra, lapis

Otheos, in your name save me. Hagios, I have acknowledged my faults to you, and I have not hidden my injustices.* Holy, holy, holy. Teach me and give me the understanding to honour, glorify, and praise you: Otheos, Elyson, judge the guilty; O Lord, O mighty Lion, overthrow those who are attacking me: Messiah, Sother, Emanuel, which means "God is with us," take hold of arms and shield, O Jesus save me, and rise up to help me,† bread, flower, light, praise, lance, mind, gate, rock, gemstone, O Athanatos, "draw your

* Psalm 31:5 (KJV 32:5).
† Compare Psalm 34:2 (KJV 35:1).

Athanatos, "effunde frameam esquiros, et conclude adversus eos qui me persecuuntur," Iesu salvator, dic animae meae, salus tua ego sum: verus panton pantastron creatori, ne tradideris me in manibus inimicos meos, sabaoth, "eripe me de inimicis meis, deus deus et ab insurgentibus in me libera me." Flecte pias auras [*aures] Christe ad praeces meas, et veni, et libera me ex affligentibus, et calumniantibus me. Iesu, vidi [*vide] angustias et miser[i]as, quas pro peccatis meis digne patior, et a peccato meo munda me: accelera et asperge me hissopo stilantis [*stillantis] gratiae tua [*tuae], ut spiritus fornicationis in me potenter extinguat, et ad omne opus bonum perceneratur [*perseveranter] accendat per virtutem patris, [et] filii, et spiritus sancti qui es eternus, et sine fine regnas in secula seculorum, Amen.

sword, Ischiros, and block the way of those who persecute me,"‡ O Jesus our Saviour, say to my soul "I am your salvation," O true Panton Pantastron Creator, deliver me not over to the hands of my enemies, Sabaoth, "deliver me from my enemies, God O my God, and defend me from those who rise up against me."§ Turn your holy ears, O Christ to my prayers, and come and free me from my afflictions and false accusations. O Jesus, witness my anguish and misery, which I rightly suffer because of my sins, and cleanse me from my sins. Hasten and sprinkle me with droplets of hyssop of your grace, in order that the spirit of fornication is forcefully extinguished from me, and enflame me to be steadfast in all good works, through the virtue of the Father, and of the Son, and of the Holy Ghost. You are eternal, and you reign unto the ages, world without end. Amen.

‡ Compare Psalm 34:3 (KJV 35:3).
§ Psalm 58:2 (KJV 59:1).

+ Agla + pentagrammaton + on + Athanatos + anasacron + on + pentateon + fama + crux + agratan + grex + lux + telasustus + hominis + tomon + Tetragrammaton + Iesus + deus + dominatur + omnium + misericors + altissimis + salvator meus libera me famulum tuum J B per hec tua nomina sancta

+ Agla + pentagrammaton + on + Athanatos + anasacron + on + pentateon + fame + cross + agratan + the flock + the light + telasustus + the book + of man + Tetragrammaton + Jesus + God + master of all + merciful + most high + save me, free me your slave, J. B.,* through these holy names of yours,

* For "J. B." ELP reads "N."

qui[a] ego indignus seruus tuus sum, te vocans sed tu domine qui ubiqui es, reminiscere miseratione tuas et libera me [ab] Insidiis Inimicos meos, visibilum et Invisibilum et per hanc virtutem sancte crucis et omni sanctorum suorum [*tuorum] + Iesus ante [*autem] transiens per medium illorum ibat Iesu Christi fili [D]ei vivi + miserere mei Amen.

because I am your unworthy servant. I call upon you, but you O Lord, who are everywhere, recollect your mercy, and free me from the snares of my enemies, visible and invisible, and through the virtue of this holy cross, and all your saints. + But Jesus passing through their midst went his way.[†] O Jesus Christ, son of the living God + have mercy on me. Amen.

† Luke 4:30. This motto is frequently seen on rings, coins, and amulets.

+ Crux Christi salua me + crux Christi protege me + crux Christi ab omni malo me defende + Iudica domine nocentes me + deus fortis expugnantes mihi + deus messia[s] + sabaoth + sother + Emanuell + apprehenda arma et scutum deus sabaoth dominus n[ost]re Iesus Christus eripe me de luto et non infingat [*infigar] + deus sanctus libera me de profundo Aquarum + o salus nostra ne absorbeat me profundum maris + o athanatos ne me ardeat furor ignis + exaltatio mea ne aperiat puteus putridicnis [*putredinis] super me os suum sed os meum redemptio me aperi et conclude adversus eos qui me persecuntur + Athanatos dic animae [meae] salus tua ego sum + o tetragrammaton + ne tradideris me in manibus Inimicorum meorum + o sabaoth eripe me ab insurgentibus in me, o Iesu salvator seculi salva me + panis uiuus + flos Incommu[n]tabilis

+ O cross of Christ save me; O cross of Christ protect me + O cross of Christ defend me from all evil. + Judge them that wrong me + O God, and fight against me. + God + Messias + Sabaoth + Sother + Emanuel + Take up arms and shields. God Sabaoth,[*] our Lord Jesus Christ , deliver me. Draw me out of the mire, that I may not be held fast. Holy God, deliver me out of the deep waters. + O Our Salvation, let not the deep sea swallow me. + O Athanatos, let not the raging fires burn me. + O Exaltation, do not let the putrid well of their mouth open wide against me,[†] but open my mouth, O my redemption, and close that of those who attack me. + Athanatos, say to my soul, "I am your salvation."[‡] + O Tetragrammaton + do not deliver me into the hands of my enemies. + O Sabaoth, deliver me from those who rise up against me. O Jesus, saviour of the

* *Sabaoth*: Gk. "of hosts."
† Compare Psalm 68:15–16 (KJV 69:14–15).
‡ Compare Psalm 34:3 (KJV 35:3).

+ virtus et Ianua paradisi + benedictio sancte mariae virginis cum fillio tuo sit super me benedictio domini nostri Iesu Christi cum suis sanctis Apostolis sit super me + benedictio super [*spiritus] sancti sit super me + benedictio sancti trinitatis, patris et filii et spiritusancti sit super me + benedictio sancte Catherine montis <montis> sinay sit super me + benedictio omnium sanctorum angelorum arcangelorum, patriarcharum prophetarum apostolorum evangelisticarum martirum virginium monachorum, pontificum sit super me Amen.

world, save me. + Bread of Life + Unchanging Flower + Virtue and Gate of Paradise + may the blessing of the holy Virgin Mary with her Son be upon me. May the blessing of our Lord Jesus Christ with his holy apostles be upon me. + May the blessing of the Holy Ghost be upon me. + May the blessing of the holy Trinity, Father, Son, and Holy Ghost be upon me. + May the blessing of Saint Catherine of Mount Sinai be upon me. + May the blessing of all saints, angels, archangels, patriarchs, prophets, apostles, evangelists, martyrs, virgins, monks, and popes be upon me. Amen.

hagios invisibilis dominus per tuum nomen oston, obsecro te adiuua me de morte sucurrere mihi ad te clamanti[s] peccatori + Tetragrammaton sicut tu es rex regum et dominus dominantium deus pater et in alio non habeo spem nisi in te deus deus [*meus] quia<m> celestia simull et terrena gubernas et moderaris te deprecor miserere mihi peccatori et libera me J b de inimicis meis visibilis et Invisibilis domine sis miserator mihi gebam, suth, sutam, in nomine patris + et filii + et spiritus sancti + amen primum nomen dei est on secundum est othon, et quando dixit dominus fiat lux tertium nomen est lophias + in nomine

O Hagios, invisible Lord, through your name Oston, I entreat you to help me from death, and to assist me, a sinner who cried out* to you. Tetragrammaton, so as you are king of kings, and Lord of Lords, God the father, and I have no hope in any thing, except in you my God, because you govern and guide the heavens and earth simultaneously, I beg you to have mercy on me, a sinner, and free me J. B. from my enemies, visible and invisible, O Lord, please be merciful to me Gebam, Suth, Sutam, in the name of the Father, and of the Son, and of the Holy Ghost. Amen. The first name of God is On, the second is Othon, and when

* *Clamanti* ["to/with the proclaiming"]: Reading "clamantis," which fits better. ELP reads *clementi* ["to/with the merciful"], which doesn't seem to fit any better.

domini et individue trinitatis + antaciton + Iturrensis grin Adonay salua me thedes et ei et dotheos Adoney [*Adonay] Amen	the Lord said, "let there be light" [it was]; the third name is Lophias. + In the name of the Lord, and inseparable Trinity + Antaciton + Iturrensis Grin Adonay, save me Thedes, and Ei, and Dotheos *Adonay. Amen.

Per signum domine tau libera me   ["Deliver me, O Lord, by the sign + Tau."][26]

[+ Conjuration of all types of weapons][27]

In nomine patris et filii et spiritusancti Amen. In nomine sancte et individue trinitatis Amen. + coniuro vos omni[a] genera Armorum gladios cultellos bipennis, lanceas clavos omnia genera armorum et mettellorum per patrem et filium et spiritum sanctum ut non ledatis me J b neque sanguinem meum effundatis donec tertegit [*ter tetigerit] ex praeceptis meis que ceedunt	In the name of the Father, and of the Son, and of the Holy Ghost, Amen. + In the name of the holy and indivisible Trinity, Amen. I conjure you, all types of weapons—swords, knives, battle-axes, lances, spikes, all types of weapons and metals, through the Father, and the Son, and the Holy Ghost, that you may not harm me J. B., nor spill my blood. Unless I have touched them three times, and at

---

25. Tau cross from ELP.

26. Compare ELP p. 92; also compare Arthur Edward Waite, *The Book of Ceremonial Magic* (Secaucus: Citadel, 1911), 44 and figure 1.

27. Compare ELP p. 92; also compare 1623 Sicilian charms in Gaetano Millunzi and Salvatore Salomone-Marino, eds., "Un Processo di Stregoneria nel 1623 in Sicilia" *Archivio Storico Siciliano* 25 (1900): 268 and 356.

scindunt dum sunt in manu mea, sic ad manus meas omnia genera armorum prospera [ad] [22] Aliorum, pervenerunt, tunc sicut sera liquescant + Iterum coniuro vos omnia genera armorum per ferream lanceam qua longuis [*Longinus] latus domini nostri Iesu Christi perforauit exiuire [*exiere] sanguis et aqua ut me J B non ledatis neque sanguinem meum effundatis + Iterum coniuro vos per Columnam in qua dominus nostre Iesus Christus ligatus fuit et adductus ante Iudica ut me J b non ledatis neque sanguinem meum effundatis + Iterum coniuro vos per tres clavos qui manus et pedes domini nostri Iesu Christi transfiexerunt ut me J b non ledatis neque sanguinem meum effundatis + Iterum coniuro vos omnia genera armorum per carticcula [*craticulam] ferream in qua sanctus lawrentius Assatus fuit ut me J B non ledatis neque sanguinem meum effundatis + Iterum coniuro vos omnia genera armorum per gladium quo sanct[us] paulus fuit decapitatus ut me J b non ledatis neque sanguinem meum effundatis + Iterum coniuro vos per ferreu[m] ligamen quo ligata fuit beata agnes duobus annis et cum eo cruciavit + ut me non ledatis neque sanguinem meum effundatis + Iterum coniuro vos omnia genera armorum, per equuleum ferreum quo beata Agatha suspensa fuit ut me J b non

my command, they will succeed in striking or cutting while they are in my hand, but in the hands of *[22]* others they melt like wax. + Again I conjure all you types of weapons, by the iron spear which Longinus used to pierce the side of our Lord Jesus Christ, and blood and water emerged,* that you not harm me J. B., nor spill my blood. + Again I conjure you by the pillar which our Lord Jesus Christ was tied to, after being brought before the judges, that you not harm me J. B., nor spill my blood. + Again I conjure you by the three nails, which pierced the hands and feet of our Lord Jesus Christ, that you not harm me J. B., nor spill my blood. + Again I conjure all you types of weapons, by the iron gridiron on which Saint Lawrence was roasted, that you not harm me J. B., nor spill my blood. + Again I conjure all you types of weapons, by the sword with which Saint Paul was beheaded, that you not harm me J. B., nor spill my blood. + Again I conjure you, by the iron shackles with which the blessed Agnes was bound and tortured for two years, that you not harm me, nor spill my blood. + Again I conjure all you types of weapons, through the iron torture-rack on which the blessed Agatha was suspended, that you not harm me J. B., nor spill my blood. + Again I conjure all you swords and knives, arrows and battle-axes, and

* John 19:35.

ledatis neque sanguinem meum effundatis + Iterum coniuro vos omnes gladios et culltellos, sagittas et bypennes et omnia genera armorum per omnia nomina sancta dei et manifesta, + Iterum coniuro vos per septuaginta nomina dei et per sanctum nomine dei qui omne [*regit] celum et terram et omnia qua in eis sunt quid est interna [*eterna] vel huiusmodi gloria [*glorie] + et coniuro vos per sanctum nomen dei + si mandolum in quo Iosue vicit duodecem reges + Iterum coniuro vos per sanctum nomen dei Tetragrammaton + lot + ser + neot + nain + he + Iterum coniuro vos per omnia gaudia ac dolores beata Marie semper virginis + et coniuro vos per omnes apostoles evangelistas, martires et per viginti 4or seniores et per omnes doctores confessores manachos et hermitas et per omnes virgines et viduas et omnes santos et sanctas dei et per Iuramentum domini nostri Iesu Christi et

all types of weapons, through all the holy and revealed names of God. + Again I conjure you through the seventy[†] names of God, and through the sacred name of God, whereby he governs[‡] heaven and earth, and everything that is in them, and which is internal [*eternal], or of this kind of glory.[§] And I conjure you through the holy name of God + Si mandolum,[¶] by which Joshua conquered the twelve kings. Again I conjure you by the holy name of God Tetragrammaton + Lot + Ser + Neot + Nain + He. Again I conjure you by all the joys and sorrows of blessed Mary, perpetual virgin + and I conjure you by all apostles, evangelists, martyrs, and by the twenty-four seniors/elders,[**] and by all teachers, clergy, monks, hermits, and by all virgins and widows, and by all the saints of God, and through the oath of our Lord Jesus Christ, and through these true and most sacred words, with which nobody has the

---

† So also Millunzi and Salomone-Marino, eds., "Un Processo di Stregoneria nel 1623 in Sicilia" *Archivio Storico Siciliano* 25 (1900): 253–379, and ELP p. 94. Perhaps an error for seventy-two, as in the oration that follows. Cecchetelli's *Crossed Keys* p. 140 reads "seventy-two." Dumas's *Grimoires et rituels magiques* reads "soixante" (sixty), p. 67, column 2.

‡ *Qui omne:* Reading *qui regit* as in Millunzi, *Archivo Storico Siciliano* 25 (1900): 358; Millunzi, *Archivo Storico Siciliano* 25 (1900): 269 and 356: *qui amat* ["who loves"]; ELP p. 94: *qui ima*t ["which but yet?"]; Dumas's *Grimoires*, p. 67: *qui aime* ["who loves"]; Cecchetelli's *Crossed Keys*, p. 140: "who governs."

§ Millunzi, *Archivo Storico Siciliano* 25 (1900): 269 and 356, and ELP p. 94 read "*eterne ... *glorie*"; Millunzi, *Archivo Storico Siciliano* 25 (1900): 358 reads: *et sunt calcolus, motus glorie* ["and they are calculated, glorious movements"].

¶ *nomen dei + si mandolum in quo Iosue vicit duodecem reges*: included in Millunzi, *Archivo Storico Siciliano* 25 (1900): 356, as *nomen Dei + et manicolum in quo Isac* [sic] *vincit duobus* [sic] *regis* ["name of God + and manicles by which Isaac conquered the two kings"]. The passage is not found in Dumas.

** *Vigintiquattuor seniores* ["twenty-four elders"]: See Revelations 4:4.

per illa vera et sacratissima verba quibus potestatem nemo habet ledendum vulnerandi atque sanguinem effundendi + ego enim transiens per medium illorum ibo + ecce crucem domini fugite per te adversa vincit leo de tribu Iuda Radex David + per signum crucis de Inimicos nostris libera nos deus noster salue + crux presiosa suspice me per eum qui pependit in te + spiritus sapientie + et intellectus + et spiritus consilii et fortitudinis + spiritus scientia + pietatis + spiritus timoris domini protege et defende me J b ab omnibus culltellus + ab eorum vulneribus et ab omnibus gladiis + et ab omnibus lanceis et ab omnibus telis et sagittas et ab omnibus generibus armorum pretege me J b + salva [me] benedic + me + sanctifica me + per signacullum crucis, vulnera omni[um] armorum anecte [*auerte] a me J b + quinque vulnere fillii dei custodiant me + hely + heloy + het + clavis + gon + eth + huc + proth + + + ceratus ++ feros + homo + Rex glorie venit in pace + verbum caro est et habitauit in nobis et videmus gloriam dei [*eius gloriam] quasi unigeniti a patre plenum gratie et veritatis Amen.

power required to strike and cause a wound or blood to flow. + I therefore passing through their midst, will go my way.* Behold the Cross of the Lord! Flee ye adversaries! The Lion from the Tribe of Judah, the Root of David has conquered, alleluia! Deliver us O our God. + Behold the precious cross, hold me up, through him who was hanged upon you + O spirits of wisdom + and comprehension + and spirits of council and strength + O spirits of knowledge + of piety + O spirits of the fear of the Lord, protect and defend me, J. B. from all knives + from their wounding, and from all swords + and from all lances, and from all darts and arrows, and from all types of weapons, protect me, J. B., + save [me], bless + me + sanctify me + through the seal of the cross, avert the wounds of all weapons from me J. B. + The five wounds of the Son of God guard me + Hely + Heloy + Het + Clavis + gon + Eth + Huc + proth + + + Ceratus ++ Feros + Homo† + O King of Glory, come in peace. + The Word was [made] flesh, and dwelled among us. We have seen [his glory], the glory of the only begotten Son, who came from the Father, full of grace and truth.‡ Amen.

---

* Paraphrase of Luke 4:30, well represented on charms and coins, as mentioned above.

† ELP p. 96: "Hely + Heloy + Het + Clavis + Egon + Eth + Huc + Proh. + Rx + Ceratas + A. + Feros + Homo." Dumas, *Grimoires*, p. 68: "heli, heloy, het, *clavis*, hegon, eth, hue. Proth, cetcras, *feros*, *homo*." Millunzi, *Archivo Storico Siciliano* 25 (1900): 357: "Egon + Heu + Proh + R/ + ceratas + A. + lotos + homo." Millunzi, *Archivo Storico Siciliano* 25 (1900): 358: "agras + tue + proh + R/ + ceratus + A. + eros + homo." Millunzi, *Archivo Storico Siciliano* 25 (1900): 270: "Egon + Heu + Proh + R/ + Ceratas + A. + Jotos + homo."

‡ John 1:14.

Precious, especially for strength [28]

In nomine sancte trinitatis et Indevidue Unitatis, patris et filii et spiritus sancti coniuro vos omnia genera armorum per patrem et filium et spiritusanctum coniuro vos bacculos gladios lanceas ences cultellos sagittas claves funes et omnia alia genera armorum per septuaginta duo nomina et per eius virtutes et potentias et per ferream lanceam cum quo long[in]us latus domini perforavit et exiuit sanguis et aqua et per ista sanctissima nomina + Ioth + hec + van + hee + ut me famulum tuum J b non ledatis neque sanguinem meum effundatis, coniuro vos omnia genera armosi supradictorum per ista sanctissima nomina dei + hel + ya + hye + eado + Ebore + Eloym + Agla + Agiel + Azez + sadon + esul + helox + holoyx + delis + yevi + yacerdel + yosi + helym + rasael + paliel + manuel + oneha + dilaton + axday + alma + panix + Alim catinal + utanzaraf + zalphi + eala + ealsali + saffna + hictimi + sed + dar + agla + aglaia + pamiel + paninon + oniel + on + homon + eteoi + lestram + panteon + bamboy + ya + Emanuell + yoth + Intasi + om + via + caliphlon + ysrael + mel +	In the name of the holy Trinity and undivided Unity, Father and Son and Holy Ghost. I conjure you all types of weapons, by the Father and Son and Holy Ghost. I conjure you clubs, short swords, lances, long swords, knives, arrows, nails, ropes, and all other types of weapons, by the seventy-two names and by their strength and power, and by the iron lance which Longinus used to pierce the side of the Lord and draw blood and water, and by this most holy name: + Ioth + Hee + *Vau + Hee + that you will not strike me, your slave J. B., nor draw my blood. I conjure all types of weapons mentioned above, through these most holy names of God: * Hel + Ya + Hye + Eado + Ebore + Eloym + Agla + Agiel + Azez + Sadon + Esul + Helox + Holoyx + Delis + Yevi + Yacerdel + Yosi + Helym + Rasael + Paliel + Manuel + oneha + dilaton + axday + alma + panix + Alim Catinal + Utanzaraf + Zalphi + Eala + Ealsali + Saffna + Hictimi + Sed + Dar + Agla + Aglaia + Pamiel + Paninon + Oniel + On + Homon + Eteoi[†] + Lestram + Panteon + Bamboy + Ya + Emanuell + Yoth + Intasi + Om + Via +

* Compare *Liber Sepher Razielis*, Seventh Semiphoras, in Peterson, *The Sixth and Seventh Books of Moses*, 268–269.

† No dot over the "i."

---

28. This prayer can be found on ELP p. 107.

eyel + piel + patriteron + safaron + lenion + yael + ut me famulum tuum J b no[n] ledo [*ledatis] neque sanguinem meum effundatis os non comminuetis ex eo "dextera domini fecit virtutem dextera domini exaltauit me non moriar sed vivam et narabo opera domini castegans castigauit me dominus et morte non traddit me" Amen benedicamus domino deo gratias.

Caliphlon + Ysrael + Mel + Eyel + Piel + Patriteron + Safaron + Lenion + Yael +* that you not strike me, your slave J. B., not draw my blood. Crush not my bones. "The right hand of the Lord has created strength. The right hand of the Lord has exalted me: I shall not die, but live, and proclaim the works of the Lord. In chastising me, the Lord has punished me, but did not hand me over to death."† Amen. May we bless the Lord. By the grace of God.‡

* Dumas's *Grimoires* p. 69: *Hel, Ya, Haye, Yac, Va, Adonai, Cados, Ebrore, Heloina, Agla, Agiel, Azoz, Sadon, Esul, Heloi, Helox, Heloix et Delis, Veni, Jacer, Del, Yosi, Helim, Rosaël, Sasael, Paliel, Mammier, Oucha, Dilaron, Zaday, Alma, Davix, Azim, Catinal, Vransara Fi, Zaphi, Ela, Calfasi, Saffua, Hictimi, Sed, Dar, Agla, Aglaja, Pamiel, Panuion, Oniel, On, Homon, Oreon, Lestram, Pantheon, Bambry, Ya, Emmanuel, Voth, Julaf, Oin, Via, Caliph, Leo, Israël, Miel, Eyel, Pyel, Patriteron, Sazaron, Lenion, Yael, Eyel, Lulapti, Calsali, Yeni.* ELP p. 108–9: *hei + ya + hye + yae + va + adonay + cados + oborel + eloym + agla + agiel + azel + sadon + esul + heloy + heloyn + delis + + yeuy + yacer + del + yosi + helim + rasuël + rasaël + palile + mammiel + oncha + dilaton + xaday + alma + pavix + alim + cutival + utauzaraf + zaphi + cala + carsaly + faffua + hictimi + sed + der + agla + aglaia + pamiel & pannion + oniel + on + homon + oreon + lestram + panteon + bamboy + ya + emanuel + yoth + lulaf + on + via + caliph + lon + ysraël + miel + cyel + pyeel + patriteron + fafaron + leuyon + yael.*

† *Psalm 117:15–18 (KJV 118:15–18).*

‡ There is a note pencilled in marg. next to this paragraph reading: "this left out."

Prayers [29] against all worldly dangers

The apostle Saint Thomas and Leonard [30] wrote to Charles, king of France, saying: "Whoever wears these names on himself cannot be harmed by their mortal enemies, nor will he be able to harm them. And note, this writing contains a name Agla, a name of Christ, and it is said that whoever sees, speaks, or carries it, will not die an evil death that day, and if any sick person wears it around their neck, they will enjoy health, and a pregnant woman who ties it over her stomach will be free of pain.

---

29. Compare ELP pp. 109–110.

30. This text is not clear in Folger, so we have followed the reading from Dumas, *Grimoires*, 69.

In nomine patris + et fillii + et spiritusancti + Amen surge causa ad iuvandum nos et trinitas atque indiuisa unitas + unus deus + sabaoth + Adonay + coteraton + yson + son + lon + con + son + osiam + solus + vita + via + veritas sapientia + ego sum + qui sum qui est + agnus + ouis + vitulus + serpens + Aries + leo + vermis + sol + Agla + Imago + panis + vita + flos + mons + Ianua + fons + petra + lapis + angelus + pastor + propheta + sacerdos + sanctus + Imortalia rex maior + primus sum + secundu[s] leo + tertius flos + quartus obise + quintus terre + sextus premax + septimus sagal + octauus bethelen + nonus Tetragrammaton + desimus seloy + undecimus hely + duodecimus legon + athanatos + heloy satus + ecanto + himas + Eleison + salvator + α + et ω + primogenitus + principium + paracletus + mediator + verbum + ysquiros + gloria + lux + mundus + Angularis + sanctus + et Imortali + Iesus + pater + filius + omnipotens + spiritusanctus + misericors + candor + eternum creator + redemptor + magni consilii + Angelus + trinus + et unus deus + dominancium + deus deorum + deus Ineffabilis + deus Incomprehensibilis + Iudex Iustus +

In the name of the Father + and of the Son + and of the Holy Ghost + Amen. Arise for our cause, and help us, and The Trinity and undivided Unity + One God + Sabaoth + Adonay + coteraton + yson + son + lon + con + son + osiam + only + Life + The Way + The Truth, Wisdom + I am + who I am + who is + Lamb* + The Egg + The Calf + The Worm + Aries + Leo + The Ram + The Sun + Agla + The Image + The Bread + The Life + The Flower + The Mountain + The Gate + The Fountain + The Rock + The Stone + The Angel + The Shepherd + The Prophet + The Priest + Holy Immortal Great King + The First I am + The Second Lion + The Third Flower + The Fourth The Bolt + The Fifth The Earth + The Sixth Premax + The Seventh Sagal + The Eighth Bethelen + The Ninth Tetragrammaton + The Tenth Seloy + The Eleventh Hely + The Twelfth Legon + Athanatos† + Heloy satus + Ecanto + Himas + Eleison‡ + Saviour + The Alpha and Omega + First Born + The First + The Paraclete ("Advocate") + The Mediator + The Word + Ischiros§ + Glory + Light + The World + The Corner + Holy + and Immortal + Jesus + Father + Son + Almighty + Holy Ghost + Merciful + Whiteness + eternally The Creator +

---

* LIH has a shortened version of this.
† *Athanatos*: Gk. "immortal."
‡ *Eleison*: Gk. "have mercy."
§ *Ischiros*: Gk. "mighty."

| | Redeemer + Great Advisor + Angel + Threefold + and One God + being Master + God of Gods + God ineffable + God incomprehensible + Just Judge +. |

| et semper in praelio in mari vel in aqua gedebilone S C q. p. et semper itur [23] In bello rex Iudiorum miserere nobis ille luya [*alleluya] precor sanctissime domine deus per tuu [*tua] [??] sanctissima nomina deprecor te ut exaudeas me et custodias me ab omni malo ab omni periculo et adversitate diaboli ut eruas me hic et in futurum deus Abraham, deus Isaac, deus Iacob, deus Angelorum deus Archangelorum deus apostolorum deus martirum deus confessorum deus virginum deus omni sanctorum, deus hatharatorum et omnes sancti et sancte dei et Electe [*electi] dei intercedant pro me J b ad dominum deum nostrum Jesum Christum qui pius et clemens qui mitis et humilis corde qui non vult mortem peccatoris nec delectatur in perdicione peccatorum Amen | And always have mercy on us in battle, by sea or water, Gedebilone S. C. q. p.* and going [23] to war. O king of the Jews, have mercy on us, alleluyah. I pray O most holy Lord God, through your most holy names, I beg you to hear me, and guard me from all evil, from all danger, and from the adversity of the devil, that might threaten me now or in the future. O God of Abraham, God of Isaac, God of Jacob, God of the angels, God of the archangels, God of the Apostles, God of the martyrs, God of the clergy, God of the virgins, God of all the saints, God of the Hatharats (?),† and all the saints and elect of God, who intervene for me J. B. before our Lord God Jesus Christ, who is kind and merciful, who is gentle and humble of heart, who doesn't wish the death of a sinner, nor delights in the destruction of sinners. Amen. |

* ELP reads "Gedebelone S. E. Q. P." meaning unknown.

† *Hatharatorum*: Perhaps *patriarchorum* ["of the patriarchs"] best fits the context. ELP p. 112 reads *Catharactorum*; Dumas's *Grimoires* reads *Cataractes* ["waterfalls"].

Prayer against arrows [31]

| Coniuro te sagittam per charitatem et per flagellacionem dominum nostri Iesu Christi o sagitta sta per celum et terram et stellas et planetas o sagitta sta | I conjure you, O arrow, by charity, and by the whipping of our Lord Jesus Christ. Halt, O arrow, by the heavens and earth and stars and planets. Halt, O |

31. ELP p. 116. Compare Willy Louis Braekman, *Middeleeuwse witte en zwarte magie in het Nederlands taalgebied: gecommentarieerd compendium van incantamenta tot einde 16de eeuw* (Gent: Koniklijke Academie voor Nederlandse Taal- en Letterkunde, 1997), 302.

per sepulcrum dominum nostri Jesu Christi o sagitta sta per resurrectionem dominum Jesu Christi o sagitta sta per celum et terram et stellas et planetas celi et universa que in celo et in terra sunt et per trimendum die Iuditii et per virginitatem corporis domini nostri Iesu Christi et corporis gloriosissima virginis mariae o sagitta sta per sanctissima trinitate Amen.	arrow, by the tomb of our Lord Jesus Christ. Halt, O arrow, by the resurrection of our Lord Jesus Christ. Halt, O arrow, by the heavens and earth, by the stars and planets in the heavens, and by the worlds which are within the heavens and earth, and by the terrible Day of Judgment, and by the virginity of the body of our Lord Jesus Christ, and by the glorious body of the Virgin Mary. Halt, O arrow, by the most Holy Trinity. Amen.

If you are uncertain about the words written above, you can attach them to the neck of some animal, and then bring them to a place where you can test it, and you will see that they will not be harmed.

Pax domini nostri Iesu Christi mecum sit cum potestate heliae prophete, o sagitta sta o sagitta per virtutem sancte marie virginis et per caput sancti Iohannis baptista et per duodecem apostolos et per 4or evangelistes et per martires et confessores virgines et vidas dei et angelos et arcangelos dei o sagitta sta per deum vivum per deum verum et per deum sanctum et per illum deum qui ex nihil[o] cuncta creavit o sagitta sta per annunciacionem domini nostri Iesu Christi o saggita sta per ineffabile memoria Iesu Christi ut non noceas mihi famulum dei J B . 2. + 1 + q + g . 2.2.2 . 1 . m . α + et ω + Emanuell + non intret gladius in carnem meam, sit natus [*nutus]	The peace of our Lord Jesus Christ be with me, with the power of the prophet Elijah. Halt, O arrow. O arrow, by the virtue of the holy Virgin Mary, and by the head of Saint John the Baptist, and by the twelve apostles, and by the four evangelists, and by the martyrs, confessors, virgins, widows, angels, and archangels. Halt, O arrow, by the living God, by the true God, by the holy God, by that God who created [all things] from nothing. Halt, O arrow, by the annunciation of our Lord Jesus Christ. Halt, O arrow, by the ineffable memory of Jesus Christ, may you not harm me, a servant of God, J. B. 2. + 1 + q + g . 2.2.2 . 1 . m . Alpha + and Omega + Emanuell +

per Iesum gubernatorem meum dominum nostrum Iesum Christum ut non habeat gladius potestatem in famulum tuum J b Amen. //	May the sword not enter my flesh, it is deflected by Jesus my governor, our Lord Jesus Christ, that the sword has no power over your servant, J. B. Amen.

Iudica deus nocentes me expugna impugnantes me, aprehenda arma et scutum et surge [*exsurge] in adiutorum meum [*mihi.] et in auxilium mei famulum dei J b + amen + tate + aiti + aitæti + custodiat me famulum tuum + ab omni malo et periculo mortis Amen	Judge those who harm me; overthrow those who fight against me. Take up arms and shield, and arise to help me,* and assist me, J. B., a servant of God. Amen. + Tate + Aiti + Aitaeti + Protect me your servant + from all evil and mortal danger. Amen.
* Compare Psalm 34:1–2 (KJV 35:1–2).	

+ Christus regnat + Christus imperat + Christus + fregit in me sit et franget gladium istum qui contra me pugnat + o sagitta sta per lanceam et omnia arma omnium inimicorum meorum visibilum et invisibilum non noceat mihi famulo tuo J b Amen	+ Christ rules + Christ commands + Christ + caused this sword to break when it struck me, and will break the sword of all those who fight against me. Halt, O arrow, by the lance [???],* and all weapons of my enemies, visible and invisible, so they won't harm me, your servant J. B. Amen.
* Something seems to be missing here.	

Whoever carries the previous prayer, may fear no enemies, nor being harmed by their swords, arrows, or any of their weapons, nor the snares of the devil, nor enchanted weapons, nor poisons, nor being harmed by unclean spirits, but will be safe at all times and in all places. +++ And if you are sceptical, you can attach these prayers to the neck of a cock, and you will see that no weapon will be able to harm it.

Barnasa + leuitas + bucella + buella + agla + agla + tetragrammaton + Adonay + domine deus magne et mirabilis, anima [*adiuva] famulum tuum J b indignum ab omnium periculum mortis corporis et	Barnasa + leuitas + bucella + buella + agla + agla + Tetragrammaton + Adonay + O Lord God, great and wonderful, help me your unworthy servant J. B., from all mortal danger of body and

animae, et ab omnibus insidiis inimicorum mearum visibilum et invisibilum + decem sunt nomina quibus apellatur deus in quocunque + nomen deus + [Euau +] <crux +> Elu + Eloy + Ela + adanay [*Adonay] + corpus Christus cogi + sabaoth + nania [*nomina] + crux [+] hec prosunt familo [*famulo] dei J b hoc enim est corpus meum + et [*ut?] diligat me + Amen +

soul, and from all traps of my enemies, visible and invisible. + There are ten names whereby God is known everywhere + the name Deus (God) + [Evau] + Elu + Eloy + Ela + Adonay + Corpus Christi (the Body of Christ) + Sabaoth + Nania + Crux (the Cross) +. These are of benefit to the servant of God, J. B. This is my body + and he loves me + Amen.[*]

> [*] Compare Millunzi, *Archivo Storico Siciliano* 25 (1900): 267: *"... in quocumque nomine Deus: + Evau + Eloi + Eli + Ada + Adonai + Corpus Christi + Logi + Sabaoth + Lomina + Crux +"*

Coniuro vos omnia arma cum quibus occi[si] sunt omnes sancti martyres praecipio vobis per merita sanctorum omnium ut non habeatis potestatem sturdendi [*scindendi] ca[r]nem meam nec sanguinem meum spergendi [*spargendi?] nec offendendi famulum dei J b nec in aliquo ledendi + crux et passio domini nostri Iesu Christi sit in memoria et in defentionem mea[m] + pax et benedictio domini nostri Iesu Christi sit semper mecum + o sagitta sta per virtutem beate<m> Marie virginis et per caput sancti Iohannis baptista[e], per apostolos, martires, confessores virgines et viduas per angelos et arcangelos + o sagitta sta per annunciacio[n]em domini nostri Iesu Christi [+] o sagitta sta per coronam spineam qua portata

I conjure all of you weapons which have killed all the holy martyrs; I command you by the merits of all the saints that you have no power to pierce my flesh, nor spill my blood, nor strike your servant J. B. with any injury. May the cross and passion of our Lord Jesus Christ be in my memory, and in my defense. + May the peace and blessing of our Lord Jesus Christ be with me always. + Halt, O arrow, by the virtue of the Virgin Mary, and by the head of John the Baptist, and by the apostles, martyrs, confessors, virgins, and widows, by the angels and archangels. + Halt, O arrow, by the annunciation of our Lord Jesus Christ. + Halt, O arrow, by the crown of thorns worn on the head of our Lord Jesus Christ. +[*] Halt, O arrow, by the

> [*] ELP p. 121 adds: *O sagitta sta per captionem, & flagellationem Domini nostri Jesu Christi* ["Halt, O arrow, by the capture and whipping of our Lord Jesus Christ"]. This fits the context.

[*posita?] fuit in capite domini nostri Iesu Christi [+]o sagitta sta per clavos qui perforavit manus et pedes dominum nostri Iesu Christ[i] o sagitta sta per vulnera, domini nostri Iesu Christi per resurrectionem Iesu Christi ut non posset [*possit] ledere me famulum dei J b + in nomine patris + et filii + et spiritusancti + Amen +	nails which pierced the hands and feet of our Lord Jesus Christ. Halt, O arrow, by the wounds of our Lord Jesus Christ, and by the resurrection of Jesus Christ. Thus may you not harm me, J. B., a servant of God + in the name of the Father + and the Son + and the Holy Ghost + Amen.
obsecro te domine fili dei viui per sanctam crucem tuam ut dimittas peccata mea + per sanctam crucem tuum custodi caput meum per venerabilem [crucem] tuam custodi pedes meos et omnia membra mea, et tribue mihi veniam et vitam eternam + sancte deus sanctiffica me fortis deus fortifica me Imortalis deus miserere mei famuli [tui] J b quia peccata mea multa sunt aput te et non suum [*sum] dignus vocare seruus tuus propterea deprecor te ut mittas in cor meum amorem celestium qui vives et regnas deus per omnia [secula seculorum] amen.	I beseech you O Lord, son of the living God, by your holy cross, that you forgive my sins + by your holy cross guard my head; by your venerable cross guard my feet and all my limbs, and grant me favour and eternal life. + O holy God, make me holy; O strong God, strengthen me; O immortal God, have pity on me, your slave J. B., though my many sins make me unworthy to be called your servant. Therefore I beg you to send the celestial love into my heart, who lives and reigns for all [eternity]. Amen.
Abba pater miserere mei + o filii + o sancte spiritus meu [*mecum] sis eme [*eripe] me ab omnibus adversarii meis + coniuro te gladium per sanctem sacerdotem veteris testamenti qui intraduxit	O Abba* father, have mercy on me + O Son + O Holy Ghost, may you be with me. Deliver me† from all my adversaries. + I conjure you, O sword, by the holy priest of the Old Testament, who

* *Abba*: Aramaic for "father."
† ELP p. 122 reads *erue me* ["destroy me"], which is more problematic.

maria et dominum nostrum Iesu Christum in templem dicentem tuam ipsius anima[m] doloris gladius [per]transibit ut non posset ledere famulum dei J b coniuro vos lapides per beatum stephanum protomartirum qui iudei lapidaverunt qui statuit pro suis persecutoribus exorare dicens ne statuas illis hoc peccatum quia nessiunt [*nesciunt] quid faciunt ut non possit ledere me famulum dei J b + In nomine patris + filii + et spiritusancti + Amen.	introduced Mary and our Lord Jesus Christ in the temple, saying "a sword of grief has pierced my soul,"* that it will not be able to harm me, J. B., a servant of God. I conjure you, O stones, that you can't harm me, J. B., a servant of God, by the blessed Stephen, the protomartyr,† who the Jews stoned, who pleaded on behalf of his persecutors, saying "judge them not for this sin, for they know not what they do." In the name of the Father + and of the Son + and of the Holy Ghost. Amen.

* From "Ad Matutuinum" in *Officium parvum de septem Doloribus B. V. M.* (Little Office of the Seven Sorrows of the B. V. M.).
† Acts 7:58.

These were the words which Pope Leo sent to the emperor and King Charles the Great (Charlemagne), and its virtue has been proven. Whoever therefore carries this on his person, or reads it out loud, or causes it to be read, that day will avoid the danger of an evil death, whether by fire, or by water, or suffer any misfortune, but will die in honour and old age, and if any pregnant woman carries these words on herself, she will have a short labor, and will not be able to go to ruin. And the words are as follows: [32]

32. Compare Scot, *The Discouerie of Witchcraft*, 132. Also Thomas Bartholin, *Thomae Bartholini Acta Medica et Philosophica Hafniensia (Hafniae: Haubold, ann. 1674, 1675, 1676)*, 97; compare also W. Sparrow Simpson, "On the Measure of the Wound in the Side of the Redeemer, Worn Anciently as a Charm; and on the Five Wounds as Represented in Art," *Journal of the British Archaeological Association* 30 (1874): 357–374: "Thys epystell of our Savyour sendeth our holy father pope Leo to the emperour Carolo magno, of the whiche we t'yndest wryten who that bereth thys blessynge upon hym, and sayth it ones a daj'e, shall obteyne .xl. yeres of pardon and .lxxx. lenttyge, and he shall not perysshe wyth soden deth."

[24]

Crux Christi est quem semper adoro + crux Christi sit in imper orta (?) et vera salus + crux Christi [superat] omnem gladium + crux Christi superat [*soluit] vincula mortis + crux Christi [sit] pro me + crux Christi sit admirabile signum + crux Christi sit mihi potestas + crux Christi spondeat omne bonum mihi + crux Christi liberat me ab omni malo presenti et futura + per hoc signum crucis sit mihi dividuae [*diuinae] gratie omnes intercessio + crux Christi auferret a me omnes adversitates huius mundi + crux Christi sit mecum et salvet me ante me et post me quia antiqu[u]s diabolus ubi te videt a me recedat + per crucis hoc signum + fugia[n]t a me omnes malignos spiritus + per heloy + Tetragrammaton + dyday + panta + yeto + esbray + Iesus ante transiens per medium illorum ibat + fons + principium + finis + veritas + omnipotens + Iesus in nomine patris + et filie + et spiritusancti + amen.	The Cross of Christ* is that which I adore. + The Cross of Christ is … (?)[†] and true safety. + The Cross of Christ [overcomes] all swords. + The Cross of Christ overcomes the bonds of death. + The Cross of Christ is for my behalf. + The Cross of Christ is a sign worthy of admiration. + The Cross of Christ is my strength. + The Cross of Christ promises all good for me. + The Cross of Christ delivers me from all evil present and to come. + Through the Cross of Christ I obtain divine grace. All intervention.[‡] The Cross of Christ takes away all adversity of this world from me. + May the Cross of Christ be with me and save me. May it be before me and behind me, so that if that ancient devil sees it, he will back away from me. Through this sign of the Cross all evil spirits flee from me. + Through Heloy + Tetragrammaton + Dyday + Panta + Yeto + Esbray. + Jesus passed through their midst, and went his way.[§] + The Fountainhead + The Beginning + The Ending + The Truth + Almighty + Jesus. In the name of the Father + and the Son + and the Holy Ghost. Amen.

* There are variations of this prayer in various *Horae*, for example *Horae ad usum Romanum*, Det Kongelige Bibliotek, MS. GkS 1612, c. 1490–1500, fol. 34r. See also Richard Rolle, *Yorkshire writers* vol. 1 (London: S. Sonnenschein, 1895), 376. ELP p. 125. Compare Clm 849, fol. 97r, in Kieckhefer, *Forbidden Rites*, 329.

† ELP p. 125: *fit in porta* ["makes a gateway"]. Most parallel passages do not contain anything corresponding to these words.

‡ (?) Text seems to be corrupt here.

§ Luke 4:30.

These are the names of almighty God, our Lord Jesus Christ, which are extracted from other similar names. Whoever carries these on himself will succeed in business, and cannot be captured at any time or charged with treason. Likewise if it hung on the neck of anybody they will be esteemed by all, and these are the words following:

+ Anthos + Anostro + noxio + boy + Eloy + Apen + Agla + Agipa Ysquiros +[33]

These are the words which Adam spoke when he was in hell or Limbo. Whoever carries them on himself, or has beseeched God and said them for seventy-three years, no enemies will be able to ambush him on a journey. And if he carries these words or names upon himself, he will not be able to be captured. "+ Valeanda Zasac +" nor will he be able to be assaulted, but will prevail through the grace of his soul, and these names must be written on paper, and you will be able to pass by your enemies.

Adonay + I + + + + + principium + finis + unctio + sapientia + veritas + spes + paracletus + ego sum qui sum + fons + mediator + hagios + ovis vinculum + pes + leo + panis + tolos [*tellus] + manus + lapis + angularis + petra + alma + sponsus + pullus + dietas [*deitas] + verax + teternium + gratia + veritas + pax + fons + aritayt + amor aleluya + Amen + unitas + fortitudo + novissimus + omnipotenti + matheus + Iohannes + marcus + lucus +	Adonay + I +++++ The Beginning + The End + ointment + wisdom + The Truth + The Hopes + The Advocate + I am who I am + The Fountain + The Mediator + holy + The Sheep, The Bond + The Foot + The Lion + The Bread + The Earth* + The Hand + The Corner-stone + The Rock + The Nurse + The Promised One + Pure (?)† + The Deity + Truthful + teternium (?) + Grace + Truth + Peace + Source + Aritayt (?)‡ + Love + Halleluya + Amen + Unity + Strength + Newest + Almighty + Matthew + John + Mark + Luke +.§

* The Earth: reading *tellus* for *tolos*, but perhaps *flos* ["The Flower"], as on Folger p. 22, which would also fit with Notker the Stammerer's (c. 840–912) list in John Ferguson, *Clement of Alexandria* (New York: Twayne Publishers, 1974), 104. Another possibility is *tholos* ["the dome"], which would fit better with "cornerstone." It is also tempting to speculate that *manus* ["the hand"] is a mistake for *mons* ["the mountain"]. ELP: telos.

† *Pullus*: "Chicken, small animal, or colt." Hughan, "The Magic Scroll. Described by Bro. W. J. Hughan," *Ars Quatuor Coronatorum: Transactions of the Quatuor Coronati Lodge No. 2076 London* 16, no. 2 (1903): 132–156, here reads *perillus*, perhaps for *perillustris* ["shining"]. Dumas's *Grimoire* p. 75 and *Crossed Keys* p. 161 read "the child," presumably Latin *puellus*.

‡ Hughan: *Alithay*; ELP: *Atitay*.

§ ELP pp. 127–8. W. J. Hughan transcribed an almost identical German text in Anonymous, "The Magic Scroll," *Ars Quatuor Coronatorum*, vol. 16 (London: Quatuor Coronati Lodge, 1903): 135: "*Adonai + Principium + Finis + Unitas + Sapientia + veritas + spes + paraclitus + ego sum qui sum + fons + mediator + agios + ovis + vinculum + leo + tellus + manus + lapis angularis + petra + alma + sponsus + perillus + deitas + verax + Dexter + Fons + pax + Alithay + amor + Alleluia + Amen + Unitas + Fortitudo + Novissimus + omnipotenti + matheus + Iohannes + marcus + lucus.*" Ferguson, *Clement of Alexandria*, 104, provides Notker the Stammerer's somewhat similar list of the names of Christ: "Messiah, Saviour, Emanuel, Sabaoth, Adonai, Only-begotten, Way, Life, Hand, Likesubstanced, Beginning, First-born, Wisdom, Virtue, Alpha, the Head, the last letter Omega, Fount and Origin of God, Paraclete, Mediator, Lamb, Sheep, Calf, Snake, Ram, Lion, Worm, Mouth, Word, Splendor, Sun, Glory, Light, Likeness, Bread, Flower, Vine, Mountain, Door, Rock, Stone, Angel, Bridegroom, Shepherd, Prophet, Prince, Deathless, Sure, God, All-Ruler, Equal."

33. ELP p. 126: "*Authos + à nostro + noxio + bay + gloy + apen- + jagia + agios + hischyros.*"

These most holy names are for the protection of my soul and body, from all evil, in the name of God and the holy Mary, and in the name of Saint Aloysius, which names King Fabricius carried upon himself, and he bequeathed to King Aloysius who himself carried it upon his person, so that we was not able to be killed nor captured.

And if you wish to test this, put it upon any (beast) which is to be butchered.

+ + + + + + + pathay + vay + adonay + in nomine patris et filij et spiritusancti + Iesus autem transice per medium illorum ibat + o + var + adaf + malarum terrarum negat + verbum car[o] factum est + et habitauit in nobis + Christus, Tetragrammaton + qui ait illi sit in sanctum [*factum?] felix + Amen + lex + Amen + Iesu quem queritis ego sum, si videbas fuit [*furem] currebas cum eo et cum adulteris portionem tuam, ponebas os tuum obundavit [*abundavit] malicia et lingua tua concinabit [*-bat] dolos + et benedic hereditati tue + laus deo + + Amen. +	+ + + + + + + Pathay + Vay + Adonay + in the name of the Father and of the Son and of the Holy Ghost. + But Jesus passing through their midst went his way.* + O + Var + Adaf + malarum terrarum negat.† + The Word was made flesh + and dwelled amongst us.‡ + Christ, Tetragramaton + who said to that one, in holiness he may be fruitful. + Amen. The law. + O Jesus, who are you seeking? I am, "When you saw a thief, then you joined with him, and partake with adulterers. You use your mouth for evil, and your tongue frames deceit."§ + and bless your inheritance. + Praise God. + Amen.

* Luke 4:30.
† O + Var + Adaf: The final f looks altered. It may originally have been an r. ELP reads "o + var + adar." malarum terrarum negat ["of the bad earth (he/she/it) denies"].
‡ John 1:14.
§ Psalm 49:18–19 (KJV 50:18–19).

Here endeth the little book

The Rest as Follows[34]

Coniurati, festinate venire et obediri [*obedire] preceptori vestro, qui vocatur octinomos.	Having been conjured, hasten to come and obey your master, who is called Octinomos.

34. In marg.: anchor glyph. In space before the new prayer is the anchor glyph repeated and in pencil in sec. man.: "from page 20 at the bottom." This section resumes the excerpts from H.

This being finished, you should whistle towards the four directions of the world, and you will immediately see great motions. And when you see this, you should say:

quid tardatis quid moramini quid facitis? praeparate vos, et obedite præceptori vestro in nomine domini Bathiat [*Bathat] + vel Vachat + super Abrac ruens + superveniens, Abeor + super Aberer +	Why do you delay? What is delaying you? Prepare to obey your master, in the name of the Lord Bathat or Vachat + rushing upon Abrac + Abeor coming upon Aberer. +

Then immediately they will come, in their own proper form. And when you see them near the circle, show them the pentacle covered with fine consecrated linen, [and uncovering it, you should say:

Ecce conclusionem vestram,] nolite fieri inobedientes,	Behold your conclusion] if you are disobedient.

And suddenly you will see them in a peaceable form. And they will say to you, "What do you desire, because we have been prepared to fulfill all your orders, because the Lord has subjugated us to this."[35]

And since the spirits have now appeared, say:

bene veneritis spiritus vell reges nobilissimi: quia vos vocavi per illum cui omne genu flectitur, celestium terrestrium et Infernalium cuius in manu omnia Regna Regum sunt: nec est qui suae contrarius esse possit maiestati. quatenus constringo vos, vt hic ante circulum visibiles, affabiles permaneatis: tam diu tamque constantes, nec sine licentia m[ea] recedatis, donec meam sine fallatia aliqua et veredice [*veridice] perficiatis voluntatem, per potentiae illius	Welcome O spirits, or noble kings, because I have called you through him before whom all beings bend their knees—even celestial, earthly, and infernal beings—in whose hands are the powers of all kings. Nor is there any who contradict his majesty. As long as I constrain you, remain before this circle, visible and courteous. Do not depart without my licence, until you have fulfilled my wishes truthfully and without deceit, through the power and virtue of Him

---

35. *Pete quid vis, quia nos sumus parati complere omnia mandata tua, quia dominus ad hec nos subiugauit.*

virtutem, qui mari posuit terminum suum, quem praeterire nemo potest, et lege illius pontetiae [*potentiae] non pe[r]transit fines suos, dei scillicet Altissimi Regis, domini qui cuncta crea[uit,] Amen.	who divided the sea from the land, whom nobody is able to disregard, and through the power of his law not passing beyond his boundaries, namely God's, the most high king, the Lord, who created all things. Amen.

Then command whatever you wish, and it will be done. Afterwards, licence them to depart as follows:

In nomine patris, filij et spiritus sancti, it[e] in pace ad loca vestra et pax sit inter nos et vos, parati sitis venire vocati	In the name of the Father, Son, and Holy Ghost, go in peace to your own places, and let there be peace between you and us, and be prepared to come when you are called.

This what Petrus de Abano has said regarding the *Elements of Magic*. But in order to make it easier to understand the plan for a circle, I will provide a specific example. Therefore, if you wish to make a circle for the first hour of Sunday in the springtime, it should be in the manner of the subsequent figure.[36]

[25]
Before you call or consecrate, say the Lord's Prayer

Our Father which art in heaven, hallowed be thy name; thy kingdom come, thy will be done in earth as it is in heaven. Give us this day our daily bread and forgive us our trespasses, as we forgive them that trespass against us, and lead us not into temptation, but deliver us from evil, for thine is kingdom, power, and glory forever and ever. Amen.

Hail Mary

Salve˙ [sic] maria gratia plena dominus tecum benedic[t]a tu in mulieribus et benedictu[s] fructus ventris tui Amen et ne nos Inducas in tentatione sed libra a nos a malo.	Hail Mary full of grace, our lord is with thee. Blessed art thou among women, and blessed is the fruit of thy womb. Amen. And lead us not into temptation, but deliver us from evil. Amen.
* Evidently a mistake for *Ave* ["Hail"].	

36. The figure is not given in the text at this point, but can be found below on Folger p. 133 and also H.

Another Hail Mary

Ave maria gratia plena, dominus tecum benedicta [tu] in mulieribus et benedictus fructis [*fructus] ventris tui dominus noster Iesus dulcissimus Amen. sancta maria mater dei ora pro nobis [peccatoribus,] nunc et in hora <nostris> [mortis nostrae. Amen].	Hail Mary, full of grace, the lord is with thee. Blessed art thou amongst women, and blessed is the fruit of thy womb, our sweet Lord Jesus. Amen. Holy Mary, Mother of God, pray for us [sinners], now and in the hour of [our death]. Amen.

The Creed

Credo in deum patrem omnipotentem creatorem celi ac terræ et in Iesum Christum dominum nostrum fillium eius unicum qui conceptus est a [*de] spiritu sancto natus ex maria virgine passus sub p[ontio] pilato crucifixus mortuus et sepultus discendit ad Inferos [*Inferna] 3io die resurrexit a mortuis et in celum [*ad celos] asscendit sedet ad dextrum dei patris omnipotentis inde venturus est <ad> Iudicandum [*Iudicare] vivos et mortuos credo in spiritum sanctum sanctam ecclessiam catholicam sanctorum communionem peccatorum remissionem carnis resurrectionem et vitam eternam. Amen.	I believe in God, the Father almighty, maker of Heaven and Earth, and in Jesus Christ his only son, our Lord, who was conceived of the Holy Spirit, born of the Virgin Mary, suffered under Pontius Pilate, was crucified, died, and was buried. He descended to hell, and on the third day was resurrected from death, and ascended into Heaven, where he sits at the right hand of God the almighty Father, there to judge the living and the dead. I believe in the Holy Ghost, in the holy Catholic Church, in the communion of saints, in the remission of sins, the resurrection of the body, and life everlasting. Amen.

Psalm lxvii [37]

God be merciful unto us, and bless us, and show us the light of his countenance, and be merciful unto us.

That thy way may be known upon Earth, and thy saving health among all nations.

Let the people praise thee, O God; yea, let all the people praise thee.

---

37. Psalm 66 (KJV 67). This Psalm is used in the *Clavicula* for constructing the circle, clothing, and consecrating the place. The translation here follows exactly that in *The Great Bible* (1540).

O let the nations rejoice and be glad, for thou shalt judge the folk righteously and govern the nations upon earth.[38]

Let the people praise thee, O God; let all the people praise thee.

Then shall the earth bring forth her increase, and God, even our own God, shall give us his blessing.

God shall bless us, and all the ends of the world shall fear him.

Psalm liiii [39]

Save me, O God, for thy name's sake, and avenge me in thy strength.

Hear my prayer, O God, and harken unto the words of my mouth.

For strangers are risen up against me, and tyrants which have not God before their eyes, seek after my soul.

Behold God is my helper: the Lord is with them that uphold my soul.

He shall reward evil unto mine enemies; destroy thou them in thy truth.

An offering of a free heart will I give thee and praise thy name, O Lord, because it is so comfortable.

For he hath delivered me out of all my trouble, and mine eye hath seen his desire upon mine enemies.

Psalm cl [40]

Yield unto God the mighty Lord praise in his sanctuary.

And praise him in the firmament that shows his power on high.

Advance his name and praise him in his mighty acts always.

According to his excellency of greatness, give him praise.

His praises with a princely praise, of sounding trumpets blow.

Praise him upon the viol, and upon the harp also.

Praise him with timbrel and with flute organs and virginals.

With sounding cymbals praise ye him, praise him with loud cymbals.

What ever hath the benefit of breathing, praise the Lord.

To praise the name of God the Lord, agree with one accord.

---

38. In marg.: "w" glyph.

39. Psalm 53 (KJV 54). This Psalm is used in *Clavicula* for constructing the circle and for consecrating the pentacles, the place, water, wax, and earth. Wording again follows *The Great Bible*.

40. Psalm 150 (KJV 150). This Psalm is used in *Clavicula* for consecrating candles. This is a choral adaptation of the Psalm, under the title "Yield unto God," attributed to the mid-sixteenth century composer Thomas Caustun, of which only one other manuscript copy is known to exist, the other being in the Chirk Castle part-books at the New York Public Library. See Peter le Huray, "The Chirk Castle Partbooks" *Early Music History* 2 (January 1, 1982): 17–42, doi:10.2307/853761.

Psalm cxxxviii [41]

I will give thanks to thee, O Lord, with my whole heart; even before the gods will I sing praises unto thee.

I will worship toward thy holy temple, and praise thy name because of thy loving kindness and truth, for thou hast magnified thy name and thy word above all things.

When I called upon thee, thou heardest me, and induedst my soul with much strength.

All the kings of the earth shall praise thee, O Lord, for they have heard the words of thy mouth.

Yea, they shall sing in the ways of the Lord: that great is the glory of the Lord.

For though the Lord be high, yet hath he a respect unto the lowly; as for the proud, he beholdeth them afar off.

Though I walk in the midst of trouble, yet shalt thou refresh me; thou shalt stretch forth thy hand upon the furiousness of mine enemies, and thy right hand shall save me.

The Lord shall make good his loving kindness towards me; yea, thy mercy, O Lord, endureth forever. Despise not the works of thine own hands.

[26]

Psalm li: misere mei deus [42]

Have mercy upon me, O God, after thy great goodness, according unto the multitude of thy mercies do away mine offenses.

Wash me thoroughly from my wickedness and cleanse me from my sin,

for I do acknowledge my faults and my sin is ever before me.

Against thee only have I sinned and done this evil in thy sight, that thou mightest be justified in thy saying, and clear when thou art judged.

Behold, I was shapen in wickedness, and in sin hath my mother conceived me.

But lo, thou requirest truth in the inward parts, and shalt make me to understand wisdom secretly.

Thou shalt purge me with hyssop and I shall be clean; thou shalt wash me, and I shall be whiter than snow.

Thou shalt make me to hear of joy and gladness, that the bones which thou hast broken may rejoice.

Turn thy face away from my sins, and put out all my misdeeds.

---

41. Psalm 137 (KJV 138). Wording is again from *The Great Bible*.

42. Psalm 50 (KJV 51). This is one of the Seven Penitential Psalms, used widely in magical and spiritual (e.g., OBVM) literature. The wording again follows *The Great Bible*.

Make me a clean heart, O God, and renew a right spirit within me.

Cast me not away from thy presence, and take not thy holy spirit from me.

O give me the comfort of thy help again, and stablish me with thy free spirit.

Then shall I teach thy ways unto the wicked, and sinners shall be converted unto thee.

Deliver me from blood guiltiness, O God, thou that art the God of my health, and my tongue shall sing of thy righteousness.

Thou shalt open my lips, O Lord, and my mouth shall show forth thy praise,

for thou desirest no sacrifice, else would I give it thee, but thou delightest not in burnt offerings.

The sacrifice of God is a troubled spirit: a broken and contrite heart, O God, shalt thou not despise.

O be favourable and gracious unto Sion; build thou the walls of Jerusalem.

Then shalt thou be pleased with the sacrifice of righteousness, with the burnt offerings and oblations. Then shall they offer young bullocks upon thine altar.

Psalm xliii: [43] iudica me deus

Give sentence with me, O God, and defend my cause against the ungodly people.

O deliver me from the deceitful and wicked man,[44]

for thou art the God of my strength. Why hast thou put me from thee, and why go I so heavily, while the enemy oppresseth me?

O send out thy light and thy truth, that they may lead me and bring me into thy holy hill and to thy dwelling,

And that I may go unto the altar of God, even unto the God of my joy and gladness, and upon the harp will I give thanks unto thee, O my God.

Why art thou so heavy, O my soul, and why art thou so disquieted within me?

O put thy trust in God, for I will yet give him thanks, which is the help of my countenance and my God.

Psalm xlvii: omnes gentes [45]

O clap your hands together, all ye people; O sing unto God, with the voice of melody.

---

43. Psalm 42 (KJV 43). Wording from *The Great Bible*.

44. In marg.: "w" glyph.

45. Psalm 46 (KJV 47). Wording from *The Great Bible*. Used in *Clavicula* for constructing the circle and consecrating wax or earth.

For the lord is high and to be feared; he is the great king upon all the earth.

He shall subdue the people under us, and the nations under our feet.

He shall choose out a heritage for us, even the worship of Jacob whom he loved.

God is gone up with a merry noise, and the Lord with the sound of the trumpet.

O sing praises, sing praises unto our God: O sing praises, sing praises unto our king.

For God is the king of all the earth: sing ye praises with understanding.

God reigneth over the heathen; God sitteth upon his holy seat.

The princes of the people are joined unto the people of the God of Abraham; for God which is very high exalted doth defend the earth as with a shield.

Psalm cxxi: [46] leuaui occulos

I will lift up mine eyes unto the hills from whence cometh my help.

My help cometh [even] from thee, Lord, which hath made heaven and earth.

He will not suffer thy foot to be moved, and he that keepeth Israel,[47] will not sleep.

Behold he that keepeth Israel shall neither slumber nor sleep.

The Lord himself is thy keeper; the Lord is thy defense upon thy right hand,

So that the Sun shall not burn thee by day, nor the Moon by night.

The Lord shall preserve thee from [all] evil; yea, it is even he that keepeth thy soul.

The lord shall preserve thy going out and thy coming in, for this time forth for evermore. Amen.

[27]

After thou hast read the Psalms, then go forward with this work: After duly[48] completing the circle, sprinkle it with holy or lustral water, and say:

Asperges me domine hissopo et mundabor: lavabis me et super nivem dealbabor.	Thou shalt purge me with hyssop, and I shall be clean: thou shalt wash me, and I shall be whiter than snow.[*]
[*] Psalm 50:9 (KJV 51:9). Translation from *The Great Bible*.	

---

46. Psalm 120 (KJV 121). Wording from *The Great Bible*.

47. Wording in *The Great Bible*: "keepeth thee."

48. Compare H. p. 106.

The blessing of the fumigations [49]

Deus Abraham, deus Isaac, deus Jacob, benedic hu[n]c creaturas, specierum, ut vim et virtutem odorum suorum amplient, ne hostis nec phantasma in eas intrare possit per dominum nostrum Iesum Christum, &c.	O God of Abraham, God of Isaac, God of Jacob, bless these creatures of spices, in order that the strength and virtue of their scents may grow, so that no enemies nor phantasms may be able to enter, through our Lord Jesus Christ, etc.

Then sprinkle them with the holy water.

The exorcism of the fire

The exorcism of the fire on which the fumigations are placed. The fire which is used for suffumigations, it may be in a new clay or earthenware vessel, which should be exorcised in this manner:

Exorcizo te creatura Ignis per illum [per] quem facta sunt omnia ut statim omne phantassma Eiicias a te ut nocere non possit in aliquo,	I exorcise you O creature of fire, by him through whom all things have been made, that all phantasms may immediately be ejected from you, so that it will be unable to harm anybody.

Then say:

benedic domine creaturam istam Ignis, et sanctifica, ut benedicta sit, in colla[u]dationem nominis tui sancti ut nullo nocumento sit gestantibus nec videntibus, per dominum nostrum Iesum Christum.	Bless O Lord this creature of fire, and sanctify it, for the praise of your holy name, so that no harm may come from bearing or seeing it, through our Lord Jesus Christ.

Concerning the garment and pentacle, and their use

The garment should be that of a priest if possible; if not, let it be made of fine linen. Then take a pentacle made in the day and hour of Mercury, when the Moon is increasing. It should be made of kidskin parchment, but first say over it a mass of the Holy Ghost, and sprinkle with baptismal water.

---

49. Another version of this blessing can be found below, Folger p. 98.

The oration to be said while putting on the garment

Ancor, Amacor, Amides, Theodonias, Anitor, per merita Angelorum: tuorum sanctorum domine Induam vestimenta salutis: ut hoc quod desidero, possim per ducere ad effectum per te sanctissime Adonay, cuius regnum permanet per omnia secula seculorum, Amen.	Ancor, Amacor, Amides, Theodonias, Anitor, by the virtues of your holy angels, O Lord, I put on the garments of salvation, that this which I desire I will be able to bring about, through the most holy Adonay, whose kingdom endures for all the ages. Amen.

[T]o consecrate all instruments [50]

O mighty and merciful God, which in the finger of thy deity, hast healed all kind of plagues and hast restored the diseased to their former health, grant now, I do beseech thee, that these instruments may be touched, blessed, sanctified, and hallowed by thy deity; that the draught drawn with the same in the dignity of thy name may serve effectually to my operation by him that liveth for evermore. Amen.

Another prayer [51]

O God, despise not the petition of wretches nor the voice of them which cry unto thee. Grant, I beseech thee, that when I invocate thy mercy, we may feel thy deity healthful unto us and assistant in all things through Jesus Christ our lord. Amen.

Another prayer [52]

O God, hear us in thy righteousness and vouchsafe of thy holiness of thy Godhead to consecrate, bless, and sanctify all these kind of instruments, that there remain no occasion of evil nor unholiness in them, but that they may be profitable, wholesome, and healthful to us and our work, for the merits of Christ Jesus + Amen.

Another

Increase, we beseech thee almighty God, the gifts of thy deity in sanctifying, hallowing, and blessing of these instruments that no wicked spirits have power or be

---

50. Not in H. The presence of multiple possible rituals for consecration is unusual.

51. In marg.: "w" glyph.

52. In left marg.: "w-."

able to resist us, through thy holy and blessed inspiration of power and virtue into them and us, that they and we may be more effectual and powerful to constrain, bind, and compel all spirits to our obedience through thy divine grace and power, and bring them to our obedience. Grant this, O Lord God, for Jesus Christ's sake, which liveth and reigneth with thee ever one God, world without end. Amen.

Another [53]

Benedic<ti>o te N per deum vivum per deum verum per deum sanctum per deum qui tibi specialem virtutem dedit ut consecratum et confirmatum existas virtutem et efficatiam potenter suscipias et retineas ad quod te duximus consecratum benedico te insuper Iesus Christ fillium eius unicum dominum nostrum qui te corrustantem diaphonumessae voluit et mittere figuras, et per reflectionem varias [*varians] demonstrare.	I bless you N., by the living and true God, by the holy God, by the God who has given you special virtue, that you may prove to be consecrated and confirmed, and you may potently accept and retain the virtue and efficacy of the consecration which we have performed. I bless you. In addition, Jesus Christ his only son our Lord, who has ordained your glittering translucent medium, and to send shapes, and to show through varying reflection.

Another

Tu deus omnipotens Invocationibus nostris clemens adesto et ut hanc N de celestia harmoni[a] tue claritatis benignus infunde tu[,] hoc N tuore [*tu ore?] benedicto ut per / [In margin: [D]e usum communionem / et in eo] / descendat in hoc N virtus spiritus sancti N scientiam representandi spiritus exorzizatorii / Imperio, obediendi mitissime fecundet	O all-powerful merciful God, be near our loving invocations, and as you pour the celestial harmony of your gracious clarity* into this N., with the blessed sight [*pronunciation?]† that through [In marg.: the use of the communion / and in it] / may descend into this N. the virtue of the Holy Ghost, the knowledge required to make manifest the exorcised
* Perhaps a mistake for *charitatis* ["charity"]. † Translation uncertain. The Latin is corrupt here.	

---

53. This seems to be specific for consecrating the scrying medium.

effectum ut omnium hominis quod te habeat habet potestatem contra omnes malignos spiritus per virtutem domini nostri Iesu Christi + fillii dei. Amen.	spirit. / With the command, obeying most agreeably, that it may be made more effective, in order that all mankind may have your power against all spiteful spirits through the virtue of our Lord Jesus Christ + the Son of God.

[28]

The Athanasian Creed [54]

Whosoever will be saved, before all things it is necessary that he hold the catholic faith; which faith, except everyone do keep holy and undefiled: without doubt he shall perish everlastingly.

And the catholic faith is this: that we worship one God in trinity, and trinity in unity.

Neither confounding the persons nor dividing the substance,

for there is one person of the Father, another of the Son, and another of the Holy Ghost.

But the Godhead of the Father, of the Son, and of the Holy Ghost, is all one: the glory equal, the majesty coeternal.

Such as the Father is, such is the Son, and such is the Holy Ghost.

The Father uncreate, the Son uncreate, and the Holy Ghost uncreate.

The Father incomprehensible, the Son incomprehensible, and the Holy Ghost incomprehensible.

---

54. This well-known prayer is also called the *Symbolum Athanasianum*. Among other magical texts, it can be found in LIH, chapter XIII, seventh prayer, p. 74.

The Father eternal, the Son eternal, and the Holy Ghost eternal.

And [yet] they are not three eternals, but one eternal.

As also there be not three incomprehensib[le]s, nor three uncreated, but one uncreated, and one incomprehensible.

So likewise the Father is almighty, the Son almighty, and the Holy Ghost almighty.

And yet they are not three almighties, but one almighty.

So the Father is God, the Son is God, and the Holy Ghost is God.

And yet they are not three gods, but one God, so likewise the Father is lord, the Son lord, and the Holy Ghost lord.

And yet not three lords, but one Lord.

For like as we be compelled by the Christian verity to acknowledge every person by himself to be God and Lord,[55]

so are we forbidden by the Catholic religion: to say there be three gods or three lords.

The Father is made of none, neither created nor begotten.

The Son is of the Father alone: not made nor created, but begotten.

The Holy Ghost is of the Father, and of the Son, neither made, nor created, nor begotten, but proceeding so there is one Father, not three fathers, one Son, not three sons, one Holy Ghost, not three holy ghosts.

And in this Trinity none is afore or after other: none is greater or less than another.

But the whole three persons be coeternal together and coequal.

So that in all things as is aforesaid: the unity in Trinity, and the Trinity in unity is to be worshipped.

He therefore that will be saved must thus think of the Trinity.

Furthermore it is necessary to everlasting salvation: that ye also rightly believe in the Incarnation of our Lord Jesus Christ.

For the right faith is that we believe and confess: that our Lord Jesus Christ, the Son of God, is God and man.

God of the substance of the father, begotten before the worlds: and man of the substance of his mother, borne in the world.

Perfect God and perfect man: of a reasonable soul, and human flesh subsisting.

Equal to the Father as touching his Godhead, and inferior to the Father, touching his manhood.

Who although he be God and man: yet is he not two, but one Christ.

---

55. In marg.: "w" glyph.

One not by conversion of the Godhead into flesh: but by taking of the manhood into God.

One altogether, not by confusion of substance: but by unity of person.

for as the reasonable soul and flesh is one man: so God and man is one Christ

Who suffered for our salvation: he descended into hell, rose again the third day from the dead.

[He ascended into heaven, he sitteth on the right hand of the Father, God Almighty,

from whence he will come to judge the quick and the dead.]

At whose coming all men shall rise again with their bodies: and shall give account for their own works.

And they that have done good, shall go into life everlasting: and they that have done evil, into everlasting fire.

This is the Catholic faith, which except a man believe faithfully, he cannot be saved.

Gloria patri filii et spiritus sancti sicut erat In principium ["Glory be to the Father, Son, and Holy Ghost, as it was in the beginning"].

[29]

The Gospel of Saint John

In the beginning was the Word, and the Word was with God and the Word was God. The same was in the beginning, with God, all things were made by it, and without it was made nothing that was made. In it was life, and the life was the light of men. And the light shineth in the darkness, but the darkness comprehended it not. There was a man sent from God whose name was John. The same came as a witness to bear witness of the light, that all men through him might believe. He was not the light, but was sent to bear witness of the light. That [that light] was a true light, which lighteth all men that come into the world. He was in the world, and the world was made by him, and yet the world knew him not. He came unto his own, and his own received him not, but unto as many as received him, to them gave he power to be the sons of God, in that they believe on his name which were born not of blood, nor of the will of the flesh, nor yet of the will of man, but of God. And the Word was made flesh and dwelt among us, and we saw the glory of it as the glory of the only begotten son of the Father, which word was full of grace and verity. John bare witness of him, and cried, saying: this was he of whom I said he that cometh after me, is preferred before me: for he was before me, and of his fullness have all we received, grace for grace, for the law was given by Moses but grace and truth came by Jesus Christ. No man hath seen God at any time: the only begotten son which is in the bosom of the

Father hath declared him. Then this is the record of John when the Jews sent priests and Levites, from Jerusalem to ask him, "Who art thou?" and he confessed and denied not, saying plainly, "I am not the Christ." And they asked him, "What then art thou, Elias?" and he said, "I am not." "Art thou the prophet?" and he answered, "No." Then said they unto him, "Who art thou, that we may give an answer to them that sent us? What sayest thou of thyself?" He sayeth, "I am the voice of him that crieth in the wilderness, 'Make straight the way of the Lord,' as said the prophet Esaias [Isaiah]." Now they which were sent were of the Pharisees, and they asked him and said unto him, "Why baptisest thou then, if thou be not the Christ, neither Elias, nor the prophets?" John answered them, saying, "I baptize with water: but there is one among you, whom ye know not; he it is that cometh after me, whose shoe latchet I am not worthy to unloose." These things were done in Bethabara, beyond Jordan, where John did baptise.[56]

How you can speak with your own good angel whenever you wish [57]

In the name of the Lord, here begins the treatise on how to converse with your own good angel.

In the name of the holy and indivisible Trinity, here begins the prayer to your own angel, who are appointed as guardians of humanity.

First, you should be well confessed, and fast on bread and water for three days. You should not eat until stars can be seen in the sky, or in any event until the day is done, and give a coin to the poor in the name of the Trinity, and say prayers devoutly, and go to a secret location (facing the church if you can see it, or else in a vestibule or facing the East), and all along the way that you have chosen, you should appear gracious, quiet, and discreet, cautiously hiding yourself, lest anyone observes or detects your secret doings, lest it be ridiculed, and your work hindered.

Then you should greet seven times with the Lord's Prayer and the Creed, and the following verses:

---

56. In left marg.: "w-."

57. Handwriting changes. Although the handwriting in this section is neat, the Latin is somewhat corrupt, and there are extensive corrections. An uncharacteristically large marg. is marked out. Harley 181, fol. 19r (sixteenth century), contains another exemplar of this text. Stephen Clucas, *John Dee: Interdisciplinary Studies* (Dordrecht, Netherlands: Springer, 2006), 241 and footnote 104, quotes from this text as being from *Ars Notoria*, but it is not actually part of *Ars Notoria* proper. Sloane 1727, fol. 59, has a somewhat shortened version.

| Increatus Pater, increatus filius, increatus spiritus sanctus, aeternus pater, aeternus filius, aeternus spiritus sanctus, | O uncreated Father, uncreated Son, uncreated Holy Ghost, eternal Father, eternal Son, eternal Holy Ghost, |

And [this prayer]:

| Omnipotens sempiterne deus, qui felicem animam humanam induisti et plasmasti ad similitudinem tuam, creasti addens unicuique corpori spiritum proprium et veracem ad custodiendum illum et defendendum ab incursibus spiritum malignorum, et illusionibus illorum, Te suppliciter rogo, et deposco clementissime pater, [30] omnipotens, et obsecro, per filium tuum Dominum nostrum Jesum Christum in cujus potestate, consistunt omnia, ut ego miserimus et indignus famulus tuus, hanc potestatem obtinere merear ut nomen proprij Angeli mei audire, et intelligere possim, et ejus virtutibus roboratus omnia Corporis et animae nocumenta per ejus visionem et defensionem fugere viriliter et veraciter merear, prestante domino nostro Jesu Christo, qui sedit in altissimis et aque cuncta disponit, Cujus Regnum et potestatem permanent in secula seculorum. Amen. | Almighty eternal God, who has placed on the blessed human soul your own likeness, adding each spirit to its own proper body, and for truly guarding it and defending it from the assaults of evil spirits, and their illusions.* I humbly ask and beseech you O merciful Father [30] almighty, and implore through your son our Lord Jesus Christ, in whose power all things endure, that I, a most wretched and unworthy servant of yours, may be found worthy to obtain this power to enable me to hear and understand the name of my own proper angel, and strengthened by his virtues, through his vision and defence, all harm of the body and soul have fled, may I merit this powerfully and truly, through our Lord Jesus Christ, who sits on the highest and disposes all things, and whose kingdom and power endures forever. Amen. |
| * Or "mockery." | |

Afterwards, prostrate yourself facing East, saying the Seven Penitential Psalms, with the seven Sabbath orations, and the same number of Creeds, begging humbly and saying,

Deus qui cuncta abscondita intueris, omnia opera occulta recordaris, et nihil latet in animis omnium creaturarum quod tu non novisti, te suppliciter deprecor ut ab omnibus perturbationibus liberatus secure tuum auxilium implorando: effectum petitionis meae consequi merear qui vivis, et regnas cum deo patre, in unitate spiritus sancti, deus per omnia secula seculorum Amen.	O God who beholds all secrets, records all hidden works, and nothing is hidden within the souls of all creatures that you have not learned, I humbly beg you to be freed from all disturbances through the security of your help, that our requests may be fulfilled through you who lives and reigns with God the Father, in unity with the Holy Ghost, [one] God forever and ever. Amen.

Afterwards, raise yourself onto your knees with good devotion, while saying:

Angele sancte, qui in conspectu altissimi dei stas semper, et mihi misero traditus es, ad me custodiendum, et defendendum me, et in necessitatibus ad subveniendum mihi, [te] suppliciter deposco, ut nominis tui titulum, ab Aucthore omnium, tibi traditum mihi revelare nullatenus forundes [*formides] ut nomine tuo sancto invocato et nominato, responsa vera [accipiam] et munera tuae sublimationis percipiam, ut de omnibus, quae desid[e]ro, mihi venias et compareas responsurus, per eum, qui venturus est iudicare vivos, et mortuos et saeculum per ignem Amen.	Holy angel, who stands always in the sight of the most high God, and who has been handed over to wretched me, to guard me and defend me, and rescue me in times of need, I humbly ask that you reveal to me the title of your name, given to you by the Author of all things, in nowise be terrified, so that with your holy name invoked and named, [I may receive] true answers and I may perceive the gift of your deliverance, so that you may come and appear to me, answering all that I desire, through him who will judge the living and the dead and the ages through fire. Amen.

Then stand and say this prayer:

Pretende domine, famulo tuo dextram Caelestis auxilii vitae [*ut te] tota virtute [*corde] perquirat, et qui digne postulat, consequi mereatur [*assequatur] per Christum dominum nostrum Amen amen (pater nostor [sic]) Aue maria	Stretch out, O Lord, the right hand of your heavenly assistance to your servant, that he may seek you with his whole strength, and obtain that which he faithfully asks, through Christ our Lord. Amen,* Amen. (Our Father...) Hail Mary...

* This text is found in "the form of clothing" in the *Manual of the Brothers and Sisters of the Third Order of Penance of St. Dominic* (London: 1852), 126: *Pretende, Domine, famulo tuo dexteram tui celestis auxilii, ut te tota corde perquirat, et que digne postulat, assequatur. Per Christum dominum nostrum.*

Et ne nos inducas in temtationem, sed libra nos a malo;	And lead us not into temptation, but deliver us from evil.

Saluum fac populuum tuum, Domine + Deus sperauit autem in te. mitte ei (vel mihi,) domine auxilium de sancto. Et de Sion tuere eos (vel me) esto ei (vel mihi) domine turris fortitudinis a facie inimici. Pater de Caelis deus misere mihi vel nobis.	O Lord God, save your people. But my trust is in you. O Lord, send to him (or to me) the help from the holy, and from Sion, to protect those (or me), O Lord, a tower of strength against the face of the enemy. God, the Father in heaven, have mercy on me (or us).

And *recite the whole Litany.[58] Which said, say this prayer:

[31]

Succurrite mihi Sancti Angeli dei devocionibus vestris santificate plebem: Benedicite, et nos homines in pace custodite. Amen	Assist me, O holy angel of God, with your devotions. Sanctify the common people. Bless and guard us men in peace. Amen.

This done, you may sit (with bent knees), and humbly listen if you are being addressed by him, because if you are clean and sincerely confessed and contrite, a light

---

58. Ms: "sit tota Letania" reading "*dic tota Letania." There are a number of Litanies that include these words, but according to Sloane 1727, the Litany of the Saints (from the *Book of Hours*) is intended. *Pater de caelis, Deus, miserere nobis. Fili, Redemptor mundi, Deus, miserere nobis. Spiritus Sancte, Deus, miserere nobis. Sancta Trinitas, unus Deus, miserere nobis* ["God, the Father in Heaven, have mercy on us; God the Son, redeemer of the world, have mercy on us; God the Holy Spirit, have mercy on me; Holy Trinity, One God, have mercy on us"].

will encompass you, like a bedewed wind,[59] and the angel will say, "I am N. who always stands in the sight of God, and departs not from your body until I bring your most noble soul into the place of rest and growth."[60]

Then turn towards whichever direction you hear him, and converse with him about whatever seems good. And so too whenever you wish to converse with him, you may call him with his own proper name. And so he will protect your life and business from all harm, guard your body in this world, and after this life, he will personally bring your soul to God.

Prayer for one's angel

Obsecro te, Angelici [*angelice]: Spiritus cui ego ad prouidendam emissus [*commissus] sum ut custodias me indesinenter, et protegas me, ab incarsu [*incursu] diaboli, vigilantem, et dormientem, nocte et die, horis continuis, ac momentis conferre [*confove] mecum ubicumque fuero [*iero], comitare mecum[.] repelle a me omnem temptationem Sathanae; et quod mea non exigant [*extingunt] merita tuis precibus obtine<re> apud misericordissimum Judicem ut [nullum] in me vel loci non habeat contrariae virtutis adimixtio. Cumque me coruptam [*per abruptam] viciorum devia [*devium] errare [*esse] *prospexerii: ad redemptorem meum, me reducere Satagas,*	I beseech thee,* angelic spirit, to whom I by providence have been entrusted: that thou guard me unceasingly, that thou protect, watch attentively, and defend me from every attack of the devil while I am waking and sleeping, by night and by day; for hours and moments without interruption cherish me and watch over me, and accompany me everywhere I go. Avert from me every temptation of Satan, and that which my merits do not extinguish, by thy prayers hold fast before God, the most merciful judge, so that [nothing] of a contrary strength may have a place in me. And whenever thou hast *fore*seen me wandering through the steep places of vices, trouble thyself to lead me back to my redeemer.
*et in quacunque angustia, et tribulatione, et tristitia me esse prospexeris, auxilium Dei omnipotentis tuo optentu [*obtentu] s<i>uper me esse sentiam*[†] Precor	And in whatever distress and trouble thou beholdst me to be, may I feel the help of almighty God approach by means

---

* This prayer is from the book of hours. Translation based on http://medievalist.net/hourstxt /suffrage.htm. Italics indicate where text varies from the text in Hours.

† This line is written *supra linea*.

---

59. Sloane 1727: "a goodly wind shall compasse you about."

60. Sloane 1727: "rest & quietnesse."

in nomine domini nostri, Jesu Christi ut si fieri potest [*possit] notum facias mihi finem meum, et cum de [hoc] corpore adductus [*eductus] fuero: non admittas [*dimittas], (vel ne addmittas) malignos spiritus me terrere, aut illudere, nec in foveam desperacionis: inducere [*incidere]: Non me derelinquas donec me perducas [*perduxeris] ad visionem conditoris mei, qui me ad custodiendum, tibi comisit, ut personaliter cum omnibus sanctis interventis tuo, merear laetari praestante eodem domino nostro Jesu Christo, qui cum Deo patre, et Spiritu Sancto, viuit et regnat Deus per omnia secula seculorum. Amen.	of thy covering over me. I pray thee, *in the name of our Lord Jesus Christ*, that, if it can be done, thou makest my end known to me. And when I shall be drawn forth from this body, do not allow evil spirits to frighten me or make sport of me, nor allow me to fall into the pit of desperation. And do not abandon me at all until thou hast led me to the sight of my creator, *who has appointed you to guard me, so that you would personally intervene with all the saints, that I may merit to rejoice with them, through our Lord Jesus Christ, who lives and reigns with God the Father, and with the Holy Ghost*, world without end. Amen.

[32]

[+ The method of the glass or stone]

[....]

glorious [61] hands and feet, and with a crown of thorn wast crowned, and in thy most [????] pains wast given to thee esell [62] and gall to drink, which with a spear wast

---

61. Primary handwriting resumes. Earliest foliation seems to read "18," which would indicate a loss of three folios. Early pagination on the other hand indicates a loss of two pages *following* this one, but there doesn't appear to be a gap in the text at that point. Fortunately a close parallel can be found in Sloane 1727, 5r, which starts as follows: "**The method of the Glass or stone.** First haue a glase or stone fayer cleane and sound without Cracke or Blemish: then must you haue oyle oliue to anoynte the stone withall, then must you confese yourself to god almighty with some Confession, and then say *Meserere mei deus* [=*miserere mei deus* (PS50/KJV51)], and read some good prayers or spsalmes then Concecrate your book and your stone together, and then concecrate your oyle and all instruments nesessary for your worke. Here followeth the Consecration of your stone and Berill and Booke: First say one pater noster, one Ave Mary; one Creed. then say *dominus vobis cum spiritu tuo* / O god of Abraham, god of Isack [=Isaac], god of Jacob, god of Elie; god of Toby, god of Angells, god of profetts, god of Marters [=martyrs], & god of Confessors, god of virgins, god of all good liuers; which hast given vertue unto stones, words and hearbs; I pore siner am imbold need through the multitude of thy great and manyfold; mercyes, to besech thy euerlasting maiesty to consecrate this Booke and pretious stone, and that thor wilt voughtsaft to send thy blessing upon them, & to blesse them with the dew of thy heauenly blessing, and in blessing this stone, to giue such a vertue unto it, that all spirits appearing in this cristal stone may be obedient unto me in all things, of all things that I shall demand of them, by the O god the Creator of all things, and blesse this booke and this stone O Lord Jesu Crist, the son of the euerliueing god, which by the will of the father together working with the holy gost by the death and passion and blood sheding hast quitened (?) the world...."

62. *Esell* (=*aisliche*): "vinegar." See Matthew 27:34.

thrust in[to] thy right side, where out did run plenteously of blood and water for the redemption o[f] the whole world, which hast risen again the 3rd day, hast spoiled hell and hast ascen[ded] into heaven, and from thence shall come to judge the quick and the dead and the world by f[ire], and by all those thy miracles which thou hast done here, O merciful Jesu, the petition of me, thy unworthy servant N.,[63] as thou hast heard the merits and prayers of thy blessed Mother, so hear the prayers of me, [a] poor and wretched sinner, by the merits and pray[ers] (?) of thy Blessed Mother, the Virgin Mary, and of all sanctes[64] and saints, and by the virtue of thy sacrament of thy body and blood, and by thy virtue and power I beseech thee, and of thy grace and mercy do crave, by thy divine virtue and power, that th[is] day this book may be consecrated and confirmed with this stone and consecrate tho[u] + and blesse thou + ratify and confirm them so that they may be firm and surel[y][65] consecrated forever to remain, so that every time and place wheresoever all the consecrations, conjurations, invocations, and all the words which are contained in this bo[ok] and written therein and thy true virtue and power and thy holy divination and full and perfect libert[y]. O Lord Jesus Christ, I do beseech thee, grant that all spirits which I shall call into th[is] stone with this book may visibly, plainly, and aptly appear unto the sight of min[e] own eyes, so that I may see and discern them as plainly as thou wast seen of th[y] disciples after thy resurrection and at thy glorious ascension into heaven from Ga[li]lee grant this good Lord as thou sheddest blood and water for me and all mankind & c. a[men.] (?)

[Take th]e (?) book in [your hand and] (?) say

Bless thee + the Father, bless thee + the Son, bless thee + the Holy Ghost, bless thee holy Mary, mother of our Lord Jesus Christ; bless thee all the holy company of heaven; bless thee all holy angels, archangels, cherubim, [seraphim,] patriarchs, prophets, apostles, martyrs, confessors, innocents, and virgins, bless thee, and I by the authority of our Lord Jesus Christ and of his holy apostles Peter and Paul and by the authority of the holy Catholic Church militant here on earth do bless, consecrate, and confirm this book and this stone, in the name of the Father + and of the Son + and of the Holy Ghost + Amen.

---

63. N.: Here the operator substitutes their name.

64. *Sanctes*: (female) saints.

65. No sign of the *y*, though there's space for it.

[Then after t]he consecration [of your book and] stone what spirits [soever …]ll you may call [with this Call] if he come not [at the first, c]all till he come [and doubtless] but he will [com]e[66]

I, N., the servant of God and son of N., and I do conjure thee or you spirits, and I do comman[d] you that you be ready and obedient unto all my commandments both ministering and serving unto me to fulfill all my will and pleasure. I conjure thee, N., by the Father, the Son, and the Holy Ghost, and by him which is Alpha and Omega + the beginning and the end by the dreadful day of doom, by the virtue of the living God and by all the names of God both effable and ineffable, so that thou appear in this precious stone or glass in this hour and that quickly without any tarrying so that thou come and that in thine own person truly in a beautiful shape visibly, plainly, aptly, and distinctly unto the sight of mine own eyes[67] and show unto me visibly and to all that stand by me that we may plainly see thee by my commandment and conjuration and by all thin[gs] which I shall command thee, and if thou do not, I, N., the servant of God the son of N., by the virtue of God omnipotent and of all his saints, I condemn thee into hell and int[o] the fire everlasting unto the last day of judgment. Fiat, fiat, fiat. Amen.

Except thou come quickly unto me and make me a true answer before thou dep[art] of all things that I shall demand of thee, and I command thee that all ways and without tarrying to come <to come> and certify me and obey unto my words and fulfill my commandments at all hours and times that thou be obedient and obey me justly and truly, even as truly as Christ Jesus did obey and fulfill the commandments of his father. And further I conjure thee by God omnipotent, by Jesus Christ his Son, and by the Holy Ghost, by the Holy Trinity, and by the virtue of his substance by the holy providence of God which he had in his mind before he made the world, and by his goodness by which he made all things, and by that wisdom when he hath set the heavens above and hath divided the earth from the waters, by heav[en], earth, and the sea, and by all things in them contained by the height of the heaven and by the deepness of the sea, by the 4 elements, and by the virtue and by the secrets' virtues which secrets are hid in them, by his merciful working, and by the power whereby God created the world, the lights, the days, and the nights, and by the angels and archangels, and by thrones and dominations, by principalities and powers and virtues, by cherubim and seraphim, and by all their offices and powers, and by those which bear rule ove[r] other powers and them which are under their powers by the

---

66. The missing words are covered up by repair work, but supplied in pencil underneath.

67. Note that the caster wants the spirit to be visible to him, instead of a seer.

firmament of heaven, and by all the heavens and by all that are in them, and by all that are in heaven and under heaven, and by all things which almighty God hath created to the laud and praise of his name and of his majesty. I conjure thee, N., by the twelve patriarchs and by the twelve prophets and their prayers, and by the twelve apostles [35] [68] and by the 24 elders[69] and their crowns and garlands [gap] of majesty and by thron[e] of God, and by the golden altar which is before the eyes of God, and by the golden censers, by the voi[ce] and thunders which proceed of the throne of God, by the passions of merits by the me[rit] (?) of confessors and of all holy priests, and by their holiness, and by the holiness of wid[ows] and virgins, and by all those which praise and worship God, that you come into this stone without any tarrying and show thyself visibly in this crystal stone which I hav[e] consecrate[d] for thee, and that I and those that stand by me may see thee as plainly as Mary Magdalene saw the vision in the garden when she went to visit the bo[dy] of our saviour Christ Jesus and as plainly as Jesus appeared unto his disciple[s] after his resurrection and as plainly as Jesus Christ was seen to the men of Galilee in his glorious ascension, and this I charge and command thee by the everlasting majesty of God and the ministry of the Holy Trinity and by the birth, dea[th], and passion of Christ and by the glorious resurrection and ascension of Christ, by the preachi[ng and] fasting and temptation of Christ, by all the pains and merits of Christ, I conjure thee, N., by him which is Alpha and Omega the beginning and the end, and by these holy names of God El + Ely [+] + Theos + Adonay + Tetragrammaton + Mescias + Sother + Emanuell + Jesus + Fortis + Fons + Salvator + Gloriosus + Bonus + On + Unigenitus + Via + Vita + Manus + Homo + Usyon + Primogenitus + Sapientia + Virtus + Caput + Finis + Fons + Origo + Paracletus + Mediator + Agnus + Ovis + Vitulus + Serpens + Aries + Leo + Vermis + Os + Verbum + Splendor + Sol [+] Gloria + Lox + Ymago + Panis + Flos + Vitis + Mons + Ianua + Petra + Lapis + Angularis + Angelus + Sponsus + Propheta + Sacerdos + Past[or +] Athanatos + Kyros + Theon + Panton + Craton + Ysus + that thou appear in this crystal. I conjure thee, N., I bind and adjure thee by the goodness of our lord Jesus Christ, by his incarnation, by his nativity, by his circumcision, by his baptism, by his fasting, by his humility, by which he washed the feet of his disciples and by his cross and passion which he suffered by the crown of thorn[s] which[70] he bare on his head, by the nails wherewith his hands and his feet were pierced, and by the spear which was thrust into his side, by the water and blood t[hat] flowed out of his side, and by the sweet prayer which he made to his father, and

---

68. Although the pagination jumps from p. 32 to p. 35, there is not a gap in the text.

69. The first line of this page in a later hand seems to have been supplied at the time of repairs.

70. In marg.: "w" glyph.

by his so[ul] which departed from the body he commended into the hands of God his father, and by th[e] virtue by which the veil of the temple did rend, the Sun was darkened, and dark[ness] was upon the whole earth, and the graves opened and the dead bodies of many did[st] rise and were seen by these and all other holy acts of God. I conjure thee N. that thou come and appear in this stone in this present hour quickly and without any tarry[ing], and that you appear truly and that in thine own proper person in form of a man vis[i]bly unto the sight of mine own eyes, so that I may see and discern thee and to show me the truth of all things that I shall demand of thee without deceit, fraud, guile, and without hurt of me or any other that ever God created, neither shall thou have power to hurt or crack this stone, nor me nor any other creature, in mind, soul, nor body, neither shalt thou lie, cavil, nor deceive me, nor depart fro[m] my presence nor commandment, until thou have answered me justly and tru[ly] and hast showed unto me plainly and distinctly all things which I desire to know, see, or hear at this time present, and that I do licence thee to depart to (?) this I adju[re], conjure, and bind thee, and command thee by the virtue and power of him which shall co[me] to judge the quick and the dead and the world by fire. Fiat, fiat, fiat. Amen.

Say as followeth three times if he come not at the first, and then straight ways he shall come.

In Nomine patris veni In nomine filii veni In nomine spiritus sanctus veni In nomine sanctis trinitatis tibi dico veni In nomine summi omnium creaturas veni ad me et visibil[iter] appare mihi in hac hora sine aliquo nocumento et lesionem ac gravamin[e] corpore et animae vell alium et omnem desciderium meum ad-imple I[n] nomine patris [et] filii et spiritus sancti amen.	In the name of the Father, come! In the name of the Son, come! In the name of the Holy Ghost, come! In the name of the holy Trinity, I say to you come! In the name of the highest of all creation come and appear visibly to me this hour, without any trouble, malice, or harm to body or soul or anything else, and fulfill all my desires in the name of the Father and the Son and the Holy Ghost. Amen.

But if the spirit rebel and will not be obedient unto thee, then constrain him with the vinculum as followeth

Hearken O thou spirit N., I conjure, adjure, bind, and exorcize thee by the most high mighty name of God our Lord + Tetragram[m]aton + Jehovah + I exorcise thee and command thee that thou tarry not, but come in all plainness and effability and plainly, that I may see thee without deformity. I exorcise thee N. and mighti[ly] command thee by him which said and it was done, and by all the holy names of al[mi]ghty God which hath been, are, and shall be, recited in his fear and to your condemn[ation]. If you be disobedient and rebel, I charge, conjure,[71] and command thee in the nam[es] and by the name + Adonay + Aloe + Alion + Sabaoth + Saday + which is the Lord God [on] high and king omnipotent of Israel, which said, "Let us make man according to our likeness and let him bear rule over the works of our hands," and by the nam[e +] y + et v + which Adam heard[72] and spake, and by the name Gyn which Noah heard and spake with his family after that he was from the flood, and by the name + y + N + et X + [which] Abram heard and did know God, and by the name Joth which Isaac[73] heard and was deliv[ered] from the hand of his brother and by the name Tetragrammaton + which Jacob h[eard][74] [36] of the angel striving with him, by the name Sabaoth which Moses names and the waters of Egypt turned into blood, and by all these holy names of the living and true God + Adonay + Saday + Athenatos + Kyros + Emanuell + Joth + Heth + Hee + Vau + and by the nine heavenly candles[75] which was revealed unto Solomon, that thou appear in this stone without any further delay, as thou wilt answer at the dreadful day of doom, and if thou be disobedient and will not appear as before I have commanded thee, I, by the authority of Jesus Christ, of his apostles Peter and Paul, and of the holy Catholic Church militant here in earth, shall and will excommunicate thee and deprive thee from all dignities into the deepest pit in hell, and there shalt thou remain in everlasting chains of fire and brimstone where shall be weeping and gnashing of teeth forever, except thou come presently speedily and show thyself openly plainly in this stone and remain and be there until I give thee leave to depart, and all ways to be willing and ready to come and obey me at my commandment to fulfill my will and all my desires. This I bind, charge, and command thee by the name Pneumaton[76] and in the wonderful might of the great name Pneumaton [sic] which Moses named and the earth opened her mouth and swallowed up Dathan and Abiron and all their generation and people. So by the virtue of the same name Pneumaton I condemn thee N.

---

71. Compare Additional MS. 36674, cap. 3.

72. Compare H. conjuration of the spirits of the air.

73. Isaac was the father of Jacob and Esau.

74. Another version of this text can be found on Folger p. 113.

75. No doubt referring to the important medieval Solomonic treatise *De novem candariis*. Forthcoming edition by Micrologus. (*Candariis* does not mean candles.)

76. Corresponds with "Pneumaton" in Bayerische Staatsbibliothek, MS. Clm 849 (Kieckhefer, *Forbidden Rites*, 291), and "Primeumaton" in H., here spelled "Newimaton," but later in the prayer it is twice spelled "Newinaton."

into everlasting pain and torment except thou appear visible here before me in this crystal as I before have commanded thee, and that thou do come now and at all times and obey me. I charge, command, bind, and constrain thee by the virtue of him that is glorious and everlasting, whose seat is of flaming fire, the wheels thereof glistering[77] beams of lightning and fire, and by the judgment seat by which I most straightly charge and command thee that, most quickly and without any tarrying, thou do prepare thyself to come from all places in the which thou now art and come withou[t] any tarrying from mountains, valleys, and hills, fields, seas, and floods, broangkes,[78] ponds, and marrises,[79] streets, baths, and market pits, cestrons,[80] greens, floors, tors, and lands, and from places of heaven and hell and earth wheresoever thou be that thou come to me without any tarrying, I chiefly and manfully command thee by[81] the name and in the name which Moses heard of the most holy and omnipotent God from the midst of the burning bush and was astonied, and by the name and in the name that the Israelites heard upon the mount of Sion and they died for fear, and by the name Burne + which the sea heard and it parted in sunder, and by the name and in the name that the fire heard and was divided, by the name and in the name that the stones heard and they burst, that thou come from the 4 parts of the world and from the place in which thou art and appear plainly in this crystal stone to the sight of my own eyes upon pain of everlasting condemnation, if thou refuse to come and obey me by him that shall come to judge the quick and the dead and the world by fire. Fiat, fiat, fiat. Amen.

If he come not, say as followeth

I conjure thee, spirit N., by the virtue of our Lord Jesus Christ almighty and by all his holy names, that ye go and be damned in hell into the fire everlasting. I bid and command and condemn you into the pains everlasting and all the righteous blood which hath been shed from the death of the righteous Abel unto this day be indeed to you a just cause to condemnation everlasting, there to remain for evermore. Amen. And again I condemn thee into fire everlasting and command you to be put into hell by the virtue of the true and living God, and by the power that God hath over thee, that thou be always bound in hell in fiery chains and sustain the great pains of fire until in this precious stone you appear and accomplish my will. Amen.

---

77. Glistering: glittering.
78. Broangkes: brooks.
79. Marrises: marshes.
80. Cestrons: cisterns.
81. In marg.: "w" glyph.

If he will be rebellious and not come, say this constraint, but always beware whether he appear, and [rea]d no further, for [there is da]nger to constrain [and cond]emn him that doth [willin]gly appear according [to thy] mind, but if he [ap]pear not, say:

Thou spirit N., thou knowest tha[t] Christ liveth, Jesus Christ overcometh, Christ reigneth, Christ ruleth in heaven, in earth, in water, in hell, and in all other places wherefore by the virtue of God, I conjure thee by the power of God. I adjure thee by the will of God, I bind thee by the commandment of God, I charge thee and command thee by these holy names of God + Messias + Sother + Emanuell + Sabaoth + Adonay + Unigenitus + Via + Spes + Homo + Usyon + Saday + α + et ω + Christus being flesh and Jesus the son of the Virgin Mary which shall come to judge the quick and the dead and the world by fire. I commit and betake thee into the hands and custody of these infernal spirits, that is Lucifer, Sathan, Beelzebub, Facieton, there to be burned with fire and brimstone until thou have appeared unto me and fulfilled my will and commandments. Amen. Harken, O thou spirit N., I charge thee to appear in pain of everlasting condemnation, and be sure that if thou wilt not obey me to do that I shall command thee, but wilt be disobedient unto my words, I, by the authority of Jesus Christ and of the holy Catholic Church, shall pronounce the great and general curse against thee to thy utter condemnation, deprivation, and expulsion from all thy company, fellowship, and dignities into everlasting darkness. Therefore I give thee warning and advertise thee that thou be ready withou[t] any tarrying to show thyself in this precious stone and do all that God hath given thee power to show me, tell me, and do for me, and be ready at my commandment, fiat, fiat, fiat. So be it. Amen.

[This] is the general curse [again]st all spirits that [....] rebel

O thou spirit N., because thou hast rebelled and not obeyed the word of almighty God, now the curse of almighty God the Father, the Son, and the Holy Ghost come upon thee, the curse of the Holy Trinity, all the holy company of heaven curse thee, all holy angels, archangels, patriarchs, prophets, apostles, martyrs, confessors, all holy innocents and virgins curse thee, all the faithful people dispersed throughout the whole world curse thee, all the holy men of the holy church curse thee, and I, N., the son of N. and N.,[82] the servant [37] of the everlasting God, by the authority of the Holy Trinity, God the Father, the Son, [and] the Holy Ghost and of the holy apostles Peter and Paul and of [the] holy Catholic Church in which I was regenerate in the holy font of baptism, I do curse thee, thou rebellious spirit into the pit of hell, there

---

82. Note that both father and mother are used here.

to take part with all the cursed, wicked, and disobedient spirits there to remain forever, without thou appear visible in this precious stone unt[o] the sight of mine own
eyes and do whatsoever I shall command thee without any further tarrying, and so
done I shall pray for thee to God[83] that thou mayest be restored unto all thy dignities
and offices which thou hast given thee by him & c. *Fiat, fiat, fiat.* Amen.

Thus, far gentle reader, I have showed thee the perfect way of this art which is
most noble, for it is proved to be true, perfect, and good and therefore thou mayest
not doubt but proceed unto it with a manly face and good comfort.

[If the] spirit rebel and will not [appea]r when he is come [and] will [not ob]ey thee, do as followeth

Take pen and ink and write the name or names of the spirit or spirits on virgin
parchment, and have sulphur and other foul scents, and make a fumigation, saying:

Coniuro te ignis per illum qui con-cremesscere fatiet orbem quod tu hunc \<spiritus\> spiritus B combures et [cale] facias ita ut sua persona senciat in æter-num.	I conjure you, O fire, by him who made the world tremble, that you burn and heat up this spirit B., so that he will feel it personally eternally.

And holding the paper with the name or names over the smoke, say:

Quia tu non obediisti mandatis do-mini dei tui nec precepta eius custodis nec mihi appare voluisti, qui sum etiam min[…] seruus eius ad respondendum mihi quare omnino excommunicabo te et nomen tuum hic positum sine scrip-tum athanatizabo [*anathematizabo] qua propter (properter?) in nomine dei et authoritatis domini nostri Iesu Christi et omnium sanctorum eius sis maledic-tus excommunicatus et nomen tuum scriptum hoc materiali igne comburetur	Because you have not obeyed the or-ders of the Lord your God, nor the warnings of his custodian, nor have been willing to appear to me, nor respond to me, who is also his servant, wherefore I will excommunicate you completely, ban-ish your name here placed or written, which I carry in the name of God and the authority of our Lord Jesus Christ and of all his saints, may you be cursed, ex-communicated, and your written name will be burned up by this material fire

---

83. An unusual addition not present in other magic texts.

ex in fetidis rebus suffumigabuntur ita te spiritum B in nomine dei in profundum puteum abissi ign[is] et sulffuris virtute dei proiicio ubi remaneas usque ad diem Iudiciij [sic] et nunquam sit recordatio de te ante faciem dei vivi qui venturus est Iudicare vivos et mortuos et seculum per ignem amen. /	burning from stinking things; so too I cast you down, O spirit B., into the stinking pit of fire and brimstone, by the power of God, where you will remain until the Day of Judgment, where you can never be recalled before the face of the living God, who will come to judge the living and the dead and the world by fire. Amen.

Then cast the paper into the fire sprinkled with brimstone, and if he burn in chains of fire and brimstone, he will break the binds and come unto thee, for the chains themselves will burst at the hearing of this great sentence pronounced.

But when you will deliver him from pain, say nothing, but write his name again and burn it with sweet smelling odours, and this way may you bring a[ny] spirit to obedience without doubt. Your fire must be of consecrated wood of eglantine. This being with authority is the greatest secret that belongs to art.

Finis.[84] ⤆

[38]

[To] have a spirit in a glass

Take a clean towel[85] and lay it upon a fair table and upon that lay thy glass, and say this oration following.

---

84. In left marg.: "w-."

85. Compare Additional MS. 36674, 39v and 66r, and also Sloane 3850, 79v. Additional MS. 36674, 39v, is the closest parallel, but it is unfortunately much damaged. Additional MS. 36674, 66r, and Sloane 3850, 79v, represent a second version.

Prayer [86]

Omnipotens sempiterne deus adesto magna[e] pietatis* tue misteriis, adesto piis Invocationibus nostris ut speculum istud quod in tuo nomine bene + dicere facti fuere + digneris sanctificare [+ut] intendimus /[spir]itum tuae Benedictionis admitte [*emitte] ut super eum et in eo spiritum tuum benedictum infundas ut [*et] quod humilitates [nostrae] gerendum est misterie [*ministerio] tue virtutes [*virtutis] impleate [*compleatur] effectus [*effectum.] et licet nos tantum [*tantis] ministerium [*mysteriis] exequendis sumus [*simus] indigni.	O almighty and eternal God, be present at these mysteries of your great kindness; be present at our devout invocations, so that you may deign to make this mirror worthy to be blessed in your name, which we strive to sanctify, to send out your spirit of blessing,‡ and pour over it your blessed spirit, that what is to be done by our humble ministry may be accomplished by the effect of your power, although we are unworthy to perform such great mysteries.

* "Potentia" is written above this word.
† Underlined words are written in marg. *sec. man.* Apparently they indicate missing text meant to be inserted here, as seen by comparing with Additional MS. 36674, 39r. They do not occur in the other two analogue texts consulted.

[tu] tamen gratie tue dona non deseras [*deserens] ut [*etiam] ad nostras preces aurem [*aures] tuum [*tuae] pietates [*pietatis] inclines [*inclinas] ut hoc speculum quod in tuo nomine bene + dictus per virtutem sanctific[ati]onis tue accipiat et perfectum fiat receptaculum in hocque obtamus ut creaturas tuas angelicas quas in tuo sacro nomine ad presentium preteritorum et futurorum certificationem vere dicamus [*veritatem] et scientiam perffectam invocare	Yet as you do not abandon the gifts of your grace, so incline the ears of your goodness to our prayers, that this mirror which is blessed in your name, by the power of your holiness, may accept and become a perfect receptacle for accepting your angelic creatures in your holy name, to show a demonstration of the past, present, and future of a true* and perfect knowledge, that we may be able to call upon your ineffable grace, without ambiguity or accusation, whatever

* So additional MS. 36674 and Sloane 3850.

---

86. There are extensive corruption and corrections, which make this page difficult to read. It seems to be a strained adaptation of the highly poetic and elaborate baptism rite in the Gelasian Sacramentary and the Stowe Missal, e.g., F. E. Warren, *The Liturgy and Ritual of the Celtic Church* (Oxford: Clarendon Press, 1881), 207–216.

proponimus [*possimus] tua[m] gratiam ineffabilium sine ambiguitate vell delacione quam quae occulis nostris radiis visibiliter representat per dominum nostrum Iesum Christum q 4 9 v f r m v s p st p* sanctum deus per omnia secula seculorum amen.	it visibly manifests with rays to our eyes, through our Lord Jesus Christ, who lives and reigns with you in unity with the Holy Ghost, God forever and ever. Amen.

* Perhaps corrupted version of H.: *qui tecum vivit & regnat in unitate spiritus sancti Deus per omnia secula…*

The Consecration

Deus qui hoc speculum ex materia fragili in [*ad] usum humani generis fieri per misisti ut lucidantibus radiis spiritus multiplices diffunderes intuentium effigies varios iudicaret respice clementer in faciem istius specudi [*speculi] et multiplica in eo benedictiones tuas quas gratie tue effluentes impetu letificas animam tuam ut tua[e] maiestates imperio sanct [*sumat] unigenit[i] [+tui] gratiam spiritus sancti [*spiritu sancto] qui per sanctum in arthanum [*arcanum] claritatis et luminis adunctiones [*admixtione] fecundet ut sanctificatione accepta et oncepta [+per] angelos vere dicas [*veridicos] quos in tuo nomine [*tui nominis] <et> virtute intendimus invocare propter assuntam [*assuetam] [+ tuam misericordiam] atque naturam intuentibus representet procull ergo [+ ab] huic speculo In bent[??]te [*benedicto] domine lucidissime et verissime omnis spiritus Immundus abstedat	O God, who permitted this mirror to be made from fragile matter for the use of human kind, in order that he may judge by the illuminating rays, the different multi-layered appearances observed by looking at its different shapes; look kindly on the face of this mirror and multiply your blessings in it, that the inrush of your abundant grace gladdens the soul, as with the command of your greatness, in order that it may obtain grace from your Holy Ghost, which through the holy secret* mixture of clarity and light, He (the Holy Ghost) may make this mirror fruitful, that a sanctifying energy being accepted and conceived in it, through your truthful angels, whom we intend to call upon through the power of your name, because of [+ your] usual [+ mercy] † and nature, it may represent by looking at.
	Therefore O Lord, may all unclean spirits depart far from this blessed mirror,

* Following Additional MS. 36674, 39v, and other witnesses.
† So Additional MS. 36674 and Sloane 3850.

[*absistant] procull tota nequitia diabol-ica fraudis et deceptionis absistat sit hoc speculum libera creatura ab omni im-pugnator incurssu et totius falaciis pur-gata dysessorum (?) speculum lucidissi-mum dubia et incerta declara angelos statim resseruans occulta et ignota de clarissime manifestas ut omnis homo in hoc speculo respiciens operante in eo spiritus sanctus perfecte certifacionis de questitis efficaciam consequator, unde [*inde] bene+dicete [*bene+dicito] speculum + per deum vivum + per deum + verum + per deum sanctum + per deum qui te specialem virtutem spe-cies representanti attribuere ut consecra-tur et confermat [*consecratum et con-firmatum] existes virtutem efficacem potentiam suscipias et retineas ad quod te duximus consecrat [*consecratum sis] bene+dicete in super per Iesum Chris-tum <dominum et> filium eius unicum dominum nostrum qui te constantem diephunum esse voluit et Imittere figu-ras et per reflectiones varias demon-strarum [*demonstrare] te deus omnip-otens Invocacio[ni]bus, nostris clemens adesto et et [*in] istud speculum de cel-istis armonia tua claritatis benignus in-fundes tu hoc speculum tuo ore benedi-cito ut per te ustum (?) commicionem et in eo angeli tui compresentes de quesites nostris nos reddent efficacitur certiores.

most clear and true; may all devilish wickedness, delusions, and deceptions withdraw far from this mirror. May the creature of this mirror be free from all attacks, assaults, and purged of all de-ceits and immune from all treachery, and may your divine light surround it, so that all doubts and uncertainties are indicated, that your angels may reveal* very clearly that which is hidden or doubtful, so that anyone who gazes into this mirror may operate in it, O perfect Holy Ghost, and successfully understand what he asks about with certainty.

Therefore I bless you,† O mirror + by the living God, + by the true God, + by the holy God, + by the God who has granted you special power for showing appearances, so that being consecrated and strengthened you may accept and retain the power for which we have di-rected you. Be blessed and consecrated through Jesus Christ his only son our Lord, who has wished you to be consis-tently translucent and to send in the shapes and to demonstrate through dif-ferent reflections with invocations to you almighty merciful God, be present with us, and infuse into this mirror the celestial harmony of your good clarity, speak with your mouth the benediction [+ of this stone], so that through you, for the common use of people, and may your angel be present in it to reliably an-swer our questions.

---

* In marg.: "after drops 5 parts say" (?).
† Another version of this text can be found on Folger p. 27, labeled "alia."

After this is done, put five drops of olive oil in [the glass] like a *cross, and then say this:

Descendat in hoc speculum virtus spiritus sancti conthenzus conthenzuus [*concitetur] speculi scientium representandi mitissimum ferum dit' [*mitissime secundet] effectum ut omnium dubitorum redant certitudo, ut omnis homo in hoc speculo inspiciens vere scientum et certitudinis perfecte se gaudeat informacionem et demonstracionem inpetrasse [*imperasse] per te ipsum dominum qui vivas et regnas et imperas in secula seculorum amen.	May the power of the Holy Ghost descend into this mirror. May it stir up the knowledge manifested in the mirror, that is may further the effect most gently, so that all doubts are resolved with certainty, so that all people gazing into this mirror may themselves enjoy true knowledge and perfect certainty, and command* of the information and demonstration, through you, O Lord who lives and reigns and rules forever. Amen.

* So Additional MS. 36674 and Sloane 3850

After this, take five drops together on thy thumbs, and make a cross and say these words following:

Per istum [*istam] uncionem sit speculum consecratum et benedictum et sanctificutum [*-catum] quae habeat perfectam potestatem ad dimonstrandum nobis angelos quos desideramus in nomine patris et filii et spiritus sancti amen.	Through this anointing may this mirror be consecrated, blessed, and sanctified, so that it may have the perfect power we desire for revealing the angels to us, in the name of the Father and of the Son and of the Holy Ghost. Amen.

After that, make a sufflation,[87] and say, "*Discendat in hoc speculum*" ["descend into this mirror"] as above [88]

After that, wash the glass with wine and holy water and mizes[89] of white bread and after put all in the fire and so the efflor[a]tion assized[90] gladly spirits shall appear and answer openly to all things.

---

87. A sufflation (or in this case an insufflation) is a ritual blowing commonly done in Catholic orthopraxy during the baptism ceremony. Its purpose therein is to "blow away the devil" and "breathe in grace."

88. Additional MS. 36674: "Through this sufflation, descend into this mirror ..." and repeats the rest of the prayer as above.

89. Mizes: crumbs (compare Latin *mica*).

90. Assized: placed.

Then say before the glass:

Coniuro te effloratem per nomen bal-sabu per sancte mater recratatruda morma instillata camnita (?) per crubem magtia minum per sufflitutiam [*sufflentiam] maximam per optimam consuitudinem per omnia cadaura per inferna tributa per sanctam mariam magdelenam per beatam margeretam per caput sancti Ioh[ann]is baptismi per petrum et paulum per virtutem domini nostri Iesu Christi ut in isto specculo continue [*continuas] ad omnia interrogatoria respondebit [*respondeas].	I conjure you, O exhalation, by the name Balsabu, by the holy Mother Recrata truda morma instilled *camnita (?)* by *crulem magtia minum*, by the greatest sufflation, by the best practice, by all *cadaura*, by the infernal tributes (?),† by the holy Mary Magdalene, by the blessed Margaret, by the head of the holy John the Baptist, by Peter and Paul, by the virtue of our Lord Jesus Christ, that you join to this mirror to respond to everything that is asked.
* Manuscript has "caita" with a macron above it. Additional MS. 36674 and Sloane 3850 read *per fantasmatis cauta* ["by the concerns of the phantasm"]. † None of the three versions consulted make much sense: Additional MS. 36674: *Ne Truda, Truda Normay instillator, Coniuro te Essleracon per nomen Belfalit per fantasmatis cauta per Cruelon istam magnam, per sufflentiam maximam*; Sloane 3850: *Ne Truda Truda Normay instillator coniuro te Essleracon per nomen Belfalum* etc. as in Additional MS. 36674.	

After this he shall soon appear, with a voice saying and doing all things to thy will. [Then] if he wishes, the master should licence him [to depart].

Experiment of invisibility [91]

Now I will speak about invisibility. Therefore on the day and hour of Jupiter make the same circle that you made for love,[92] and enter the circle with your instruments. Moreover, you should have had your bed properly and beautifully made up, and

---

91. In pencil in marg. (old hand): "… Lib' 9 (?), fol. 99 ….haue (?) this experiment." Compare slightly more elaborate versions in Sloane 3853, fol. 36r ff and 119v ff, Sloane 3885, fol. 50r ff, and Mun. A.4.98, 72 ff and 78 ff. Another variation can be found in Sloane 3853, fol. 119v ff, and Wellcome MS. 110, 79r. On a similar operation involving Queen Sympilia and her retinue, see Greenfield, *Traditions*, 214, and A. Delatte, *Anecdota Atheniensia* I (Paris, 1927), 433 lines 9–21, and a recent translation by Ioannis Marathakis, *The Magical Treatise of Solomon or Hygromanteia* (Singapore: Golden Hoard Press, 2011). There is also a short version in Peterson, *Grimorium Verum* (2007), 44.

92. The experiment for love immediately precedes this in Sloane 3853 and Sloane 3885, and evidently in the prototype being used here.

equipped with clean linens.[93] And the circle thus well prepared, face south in such a way that the middle of the table is beyond the circle. Say the same conjuration, extending your scepter here (i.e., towards the south), and only you should be operating.[94]

Coniuro vos spiritus Micoll titam et burfex o virgines gloriose per infinitam dei patris potentiam per infinitam filii sui sapientiam per infinitam sancti spiritus clementiam et per beatissimam virginem mariam et per omnem celi melitiam et per tremendum diem Iudicii
 	
   coniuro etiam vos virgines per omnes spiritus Iouis omni mundo et per emanacionem sanguinis a latere crucifixi per cissuram templi et veli et per obstritaconem [*obscuracionem] solis in eius mortis et per mortuorum resurrectionem et per virginitatem humilem et fecunditatem beatissimum genetricis dei et per omnia nomina sua et per omnia nomina domini nostri Iesu Christi et per illud ineffabile nomen quod in sceptro meo hic in sculptur est et in anulo meo
	I conjure you, O spirits Micoll, Titan,* and Burfex, O glorious† maidens by the infinite power of God the Father, the infinite wisdom of the Son, and by the infinite mercy of the Holy Ghost, and by the blessed virgin Mary, and by all the hosts (or army) of heaven, and by the terrible Day of Judgement.
	
	   I also conjure you, O three maidens, by all the spirits of Jupiter, and by this sigil of Jupiter which I show here, and by the flowing of blood from the side of Jesus at his crucifixion, and by the tearing of the veil in the temple, and by the darkening of the Sun at the time of his death, and by his resurrection from death, and by the humble virginity and fertility of the blessed Mary, mother of God, and by all her names, and by all the

* Sloane 3853: "Aricol or Micol, Tytarit or Titan, and Bursex or Burphax." Compare "Florella, Mical, and Tytan" in Sloane 1727, fol. 37r. Sloane 3853, fol. 119v: "Meillia, Catillia, et Sabillia." Sloane 3885, fol. 50v: "Michael [sic] Titan et Burfax." Sloane 3846, 31v: "Mycholl, Setan, & Burfax." Mun. A.4.98, 72, reads "Michol titan et burfax," but on p. 78 "Micob" etc.
† Sloane 3853, fol. 36v, and Mun. A.4.98, 72: *generose* ["noble"].

---

93. Sloane 3853 adds: *Et facias circulum circo lectum tuum, et habeas mensam nouam quam in primo tractatu diximus ad latitudinem cubiti unius. Et sint suppositoria eiusdem mense de lignis lauri habeasque mappam nouam lota in aquam rosaica. Et tres cultellos novos cum manubriis albis & sanctificatis & 3es ciphos plenos aquam pura cum tribus peruis panibus paratis iuxta circulum* ["And you should make the circle around your bed, and have a new table which we spoke of in the first treatise, with a width of one cubit. And this table of laurel should be placed beneath a new tablecloth washed in rose water. And three new knives with white handles, and consecrated, and three cups filled with pure water, and furnished with three small breads, beside the circle"]. Mun. A.4.98, 72 ff, is similar.

94. Sloane 3853 and Mun. A.4.98: *Sic que medietas mense sit infra circulum quibus bene preparatis verso vultu ad austrum protendendo sceptru ad austrum Sol existens in circulo dicas prima coniurationem* ["And thus the middle of the table should be beyond the circle. With this well prepared, turn and face the south, stretching out your scepter towards the south, the sun rising in the circle, you should say the first conjuration"].

mirifice in signiter [*insignitum] quatenus mihi visibilitater venietes et annulum invisibilitates mihi aportare festinatis et mihi solacium que poteritis in omnibus preparatis et meum velle cum effectu perficere non desinatis et sine fictione fallatia, vell mora mihi celeriter apparetei ut una ex vobis quacunque eligero in hoc lecto sanctissimo quiessere se festinat et ut omnes terrarum populi sciant quam mirabile sit et gloriosum nomen deus sacratissimum ipso prestante qui veniet Iudicare seculum per ignem amen.

names of our Lord Jesus Christ, and by that ineffable name which is carved on my scepter, and marked on my wonderful ring,* that you come to me visibly, and hasten to bring me the ring of invisibility, and comfort me in all things which you are able, and prepare to fulfill my will without stopping and without fabricating, deceit, or delay, quickly appearing to me, and that one of you, whichever I will select, will hasten to rest herself in this most sacred bed, and in order that all the peoples of the earth may know what a miracle is, and (by) the excellent and glorious and most sacred name of God himself, who will come to judge the world by fire. Amen.

* Sloane 3853, fol. 38v, says the ring should have the name Tetragrammaton engraved on it. There is a drawing of it on fol. 53r showing Hebrew lettering and crosses. Design for the ring (pictured below), according to Sloane 3853.

[39]

With this complete, if they don't come, then repeat,[95] and doubtlessly they will come, and they will not fear the circle nor touch the scepter, but they will immediately put themselves around the table, paying respects to you. But you should not leave the circle because of this, but sit. Nor eat with them, but you will see them hasten to eat, and a glorious table, well-equipped with all foods possible, and they will often offer you drink and wine. But one of them, the most pretty, and the smallest,

---

95. Sloane 3853 and Mun. A.4.98 add: *3a vice* ["three times"].

will not speak to you, nor will she face you, but will stand away from the others, so that you will be able to offer her the top of the sceptre,[96] which if she doesn't fear, give to her to kiss (while remaining in the circle), and you should say as follows:

Coniuro te virgo pulcherrima per coniurationem et verba virtute quorum huc venisti quatenus mihi dato anulo invisibilitatis mihi visibiliter ad hunc lectum accedere sine mora festines et nuda ibidem quoque iaceas et mihi omne solatium facias quod poteris sine fraude vell damno vell illusione vel lesure corporali nec recedes quousque licentiam tibi voluero concedere quia te elego in meam et astringo te horum virtute verborum prestante domino nostro Iesu Christo qui viuit et regnat deus amen.	I conjure you, O most beautiful maiden, by the conjuration and words by whose power you have come here, that you give me the ring of invisibility. Hasten to approach this bed without delay, visible to me, and likewise lie down naked in that place, and provide me with all comfort which you are able, without fraud or forfeiture or illusion or physical injury, not leaving until such time as I wish to grant your freedom, because I select you as mine, and bind you by the power of these words, with our Lord Jesus Christ as our guide, who lives and reigns, God. Amen.

Having finished this, you should sit down, and she herself will give you a ring of invisibility, and immediately afterward she will laugh a little. And without delay the others will indignantly stop dining, whereupon when you see this, you are free to bid them depart in peace. Then you may go to the bed, and lie down nude, you on your right side, and she on her left side. And you can know her and do whatever you wish with her, because without doubt she is a woman, nor will she be able to harm you if she has been bound, and never have you had a more gentle or amorous creature in bed, for I have tried this many times.[97] Nevertheless, she is willing to speak little[98] to you, nor may you inquire from her whether she is a woman or some spirit.[99]

But be careful that you ask her for the ring, and everything else you wish, the first time you call them, before you go to the bed, because she will try to cheat you, saying "I cannot grant your petitions yet, but if you lie down with me, I believe I will satisfy you well enough." However, after enjoying her company in bed, you will no longer be

---

96. Following Sloane 3853: *vel [*nec] tibi loquetur nec tibi vultum faciet ad quem secrecius quo poteris ad os eius septri summitatem offeres.*

97. Wellcome MS. 110 adds: *et socius meus similiter* ["and my associate has likewise"].

98. Wellcome MS. 110 adds: *vel nihil* ["or nothing"].

99. Wellcome MS. 110 adds: *seu corpus [f]antasticum* ["or phantastical body"]. This is reminiscent of the tale of Lohengrin. Presumably, if you ask her about her nature, you will lose her forever.

able to compel her, because you will then be impure. When all is done, you may permit her to depart, and you may lie down in your bed in the circle until morning.

The end.

The licence (or releasing) of any spirit

O tu spiritus N qui es creatura dei te coniuro per virtutem omnium sanctorum nominum dei, et per omnia nomina sanctorum angelorum archangelorum patriarcharum prophetarum apostolorum evangelistarum martirum confessorum atque virginum et per virtutem sanctissime genetrices dei marie, ut vadas de [*ad] quibus venisti sine nocumento corporis mei vell alicuius animalis in toto mundo et paratus esto ad me venire quando te invocavero per virtutem huius nominis dei + Tetragram[m]aton + vade in pace absque ulla tempestate, aut ullo malo faciens in nomine patris, et filii, et spiritus sancti amen. / et dic in principio &c.	O you spirit N., who is a creature of God, I conjure you by the virtue of all the holy names of God, and by all the names of the holy angels, archangels, patriarchs, prophets, apostles, evangelists, martyrs, confessors and virgins, and by the virtue of the most holy mother of God Mary, that you rush from [*to] wherever you have come from, without harming my body, or any animal in the whole world, and be prepared to come to me when you are invoked, by the virtue of this name of God + Tetragrammaton + Go in peace, without any storming, and without doing anything bad, in the name of the Father, and the Son, and the Holy Ghost. Amen.

And then say "In the beginning..."[100]

A general rule, when that you call a spirit first and he appear: when he is come, ask
him nothing, but charge him to be obedient to that book forever after: and at that
ti[me] ask him no more, but licence him until another time, and when thou wilt call
h[im] again, and he shall tell and be ready to give thee a true answer at all times of all
things.

---

100. John chapter 1.

This is the consecration of the circle [101]

Coniuro te circulum et consecro locum istum per illum vivum et verum deum creatorem celi et terri qui istum circulum et locum per ipsum creatorem celi et terre qui hista nomina the[os +] Iskiros + athanatos + Ioth + atheo + sabaoth + pheabaoth + hele + hubiet + ad[...] + antrielle + amarelle + condonelle + agios + chebenas + thele[as +] ymas + ban + hen + hely + en + vaus + ethen + bury + tallens + Sem[...] nomine + Ianayara + et per omnia nomina sanctissima dei nota et ignota sit locus iste circulus iste ex dono gracie omnipotentis altissimi dei, benedictus + et consecratu[s] sanctifi+catus et custoditus societate omnium sanctorum evangelistarum martirum p[atri]archarum prophetarum principatum potestatum consumatus [*confirmatus] et consiliatus circul[us] vel locus iste quatenus virtutem potestatem et sanctitatem suam capiat in signo dei v[ivi et veri] et a sancta cruce Christi et a sancta maria matre domini nostri Jesu Christi plena gracie co[nse]cratus itaque quod per [*ingredi nec intra] circulum istum terrores trimores [*timores] tempestates aliquo modo cause [*nobis] nocendi non valiant in ferre [*valeant inferre] ipso adiuuante et circum cidente [*defendente], cui celest[ia] terrestria et infernalia subiciuntur. amen	I conjure you, O circle, and consecrate this place by that living and true God, creator of Heaven and Earth, and indeed this circle and place, by these names of the creator of Heaven and Earth The[os +] Iskiros + Athanatos + Ioth + Atheo + Sabaoth + Pheabaoth + Hele + Hubiet + Ad[...] + Antrielle + Amarelle + Condonelle + Agios + Chebenas + Thele[as +] Ymas + Ban + Hen + Hely + En + Vaus + Ethen + Bury + Tallens + Sem[...] the name + Ianayara + and by all the most holy names of God, whether known or unknown. May the site of this circle be granted the gift of the grace of the almighty and most high God. May it be blessed and consecrated, sanctified and guarded by the company of all saints, preachers, martyrs, patriarchs, prophets, [Angels, Archangels, Dominations,] Principalities, Powers, strengthen and restore this circle or place so that it may take on virtue, power, and holiness from the sign of the living and true God and from the holy cross of Christ and from the holy Mary, mother of our Lord Jesus Christ full of grace, consecrated therefore so that no terrors, fears, and tempests may be able to enter this circle, or harm us in any way, that it may be strong for helping and defending us, which all heavenly, earthly, and infernal powers are subject to. Amen.*
* There is corruption in all three versions consulted, but this seems to be the general sense of the passage.	

101. In marg.: "...s is more perfect ... ar after in this booke ...d also in the booke ... th came out of order. / fol. 61." In later (pagination) hand: "107." Compare with "consecratio circuli" on p. 97. Compare also Sloane 3853, fol. 68r.

Consecration of the holy water [102]

Asperge [*Aspergo] te equa [*aqua] benedicta in circulo et in loco omnipotentis dei qui te aqua facit benedixit et conse+cravit et dedit potestatem famulis suis sacerdotibus precipue con[secrare] qui est pater et filius et spiritus sanctus, et ego te aqua benedict' [*benedico] Invoco et exorziz[o] in nomine dei et sancte matris Ecclesie et maria matris eius nec non in nomine et virtu[te] eius et omnium sanctorum et sanctarum eius cum omni celesti consertio ut tu aqua sis consecra[ta] per illum deum qui te fecit et consecrari iussit sis omnibus nobis protectio et defentio a[b] omnibus diaboli tempestationibus [*temptationibus] et infestationibus insidiis et fraudibus potestate sancti spiriti nobis qui misericordia suam posse ubique ad omne dignetur per Christi dominum nostrum am[en.]	I sprinkle you, O holy water, in the circle and in the place of almighty God, who made you blessed and consecrated, and has given power to his servants, especially to the priests to consecrate [it in his name],* who is the Father, Son, and Holy Ghost, and I bless, invoke, and exorcise you, O water, in the name of God, and the holy mother Church, and Mary his mother, and besides in his name and virtue and of all the saints male and female, with all the celestial assembly, in order that you, O water, may be consecrated through that God who has made you, and ordered you to be consecrated for our protection and defense against all temptations of the Devil, and against his assaults and snares, by the power of the Holy Ghost, who is merciful to us, and may it be deemed worthy everywhere and for everything, through Christ our Lord. Amen.

* Following Sloane 3853: *dedit potestatem sacerdotibus precipue in diebus dominicis in ecclesia sua illam Aquam in nomine suo bene+dicere & sancti+ficere qui est pater ...* ["he gave power to the priests, especially on Sundays in his Church to bless and sanctify that water in his name, who is the Father" etc.]

In order that the spirits don't have the power to harm you, these names are written on your chest or in your hand.

Here are the most holy names which make the spirits speak:

+ Emanuell + sabaoth + on + messias + sother + Agla + Adonay + + yana + you + Tetragram[m]aton + semephoron + vay + any + eye + ass[...] + essereayeey + Adonay + sabaothe +	+ Emanuell + Sabaoth + On + Messias + Sother + Agla + Adonay + + Yana + You + Tetragram[m]aton + Semephoron + Vay + Any + Eye + Ass[...] + Essereayeey + Adonay + Sabaothe +

102. From Book of Consecration; compare Sloane 3853, fol. 67.

[40]  103

It is good to have these names written on your chest, or in your hand when you conjure the spirits.

Concerning Baron[104]

Take a sheet of parchment made from unborn dog, and write on it these characters ᙄᙅ ᙄᑕ ᖇᐁᒿ ᖯ ᙭ ᥱᒿ with the blood of a lapwing,[105] but if you are unable, with the blood of a magpie.[106] Then hold the paper in your hand, and recite Psalm 51 ("Have mercy on me, O God...."[107]) three times. Then say the conjuration which concerns the spirit Baron.

When any (?) spirit appeareth, say this:[108]

I conjure thee, spirit N., now that thou art appeared to me by Almighty God, and by all his virtue, might, and strength, and by all the virtue which he hath in heaven, in earth, and in the sea, and under the earth, and by the high name of God + Agla + that thou be obedient unto me and serve me, saying ever to me the truth in all things that I shall ask thee. I conjure thee by the dreadful day of doom that thou make no lies to me nor false imaginations, neither use any false wiles, but ever tell the truth and give to me a true answer of all that I shall require of thee. *Iterum* ["again"], I conjure thee by the holy names of God Pneumaton + that Moses named when the earth swallowed Dathan and Abyron, right so in the same name, I conjure and command thee to speak unto me meekly, lowly, and gently and openly in a man's voice, and say the truth of that I shall ask thee, *fiat, fiat, fiat*. Amen. And if thou withstand my will and com-

---

103. Stylized Pseudo-Hebrew Tetragrammaton—Hebrew letters—"Yod-He-Vau-He- Nun? / Yod-He-Vau-He/."

104. Compare below Folger p. 134 and again p. 175. Compare also Wellcome MS. 110, 39v, where the spirit is named "Barachin," and Sloane 3853, 215r, where it is called "Baraham or Baron."

105. Latin reads *upupa*, which generally means hoopoe *(upupa epops)*, but this manuscript elsewhere (Folger pp. 56 and 167) translates it as "lapwing." The editors strongly condemn mistreating animals.

106. Or perhaps *pici* ["woodpecker"], but JHP doesn't recall seeing the latter used in magical texts.

107. Psalm 50 (KJV 51).

108. In faded lighter (red?) ink in marg., mostly illegible: "[??]s exp'is [?]rifer / [.]tr set do[??]nis in th[?]a / [.]et hearap'e[?] p 177 / so it is fol. 59 lib. /[??]er."

mandments in word or deed, by day or night, here or elsewhere, now or at any time hereafter, I condemn thee by name N., by all the might of God and our lady Saint Mary and of all the company in and of heaven, by the pain, death, and passion of our Lord Jesus suffered, and by the virtue of his blessed flesh and blood, and by the virtue of all the holy names that I afore here have named and read. I command and bind thee to the deep pit of hell: there to remain till the day of doom except thou give me anon a grant of my asking in all things that thou mayest do.

Bind him by this oath, and make him say after thee these words:

I, N., swear by God, by the Holy Virgin Mary, mother of Almighty God, and by all the company of heaven that I will be ready to thee, N., by day and by night, to say and to do truly, without leasing or subtlety or guile, that I can or may and that without circle, character, [or] conjuration when thou wilt call me.

The experiment of Baron

Experiment of Baron,[109] who is said to be good for hidden treasure, and he is able to do many other things. You may operate at any day or hour of the day or night, in the bedroom of the house, or out in a field, either alone or with two or three associates, but alone is better. Make a circle in the earth,[110] but when you have spoken with the spirit once with the circle, you will not need it again. In the first place, when you wish to operate, you must fast for three days on bread and water, and abstain from sexual gratification, and cut your nails, both hands and feet. Then take the skin of an unborn cat,[111] and make four pieces of paper, and write these characters with the pentacle of Solomon to what purpose they will be dedicated, with the blood of a lapwing, … (?), or in whichever part you place one piece of paper, …, then hold the paper in your right hand and say Psalm 51 ("Have mercy on me, O God") three times. Then say:

---

109. Compare also Sloane 3853, fol. 215r.

110. Sloane 3853 adds "with the sword."

111. Instead of *catti* ["of a cat"], Sloane 3853 reads *canis* ["of a dog"], and "Concerning Baron" above does as well.

The invocation of Baron

Coniuro te spiritum qui vocaueris baron per fidem quam debes socio tuo prevat et per virtutem domini nostri Iesu Christi filii dei viui puri, et misericordissimi et per illum angelum qui in tuba canet in die Iudicii, et dicet venit venit venit et per omnes angelos et archangelos thronos et ducatus [*dominaciones] principalitates [*principates] potestates cherubin et seraphin, et virtutes,	I conjure you,* O spirit who is called Baron, by the loyalty which you owe to your personal servant, and by the strength of our Lord Jesus Christ, son of the living God, pure and merciful,† and by that angel who will sound the trumpet on the Day of Judgement, and will say "come, come, come," and by all Angels and Archangels, Thrones and Dominations, Principates, Potestates, Cherubin and Seraphin, and Virtues.

* Compare Sloane 3853, fol. 224r; Wellcome MS. 110, fol. 39v, 43r.
† Sloane 3853: *dei viui et veri & pii misericordissimi* ["living and true and blessed God most merciful"]. Wellcome MS. 110: *dei viui ac veri et misericordissimi.*

Coniuro te baron per po[e]nas domini nostri Iesu Christi et per pat[i]bulum crucis in qua suspensus <est deus> [*fuerit, et] per claues quibus affixus est cruci et per lancea[m] qua latus eius perforatus est, et per sanguinem et aqua[m] que de lattere eius effluxerunt, et per transiuit et per mortem et resurrectionem et ascentionem eius et per sempiternam graciam spiritus sancti par[a]cleti, et per anulum et sigillum salomonis, et per vinculum salomonis, et per angelos et per virtutem qua sol obstatus est [*obscuratus erat] et petre cesse sunt, et monumenta apereta et sunt	I conjure you, O Baron, by the condemnation of our Lord Jesus Christ, and by the yoke of the cross on which he was suspended, and by the nails which attached him to the cross, and by the lance which pierced his side, and by the blood and water which flowed from his side, and by <crossed> [*the crown of thorns which he wore on his head],* and by his death and resurrection and ascension, and by the eternal † grace of the Holy Ghost, the Paraclete, and by the ring and sigil of Solomon, and by the bond of Solomon, and by the angels,‡ and by the power which obscured the Sun, broke up

* Following Wellcome MS. 110: *per coronam spineam quam in suo capite portauit.*
† Wellcome MS. 110: *septiformam* ["seven-fold"].
‡ Probably a corruption of l*apidem angularem*, which appears in parallel passages in this text Folger pp. 134 and 175.

et multa corpa sanctorum qui dorm- ierunt surrexerunt, per virgam quea [*quae] mare apparuit, et per virgam A[a]ron et archum federis per tronum dei viui, et per thuruludum [*thuribu- lum] auream et per altare aureum que qui est ante occulos eius et per premissas [*mensus] <et per missas> pro posito- rum [*positionum], et per sanctum sanctorum	the rocks, and opened the tombs and caused the bodies of many saints who had slept to rise up,* and by the staff which parted the sea, and by the staff of Aaron, and by the Ark of the Covenant, and by the throne of the living God, and by the golden censer, and by the golden altar which is before his eyes, and by the weighing of the facts, and by the holy of holies.†

* Matthew 27:51.

† Based on parallel text on Folger p. 175. Wellcome MS. 110 reads *per omnes missas prophetarum et apostolorum* ["by all the Masses of the prophets and apostles"]. Since this is evidently structured on Revelations 8:3, it originally probably read something like *per omnes preces prophetarum et sanctorum et sanctarum* ["by all the prayers of the prophets and saints"].

Coniuro te spiritus qui vocater [*vo- catur] baron per glorisum virginem mariam matrem domini nostri Iesu Christi qui dei filium portavit et sanctis- simum nomen eius, ⟨et latus eius⟩ et latus [*loc] eius gloriose [*gloriosi] vir- ginis et uberaque dominus proprio ore suscepit et succit, qui vocatur, Alpha et Omega + ya + haday + Emanuell + sa- baoth + Arphaxat + et per hoc nomen sanctum dei semafores + et per hoc nomen Adonay + quod dominus media nocte clamauit ad qua vocem omnes mortui boni et mali in Ictu oculi resur- gent, et per nomen Sother + in quo fa- ciet dominus omnes lapides terra<u>m	I conjure you, O spirit who is called Baron, by the glorious Virgin Mary, mother of our Lord Jesus Christ, who carried the son of God, and by his most holy name, and by the milk of the glori- ous virgin, which the Lord accepted into his own mouth from her and from her breasts, he who is called Alpha and Omega + Ya + Haday* + Emanuel + Sa- baoth + Arphaxat + and by this holy name of God Semiphoras + and by this name Adonay + which the Lord pro- claimed in the middle of the night, which being called, all the dead—good and evil—will be raised up in the blink of an eye, and by the name Sother† + by

* Likely an error for "Ya + Saday." The parallel text on Folger p. 175 reads "Vasaday." Wellcome MS. 110 and Sloane 3853 both read "Ya."

† Compare Sloane 3847, fol. 16r ff, Wellcome MS. 110, fol. 37r.

et omnia edificia una die unum adversum altrum distruere, et in simull debellare, et tunc [41] diciter umentibus [*dicent viuentis] montibus cadite super nos a [*et] facere [+ benedictionem] sedente [*sedenti] super<a> thronum e[t] per hoc nomen ineffabile quod est Ya in quo dominus noster pacter [*peracto] Iudicio diabolum cum tota corpore suo, et cum omnibus impiis suis in carcere[m] et in stagnum ignis et sulphuris precipitabit, et dominus cum suis electis cum gloria triumphali in celestium patriam reuertetur, coniuro te exorzizo te Baron ut sis spiritus benignes [*benignus] et humilis in omnibus mihi serui es [sic] socijs tuis per benedicionem dei in firmento celi, et per laudabilem et mirabilem ascencionem eius et per gloriosum Iudicium eiu[s] et formidabile vel formicabile in secula seculorum.

which the Lord made all stones of the earth, and all buildings, to demolish one opponent after another, and likewise to vanquish them, "and then [41] the living will say to the mountains, fall upon us, and to the hills: cover us,"* and make (a benediction) "to him who sits on the throne,"† and by this ineffable name which is Ya, by which our Lord will carry out judgment on the Devil with all his congregation, and all his wicked will be thrown into prison and into the lake of fire,‡ and the Lord with his chosen, and the triumphant glory of the Heavenly Father will be restored. I conjure you, O Baron, that you be benignant and humbly serve me in all things, along with your associates, by the blessing of God in the firmament of Heaven, and by his praiseworthy and miraculous ascension, and by his glorious judgment, and terrifying or tingling (!) forever and ever.

* Luke 23:30.
† Revelations 4.9 and 6:16.
‡ Revelations 20:9.

Coniuro te iterum Baron per angelos et archangelos dei et omnes celos dei, coniuro te Baron per aquas qui super celos sunt, et per omnes virtutes dei, et per solem et lunam, per Imberem et rorem et omnes spiritus domini coniure [* coniuro] te per ignis estum frigus, et estatem glacies et viues [*niues,] noctes, et dies, per fulgura et nubes coniuro te Baron per terram et 4 elementa coniuro

I again conjure you, O Baron, by the angels and archangels of God, and by all the heavens of God. I conjure you, O Baron, by the waters which are above the heavens, and by all the powers of God, and by the Sun and the Moon, by the rain and the dew, and by all the spirits of the Lord. I conjure you by the fire and the raging heat, by the winter and the summer, by the ice and snows, by night

te Baron per montes et colles et per omnia gernimanta [*germinantia] in terr[a.] Coniuro te baron per volucres celi, per omnes bestias et pecora et omnes filius [*filios] homi[num.] Coniuro te Baron per Isralem et omnes sacerdotes et servos dei, et per omnes spiritus et animas iustorum dei, et omnes sanctos et humiles corde, coniuro te Baron per pulmonem et epac domini et per omnia membra dei, et per quinque vulnera dei, et per septem sacramenta ecclesie dei, ut scito [*cito] venias hunc coram me et sociis meis in forma humana et facias et compleas quecunque dicam tibi.

and day, by the lightning and the clouds. I conjure you, O Baron, by the earth and the four elements. I conjure you, O Baron, by the mountains and hills, and by all that sprouts forth on the earth. I conjure you, O Baron, by the birds in the skies, and by the beasts and cattle, and by all the children of mankind. I conjure you, O Baron, by Israel, and by all the priests and servants of God, and by all the spirits and souls of the just of God, and by all the saints and those of humble heart. I conjure you, O Baron, by the Lord's lungs and liver, and by all the internal organs of God, and by God's five wounds, and by the seven sacraments of God's church, that you quickly come to me in person in human form, and to my associates, and accomplish and fulfill whatever I ask you.

And immediately that spirit will come, who is wise and obedient in all things.

When you wish to operate, write these characters with the blood of a lapwing:[112] *ʃ·η·ɪ·ʃʃ·Ƈ·ν·ʃ·Ɂₒ+·Ƈ·ṅ·ʒ·Ƙₒ·ʃ·ꞙₙʃʃo͂·ʓ·ⱬ͜ᴜ·ͤℓβ·* Hold these characters in your right hand, and say the whole Psalm "Have mercy on me, O God"[113] three times, and then begin, and he will tell you whatever you wish, and come in human form, or however you wish. Then make your interrogation, and he will respond to you. And if you wish he will bring a virgin girl, that you may have conjugal relations without harm, and he can point out hidden treasure, and can make discord or harmony between men and women, and can do many other things. Your petition complete, Baron himself will say to you, "give me [leave." Then give him his freedom, and][114] order him that he should come and respond to you when called by conjuration, whether in the house or outside, and whatever hour you wish to have him, and

---

112. Latin *upupa*, but see note on Folger p. 40.

113. Psalm 50 (KJV 51).

114. Restored per parallel text on Folger p. 176, and to complete the sense.

then say to him that he can retire in peace, in the name of the Father, and the Son, and the Holy Ghost. Amen. [115]

A bond for a spirit who is rebellious and won't appear

Maledicti summe trinitates, et individue unitates patris, et filii, et spiritus sancti discendat super vos N. eo qui desedere nolite, vel coram nobis apparere recus[at] conculcat capita vestra humilitas, et virgintas beate marie virgines lig[ent] et destruant vos omnea merita, et intercessiones omnium sanctorum angelorum, archangelorum patriarcharum, prophetarum apostolorum evangelistarum innocentiam martirum conffessorum atque virginum et omnium electorum dei qui ab initio mundi fuerunt usque in hanc horam confundant vos omnia sacramenta eccl[es]ie dei destruant et interficiant vos omnes vires, et potencie dei sumi trinitate [+ per] passionis [*passiones] domini nostri Iesu Christi et per eius resurrectionem in ignem eternum mittaturos [*mittereris] Iubeo Ibidem duriter tormentari multiplicantur si[s] vos omnes dolores mundi et infernorum semper sitis infernis ignis ligati et penam ignis ibū [*ibi] sustinatis, nisi thesaurum hic in terra subpositum et recondit nobis statim dederitis et in nostra potestate ac regimine relinquerite, et permisseritis vel sic mihi obedierite [*obedire] mihi feceritis nisi mihi statim appareti[s] hic ante circulum, etc ut vis et multiplicantur super

The curses of the ultimate Trinity, and indivisible Unity, Father and Son and Holy Ghost, descend upon you, O N., one who has been unwilling to descend, and refuses to appear to us in person, they tread upon your head. May the humility and the virginity of the blessed Virgin Mary bind and destroy you. May and all the merits and the intercession of all saints, angels, archangels, patriarchs, prophets, apostles, evangelists, innocents, martyrs, confessors, and virgins, and all the elect of God, who have been clean from the beginning up to this very hour, confound you. May all the sacraments of the church of God demolish and destroy you. May all the powers and forces of the highest God and Trinity. By the passions of our Lord Jesus Christ, and by his resurrection, may you be sent into eternal fire. I order you to be harshly tormented in that place, and your pains be multiplied with all the pains of the world and of hell. May you be bound always in chains of fire, and there sustain pains of fire, unless you immediately grant to us the treasure hidden beneath this ground, and relinquish it into our power and control, or otherwise obey me, (or unless you immediately appear to me before this circle, etc.) Unless you

---

115. Compare Sloane 3853, fol. 215r.

vos maledictus spiritus omnes dolores supradicti sicut arene maris et stelle celi donec peticiones et disider[i]um nostrum sine mora perimpleueritis et hoc absque damno aliquo anima[rum] nostrarum aut corpor<or>um, fiat fiat fiat amen.

satisfy my wishes, O cursed spirit, I will multiply your punishment with all the pains mentioned above, as the sands in the sea and the stars in the sky, unless you fulfill our petitions and desires without delay, and this without any forfeiture of our souls or bodies. Fiat, fiat, fiat. Amen.

Prayer [+ of purification]

O pie exaudibilis deus, et domine sancte pater omnipotens eterne deus et miserico[rs] deus qui cuncta creasti et omnia cognostis tu sis que [*et scis quod hoc] non facimus propter vel causa proband virtutem tuam sed causa obtinend, et habendi thesaurum his inffossum atq[ue] sepultum ergo / obsecro te domine per tuam misericordium, et potentiam et pietatem e[t] per ineffabilem venerabilem, et trimendum nomen tuum + Ioth + per quae tremet sanctum seculum cuius pauore obediunt omnes creature mihi trubuere digne[ris] ut ex hac operacionem propter tua sanctissima et inficatissima [*infinitissima] verba tua hunc thesaurum quali sanctum quae sat citissimum habeamus per illud sanctissimum nomen tuum Adonay + cuius regnum permanet in eternum sine fine. amen.

O blessed God,* worthy of being heard, and holy Lord, Father almighty eternal God, and merciful God, who has created all things and knows all things, know that we do this not to tempt your power, but to obtain our petition, and this treasure which is buried and hidden. Therefore I entreat you, O Lord, by your mercy and power and pity, and ineffable venerability, and by your terrifying name + Ioth + at which all creatures tremble with fear and obey. Deign to grant me success in this operation, because of your most sacred and infinite words, that we may have this treasure very quickly, through that most sacred name of yours, Adonay + whose power persists forever without end. Amen.

* Compare *Clavicula*—Aubrey 24, 73v; Additional MS. 10862, 19v; Michael 276, p. 23; Mathers, *The Key of Solomon the King*, book I chapter 5.

[42]

When you have finished, say the following prayer, and the Gospel of St. John.

Deus propicius esto mihi peccatori miserimo et custos sis mihi omnibus diebus vite me deus Abraham deus Iacobus miserere mei, et mitte mihi adiutorum sanctum michalem arcangelum gloriosissimum qui defendat me hodie, et protegat me ab omnibus Inimicis meis visibilibus et invisibilibus sanctum michalem archangelum defende me in praelio ut non periam in tremendo	O God, be favourable to me, a poor sinner, and guard me all the days of my life. O God of Abraham, God of Jacob, have pity on me, and send the help of your holy and most glorious Archangel Michael who defends me today, and protects me from all my enemies visible and invisible. Archangel Michael, defend me in battle that I may not die in terror.

Iudico, michaell sancte archangelem Christi per gratiam qua meruisti a domino te deprecor per unigenitum deus dominum nostrum Iesum Christum ut eripias me hodie, et omne tempore a periculi mortis et ab insidiis demonum sancte michaell sancte gabriell sancte uriell sancte raphaell sancte thobiell sancte barachiell sancte cherubin sancte saraphin et omnes sancte virtutes celorum ut mihi per summam potentiam dei prestetis auxilium deus det mihi gratiam ut null[us] Inimicus me condemnare posset, nec in via, nec in domo, nec in coniuio, nec extra domum vigelantem, nec dormientem, nec morte subitanea, nec aliquomodo perturbare, ecce crucem + fugite partes adverse vicit leo de tribu Iuda ex sterpe [*filius] david	I proclaim, Michael, holy archangel of Christ, by the grace which you have merited from God, I entreat you by the only-begotten son of God, our Lord Jesus Christ, that you rescue me today, and at all times, from mortal danger, and from the snares of the demons. O holy Michael, holy Gabriel, holy Uriel, holy Raphael, holy Thobiel,* holy Barachiel, holy cherubim, holy seraphin, and all the holy powers of Heaven, may you grant help by the highest power of God. May God give me grace, that no enemy will be able to condemn me, not on the road, nor at home, nor drowsy, nor outside the home, waking nor sleeping, nor sudden death, nor to disturb me in any way. Behold the cross + Flee ye adversaries! The lion from the Tribe of Juda, the

* An angel who turns up repeatedly in fifteenth-century sources. If there were to be a seventh angel here, it would likely be Raguel, with whom he appears elsewhere.

radix Iesse. all[elui]a all[elui]a salva me qui per crucem et sanguinem tuum redemisti me, auxilia me deus meus Agros Agros crux + Christi salva me crux + Christi protege me crux + Christi + defende me. / Iesu tua passio sit mihi protectio amen.	root of David, son of Jesse has conquered. Alleluia, alleluia, alleluia. Save me; by your cross and your blood you have redeemed; help me, O my God, Agros Agros,* the cross + of Christ saves me, the cross + of Christ protects me, the cross + of Christ defends me. O Jesus, may your suffering be my protection. Amen.

* This is almost certainly a mistake for *Agios, Agios*: Gk. "holy, holy," as in parallel text on Folger p. 52.

A vincle [116] or call

I conjure thee [117] spirit by the living God, by the true God, and by the holy God, and by their virtues and powers which have created both thee and me and all the world, I conjure thee N. by these holy names of God + Tetragrammaton + Adonay + Algramaye + Saday + Sabaoth + Planaboth + Panthon + Craton + Pneumaton + Deus + Homo + Omnipotens + Sempiternus + Ysus + Terra + Unigenitus + Salvator + Via + Vita + Manus + Fons + Origo + Filius + and by their virtues and powers, and by all their names by which God gave power to man both to speak or think. So by their virtues and powers I conjure thee spirit N., that thou immediately appear here before me in the circle appointed for thee, visible unto me without any tarrying or deceit, quietly and peaceably, without hurting, harming, frouting, fearing, or in any wise annoying of me or any of God's creatures whatsoever. I conjure thee thereto, by the excellent name of Jesus Christ Alpha and Omega, the first and the last, for this holy name of Jesus is above all names: for in this name of Jesus every knee doth bow and obey, both of heavenly things, earthly things, and infernal, and every tongue doth confess, that our lord Jesus Christ is the glory of the father, neither is there any other name given unto man whereby he must be saved. Therefore in the name of Jesus of Nazareth, and by his nativity, circumcision, baptism, fasting, and temptation, [118] by his agony and bloody sweat, by his cross and passion, by his precious death and burial, by his glorious resurrection and ascension, and by all that appertaineth unto his passion and by their virtues and powers, by his coming in the dreadful day of doom: I conjure

---

116. Vincle: bond.

117. Scot, *Discouerie of Witchcraft*, 233.

118. This list is much more elaborate than that in Scot, *Discouerie of Witchcraft*, providing evidence of an independent transmission.

thee, thou spirit N., that thou appear to me visible in that circle appointed there for thee, without any dissimulation, harm, or annoyance in manner and form aforesaid in human form and shape. I conjure thee, spirit N., by the blood of the innocent lamb Jesus Christ which was shed for me upon the Cross for all those that do believe in the virtue of his blood shall be saved. I conjure thee N. by the virtues and powers, and by all the royal names and words of the living God by me pronounced, that thou be in all things obedient unto me and to my words rehearsed. If thou refuse this to do, I, by the virtue and power of the Holy Trinity do condemn thee into the place where there is no hope of remedy or rest but everlasting horror and pain there dwelling and a place where there is pain upon pain daily, horribly, and lamentably thy pain to be there augmented as the stars in the heaven and as the gravel or sand in the sea, except thou spirit do appear unto me visibly immediately in that circle quietly, as is aforesaid, in human form, and not alter thy shape. I charge thee upon pain of everlasting condemnation, I conjure thee spirit N. by the golden girdle which girded the loins of our lord and saviour Jesus Christ,[119] so be thou spirit bound into the perpetual pains of hellfire, for thy disobedience and unreverent regard that thou hast to the holy names and words of the living God by me pronounced and his precepts. I conjure thee N. by the two-edged sword which John saw proceed out of the mouth of the almighty and so thou spirit N. be torn and cut in pieces with that sword, and be condemned into everlasting pain where the fire goeth not out and where the worm dieth not. I conjure thee N. by the heavens and by the celestial city Jerusalem, and by the earth, and by the sea, and by all things contained in them, and by their virtues and powers. I conjure thee by the obedience that thou dost owe unto thy principal prince and except that thou do appear visibly in this circle in my presence here immediately as is aforesaid, let the great curse of God, the anger of God, the shadow of darkness and of death, and of eternal condemnation be upon thee for ever and ever, because thou hast denied thy faith, thy health, and salvation. For thy great disobedience thou art worthy to be condemned; therefore let the divine Trinity, Thrones, Dominations, Principates, Potestates, Virtues, Cherubim and Seraphim, and all the souls of saints both of men and women condemn thee forever and be a witness against thee at the day of judgment, because of thy disobedience, and let all the creatures of God and of our lord and saviour Jesus Christ, say thereunto. Amen, Amen, Amen.

---

119. Revelation 1.

[43]

A conjuration of obedience

I conjure thee spirit, that there standeth or appeareth by the infinite word of God, by the great goodness of God, by the which he made man to his own image and likeness, and by his justice and judgments cast you and your fellows for sin, pride, presumption, and disobedience out of heaven into hellfire to be damned. I conjure you also by his abundant mercy and goodness by the which he saved us and redeemed us. I conjure you by the virginity of the Blessed Virgin Mary, mother of our lord and saviour Jesus Christ, and by the obedience of our lord and saviour Jesus Christ to his father and mother, and by his holiness and meekness, that thou be as meek unto me as the lamb before the shearer, and as meek as Jesus Christ was when he suffered himself to be taken and bound and sent to Caiaphas, and as obedient unto me as Christ Jesus was when he suffered himself to be bound to the cross and nailed thereto suffering most grievous torments, and sweating both water and blood for the redemption of mankind. I charge thee and I conjure thee by all the powers of God and by all his holy names, by the which thou wast compelled hitherto, and here to come that thou be as obedient unto me as the walls of Jericho were, which fell down without stroke of hand after they were compassed of the people of God seven times, and as obedient unto me as the wind and the sea that became calm and the foul spirits came forth and possessed the swine at the commandment of Christ Jesus, and as obedient as the hail, rain, lightning, thunder, grasshoppers, frogs, thick darkness, botches, blains, and sores were at the lifting up of Moses's hands to come into the land of Egypt as obedient as the Red Sea that divided itself and as obedient [sic] as the Sun and Moon that stood still by the will of God at the commandment of Joshua, and as obedient as the bears and fire were by the will of God to obey the commandment of Elijah,[120] and hereunto I bind thee by Jesus Christ and by his power, and by all that is aforesaid and by the names of God Elgrah + Ebanher + Agla + Goth + Ioth + Othie + Venoth + Nabrat + Nayoth + Nath + by the which Solomon the king did bind up the Devil, and spirits in the brasen pans, so do I bind thee to my obedience.

A band to bind them into the triangle or ring

I conjure and bind thee by the power of God into this △ as fast as Christ Jesus was bound by the Jews in his humanity when he was sent unto Caiaphas and Pilate, and by the Cross of Christ Jesus so fast and sure do I bind thee as himself was bound to the Cross and nailed thereto in his humanity when he shed both water and blood

---

120. The incident with the bears actually involved Elisha, not Elijah. See 2 Kings 2:23–24.

and suffered most grievous pains on the Cross for the redemption of the world, yea, I bind thee as fast as the body of Christ Jesus was bound in the linen cloths when he was laid into his sepulchre and I sigillate[121] thee into this Δ as Christ Jesus his body was sigillated and shut up in his sepulchre, and I sigillate thee by his holy name Phaa + by and in the which God sigillated the heavens, the earth, the seas, and all therein, setting them their bonds the which they may not pass. And I bind thee to thy obedience by and in the virtue of the name of God Zechellote vell lechellote + Ysmas + by and in the virtue of the which God hanged the earth upon the waters that it should not move at any time.

Yea, I conjure and bind thee by and in the virtue of the holy name of God + Kachionader[122] by the which God set, placed, and bound the Sun, the Moon, and the stars in the height of Heaven to keep their course obediently forever, so long as the world end.

Yea, I bind thee by and in the virtue and power of the holy names of God + Degeron + or + Gegeron + by the which Moses bound the Red Sea that it stood as still as a stone on both sides like a wall while the people of Israel passed through.

And I bind thee by and in the virtue and power of the holy names of God, Hachio • Nad[a][123] Valislior + vel Hachionada + Balizer +[124] by the which Josua bound the Sun that he stood still on Aaloth and the Moon stood still on Gibeon, and they durst not move till he had fought the battle of the Lord and had slain the mighty king of the Amorites.

And I bind thee by and in the virtue of the holy name of God Panteon + the which Moses named and brought darkness on all the land of Egypt.

I bind thee in and by the virtue of the name of God + Pancraton + the which Elias named and the heavens were bound up and shut fast that it rained not on the earth in three years and six months.[125]

And I bind thee up by and in the virtue of the name of God + Baruch + the which Daniel named in the lion's den, and the lion's mouths were shut and bound up that they could not open them to hurt him.

---

121. I.e., seal.

122. Compare LIH name 53: Achionadabir?

123. Compare Sloane 3846, 26r.

124. 67 Moses: *bachando, beltzlior, dealzhat; Razielis: Bachianodobalizlior, & thus bachiocoiodobaliz hac.*

125. James 5:17–18. Recounted by Agrippa in OP Book 3, chapter 64.

[44]

And I bind thee by and in the names of God + Spargontio + Emanuell + by the which Shadrach, Mesach, and Abednego called on the lord in the fiery furnace, and the fire was bound that it could not hurt nor touch them.

Iterum ["again"] I conjure and bind thee by and in the virtue and power of the holy name of God + Messias + by the which the great and mighty whale was bound not to hurt Jonah being in his belly three days and three nights, but to be obedient and serviceable to the will of God to cast him up upon the dry land safe and sound.

And I bind thee up and sigillate thee by the names + Elgrah + Ebanher + Agle + Goth + Joth + Othie + Venoch + Nabrat + Nayoth + Nath + by the which Solomon did bind the devils and spirits and shut them up in the brasen pans for disobedience.

Yea, I bind thee in the name of God + Abeneton + by and in the which God shall humble and make low the hills.

And in the name of God + Praigmon + by the which God shall darken the Sun and the Moon and shall make all the stars to fall from heaven.

Et per nomen et in nomine + Sabaoth + in quo deus ad Iudicium veniet cum angelis *and like an emperor shall triumph in his glory,* et angeli paribunt, et omnia elementa turbabuntur tempestate ignis sulfuris et frigoris mixto.	And by the name and in the name of + Sabaoth + in which God will come with his angels for judgment, *and like an emperor shall triumph in his glory.* And the angels will attend, and all elements will be disturbed by the season of mixed fire, sulfur, and cold.*

* The passage seems to echo the twelfth century Honorius Augustodunensis, *Elucidarium*, bk. III, chap 51, in Parker, Elizabeth C., and Mary B. Shepard. *The Cloisters: Studies in Honor of the Fiftieth Anniversary* (New York: Metropolitan Museum of Art, 1992), 174: "*Ita Christus in ea forma qua ascendit cum omnibus ordinibus angelorum ad judicium veniens; angeli crucem ferentes ... omnia elementa turbabuntur, tempestate ignis sulfuris et frigoris mixtim undique furente....*"

Et per nomen, et in nomine + Jehovah cui omni genu flectitur tam celestiam quam terrestium et per nomen et [in] nomine + Tetragramaton + Jehovah + in quo est plasmatum omne seculum quo audito elementa corruunt Aer	And by the name and in the name of + Jehovahh at which all knees bend in Heaven and on Earth, and by the name and in the name of + Tetragrammaton + Jehovahh* + in which is formed all the ages, which being heard, all the elements

* H. p. 121.

concu[t] itur mare retrogradatur terra tremit ignis extinguitur omnesque exercitus celestium terrest[r]ium et Infernorum tremuit [*tremunt] turbantur et corruu[n]t.	are overthrown, the air is shaken, the sea runs back, the fire is extinguished, the earth trembles, and all the heavenly, worldly, and infernal hosts tremble, are troubled, and are confounded.

Et per illum qui sedet super sedem Aemaelion et venturus est Iudicare vivos et mortuos et seculum per ignem.	And through Him who sits upon the seat Aemaelion, and will come to judge the living and the dead and the ages by fire.

Et per hac nomina que maxima sunt in Arte nigromantica + balsac + super balsac + sarye + sarapye + pamulion + de sede sarapais in potestate Aye + per que aque restant et elementa concutinatur vel non comitantur et per hec septima nomina dei largia + gaaghum + levalogni lavafarim + vbalgana + haia + layazogin + layarosin + layaschesyn + per qui ligantur Omnia	And through these names which are great in the art of Nigromancy + Balsac + over Balsac + Sarye + Sarapye + Pamulion + down from the seat Sarapais* in power Aye + by which the waters stay back, and the elements shook violently, or not intermingle, and by these seven names of God: Largia + Gaaghum + Levalogni lavafarim + Vbalgana + Haia + Layazogin + Layarosin + Layaschesyn† + by which all things are bound.

* Compare Wellcome MS. 110, 43v: *et per omnia nomina istorum que sunt maxime dei Nigromantie artis, s, balsarum super Balsak paulin, in potestate Orye Saraye de sede Sarparis quibus nominatis aque restarent a cursu s[??].* This seems to be a variant or degenerated version of H.

† Obviously not seven. Might these be corrupted from the seven names of God on Sigillum Dei: Narath, Libarre, Libares, Layaly, Lyalg, Ueham, Yalgal?

and I bind and conjure thee by these seven glorious names of God + legethomonon + ledelegna + ledeforon + Arbelgenorochon + lederogaon + ledepoten + ledeseleson + per que deus creavit, et sigillavit celum et terram et mare et omnia que in eis sunt, et sub pena legechomon + leolagnah + leoferon + Abelgenochon	And I bind and conjure thee by these seven glorious names of God + Legethomonon + Ledelegna + Ledeforon + Arbelgenorochon + Lederogaon + Ledepoten + Ledeseleson + by which God created and sealed Heaven and Earth and the sea, and all that is in them, and under penalty Legechomon + Leolagnah

+ leoeragaron + leoeruchon + leoseleson + Aelchion + Emandiol + ferlilioh + murdiell + melchion Edulthiol + muriol + layahymnum + laialagan + layasim + vbafganarythin + layagirym + layaratyn layasalasyn + layagemyn + lagha + layasuryn + vbalgamargthin + levalegin + layaselefyn, et subpena damnationis eterna, et deprivationis, verem ab officies a locis a dignatibus vestris.	+ Leoferon + Abelgenochon + Leoeragaron + Leoeruchon + Leoseleson + Aelchion + Emandiol + Ferlilioh + Murdiell + Melchion Edulthiol + Muriol + Layahymnum + Laialagan + Layasim + Vbafganarythin + Layagirym + Layaratyn Layasalasyn + Layagemyn + Lagha + Layasuryn + Vbalgamargthin + Levalegin + Layaselefyn, and under penalty of eternal damnation, and depriving you from all your offices, place, and dignities.

The malediction

As God almighty cursed the earth at the fall of Adam that it lost his former force and strength, so do I in the name of God almighty, by the power that he hath given me, I do curse thee N., that thou also hereby lose thy former power and strength.

And as he deprived Adam from the joys of paradise, and cast him out into the vale of misery from joy to sorrow, from ease to pain, from imperial rule and dignity to bondage and servitude, from life to death and everlasting damnation, so do I deprive thee of all thy offices, rule, powers, and dignities, and I do cast thee for thy disobedience into the dark dungeon of hell under the depth of all waters, into the damnable pit of everlasting sorrow and pain, into darkness without light, into sorrow without comfort, into bondage perpetual, into prison without liberty, where there is nothing but weeping, and wailing, and gnashing of teeth, where the wrath and curse of God be, and remain upon thee forever. Amen.

And I also curse thee as God cursed the serpent that deceived Eve, saying, "Cursed be thou, for thy pride, presumption, falsehood, and deceit, upon thy belly shall thou go, and the dust of the earth shall be thy food." So likewise be thou cursed for thy disobedience, presumption, and deceit, and condemned into hellfire and pain perpetual as is aforesaid.

And as the Lord God plagued and cursed Cain that he fled far from His presence, so be thou cursed and plagued that thou flee far from the presence of God of his angels and of me, and from the presence of all spirits and creatures: into painful darkness perpetually where thou shalt remain forever, without joy, ease, or comfort, [45] and as the blood of that blessed Abel shed by that accursed Cain cries to the Lord God out of the earth for vengeance against Cain, even so do I cry unto thee, O Lord God, that thou lay thy plagues, punishments, and wrathful indignation upon these disobedient, deceitful, and accursed spirits + for their pride, stubbornness, and dis-obedience to me at these and at other times, and to thy holy names by which they have been invoked and called.

And as the Lord plagued Judas for his treachery and deceit and caused him to break in sunder that his bowels fell out with pains and torment, so God plague and torment you, rend and tear you asunder with infernal pains and plagues perpetual in his fury and wrathful indignation, utterly confounding forevermore.

And as Judas was deprived of his office, place, authority, and apostleship for his transgression, so God and I, by the power that God hath given me, do utterly deprive thee of thy authority, office, rule, power, and dignity, for evermore utterly confound-ing thee with Judas.

And as Christ cursed the fig tree, which presently withered and dried up, saying, "Nevermore, fruit grow upon thee," so in the name of God and in his behalf do I curse thee into hellfire, never to be restored to liberty, and the curse of God almighty be upon thee, and remain upon thee for evermore.

And as Christ Jesus, being on the cross, cried unto his Father, "Eloy + Eloy + Eloy +," so cry I unto thee, O Lord God omnipotent, for help and power, saying, "Eloy + Eloy + Eloy +." Send down thine angels, O my God, to bind up in pain and darkness perpetual these disobedient, deceitful, and accursed spirits for their stubbornness and disobedience.

And as the veil of the temple did rend asunder, so let them be rent with pains, and as Christ Jesus did rend and tear hell and break all the bands asunder wherein man was bound to perpetual damnation for sin and transgression of the commandments of God, so do I, by the power of God unto me given, rend and tear you and bind you up perpetually into pains perpetual and torments everlasting.

And I also curse you and deprive you of all liberty, dignity, power, and authority, rest, [and] ease by and in the name of God + Primeumaton + which Moses the man of God named, commanding the earth to open her mouth wide and to swallow up Dathan, Corah, and Abiron quick into hell for their disobedience.

And as the Lord in his wrathful indignation opened the heavens and rained down great floods upon the earth to the utter destruction of all mankind, Noah and his family excepted, and as he rained down fire and brimstone from heaven, and burned and utterly confounded, and destroyed Sodom, Gomorrah, Zeboiim, Zoar, and Adma,[126] and confounding Babel, with the pride of Nimrod, and rained blood, hail, storm, and tempest in Egypt, and brought many grievous plagues thereon to the de-struction thereof, and destroyed Pharaoh and his host in the Red Sea, so the Lord God pour out his wrathful indignation, vengeance, and plagues upon you to your utter overthrow and destruction, bringing all the plagues of Egypt upon you, and rain

---

126. See Genesis 14:2.

down upon you storms, hail, ice, snow, vapor, fire and brimstone, darkness, lightning, thunderbolts, and wrathful indignation, fury, vengeance, damnation, pains, torments, confusion, disdain, anguish, sorrow, heaviness, desolation, and utter imprisonment, and bind you up fast under the depth of all waters, in darkness and pain perpetual until the day of doom, utterly confounding you with the old world with Nimrod and Babel, with Sodom, Gomorrah, Zeboiim, Zoar, and Adma, with Pharaoh and his host, and with Dathan, Korah, and Abiram, and let his everlasting curse and indignation remain upon you for your disobedience and utterly confound you and bind you up as is aforesaid for evermore.

Grant this, O Lord God Father, for Jesus Christ's sake, which [=who] died for the sins of the people and now liveth and reigneth with thee in the unity of the Holy Ghost, ever one God in glory, majesty, and power, to whom with the Father and the Son and the Holy Ghost be rendered all praise, wisdom, power, dominion, imperiality, and eternity forever more, world without end. Amen, Amen, Amen. Fiat, fiat, fiat.

Curse them three times, hereby saying this curse three times over, and no spirit shall have power to withstand thee.[127]

[46]

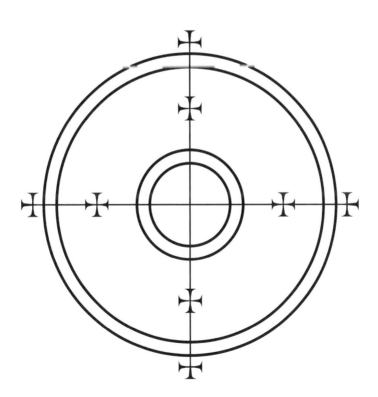

---

127. In marg.: anchor glyph. It is repeated under the text as well.

[47]

To speak with a spirit in thy bed [128]

In the day of Mercury, go to thy bed alone in some fair chamber, and have a wax candle burning by thee, and you must have lignum aloes at your head, and say these words three times:

These be the words

Holy, holy, holy, our Lord Jesus Christ was betrayed on a Wednesday; holy, holy, holy, upon the Thursday our Lord Jesus Christ was held and scourged; holy, holy, holy, upon a Friday, our Lord Jesus Christ was hanged, whipped, and buried; holy, holy, holy, with all thy saints, send to me thy messenger.

When thou wilt work this, you must fast with bread and water and confess yourself to God, and after you have said this above three times go to bed and thou shalt see a bearded man come to thee, then ask his name, which is Balancus, and demand of him what thou wilt and he will answer.

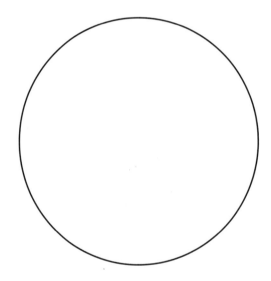

---

128. This page is in a different handwriting, and very neatly and carefully written.

[48]

[+ Diagram for winning at games] [129]

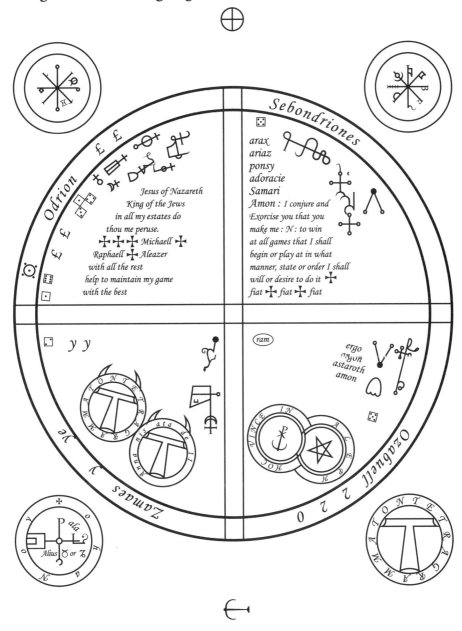

---

129. Text includes: Upper Left: "Odrion / Jesus of Nazareth King / of the Jews / in all my estates do thou me peruse. +++ Michaell +Raphaell + Aleazer with all the rest, help to maintain my game with the best." Upper Right: "Sebondriones / arax / ariaz / ponsy / adoracie / Samari / Amon: I conjure and exorcise you that you make me :N: to win at all games that I shall begin or play at in what manner, state, or order I shall will or desire to do it + fiat + fiat + fiat." Lower Left: "y g / TE TRA GRAM MATON AN NA NIS ATA DE II / Zamaes." Lower Right: "ergo / argon / astaroth / amon / Hoc vince in ["in this you conquer"] / ALEPH / Ozabuell 220."

[49]

This table is to know what planet doth rule every hour, both day and night, the use whereof is this: At the left side be the governor of the day; at the right side be governors of the night; in the uppermost place in the table be the governors of the whole day, which stand in place for the names of the days also.

Planets governing the day be these which follow:	☉	☽	♂	☿	♃	♀	♄	Planets governing the night be these which follow:
♌ ☉ ♌	1	12	9	0	10	0	11	♃
♈ ♀ ♎	2	0	10	0	11	1	12	♂
♊ ☿ ♍	3	0	11	1	12	2	0	☉
♋ ☽ ♋	4	1	12	2	0	3	0	♀
♑ ♄ ♒	5	2	0	3	0	4	1	☿
♐ ♃ ♓	6	3	0	4	1	5	2	☽
♈ ♂ ♏	7	4	1	5	2	6	3	♄
♌ ☉ ♌	8	5	2	6	3	7	4	♃
♈ ♀ ♎	9	6	3	7	4	8	5	♂
♊ ☿ ♍	10	7	4	8	5	9	6	☉
♋ ☽ ♋	11	8	5	9	6	10	7	♀
♑ ♄ ♒	12	9	6	10	7	11	8	☿
♐ ♃ ♓	0	10	7	11	8	12	9	☽
♈ ♂ ♏	0	11	8	12	9	0	10	♄
Governors of the day								Governors of the night

[50]

Moses, David, Solomon, Hermes, Cyprian, Lombard, Bacon They and divers and others say best in philosophy in magic and also in necromancy etc., saying that where it is in himself, and there is no doubt that superior things to inferior and inferior to superior do make answer and agree, and our chief worker is God, only from whom all marvelous works do ascend, even as all things be created of one only substance and of one disposition whose father is the Sun and whose mother is the Moon, the which carried him in her womb through the air, and of her speaketh Hermes, the father of all creatures, the treasure of marvels, the giver of virtues, the virtue of superior things overcometh all things. These most wise philosophers hath set forth a book of four things. One is of stars, [+ one is of] herbs, [+ one is of] stones, and [+ one is of] figures, and that to the[130] introduction of four of the most excellent sciences, one is astronomy, [+ one is] physic, [+ one is] alchemy, and [+ one is] magic. These be the most profitablest sciences, by the which a man may soonest help himself, for astronomy is the root of all things and showeth the secret of workings, and physic discerneth the nature within and without, and it helpeth thee quickly of minerals and helpeth thee and preserveth thee wholly and clean and giveth judgment of the qualities of minerals the mutability of kind of stones, salt, and metals, and that with the producing of one metal out of another, and that by examination of roots of nature, and that maketh everyone to know another thing and that by magic, by magnitude and power, for magic excelleth in this and in all other arts, for he divideth the spiritual possibility in binding and calling of spirits, and with their power and by them he doth incredible marvels and that to mankind, this art magic is called of the wise, the solace, and utility of philosophers of the which our Allcamus,[131] the philosophers in the desert.

Planets which be good and evil

     ♀ ♃   which be good

     ♄ ♂   be evil

     ☽ ☉ ♃   be indifferent

The hours of the Sun and Venus are nevertheless best for performing all experiments of love and grace (or influence).

---

130. In marg.: "w" glyph.

131. Allcamus: Unknown.

Signs that be good to work

♈ Aries	♈ ♌ ♐ be fiery signs	♈ ♊ ♎ ♑
♒ Aquarius	♋ ♎ ♒ be airy signs	♉ ♌ ♏ ♒
♍ Virgo	♊ ♏ ♓ be watery signs	♋ ♍ ♐ ♓
♊ Gemini	♉ ♍ ♑ be earthy signs	
♎ Libra		
♋ Cancer	♈ ♌ ♐ be east	♈ ♉ ♓ ♏ ♎ ♍
♉ Taurus	♋ ♎ ♒ be west	♒ ♑ ♐ ♌ ♊ ♋
♌ Leo	♊ ♏ ♓ be north	
♐ Sagittarius	♉ ♍ ♑ be south	
♑ Capricorn		
♓ Pisces		
♏ Scorpio		

[51]

John's gospel [132]

In principium [*principio] erat verbum et verbum erat apud deum et deus erat verbum Hoc erat in principio apud deum. Omnia per ipsum facta sunt, et sine ipso factum est nihill quod factum est in ipso vita erat, et vita erat Lux hominum; et Lux in tenebris lucet, et tenebres [*tenebrae] eam non comprehenderunt. fuit homo missus a deo, cui nomen erat Iohannes. hic venit in testimonium ut testimonium perhiberet de lumine, ut omnes crederent per illum non erat ille Lux, sed ut testimonium perhiberet de lumine <ne>. Erat Lux vera quae illuminat omnem hominem venientem in <hunc> mundum. In mundo erat, et

In the beginning was the word, and the word was with God: and God was the word. The same was in the beginning with God. All things were made by it, and without it, was made nothing that was made. In it was life, and the life was the light of men, and the light shineth in darkness, and the darkness comprehended it not. There was sent from God a man, whose name was John. The same came as a witness to bear witness of the light, that all men through him might believe. He was not the light: but was sent to bear witness of the light. That light was the true light, which lighteth every man that cometh into the world.

---

132. Another version of this text is found above, Folger p. 29.

mundus per ipsum factus est et mundus eum non cognovit. In propria venit et sui eum non receperunt quotquot aute[m] receperunt eum, dedit eis potestatem filios dei fieri, his qui credunt in nomine eius, qui non ex sanguinibus, neque ex voluntate carnis, neque ex voluntate viri, sed ex deo nati sunt, et verbum caro factum est et habitavit in nobis, et videmus [*vidimus] gloriam, eius gloriam quasi unigeniti a patre, plenum gratie et veritatis.	He was in the world, and the world was made by him: and the world knew him not. He came among his own, and his own received him not. But as many as received him to them gave he power to be the sons of God: even them that believed on his name: which were born, not of blood nor of the will of the flesh, nor yet of the will of man: but of God. And the same word became flesh, and dwelt among us: and we saw the glory of it, as the glory of the only begotten son of the father, full of grace and truth.

Protection against thieves[133]

Deus antem [*ante] transiens per medium illorum, Ibat + Iesus Christus + benedictus deus quotidie prosperum iter facit deus salutaris noster + Iesus obstine\<n>tur occuli eorum ne videant, et dorsum eorum in curva Iesus. effundas super eas iram tuam, et furor Ire tue comprehendat eos + "Irrnat [*Irruat] super inimicos meos formido et pavor in magnitudine brachii fiant imobiles quasi lapis," donec pertranseat famulus tuus + quem redemisti + dextera tua magnificata est, in virtute domini percuciet Inimicum, in multitudinem virtutis tuae deposuisti omnes adversarios meos +	But God [*Jesus] passing through their midst, went his way.* + Jesus Christ + Blessed God makes the daily journey prosperous. O God of our salvation + Jesus established that their eyes will not see, and their backs bent, Jesus. Pour out your anger over them, and may the furor of your wrath seize them firmly. + "May fear and dread beset my enemies, in the greatness of your arm: let them become immovable as a stone" until your servant passes by, + whom you have redeemed +.† Your right hand is magnified in power, O Lord, and will beat the enemy. In the multitude of your power you have
* Luke 4:30. Used elsewhere in this text.	
† Compare Exodus 15:16.	

---

133. Another version of this text is found above, Folger p. 21. In right marg.: "11." In left marg.: "5." Note date May 8, 1577.

Iesu eripe me et ab insurgentibus in me libera me + Jesu custodi me, el [*et] de manu peccatoris el [*et] ab hominibus iniquis eripe me + Jesum "eripe me de operantibus iniquitatem et de viris sanguinum salva me" + gloria patri + Anthos + Anostro + Moxio + Bay + Gloy + Apen + Agia + Agias + yskiros + octovo maye 1577.	put down all my enemies +.* O Jesus, deliver me and defend me from those who rise up against me† + O Jesus, guard me from the hands of the wrongdoers, and deliver me from unjust men.‡ + O Jesus, "deliver me from those who work iniquity, and save me from bloody men."§ + Glory be to the Father + Anthos + Anostro + Moxio + Bay + Gloy + Apen + Agia + Agias + yskiros + May 8, 1577.

* Compare Exodus 15:6–7.
† Compare Psalm 58:2 (KJV 59:1).
‡ Compare Psalm 139:5 (KJV 140:4).
§ Psalm 58:3 (KJV 59:2).

The priest says, be willing to confess [134]

Benedicite pater, Res[ponsat] Sacerd[os], dominus sit in corde tuo, et in Labiis tuis ad confitendum omnia peccata tua, In nomine patris et filii et spiritus sancti Amen.	Father, let us bless. (The priest responds:) May the Lord be in your heart, and on your lips for confessing all your sins. In the name of the Father, Son, and Holy Ghost. Amen.

Confiteor deo ceeli beate Marie virginis, et omnibus sanctis tuis, O deus et coram vera Maiestate tua, quia peccaui minius [*nimius] Superbia in vana gloria, in extollentia onulorum [*oculorum] et vestium ac fortitudinem, In inviduam et odio, In avaritia, tam honoris Alterius, quam pecuniae, In Tristitia de bonis et honore Alterius, In ira, et Iracundia, In	I confess* to God in heaven, to the blessed Virgin Mary, and to all your saints, O God, and the presence of your true majesty, because I have sinned greatly in my pride, in haughtiness of eyes and clothes and firmness, in envy and hatred, in coveting the honours or money of another, in being sad about the good or honours of another, in anger

* Compare parallel version on Folger p. 102, plus Mathers, *The Key of Solomon*, 1.4; Aubrey 24, fol. 68r; Additional MS. 10862, fol. 16r; Michael 276, II, p. 19; Sloane 3847, 8v. In marg.: "w" glyph.

134. From the Catholic Church, *Brevarium Ad Usum Insignis Ecclesiae Sarum* (Cambridge: Cambridge University Press, 1879), Fasciculus li., 479. In right marg.: "12."

ventris gule, et comestionibus superluis [*superfluis], In fabulis vanis et ebrietatibus gulosis, In osculi et amplexionibus et palpationibus [*palpantibus] Immundis, et in multis Aliis generibus sive actibus luxuriosus, In periuriis, furtis, et homicidiis, in extortacionibus per vis et adulacionibus malignis, In deceptionibus proximorum, et oppressionibus pauperum, In indicii timerariso [*temerariis] falsis et Impiis, In mendaciis et iuramentis multimodis, In detractionibus et discordiis Seminandis, in derisionibus et maledictionibus variis vigiliis et ludis, salutis anime meo contrariis, In transgresionibus preceptorum tuorum, et odio proximi, In dando mala exempla mihi subditis, In non visitando infirmos et desolatos, In vivendo, In bla-[s]phemando alios, et in malum swadentibus consentiendo, In male redendo tibi deo creatori meo gratias et orationes de bonis et quas mihi concessisti.

and irritability, in gluttony and excessive consumption, in empty chatter, drunkenness, and gluttony, in impure kissing, embracing, and touching, and many other kinds or acts of wantonness, in perjury, theft, and homicide, in extortion by force, and spiteful flattery, in deceiving neighbours and oppressing the poor, in rash, false, and wicked testimony,* in lying and many kinds of swearing, in slander and planting discord, in mocking and cursing the different vigils and (instead) gaming, against the salvation of the soul, in violation of your teachings, in hatred of neighbours, being a bad example to my subordinates, in not visiting the sick and desolate, in living (with gluttons and wantons),† in blaspheming others, and in urging others to do the same evil, and in badly disregarding the gratitude and prayers owed to you, God the creator, and the good which you have granted me.

* Parallel passages read *iudicii* ["judgment"].
† Compare Folger p. 102.

Confiteor Tibi o pater quia non solum peccaui in omnibus peccatis supradictis set in omnibus alliis quibus humana fragillitas cogitando, Audiendo, videndo, loquendo, delectando concupiscendo peccare potest. Et ideo tibi domino meo ceeli et terre creatori potentissimo veniam de omnibus peccatis per me factis et commissis humiliter deposco ut non gaudeat super me Inimicus

I confess to you, O Father, not only because I have sinned in all the ways mentioned above, but also in all the ways of human frailty, in thinking, hearing, seeing, speaking, pleasure, lower passions, and all the ways that one can sin. And therefore I ask pardon from you, O my Lord, most powerful creator of the heavens and the earth, for all sins committed by me and brought about, beseech that

meus et non glorietur adversum me in die Iudicii Accusans mea peccata et celera [*scelera] tacuisse, et confessum non fuisse sed sit gaudium de me in coelo sic de aliis iustis et confessis, et me mundus et confessus de peccatis meis coram tuam presentiam altissime pater omnipotens per tuam clementiam, da mihi ut obedire possim, et cognoscere omnis spiritus quos invocare voluero et concedo [*concede] mihi potestatem ut possim complere meam omni modam [*modum] voluntatem per gloriosissimam magestatem tuam inqua gloriosissime regnas et regnaturus es in secula seculorum Amen.

my enemy may not rejoice over me, nor stand against me on the Day of Judgement, accusing my sins and crimes left unmentioned and unconfessed, but give me eternal joy in Heaven, with the other just and confessed, that I may face you in person, pure and confessed of all my sins, O most high Father, through your mercy, that I may be able to obey, and recognize all the spirits which I wish to invoke, and grant me the power to fulfill my will in all ways, by your most glorious majesty, whereby you reign most gloriously, and will reign forever and ever. Amen.

Then the priest says [135]

Misereatur Tui omnipotens Deus et dimittat tibi omnia peccata tua: liberata ab omni malo concede te voluntatem et desiderium tuum, conservet et confirmet in bono et ad vitam, perducat eternum Amen, et [*per] meritum passionis domini nostri Iesu Christi Souffragia sanctae matris ecclesie, bona que fecisti, et <aquam> [*quae] per dei graciam facies sint tibi in remissionem peccatorum tuos Amen.

May almighty God have mercy on you, forgive all your sins, and deliver you from all evil, grant you your desires and wishes, conserve and strengthen you in goodness and lead you to eternal life. Amen, by the merits of the passion of our Lord Jesus Christ, the prayers of our holy Mother Church, the good which you have done, and by the grace of God that you will do hereafter, be to you for the remission of your sins. Amen.

135. From the Sarum Breviary of 1531, cited in George Harford, *The Prayer Book Dictionary* (London: Sir I. Pitman, 1912), 2. In marg.: "13."

Then he gives absolution

Dominus noster Iesus qui est summus pontifex per suam piissimam misericordiam te absolvat, Et ego Auctoritatem mihi concessa absolvo te, primo a sentencia minoris excomunicationis si indigeas, deinde absolvo te ab omnibus peccatis tuis, In nomine patris et filii et spiritus sancti Amen.	Jesus our Lord, who is the highest pontiff, by his most pious mercy, absolves you. I, by the authority granted me, absolve you first from the sentence of minor excommunication[*] if you need it, and then from all your sins, in the name of the Father, and the Son, and the Holy Ghost. Amen.

* Lesser excommunication involved temporary suspension of participation in the sacraments of the church.

For special penance, say the seven penitential Psalms, etc. [136]

Actiones nostras quesimus [*quesumus] domine aspirando preveni et adiuvando prosequere, ut cuncta nostra operatio <et> a te semper incipiat, et per te [in]cepta finiatur. Amen. Dignare me domine die isto, sine peccatis custodire, dirige gressus et actus meos hodie per semitas iustitie tuae<eri> sic tua iustitia adesto fragilitati me[a]e ut in nulla te re capitalliter offendam. Amen.	Direct our actions, we beg you, O Lord, by your holy influence, and carry them on by your assistance, that every prayer and operation of ours may always begin with you, and through you be ended. Amen. Deem me worthy this day, O Lord,[*] guard me from sin, direct my steps and my deeds this day, by the paths of your justice, thus your justice will be present in my fragility, so that I will in no mortal way offend you. Amen.

* Edgar Hoskins, *Horae Beatae Mariae Virginis; Or, Sarum and York Primers, with Kindred Books, and Primers of the Reformed Roman Use Together with an Introduction* (London: Longmans, Green, 1901). Church of England, *Private Prayers, Put Forth by Authority During the Reign of Queen Elizabeth* (Cambridge: University Press, 1851), 244.

---

136. This prayer appears in the *Liturgia Horarum (Liturgy of the Hours)* and other medieval collections of prayers. A slightly different version is found in the *Rituale Romanum (Roman Ritual)*. Other magic texts incorporate it as well, including LIH VI (prima oratio); Sloane 3851, fol. 2r; and Kieckhefer, *Forbidden Rites*, 252.

[52]

Surgite Sancte de mantioni-
bus vestris loca sanctificata
nobis et omnes spiritus qui hic
fuerunt benedicite, et nos humiles peccatores in pace custo-
dite per crucis hoc + signum fugiat procull omne malignum, et
per idem signum salvetur
quotque benignum.

Domine esto nobis turris fortitudinis
a facie inimici, exurge, domine adiuva
nos, et libera nos propter nomen tuum.
Amen.

Benedicite <me> pater, Res[ponsus:]
dominus sit in corde meo et in labiis meis
vere confitendum et declarendum, omnia
peccata (?) mea in nomine patris etc.

[52]

Arise O holy ones from your lodg-
ings, and bless this place of ours, and all
spirits who have been here, and guard us
humble sinners in peace, through this
sign of the cross may all evil flee, and
through the same sign + let everything
that is kind and good be preserved.

O Lord, be a tower of strength to us
in the face of our enemies. Arise O Lord
to help us, and deliver us for your name's
sake. Amen.

Father, let us bless. Response: May
the Lord be in my heart and on my lips,
truly confessing and declaring all my
sins, in the name of the Father, etc.

Confiteor deo [et] beate Marie virgine et omnibus sanctis factis in verbis,
in cogitatione et locutione in dilecta-
tione maria et omnes sanctos et sanctas
in polucione in *isaie* [*mentis et corpo-
ris] in concensu, in tastu [*tactu], audi-
tas, risus, visus, verbo ore, mente, corde,
et opere participando, cum excomunica-
tis et in cunctis aliis viciis mea mala mea
culpa, me gravissima culpa, et ideo
deprecor sancta dei orare pro me.

I confess all my sins to God* and to
the blessed Virgin Mary, and all the
saints, in thoughts and words and deeds
and speech, in enjoyment, in pollution
of mind and body,† in feeling, touching,
hearing, laughter, seeing, word of
mouth, with the mind, with the heart,
and participating in the work with an
excommunicated person, and with all
my other sins, through my sin, my sin,
my most grievous sin, and therefore I
beg for saint Mary, and all the saints of
God—male and female—to intercede
and pray for me.

* Another version of this confession can be found below on Folger p. 104.
† So the prayer books with closest parallels.

Misreator [*Misereatur] nostri omnipotens deus et dimittat nobis omnia peccata nostra liberat [*liberet] nos ab omni malo conservat et confirmet in bono et ad vitam perducat nos eternam. Amen.	May almighty God have mercy on us, and dismiss all our sins, and deliver us from all evil, and preserve and strengthen us in goodness, and lead us to eternal life. Amen.

Deus propicius esto mihi peccatori, et custos sis omnibus diebus vite mee, deus Abraham, deus Isaac, deus Iacob, miserere mei et mitte mihi in adiutorium meum, sanctum Michalem arcangelum qui me defendat et protegat ab omnibus inimicis visibilibus et invisibilibus, et sancte Michael Arcangele dei per gratiam quam meruisti habere te deprecor, per unigenitum filium dei omnipotentis et dominum nostrum Jesum Christum ut eripias me hodie periculis mortis, sancte Michael, sancte Gabriel, Sancte Raphael, Sancte Cherubine, Sancte Seraphin omnes Angely et Archangely dei precor vos omnes virtutes celorum ut mihi plenam potestatem deo, ut nullus Inimicus me condemnare possit, nec in via, nec in domo, nec in aqua, nec in igne, nec in bello, nec in lecto, nec in gladio, nec morte subitania, nec vigillando, nec dormiendo, nec manducando, nec bibendo, nec ullo modo, per signum + domini nostri Iesu Christi fugite partes adverse vincit Leo de tribu	O God, have mercy on me, a sinner,* and may you guard me all the days of my life. O God of Abraham, God of Isaac, God of Jacob, have mercy on me and send the holy archangel Michael to help me, defend me, and protect me from all enemies visible and invisible. O holy Michael, archangel of God, through the grace which you have merited, I beg you to intercede for me, by the only-begotten Son of almighty God, and our Lord Jesus Christ, that you rescue me this day from mortal peril. O holy Michael, holy Gabriel, holy Raphael, holy Cherubim and Seraphim, and all Angels and Archangels of God, I pray all you powers of Heaven, that (you send) the full power from God, that no enemies will be able to condemn me, not on the road nor at home, neither in the water nor in fire, neither in war nor in bed, not with a sword, not with sudden death, not waking nor sleeping, not eating nor drinking, not by any means, by the sign + of our Lord Jesus Christ. Flee ye adversaries!

* Luke 18:13. "O God, be merciful to me a sinner." Used by John Dee, *A True & Faithful Relation of What Passed for Many Yeers between Dr. John Dee… and Some Spirits* (London: Printed by D. Maxwell for T. Garthwait…, 1659), *Book of Hours,* adapted in Orthodox "Jesus Prayer" practice. In marg.: "w" glyph.

Iuda david aleluia, salvator mundi adiuva me salva me quia per + tuam et sanguinem tuam redemisti me, salva me in omni tempore et in omni tribulatione O Agios + Otheos + Agios + Iskiros + Agios + Athanatos + Crux Christi + adiuva me in omni tempore, ab omni tribulacione et in omnibus diebus vite mee I[n] nomine patris et filii et spiritus sancti Amen.	The Lion from the Tribe of Judah, David, Hallelujah! O Saviour of the World! Help me, save me, because by your cross and your blood you have redeemed me. Save me from all troubles and at all times. O Agios + Otheos + Agios + Iskiros + Agios + Athanatos + Cross of Christ + Help me at all times from all troubles, all the days of my life, in the name of the Father and the Son, and the Holy Ghost. Amen.

Seven Angels

Who that will work must not be unmindful of the seven angels, for doubtless some angels be upon the seven heavens and upon the seven planets and upon the seven days of the week, and upon the seven metals and upon the seven colours and upon the seven works having great power, which seven angels are these.

Raphaell + Gabriell + Samaell + Michael + Saquiel + Anael + Capcyel +

Upon these angels he must call upon in the seven days early, in this manner or such like.

---

137. Pentagram with characters. The first three glyphs are fairly clearly "a g l." The last one (8 o'clock) seems to be a lower case Greek "omega." The one at the bottom is most uncertain, probably a Greek pi, but the result is not something JHP recalls seeing elsewhere. "a g l a +" is fairly common, and of course "e l / ely" in LIH. Mathers, *The Key of Solomon* has a somewhat similar diagram in Figure 9, the first Pentacle of Mercury, which includes the name "Agiel."

O Angely supradicty sanctis, me quovis quam volo querere adiutores et mihi in omnibus adiutores.	O holy angels mentioned above, come to my aid in anything that I seek, and help in all things.

If you wish to test experiments

Understand the times, hours, phase of the Moon, from the conjunction to the opposition, but you can test experiments in the waning Moon but not after the opposition, but not thoroughly, wherefore it is necessary for you know well the progression of the Moon, it is best if you complete it during days 2, 3, 4, 5, 6, 10, 12, or 14. You must complete it well within the day.

Note: If you wish to write the experiments 20 times the Moon (?) before sunrise, or 4 times after the setting sun, but read the conjuration aloud while facing east.

The sixth time the conjuration after sunset facing west.[138]
The eighth time face towards the south until sunset.
The tenth time after sunset face towards the north.

Note well thou must not work in this craft every day and every hour, but thou must well behold the ☽ increasing and of number as of 2 or 4. 6. 8. 10. 12 or 14 and in none other in the ☽ to the next ♂ conjunction.

---

138. In marg.: "w-."

Epilepsy spell [139]

It is said the ring, which I have seen, you may make thus of silver. The inside should be inscribed in this manner: + Dabi + Habi + Haber + Hebr + no epileptic fits will afflict you when placed on the finger.[140]

I have seen a headache cured by wearing a hand-written document as shown at the side (*below), when the patient perceives no relief from medicine, recite aloud three times the Lord's prayer. To relieve a headache,

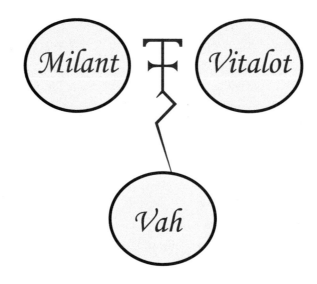

---

139. See Henry Charles Lea, *Materials Toward a History of Witchcraft* (New York: Thomas Yoseloff, 1957), Part 2, 438: "Cardan gives the opinion of those who believe that demons can visit us likewise say that morbus comitialis can be relieved by a silver ring inscribed + *Dabi* + *Habi* + *Haber* + *Hebr* +. Cardan has seen a headache cured by wearing a paper inscribed *Milant Vap Vitalot* while repeating the Lord's prayer thrice." (It appears that the transcription of Lea and Howland is in error; all editions JHP has seen read "Milant *Vah* Vitalot.") The same headache cure is also repeated below, Folger p. 208. The *Grimoire of Honorius* repeats the same per the translators David Rankine and Paul Harry Barron, *The Complete Grimoire of Pope Honorius* (London: Avalonia, 2013), 152.

140. There is a slightly more elaborate version of this spell recorded in C. LaVielle, "Erreurs et Préjudés Populaires Concernant La Médecine" *Bulletin de La Société de Borda* 20, no. 1 (1895): 128: "Prendre un anneau en pur argent et dans son châton vous enchâsserez un morceau de corne de pied d'élan; puis vous choisirez un lundi de printemps auquel la lune sera en aspect bénin ou en conjonction avec Jupiter ou Vénun, et à l'heure favourable de la constellation, vous graverez en dedans de l'anneau ces mots: Dabi, Habi, Haber, Habi. En portant continuellement cet anneau au doigt, vous n'aurez plus de crise." Also in *Secrets merveilleux … le Petit Albert* (1782), 228.

A	B	C	D	E	F	G	H
1	6	20	23	12	9	12	3

I	K	L	M	N	O	P	Q	R
6	15	5	12	3	3	2	23	22

S	T	V	X	Y
13	21	18	16	6

[53]

1. First take the days of the age of the Moon

2. Secondly the number of the planets in what day they do fall

3. And the number of the proper names even as you and they be called in the ABC ~ [141]

4. And then begin to say, "*Christus deus homo.*" ["Christ, God, Man"]

5. And you must take away[142] at once in number until the end of your number and look what remaineth.

Note: If *Christus* remain, go freely; if *deus*, there will be some let [143] (?); if *homo*, it is very evil and dangerous.

Of the intelligences, numbers, and names of the planets [144]

In order that we may recognize the nature of these intelligences, of the bodies which by themselves are ruled, the powers should be known.

☽ The Moon therefore governs the elements and the bodies of living creatures. The order of Angels, i.e., messengers, preside over these. The prince of these is Gabriel, i.e., "the endurance (or strength) of God." For by means of the light of the Moon, all things are conveyed to us out of the sky, and it is the most endurable in life.

☿ Mercury presides over all comprehension and perception. The order of Virtues presides over Mercury, whose chief is Raphael, that is "the medicine of God." For with the medicine of human beings, it is the perception with comprehension, by which the virtues in us are brought together.

---

141. In marg.: "16."

142. There is a space in the manuscript. Perhaps "9" is missing.

143. Let: a hindrance or obstacle.

144. Cardano, *De subtilitate libri XXI* (1663), http://archimedes.mpiwg-berlin.mpg.de/cgi-bin/toc/toc .cgi?page=309;dir=carda_subti_016_la_1663;step=textonly.

♀ Venus, is the mother of pleasure and delight, and she enjoins us toward producing offspring. The order of Dominations is placed in charge of them, namely the power of guarding each species. But guarding is completed with the generation, the generation with lying together, and lying together with love. The highest of those which are in charge of Venus is Anael, who is called "the Grace of God." Indeed he is the grace of God, to be loved and to love, to join the fertile, and beget offspring, moreover beauty itself, and charm.

☉ To the Sun has been given all life: In charge of that is the order of Archangels, that is, the first messengers: For all virtue descends from the Sun through the Moon. Of these first Michael, i.e., "who is like God?" Nor is anything else comparable to the Sun, from which also the Sun is said to be unique.

♂ Mars provides strength and boldness, lest we live in perpetual fear. The order of Potestates (or Powers) is in charge of these: For in strength is power, and Power is joined with strength. The prince of the Potestates is Samael, i.e., the "hearing of God:" For power and strength have been placed in the hearing of God.

♃ Jupiter is that whereby everything is mixed and moderated, wherefore abilities and strengths, whose order of Principalities is established in moderation and temperance: Their prince is Sachiel, i.e., "the quiet of God:" For in moderation and with temperance we acquire quiet: The same is the author of tranquillity, of time, of peace, and of happiness.

♄ But Saturn gives firmness, and it mixes proportionately the moisture and the heat of the others, and that is believed to be on account of the coldness and the dryness of death, and the Lord of the Dead. The Thrones guard him: For by him the powers are strengthened, and whatever durability they have: The throne indeed is the seat. Of this therefore the lord is called Cassiel, i.e. "the hopes of God:" For durability brings hope and security.

The rulers of the Eighth Sphere are the Seraphim, i.e., "burning ones." and indeed those lights are seen to burn much of that sphere. But Cherubim, i.e., "knowing," preside in the first heaven.

[The] parchment [145]

To write any experiment, the best virgin parchment is *vellum vitulino*,[146] parchment of silk, of a lamb, of a virgin kid or a fawn, but provided always that the beast be not dead, but killed according to order.

---

145. In right marg.: "19."

146. *Vellum vitulino*: parchment made from the amniotic sac of an unborn calf.

[The] ink

The ink wherewith you must write must be of a clean glass, gum[,] vitriol, mastic, frankincense,[147] and crocus, and tempered with white wine, and the third day when it hath taken residence, let it be cleansed, then put thereto a little *algabay*, and *abnea* [storax], and fine musk, amber, balsamum myrrh, and lignum aloes, and boil it with mastic, and do further as in the second leaf of Sepher Raziel thou art admonished, with this ink thou shalt write the holy names of God.[148]

[The p]en

The pen, with which the holy names of God must be written, must be of a green reed, which must be gathered before the Sun arise. He that gathereth it must be clean washed in pure running water, or quick well, and clothed in clean clothes. When this reed is gathered as near as may be let the Moon be in cauda draconis or in Jupiter, for they be therefore true and good, and further do as the third leaf of the book aforesaid teacheth thee.

[Wr]iting

When thou writest any invocation to work by, thou shalt hold thy face towards the east, and write from morning until midday that thou eat, and after thou hast eaten and drunk, thou shalt write no more that day. Note that the writing is of most force when the Moon is even, as 2, 4, 6, and also in the day of Moon, Mercury, or Jupiter, but beware of Saturn and the Sun, and Solomon says, if thou put to thy ink the blood of a vulture, turtledove, or of a gander, that shall be much better and have more virtue.

[54]
Seven planets, twelve signs, thirty days

Note there be 7 brethren, which have among themselves 12 realms to be divided, and in each realm be 30 cities, and in every city 60 castles, and in every castle, 60, caldee 1 field or wild towns.

Aries, Leo, and Sagittarius	have power in the	East	Choleric: Fiery
Taurus, Virgo, and Capricorn	have power in the	South	Melancholy: Earthy
Gemini, Libra, and Aquarius	have power in the	West	Sanguine: Airy
Cancer, Scorpio, and Pisces	have power in the	North	Phlegmatic: Watery

---

147. Many of the herbal identifications below are taken from Don Karr's and Stephen Skinner's edition of the *Sepher Raziel, Also Known as Liber Salomonis* (Singapore: Golden Hoard Press, 2010).

148. In marg.: "w-."

The nature of the seven planets [149]

♄ Saturn in Hebrew called Sabday. He is first and the highest planet, whose nature is cold and dry, whose complexion is melancholic, an enemy to mankind. Masculine, he hath two houses as Capricorn and Aquarius. If he be lord of the nativity, he maketh the children of proud heart, lofty in honours, sad, keeping anger, upright in counsel, disagreeing with their wives, malicious, of stature lean, pale, slender, and hard favoured, thick lips, wide nostrils, and cold of nature. He is of slow motion, for he performeth his course but in thirty years. He governeth in man's body the right ear, the milt, the bladder. He hath dominion over the phthisic, catarrh, palsy, dropsy, quartan ague, consumption, gout, leprosy, morphew,[150] canker, flux, and griefs of the spleen. He signifieth fathers, wroth, and discord in lands.

♃ Jupiter in Hebrew is zedec. He is of nature warm and moist, and is said to be temperate, for that he is between old [*cold?] Sabday and hot Madyn, whose complexion is sanguine. He is a friend to nature and to mankind, masculine of the day, and is called the greater fortune. He hath two houses: Sagittarius and Pisces. He is meetly slow of motion, performing his circuit but in twelve years. He governeth in man's body the liver, the lungs, ribs, midriff, gristles, blood, and seed. He hath dominion over the king's evil, pleurisy, infection of the lungs, apoplexy proceeding of blood cramp, great headache, heart burning, and other diseases rising of blood. If he be lord of the nativity, he maketh the children born to be of noble courage, trusty, achieving great exploits, merry, glorious, and honest, of stature fair and lovely coloured, gentle eyes, thick hair, stately in going, very loving both of wife and children. He signifies good, honour, and virtue.

♂ Mars, in Hebrew is Madin. His nature is immoderate, hot, and dry, his complexion choleric, masculine of the night, evil disposed and termed the lesser fortune. He hath two mansions: Aries and Scorpio. He is indifferent, quick of motion, performing his course in two years. He governeth in a man's body the left ear, the gall, the reins, and cods.[151] He hath influence in the tertian fever, pestilence and continual ague, ringworm, megrim,[152] rottenness, untimely deliverance, breaking of veins, and all diseases caused by choler. If he be lord of the nativity, he maketh the children born rough, wild, fierce, invincible, bold, contentious, obscure, easy to be deceived, of stature indifferent, lean, hard faced, redheaded, small eyed, delighting to burn and destroy, subject to breaking their limbs and violent death, or else to fall down from an high place. He is evil, loose, and breme,[153] a ravisher and a liar.

---

149. Compare http://www.ajdrake.com/e211_spr_05/materials/guides/med_humors.htm.

150. Morphew: discolored skin lesion.

151. Cods: the scrotum.

152. Megrim: migraine.

153. Breme: fierce.

⊙ The Sun, in Hebrew is Haminam. His nature is hot and dry moderately. He is life and light of all other planets, masculine, of the day, good fortune by aspect, but evil fortune by corporal conjunction.[154] He is quick of motion, finishing his course in 365 days and almost six hours. He governeth in man's body the brain, marrow, sinews, the right eye of a man, and the left eye of a woman. He hath rule in all the hurtings of the mouth, in distillations of the eyes, and in all hot and dry diseases, which proceed not of choler. He hath only but one mansion, i.e., Leo. If he be lord of the nativity, he maketh the children born trusty, lofty, wise, just, courteous, religious, and obedient to their parents, of person corpulent, their hair inclined to yellow, tall, large limbed, doing all things with a grace, and if this planet be well placed, he causeth long life. All other planets dread him, for he is most strong.

♀ Venus, in Hebrew fair Noga, whose nature is cold and moist temperate, whose complexion is phlegmatic, feminine of the night, and is called the lesser fortune, but of inclination well-disposed to mankind. She is of a swift progression, absolving her revolution in one year. She governeth in man's body the loins, kidneys, buttocks, belly, flanks, and matrix. She beareth rule over all cold maladies and moistness in the liver, heart, and stomach, and specially in women about their privities. She hath two mansions: Taurus and Libra. If she be lady of the nativity, she maketh the children born pleasant, merry, given to pleasures, lovely, lecherous, just, inviolable keepers of faith and friendliness, of stature tall, comely, white, fair, having wanton amiable eyes, gentle looks, thick and soft hair, sometime curled dancers and delighted in music, and for the most part, they are fat and fleshly, and singing mirth and gladness, and very pleasant among women.

[55][155]

☿ Mercury, in Hebrew is Cocab, and of them is called the writer and fore speaker whose nature in all respects is common and convertible, masculine with masculine, and feminine with feminine, hot with hot and cold with cold, moist with moist, dry with dry, good fortune with fortune, and best with a good aspect or conjunction. He is of a swift motion, performing his course in one whole year. He governeth in man's body the tongue, memory, cogitation, hands, and thighs. He hath dominion over the pleurisy, madness, melancholy, falling sickness, cough, rheum, and the abundance of distilling spittle, and generally all thoughts are subject unto him and he hath two mansions, Gemini and Virgo. If he be lord of the nativity, he maketh the

154. Corporal conjunction: the appearance of two planets close to each other.
155. There is a tiny hexagram in the center top of the page.

children stout, wise, and apt to learn, modest, secret and eloquent, of person small, lean, pale of visage, smooth haired, fair eyed, hard and bony handed.

☽ The Moon in Hebrew is Labona, and of some called Malx, whose nature is cold and moist, feminine, and of the night, conveyer of the virtue of all other planets. She is passing swift of motion, finishing her course in 27 days, 7 hours, and 44 minutes. She governeth in a man's body the brain, the left eye of a man, and the right eye of a woman, the privy parts of a woman, the stomach both in man and woman, the belly and generally all the left parts of the body. She ruleth the palsy and the writhing of the body, displacing of members, obstruction of sinews, with infirmities proceeding of cold and moisture. She hath but one[156] house only, Cancer. If she be sovereign of the nativity, she maketh the children born honest, honourable, the inconstant loving moist and wet places, and given to see strange countries, of stature tall, white, and effeminate virtue.

Soli deo, laus honor et gloria. ["To God alone be praise, honour, and glory."]

These seven planets of wise men are called the keys of the world, and every of these may do in his hemisphere in his empire as emperor in his empire or prince in his kingdom.

Solomon sayeth, the prophets calleth them brethren; he calleth them seven quick-sprites, somewise men the seven lamps burning, or seven candlesticks of light and of life, others seven heavenly bodies which we commonly call seven planets or stars.

Note[157] that it were a great destruction and confusion in land and in sea, and in the elements if any of the bodies above were broken or were evil entreated, for if one of these failed, the earth should come again to his first state and all the elements should be consumed.

☉ If the Sun should be destroyed, each life and each soul should be destroyed.

☽ If the Moon were destroyed, the ligatures or buildings of the sea should be destroyed.

♄ Know you that ♄ is earthy and holdeth all the earth in a balance that it shall not move.

♃ Jupiter holdeth the air.

♂ Mars, the fire, the Sun, the day, and men.

♀ Venus holdeth the fair parts of the world.

☿ Mercury, reasons, Moon, the earth, sea, and waters.

---

156. *Sec. man.*

157. In right marg.: "27."

♄ Saturn joyeth[158] in the twelfth house.[159]

♂ Mars in the sixth.

☉ The Sun in the ninth.

♀ Venus in the fifth.

☿ Mercury in the ascendant in the first house.

☽ The Moon in the third house.

Seven precious stones which were in the crown of Zepheraziel.*	The Names of 24 stones	24 Notable good herbs
1. Red carbuncle.	1. A carbuncle.	1 Acill almalit i.e., Corona regia, or Rosemarinus.
2. Emerald.	2. Topaz.	2. Artemesia.
3. Sapphires.	3. Emerald.	3. Canabus.
4. Beryl.	4. Jagnucia.	4. Fleniculus.
5. Topaz.	5. Crisopasuis.	5. Cardamomum.
6. A Jacinth.	6. Saphirus.	6. Anisum.
7. Adamant.	7. Beryl.	7. Coriandrum.
	8. Onyx.	8. Petersilum.
	9. Sardus.	9. Ypericon or hipericon
	10. Crisolitus.	10. Apium
	11. Elithopia.	11. Coriandrum of the second kind.
	12. Christallus.	12. Saturea.
	13. Cornelua.	13. Sancta.
	14. Jaspis.	14. Serpillum.
	15. Yris.	15. Maiorana.
	16. Coralus.	16. Dragnucia.
	17. Persius.	17. Nepita.
	18. Catell.	18. Luna.
	19. Celonites.	19. Salma.
* Karr, *Sepher Raziel: Liber Salomonis*, 2010, edited from Sloane 3826, fol. 16v.		

158. Joyeth: to be in the house where the planet has greatest influence.

159. Jupiter is omitted from this list.

	20. Calcedonis.	20. Savina.
	21. Cerammnuis. (Ceramuris?)	21. Nasturcium.
	22. Metestus.	22. Cannaferula.
	23. Magnetis.	23. Calamtum.
	24. Adamant.	24. Cicoria. vide in Zephar Raziell folii 22 23 24.*
* Karr 16v.		

[56]

Twenty-four beasts having power over stones and herbs and commonly called visions

.1. Fire, the body of the Sun, called a quick fire.

.2. The mist or cloud.

.3. A spirit or souls of bodies.

.4. The wind, called a quick air.

.5. A fantasy or shade.

.6. Demon.

This was [160] formed of pure matter without corruption, and is immortal and for-ever enduring, but now hath taken thickness and darkness of the earth, and dwelleth in darkness and obscurity. He hath power to take form or shape of what he will in the earth after the will of the creator, as the Sun, the Moon, the stars, angels, cloud, fowl, beast, fish, man, reptile, or any other etc., and for our uncleanness they are become furies, and therefore the invocating of them, their appearing, constraining, binding, and loosing must be done with all pureness and cleanness, first with orison, fasting, and praising God, fumigation, etc.

These are like the body of the Sun, otherwise call birds, or animals of the air

.7. *Aquila* an eagle. 1

.8. *Vultur,* or a vulture. 2

.9. *falco,* i.e., a falcon. 3

---

160. Compare Raziel in Sloane 3846, 139r.

.10. *Turtur* ["a turtledove"]. 4

.11. *Upupa*, i.e., a lapwing. 5

.12. *Ciconia*, i.e., a haysoncke.[161] 6

The wing concerning the fishes of Mars, and others, etc.

.13. *Balena* ["a whale"]. 1

.14. *Delphine* ["a dolphin"] king of the sea. 2

.15. *Cancer* ["a crab"]. 3

.16. *Pisces claves or sepia*, ["a cuttlefish"]. 4

.17. *Murena* ["an eel"]. 5

.18. Renaviridis[162] 6

The wing concerning animals or beasts of the earth

.19. Leo, an lion. 1

.20. Elephauñt, an elephant. 2

.21. Ceruus, a hart. 3

.22. Cattus, a cat. 4

23. Mustella, a weasel. 5

.24. Talpa, a want.[163] 6

For the virtue of these, look in Sepher Raziel.

Of suffumigations called incenses[164]

Note as there be seven heavens, seven stars, and seven days in the week, so there be seven suffumigations which holdeth with them the virtue of the seven stars, and maketh glad the spirits of the air, the angels of heaven, and the devils etc.

♄ Incenses of the Saturday ought to be made of all good things, and well smelling roots as costus and frankincense etc.

☉ Incenses of Sunday is mastic, musk, and other good gums.

---

161. Ciconia: stork. Haysoncke: a hedge-sparrow. These are two different birds.

162. Renaviridis: green frog.

163. Want: a mole.

164. Compare below, Folger p. 93; Razielis; OP Book 1, chapter 44. In marg.: "w" glyph.

☽ Incenses of Monday is myrtle leaf and bay laurel and other leaves of good odour.

♂ Incenses of Tuesday is sandalwood, red, black, and white, and all such trees as aloes, cypress, etc.

☿ Incenses of Wednesday is of cinnamon, cassia lignea, laurel bark, and mace and other good rinds.

♃ Incenses of Thursday is nutmeg, cloves, and citrus, and the rind of oranges dry powdered and other fruits of good savour, etc.

♀ Incenses of Friday is musk, roses, violets, and crocus and other flowers of good savour and in the contrary to the contrary put you all incenses, stinking.

☜ Note that each incense of good odour gathereth together his spirits, after that his nature, his colour, his strength is. This we see that all suffumigations are made of roots, trees, rinds, leaves, flowers, fruits, and gums.

Acill. There is an herb called Acill almalit, i.e., corona regis or rosemary. The house that is suffumigated therewith, no devil nor spirit hath power over the same. Peony hath the same virtue.[165]

Cannabis ["hemp"]. Anoint thee with the juice of cannabis and the juice of archangel ["white nettle"] and before a mirror of steel call spirits, and thou shalt see them and have power to bind and to loose them.

Fennel. The fume of fennel chaseth away spirits.

Cardamom. Cardamom giveth gladness to him that useth it, gathereth together spirits, and when thou invocatest any spirits, eat thereof or make fume of it.

Anise. Take the herb anise and join to camphor, and thou shalt see spirits [that] shall (?) dread thee. It profiteth much to the achieving of secret and privy things.[166]

Coriander. Coriander gathereth spirits together. A fume being made thereof with *Apio*[167] *nisquio* [*jusquianus*, or "henbane"] and *lazias*[168] *cictuta* [*cicuta*, or "water hemlock"] urgeth spirits and therefore, it is said, *herba spirituum*.

Parsley. This herb chaseth away the spirits of roches.[169]

---

165. The next in Raziel is Artemisia, which is missed here.

166. Frederick Hockley copied the experiments for cannabis, fleniculus, and avisum into a private magical tract written for a client around 1825. See Hockley, *Experimentum*, 3.

167. Apio: either honey or a plant of the genus Apio, such as celeriac or parsley.

168. Lazias: unknown

169. Roches: possibly "riches," or a term for a seam of metal, presumably in this place precious. Spirits were believed to guard both.

Ypericon ["**hypericon**"]. *Ypericon,* the juice mixed with crocus, artemesia, and valerian root is very good to write withal, for the obtaining of friendship, either of a prince, of spirits, of the air and devils, and if ye do thou shalt obtain that thou covetest.

Apium.[170] *Apium,* hath great power upon winds and devils and fantasies.

[57]

Vazebelib ie. Martagon.[171] *Apium, insqrino* ["henbane"] and artemesia, being made in suffumigation by seven nights with *fagar Almaits* roots, dried, and tempered with *Aqua lapides,* gathereth spirits together, and being environed with any evil, suffumigate thyself therewith, and thou shalt see many wonders, as fantasies and devils of diverse manners, etc.

Savory. Savory is an herb which, being born about one, giveth grace and good fortune, especially in the day of Venus.

Dragnutia.[172] The herb *Dragnutia,* if it be gathered when the Sun is in the first degree of Cancer and the Moon beholdeth Mercury, or is in the house of Mercury, if thou touch closures or locks therewith, they shall be opened to thee. Hermes sayeth that it gathereth together wind and spirits if mandrake and Capillis dezoara be joined therewith.

Luna. This herb *luna,* i.e., the seed thereof, parsley, *Azartochona,* and the root of violet and axii, maketh to see in the air things to come and to say many prophesies, being made in a suffumigation.

Salma ["**salvia, or sage**"]. *Salma* defendeth a place from evil spirits, and is very good for a man in health to carry about with him, but not for a sick man.

Colamton ["**calamint, or pennyroyal**"]. This *Colamton,* mint, palma Christi, i.e., peony, being suffumigated, taketh away evil spirits from any place, and defendeth a man against fantasies.

To defend treasure from finding [173]

Take *Coriandrum* of the second kind, which maketh one to sleep, and adjoin thereto crocus, henbane, and *Apio,* and grind them together and temper them with chicory, water hemlock, and make a suffumigation thereof, and suffume the place

---

170. Apuim: see note for apio, above.

171. Vazebelib i Martagon: two spirits to be summoned via the concoction that follows, according to Raziel.

172. Karr has Dragantia linked to either columbrina or adderwort.

173. In right marg.: "23."

where thou wilt hide any treasure in, when the Moon is joined with the Sun in *angulo terre* ["the earth angle"], and that treasure shall never be found and who that would take the same away shall be made fools. Note that in the laying or hiding of the same treasure thou suffumest them with frankincense, musk, chicory, lignum aloes, *cosso,* ever more devils will keep that place and evil winds, and know you that it may never be dissolved or for-done[174] again without an image made thereto by the point of stars.

To constrain and bind devils

Take the herb *sancta*[175] and bear it reverently, for it defendeth the place where it is from evil things, for with this prophets made dead men to speak that were dead many days. In place where this herb is, spirits have no might. It giveth men power to obtain their desire.[176] This herb, put upon the place where devils be enclosed, it constraineth them and bindeth them, lest they might have power to depart away, and Solomon said, "I found in the *book of hermits*,[177] that who that taketh water in the hour of the night and goeth upon the tomb of a dead man, with whose spirit he would have speech withal, cast the water upon the tomb with the herb hyssop, and let the water be suffumed with costus, chicory, and musk, and say, "*Surge, surge, surge* ["arise, arise, arise"], O thou spirit, and come and speak with me." This do by three nights, and in the third night he shall surely come to thee, and shall speak with thee, and confer with thee of what thing thou wilt. This is proven. Glory to God, always and everywhere.

To see spirits, etc.

Take the herb fleabane, *sicorda* [chicory?], *garmene,* and the tree that swimmeth which is said *arbor cancri* ["crabtree"], and *malie* with *rore madii*, and with the tree that showeth by night called *herba lucens* ["the shining herb"], and with these make an ointment and put thereto the eyes (?) of a whelp and the fat of a hart, and anoint thyself and it will make open the air unto thee, that thou mayest see spirits in the clouds of the heavens, and all so there by thou mayest go surely, whither thou wilt, in one hour.

---

174. For-done: undone, destroyed.

175. The Latin Raziel gives *Centaurea*, a considerably sized genus.

176. In marg.: "w-" glyph.

177. I.e., the early astrological treatise *Liber Hermetis*. See Sloane 3847, fol. 84–100.

That one shall prosper in his affairs

Take catnip, marjoram, *athanasia*, clover, sage, *perunita*, ivy, artemisia, and hyssop gathered, the Moon increasing, the day of Jupiter. And in the morrow when the [+Sun] waxeth[178] from the first degree of Aries, until the first of Cancer but when you gather them be clean, and laved or washed, and stand thy face toward the east, and gather them, and be assured the hour and place is amended where these herbs be is mixed, and put them upon the gate of the house and thou shalt profit evermore.

To win favour of princes, etc.

Take the herb juniperus sabina, which as some say, is a tree of love and delectation, is join with crocus, lingua, snake tongue, and somewhat of periwinkle, and put it in a ring of gold, and then thou mayest go surely before the king, or before whomsoever thou wilt, but if thou put the stone with it that is called topaz,[179] or else beryl. This ring must be made when the Moon is joined with Jupiter in trine from the Sun and then it is called "the ring of the Sun." It preserveth health; it giveth favour and grace, and procureth honour.[180]

To see devils or spirits

Take the herb giant fennel, which is dreadful and grievous and very strong in operation. Take the juice of it, the juice of cicute, or water hemlock, henbane, *tapsibarbati*, red sandalwood, and black poppy. With this confection made, thou mayest fume what thou wilt, and thou shalt see devils and strange things, and if *apium* were joined therewith. Know that, from each place suffumed, devils should fly, etc., see in *Sepher Raziel* fol. 13.

[58]
To bind and loose spirits [181]

Take chicory and join with *trigon* and cinquefoil, hypericon, urtica, or stinging nettle, verbena, and *albeate* together, and bear them at thy neck, and under thy feet. Put seven-knotted grass and seven-leaved grass [the above], *martagon* and domestic

---

178. So Razielis, Karr p. 78.

179. So Raziel; Folger: topzins.

180. In right marg.: "24."

181. In marg.: "+."

lily and *silvestri* [182] and the herb angelica, for he that hath these under his feet, or sitteth upon them, and hath the others in his neck, and hath seven rings of seven metals in the figures,[183] know ye that he shall have might in binding and in loosing and in chanting, and to do both good and evil in all places, and make you suffumigation of the these nine things: white frankincense, *thimiamate*, mastic, musk, lignum aloes, *cassia*, and cinnamon, and therewith suffumigate every of the things abovesaid, saying, "Raphaell, Gabriel, Michael, Cherubine, Seraphin, Ariell, paritaseron, Micraton, Sandelon, *complete meam petitionem et meam voluntatem* ["fulfill my petition and my will"]," and they shall fulfill it. These be the chiefest names of the nine orders of angels.

Upupa [184]

Upupa, a lapwing, hath one bone in his wings which gathereth together devils and spirits of the air, the property of him is, that who so taketh the heart of him and wrappeth it in honey, and then as soon as he may swallow it and drinketh the milk of a white cow or red, know that it maketh a man say things to come, and who that cutteth off the neck thereof where a cock croweth not neither may be heard, neither the voices of a hound neither where wheat is sown, and when he cutteth of the neck, let him call devils and let him bear with him the half deal of the blood, and with the other half, anoint himself and ever more one of the devils shall go with him, viz., he whom he calleth and he shall tell him many things, etc.

To subdue spirits

Ciconia, a stork, who that slayeth him in the day of the Moon, and take the blood of the heart of and anoint himself therewith, and eateth the flesh with fennel seed, cardamom, and cloves, and suffumigateth himself with good odours as frankincense, mastic, and cinnamon, with such others, he shall have grace of enchanting, of conjuring and constraining spirits of the air, etc.

♃[185]------------------------

---

182. Silvestri: possibly white bedstraw or a variety of rye.

183. Error for fingers?

184. In marg.: "0."

185. In marg.: circled "+" glyph.

Note that they that suffumigate observe or ought to do seven things, for so Solomon said the hermits did, and attained to their desire.

1. They used abstinence or fasted.

2. They washed and cleansed themselves.

3. They did alms.

4. They slew and cast blood into the fire.

5. They pray much in hours, i.e., times in the day and times in the night.

6. They made fumigation with good things and well smelling as above, and thereby attained to their petitions, by the commandment of the creator.

7. They slew and burned all.

Suffumigating

The manner of the suffumigating a man's self: It ought to be made in seven manners, i.e., towards the east, west, north, and south, towards heaven above, and towards the earth beneath, and the seventh time all about, and ever more as oft as any man doth is let him address his mind unto God and pray, and he may have his will fulfilled.

Now we speak of the suffumigations of the four parts of the world, and of the four elements, for the part of the east and the fire serveth amber, musk, and white wax, i.e., with wax for the part of the south and the earth *Algalia almea and Tiriaca* ["*abelmoschus (musk mallow)*, almea (balsam of storax), and theriac"], for the part of the west and the air, balsam, camphor, and olive oil, for the [part of the] north and the water, lignum aloes, nutmeg, and mace.

The[186] master that worketh must purify himself by seven days before the work. He must wash himself; he must eat nothing of theft, neither of raven, neither of evil party, neither any thing unclean, neither that as is fallen to death, neither of any beast of four feet, nor of none other, and he must eschew from evil malice and falsehood. He must not drink wine nor eat fishes nor anything with blood goeth fro. He must not join to a woman to pollute himself, nor menstruate, nor enter into a house where is a dead man, nor go to the grave of a dead man, nor by him that suffereth and the law hath condemned. Avoid pride, be clean, continue in prayer, keep thy tongue from slandering, lying, and swearing, fast truly, keep thy bed warily, and avoid sin. Light thy house with prayer, praise ye angels, do alms, remember the needy, and forget not the works of mercy and be not joined to evil men. Clothe thyself with clean clothes, trust

---

186. In left marg.: "w" glyph; in right marg.: "16."

in God, be faithful, have a good hope, and use appellation in all necessities to the Creator, and no doubt but thou shalt obtain that by petition thou desirest.

Who that by Semoferas[187] will do anything must observe seven things. First meekness, truth, patience, abstinence, trust, charity, and mercy.

[59]

Semoferas:[188]

Here followeth the names of Semoferas which God gave to Adam in paradise, in which be four letters compared and likened to the four parts of the world, to the four elements, to the four complexions, and to the four natures of beasts, and these be they.

ל ֵה ֵה ו ֵה ֵה ֵה ו ֵה ֵ. ֵ.

These letters must be named piteously, devoutly, and meekly.

Solomon sayeth that there be seven Semoferas.
1. The first, when Adam spake with the Creator in Paradise.
2. The second, when Adam spake with the angels.
3. The third, when Adam spake with the devils.
4. The fourth, when Adam spake with men, fowls, fishes, reptiles, and wild beasts.
5. The fifth, when he spake with seeds, herbs, trees, and growing things upon Earth.
6. The sixth, when Adam spake with winds, and the [four] [189] elements.
7. The seventh, when Adam spake with the Sun, the Moon, and the stars. By this Semoferas Adam did whatever he would, which Semoferas was given unto him when the Creator inspired grace into him.

1. The first Semoferas is when the Creator formed Adam in Paradise,

is as much to say as Yana, in great necessity who that meekly and devoutly calleth upon this name, no doubt but he shall have grace and help.

---

187. Compare Razielis, 153v.

188. In left marg.: "+"; in right marg: "27." Compare transcription of *Razielis* in Peterson, *The Sixth and Seventh Books of Moses*, 267 ff, which is virtually identical.

189. So Razielis. There is a space, presumably to switch to red ink.

2. The second Semoferas is when Adam spoke with the angel which brought unto him these letters  i.e., Yseraye.[190] This name thou shalt name when thou wilt speak with the angels, and without doubt it shall avail thee much in thy work.

3. The third Semoferas is when he (Adam) spoke with demons and with dead men, which to every of his questions, sufficiently answered, viz., Adona, Sabaoth, Adonay, Cados, Addona Amora.[191] These thou shalt name when thou wilt gather together winds, devils, or spirits.

4. The fourth Semoferas is when (Adam bound) animals and spirits, and whatever. With this Semoforas, Adam bound and loosed spirits, beasts, fowls, and fishes, etc. Langume, Lamazirin, Leuagelayn, Lagri, Lanagala, Lematozim, Layfyalafyn. When thou wilt bind or loose, thou shalt name these.

5. The fifth Semoferas is when (Adam named) animals and whatever. The fifth is when he named the seven natures, with which he bound herbs, seeds, and trees. Liaham, Lialgana, Liafar, Vialurab, Lelara, Lebaron, Laasalilas, etc.

6. The sixth Semoferas is of great virtue and power i.e., Letamynyn, Letaglogen, Letafyryn, Babaganarityn, Letarimitim, Letagelogrim, Letafatazin. These names thou shalt name when thou wilt that the elements or winds shall be helping unto thee, etc.

7. The seventh Semoferas is of great virtue and power, for they be names of the Creator which ought to be named in each thing and in every work, Elyaon, Yaena, Adonay, Cados, Ebreel, Eloy, Ela, Egiel, Ayom, Sath, Adon, Sulela, Eloym, delyom, Yacy, Elym, Delis, Yacy, Zazael, Paliel, Man, Myel, Euola, Dilatan, Saday, Alma, Papyn, Saena, Alym, Catinal, Uza, Yarast, Calphi, Calsas, Safna, Nycam, Saday, Aglataon, Sya, Emanuell, Joth, Zalaph, Om, Via, Thau, Domyfrael, Muel, Lalialens, alla, phenor, Aglata, Tiel, Piel, Patriceion, Cepheron, Baryon, Yael. These thou shalt name every time when thou workest upon the four elements, and whatever thou wilt do by them, it shall be done, etc.

[60]

The Semoferas of Moses

Here begins the Semoferas which the Lord gave to Moses, and it is divided into seven chapters of which the first is.

---

190. Perhaps AshR AHIH, i.e. "Asser Eheie," one of the names of God of seven letters.

191. This is similar to Sloane 3826, 54v, which reads "Adona Sabaoth Adonay Cados Addona Annora"; Sloane 3846 reads "Adonay Sabaoth, adonay cados, addonay amiora."

l. When Moses ascended the hill and spake with the flame that environed the bush and the bush burned not nor was not consumed.

2. The second, when he spake with God in the hill.

3. The third, when he divided the Red Sea etc.

4. The fourth, when the yard [192] was turned into a serpent.

5. The fifth are the names which were written in the forehead of Aaron.

6. The sixth when he made the brazen serpent, and the calf, and when he smote the Egyptians with plagues.

7. The seventh when he rained manna in the desert, and drew out water forth of the rock, and led the children of Israel from captivity.

Chapter 1

Maya, Afi, Zye, yarimye, Vue, Bace, Sare, Buire, maa, yasome, roy, Lyly, Leoy, Yly, Yre, Cy, Loy, zolye, Lee or see, Loace Cadeloy, Vle, Meharamehy, ry, hy, fossa, tu, Nimi, Sehie, nice, yelo, habe, vele, hele, ede, quigo, ramye, habe these name devoutly etc.

Chapter 2

Abguicam, Loaraceram, Naodicras, Pecarcecay, Acaptena, Yeger, Podayg, Saccocicum. These be the names with God said to Moses when he ascended the hill and spake with him. These be the names with which the Temple of Bozale was founded. These be the names of the prophets, wherewith the angels sealed the [four] [193] parts of the world. By these are many miracles to be done, but they must be named chaste and clean.

Chapter 3

Eva, Elaye, syec, helame, Macie, Lehahu, Lelahu, Aliale, Cure, Azaye, Boene, hyeola, ysale, Mabecha, Avayha, Ye, Ye, Malece, Amare, Loena, quleye, Lyeneno, leyane, habana, nechee, hycers.

---

192. Yard: staff.

193. Folger omits.

Chapter 4

Micracon, Indy Xeddem, Pcddem, roexi, saconits, patrint, piston, ycymor, hygaron, ygnyron, Temgaron, Mycon, Micondasnos, Castas, Laceas, Astas, yecan, Cina, Tabluist, Tablanac, Zacuss. These names when thou wilt have thy question fulfilled.

Chapter 5

These names were written unto the people, of Aaron, when he spake with the Creator, Saday, hayleos, loez, Elacy, Citonii, hazyhaya, yeynimese[y], Accida, bacuc huadonemi, eya, hiebu, ven, vaha, oyaha, eye, eye, ha, hia, haya, zahia, hahya Eyey, yaia, El, Ebehel, va, va, va. Keep well these names, for they be of great virtue, and by them thou mayest achieve what thou demandest of the Creator.

Chapter 6

Yana, Yane, Sya, Abibhu, Vanohia accenol, Tivgas, Yena, Eloym, Ya, vehu, yane, hayya, vehu, Ahyaenia. With these names thou shalt destroy evils, and all enchantments, but presume not to name them vainly.

Chapter 7

Saday, Saniora, Ebon, Pheneton, Eloy, Eneyobcel, Messias, Jahe, Yana, or Eol[yen]. By these thou shalt do many marvels, and if thou be in any anguish, name these names, and no doubt but thou shalt feel their virtue. Then say, these names, before rehearsed being named, *Deus viue verax magne fortis potens pie sancte munde, omni bonitate plene, benedicte domine benedictum nomen tuum, tu completur nostram, compleas questionem, tu factor, fac nos ad finem nostri operis,*[194] *elargum, tu s[ancte] et miserationis, nobis miserere nomen tuum Yesaraye sit per verbum benedictum.* Amen.[195] God quick, very great, strong, mighty, meek, holy, clean, full of all goodness, blessed Lord, be thy name, thou fulfiller, fulfill our question, thou Maker, make us to come to the end of our work, thou holy and merciful, have mercy on us. Thy name Yesarie, be it blessed by words. Amen. Jesaraye is as much to say, as God without beginning and without ending. Angila is the name of a prophet, and properly written in gold, and

---

194. Razielis adds: *pervenire tu largitor nobis integru complementum nostris operis.*

195. Translation follows in the text. JHP translation: "O God living, true, strong, great, mighty, pious, holy, pure, full of all goodness, blessed Lord, blessed be your name, you O fulfiller, fulfill our question; you, O maker, make us come to the end of our work; O bountiful, holy, and merciful one, have mercy on us through your name Yeseraye through the blessed word."

whosoever beareth it upon himself shall not during the time he beareth it, need to fear sudden death.[196]

♃------------------------

Four great names

These four names of God are of great virtue, for prophets were wont to bear them written in precious stones: Joac + Jona + Eloy + Yena + and whoso beareth them written in virgin parchment in letters of gold shall not lack living, clothing, nor worship, so long as he beareth them upon him.

[61]

A name to get victory

These be the names with which Joshua made the Sun to stand still in his place against his proper nature,[197] whereby he overcame the Gabionites and thirty-four kings: Bachionodo balizlior.

This name giveth vengeance of enemies, and whoso beareth it with him, a prison may not hold him, neither in battle he may not be overcome of any man.

To remove wrath and sorrow

This name, Hacedion or Hachedion, removeth wrath and sorrow, and increaseth gladness and love.

For victory

This name, Mephemyphaton + whoso beareth upon him shall not easily be overcome.

These be seven high great names and virtuous, which name when thou wilt ask any thing, and thou shalt obtain, but choose good times and hours.

---

196. This is the end of the material from Razielis proper. The following section, from "Four great names … Bycol, Ycos" are a separate text sometimes appended to it. In Sloane 3846, 158r, this short text is titled "Here beginneth names that be necessary to euerich Christen man."

197. Joshua 10:12–13.

Comiceron.			Hyeyady.	On.	Onoytheon.
Sedalay.			Aneyym.	Jesus.	Stimulamaton.
Tohomos.			Valayeyl.	Christus.	Alzaphares.
Zofyn.			Selaleyl.	A & Ω.	Tetragrammaton.
Agata.	*Soli deo honor et gloria.*		Maynaceel.	El.	Elioram.
Bycol.	["Honour and glory to God alone."]		Vassaliel.	Ely.	Egirion.
Ycos.				Eloy.	Istion.
				Eloye.	Orchona.
				Elyon.	Usiormis or Usior.
					Ormis.

Onelabiasin.	Emanuell.	Ya. Ya.	Yayn.	*Alpha. et Omega.*
Noyin.	Sabaoth.	Ye. Ye.	Deg.	*Principium. Finis.*
Messias.	Adonay.	Joth.	Eloye.	["Alpha and Omega,
Sother.	Egge.	Theos.	On.	beginning and end"]

+

The consecration of the ring

Hoccindinos + Osytheon + Stimulamaton + Elioram + Messias + Sother + Emanuel + Sabaoth + Adonay + Panthater + Primellus + Grabaton + **per hec** sanctissima et alia nomina qui non licet nominare, te suppliciter expostulo ut presente Annulo qui sapientissimus Salomon instituit et quo in suis experimentis usus et super omnia demonia et malignos spiritus virtutem efficaciter obtineat et eos ad libitum suum per huius Anuli virtutem exorcizator constringat eaque in omnibus experimentis suis qui sotiis salus sit et protectio per te deum qui omnium es refugium et virtus, gloria et potestas per eterna scta [*saecula] Amen.	Hoccindinos + Osytheon + Stimulamaton + Elioram + Messias + Sother + Emanuel + Sabaoth + Adonay + Panthater + Primellus + Grabaton + by these holy names, and by other names which it is not permitted to name, I humbly urge you, that this ring which is here present, which the wise Solomon prepared and used in his experiments, and obtained effectual power over all demons and evil spirits, and he was able to exorcise them at his pleasure through the power of this ring, and he was able to bind them fast in all his experiments, and may it be salvation and protection to the associates, through you, O God, who are the refuge of all, and the virtue, glory, and power, through the eternal ages. Amen.

After that these Psalms should be said: Psalm 120: I have lifted up my eyes...; Psalm 112: Praise the Lord, ye children...; Psalm 129: Out of the depths....[198]

Before this, for three days time, you may eat, but abstain from all impurity, and place it on the altar while celebrating three Masses, and then return the ring to a clean place and with fragrances such that the power is greatest. It is proven, not only for the present operation, but also previous ones, with all the necessities brought together, we have no doubt. And with this the consecration of the ring is accomplished. The end.

Days most expedient to work any marvels on [199]

1 The 1 day of the month is good to begin all manner of things.
2 The 2 for hate and enchantment against enemies.
3 The 3 is right naught.
4 The 4 to enchant and conjure wicked spirits.
5 The 5 to go invisible, and enchant against enemies.
6 The 6 for theft and knowledge of hidden goods.
7 The 7 naught.
8 The 8 for love of virgins.
9 The 9 naught.
10 The 10 naught.
11 The 11 at the afternoon, to enchant.
12 The 12 for theft.
13 The 13 for love.
14 The 14 to go invisible.
15 The 15 naught.
16 The 16 for discord.
17 The 17 for love of women.
18 The 18 for the theft.
19 The 19 for hate.
20 The 20 naught.
21 The 21 to go invisible.
22 The 22 for love.
23 The 23 for discord.
24 The 24 naught.
25 The 25 for enchantments.

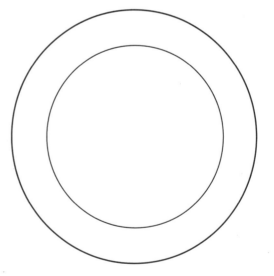

---

198. In the KJV these Psalms are numbered 121, 113, and 130.
199. In left marg.: "w-" glyph; in right marg.: "37–38."

26 The 26 both for love.

27 The 27 both for love.

28 The 28 both naught for love.

29 The 29 both naught for love.

30 The 30 against enemies.

31 The 31 *Idem cum principio. deo semper et ubique gloria, laus et honor* ["The same as in the beginning. Glory, praise, and honour to God, always and everywhere."]

[62]

A malediction for the fire [200]

Coniuro te ignis per illum qui orbem contremere facit quatinus spiritum illum N callefacias et comburas ita quod in sup persona sentiat eternaliter fiat fiat fiat.	I conjure you, O fire, by him who made the world tremble, that you will heat up and burn that spirit N., that he may perceive his eternal sentence. Let it be so; let it be so; let it be so!
Maledictus et blasphematus sis perpetualiter et in pena eternaliter, et nulla requies sit in te in aliqua hora nec die nec nocte, si statim non eris obediens verbis, que diciuntur [*dicentur] de illo, qui tremere facit orbem, et per hac nomina istorum nominum, quibus omnibus creatura humilliter obedit, et pavore, ac timore, omnis eorum creature contremiscit, et in eis tonitr[u]na, et fulgura, sunt creata, que te et tuo subditos destruant: qui sunt hac + Adepleniton + Perasac + patir + ffome + lameth + mem + memene + sameth + ay + ey + ffy + Asade + Costin + vod + per ista nomina	May you be cursed* and reviled forever, and suffer eternal punishment, and may you have no rest at any time of the day or night, if you do not immediately obey those words, which spoken make the world tremble, and by these names, the same names which all creation humbly obeys, and all creatures tremble with fear and dread, and by which the thunder and lightning were created, which will destroy you and your subordinates, which are these: + Adepleniton† + Perasac + Patir + Ffome + Lameth + Mem + Memene + Sameth + Ay + Ey + Ffy + Asade + Costin + Vod + By these names

* In marg. in pencil: "also page 108."

† This is of course the Hebrew alphabet, here corrupted beyond recognition, as evident from parallel texts, e.g., Bodleian Library MS. Michael 273, 56.

---

200. Another version of this curse can be found on Folger p. 108, also Mathers, *The Key of Solomon*, p. 42.

te N. maledicimus et privamus ab omni-	I curse you N., and deprive you from all
bus graciis et habitibur [*habitabatur] et	grace, and from any place you may have
priorum virtutem in stagnum Ignis et	inhabited, and from any prior powers,
sulphuris, ut hostem in profundum	and relegate you to the lake of fire and
abissi, te religamus eternaliter nunc et in	sulphur, and into the deepest abyss, now
eternum, sic fiat sic fiat.	and forever. Let it be thus. Let it be thus.

If he come, rewrite his name, and make a fragrant fire, and perfume it with fragrant spices.

This is to be done if the spirit has been rebellious against the exorcist and is unwilling to come, then write their names on paper, and soil it with mud, and a fire should be kindled with sulfur, pitch, horn, asafoetida, and other foul smelling things, saying as above.

Another for the fire for the four kings

Coniuro te ignis et exorciso te illum qui orbem contremere facias ["I conjure you, O fire, and exorcise you, by Him who makes the world tremble"], and by him whose presence made the infernal powers to tremble and quake, that thou O fire and angel of the most high God be now and from henceforth and that forever maledicted and accursed, and inasmuch as in thee lieth, grieve, torment, waste, and burn these names of these obstinate spirits, stubborn and unbelieving kings, and wicked mates of that great and unhappy prince Lucipher, i.e., Oriens, Amaymon, Paymon, et Egyne so that as thou, O fire, doth grieve and vex their names etc., so their proper shapes and forms most accursed may be afflicted and that most acerbitly in the bottomless pit, deep dungeon and odious stinking lake, which continually, and that without ceasing, leaveth not off to burn with unquenchable fire, mixed with sulfur, pitch, and other matter increasers of those flashing flames, being just and due plagues of God ordained, and for their merits and desserts, i.e., Oriens, Paymon, Amaymon and Egione, most justly provided, O fire, the Father curse thee, the Son curse thee, the Holy Ghost curse thee, all Angels curse thee, Archangels, Cherubim, Seraphim, Powers, Potestates, Principates, and Dominations curse thee, all holy patriarchs, prophets, apostles, martyrs, confessors, and virgins, curse thee, O fire, all the powers of heaven and elects of God curse thee,[201] and I now by the licence of God curse thee, by the licence, com[b]ina-

---

201. The almost identical curse on Folger p. 109 rearranged the phrase "The lycences, coniurationes, threates, & indignations of God curse thee." The crossed out "the" might be evidence of editing here.

tions of threats and indignations of God curse thee, and I now by the power and authority of Aaron, the great priest of God, of my own priesthood, and by the virtue of all priests, that have been, now are, and hereafter shall be in the Church of God, here and in all places, in all times and in all ages, now and forever, curse thee. The curse which fell upon Cain, the whole world, and Judas, curse thee, all benedictions and blessings of God the Father, etc., curse thee and curse thee again, and make thee of such power, that thou mayest persecute, vex, waste, burn, torment, scald, scorch, and continually burn the names of those rebellious and wicked spirits that they may be urged thereby to come, to run, and to appeal to me for aid and help requiring to be released of their unspeakable anguish, sorrow, and unspeakable punishment and hellish torment and tortures, and that by the power and virtue of our Lord Jesus Christ, who is *via sine devio, veritas sine nubulo, et vita sine termino, cui laus est et potestas honor virtus et gratiarum actio, gloria et victoria, qui vivet e[t] regnat, et imperat in Trinitate perfecta gloriosus deus per infinita secculorum seccula Amen. fiat, fiat.* ["a way without deviation, truth without a cloud, and life without end, to whom is praise and power, honour, strength, and act of grace, glorious and triumphant, who lives and reigns and commands, glorious God in perfect trinity, forever and ever. Amen. May it be so, may it be so, may it be so."] [202]

With penalty inflicted [203]

O N convertate deus in infernum Psalm. 9 verse 18. pluat deus super te laqueos ignis sulphur et procellas O N verberet te deus virga ferrea et tanquam vas figuli confringat O N confundat te deus, veniat Mors super te et descendas in infernum vriens, deducat te deus in puteum interibus [*interitus], Confringat deus caput tuum, et verticem capilli tui [+ perambulantium] in delictis, tuis, obsturentur occuli tui Ne videas et dorsuntum [*dorsum tuum] in curvetur semper, Effundat deus super te Iram	O N., God will return you to hell. God shall rain snares upon you, fire, brimstone, and storms, O N., God shall flog you with an iron rod, and shall break you into pieces like a potter's vessel. O N., God shall confound you. Death will come to you, and you will descend alive into hell. (Psalm 9:81) God shall bring you down into the pit of destruction. God shall shatter your head, the hairy crown of you who walk in sin. Your eyes will be darkened that you see not, and your back will always be bent.

---

202. In left marg.: "+."

203. Another version of this curse can be found on Folger p. 161. In marg. in brown ink: "4o–o." The whole of this curse is assembled from passages from the Psalms, recounting all the bad things therein which God inflicts on the wicked. See Psalms 9:18, 10:7, 2:9, 24:3, 54:16, 54:24, 67:22, 68:24–25, 68:27, 69:4, 82:14–18, 87:17, 88:33, 88:47, 96:3, and 139:11. KJV numbers them 9:17, 11:6, 2:9, 25:2, 55:15, 55:23, 68:21, 69:23–24, 69:26, 70:3, 83:13–17, 88:16, 89:32, 89:46, 97:2, and 140:10.

suam et furor eis te comprehendat, per-cutiat [*percutiet] te deus et persequatur te, et super dolorem vulnerum tuorum addat Avertat te deus retrorsum et erub-escas, ponat te deus ut rotam et ut scipu-lam ante faciem venti, sicut ignis qui comburit silvam, et sicut flamma com-buriens montes, persequatur te deus in tempestate sua et in ira sua turbet te, Im-pleat deus faciem tuam ignominia ut obedias nomini illius o N conturbat te ut pe[reas] in seculum seculi. Transeat te in ira domini, et terroris eius te conturbent, visitet te deus in virga iniquitates tuas, et in verberibus peccatta tua, Ira dei exard-escat [in] te tanquam ignis. Ignis ante deum, procedat, et in circuitu inflammet te, cadant super te carbones in ignem deiiciare, in miseriis non subsistas.

God will pour out his anger upon you, and his wrath will seize you. God will strike you and persecute you, and add grief to your wounds. God will turn you backwards, and you will blush in shame. God will place you like a wheel, and like straw before the face of the wind, like a fire which burns wood, and like a flame burning mountains. God will take ven-geance on you in his tempest, and shall trouble you in his wrath. God will fill your face with shame, that you will obey his name. O N., he will confound you, so that you will perish forever. The wrath of the Lord has come upon you, and his terrors have troubled you. God will visit you in your iniquity with a rod, and your sins with lashes. God's anger will flare up against you like fire. A fire shall go be-fore God, and shall burn you. Burning coals will fall upon you; in misery you will not be able to stand.*

[63]

+

A suffumigation that rejoiceth spirits

Amber, lignum aloes, costus, musk, crocus, blood of a lapwing, frankincense. These be meat, drink, and gladness to the spirits of the air, and gathereth them to-gether and urgeth them to appear, as sayeth Hermes.[204]

Greek incense, mastic, sandalwood, galbanum, *muscha lazerat*, myrrh, and amber. These fumigations be collectors of spirits and placators of them.[205]

---

204. From Raziel, e.g., Sloane 3846, 140r, and Karr, "Liber Lunae and Other Selections from British Library MS. Sloane 3826," (2010), 179. Quoted in OP Book 1, chapter 43. This section is repeated on Folger p. 107.

205. Raziel, Karr, "Liber Lunae," (2010), 190.

Thus evermore reigneth these planets [206]

ħ ♑︎♒︎ First Saturn.

♃ ♐︎♓︎ Then Jupiter.

♂ ♈︎♏︎ Then Mars.

☉ ♌︎ Then the Sun.

♀ ♉︎♎︎ Then Venus.

☿ ♍︎♊︎ Then Mercury.

☽ ♋︎ Then the Moon.

ħ Saturn is lord on Saturday.	ħ♃♂☉ et ♀ are masculine, i.e., mankind
♃ Jupiter is lord on Thursday.	♀☽ are feminine, i.e., womankind.
♂ Mars is lord on Tuesday.	ħ♂☽ Are evil planets
☉ The Sun is lord on Sunday	♃☉♀ Are good planets
♀ Venus is lord on Friday.	☿ is changeable i.e., indifferent viz.
☿ Mercury is lord on Wednesday.	good with them that be good, and evil
☽ The Moon is lord on Monday.	with them that be evil.

ħ is cause of dearth, death, and peace.

♃ is cause of long peace, rest, and virtuous living.

♂ is cause of dryness, debate, and war.

☉ is cause of life, health, and waxing.

♀ is cause of lusty love and lechery.

☿ is cause of much speech, merchandise, and sleight.

☽ is cause of moistness, great waters, and violent floods.

---

206. In left marg.: anchor glyph; in right marg.: "42."

[64]

♄ The highest and slowest in proper motion, cold, dry, and pale, like unto lead colour, requiring thirty years to end his course.

♃ Jupiter is next under ♃, temperate, fair, and bright; his course is performed in 12 years.

♂ Mars is hot and dry, of fiery colour, and in 2 years endeth his course.

☉ The Sun is placed in the middle of all planets, most clear and bright, the well of pure light, every year finishing his course.

♀ Venus is next to the Sun, cold and moist, and clear, yea, more brighter than Jupiter. Her course is like unto the Sun, never above 48 degrees from the Sun. She is called the morning star when she goeth before the Sun; coming after the Sun, she is named the evening star.

☿ Mercury is next under Venus, somewhat shining, but not very bright, never above 29 degrees. From the Sun his course is like to Venus or to the Sun motion.

☽ The Moon goeth about within 30ti days.

For more plainness of that which is opened, now shall follow a figure, by the which ye may perceive how the orb of the one planet compasseth the other, also how these planets are placed in heaven, yea, which planet is highest from the Earth, and which is nearest unto us.

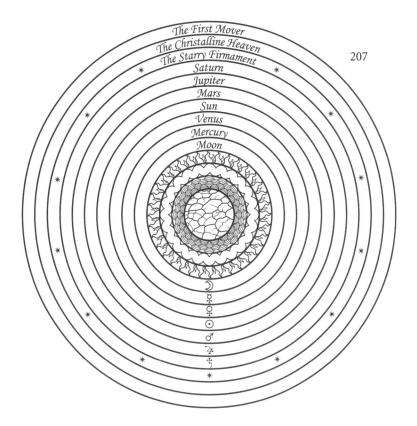

These seven planets are seven planets, moveable stars. The twelve signs take great power and might of them, and as some affirm, the planets of the twelve signs, so that the planets be to the signs as the soul is to the body, and the signs to the planets as the body to the soul, for like as the body may do naught without the soul, no more may a sign without the seven planets.

[65]

Here followeth a table of every thing of every sphere by himself

To know if a man or woman be sick, whether he or she shall live or die.

1. In the third sphere is contained three things: the first to know if a woman be with child and whether it be a man or a woman. 2.[208] The second treatise of the same,

---

207. Geocentric Universe: "The first Mover / The christalline heaven / The starry firmament / Saturn / Jupiter / Mars / Sun / Venus / Mercury / Moon, elements (fire, air, water, earth)."

208. The rest of this paragraph is in marg.

and also, if two men fight, whether of them shall have the victory. [3. ..]ence whether / [??] shall speed / [??] or no

The second to know who shall die first of a man or his wife.

The third if a man be blind, to know in which eye it is, although you never saw it.

Fourth to know under what sign or planet any man is born.

Fifth to know whether a man shall speed in his journey or no.

Sixth to know of life or death, if any man be sick, to know who shall die first of man or his wife, to know if one lie or not, to know whether a man shall come or go safe to any place, to know if one studieth, if one take a benefice, also, if to plead at the bar in the law, who shall overcome.

Seventh to know if a servant be run away, whether he shall come again or no; also if one be sick, whether he shall recover; also if one shall have good fortune in play or gaming.

First take the letters of his name that is sick, and the number that goeth by the letters in his name, by the sphere following, and make thereof a sum and of the age of the Moon how old she is, and the number of that day that he sickened on, and put all the sums together, and of the sum take out thirty as oft as you may, and if you find the remainder in the middle circle above, he shall shortly amend. If you find it in the right side, he shall long languish in it, but in the left side, speedy amendment cometh, so in like manner the contrary holdeth in the nether part, if it be found there. The figure followeth.

Deo semper et ubique gloria ["Glory to God, always and everywhere"]

[66]

An example of the sphere following, how you shall work, and with all other as with this: if there be a man or woman fallen into sickness, look what day he sickened thereof, and take that day as it stands in the sphere, and the number of the age of the Moon on the same day, and the number of the sign in which the Moon is in at the same time, and the number of the letters of his proper name, and put them all together, and then divide them by thirty and look the remainder in the sphere, and if you find it in the over part of the sphere, he shall live long, but and if in the nether part, he shall die, likewise do by champions that shall fight.

Deo semper et ubique gloria ["Glory to God, always and everywhere"]

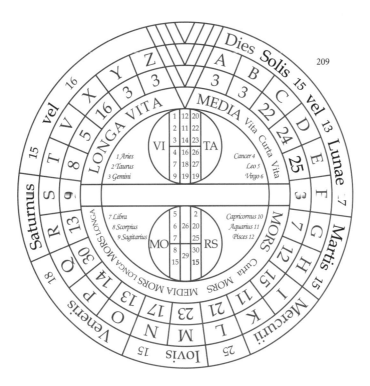

The twelve signs should stand in the figure.

---

209. Outer circle reads: *Dies Solis 15 vel 13, Lunae 17, Martis 15, Mercurii 25, Iovis 15, Ven[e]ris 18, Saturnus 15 vel 16* ["Day of the Sun 15 or 13, of the Moon 17, of Mars 15, of Mercury 25, of Jupiter 15, of Venus 18, of Saturn 15 or 16"]; second circle has Latin alphabet from A to Z; third circle has numbers corresponding to the letters; fourth circle: *Media vita, Curta vita, Mors Curta, Mors Media, Mors Longa, Mors Longa, Longa vita* ["Medium life, short life, short death, medium death, long death, long death, long life"]. Inside top has *Aries 1, Taurus 2, Gemini 3"* / circle with VITA ["LIFE"] and numbers / *Cancer 4, Leo 5, Virgo 6*. Inside bottom: *Libra 7, Scorpius 8, Sagitarius 9"* / circle with MORS ["DEATH"] and numbers / *Capricornus 10, Aquarius 11, Piscis 12*. For other instances of this operation, see Joanne Edge, "Licit magic or 'Pythagorean necromancy'? The 'Sphere of Life and Death' in late medieval England," *Historical Research* 87, no. 238 (2014): 611–632.

[67]

To make a thief not to depart out of the place where he would steal [210]

In the name of the Father, and of the Son, and of the Holy Ghost. Amen. This place I beset within and without, and all the place round about. If there come any thief to fetch goods away, set the holy place before and behind them, of the right side and left side and round about them, and cause them to tarry till I hither again come, by Mark, Matthew, Luke, and John, these, as fast bind you one to one as ever Saint Bartholomew bound the devil with the hairs of his head.[211] Then so still as he stood, so still stand these in and by the virtue of the blessed and holy Trinity, and that until I again come and bid them begone. And say three Our Fathers, three Hail Marys, and three Creeds. In the name of the Father, and the Son, and the Holy Ghost. Amen.

The circle for this work

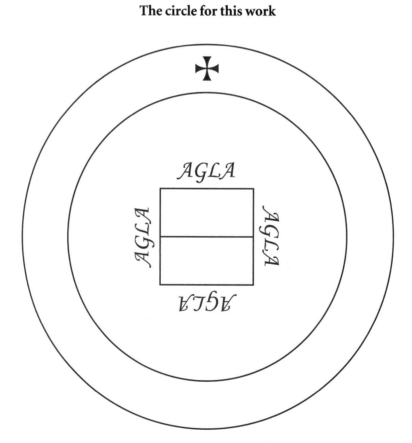

---

210. At top of the page: "6" and the circled "+" glyph (⊕) in brown ink; in left marg.: "56."

211. See above: There are two similar references to St. Bartholomew, but there they state he bound the devil with the hairs of his beard.

The names of the seven sisters of the fairies [212]

Lillia (1), Restillia (2), Faca (3), Folla (4), Africa (5), Julia (6), Juliana (7)

Here beginneth the most true and profitable experiment for to make a thief to come again with that which he hath stolen, at the will of the master. [213]

There be four kings reigning in four diverse parts of the world, that is to say, east, west, north, and south, under which four kings be four spirits as it were bishops. The power of the said four kings etc. are in the four elements, viz., air, fire, water, and earth, and these spirits have power to bring again the thief with his stolen goods, whither so ever the master will have him, at the reading of this experiment.

Thou must on the Monday at the waxing of the Moon, or on the Wednesday go and be clean shriven, even as clean (I mean as thou shouldst presently die), and then before the Sun arise go and hear a Mass of the Holy Ghost, and then go into a secret place into a wood where no man useth to come and make a plate of lead, in manner of this form, which after ensueth, and write in the midst this name Satan, then write round about above this manner, Satan, the goods stolen, the name of the owner, man or woman, and whatever it be that is stolen: gold, silver, or cattle, etc.

Then make four diverse plates, each by himself, and write the name of the spirit and his sign by him, the name Teltrion in the east, the name Spyrion in the west, the name Boytheon in the south, and the name Mayeryon in the north, and then set the great plate between them, all four with the names of Satan, and the stolen goods by him, and the owner of the goods, and then a little way aside make a round circle and stand therein and say this conjuration.

---

212. There is more information on these fairies on Folger p. 81. Sloane 3853, 143v, gives the names of the *septem sorores* ["seven sisters"] but only six of the seven: "lilia, Restilia, Foca, Affrica, Iulia, Iuliana." This is in a charm for "expulsion of elves and fairies." Sloane 1727, 23v, has the equivalent charm in English, and gives seven names: "lilia, Restilia, foca, fola, Afryca, Julia, Venulia" These names are also listed in *Janua Magica Reserata* (in Sloane 3825) as "Lillia, Restilia, Foca, Tolla, Affrica, Julia, Venulla." See also the article by Frederika Bain, "The Binding of the Fairies: Four Spells" in *Preternature: Critical and Historical Studies on the Preternatural* 1, no. 2 (2012): 323–354. Bain includes a transcription of Folger MS. Xd 234 (ca. 1600), giving their names as Lilia, hestillia, fata, sola, afrya, Africa, Iulia, and venulla (variant: Venila).

213. Compare Sloane 1727, 50r; Sloane 3824, 16v; Sloane 3853, 73r; Wellcome MS. 110, 99v; Rawlinson D. 252, 124r. In marg.: "This exp. is also in the ould parchment booke." In right marg.: "56 b." Mun. A.4.98, 78, has their names as Lillia, Restillia, Foca, Folla, Afficia, Iulia, and Remilla.

[68]

O vos spiritus Theltrion, Speryon, Boytheon, et Mayeryon, vel Maorys, quorum nomina sunt hic scripta, Coniuro et exorciso vos spiritus per deum verum per deum sanctum et per omnia sancta nomina domini nostri Iesu Christi, quibus patriarchae et prophetae eum invocaverint et ipse iuvabat eos, et per excellentissime nomen dei + Tetragrammaton + et per omnia que de deo dicta sunt, et dici possunt, et per virtutem omnium sanctorum et sanctarum, et per dissipulorum et Innocentes, et Martiros, et novem ordines Angelorum et per Angelos et Archangelos dei, et per Thronos atque Maiestates, principatus virtutes et potestates, et per Cherubine et Seraphine, et per omnes spirituum ordines, et per prophetas [et] per patriarchas, et per apostolos et per Evangelistas et dissipulos et Innocentes et per Martyros et confessores, et per Monachos, et per heremites, et per omnes virgines, et per omnes viduas, et per omnes sanctos et sanctas dei, et per vicinos, per Caelum et Terram per Solem et Lunam et Stellas Caeli, et per undas Maris, ut ubicumque Citis vel in aqua, vell in ignem vel in aere, vel in terra conveniatis in unum locum, in quo illi latrones, et illos reduxeritis, et reducere faciatis, cum tali re N et N et ut deliberantur in tali loco N, et taly tempore N.

O you spirits Theltrion, Speryon, Boytheon, and Mayeryon or Maorys, whose names are here written, I conjure and exorcise you spirits by the true God, by the holy God, and by all the holy names of our Lord Jesus Christ by which the patriarchs and prophets called upon him, and he helped them, and by the most excellent name of God + Tetragrammaton + and by all the words spoken by God, and those yet to be spoken, and by the power of all the saints—male and female—and by the disciples, the innocents, and martyrs, and the nine orders of angels, and by the angels and archangels of God, and by the Thrones, Greatnesses [*Dominations], Principalities, Virtues, and Powers, and by the Cherubim and Seraphin, and all other orders of spirits, and by the prophets, patriarchs, apostles, evangelists, disciples, innocents, martyrs, confessors, monks, hermits, and by all virgins and all widows, and by all the saints of God, and by the neighbours, by heaven and earth, by the Sun and Moon, and the stars in the heavens, and by the waves of the sea, that wherever you move, whether in water or fire or air or in earth, that you will assemble together in one place those thieves, and lead them back, and make them return, with these things: X and Y, delivered to this place: X, at this time: X.

Coniuro vos spiritus Teltryon in Oriente, Speryon in Occidente Boetherion in Meridie, et Mayeryon in attentrionale [*septentrionale!], Coniuro vos per Regem vestros ut mihi obediatis et voluntatem et desiderium meum impleatis, sine lesione corporis vel anima mea, vell illius vel illorum per omnia sancta nomina domini nostri Jesu Christi Mess[i]as + Sother + Emanuell + Sabaoth + Adonay + et Helyon + Ananizapta + Elyzar + et coniuro vos per predicta nomina sacra dei, ut non requiescatis in 4or Elementis, hoc est nec in igne nec in aqua, nec in Aere, nec in Terra, donec illos vell illum, cum talibus rebus, et tali die et hora, et tali in loco reduxeritis per virtutem omnium celestium, terrestrium, et inferrorum, et in ignem eternum vos mitti, vos iubeo, et in catenis Igneis, donec impleatis per vera signa, et caracteres, et per Satan, cui debetis obedire, et per omnia mundi elementa et per earum virtutes, vel per 4or mundi plagas, et per Luciferem inferni potestatem, et per omnes herbas, et arbores Lapides que preciosos, per vincula Salamonis, et per omnia Caelestia, Terrestria, Infernalia.

I conjure you spirits Teltryon in the East, Speryon in the West, Boetherion in the South, and Mayeryon in the North.* I conjure you by your king, that you obey me, and fulfill my wishes and desires, without harm to my body or soul, or to that one or those ones, by all the holy names of our Lord Jesus Christ, Messias + Sother + Emanuel + Sabaoth + Adonay + and Helyon + Ananizapta[†] + Elyzar + and I conjure you by the afore-mentioned sacred names of God, that you rest not in the four elements: Not in the fire, nor the water, not in the air nor the earth, until you lead back that thief or thieves with such things, and in such a day and time, and in such a place, by the power of all celestial, terrestrial, and infernal beings, and I order you to be sent to eternal fire, and in fiery chains, until you satisfy me by a true sign and characters, and by Satan, who you must obey, and by all the elements and all their powers, or by the four plagues of the world,[‡] and by Lucifer, the power of hell, and by all herbs, trees, precious stones, by the bonds of Solomon, and by all celestial, terrestrial, and infernal beings.

---

* Compare Sloane 3853, 73v: *Theltryon, Spireon, Beytheon, Machyreon;* Sloane 3853, 89r: *O vos spiritus Teltrion + Sireon vel Spirion vel Spirdon + Bethereon vel Betheron + Mahireon vel Mahereon +;* Sloane 3824, 16v: *Theltryon , Sperion, Mayerion, Boytheon.*

† The magic word *Ananizapta* is found in charms, rings, and amulets at least as early as the fourteenth century. See Don C. Skemer, *Binding Words: Textual Amulets in the Middle Ages* (University Park, PA: Pennsylvania State University Press, 2006), 155 note; Thomas Roger Forbes, "Verbal Charms in British Folk Medicine" Proceedings of the American Philosophical Society 115, no. 4 (1971): 293–316. Another example is a charm against the "falling evil" (i.e., epilepsy) in Scot, *Discouerie of Witchcraft*, Book 12, chapter 14.

‡ Revelations 8:7–12?

And if thy work come not to effect at the day and hour, bury all thy plates in the earth until it come again, and truly thou shalt not fail, but have it again within short space after.

This is the circle of the experiment [214]

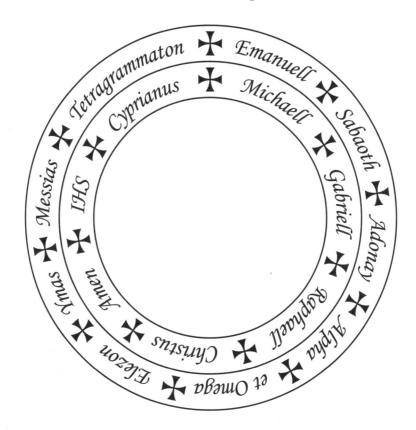

---

214. Text reads "Messias" and Greek "IHS," a very common abbreviation for "Jesus." Another exemplar for this can be found in Sloane 3824, which reads *Eleyson, Asmus, Messias, Tetragrammaton, Emanuel, Sabaoth, Adonay, Alpha et Omega, Michael, Gabriel, Jesus Christus, Amen, Ihys, Cyprianus.*

[69]

This is the figure of this preceding experiment [215]

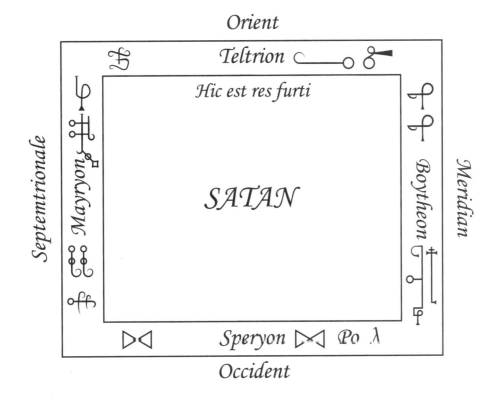

God send thee to thy end both health and wish at will, that I thy faithful friend may see thee prosper still.

Of all good things the world brings forth, a faithful friend is thing most worth.

Yet I live in hope to win our lady's grace, to speak for mercy to her lord, when she shall be in place

in utraque fortuna fidelis ["in each chance faithful"]

The earth profiteth none (?) that I pass for but one.

---

215. Figure includes words *hic est res furti* ["here are the things stolen"]; according to the instructions at the beginning of this experiment, you should list both "the stolen goods byely by the name Satan" and "the owner of the goods." In right marg.: "57"; in left marg.: anchor glyph.

[70]

To be said before the invocation [216]

O Lord Jesus Christ, King of Glory, God of all celestial virtues, holy father and marvelous disposer of all things, which from God the Father camest human into the world, that thou wouldst loose the world from sin, and show unto man true judgments, which without beginning and without ending art one God and true to remain Alpha and Omega, the first and the last, the beginning and the ending, which of the Blessed Virgin Mary hast willed to be borne, in whose sight all thing visible and invisible, by whose presence the eyes do behold, and from whom no secret is hid, and unto whom every heart is open, to whom every soul do confess itself and every tongue do speak, to whom all things doubtful, unknown, and hid is manifest and certain, of whose unspeakable sweetness the heavens and the earth be full, to whom all secrets, heavenly, earthly, and infernal, be known, I do beseech thee, hear me, and help me, and be unto me meek and merciful in this present work, and for the love and merit of thy bitter death and passion, vouchsafe of thy great mercy and unspeakable power, to be my protector, shield, and defender against the malice, illusions, and crafty assaults of all unclean and wicked spirits, so that at no time they may have power to hurt or harm me, and grant also most benign and merciful Jesu that N., a spirit of great power, may through thy omnipotent might, descend by the beams of heavenly light unto me, thy poor servant N., and that he by the calling of thy holy name may by perfect demonstration reveal and show unto me N. all things that I shall demand or ask of him and to fulfill my desire. This grant, O merciful God, for the bowels of thy mercy's sake, for thou art our God whose power is unspeakable, whose kingdom is everlasting, and of all creatures glorified, world without end. Amen.

To be said at the beginning and ending of every work [217]

O the most high and the very true God, the great and merciful God of exceeding much might, O holy, holy, holy, pure, and replenished with all goodness, O God blessed art thou and blessed be thy holy name, for thou my God art he which art the fulfiller of this my prayer and of all my desires. O thou my Lord and God, now suffer me to have this my desire to be accomplished and fulfilled, and that now through thy merciful goodness, to me N. now and forever, so be it, and thou my Lord God in Trinity and that through thy most holy Name + Tetragrammaton[218] + יהוה Agla + Saday +

---

216. In right marg.: "58."

217. In left marg.: "w" glyph; in right marg.: "59."

218. Compare Raziel in Peterson, *The Sixth and Seventh Books of Moses,* 269–270; compare also Folger p. 17.

haley + Kes + El + Amye + Semy + hasy + hayn + yenmissye Sacodere + barew + Adanahew + Eya + hey + hew + hew + va + ha + Eye + Eye + Eye + ya + ya + ya + Ebel + El + El + Ahey + A + ha +A + hue + Ahue + Ahue + Ahue + va + va + va + vadua + ylaye + Alenda + Le + Ane + hy + he + ha + ysale + ne + he + ha + Araya + Acamine + leena + quiloso + lyeneno + pheale + neale + ye + ye + malahe + huana + Nethe + heyrete + hasyonada + Balysany + Methe + pheniphatoll + comythomo + sedalaye + Thro + Thro + Thro + homos + zepny + Aglatha + Byell + Ioell + Sacomith + paconith + pyfam + ytomor + hygarom + ynquiron + cengaron + myron + mycon + Dasnot + Cassas + Iatas + yeton + eya + Rabba + Rab + Raba + man + Sarus + Eyesarey + Agla + yana + Maysay + Sye + sere + Myge + Mehatae + Sare + Maasame + evana + Ate + Dacye + byne + Rahew + yabe + Astrolye .l. roe + saye + Gole + Maha + samoer + Bybyloey + ybyyre + Lylay + Raby + lee + velsee + leace + cade + lethe + [by + yre + tylay + Raby + lee + vel + see + leace +Cade + lethe +] [219] lyhele + meamare + tyrya + hyse + Saquiel + Mum + seymee + yele + habe + l [220] hele + Amye + hara + eyesserye + [Agios + Iskiros + Athanatos + Agla + On + Tetragrammaton + Jehovah +] O thou my God, and by thee, and by all these holy, fearful, and honourable names, being full of all honour and glory and praise, suffer me now to bring to good end and effect is my bold enterprise and attempt, O Tetragrammaton + O Agla + pater kyrie + Adonay + O thou the Creator, Redeemer, Saviour, and Sanctifier of me, N , and also of all creatures, O thou + El + and Eloye + of incomprehensible majesty. Now forsake me not, poor sinful wretch that I am, now ne [=not] yet in the time of my necessity, although that I am guilty in the faith over (?) my doings, oh yet I ask mercy and forgiveness of thee, Jesus Christ, and here I desire thee my God to be my help and comfort, and the very God that heareth me in general, as well in words as cogitations and thoughts, O God of Abraham, O God of Isaac, O God of Jacob, O thou my great and mighty God, now hast thee to help me, O thou my God, the which didst deliver Daniel out of the den of lions, and the three children Shadrach, Meshach, and Abednego out of the burning furnace, O thou my God the which didst redeem Susanna and that from the false accusation of the <of the> great crime and shameful slander, O thou my God that didst defend Tobias from his enemies, O thou my God, deliver me N. from the great burden of my sins, and from all my enemies, and from all evil misfortunes, O thou my great and living God, I, N., now desire thee most heartily to give me power and strength over this spirit N. and over all spirits and [71] that I may overcome this spirit N., subdue him, and bring him to my obedience, and that now forthwith that he may obey me, now and at all

---

219. Sections in [ ] is found on Folger p. 17 but omitted here.

220. The "l" probably means *vel* ["or"] here.

times, although it be against his will, and that it may now so be, and that through the power of Jesu Christ. O Jesus of Nazareth, king of Jews, suffer that this spirit N. may now fulfill my will and petition, and that as near as he may, and that this spirit N. to come forthwith here to me to do my will and mind. O thou my God in Trinity, in thee is all my trust, now suffer me not to be led with no illusions of this spirit nor none others, nor that he etc., to hurt me in body, mind, nor soul, O God of Angels, Archangels, Cherubim, Seraphim, Principates, Thrones, and Potestates, Dominations, and Powers, O God of all patriarchs and prophets, O God of the Apostles, martyrs, confessors, virgins, O God the Father, O God the Son, O God the Holy Ghost, O God the Father of our Lord Jesus Christ, I, N., do call on thee now and on thy holy names, and now most heartily desire thy benign and glorious majesty, that thou my God wilt now vouchsafe to grant me thy help and aid against this spirit N. and vouchsafe to keep me both from him and all mine enemies and other mischances, and that now forthwith I may have this spirit in obedience, and that as thou art the very God in Trinity, now to grant to me N., and that by thy mighty power and virtue and great strength of Jesus Christ of Nazareth, and by thy holy name + Tetragrammaton + and by all the most holy and glorious names of God, and by the speaking and hearing of all thy holy and elect names and by Tetragrammaton + by all these and the rest of the holy names of God the Father, the Son, and the Holy Ghost, three persons and one God in Trinity, and thou the ruler of all these and of all things, the which livest and reignest one God in Trinity for ever and ever. O thou my God, send me now and grant me thy blessed help, and suffer me here to have this spirit N. to appear here to me in a fair form, which by invocating of him I shall appoint him, and to fulfill my request and desire, and that through the blessed name of thee the most high God I desire it, and I desire it for our Lord Jesus Christ his sake,[221] so be it. Amen. And in the name of the merciful God of Israel, and of paradise and of heaven and of earth, and of the seas, and of things beneath the earth, and of all creatures + now to be with me N. and with these words, letters, and characters, and with these names and with this my desire or great petition now forthwith here to be fulfilled, and that by the sufferance of the great and everliving God so be it + In the name + of the Father and of the Son + and of the Holy Ghost + three persons in Trinity, so be it. Amen.

---

221. In left marg.: "w-" glyph.

This done to your other business, etc.
[+ prayers of purification and consecration] [222]

Deus unus, Deus Iustus, deus fortis, deus magnus, deus potens, deus sine fine, deus perfectus omnium bonorum, domine Jesu Christe qui de sinu patris in uterum virginalem mirifice descendisti, et cum hominibus in terra apparuisti, qui et beato Johanni pectus tuum dormienti secreta celorum revelasti, et de sanctissimi pectorum de portare fecisti, ac secreetis celestibus eum super omnes mortales inspirasti, per spiritum sanctum super Apostolos tuos descendere fecisti, et eos per uniuersum mundum in nomine unigenitus filii tui predicare et baptizare voluisti, tu qui hec et multa alia fecisti, habe pacientiam in me et largire mihi in hec vel istud magnum misterium, quod ego infirmus peccator simplex et humiliter te peto quarinus in te virtuta tua et miserecordia, per intercessionem beate gloriose et intimerate virginis Marie Matris Domini nostri Iesu Christi filii tui unigeniti, hoc opus perducere valeo ad effectum quod opto, et desiderio quod tua gratia mihi deducte facere valeam ut spero et credo firmiter viz, ad cortandum et cogendum spiritus nec non benedicere et sanctificare dignare hoc presens opus scriptum ut ista verba verba [sic] per totumque ei vell eis convenient ac ei vel eis convenire poterint ut in nomine patris et filii et spiritus sancti virtutes quas optinere debeat re (?) optineat, et in se ad

Only God, just God, strong God, great God, mighty God, God without end, O God, perfection of all good, O Lord Jesus Christ, who descended from the bosom of the Father into the womb of the wonderful virgin, and appeared on the earth before mankind, and which you revealed to the blessed John, your *beacon (?), the secrets of heaven, while he slept, and from the most holy … (?) you have made, and you have inspired him with the heavenly secrets beyond all other people, through the Holy Ghost you have made to descend upon your apostles, and through them to the whole world, in the name of your only-begotten Son you are announced, and you have wished to baptize, you who have done this and much more, have patience with me, and grant to me *this or that* great mystery, because I, a weak sinner, simple and humble, beg you according to your virtue and mercy, through the intercession of the blessed, glorious, and God-fearing Virgin Mary, mother of our Lord Jesus Christ, your Son, that I may have the strength to accomplish this work which I desire, by your grace, namely, for constraining and assembling the spirits. Deign to bless and sanctify this present written work, that all your words which are collected together, so that in the name of the Father and of the Son and of the Holy Ghost it may hold

---

222. In right marg.: "61."

coartandum et cogendum convincere scernere, excitare, constringere, congregare, dispergere, pacificare et ligare, venire facere et respondere, stare, et recedere, humiliare et obedire solvere et includere, damnare, ac sine spe salvacionis ingravissimis pene infernalibus piicere et usque ad diem Iudicii, a facie huius (?) seculi dampnare a aeris, igneas aquaticos, terreas, et infernales potestates et omnes spiritus et anime, a celo usquae in profundissimum lacum abissi, mihi inobedientes ac voluntati in de resistentes, nisi obedientes preceptis meis quam docum que mihi placueris, et cum eis opus habuero ac eis coniurare et convocare, et invocare voluero, et per istud presence scriptum vel ista verba in hoc volumine contenta per te sanctissime + Adonay + in maiestate divina sedens Trinus et unus deus domine dominantium per infinita secularum seccula Amen.

the virtue and power for confining and compelling (the spirits), to conquer, to overthrow, to arouse, to constrain, to gather and disperse, to pacify and bind, making them come to answer, to remain and to depart, to be humble and obey, to release and to shut up, to condemn, and expel without hope of salvation into the most dire pain of hell, until the Day of the Judgement. … (?) of the earth, from the aerial, fiery, aquatic, terrestrial, and the infernal powers, and all spirits and souls, from Heaven all the way to the deepest pit of the abyss, if you are disobedient to me and resist my will … (?) I have determined to conjure, assemble, and invoke, and by this same present book, and by these words contained in this book, through you, O most holy + Adonay + sitting in divine majesty, threefold and one God, Lord of Lords, forever and ever. Amen.*

* This whole paragraph is corrupt and translation uncertain.

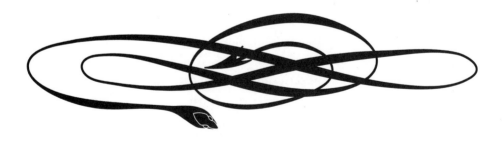

[72]

O Glorissim. Regina Angelorum et omnium celorum dominam mundi, et omnium sanctorum, Imperatrix inferni et omnium infernorum, et misericordissima adiutrix donatorum tuorum ad te confugio, adiuva me misericordissima domina quoniam labor meus non sufficit sine te, et quia peccata mea impediunt me, et merita mea non adiuvant ad tam multa et maxima, et incomperabilia dona qui desidero et peto sine multis et maximis auxiliis ea optinere non valde unde te in primis in vita gratia Ianua vite exordium salutis humane mater pietatis et misericordie benignissime imploro et in voce in adiutorium meum et auxillium hodie et nunc et in omni tempore ut possim obtinere qui nunc desidero si placeat deo, et tibi, expedit anime meo, Amen Amen.

O most glorious queen of the angels,[*] and of all the heavens, she who commands over[†] all the world and all the saints, empress of hell and all the inhabitants of hell, and most merciful helper of your givers, I take refuge in you. Help me most merciful mistress, because my effort is not sufficient without you, and because my sins hinder me, and my merits are not of much help, and the incomparable gifts which I desire and beg for, cannot be obtained without great help and support from you, foremost in life, gateway of life, the beginning of human salvation, most generous mother of piety and mercy. I implore you to be my help and aid, now and at all times, so that I will be able to obtain what I now desire, if it pleases God, and you, release my soul. Amen, Amen.

[*] In right marg.: "62."
[†] *Domina*: i.e., female authority, equivalent of lord or master, but "lady" or "mistress" are both too easily misconstrued.

In nomine Domini nostri Jesu Christi, patris et filii et spiritus sancti, Amen. Sancta trinitas inseperabilis unitas, te invoco ut sis solus defencio et protectio corporis mei et anime munc [*nunc] et in perpetuum, per virtutem Sancte + Crucis domini nostri Iesu Christi et passionis et orationes sanctissime Matris tue Marie, et omnium sanctorum sanctarum ut mihi concedas

In the name[*] of our Lord Jesus Christ, the Father, and the Son, and the Holy Ghost. Amen. Holy Trinity and inseparable Unity, I call upon you, that you may be the only defense and protection of my body and soul, now and forever, by the power of the holy + cross of our Lord Jesus Christ and by the passion and prayers of the most holy Mary, your mother, and all the saints, that you grant

[*] Compare Weyer, *Pseudomonarchia Daemonum*.

graciam tuam atque pietatem [*potestatem] divina[m] super omnes malignos spiritus ut quoscunque in virtute sanctorum nominu tuorum invocavero sctami [*statim] ex omni parte ad me conveniant et voluntatem meam perfecte impleant non mihi nocentes neque terrorem inferentes, sed potius pie obedientes mihi minissrantes [*ministrantes], et tua divina virtute mandata mea perficiat, per te Iesu Christi cui est laus et honour in secula seculorum Amen.	me your grace and divine power over all evil spirits, so that whichever of them I call upon by the power of your sacred names, they will immediately come together from all parts of the world, and fulfill my will completely, bringing no harm nor terror to me, but rather religiously obeying me diligently, and with your divine power he will complete my orders, through you, O Jesus Christ, to whom be the praise and honour forever and ever. Amen.

Then say, sitting on thy knees, as followeth

Deus Deus meus Respice in me, et misere mei et ne abneges mihi quicquid a te petam quod pluribus aliis consesisti [*concessisti] et ne respicias ad universa delicta mea quibus peccaui te domine non negavi, propter exaudi preces famuli tui N. et presta ut in presenti experimento per virtutem nominum sanctorum tuorum veritatem invenire merear qui vivis et regnas deus per omnia secula seculorum amen.	O God my God, look back upon me* and have mercy on me, and do not refuse to me whatever I desire from you, because you have granted many things to others, and do not look back at all my faults with which I have sinned. I have not denied you, O Lord, for you hear the prayers of your servant N., and permit that I am worthy to discover the truth in the present experiment, by the power of your holy names, who lives and reigns, God for all ages. Amen.
* Compare Sloane 3853, fol. 57r.	

Everlasting God, Creator [223] of all things, in whose hands lieth the disposition of all times and seasons, qualify, O Lord, I do beseech thee, the inclinations of thy creatures, i. heaven, earth with all constellations and planets with such natural and kindly moderation, as may most serve to the obtaining of our purpose and weighty attempt, so that they work such force in all places that by them the spirit N. may be urged and enforced to obedience, and the rather by their powers I may obtain and have my will and desire, and also that those creatures aforesaid may serve to the commodities,

---

223. In left marg.: "w-" glyph; in right marg.: "63."

health, and welfare of all mankind: so that we receive not only our desire and request by way of petition of this spirit N., but also by them we may possess and have the fruits of the bare earth to our comfortable sustentation, and thereby prompted duly to the honouring and praising of thy holy and reverend name, therefore, mortify within us, O Lord, the old roots of our native iniquity, killing them, as it were, with the winter of cold lust to ensue them: so we the seed of thy grace within us, that we may spring up in all goodness: send us the fervency of the spirit that we may show forth ripe and perfect fruits of a lively faith, that when it shall be thy good pleasure, to appoint thy final harvest or vintage, thou wilt vouchsafe to bring us into thy joyful barn, like good and cleansed corn, like ripe and profit grapes, which is to say into thy everlasting kingdom there to rest with thy chosen Abraham + Isaac and Jacob, in all eternity. So be it. Amen.

Soli, laus, honor, et gloria. Finis. ["To him only be praise, honour, and glory. The end."]

[73]

Officium de spirittibus

The offices of spirits

There be four kings of the air: Orience king of the east, Paymon king of the west, Amaymon king of the south, and Egine king of the north.

And there be three devils, and that in the Art of Nigromancy: viz., Lucipher, Bellzebub, Satan.

1. Lucipher is the father of all devils. He may not be called, for he is in the depth of hell, yet by him as by Tantavalerion, other devils may be conjured and bound, for all devils do reverence and worship this devil Lucyfer, and that with a kind of majesty, they do all obey him, for so hath God ordained and appointed to them.

2. The second is called Bell, the which is Bellsabube, and he is the prince of devils. This Bell before the time of Solomon was thought to be the God Charon, whose idol was worshipped, and he was of the order of Cherubim, and 1,000,000s of devils or wicked spirits do minister unto him. He appeareth very beautiful, and giveth to the master that calleth him gold and silver, and maketh expert in sciences. He appeareth well for half an hour, and giveth of each demand a true answer. He giveth a servant or familiar which shall be in service very dutiful, during a man's life, but Nota he hath one proper Invocation by the which he shall be called by: otherwise he hath been wont to slay the master conjuror, and that in his circle, unless he did suffumigate

himself well, and that with amber, lignum aloes, and mastic, and he must be called towards the east, wherein he must be urged to do his office and duty.

3.[224] The third devil or spirit is Satan, the which was of the order and throne of the Cherubim, who that likewise, after 1,200 years, intendeth to come again and possess his former place, which is not to be believed. He is wont to ask of the master conjurer that he should with Solomon pray the Creator, that he may come to his Throne again, but he that is master shall say that he fell not of his own will, and for that cause he abideth in the air, and is not cast into hell. Bu[t] let the master take good heed that he do not obey him in his request, and when the master will depart with him, let him say,

"I here beseech my God, that if it be given to thee by him and that from above, that thou mayest be again restored to thy former place or throne, so be it."

Note that Satan abideth in an obscure air, and that the four princes or the four kings, unto which king's power is given to hurt the land, the seas, the trees, and they be of the orient. These four kings are Orience, Paymon, Amaymon, and Egin. Satan knoweth the virtue of these kings, and it was he that tempted our fathers in the desert or wilderness, making them disobedient to God's will. He hath power to kill, to destroy, to make blind, and to do many mischiefs, God defend us. Amen.

East

4. Orience the king appeareth with 100 or 200 legions, and that fair with a feminine countenance, and a goodly crown upon his head. He rideth upon an elephant, having before him trumpets, shawms,[225] and much minstrelsy, of diverse instruments, and when he is called, he cometh with other great kings, but Note and if he be called alone, he then appeareth in the likeness of an horse, that is of the Throne, having of an horse the very shape, and when that he is sacrificed unto or offered unto, then he taketh such a shape as the master will, and he doth willingly receive the sacrifice or offering. He giveth well nigh an answer to all demands and questions, and telleth the truth of things past, present, and to come, and if that he be angry, he will vex all them that do not sacrifice unto him, except that he do give money or teach sciences, and then he is compelled, and that by divine power to the contrary. He hath power to consecrate books, and he knoweth all experiments, and hath power to teach them, and there is a king under him whose name is Baall, and his office is to teach a man all manner of sciences, and maketh a man to go invisible, and hath under him 250 le-

---

224. In marg.: "w" glyph.

225. Shawm: a woodwind instrument like an oboe.

gions, yet at the first you must constrain a spirit called Femell, who is the messenger of the east. Note, let the master say:

O thou Bellfarto or Bellferit, the which is the messenger of the king of the east, I conjure thee, and that by the living God, and by the blessed Virgin Mary Mother of our Lord Jesus Christ, and by the thrones of angels, and by the blessed Apostles, and by the saints of God, that now presently and without any delay or tarrying, the same spirit which is called Femell that thou make or cause to appear, and obey my will, and do my commandment, and that with all speed, so be it.

[74]

South

5. Amaymon the king is of the south, and is great and mighty, and he appeareth in the likeness of an old man with a great beard, his hairs like to a horse's hairs. He hath a bright crown on his head and rideth upon a fierce lion roaring, and he shaketh a rod in his hand and his ministers go before him with all manner of instruments and music, and he cometh with other three kings, and he gladly doth receive sacrifice and burnt offerings and gifts. He maketh answer to all things, and maketh a man wonderful cunning and expert in philosophy, and in the art notaria,[226] and he giveth the best acquaintance with nobility, and confirmeth the doings thereof, as dignity and promotion. He may well be kept in obedience one hour, during which time he may be used, but let the master turn into the south to receive him, and that gently and eke[227] with pleasantness, and declare unto him the thing thou wouldst have taken in hand, and hold thou thy ring upon thy face, and he will do thy will, and call thou him in a fair air, or day, and look that thou have the ring of Solomon, and the stole and the ausipites or coronepes.[228] He cometh with all manner of invisibility, and a great company with him, and therein be kings, i.e., Emlon, Ocarbydatonn, and Madyconn. These kings be messengers of the king of the south, to whom shall be said:

"I conjure you now by God, and by St. Mary, his son Christus' mother, and by the thrones and choirs of angels, and by the death and passion of our Saviour Jesus Christ, and by Abraham, Isaac, and Jacob, and by Moses, Ely, Enoch, and David, and by holy Shem, Noah, and Lot, and by Elizabeth, Katherine, and Margaret, and by all the prophets, Isaiah, Jeremiah, Ezekiel, Daniel, Habakkuk, Zachariah, Malachi, Zephaniah, Joel, and Abdy [Obadiah?], that now shortly, without any tarrying, you cause

226. Art notaria: Likely the notory art, a magical procedure to aid in memory and learning. See Julien Véronèse, *L'Ars Notoria Au Moyen Âge* (Firenze: SISMEL edizioni del Galluzzo, 2007).

227. Eke: also.

228. Unknown.

the same spirit Emlon, that he shortly and speedily come to me, obey me, and fulfill my will and desire. I charge and command you by our Lord Jesus Christ that you yield him to me and that without any delay or tarrying." This, when he cometh, may tarry from twelve at noon till midnight.

West

6.[229] Paymon the king; he appeareth and speaketh with a hoarse voice, and he being called is more obedient to the will of Lucifer than of any of the other kings be, and thou compel him by divine power, then he appeareth in the likeness of a soldier, yet when that he cometh to the presence of the m[aste]r, he maketh variance still. He rideth upon a dromedary or a camel, and is crowned with a bright crown, and hath the countenance of a woman,[230] and before him goeth a band of men, and that with trumpets and all kind of instruments, and Paymon himself speaketh with his tongue, yet the master shall cast to him a paper wherein it is written, that he shall speak plainly and distinctly, that the master may understand what he sayeth, and so then he will,[231] and there is Belferth, the messenger of the king of the west, and there is Belial, a king, and Baasan, a king, and they do make a man to go invisible, and Rombalence or Ramblane. These may appear from the third hour to the twelfth hour following. Then say, "And thou Alphasis, I conjure thee, and that by the most meek Lord our Saviour Jesus Christ, and by the sphere that clave his heart asunder, and that to the redemption of all mankind, and by the nails that pierced his blessed hands and feet, and by all the virtues of God, and by all the holy names of God, Agios + Yskiros + Athanatos + Otheos + Alpha + and Omega + Agla + El + Tetragramaton + that now shortly and that, without any tarrying, this same spirit Alphassis to be here ready, and to do all that I here shall command him to do, for me N. and that you now here do yield him unto me, and that without delay or long tarrying, and here to fulfil my petition and desire. So be it."

North

7. Egyn the king, is of the north, and appeareth in the likeness of a man, and his face is very clear. His nostrils are very sharp like a sword, and out of his mouth co-

---

229. In marg.: "w-" glyph.

230. Interestingly, all the spirits appearing female are actually considered male. See discussion of whether evil spirits can be female in Johannes Trithemius, *Ioannis Tritemii Liber octo quaestionum ad Maximilianum Cesarem* (Oppenheym: impensis Joh. Hasselberger, 1515). The discussion is in questio sexta ["question 6"]. (Pages are not numbered, see http://www.literature.at/viewer.alo?obj id=11936&viewmode=fullscreen&scale=3.33&rotate=&page=48.)

231. Compare Paimon, Peterson, *The Lesser Key of Solomon*, 10–11.

meth flames of fire, and he rideth upon a dragon, and he is crowned with a crown of precious stones, and in his cheeks he beareth two tusks, and he beareth on his right side two hissing serpents shining, and he cometh with a great noise and clamour before him go sundry kinds of musical instruments and sweet organs, and he teacheth perfectly all physic, and singing, and the art Notaria, and the art of Nigromancy, and the art memorativia, and he speaketh of and [232] in diverse parts of the world, and of things to come, past, and present, and of certain secrets, and hid things, and of the being and compacting of this world, and what the earth is, and whether the water may sustain the earth or the earth the water, and he telleth what a bottomless pit is called, commonly the Abyss, and where it is, and what the wind is, and from whence it cometh, and he giveth very good acquaintance and dignities, prelateships and confirmeth the same, and maketh consecration of books and other things, and giveth true answers of all questions and demands, and thou must look to the north when thou callest him, and so soon as he appeareth, show him the Seal of Solomon, and his ring, and forthwith he will fall down to the earth and will worship the master, and the master shall take and thank him therefore, and he hath 12,000 legions, and causeth a man to win at all manner of games, and Rodabell, or Radabelbes, be the messengers of the king of the North.

"O thou Lambricon, vel Lambracaron, kings of the north etc., they may come from midnight to the morning, I conjure thee, and that by the meek Lord Jesus Christ, and by him which hath made of naught all the world and all and every thing therein, and by Mary Magdalene, and by the Virgin Saint Katherine who slew Kwphin[233] your brother, and by the crown of thorn that our saviour Jesus Christ had on his blessed head, and by the spear that he was pierced with to the heart, and by the nails wherewith his blessed hands and feet were fastened to the + of tree, [75] and by these precious names La + Ya + Gala + Layagom + Vlba + Garanitom + Lasam + Sarym + Lassa + Ioratom + La + Ya + Lasary + that you now shortly, and that without any delay or tarrying, that this spirit by name Rodabell vel Radebelbes now to be here, ready and obedient to all my will, and that now herein you obey to me and that without any tarrying."

Then say the conjuration that to the four kings doth appertain begin, then conjure those four messengers without fear, saying thus: "O Femell, Alphassis, Emlon Rodabell, I conjure you, etc.," as is aforesaid.

8. Fersone[234] is a king and appeareth in the likeness of a man, having the face of a lion, and he hath 40 playing before him, with trumpets and other instruments, and he knoweth all things past, present, and to come, and knoweth all the places where

---

232. Perhaps "work" omitted?

233. Unknown from the history of the saint.

234. Compare Weyer, *Pseudomonarchia Daemonum*, spirit #11: Purson alias Curson.

any treasure is hid, and showeth it willingly, and he desireth sacrifice, and that is of a brasen made [maid?], and he hath under him 72 legions.

9. Ebeyeth, a king and a great ruler; he appeareth with a crown or diadem, and there is nothing seen of him but his head, and he cometh with minstrels afore him, and he teacheth what spirits be best for familiars, and giveth true answer, and he hath under him 80 legions.[235]

10. Harchase is a great king, and appeareth like a fierce bear, and he maketh a man to go invisible, and showeth all places, where treasure is hid, and he hath under him 26 legions.

11. Gorsyar is a king, and appeareth having a lion's face, and he is crowned with a diadem, and bearing in his hand a fierce viper, and he rideth upon a bear, and before him cometh trumpets, and he knoweth all things, and where hid treasures be, and he will willingly appear, and will answer to all hid and secret questions, and of hid things, and hath under him six legions of spirits.[236]

12. Skor [237] is a great king and appeareth like a curlew,[238] and he doth fetch money out of kings' houses, or out of any house or place, and he will carry it there as thou commandest him, for he is true and faithful, and that in all his doings that he is commanded, and he hath under him ten legions.

13. Garsone the king; [239] he appeareth like a man, and he knoweth things past, present, and to come, and telleth where is treasure hid, and he giveth true answers, and that of things that be secret and divine of the Deity, and of the creation of the world, and hath under him seven legions.

14. Tamon, [240] a great king; he appeareth like a goat. He teacheth to find treasures that are hid in the earth, and to find precious stones, and to find minerals and hid money, and he speaketh foully and evil favouredly, and without discretion, unless that he be constrained to the contrary thereof, and he hath under him 50 legions.

15. Varbas or Carbas [241] a great prince or king; he appeareth like a fierce lion, yet when he cometh before him that calleth him, then he taketh on him the form of a man, and he giveth true answers of secret and hid things, and teacheth to heal sick

---

235. In marg.: "Hee geveth true answeares and what familiars are best."

236. Compare Sloane 3853, fol. 257r: Gorsior; Wellcome MS. 110, fol. 32r: Gorsyer.

237. In marg.: "A carrier."

238. Curlew: a wading bird native to Great Britain.

239. In marg.: "A good & true spirit."

240. In marg.: "w-" glyph.

241. In marg.: "A good phisiection."

people, and he excelleth in the teaching of nigromancy and he causeth to be changed, and that from his right physiognomy, and he hath under him 26 legions.[242]

16. OGya, a great prince; appeareth like a viper, having teeth, and two great horns, and bearing a sharp sword in his hand, and he giveth true answers, and that of all things that is demanded of him, and he hath under 35 legions.

17. There is one Skor a great prince; he appeareth like a dog and hath a strange voice, and he is marvelous in his working, for he will take away the enemies' sight, the which is against the caller, and he will bring money out of kings' treasures, and out of other places, if he thereto be commanded, and he fetcheth and carrieth all things, and is very faithful in all his doings, and namely to his caller, and he hath under him 46 legions.[243]

18. Drewchall is a great prince or a king; and his office is to win holds,[244] and to cast them that keepeth them into a sleep, and he maketh to appear a great army of harnessed men in the field, and he himself appeareth like a great hart, and that with horns, and hath under him 36 legions.

19. Gloolas,[245] a great king or prince; he appeareth like to a dog having wings, and he is the chief leaders of murderers,[246] and knoweth things past, present, and to come, and he giveth knowledge of friends and of enemies, and maketh a man to go invisible, and so long as the caller or master will, and hath under him 20 legions.

[76]

20. Forcase [247] a great prince; he appeareth like a great man, and he knoweth the virtues of all herbs, and also of stones, and he giveth again the sight that was lost, and telleth the places of treasures, and giveth true answers, and hath under him ten legions.

21. Rewboo, a great prince; he appeareth like a knight, and he giveth true answer of things that he is demanded of, and he giveth him that calleth him gold and silver, and hath under him 29 legions.[248]

---

242. Compare Marbas in Peterson, *The Lesser Key of Solomon*, 9.

243. Compare Sloane 3853, fol. 257r: Scor?

244. Hold: fortress.

245. Compare Sloane 3853, fol. 257v: Glolas; and Weyer, *Pseudomonarchia Daemonum*, spirit #18: Glasya labolas.

246. Weyer, *Pseudomonarchia Daemonum*: homicidarum.

247. Compare Weyer, *Pseudomonarchia Daemonum*, spirit #29: Forras or Forcas.

248. Compare Sloane 3853, fol. 258r: Robo.

22. Coolor,[249] a great prince; he appeareth like a child, and he hath wings like to a goshawk, and he rideth upon a dragon that hath two heads, and he giveth true answers for hid treasures and he hath under him thirteen legions.

23. Hanar, a great prince; he appeareth in a flame of fire, and will take on him the form a man, and he is cunning in astronomy, and telleth where treasures be that are kept with spirits, how many they be and what they be, and he giveth favour to the master, and under him be eight legions.

24. Hooab, a prince, a great governor; he appeareth like a black bird, yet when he taketh the shape of a man, then he is a leader of women, and he maketh them to burn in the love of men, and if he be commanded, he maketh them to be turned into another shape, while that the men and they may come together, and he hath under him 26 legions.

25. Doolas, a great prince; he appeareth like a child and wings like an angel. He rideth upon a dragon having two heads, and giveth true answer of hid treasures, and he keepeth all treasures where the serpents or drakes[250] be seen to appear, and he giveth and appointeth the places where treasure is to all spirits to keep, and he giveth a man all manner of household spirits, and without him, none can do it, and he giveth to the master all manner of serpents, and hath under him 20 legions.

26. Formecones is a great prince, and appeareth like a bull, and when the master will, he taketh the form of a man, and he maketh one marvelous cunning in astronomy and in all other liberal sciences, and he giveth the master wisdom, and he knoweth best the virtues of herbs and stones, and he bringeth lunary and precious stones, and hath under him 36 legions.

27.[251] Tamor or Chamor, a prince; he appeareth in a fiery flame, and deluding the sight, and so blindeth the lookers on, and that with notable delay, and when he is compelled, he taketh the form of a man, and he is excellent in astronomy and in all other liberal arts, and he giveth the best acquaintance and the favour of great men and princes, and he telleth places where treasure is, that be not kept with spirits, and under him is legions 34.

\-- lilecester [252]

---

249. Compare Weyer, *Pseudomonarchia Daemonum*, spirit #50: Volac.

250. Drake: dragon.

251. In marg.: "w" glyph.

252. Lilecester: Likely a variant of Leicester. If so, it might signify a break in the manuscript, indicating that the information before was copied from a book from that place.

28. Lewteffar or Falcas, a great prince; he appeareth like a monster, and he speaketh homely,[253] and he healeth all sickness and diseases, and he maketh one to seem as though he were mad, and one to rise against another, and in five days he teacheth on every part that is of necromancy, and he knoweth every part of free lone (love?),[254] and he enticeth woman most to pride. He is a liar and will not confess himself to be Abarak, but he sayeth that he is one of the four kings. First he desireth sacrifice, and he telleth of goodly things, and he fetcheth treasure or money, and he rideth upon a fiery dragon, and he hath starry eyes, and a head of a devil, the tail of a viper, and the hands of a bear, and the feet of a mole, and he speaketh of great things, and his breast is open and his breath stinketh, and his breath is fiery and he is crowned with a rainbow, and he looketh downward, and he loveth music, and he appeareth in the seventh hour, and he carrieth always in his forehead an eye, and first he appeareth, and that laughing, and he be vexed, then is he very desperate, and he never entereth into running water, and his voice is very hoarse, he doth make a man skillful in astronomy and astrology, and in geomancy, and in all other the liberal sciences, and getteth men the love of women, and giveth dignity and promotion, and confirmeth it and many other things. He fetcheth money or gold from any place he is appointed, and bringeth it anywhere the master will command him, and hath under him 20 legions.

29. Dyelagoo,[255] a great prince; he appeareth like a beautiful angel, and is very trusty in all things he is commanded by the master, and he maketh one invisible, and maketh one to transform themselves into another shape, and willingly, he giveth the love of women, and telleth the places of hid treasures, and giveth favour of friends and enemies, and under him he hath 20 legions.

30. Barbaryes, a great prince; he appeareth like an armed soldier, and he beareth in his hand a spear with a banner, and he getteth best friends and that to withstand the enemies of the master, and he causeth the enemies to lose their sight, their hearing, and their strength, and if it please the master, it shall be so, and he maketh one wise and bold, and he hath under him 50 legions.

[77]

31. Porax[256] a great prince and a strong; he appeareth like an angel, and yet black and very dark, and he hath power in building of places and houses, and in dissevering[257] of lands, woods, and waters, and in the planting of fruit trees, and in sowing of

---

253. Homely: plainly.

254. If this reading is correct, this is a century before the term "free love" came into usage.

255. In marg.: "Very trusty in all things."

256. In marg.: "Dukes."

257. Dissevering: division.

seeds, and he knoweth the virtue of herbs, and teacheth to still waters, and hath under him nine legions.

32. Acharos, or Aharas, a duke;[258] and he is under the king of the east. He appeareth willingly like an old man, and his office is to teach all languages, and he causeth them that be run away to come again, and under him are 29 legions.

33. Amada, a duke; he appeareth like a monstrous beast. He giveth true answer of things past, present, and to come, and hath under him 42 legions.

34. Barton is a great duke; he appeareth like a great bear having a dragon's tail, and he is very expert in the virtue of herbs and precious stones, and will carry one from region to region, and that swiftly and safe and hath under him 30 legions.

35. Allogor,[259] a duke; and appeareth like a fair knight, and beareth in his hand a spear with a banner, and giveth true answers, and he openeth all doubts, and showeth how they may be brought to pass, and what shall happen, and under him he hath legions 30.

36. Globa, a duke; he appeareth like a man. He is the chiefest ruler of women, and to make them to burn in love with men, and he maketh women to be barren and to have no children, and he hath under him 20 legions.[260]

37. Marshiones, a duke; he appeareth like to a strong man, having a serpent's tail, and he is expert in herbs and stones, and he will carry one from country to country, and that swiftly and without hurt, and hath under him 30 legions.[261]

38. Bartyn a strong duke; he appeareth like a bear, and knoweth herbs and stones, and will carry one quickly where he will be, and hath under him 20 legions.[262]

39. Kayne, a duke; and appeareth like a raven, and after to take the form of a man, and a counselor to steal, and doth carry treasures from kings' houses, and will leave it there as the master will, and he giveth favour both of friends and enemies, and hath under him 20 legions.

40.[263] Rewsyn a duke; and appeareth like a beautiful woman. He knoweth things past, present, and to come, and he causeth one that, after he is departed out of this world, then he causeth one of his ministers to enter into his body, and to speak with one of his kind, or with any others, and he hath under him ten legions.

---

258. In marg.: "dukes."

259. Compare Weyer, *Pseudomonarchia Daemonum*, spirit #12: Eligor or Abigor; and Boudet, "Les Who's Who Démonologiques," spirit #18 of Cambridge, Trinity College MS. O.8.29: Abugor. Compare also Sloane 3853, fol. 257r: Algor.

260. Compare Sloane 3853, fol. 257v: Globa.

261. Compare Sloane 3853, fol. 258r: Merchius.

262. Compare Sloane 3853, fol. 257r: Bertin; Wellcome MS. 110, fol. 32r: Virtyn.

263. In marg.: "w" glyph.

41. Gemyem, a strong duke;[264] appeareth like a fair woman and crowned with the crown of a duchess, and rideth upon a camel, and giveth true knowledge of things past, present, and to come, and of hid treasures, in the which places do appear half women, and he is a prince, and a companion of the love of women, and especially of maidens, and under him are 42 legions.

42. Friblex, a great duke and a marquis; and appeareth like an angel. He is both meek and true, and that in all commandments of the master, and therefore he is called Friplex [sic], and is the more mighty, and hath under him six legions.

43. Soonek, a great earl; [he] appeareth like a cruel bear, and yet by the master he taketh the shape of a man, and giveth the understanding of voices, and that of all creatures, and of all wild beasts, and teacheth all manner of languages and to understand them, and knoweth that is past, present, and to come, and he will declare where treasures be, and hath under him 18 legions.

44. Moyle, a great marquis; he appeareth like a lion, and hath wings like a griffin, and when the master will, he taketh the form of a man, and he maketh one witty and perfect in all sciences, and giveth victory upon enemies, and in feats of arms maketh one expert, and giveth favour of great men, and giveth true answer of all things secret, and he hath under him 13 legions.

45. Geyll a great earl; appeareth like an elephant, and taketh the form of a man, and speaketh with a hoarse voice, and ruleth all wild beasts, and willingly he giveth of them to the master, and he fetcheth money and gold, and that from any place that the master will, and carrieth it where the master will command him, and leaveth it for the master, and he giveth the best acquaintance and dignities and confirmeth it, and hath under him 50 legions.

46. Deydo alias Deyoo, a great earl; and appeareth like a child. He maketh trees to flourish, and to grow green, and that out of time, and he maketh a man perfit[265] in all the liberal sciences and in the mathematical science, and giveth the understanding of all languages, and causeth a man to speak them well, and perfectly, and hath under him 414 legions.

---

264. Compare Weyer, *Pseudomonarchia Daemonum*, spirit #51: Gomory. Also compare Sloane 3850, fol. 77r, spirit number 1, and Additional MS. 36674, fol. 64r, number 1: *Gomory dux fortis & potens, apparet ut mulier pulcherrima ac ducali cingitur corona, in Camelo equitans, bene & vere respondet de praeterritis, praesentibus & futuris, & occultis thesauris ubi lateant, conciliat amorem mulierum & maxime puellarum, imperat legionibus viginti sex.*

265. Perfit: proficient.

[78]

47. Sogan or Sogom, a great marquis; appeareth like a pale horse, and spea-keth with a hoarse voice, and he putteth souls out of the place of pains which some call purgatory, and he is free, and appeareth in what shape that the master will, and answereth truly and desireth a sacrifice, and rejoiceth therein, and he teacheth the mathematical science marvelously. He instructeth in wisdom and philosophy. He maketh the souls of the dead to appear before the master, and namely the souls that are nigh to the waterside or the seas, and that in a certain purgatory, which is called, the lawful affliction of souls, and what souls so ever appear before the master, they shall come in the shape of airy bodies, and evidently appearing in the form the which they first had, and they have power to answer questions, and that in the presence of the master, and hath under him 36 legions.

48. Royne, a great earl; and appeareth like a soldier, and he continually pro-cureth venery, and that between a man and his wife, and his face is like a lion, and he rideth upon a black horse and dividing a snake with his arms or arm, and he buildeth great towers, and that willingly, and houses, and bulwarks of war, and he destroyeth enemies, and their houses, and he consecrateth books and other things, and telleth of hid treasures and secrets, and under him are 26 legions.

49. Sowrges, a great marquis; and governeth in the parts of Africa and teacheth best grammar, logic, rhetoric, and divinity, and telleth the places of treasures, and openeth the same to the master, and he maketh one to pass the seas, waters and floods safe, and in a privy safeguard, and that in a most swift course. He maketh a man to ride in the same journeys upon what him list,[266] whether he will in a ship or on a horse or boat, and he himself appeareth like a knight riding upon a horse, and that with three heads, one like a horse, one like a bird, and one like a fish, and hath under him 26 legions.

50. Bryman or Myniciorom, a great earl; appeareth like a little goose. He speaketh with a very pleasant speech, and is most excellent in herbs and stones, and of flowers, fishes, birds, beasts, and in metals, woods, and waters, and he maketh one invisible, and that from time to time, and he causeth men to sleep continually and that till they die, and desireth a sacrifice, and hath under him 30 legions.

---

266. Him list: what he wishes.

51.[267] Barbates or Barbares,[268] a lord and a great viscount; he appeareth like a shooter, or forest man, with 4 minstrels and bearing 4 trumpets, 1 of gold, 2 of silver, 3 of brass, 4 of ivory. He is the guide of many rulers, and truly teacheth to understand birds, and the barking of dogs, and the howling and crying of all other beasts, and he telleth of innumerable treasures that be hid, and hath under him 29 legions.

52. Goorox, an earl; he appeareth like a bull, and sometime like a man, and he hath great knowledge in astronomy and all manner of liberal sciences, and he knoweth the virtues of herbs and stones, and under him are 30 legions.[269]

53. Barbares,[270] an earl; he appeareth like a sagittary, that is, half a man and half a beast,[271] and showeth the places where treasure is hid, and hath 26 legions.

54. Annobath, a lord and governor; appeareth like an armed knight, and rideth upon a pale horse, and he is crowned with a double crown, and beareth in his hand a warlike spear, and he teacheth the knowledge of necromancy, geomancy, and chiromancy, and the art magic, and telleth of treasures, and who keepeth them, and how they may be come by, and he giveth true answers, and that to the master, and hath under him 18 legions.

55. Gemmos,[272] a strong lord; appeareth like a knight, his horse is red, and he speaketh with a strong voice, and he teacheth how all kind of metals may be turned into pure gold, and he knoweth the virtues of herbs, and precious stones, and he teacheth physic and logic, and giveth true answer of things stolen, and he was of the order of the Archangels, and therefore he is of the greater force, and hath under him 27 legions.

56. Ansoryor or Antyor,[273] a lord; and appeareth like a warlike knight, riding upon a pale ass, and he beareth in his hand a viperous eagle, and he is very excellent in physic, and in micromancy [sic], in pyromancy, hydromancy, and in all arts, and giveth true answers of things past, present, and to come, and knoweth the natures and properties of herbs, stones, and trees, and giveth to one every liberal art, and that to the m[aste]r and maketh him perfect therein in seven days, and desireth sacrifice, and thou bind him not well, he will deceive the master, and hath under him 20 legions.

57. Noocar, a noble lord; and appeareth like an old man, walking with a staff, and is obedient to the master, and willingly showeth all things, and the secret places of

---

267. In marg.: "w" glyph.

268. Compare Weyer, *Pseudomonarchia Daemonum*, spirit #6: Barbatos.

269. Compare Sloane 3853, fol. 257v: Corax; Weyer, *Pseudomonarchia Daemonum*, spirit #15: Morax.

270. This spirit is suspiciously close to #51.

271. Sagittary: in particular, a centaur.

272. In marg.: "Philosyphers stones" and *sec. man.*: "A good phisition."

273. In marg.: "A good phisicion but yet deceitfull."

treasures and the treasures which be kept under Saturn or Mercury, or shall be made under the lot of other planets, and of all other he teachest [sic] best the art of necromancy, and it ought to be done, [79] under the fortitude and direction of every planet and place, and he discerneth the force of herbs and precious stones and waters, and he loveth money, and he hath the tail of a viper, and earthly feet, and dirty hands, and the voice of a screech owl, and he looketh ever toward heaven, and he will not tell the truth, till the master compelleth him, and he hath under him 27 legions.

58. Boab or Boall, a great prelate, appeareth like a soldier, his head is like a lion, and he rideth upon a black horse, and his eyes do shine like fire, and he speaketh with a hoarse voice, and hath great teeth, like to an ox, and he giveth the knowledge for to understand the barking of dogs, and he doth transpose gold and silver, and that from place to place, and telleth of secret hid things, and under him is 44 legions.

59. Aron or Aran, a lord, and he appeareth like a man, and telleth of things past, present, and to come, and of secret hid things, and getteth favour both of friends and enemies, and getteth dignities and promotions, of this world and confirmeth the same, and that with his doings, and sayings, and he hath under him 45 legions.

60. Jambex,[274] a marquis, a captain, and a great governor; he appeareth like a woman, and speaketh pleasantly, and he liveth [sic giveth?] the love of great men, and of new men, and that willingly, and the master must make an image of wax, and in the forehead thereof, to write that love overcometh love, and thou do cause Jambex then to consecrate that image, so written, thou shalt cause a man or woman to come where that thou wilt, set that image for them to come to, and he hath under him 25 legions.

61. Fewrayn, a governor or marquis; appeareth like the countenance of a woman, and seemeth to be meek and giveth the love of women, and he teacheth all tongues and that marvelously, and truly, and hath under him nine legions.

62. Carmerin or Cayenam, a lord; he appeareth like a beautiful woman, and crowned with a double crown, and rideth upon a camel, and telleth the truth of secret treasures and specially where women be seen, and he is a prince thereof and keeper of them, and hath under him 30 legions.

63. Mathias, a lord; he appeareth like a bear, and he casteth flames of fire out of his mouth, and his office is to carry a man from country to country, and he hath under him 36 legions.

64. Pamelon,[275] a great ruler; he appeareth like a man, he telleth of things that be in the water, and of things that be in the earth, and how to come by them, and he is good and that for the love of maidens, and he hath under him six legions.

---

274. In marg.: "for an image pro amore."

275. In marg.: "w" glyph.

65. Joorex is a ruler; he appeareth like a hart and speaketh with a small voice. He teacheth to make all manner of instruments of music, and teacheth astronomy, and causeth a man to win, and that all games, and if he be enclosed in a ring and worn upon the forefinger, and hath under him nine legions.

66. Mageyne,[276] a ruler; he appeareth like a hedgehog, and is a very good companion, for he teacheth a man and helpeth him in all manner of needful business, and namely in all manner of husbandry and occupations, and hath under him 20 legions.

67. Gasyaxe,[277] is a great ruler; and appeareth like a hare, and teacheth a man to enclose all manner of spirits, and how to conclude[278] them that be but for answers, and for them that be dicers, and carders, shooting and bowling, and for the love of women, and how to make a glass that all men may see the truth therein, of all such things as they are desirous of, and he teacheth how to have a true answer of all spirits, and if the master put him into the head of a dead man, then he will teach all the art of necromancy, magic, or other sciences, and he hath under him of spirits 16 legions.

68. Barsy, a great ruler and a captain; he appear like an archer, and bearing about a quiver, and that of iron, and he is the beginner of wars, and he maketh men to shoot near unto the mark, and he hath great power thereto, and he hath under him 30 legions.[279]

69. Bartax is a ruler; and he appeareth like an old man, and his office is to tell where and in what place hidden treasure is, and who they be that keepeth it, and how it may be come by, and he hath under him four legions.

70. Vsagoo,[280] a great prince; he appeareth like an angel, and is just and true in all his doings. He giveth the love of women, and telleth of hid treasures, and hath under him 20 legions.

[80]

71. Gyell, a great count (or earl); he appeareth like an elephant and speaketh with a hoarse voice, and he bringeth forth money out of any place, palace, or house, and will lay the same in what place by the master he is commanded, and there leave it, and he hath under him seven legions.

---

276. In marg.: "A good companion."

277. In marg.: "A teacher of all artes."

278. Conclude: i.e., include.

279. Compare Sloane 3853, fol. 257v: Berci.

280. In marg.: "A true spirit." This spirit corresponds with the third spirit in Goetia in Peterson, *The Lesser Key of Solomon*, p. 8: Vassago; not found in Weyer, *Pseudomonarchia Daemonum*.

72. Syeonell, a great count (or earl); he appeareth like a fierce bear, and when the master will, he appeareth like a child, and then he teacheth best all kind of languages, and telleth where treasure is hid, and hath under him 18 legions.

73. Corsone,[281] a great count (or earl); he appeareth like a man, and a lion's face, and crowned with a diadem, and holding in his hand a viper, and he hath an earthly body, and truly and willingly he telleth where the places be where treasure is, and under him are six legions.

74. Pamelon or paynelon [282] appeareth like a knight. He doth compel other spirits to come from the four corners of the world and to appear before the master, and he giveth true answer of all things, and telleth of the unknown art, and hath under him ten legions.

75. Gemon, a valiant captain; he appeareth like a fair woman and crowned with a crown, and rideth upon a camel, and telleth of treasures hid and of things past, present, and to come, and hath under him five legions.

76. Leban, a knight and a mighty soldier; he appeareth like a giant. He carrieth men whether they will, and so doth he all other things whither the master will, and to fetch the same out of any country, and that speedily and without delay, and at the master's commandment he will carry mountains, hills, and castles, and so will he do any manner of riches, and leave it where he is commanded by the master, and hath under him of legions, 40.

77. Doodall,[283] a knight and a mighty soldier; he appeareth with a spear of gold in his hand, and he hath power to gather together other spirits, and he to take counsel with them, and that for things that have chanced against a man, etc., and to know a remedy therefore, and that before, and he hath under him six legions.

78. Geenex,[284] a knight; he appeareth like a valiant captain, and teacheth physic, and the making of rings, out of the which rings answers be given of spirits, and he teacheth how to enclose other spirits, and to make glasses wherein may be seen things lost or stolen, and he telleth how the truth of the answers of other spirits may be understood, and he appeareth and that soonest in a dead man's head, and most commonly he appeareth like a hare, and hath under him of legions 20.

79. Cornyx, he appeareth like a captain, and he hath power to call together birds, and that to one place, and to take them, and he hath under him seven legions.

---

281. Compare Weyer, *Pseudomonarchia Daemonum,* spirit #11. Also Additional MS. 36674, fol. 64r, number 5: *Purson alias Curson, magnus rex prodit ut homo facie leonina, callet praeterita, praesentia & futura, aperit occulta, thesauros detegit, familiares parit optimos, praeset legionibus 22.*

282. Note that spirit 64 was also named Pamelon.

283. In marg.: "w" glyph.

284. In marg.: "A teacher in art: and a teacher of phisike."

80. Mosacus appeareth in the form of a giant with the snout of an elephant with fiery eyes, having two heads in his breast, the head on the right breast a dog's head and on the left breast the head of an ass, and in the midst of his two arms on every arm the heads of two bloodhounds, and in his right arm a crook in compass of a sickle, but hath anothethe (another?) as it were come forth of that. He hath two eyes in the midst of his belly, and at his knees the heads of two bloodhounds. His hands and feet like the feet of a goose, but being commanded, he appeareth like a child with a red head. He giveth answer truly unto thy questions.

81. Oberyon a king; he appeareth like a king with a crown on his head. He is under the government of the Sun and Moon. He teacheth a man knowledge in physic and he showeth the nature of stones, herbs, and trees, and of all metals. He is a great and mighty king, and he is king of the fairies. He causeth a man to be invisible. He[285] showeth where hiding treasure is and how to obtain the same. He telleth of things present, past, and to come, and if he be bound to a man, he will carry or bring treasure out of the sea. His burden is 1000000 £.[286] He holds the waters and low parts of the earth ♒︎♓︎.

82. Bilgall, appeareth in the likeness of an ox but a man's head with flames of fire proceeding out of her [sic] mouth.

[81]

[+ Mycob is queen of the fairies]

Mycob is queen of the fairies, and is of the same office that Oberyon is of. She appeareth in green with a crown on her head, and is very meek and gentle. She showeth the nature of herbs, stones, and trees. She showeth the use of medicines and the truth. She causeth the ring of invisibility to be given to the invocator.

Lillia   + Restillia   + fata,   falla, Afria or Africa, Julya,   Venalla,

These seven sisters is for to show and teach a man the nature of herbs, and to instruct a man in physic; also they will bring a man the ring of invisibility. They are under Micob, the queen of fairies.[287]

---

285. Handwriting changes at this point for the rest of the paragraph. Note particularly the unusual c's.

286. JHP thinks £ here refers to how much treasure he can carry, in pounds, although it is not clear whether weight or the currency is intended.

287. For the ring of invisibility, see Folger p. 38, where the first fairy is named Micoll. Sloane 3846, 25v, includes an operation to invoke Micol, queen of the pigmies. See also Sloane 1727, 23r. In marg.: "quenn of ferres."

[+ There be four kings of spirits of the air]

Note: There be four kings of spirits of the air, the which have power and domination upon all spirits of the air, and all the parts of the world, viz., Oriens, Paymon, Amaymon, and Egine.

The first king reigneth in the east and is called Oriens, and he cometh in the likeness of an horse with a 100 heads, or as some write, with five heads, but if thou call him with his company, he appeareth with a fair favour and as a woman, riding upon an elephant and all manner of minstrels before him. He can tell all things past, present, and to come, and can prophesy truly of things to come. He can give any science earthly and earthly treasure, and he hath under him spirits innumerable, of which twelve of the best and most principal are these.

1.[288] The first is called Baall, and he hath power of love, both of man and woman, and to make a man invisible, and he appeareth in the likeness of a king, and he speaketh hoarsely.

2. The second is called Agaros; he can teach all manner of languages, and tongues. He can bring again a fugitive or one run away, and can promote to dignity and worship, and appeareth in likeness of an old man riding upon a cockadrill.

3. The third is called Barbas alias Corbas, a great chief. He can tell of all secrets, to make an old man sick, and to change a man into another shape, the shape of a beast. He appeareth in likeness of a man.

4. The fourth is called Star,[289] and he hath power to take from a man hearing, seeing, and understanding, and to bring money, whether he is commanded. He is a good and true spirit. He appeareth in likeness of a swan, and speaketh hoarsely.

5. The fifth is called Semper; he hath power to make a great sea appear full of ships, with all manner of instruments of war, to fear enemies. He can make great winds, he can rankle wounds and make worms breed in them, and appeareth in likeness of a maiden.[290]

---

288. In marg. in a later hand: "according to Scot p. 277 4to 1651" obviously referring to Scot, *Discouerie of Witchcraft*. In marg. below this is a "w" glyph.

289. In marg. in a later hand: "A good and true spirite." Compare Additional MS. 36674, fol 64r number 7: "Scor can bring money is true to the commandements of any Exorcist, he appeareth like a swanne."

290. Compare Weyer, *Pseudomonarchia Daemonum*, spirit #32: Vepar alias Separ; and spirit #42 in Goetia in Peterson, *The Lesser Key of Solomon*, 26.

6. The sixth is called Algor; [291] he hath power to tell all secrets and to give love and favour of kings, princes, and lords, and appeareth in likeness of a fair knight with spear and shield.

7. The seventh is called Seson; [292] and he can tell all things that ever hath been or ever shall be and hath power to show the place of hid treasure and to make one familiar with every man. He appeareth with a lion's face crowned with a diadem, having a venomous serpent in his hand, and rideth upon a wild boar. Nevertheless, he will gladly take a body of the air and appear in likeness of a man.

8. The eighth is called Maxayn; and he hath power to teach the virtues of all herbs, trees, and stones, and to bear a man from region to region, in a brief time. He appeareth in the likeness of a bear, with a serpent's tail, and a flame of fire coming forth of his mouth.

9. The ninth is called Neophon; he hath power to tell of all things that hath been or shall be, and of all secrets. He giveth men favour of great men, and appeaseth the enmities of foes. He giveth dignity, worship, and riches, and appeareth in likeness of a dog.

10. The tenth is called Barbais; he can teach one to understand the chattering of birds, barking of dogs, and lowing of beasts. He telleth of hid treasure, foredoeth[293] witchcraft, and appeareth in likeness of a wild archer.

11. The eleventh is called Amon; he hath power to make wild beasts tame, and tell all secrets, to get love of friends and enemies. He appeareth in likeness of a wolf, with a serpent's tail, casting fire out of his mouth, but he may appear in likeness of a man, and then he hath teeth like a dog.[294]

12. The twelfth is called Suffales; he hath power to break peace, and cause debates, strife, and battle. He is false in his answers, but if he be constrained strongly he appeareth like a spark of fire. **End of the first king.**

---

291. Compare Additional MS. 36674, fol 74, number 8: "Algor can tell of all secret things, & give loue & fauoure to all great persons he appeareth like a faire knight."

292. Compare Additional MS. 36674, fol. 64r, number 9: "Sefon can tell of things past present & to come, & hath power to shew thee where treasure is hidden, & maketh thee familiar with euery man, he appeareth in the likeness of a man. These three last are under Oriens king of the East."

293. Foredoeth: destroys.

294. Compare Amon in Peterson, *The Lesser Key of Solomon,* 10.

[82]

The second king is called

Amaymon reigneth in the south, and all spirits in the south part of the world to him are obedient. His power is to give true answer of all things, and he giveth familiarity, dignity, and riches, and by God's permission he hath power to consecrate books, etc. He appeareth in favour of an old man having a long beard and long hair hanging over his eyes, crowned with a bright crown, and rideth upon a ramping[295] lion, and in his right hand he beareth a dart. Before him cometh dancers and all manner of minstrels. He bringeth with him spirits innumerable, of whom twelve of the most noblest are these that followeth, but of all spirits in the world beware of him, for he is very perilous.

1. The first is called Asmoday; he can teach astronomy, arithmetic, music, and geometry, and to tell of all things be it never so obscure. He can cause one to go invisible, and can show the place where treasure is hid, and appeareth with three heads, one like an ass, the second like a bull, and the third like a ram, his tail like a serpent, his feet like an ass, and a flame of fire cometh out of his mouth.[296]

3. The[297] third is called Astaroth; he can teach the seven arts liberal, and to give true answer of all things past, present, and to come, and he appeareth very horribly, riding upon an infernal dragon bearing a serpent in his hand out of whose mouth cometh a great sting. Therefore suffer him not to come within your circle, for he is perilous and will put you in danger.

2. The second is called Bileth; he can teach the arts liberal, he can make consecrations as well evil as good. He teacheth invisibility.[298]

4. The fourth is called Abech; he teacheth the seven sciences, all manner languages, getteth friendship, giveth true answer of all things, and appeareth like an king, but you shall see nothing of him but his head, and before him cometh trumpeters.

5. The fifth is called Berith;[299] he giveth dignity, he turneth metals into gold and silver. He can tell all things past etc. He appeareth like a knight riding on a red horse, crowned with two red crowns. He speaketh clearly,[300] unless he be mastered and strongly constrained.

---

295. Ramping: rearing, the posture of a lion on a coat of arms.

296. Compare Sloane 3853, fol. 227v.

297. In marg.: "mistaken bileth is second and astaroth the 3d."

298. See Beleth in Peterson, *The Lesser Key of Solomon*, 12–13.

299. In marg. in modern hand: "26." Berith is the spirit #26 in Scot, *Discouerie of Witchcraft*.

300. Weyer, *Pseudomonarchia Daemonum*, adds "he is a liar," which should perhaps be supplied here to complete the sense.

6. The sixth is called Mallapas;[301] he maketh castles and towers. He can subvert and overthrow all manner of buildings and edifices. He appeareth in likeness of a raven, nevertheless he may appear by constraint like a man. His speech is hoarse.

7. The seventh is Partas;[302] and when he receiveth the shape of a man, he hath power to tell the virtues of herbs and stones, and to teach logic, to make one invisible, to restore to a man that hath lost his sight the same again, to show the place of hid treasure, and appeareth like a wood bear.

8. The eighth is called Busin; he answereth truly to all manner of questions. He can bring dead bodies from one place to another and to make one of his spirits to enter into the dead body, and to carry it about, and to speak and go at commandment, and to all manner of things done by the dead when he was living, except eating. He appeareth in likeness of a fair woman, but he speaketh hoarsely.

9. The ninth is called Oze;[303] and he hath power when he receiveth shape of a man to teach the seven arts liberal and to tell all secrets, to change a man into another shape, and he appeareth in likeness of a leopard.

10. The tenth is called Pathyn; and he hath power to make a man wise, to tell all secrets. He appeareth with three heads, bearing a serpent in his hand and a pin of burning iron in his mouth, with the which pin he may burn what place or thing he is commanded to burn.

11. The eleventh is called Cambra; he hath power to teach the virtues of herbs and stones, and to make any bird tame, and appeareth like a swan.

12. The twelfth is called Gamor; when he receives a man's shape, he can marvelously inform thee in astronomy and all the rest of the sciences. He can inform thee to have the favour of great estates, and can show treasures hid, and what the spirits be that keep the same, and he appears as a spark of fire.

The third prince or king of the spirits is called

Paymon[304] and he himself has notable power, and willingly answers to all things that you ask of him. He will speak of the state of the world, and he may give familiarity, and he may make all fishes of the sea to be obedient. He appeareth like a king with a woman's face crowned with a bright crown. He rideth upon a dromedary and after him comes a great company of spirits with all manner of instruments of melody, but

---

301. In marg.: "31" i.e., in Scot, *Discouerie of Witchcraft*.

302. In marg.: "28 Foras."

303. Spirit #55 in Scot, *Discouerie of Witchcraft*.

304. In marg. (modern): "21." He is actually spirit #22 in Scot, *Discouerie of Witchcraft*, and Weyer, *Pseudomonarchia Daemonum*.

if he be called alone, then he appeareth with two kings and speaks mystically, for he would not be understood. Nevertheless thou mayest command him to speak in thine own language. He hath infinite of spirits under him but twelve of the most mightiest be these.

[83]

1. The first is called Beliall;[305] he giveth dignity and promotion, and he giveth love and favour of all persons. He appeareth in likeness of a fair angel, riding in a chair of fire, and speaketh sweetly.

2. The second is called Bason; he maketh one invisible and wise, and will answer to all questions. He appeareth with three heads, one like a dog, one like a man, and one like a raven. He rideth upon a wild bear, and beareth upon his fist a goshawk, and out of his mouth proceedeth a flame of fire, and he speaks hoarsely.

3. The third is Gordonsor; he can tell the truth of all things, etc. and he is right mighty in the errands doing. He appeareth like a good angel having a dark face.

4. The fourth is Balath; his office is to make a whole man sick, and to take from a man his senses or wits. He maketh a man marvelous cunning in the seven liberal sciences. He may give love and dignity to all men, he can carry one from one place to another, and appeareth like a misshapen image and speaketh hoarsely.

5. The fifth is called Mistalas; he, receiving man's shape. He hath power to teach and instruct one in witchcraft and necromancy, and knoweth the virtues of herbs, stones, and trees, and appeareth like a night raven.

6. The sixth is Lecher; he knoweth the secrets of the seven sciences. He getteth friendship. He appears like a knight with a red lion's face, and he speaketh very sadly.

7. The seventh is called Zagayne;[306] and when he receiveth man's shape, he giveth wisdom, and turneth earth into any kind of metal. Also he can turn water into wine, and of a fool make a wise man, and appeareth like a wild bull.

8. The eighth is called Caleos;[307] he hath power and knowledge of infinite treasures. He maketh one beloved and purchaseth familiarity. He appeareth like a knight riding upon a crocodile, and he weareth upon his head two crowns, but he is very false in his answers, but if he be well constrained and mastered.

---

305. In marg. (modern): "22."

306. In marg. (modern): "47." Compare Weyer, *Pseudomonarchia Daemonum*, spirit #48, Sloane 3850, fol. 77r, spirit no. 2, and also Additional MS. 36674, fol. number 2: "*Zagan magnus praeses and rex, ut Taurus prodit cum alis ad modum gryphis: sed assumpta hominis forma, hominem ingeniosum reddit, transmutat cuncta metallorum genera in monetam illius ditionis, and aquam in vinum, and praeest 33 legionibus.*"

307. In marg.: "w" glyph.

9. The ninth is Cagyne or Cogin;[308] he hath being in human shape to bring any soul being not in the heavenly nor infernal power, to speak with thee. He appears in likeness of a pale horse.

10. The tenth is called Suchay; he can teach all manner of languages, and to carry one in short space from one place to another. He giveth the love of women, and is in that the most principalest, and especially of widows. He appeareth with a fair face like a woman.

11. The eleventh is Ryall;[309] who having human shape can resolve all doubts and tell all things. He can give love of women, get friends, and turn the hearts of enemies. He appeareth like a dromedary and speaketh sadly.

12. The twelfth is called Zayme; he can bring money from any place he will, or is assigned unto him, and to carry the same to any appointed place. He can in a moment show the building or situation of any plot, city, or castle, and can procure dignity and honour, and cometh like a raven.

The fourth prince or king of spirits is called

Egin and he reigneth in the North. He hath power to teach all manner of sciences and will gladly tell all secrets and the truth of things past, present, and to come. He getteth friendship and raiseth one to dignity. He can make alterations of things, he appeareth in the likeness of a man, with a bright face, crowned with a double crown, and he rideth upon a dragon, and cometh with a fearful noise, and before him cometh diverse sorts of instruments, but being called alone, he bringeth with him three kings and comes not so hastily nor so dreadfully as others. Also he hath with him infinite spirits, of which these twelve are chiefest.

1. The first is called Ozia; he can teach all manner of arts or sciences, invisibility, and give favour of enemies. He can carry one from one place to another, and that upon a sudden. He appeareth like an old man riding like an elephant.

2. The second is Vriell or Vriall;[310] he turneth one metal into another, as iron or brass into gold and silver, wine to water, or water to wine, of a fool maketh one wise,

---

308. In marg. (modern): "46."

309. In marg. (modern): "65" i.e., this corresponds with Weyer, *Pseudomonarchia Daemonum*, spirit #65 (should read 66): Vuall or Wal. Compare Additional MS. 36674, fol. 65r, number 6: *Vual dux magnus and fortis, conspicitur ut Dromedarius magnus and terribilis: at in humana forma sonat linguam Aegiptiacam grauiter: hic prae caeteris amorem maxime mulierum conciliat. Inde nouit praeterita, praesentia, and futura gratiamque confert amicorum and inimicorum.*

310. In marg.: "In mettelles. for gowld [or] siluer."

and maketh one go invisible, and he appeareth like a boisterous king and speaketh hoarsely.

[84]

3. The third is Vzago;[311] who, taking human form, hath power to make one wise and invisible, and to change man into another form or likeness. He getteth love and favour of all men, and giveth true answer of all things. He appeareth like an angel, and is right, true, and faithful in all his doings.

4. The fourth is Synoryell; and he, having human shape, teacheth to understand beasts lowing, birds chirping, and dogs barking, and all manner of languages, and can tell all things, and show the places of hid treasure, and cometh like a wood[312] bear.

5. The fifth is Fessan (Tessan?). He teacheth astronomy and arithmetic, and giveth true answer of secret things, and appeareth like a flame of fire, and speaketh hoarsely.

6. The sixth is Goyle. He maketh a man gorgeous and gay, to have the love and favour of princes. He answereth to all questions, and appeareth like a ramping[313] lion.

7. The seventh is Auras. He hath power to carry dead coarses[314] whither they be appointed, and giveth answer to all questions, and appeareth in the likeness of a wild ass.

8. The eighth is Othey; and he can upon the sudden[315] make castles, towers, and towns. He answereth truly to all things. He appeareth like to a tun of wine, and sometimes like a man, and then his eyes burn like fire.

9. The ninth is Saranyt. He can raise dead men, and cause them to take again their own shape, and to speak with men. He can teach one the seven arts or sciences liberal, and he appears like an ass with a woman's face.

10. The tenth is Muryell.[316] He maketh love between persons and can tell of treasure hid, and appeareth as a white lion.

11. The eleventh is Hinbra.[317] He giveth dignity and telleth secrets, getteth friendship, conveyeth money from place to place, and appeareth like a giant, but speaketh so small that vunethes (uim-?) one can hear or perceive him, but he is passing true.

---

311. In marg.: a glyph, and "for love." The description is different from that of Vassago above.

312. Wood: rabid.

313. Ramping: rearing, as on a coat of arms.

314. Coarses: corpses.

315. Upon the sudden: suddenly.

316. Compare Additional MS. 36674, fol. 64r, number 11: "Gamor when he doth receiue mans shape can meruaylously confirm to haue the fauours of great persons and sheweth of any treasure that is hid which any spirit keepeth."

317. Compare Additional MS. 36674, fol. 64r, number 12: "Umbra can give dignity and familiarity and tell all things to come, he can convey money from place to place if thou bid him: he is very true, he cometh loke a Gyant."

12. The twelfth is Annoboth vel Anaboth.[318] He hath power to make one marvelous expert in necromancy, and to show the place of hid treasure, and to tell who keepeth it, and if the spirit be of the north, he will drive him away. Also he can tell of wonderful strange things, and appeareth in likeness of an armed knight.

Beallphares [319] or Beallphare, an excellent carrier. He telleth of hidden treasures in the earth or of things stolen or lost and is true in all his doings. He cometh forth out of the east, for so he hath been called from the east and he appeared very (?) dutifully to God's people and his servants.

[85]

The shapes familiar to the spirits of the Sun [320]

They appear for the most part with bodies that are large and tall, bloody and thick, with a gold colour tinged with blood. Their movement is like the glittering of the sky, and the sign that they have appeared is that the one who calls them will break into a sweat.

Moreover, their particular forms are:

A king having a sceptre, riding a lion; a king with a crown; a queen with a sceptre; [321] a bird; a lion; a rooster; a [yellow or gold garment]; [322] a sceptre; a shining one.[323]

The fumigation of Sunday: Red sandalwood. [324]

The spirits of the air for Sunday are subject to the North Wind.

Their [325] nature is to procure gold, jewels, wealth of gems, as well as grace and good will. They can break down hostilities among people, grant honours (or public office) to them, and bring on or take away sickness.

The spirits that reign this day are as follows:

King Barkan, with his helpers, viz. Bybell, Mylalua, Buesaba. Here state your request and your business.

---

318. Compare Sloane 3850, fol. 77v, number 13; and Additional MS. 36674, fol 64r, number 13. In marg.: "w" glyph.

319. This note is inserted at the bottom of the page *sec. man.*

320. This wording of this section is almost identical to that in the so-called *Fourth Book of Occult Philosophy* of Agrippa. It also has parallels with Honorius, *Liber Iuratus,* CXXII ff.

321. In left marg. in late pencil: "page 1 of Theus MS."

322. There is a space in the manuscript, presumably to change pen, but so Pseudo-Agrippa.

323. Instead of *candatus,* Pseudo-Agrippa reads *caudatus* ("tailed"), which Du Cange glosses thus: *Caudatos autem dicebant, quibus ablata erat cauda.* This doesn't seem to fit the context as well.

324. Compare H. In right marg.: "170."

325. In marg.: "w" glyph.

This done by the space of one hour after, or at the discretion of the master, meekly kneeling upon your knees, call upon the angels of the day and hour after this manner.

Michael DarDiel huratapel. Estote adiutores mee petitioni, et in adiutorum mihi meis rebus et petitionibus.	O Michael,[*] Dardiel, Huratapel, be my helpers in these petitions, and help me in my affairs and petitions.
[*] In left marg.: "Cum genibus flexis" (kneeling).	

Then, invoke the angels from the four parts of the world that rule the air on that day.

Towards the East: Samael, Baciel, Atel, Fabriel, Vionatraba.

Towards the West: Anael, Pabel, Ystael, Burchat, Suceratos, Capabil.

Towards the North: Aiel, Aniel, Masgabriel, Sapiel, Matnyel.

Towards the South: Habudiel, Machasiel, Charsiel, Uriel, Naromiel.[326]

The fumigation of Sunday: Red sandalwood.[327]

After you have repeated these names in their heavens, then say,

O vos[*] omnes, adiuro atque contestor per sedem Adonay + per Hagios + Otheos + Iskiros, Athanatos, Paracletus, α et ω, et per hac tria nomina secreta Agla + On + Tetragramaton + quod hodie debatis ad implere quod cupio.	I adjure and call all you forth, by the seat of Adonay + and by Hagios + Otheos + Iskiros, Athanatos, Paracletus, Alpha and Omega, and by these three secret names Agla + On + Tetragrammaton + that you at once fulfill what I desire.
[*] In marg.: "page 5 T Ms." Compare H. p. 111–112; and Sloane 3850, fol. 78r.	

---

326. In right marg.: "171."
327. Note the duplication.

[86]

328

Made in the Day of ☉ Hour of ☉

Soll

Seale ☉

Conjuration of Sunday

Coniuro et confirmo super vos An geli fortes Dei et sancti in nomine Adonay + Eye + Eye + Eye + qui est ille qui fuit, est, et erit, Eye + Abraye: et in nomine Saday + Cados, Cados, Cados, alte sedentis super Cherubin, et per nomen magnum ipsius dei fortis et potentis, exaltatique super omnes celos Eye, Saraye, plasmatoris seculorum, qui creavit mundum, caelum, terram, mare, et omnia que qui in eis sunt in primo die, et sigillauit ea sancto nomine suo Phaa: et per nomina sanctorum Angelorum, qui	I conjure* and encourage you, ye strong and holy angels of God, in the name Adonai + Eye + Eye + Eye + which is he who was, and is, and is to come, Eye + Abray: and in the name Saday + Cados, Cados, Cados, sitting above the cherubim; and by the great name of God himself, strong and powerful, who is exalted above all the heavens; Eye, Saraye, who created the world, the heavens, the earth, the sea, and all that in them is, in the first day, and sealed them with his holy name Phaa; and by the names of
* In left marg. in ink: "w"; in pencil: "page 5 Ts"; in right marg: "171." Compare H. pp. 132–133.	

---

328. Figures shows the portrait of King Barkan, Solar pentacle, and Mars Kamea Seal—"made in the day of the Sun, hour nature & artif of the Sun / Sol." At bottom is "seal or character of Mars" from OP Book 2, Chapter 22. JHP believes the seal in this and the following six illustrations are variations of the "planetarum sigilla" found in the Magical Calendar (Harley 3420, 27v). The seal of Mars has been corrected here to the seal of the Sun.

Dominantur in quarto exercitu, et serviunt coram potentissimo Salamia, Angelo magno et honerato: et per nomen stelle, que qui est ☉ et [per] signum, et per Immensum nomen dei viui, et per nomina omnia predicta, Coniuro te Michael, Angele magne qui es prepositus diei Dominice: et per nomen Adonay, dei Israel, qui creauit mundum, et quicquid in eo est, quod pro me labores, et adimpleas omnem meam peticionem, iuxta meum velle et votum meum, in negotio et causa mea.	the angels who rule in the fourth* army, and serve before the most mighty Salamia, an angel great and honourable; and by the name of his star, which is the Sun, and by his sign, and by the immense name of the living God, and by all the names aforesaid, I conjure thee, Michael, O great angel who is chief ruler of Sunday, and by the name Adonai, the God of Israel, who created the universe, and everything that is in it, that you labor for me, and fulfil all my petitions according to my will and desire in my business and plea.†

* H. reads "primo," but "quarto" is consistent with Raziel in Peterson, *The Sixth and Seventh Books of Moses*, where the fourth heaven, Machonon, corresponds with the sphere of the Sun, and the angel Michael.
† In marg. in pencil: "See Agrippa 570."

This ended, read the invocation for the angels of every day as you shall find at the end of the invocations and offices of the seven angels.[329]

The forms familiar to the spirits of the Moon ☾

They will appear[330] for the most part with a large and tall body, soft and phlegmatic: their colour is like a dark and obscure cloud, with a swollen face, eyes red and full of water, a bald head, and teeth like a boar. Their movement is like a mighty sea storm, and the sign that they have appeared, is that a huge rainstorm appearing near the circle.

Moreover, their particular forms are:

An arrow-armed king riding a fallow. A small boy. A woman huntress with bow and arrow. A cow. A doe. A goose. A green or silvery garment. An arrow. A millipede.

The spirits of the air on Monday are subject to the West wind, which is the wind of the Moon.

The fumigation of Monday: Aloe.

329. In marg. in pencil: "p. 7 Theus Ms."
330. In right marg.: "17[.]"

[87]

Their nature[331] is to give silver; they can also carry things from place to place, to grant speed to horses, and to disclose the secrets of persons present and past.

King Harkam, his helpers, viz Bylethor, Byleth, Mylu, Acuteba.[332]

Gabriel

"Gabriel, Michael, Samael, *estote adiutores mei petitioni* etc." ["Gabriel, Michael, Samael be my assistants in this petition, etc."]

To the East: Gabriel, Gabrael, Madiel, Deamiel, Ianael.

To the West: Sachiel, Zaniel, Habaiel, Bachanael, Corabiel.

To the North: Mael, Vuael, Valnum, Baliel, Balay, Humastrau.

To the South: Curaniel, Dabriel, Darquiel, Hanuin, Anayl, Vetuel.

O vos omnes, Adiuro atque contestor etc.	O all of you, I adjure and appeal to you, etc.

---

331. Compare LIH CXX.

332. LIH: Harthan is the king, Bileth, Milalu, and Habuchaba are his ministers.

333. Figure shows the angel Gabriel, Luna Kamea Seal, Circle, and King Harkam. In marg.: "w" glyph.

Conjuration of Monday [334]

Coniuro et confirmo super vos Angeli fortes et boni, in nomine Adonay, Adonay, Adonay, Eie, Eie, Eie, Cados, Cados, Cados, Achim, Achim, Ia, Ia, fortis Ia, qui apparuit in Monte Sinai, cum glorificatione regis Adonay, Saday, Zebaoth, Anathay, Ya, Ya, Ya, Marinata, Abim, Ieia, qui Maria creavit, stagna et omnes aquas in secundo die, quasdam super celos, et quasdam in terra. sigillavit mare in alto [*alio] nomine suo, et terminum, quem [*quam] sibi posuit, non preteribit: et per nomina Angelorum, qui Dominantur in primo exercitu, qui serviunt Orphaniel Angelo magno, precioso et honorato: et per nomen stellae que est Luna: et per nomina predicta, super te Coniuro, scilicet: Gabriel, qui es prepositus diei Lune secundo, quod pro me labores et adimpleas omnem meam petitionem, Iuxta meum velle et votum meum, in Negocio et causa mea etc.	I conjure and encourage you, O strong and good angels, in the name of Adonay, Adonay, Adonay, Eie, Eie, Eie, Cados, Cados, Cados, Achim, Achim, Ia, Ia, strong Ia, who appeared on Mount Sinai, with the glorification of the king Adonay, Saday, Zebaoth, Anathay, Ya, Ya, Ya, Marinata, Abim, Ieia, who created the seas, the pools, and all waters on the second day, which are above the heavens, and in the earth, and sealed the sea in his other name, with a boundary beyond which it cannot pass. And by the names of the angels who have command in the first army, which serve Orphaniel, the great, precious, and respected angel. And by the name of the star which is the Moon. And by all the preceding names, I conjure over you, namely Gabriel, who is placed in command of Monday, which is the second day, that you work on my behalf and fulfil my all petitions, according to my will and vow, in my business and plea, etc.

[88]

♂ The fumigation of Tuesday: Pepper.

♂ The forms familiar to the spirits of Mars[335]

They appear with a long forehead,[336] yellowish,[337] and ugly in appearance, with a brownish colour, and somewhat red, with deer's antlers, and the claws of a griffin,

---

334. In left marg. in pencil: "p. 11 T [=Theus] Ms."; in right marg. in pen: "172."

335. In left marg. in pencil: "p. 13 Th. S."

336. Pseudo-Agrippa: *longo corpore* ["long body"].

337. Or irritable. The choleric humour was associated with fire and yellow bile.

bellowing like a mad bull. The sign of their appearance is that they will bring the appearance of lightning and thunder near the circle.

Moreover, their particular forms are: An armed king, riding a wolf; an armed man; a woman wearing a round shield on her thigh; a he-goat; a horse; a stag; a red garment; wool; a tapeworm.

The spirits of Tuesday are subordinate to the Eastern wind.

Their nature is to cause battles, death, murder, and burnings, and give two thousand soldiers for a while, and to grant death, sickness, and health.

King Iammas, with his helpers Carmas, Itamall, Palframen, Palframe.[338]

made in the day of the Sun,[340] hour of Mars.

Samael. Satael. Amabiel. estote adiutores mei et c.	Samael, Satael, Amabiel, **may you be** my assistants, etc.

To the East: Friagne, Guael, Damael, Calzas, Arragon.

To the West: Lama, Astagna, Lobquin, Soncas, Iaxel, Isiael, Iriel.

To the North: Rabumel, Hyniel, Rayel, Seraphiel, Mathiel, Fraciel.

To the South: Sacriel, Ianiel, Galdel, Osael, Viannel, Zaliel

---

338. LIH: Iammax the king, [and his ministers] Carmox, Ichanol, Pasfran.

339. Figure shows the angel Samael, Mars Circle, and King Iammas. The seal of Mars in black at the bottom of the image is missing from Folger, but it has been added here for consistency and completeness. In marg.: "w" glyph.

340. Perhaps Mars is meant here?

O vos omnes, adiuro atque contestor etc.	O all of you, I adjure and appeal to you, etc.

Conjuration for Tuesday

Coniuro et confirmo super vos, Angeli fortes et sancti, per nomen, Ya, Ya, Ya, He, He, He, Va, Hy, Hy, Ha, Ha, Va, Va, Va, An, An, An, Aie, Aie, Aie, El, Ay, Elibra, Eloim, Eloim: et per nomina ipsius alti dei, qui fecit aquam ar[i]dam apparere, et vocauit terram, et produxit arbores, et herbas de ea, et sigillauit super eam cum precioso honorato, metuendo et sancto nomine suo: et per nomen Angelorum dominantium in quinto ex<c>ercitu, qui serviunt, Acimoy, Angelo magno, forti potenti et honorato: et per nomen stelle, que est Mars: et per nomina praedicta coniuro super te Samael Angele Magne, qui praepositus es diei Martis: et per nomina Adonay dei vivi et veri quod pro me labores, et adimpleas omnem meam petitionem iuxta meum velle et votum meum, in negocio et causa mea etc.	I conjure and encourage you, O strong and holy angels, by the name Ya, Ya, Ya, He, He, He, Va, Hy, Hy, Ha, Ha, Va, Va, Va, An, An, An, Aie, Aie, Aie, El, Ay, Elibra, Eloim, Eloim, and by the names of the same high God, who made the water and dry land appear, and he called the dry land Earth, and he produced trees and herbs from it, and set his seal upon it with his precious, honoured, feared, and holy name, and by the name of the angels governing the fifth* army, who serve the great angel Acimoy, strong, powerful, and respected, and by the name of the star which is Mars, and by the names before spoken, I conjure over you, Samael, great angel, who is placed in command over Tuesday, and by the names (sic) Adonay, God living and true, that you work for me, and fulfill all my petitions, according to my will and my vow, in my business and plea, etc.

---

* Fifth: Quinto follows Razielis in Peterson, *The Sixth and Seventh Books of Moses*; some editions of H. read "tertio."

[89]

☿ Fumigation of Wednesday: Mastic.

The shapes familiar to the spirits of Mercury:

They appear for the most part with bodies of moderate height, cold, humid, attractive, with likeable voice, in human form, looking like an armed soldier. Their colour is translucent. Their movement is like silvery clouds. The sign that they have appeared, is that one who calls them will start shivering.

But their particular shapes are: A king riding a bear; an attractive young man; a woman holding a distaff; a dog; a she-bear; a magpie; a variable-coloured garment; a wand; a staff.

King Saba; his ministers: Hanyey, Yron, Alvedio

The spirits of the air on Wednesday are subject to the Southwest wind.

Their nature is to bring all kinds of metals, to reveal everything earthly, past, present, and future, to appease judges, to give victory in battle, to teach all experiments and rebuild destroyed knowledge, and to transmute bodies from mixed elements, conditionally, one into another. They also give sickness or health, elevate the poor, [cast down the high ones, bind] or unbind [spirits],[341] and to open locks. Such spirits have the operations of the others, but not with perfect power, but in virtue or knowledge.

---

341. Words in [ ] omitted from manuscript, but so H. and LIH, and to complete the sense.

342. Figure shows the angel Raphael, Mercury Kamea seal, circle, and King Saba. In marg.: "w" glyph.

[+ Angels of Wednesday:] Raphael, Miel, Seraphiel: *Estote adiutores mei* ["May you be my assistants,"] etc.

To the East: Mathlai, Tarmiel, Baraborat.

To the West: Ierescue, Mitraton.

To the North: Thiel, Rael, Iariahel, Venahel, Velel, Abviori, Vcirmiel.

To the South: Millet, Nelapa, Babel, Caluel (or Laquel).

Conjuration of Wednesday:

Coniuro et confirmo vos Angeli fortes, sancti et potentes, in nomine fortis, metuendissimi et benedicti, Ia, Adonay, Eloim, Saday, Saday, Saday, Eie, Eie, Eie, Asamie, Asaraie: et in nomine Adonay<e>, dei Israel, qui creavit luminaria magna, ad distinguendum diem a nocte: et per nomen omnium Angelorum deservientium in exercitu secundo coram Tetra Angelo maiori, atque forti et potenti: et per nomen stelle, que est Mercurius, et per nomen sigilli, quæ sigillatur a Deo fortissimo et honorat[i]o, per omnia predicta super te Raphael Angele magne Coniuro, qui es prepositus diei quartae: et per nomen sanctum quod erat scriptum in fronte Aaron sacerdotis altissimi creatoris et per nomina Angelorum, qui in gratia[m] salvatoris confirmati sunt: et per nomen sedis animalium habentium senas alas, quod pro me labores, et adimpleas omnem meam petitionem, iuxta meum velle et votum meum, in negotio et causa mea etc.

I conjure and encourage you, O strong, holy, and potent angels, in the name of the mighty, most fearful, and blessed Ia, Adonay, Eloim, Saday, Saday, Saday, Eie, Eie, Eie, Asamie, Asaraie, and in the name of Adonay, God of Israel, who created the great lights,[*] and distinguished day from night, and by the names of all the angels serving in the second army, in the presence of the great angel Tetra, strong and powerful, and by the name of the star which is Mercury, and by the name of its seal, which is a seal from God, most powerful and respected, and by all the previously mentioned names, and I call upon you, O great angel Raphael, who is placed in command of the fourth day; and by the holy name which was written on the front of the Aaron, highest priest of the Creator, and by the names of the angels who are well established in the grace of the saviour; and by the name of the seat of the living creatures, each having six wings,[†] that you work for me, and fulfil all my petitions, according to my will and desire, etc.

[*] Psalm 135:7 (KJV 136:7), Genesis 1:14.
[†] Revelations 4:8. The seraphin and cherubim are said to have six wings. Isa. 6:2.

[90]

The fumigation of Jupiter: Crocus (or Saffron)

The usual shapes of the spirits of Jupiter:

They appear with reddish and yellowish bodies, of medium stature, their movement is shaky,[343] their appearance is very mild, and their conversation is soothing. Their colour is rust-coloured. Their movement is flashing with thunder. The sign that they have appeared is that men will appear near the circle, who will appear to be getting devoured by lions.

Moreover, their particular forms are: A king riding a stag, with an unsheathed sword. A man wearing a mitre, with a long garment. A girl with a crown of laurel, decorated with the flowers. A bull. A stag. A peacock. An azure garment. A sword. Boxwood.

King: Forman; his ministers: Gewthren, Gewthem.[344]

The spirits of the air of Thursday are subject to the South wind.

Their nature is to acquire the love of women, cause people to be happy and joyful, pacify quarrels, calm enemies, heal the sick and make healthy persons sick, to bring or remove [+ condemnation].[345]

---

343. Latin *horribile*, which RT translates with the more common meaning, "horrible fearful," but the root *horreo* means to "move shakily." LIH: *trementissima in motu* ["very jittery movement"].

344. It is very interesting that this does not follow H., which reads "King Suth, ministers Maguth, Gutriz," but rather is closer to LIH, which reads: "Formione the king, and his ministers Guth, Maguth, and Guthryn."

345. Or losses. Following H.: *"adferre vel auferre damna."*

Sachiel. Castiel. Asasiel. esto adiutores mei etc.	Sachiel, Castiel, Asasiel,* may you be my assistants, etc.
* In marg. in pencil: "Azazel / P.L. I. 534."	

But because there have been no angels of the air reported beyond the fifth Heaven, therefore on Thursday say the following prayer towards the four parts of the world.

Ad Orientem	**To the east:**
O deus magne et excelse, et honorate, per Infinita secula. ego rogo te piisime pater etc.	O great God, exalted and honoured, through the infinite ages. I ask you most pious Father, etc.
Ad occidentem	**To the west:**
O deus, sapiens, clare et iuste ac divina clementia: ego rogo te piisime pater, quod meam petitionem, quod meum opus et meum laborem hodie debeam complere, et perfecte intelligere, tu qui vivis et regnas per infinita secula seculorum, amen.	O wise God, illustrious and just, with divine mercy, I ask you O pious Father, that my petition, that my work and my labour be fulfilled, and understood perfectly, who lives and reigns through the infinite ages, Amen.

346. Figure shows the angel Sachiel, Jupiter Circle, and King Forman. The seal of Jupiter in black at the bottom of the image is missing in Folger, but it has been added here for consistency and completeness. In marg.: "w" glyph.

Ad septentrionem	To the north:
O deus potens, fortis et sine principio. ego rogo te piissime pater etc.	O powerful God, strong and without beginning, I ask you O pious Father, etc.
Ad Meridiem	**To the south:**
O deus potens et misericors, ego rogo te piissime pater etc.	O God, powerful and merciful, I ask you O pious Father, etc.

Conjuration of Thursday

Coniuro et confirmo super vos Angeli sancti, per nomen Cados, Cados, Cados, Escher[e]ie, Escher[e]ie, Escher[e]ie, Hatim, ya, fortis, firmator seculorum, Cantine, Iaym, Ianic, Anic, Calbat, Sabbac Berifay, Alnaym: et per nomen Adonay qui creavit pisces et reptillia in aquis, et aves super faciem terre, volantes versus celos die quinto: et per nomina Angelorum |+ serventium in sexto exercitu coram pastore Angelo] sancto et magno et potenti principe: et per nomen stelle que est ♃ et per omnem [*nomen] sigilli sui: et per nomen Adonay, summi dei omnium creatoris: et per nomen omnium stellarum, et per vim et virtutem earum, et per nomina predicta coniuro te Sachiel Angele magne qui es prepositus diei Iovis, ut pro me labores, et adimpleas omnem meam petitionem, Iuxta meum velle et votum meum in negotio et causa mea etc.	I conjure and encourage you, O holy angels, by the name Cados, Cados, Cados, Eschereie, Eschereie, Eschereie, Hatim, Ya, Strong, strengthening the World, Cantine, Iaym, Ianic, Anic, Calbat, Sabbac Berifay, Alnaym, and by the name Adonay, who, on the fifth day, created the fishes and creeping things in the water, and the birds above the face of the earth, and by the names of the angels [serving in the sixth army before the angel Pastor], holy, great, and potent prince, and by the name of the star which is Jupiter, and by all his seals,* and by the name Adonay, highest God and creator of all things and by the names of all stars, and by their strength and virtue, and by the names mentioned before. I conjure you, O Sachiel, great angel, who has command over Thursday, that you labor for me, and fulfill all my petitions according to my will and desire in my business and plea.
* Probably a mistake for nomen sigilli sui ["the name of his seals"] as above, and as in H.	

[91]

♀ Fumigation of Venus: Costus.

King: Sarabotres; his ministers: Nasar, Manasa.[347]

The usual shapes of the spirits of Venus:

They will appear with attractive bodies, of medium stature, with amiable and pleasant face. Their colour is white or green, gilded from above. Their movement is like the clearest star.[348] The sign that they have appeared, is that girls will be seen playing outside the circle, calling for the one who invoked them to come and play.

Moreover, their particular forms are: A king with a sceptre, riding a camel; a girl with beautiful clothes; a nude girl; a she-goat; a camel; a pigeon; white or green garments; flowers; the herb savin.

The spirits of the air on Friday are subject to the west wind.

Their nature is to give silver, to arouse men, and incline them to extravagance, to bring harmony to enemies through extravagance, to make marriages, to gently draw men into love for women, to give or remove weakness, and to make all things that have movement.

349

---

347. Again, this follows Honorius, not Petrus.

348. Venus is commonly called "the clearest star."

349. Figure shows the angel Anael, Venus Kamea Seal, Circle, and King Sarabotres. In the marg.: "w" glyph.

Anael. Rachiel. Sachiel. estote adiutores mei etc.	Anael, Rachiel, Sachiel, be my assistants, etc.

To the east:

Setchiel, Chedisutaniel, Corat, Tamael, Tenaciel.

To the west:

Turiel, Coniel, Rabiel, Kadie, Maltiel, Hufaltiel.

To the north:

Peniel, Penael, Penat, Raphael, Raniel, Doremiel.

To the south:

Porna, Sachiel, Chermiel, Samael, Santaniel, Famiel.

O vos omnes, adiuro atque contestor etc. ["O all of you, I adjure and appeal to you, etc."]

Conjuration of Friday [350]

Coniuro et confirmo super vos sancti Angeli fortes atque potentes, in nomine On, Hey, Hey, a, Ia, Ic, Adonay, Saday, et in nomine Saday, qui creavit quadrupedia et animalia reptilia, et homines in sexto die, et Adae dedit potestatem super omnia animalia: unde benedictum sit nomen creatoris in loco suo: et per nomina Angelorum servientium in tertio exercitu coram Dagiel, Angelo magno principe forti atque potenti: et per nomen stelle, qui est Venus: et per sigillum eius, quod quidem est sanctum: et per nomina predicta coniuro super te Anaell, qui es prepositus diei sexte ut pro me labores et adimpleas omnem meam petitionem, iuxta meum velle et votum meum in negotio et causa mea etc.	I conjure and encourage you, O holy angels, strong and potent, in the name of On, Hey, Hey, a, Ia, Ic, Adonay, Saday, and in the name Saday, who created the four-footed creatures and creeping things, and men on the sixth day, and gave Adam power over all animals, from which blessed be the name of the creator in his place, and by the names of the angels serving in the third army, in the presence of the great angel Dagiel, strong and powerful, and by the name of the star which is Venus, and by its seal, because it is most holy, and by the names before mentioned, I call upon you, O Anael, who has been given command over the sixth day, that you work for me, and fulfil all my petitions, according to my will and desire, etc.

---

350. In left marg. in pencil: "p. 30"; in right marg.: "176."

[92]

The fumigation of Saturday: Sulfur

Maymon the king, his ministers:[351] Albewe, Malyke, Etheye, Alydee, Cherasa, but these be not so true as other of the other days.

The shapes familiar to the spirits of Saturn

They appear for the most part with long and slender bodies, with angry faces, having four faces, one in the back of the head, one on each cheek, and each has a beak. They likewise have faces on each knee. They have a black translucent colour. Their movement is like [the moving of the wind. The sign of their appearance is] [352] a white ground, much brighter than snow.[353]

Nevertheless, the particular forms are: A bearded king riding a dragon; an old man with a beard; an elderly woman, leaning on canes; a pig; a dragon; a horned-owl; a black garment; a sickle; a juniper.

The spirits of the air for Saturday [are subject to the southwest wind.]

Their nature is to sow discord, hatred, and evil thoughts, to give the metal lead if desired, and to kill anyone, and mutilate limbs. As above.

---

351. In left marg.: "p. 31 J Ms."; in right marg.: "176."

352. A line appears to have been accidentally omitted, but so Pseudo-Agrippa.

353. LIH: "Their bodies are long and slender, full of wrath and anger. They have four faces: one is forward, another behind, which have two large and long beaks measuring three feet, which can be seen devouring two serpents. The other two faces are on the two knees, which appear to be crying with most great mourning, and they are black in colour, and shining like a burnished mirror. Their movement is the moving of the wind with the appearance of an earthquake. Their sign is that the ground will appear to be white, covered with snow when they are invoked."

354

Cassiel. Machatan. Vriel. estote adiutores mei etc.	Cassiel, Machatan, Uriel, be my help-ers, etc.

Ad Orientem.	**To the east:**
O deus magne et excelse, et honorate per infinita secula: ego rogo te piisime pater quod me[am] peticionem, quod meum opus et meum laborem hodie de-beam complere, et perfecte intellige[re,] tu qui vivis et regnas per infinita secula seculorum, amen.	O God, great and exalted,[*] and hon-oured throughout the endless ages, I ask you, most pious Father, that my petition, that I will be able to fulfill my work and my labour today, and to understand fully, you, who lives and reigns forever and ever. Amen.
Ad septentrionem.	**To the west:**
O Deus potens fortis et sine prin-cipio ego rogo te benignissime pater etc.	O God, great, wise, illustrious and just, and the divine mercy, I ask you, O most merciful Father, etc.
[*] This duplicates Jupiter/Thursday. H. differs.	

354. Figure shows the angel Cassiel, Saturn Kamea Seal, Circle, and King Maymon. In marg.: "w" glyph.

Ad occidentem.	To the north:
O Deus Magne sapiens, clare et iuste, ac divina clementia: ego rogo te clementissime pater, etc.	O God, mighty, strong, and without beginning, I ask you, most kind Father, etc.
Ad Meridiem.	**To the south:**
O Deus potens et misericors ego rogo te magnissime pater etc.	O God, mighty and merciful, I ask you O most great Father, etc.

Conjuration for Saturday

Coniuro et confirmo super vos Caphriel vel Cassiel Machatori [*Machaton] et Seraquiell Angeli fortes et potentes: et per nomen Adonay, Adonay, Adonay, Eie, Eie, Eie, Acin, Acin, Acin [*Acim, Acim, Acim], Cados, Cados, [Ina vel] Ima, Ima, Saday, Ia, Sar, Domini formatoris seculorum qui in septimo die quievit: et per illum qui in beneplacito suo filiis Israell in hereditatem observandum dedit, vt eum firmiter custodirent et sanctificarent, ad habendum inde bonam in alio seculo remunerationem: et per omnia nomina Angelorum servientium in excercitu septimo Boell Angelo magno et potenti principi: et per nomen stelle que est Saturnus: et per sanctum sigillum eius, et per nomina predicta, Coniuro super te Caphriel qui es prepositus diei septimae, que est dies Sabati, quod pro me labores, et adimpleas omnem meam petitionem, iuxta meum velle et votum meum in negotio et causa mea etc.	I conjure and encourage, O Caphriel (or Cassiel), Machatori* (or *Machaton), and Seraquiel, strong and powerful angels, and by the name Adonay, Adonay, Adonay, Eie, Eie, Eie, Acin, Acin, Acin [*Acim, Acim, Acim], Cados, Cados, [Ina or] Ima, Ima, Saday, Ia, Sar, of the Lord shaper of the world, and on the seventh day rested, and by him who of his good pleasure decreed the same to be observed by the children of Israel, that they steadfastly guard and sanctify the same, thereby earning a good reward in the other world, and by all the names of the angels serving in the seventh host before the angel Boel, great and mighty prince, and by the name of his star, which is Saturn, and by his holy seal, and by the names previously spoken. I conjure upon you, O Caphriel, who has been placed in command of the seventh day, which is the Sabbath day, that you labour for me, and fulfill all my petitions, according to my will and vow, in my business and plea, etc.

* Machatori: so also H., but probably an error for Machaton.

[93]

[+ Directional and planetary incenses]

This being done,[355] suffumigate the four parts of the world and the four elements, east, west, north, and south.

For the part of the east and the fire serveth amber, musk, and white wax.

For the part of the west and the air serveth bathamus, camphor, and olive oil.

For the part of the north and the water serveth lignum aloes, nut, nutmeg, and mace.

For the part of the south and the earth serveth musk mallow, balsam of storax, and theriac.

Note[356] as there be seven heavens, seven stars, and seven days in the week, so there be seven suffumigations which holdeth with them the virtue of the seven stars, and maketh glad the spirits of the air, the angels of heaven, and the devils etc.

♄ Incenses of the Saturday after the opinion of Solomon, ought to be made of all good things and well-smelling roots, as costus and frankincense etc.

☉ Incenses of Sunday is mastic, musk, and other good gums.

☽ Incenses of Monday is myrtle leaf and bay laurel, and other leaves of good odours.

♂ Incenses of Tuesday is sandalwood, red, black, and white, and all such trees as cypress, etc.

☿ Incenses of Wednesday is nutmeg, cloves, and citrus and the rind of oranges dry powdered and other fruits of good savour.

♃ Incenses of Thursday[357] is cinnamon, cassia lignea, laurel bark, mace, and other good rinds.

♀ Incenses of Friday is musk, roses, violets, crocus, and other good flowers of savour, and to the contrary, contrary, put you all incenses stinking.

♄ the root ♃ the fruit ♂ the wood ☉ the gum ♀ the flowers ☿ the bark ☽ the leaves	This you may see, that each incense of good odours gathereth together his spirits: after his nature, colour, and his strength is, and further we see that all suffumigations are made of roots, trees, rinds, leaves, fruits, and gums, etc.

---

355. Compare parallel text on Folger p. 58. This section seems to be based on *Razielis*, Karr, "Liber Lunae," (2010), 100. In marg.: "177."

356. Compare Folger p. 56.

357. Note: The incenses for Wednesday and Thursday are accidentally switched. In marg: "[You] must take the odours [of] Wednesday for Thursday." Below this in marg.: "w" glyph.

Martagon [358] appium, insqrino, and artemisia, being made in suffumigation, mixed with coriander [and] cardamom, seven nights during the time of the citation, these being tempered with *aqua lapides*, gathereth spirits together.

Note that during the time that these suffumigations are in burning by the suffumigator, the master may take his ease and immediately after read the proper call of the spirits, etc., and by the space of one hour after, let the master read the invocation for Tantavalerion folii, also hemlock, henbane, and coriander burnt are good to urge the spirit a body.

Deus pater, Deu fillius, Deus spiritus sanctus ["God the Father, God the Son, God the Holy Ghost"] three persons and one great God and living God in trinity, and he is Alpha and Omega.

[+ List of Pagan gods]

1. Phoebus, is called the God of the Sun.	15. Bacchus, God of wine and excess.
2. Phoebe, God of the Moon.	16. Pan, God of shepherds and beasts
3. Apollo, God of wisdom.	17. Venus and Cupid, Gods of love.
4. Aeolus, God of the air and the winds.	18. Hebe, God of youth.
5. Aurora, God of the spring of the day.	19. Mercury, God of language, sciences, and eloquence.
6. Neptune, God of the seas and waters.	
7. Diana, Goddess of woods and chases.	20. Mars, the God of battle, and he by the sufferance of God doth change the nature of beasts.
8. Jupiter, God of riches.	
9. Juno, Goddess of riches and treasure.	
10. Ceres, Goddess of corn.	21. Hecate, Goddess of charmery and invocance.*
11. Saturn, God of gold and lead.	
12. Fortune is a variable God not a certain.	22. Morpheus, the opener of dreams.
13. Discord, the God of strife and debate.	23. Pluto, the God of hell.
	24. Minons, the Judge of hell.
	25. Cerberus, the porter of hell.
14. Isis, God of fruit.	26. Atropos, the God of death.
* Charmery and invocance: Magical arts.	

Saint Cyprian, Friar Bacon, Friar Bungi, Friar Lumbard, and others say that Lucifer, Beelzebub, Sathanas, Pluto, Minos, Asmodeus, Lamathan, Balberith, Balphegore, Baal, and Cerberus be chief rulers of hell, saving Tantavalarion, the emperor of hellish spirits.

---

358. In left marg.: "[…] quiam" (?)." In right marg.: "178."

[94]

These be they that make books and write books

I desire you, Obymero, *per noctem, et* ["by the night, and"] Symeam *et membres membris et* ["and members with members, and"] Lasys *cawtis nomis et Arypys,* ["in cautious districts and *Arypys* (?)"] that you do command in this hour, and make me, and that without any questioning, a very fair book, and in that form and shape, as that it shall be given you in commandment by me, and that it be done according to my will, at my coming in readiness, to the same book or books, and that they to be of such effect, when that I will, and that now you come to me to make true this book or books, and that now you forthwith do come here to me, and to fulfill the same, and that effectually, and thou Abrinno or Obymero, *per noctes* ["every night"], symon mobris, Laycon, Catys, Oropys, and drypys, you angels being the best writers, now do you here appear, and that in the shape of writers. Therefore in the name of the Father and the Son and the Holy Ghost, I now conjure you and that by him that created all things, and by this great and most fearful name + Tetragrammaton +[359] and by all other his blessed names, that now forthwith and that without any let or hurt, that now immediately you do come here to me and to make me such a book incontinent containing this form, and to write the same, and that now by the virtue of God, and all words, and by the virtue of these characters, that this book be written now forthwith. So be it.

Go you to some secret place, and that alone, and bear with thee quires of paper or parchment to make the book or books. Open thou thy book that thou callest them by, and say as afore, and bid them make a book of alchemy, or of art magic, conjuration, or nigromancy, or of what art or science thou wilt have it. *Finis.*

---

359. In marg.: "w" glyph.

A conjuration most necessary to the angels of each day to the obtaining of any spirit thou callest

I conjure,[360] adjure, and confirm upon you, O angels of God, mighty and good, in the name of + Adonay + Adonay, Adonay, Eye, Eye, Eye, V (?). God was, God is, and God shall be, and in the name of God, Cados, Cados, Cados, high sitting upon Cherubim, and by the great name of the strong God, high and mighty above all heavens, Eye, Saraye, the shaper of worlds, the Creator of heaven, earth, sea, and hell, and all in them that hath any being, O holy angels, I conjure and invocate you by him whose name is Jehovahh, that made the first day and sealed it with his own name Phaa, and by him which appeared in the Mount Sinai to Moses the great prophet and leader of his people Israel, whose name is Achim, Ia, and that with great glory, who made the waters, seas, floods, springs, wells, and fountains the second day, and sealed them with his own name I. that they should not pass their straits and bounds. I conjure and confirm upon you Angels mighty and holy, and that by the names of that high God, that made the third day from the water to appear dry land and called it the land, and sealed it with his own name I that it should bring forth trees and herbs of itself. I conjure you mighty angels, holy and of great power, in the name of the dreadful and blessed Ia, Adonay Eloim, Saday, Asarie, and in the name of Adonay God of Israel, that created great lights to divide the day from the night the fourth day and sealed it with his own name Phaa, that it should be unto times and tides, nights and days. I conjure you, O holy angels, by the mighty Escherie, the confirmer of worlds and by the name Adonay, that on the fifth day created fishes and all other creeping things in the waters, birds flying upon the face of the earth, and sealed it with his own name, Phaa. I conjure you, angels of great power in the name, On, Hey, Heya, Saday, and in the name Saday, that created all four-footed beasts and men in the sixth day and gave to Adam power upon them and upon all the works of his hands. I conjure you, O noble angels, strong and mighty, and by the name Acim, Ima, Sagla and Ia, the Lord of Lords, which in the seventh day rested and gave it as a law to the children of Israel to be observed as a holy and sanctified day. I conjure and exorcise you, O angels of great power, by the seven notable, coruscant,[361] and splendishing[362] stars, the Sun, the Moon, Mars, Mercury, Jupiter, Venus, Saturn, and by the great name of God, Tetragrammaton, the mighty name Agla, the wonderful name Adonay, the strong name, El, and the name On, names of singular majesty, O angels, by all these and all others

---

360. In left marg.: "9." Below that in pencil: "p. 5 J MS...." Also in left marg. in red ink are symbols for the planets or days of the week – ☉☽♂☿♃♀♄, but not lined up with text (as far as JHP can tell). In right marg.: "184."

361. Coruscant: glittering.

362. Splendishing: shining.

most reverent and high names of God both effable and ineffable, known and unknown, which I, by reason of mine imbecility and weakness, dare not to attempt as
once to be so hardy to name nor excogitate, by these *iterum atque iterum*, again and
again and so many times again as there be stars in the sky, sands on the shores, [95]
fishes in the sea,[363] and grasses upon the face of the earth, I conjure and adjure, urge
and constrain, confirm and compel, bid and command you and every of you, one and
all, jointly and severally, to give and yield unto me, as now in this perilous work your
strengths and aid, and that you command by and under the licence of your God
whose messengers to serve you, you [sic] are, that as certainly as thou, O Michael, art
appointed to ☉ to protect and govern the people of God, and that by invincible
strength, as true as thou, O Raphael, was attributed *ad Tobie, ☿ ut parentum Sanaret,
ex periculis liberat filium, et ei uxorem suam adduxerit* ["to Tobiah, ☿ that he cure his
parent, free his son from danger, and lead his wife to him"], as assuredly as thou O
Gabriel,[364] wast appointed the most joyful ambassador to the most pure, holy, and
chaste Virgin Mary, *virgo ante partum in partu et post partum* ["a virgin before giving
birth and after giving birth"], and greeting her with this undoubted salutation, *Ave
gratia plena Dominus tecum* ["Hail Mary, full of grace; the Lord is with you"], and as
Daniel received consolation from his God by thee, and Zacharie *pater Iohanes Baptiste* ["the father of John the Baptist"] for his incredulity and unbelief was stricken
dumb, and for a time lost his speech, so certainly, truly, and undoubtedly, O you holy,
mighty, and excellent angels, I beseech and pray you, yea, and I in the name of your
God whose spirits you are, I do charge and command you that you and every one of
you licence and permit all superior spirits and devils, to compel, urge, and command
this spirit N. to come speedily, and to appear visibly here in a circle for him made and
prepared with his name written therein, and that in a fair human shape and form,
even like a child of three years of age, without the molestation of the air or hurting of
any creature bearing life, annoying of beasts, or fearing of me or any of my fellows,
and that being come, he do his best to the uttermost of his office and duty to tell,
show, and declare, yield, give, and deliver to me the simple truth and nothing but the
truth of all such things I shall ask, require, or demand of him, and also if he shall be
stubborn and pertinent in contempt and not obedient to me, calling upon him by the
mighty power of your and my God, that then you cause and enforce the same spirits,
superiors, magistrates, and rulers, to punish, vex, trouble, molest, and torment him
the said rebellious and contemning spirit, with all the hellish and unspeakable pains
and languishings, and that if he be in joy, to diminish the same, and if he be in pain,

---

363. In right marg.: "185."
364. In right marg.: "☽."

to augment and multiply it, and also, O you most excellent, potent angels, I pray and beseech you to grant and yield unto me your + (?) succors that I may have power to call, to urge, to compel, to bind, to curse, to make obedient, to release, and to dismiss the same spirit N., he fulfilling my will and desire, and I conjure and straightly charge you and every of you, by all the words now spoken, and in this book written, and in the most high and secret art in nigromancy contained and by the rod of Moses, the Ark of God and most high and mighty Name of God, written in the forehead of Aaron the Priest [365] of the super excellent and honourable God, by all these I invocate upon you, O angels, and by this most terrible name and name of singular power + Tetragrammaton + that you labor for me and do your endeavour that I may have this my petition granted, my will fulfilled, and my desire accomplished, according as shall be most acceptable to the good pleasure of my God, necessary for the health of my soul, and the utility of my body, that is that this spirit N. may presently without delay visibly come and appear personally in fair and human form, *quasi puer tres annos natie* ["as if a child of three years of age"], and truly to declare, and true answers to make, to all interrogatories, questions, or demands as shall be by me or any other of my fellows or associates prepouned [366] or in any wise delivered, and that he may do his office and duty to the uttermost and nothing thereof to keep back, nor conceal from me and us, but be by God's permission, your aid and our calling upon, ready to minister the same presently, and the very time to him limited to him and assigned. This grant Good Lord God who livest and reignest in glory sempiterne without beginning and without ending, now and forever, for thy dear son's sake Jesus Christ, the everlasting and true word, the Immaculate Lamb, the saviour of mankind, and the most just judge, to whom together with the Holy Spirit sanctifier of all the elects, be praise and glory. Amen, Amen.

O Angeli supradicti, estote adiutores mee petitionis et [in] adiutorium mihi in meis rebus et petitionibus. O vos Angeli omnes, adiuro atque contestor, per sedem Adonay, per Agios Otheos, Iskyros,	O angels spoken of before, be my helpers in these petitions, and help me in my affairs and petitions. O all you angels, I adjure and appeal to you, by the seat of Adonay, by Agios, Otheos, Iskyros,
* Compare H. "On the Manner of Working."	

---

365. In marg.: "w" glyph.
366. Prepouned: propounded.

Athanatos, Paracletos, Alpha, et Omega,	Athanatos, Paraclete, Alpha and Omega,
et per hac tria nomina secreta + Agla +	and by these three secret names + Agla +
On + Tetragrammaton + quod hodie	On + Tetragrammaton + that this day
deb[e]atis, adimplere quod cupio. pro T.	you might fulfill what I desire. On behalf
B. et M. B.	of T. B. and M. B.*

| * "Pro T. B. et M. B." is in brown ink in a later hand. |

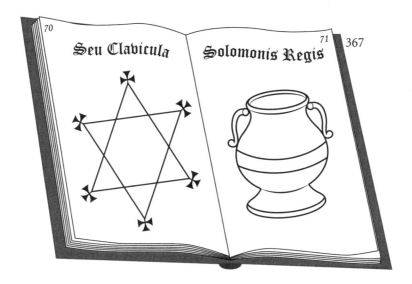

[96]

The order of the circle work

Accingimini filii potens et / estote	Be prepared, O mighty children, and
parati in hoc tempore quoniam melius	be ready now, because it is better for us
est / nobis mori in servitia dei, quam vi-	to die in the service of God, than to see
vere mala gentis / per valebunt	the calamities of the people prevail.*

| * Compare *Divinum Officium Matutinum: Accingimini filii potentes, et estote parati: quoniam melius est nobis mori in bello, quam videre mala gentis nostrae, et sanctorum.* This hymn from 1 Maccabees 3.58 is also used in the Mass on some occasions. For example, see Catholic Church, *Breviarium Romanum Ex Decreto Sacrosancti Concilii Tridentini Restitutum, Etc.* ([Cambrai]: ex Ducali Campidonensi Typographeo, 1796), 530. |

---

367. Probably added in the nineteenth century.

O filii omni tempore be / nedic deum, et pete ab eo viam vos diri- / gat, et omni tempore concilia vos in / ipso permaneant.	O children, bless God at all times, and pray that he guides your path, and at all times remain in his council.[*]

* Compare Responsorio de Tobia.

Orate fratres pro me / ut meum hoc operum pariter que vestrum, / acceptum sit Domino deo, et Illumina cor meum / et labia mea: et accipiat dominus digne hec / opera et habeam desideriis, meis Amen.	Pray, O brothers, on my behalf, that this work of mine, and also yours, may be acceptable to the Lord God, and illuminate my heart and my lips, and may the Lord accept this work that I may have my desires. Amen.

The Order of the Circle Work

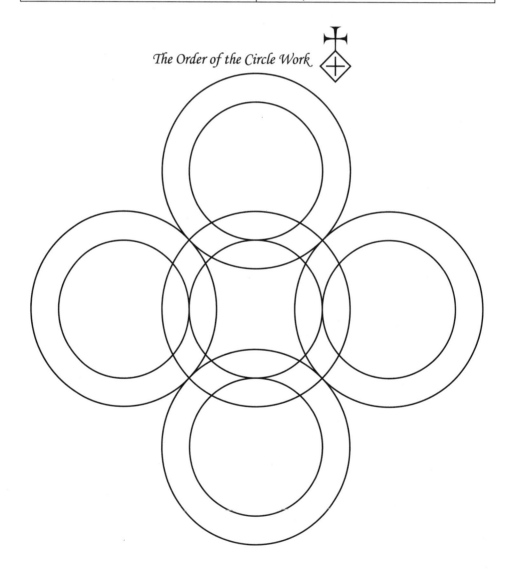

[97]

Associates say kneeling, these Psalms as follows: [368]

1. Psalm 115: I have believed, therefore I have spoken…

2. Psalm 119: I cried to the Lord in my trouble…

3. Psalm 139: Deliver me, O Lord, from the evil man…

4. Psalm 140: I have cried to you, O Lord, hear me…

5. Psalm 141: With my voice I cried to the Lord…

The consecration of the circle, the master standing in the midst [369]

Coniuro te circulum, et locum istum per illum verum deum qui istam Terram creavit, sanctifico + et consecro + te circulum, et locum istum, per ipsum Creatorem qui totum mundum de nichilo creavit et fecit, et per ista eius nomina sanctissima + Theos + Otheos + Yskiros + Athanatos + Ioth + Agla + On + Eloe + Eloy + Elyon + Ya + TETRAGRAMA-TON + et per omnia alia nomina sane tissima mihi nota et ignota sit locus iste et circulus iste ex dona gratiem [*gratiarum] omnipotentis altissimi dei benedictus + et consecratus + sanctificatus + et custoditus + et societatem omniu[m] sanctorum dei, et sanctorum Angelorum et Archangelorum, dominationum, principatum, potestatem, virtutem, cherubine, et Seraphine, prophetarum, Apostolorum, Evangelistarum, Martirum,	I conjure you, O circle, and this place, by that true God who created this Earth. I sanctify + and consecrate + you, O circle, and this place, by the Creator himself who created and fashioned the whole universe from nothing, and by these most holy names: + Theos + Otheos + Yskiros + Athanatos + Ioth + Agla + On + Eloe + Eloy + Elyon + Ya + TETRAGRAMATON + and by all other most holy names known or unknown by me, may this place and this circle by the gift of the grace of the almighty and most high God + blessed + and consecrated + and sanctified + and guarded + and the society of all of God's saints and holy Angels and Archangels, Dominations, Principalities, Powers, Virtues, Cherubin, and Seraphin, and of his prophets, apostles, evangelists, martyrs,

---

368. The Psalms are here numbered according to the vulgate. KJV numbers are 116, 120, 140, 141, and 142.

369. In right marg.: "153"; in left marg. in pencil: "I think this is in the Secretum Secretorum Ms." Compare with the "consecratio circuli" on Folger p. 39.

Patriarcharum, Confessorum, atque virginum, potenter confirmatus, et Reconciliatus Circulus et locus iste, quatinus talem virtutem habeat potestatem et sanctitatem suam capiat et optineat a signo dei vivi et veri, et a sancta Christi cruce + quod nullus spiritus malignus habeat aliquam potestatem locum aliqualiter ingredi nec inter circulum istum terrores fantasma tymores nec temptaciones aliquo modo nobis nocendo valeant inferri ipso iuvante et defendente cui celestia terrest[r]ia et infernalia subiiciuntur, per Dominum nostrum Iesum Christum fillium tuum, qui vivis et regnas deus in seccula secculorum Amen.	patriarchs, confessors, and virgins,* powerfully strengthened, and restored circle and this place, that it may have such virtue and power, and may keep and possess holiness from the image of the living and true God, and from the holy cross of Christ + that no evil spirit may have any power or place to advance into this circle, nor cause any terrors, phantasms, fears, nor temptations of any kind, nor have power to harm us, with His help and protection, to whom all powers of heaven, earth, and Hell are subject, by our Lord Jesus Christ, your son, who lives and reigns, God forever and ever. Amen.

* In marg.: "w" glyph.

Here sprinkle the circle with holy water

Surgite sancti de mantionibus vestris loca sanctifficate nobis, et omnes spiritus qui hic fuerunt benedicite, et nos humiles peccatores in pace custodite [*custodire].	Arise, O holy ones, from your dwellings; sanctify our places, and bless all spirits who have been here, and watch over us humble sinners in peace.*

* Compare this antiphon used in the dedication of churches: *Surgite sancti de mansionibus vestris loca sanctificate plebem benedicite et nos humiles peccatores in pace custodire alleluia* ["Arise, O holy ones, from your dwellings; sanctify our places, bless the people, and watch over us humble sinners in peace. Alleluia."]. Catholic Church; Martin Gerbert, *Monumenta Veteris Liturgiae Alemannicae*, Pars II (S. Blas: Typis San-Blasianis, 1777), 60.

Then say this in the four parts, etc.[370]

Per cruce + hoc signum fugiat pro[c]ull omne malignum, et per idem signum salvetur quotque benignum.	By this sign + of the cross, may all evil flee away, by the same sign may all good be preserved.

370. In marg.: "139." Compare Scot, *Discouerie of Witchcraft*, 241.

This being said and done, take the sword and do as followeth.

Take the sword and therewith make [four][371] crosses in the four parts of the world, first the east, west, south, and north, then turn to the east and say as followeth:

Oremus eas	Let us pray to them
Deus totius pietatis, autor [+ et] fundamentum qui per os unigeniti filii tui dixisti domus meam domus orationes vocabitur, hanc partem orientialem + purificari + benedicere + et sanctificare + consecrare + digneris, et adversus omnes Nove hostitias et illusione protegere digneris cum eius habitati, omnibus, per gloriosam maiestatem tuam in qua gloriosissimam regnans et regnaturus es in secula secculorum. Amen.	O God of all piety, author, and foundation, who by the mouth of your only begotten son you said "my house shall be called a house of prayer"[*] deign to + purify + bless + sanctify + and consecrate + this eastern part, and deign to protect against all unusual hostilities and illusions[†] which inhabit it, through your most glorious majesty, in which you reign and will reign most gloriously, forever and ever. Amen.
* Matthew 21:13.	
† Latin unclear; reading *"omnes novas hostilitates et illusiones."*	

Then go into the west, and with the sword crossing it, say as you continue:

Deus qui per unigenitum tuum et eius Introitum ulnas per carum (?) hierusalem sanctificasti te suppliciter exoramus, ut hunc partem occidentalem et omnes in ipso habitantes + purificari + benedicere +sanctificare + consecrare + adversus omnes malignas illusiones spiritum protegere digneris, per gloriosissime regnas etc.	O God, who through your only-begotten, as you sanctified the gates at the entrance to Jerusalem,[*] we humbly beg that you deign + to purify + bless + sanctify + and consecrate + this western part and its inhabitants, and protect against all evil deceits of spirits, by your most glorious reign, etc.
* This passage has a precursor in the *oratio introitus in eclesiam* ["prayer of the entrance into the church"] in some old monastic prayer books; see Catholic Church and Robert of Jumièges, *The Missal of Robert of Jumièges*, Volume 11 (London, 1896), 280. Also Josef Anton Mesmer, Über den Mittelalterlichen Kunstausdruck Galiläa" *Mittheilungen der Kaiserlich-Königlichen Central-Commission zur Erforschung und Erhaltung der Baudenkmale,* 6, no. 4 (n.d.): 104–5.	

---

371. There is a space, presumably to switch ink.

Into the south and say as you continue:

Deus cuius proprium infima sublivari, et in te confidentes semper cadere, te suppliciter exoramus ex dono gracie tue hanc partem meridionalem et omnes in ipso habitantes + purificare etc.	O God, whose nature is to elevate the humble, trusting in you to always raise the fallen, we humbly beg you from your gift of grace, + to purify + bless + sanctify + and consecrate + this southern part, and all its inhabitants, etc.

In the north

Domine omnipotens qui de nichillo cuncta formasti qui ad te voce clamantes benignitur exaudis, te laudamus + Te Adoramus + Te benedicimus + Te glorificamus + Te supplices + exoramus ut hanc partem septentrionale et omnes in ipso habitantes adversus omnes malignos spiritus illusiones protegere etc.	O almighty Lord who created all things from nothing, who clearly hears the voice calling out to you, and rejoices, + we praise you, + we honour you, + we bless you, + we glorify you, + we humbly beseech you, + we beg you to protect this northern part and all its inhabitants against the deceits of all evil spirits, etc.

This done, go into the midst of the circle, turning into that part the spirit is, and say

O God the Creator of all things, which hast separated heaven and earth, and hast placed the deep in the bottom thereof, and hast given original increase unto all creatures in fire, in air, in water, and earth, which hast made the Sun, the Moon, and orders of stars, which hast created angels in the appointing of light, which hast formed man unto thine own similitude, and hast inspired him with the breath of life, hast coupled Eve unto him for his wife, being formed of a rib taken out of his side, which hast cast them from the paradise of pleasure, for the breach of thy commandments, which spakest unto Moses thy servant in the midst of the fiery bush, which didst cause the rod of Aaron to wax green [98] and to bring forth buds and fruits, which opened a way unto the people of Israel, through the midst of the Red Sea, and didst therein overthrow and drown Pharaoh with his whole army, which gavest food to Elijah by a raven, which didst deliver Jonas from the belly of the whale, wherein he lay three days, which preservedst the three young men, Shadrach, Meshach, and Abednego, from the violence of the hot burning oven, which didst send thy only begotten son into the world for the salvation of mankind, which didst raise Lazarus, being dead and stinking, which gavest sight to the blind, speech to the dumb, hearing to the deaf, and restored the health to his limbs, which by his death hath restored to life the lost world, O God, which hast done these things and others innumerable that neither tongue can express, nor man's mind conceive, we humbly pray and beseech thee that thou wilt vouchsafe, with thy great might to purify + bless + sanctify + and make holy both us and our circle,[372] that it may be a place of preservation, protection, and defense for us against all wicked illusions of deceivable spirits, and that by thy holy and blessed commandment and virtue of thy Son's cross + grant Lord that they have no power over us, by thy glorious majesty, in the which thou dost and shalt reign most gloriously, now and forever and world without end. Amen.

Then cense[373] the circle with suffumigations meet and convenient, etc., but first bless both [sic] the censer, the fire, and the suffumigations.

O God,[374] which in the finger of thy deity hast healed all kind of plagues, and hast restored the diseased unto their former health, grant now, I pray and humbly beseech thee, that this N. of metal etc. may be touched + blessed + and sanctified by thy deity, that by the dignity of thy name it may serve to the operation to which it is prepared: by him which liveth and reigneth God for ever and ever. Amen.

O God, which despisest not the petitions of wretches, nor the voices of them that cry unto thee, grant we humbly beseech thee, that we invocate thy mercy, we may feel thy deity healthful unto us[375] by Christ our Lord. Amen.

O God, pour out here thy marvelousness and vouchsafe by the holiness of thy Godhead to consecrate + bless + and sanctify + this kind of instrument, that it may give in all our actions wholesome remedy.

O Almighty God, increase, I beseech thee, the gifts of thy deity over this kind of instrument, that it may more effectually by the disposition of thy divine grace serve us, that by it we may come and aspire to our desire, by Christ our Lord to whom with God the Father and the Holy Spirit be all honour and glory, power, and dominion, now and forever and ever. Amen.

Then sprinkle with holy water.

---

372. In right marg.: "139."

373. In marg.: "153."

374. In left marg.: "w" glyph; in right marg.: "154." Compare Sloane 3850, fol. 130r.

375. Echoes of LIH?

The blessing of the fumigations [376]

Deus Abraham, Deus Isaac, Deus Iacob, Benedic hunc creaturas specierum, ut vim et virtutem odorum suorum amplient, ne hostis nec phantasma in eis intrare possit, per Dominum nostrum Iesum Christum fillium tuum qui tecum vivit et regnat in unitate spiritus sancti deus per omnia seccula secculorum, Amen.	O God of Abraham, God of Isaac, God of Jacob, bless these creatures of the spices, that the power and strength of their scents may be made greater, that no enemies or phantasms may be able to enter, through our Lord Jesus Christ your son, who lives and reigns with you in unity with the Holy Ghost, God forever and ever. Amen.

Then sprinkle with holy water.

The exorcism of the fire, over which the fumigations are placed

NOTE: The fire which must be used for fumigations must be in a new clay or earthenware vessel.

Then exorcise in this manner:

Exorcizo te creatura ignis, per illum per quem facta sunt omnia, ut statim omne phantasma eijcias ate, ut nocere non possit in aliquo.	I exorcise you, O creature of fire, by Him through whom all things were made, that all phantasms may be cast out immediately, and be unable to harm in any way.

Then say:

Benedic domine creatura istam ignis, et sanctiffica + ut benedicta sit in collandationem nominis tui sancti, ut nullo nocumento sit gestantibus, nec videntibus, per dominum nostrum Iesu, Christum fillium tuum, qui tecum vivit et regnat in unitate spiritus sancti deus, per omnia secula secculorum Amen.	Bless, O Lord, this creature of fire, and sanctify it + for the praise of your holy name, that no harm may come from bearing or seeing it, through our Lord Jesus Christ, your son, who lives and reigns with you in unity with the Holy Ghost, God forever and ever. Amen.

Then let the master compass the circle seven times about, censing it and burning fumigations, saying,

---

376. Compare parallel version on Folger p. 27.

dirigatur domine ad te oratio mea sicut Incensum in conspectu tuo, elevatio manum nostrarum sacraficium vespertinum.	Let my prayer be guided* to your sight, O Lord, like incense: the lifting up of our hands, like the evening sacrifice.†
* In marg.: "154 (?)." † Paraphrased from Psalm 140:2.	

[99]

Note[377] that he shall stay in the four quarters—first east, west, north, and south—so long that he may say the whole *dirigatur* aforesaid. Which being done, cast holy water all about the circle, saying "Sprinkle me, O Lord," etc.

Then take the sword hallowed and make four crosses in the four quarters thereof and say,

Domine deus esto mihi Tueris fortitudinis contra omnium malignorum.	O Lord God, be a tower of strength to me against all evil.*
* Compare Psalm 60.	

Then go into the east and hold up your sword and cast your arms abroad and say,

Ecce signum + Nomina triumphatoris per quem vos cotidie ex pavescitis et timetis, obedite ergo mihi O N per hac verba seecretissima secretarum.	Behold the sign + the names of the triumphant, which continually cause you dread and fear. Therefore, obey me, O N., by these words—the most secret of secrets.

This done in all quarters, lay down the sword, the point towards the east, and place every man in his place, and assign unto them their office.

Then turn thy face into the east and say on thy knees as followeth:

Angelus qui mentis [*meus] es custos pietate superna, me tibi comissum serva, defenda, guberna, benedicat me Imperialis Maiestas, foveat me regalis	O angel who is my guardian, through heavenly love we are brought together, defend and guard me. May the imperial Majesty bless me; may the royal Divinity

---

377. Compare Mathers *The Key of Solomon*, I.5; Aubrey 24, f73v. In marg.: "153."

divinitas, custodiat me sempiterna deitas, protegat me gloriosa unitas deffende me Immensa Trinitas, dirigat me Ineffabilis bonitas, regat me potencia patris vivificet me sapientia, fillii, Illuminet me virtu spiritus sancti + Alpha + et Omega + deus et homo sit ista Invocatio mihi salus et protectio, Amen, amen.	favour me; may the eternal Deity guard me; may the glorious Unity protect me; may the infinite Trinity defend me; may the ineffable Goodness direct me; may the mighty Father rule over me; may the wise Son vivify me, may the virtuous Holy Ghost enlighten me, Alpha and Omega, God and Man. May I, your servant, the same one who is calling, have health and protection.*

* Compare Folger p. 181. In marg.: "w" glyph.

Then say this, making the fumigation answerable for the days.

Munda me domine ab omni inquinamento mentis et corporis ut possim mund[at]us implere hoc opus sanctum.	Cleanse me, O Lord, from all impurity of mind and body, that I may be clean to complete this holy work.*

* From the mass—order of communion.

In spritu humilitatis et in animo contritio suscipiamur domine a te: et sic fiat factum nostrum in conspectu tuo a te suscipiatur hodie et placeat tibi domine deus.	Accept us, O Lord, in the spirit of humility, and contrite heart, and grant that the act which we offer today in your sight may be pleasing to you, O Lord God.

Libera nos quesumus domine ab omnibus malis preteritis presentibus et futuris, et da pacem in diebus nostris ut opere miserecordie tue adiuti et ab ira et malignancia diaboli simus semper liberi, et ab omni perturbacione securi.	Deliver us, O Lord, from all evil, past, present, and to come, and grant us peace in our days, that with the help of your mercy, we may always be free from anger and the malice of the devil, and safe from all distress.

Veni sancte spiritus reple tuorum corda fidelium, et tui amoris in eis ignem accende. 3 tymes.	Come, O Holy Ghost, fill the hearts of your faithful, and enkindle the fire of your love in them. (3 times.)

Sancti spiritus ascendit [*adsit] nobis gratia\<m\>, que corda nostra sibi faciat habitacula.	May the grace of the Holy Ghost ascend [*be present] with us; may it make a home in our hearts.*

* Sarum Missal: *Sancti Spiritus adsit nobis gratia, quae corda nostra Sibi faciat habitacula, expulsis inde cunctis vitiis spiritalibus.*

Oremus	**Let us pray**

Domine miserere mei sana animam meam quia peccavimus tibi deus qui contritum cor et humilitatem nunquam despicis, sed potius benigniter respicis, et qui potestatem [*peccantem] non statim iudicas, sed confessionem et penitenciam et meritum expectas: te queso ut facinorum celerum [*scelerem] et omnium peccatorum meorum squalares [*squalores] abstergas per gloriosissimam Maiestatem tuam in qua gloriosissime regnas et regnaturus es in secula seculorum. Amen.	"O Lord, have mercy on me. Heal my soul, because we [sic] have sinned against you."* O God, who never despises a contrite and humble heart, but rather looks upon it kindly, and who does not quickly judge a sinner, but await their confession, penance, and redemption, I beg you to wash away the wickedness of my deeds, and the filth of all my sins, through the most glorious greatness by which you most gloriously reign and will reign forever and ever. Amen.

* Psalm 40:5 (KJV 41:4). Compare this paragraph with Véronèse, *L'Ars Notoria Au Moyen Âge*, oration "Theos patir vehemens."

Then let the master say, and the associates answer.

Kyrie eleyson.	Lord have mercy.
Christe eleyson.	Christ have mercy.
Kirie Eleyson.	Lord have mercy.
Creator omnium rerum deus, miserere nobis	O God, Creator of all things, have mercy on us.
Christe filli dei vivi, miserere nobis,	O Christ the Son of the living God, have mercy on us.
Spiritus sancte paraclite deus, miserere nobis,	O God the Holy Ghost, Paraclete, have mercy on us.
Sancta Trinitas unus deus, miserere nobis.	O God the Holy Trinity, have mercy on us.

~~Sancta Maria Mater dei, ora deum ut mi misereat nobis.~~ ~~Sancta dei genitrix ora deum ut miserere nobis.~~ ~~Sancta virgo virginum ora deum ut miserere nobis.~~ ~~Sanctem Michael ora deum ut misereatur nobis.~~ ~~Sanctem Gabriell ora deum ut misereatur nobis.~~ ~~Sanctem Raphaell ora deum ut misereatur nobis.~~ ~~Sanctem Cherubime ora deum pro nobis.~~ ~~Sancte Seraphine ora deum pro nobis.~~ ~~Sancte Virtutes ora deum pro nobis.~~ ~~Sancte Dominationes ora deum pro nobis.~~ ~~Sancte Potestates ora deum pro nobis.~~	[Crossed out:] Holy Mary,* mother of God, pray to God to have mercy on us. Holy mother of God, pray to God to have mercy on us. Holy virgin of virgins, pray to God to have mercy on us. Holy Michael, pray to God to have mercy on us. Holy Gabriel, pray to God to have mercy on us. Holy Raphael, pray to God to have mercy on us. Holy Cherubim pray to God for us. Holy Seraphin, pray to God for us. Holy Virtues, pray to God for us. Holy Dominations, pray to God for us. Holy Powers, pray to God for us.

* This seems to have been adapted from the Litany of the Saints.

~~Sancte principatus ora deum pro nobis.~~ ~~Sancte Throni ora deum pro nobis.~~ ~~Omnes sancti Angeli et Archangeli et omnes Spiritus sanctus ora deum pro nobis~~ ~~Omnes sancte patriarcharum proph- ete orate deum pro nobis.~~ ~~Omnes sancti Apostoli evangeliste dei orate deum pro nobis.~~ ~~Omnes sancti discipuli domini orate pro nobis.~~ ~~Omnes sancti domini Innocenti et virgines et vidue et omnes sancti et dei sancte dei orate deum pro nobis Amen.~~	Holy Principalities, pray to God for us. Holy Thrones, pray to God for us. All ye holy Angels and Archangels, and all ye holy spirits, pray to God for us. O holy prophet of the patriarchs, pray to God for us. O holy evangelists of the apostles, pray to God for us. O holy disciples of the Lord, pray to God for us. O holy innocents, and virgins, and widows, and all ye saints of the Lord—male and female—pray to God for us. Amen.

[100]	*[100]*
Oremus	Let us pray
~~This must the master say alone.~~	[Crossed out:]
~~Propitius esto nobis peccatoris do=~~ ~~mine, vell mihi peccatoris domine per~~ ~~Annunciacionem tuam, misere nobis~~ ~~domine,~~	This* must the master say alone:
	O Lord, be gracious to us sinners (or to me, a sinner), by your annunciation; have mercy on us, O Lord.
~~per Nativitatem tuam, miserere nobis~~ ~~domine, vel mei domine,~~	By your nativity, have mercy on us (or on me), O Lord.
~~per Baptismum tuum, miserere~~ ~~nobis domine,~~	By your baptism, have mercy on us, O Lord.
~~per ievinium [*ieiunium] tuum,~~ ~~miserere nobis domine,~~	By your fasting, have mercy on us, O Lord.
~~per omnia Miracula tua, miserere~~ ~~domine,~~	By all your miracles, have mercy, O Lord.
~~per crucem et passionem tuam,~~ ~~Miserere domine,~~	By your cross and passion, have mercy, O Lord.
~~per preciosam mortem tuam, miser=~~ ~~ere domine,~~	By your precious death, have mercy, O Lord.
~~per gloriosam Resurectionem tuam,~~ ~~Miserere domine,~~	By your glorious resurrection, have mercy, O Lord.
~~per Admirabilem ascentionem tuam,~~ ~~Miserere domine,~~	By your wonderful ascension, have mercy, O Lord.
~~per Adventum sancti spiritus pera=~~ ~~cliti, Miserere domine,~~	By the advent of the Holy Ghost Paraclete, have mercy, O Lord.

* It is not clear why this section was crossed out.

ab omni malo, libera <me> nos domine, a subitania et Improvisa morte, libera nos domine, ab omnia peccato, libera nos domine vell libera me domine, ab omni scandela et dampno, libera nos domine,	Deliver us (or me) O Lord from all evil; deliver us O Lord from sudden and unforeseen death; deliver us (or me) O Lord from all sin; deliver us O Lord from all temptations and damnation.

Oremus	Let us pray.

This must the master say alone: [378]

Deus cui proprium est misereri semper, et parcere absolucionem et ablucionem omnium peccatorum meorum nostrorum tribuere et peccatoribus veniam prestare largire, queso mihi peccatori Indulgemus remissionem, et absolucionem omnium peccatorum meorum spacium vere penitencie emendationem moris et vite, Amorem tuam gratiam et consolacionem Sancti spiritus, per gloriosam maiestatem tuam in qua gloriosissime regnas et regnaturus es in secula seculorum Amen.	O God, whose nature is to be merciful always, and to forgive and grant the absolution and washing away of all my (or our) sins, and to grant favours to sinners, I beg that you grant forgiveness to me, a sinner, and absolution of all my sins, time for true repentance and correction of life and death, along with your love, grace, and the consolation of the Holy Ghost, through your glorious majesty, who reigns most gloriously, and will reign forever and ever. Amen.

Then let the master say this:

Ascendat ad te domine deus meus omnipotens clamor meus, et exaudi orationem et deprecationem meam	Let my cry ascend to you, O Lord my God almighty, and hear my prayer and my supplication.[*]

* Compare Psalm 101:2. This series of prayers is also found in Rawlinson D. 252, 142r ff.

Miserere mei opus manum tuarum et dimitte mihi quod in te commisi [*ommisi].	Have mercy on me, the work of your hands, and forgive me for having disregarded you.[*]

* In left marg.: "w" glyph; in right marg.: "159." Latin has "*ommisi.*" Folger reads *commisi* ["I have brought together"]. JHP would expect to see "*in te peccavi*" ["I have sinned against you"].

Declara mihi gratiam et virtutem tuam: et occulta sapientie tue manifesta mihi.	Declare to me your grace and virtue, and reveal to me your hidden wisdom.[*]

* Compare Psalm 50:8 (KJV 51:8).

Et ostendo mihi Angelos et spiritus tuos iuxta desiderium meum: et fac me cognoscere illos.	And reveal to me your angels and spirits, just as I desire, and make them recognize me.

---

378. In marg.: "158."

Sis mihi domine copiosus miserecordia tua: ne peticiones mee vanae fiant.	May your mercy be abundant to me, O Lord; let not my prayers be in vain.

Benedictus es domine qui sapientiam dedisti timentibus te: qui dedistis agnitionem hominibus per quam te cognoscunt et timent.	You are blessed, O Lord, who have given wisdom to those who fear you. You give perception to them, by which they recognize you, and they are afraid.

Qui fideles tuos a Morte deffendis: in cuius etiam manu est omnia Anima vivens.	You defend your faithful from death; in his hand is the soul of every living thing.*
* Compare Job 12:10.	

Tu vero cum piis es hominibus bonum concedens: cum malis vero malum.	Truly you are with the blessed; you grant good to men, truly evil with the evil.

Tu qui servis tuis confers sapientiam: per quem omnis creature tue excolere possunt te benedictum	You who bring wisdom to your servants, through which all your creation is able to be perfected, blessing you.

Sit ergo nomen tuum super omnem benedictem: quia nomen tuum in te est, et tu in nomine tue.	Therefore may your name be blessed over all things, because your name is in you, and you in your name.

Tuum enim nomen est super omnem nomen exaltatum: et Ideo omnes Angeli et excercitus eorum, tuum nomen laudatur et honoratur.	Indeed, your name is exalted above all names, and therefore all angels and their armies praise and honour your name.

Tu vero Angelorum superiorum et Inferriorum orationem exaudis: tu omnium creaturarum es Creator, tu omnium es fortissimus, et tua fortitudo non deficiet.	Truly, you hear clearly the speech of the superior and inferior angels. You are the creator of all creatures. You are the mightiest of all, and your strength will not fail.

Tu unus es in seculo super sedem Maiestatis sedens quam omnis Angeli laudent [*laudant], benedicunt, et adorent [*adorant], glorificant, atque magnificant.	You are one in the world, sitting upon the seat of majesty,* which all angels praise, bless, adore, glorify, and extol.
* Compare Luke 25:31.	

Tuam vero vocem Angeli audiunt et Intelligunt: quamvis non te videatur.	Truly the angels hear and understand your voice, although you cannot be seen.

Tu igitur enim patre supplex exora, et in tua pietate tota mente confido: exaudi ergo peticionem meam quoniam ad te devote clamantes benigniter exaudis.	Therefore indeed, with the Father you exhort those who humbly beg, and I trust in your kindness with all my heart. Hear therefore my petition, because you hear the voice faithfully calling out to you.

Da queso domine deus meus mihi gratiam, sapientiam, virtutem, et potenciam, quatinus Angelus vel Angeli ille, vel spiritus istius N quotiens ipsum vel ipsos, Invocavero, mihi benigniter appareat, vell appareantur, et peticcioni mee veraciter satisfaciat, per gloriosam Maiestatem tuam, in qua gloriosissime regnas et regnaturas es in secula seculorum Amen.	O Lord my God, grant me grace, wisdom, strength, and power, I beg such that this spirit N., or any spirit or spirits that I may call upon will kindly appear to me and truly satisfy my petition, through your glorious majesty by which you reign most gloriously, and will reign forever and ever. Amen.

Deus meus miserere nobis, sana anima meam quia peccaui tibi non abneges vim [*uni] quam pluribus contulisti: exaudi deus orationem famuli tui N et in quacunqua die invocavero te velociter exaudi me: sic exaudisti virginem Mariam Matrem tuam.	My God, have mercy on us; heal my soul, for I have sinned against you. Do not deny to the one that which you have given to the many.* O God, hear the prayer of your servant N., and in whichever day I will call you, quickly hear me. Thus you have clearly heard the virgin Mary, your mother.
* LIH XCV; also in Kieckhefer, *Forbidden Rites*, 259.	

Suscipe clamore confitentis, audi vocem precantis seu peccatoris per merita et orationes sanctissime Marie Matris tue atque omnium Sanctorum tuorum, te deprecor ut oratio mea, et preces oris mei perveniant ad Aures pietatis tue.	Accept the cries of him who confesses,* hear the voice of the praying or the sinners, by the merits and most holy prayers of Mary your mother, and all your saints. I beg that my prayers and the requests of my mouth may reach the ears of your piety.
* Also in LIH XCV.	

After this, then say your confession.

Ne derelinquas me domine deus meus, et ne decessaris [*discesseris] a me. Intende in adiutorium meum domine deus salutis mee, fiat miserecordia tua confundar in eternum, intret in conspectum tuo oratio mea domine Inclina aurem tuam ad precem meam, domine exaudi orationem meam: et clamor meus ad te veniat	Do not abandon me, O Lord my God, do not depart from me. Attend to my help O Lord, the God of my salvation.* Let your mercy spread forever. Let my prayer enter into your view, O Lord, incline your ear to my prayer.† O Lord hear my prayer, and let my cries come to you.
* Psalm 37:22–23 (KJV 38:21–22). † Psalm 87:3 (KJV 89:2).	

[101]

Then the exorcist[379] should arrange and place both hands on the pentacle, and one of his associates should hold the book before the master with all the conjurations, and the master should face towards the four parts of the earth, saying,

Domine deus meus, esto mihi Turris fortitudinis a facie omnium spiritum malignorum.	O Lord my God, be my tower of strength in the face of all evil spirits.

Then prostrate yourself to the east, then the west, and south, and north, and before each part say these words:

---

379. In marg.: "160."

Ecce + signum et Nomina Trium-phatoris per quem vos o spiritus M. quotidie ex pavescitis et timetis, obedite ergo mihi et tu spiritus N. per hec verba secratissima secretorum, + On + Oreon + Sercon + Eloe + Eloym + Sabaoth + Elym + Ely + Adonay + Lamet + Saday + Tetragrammaton + Alpha + et Omega + principium et finis, qui est et qui erat, et qui venturus est.	Behold + the sign and the names of the Conqueror, which always* fill you with fear and trembling, O spirit N. Obey me therefore, O spirit N., through these most secret of secret words, + On + Oreon + Sercon + Eloe + Eloym + Sa-baoth + Elym + Ely + Adonay + Lamet + Saday + Tetragrammaton + Alpha + and Omega + the First and the last, who is and was and ever will be.
* The manuscript has a ∧ but with no inserted text.	

Then say, *E Deus totius pietatis* ["O God, author of all piety"] etc.[380]

Then give comfort to your associates.

Viuit dominus, et omnia que vivunt in ipso vivunt, qu[e] dat universus ["The Lord lives, and all things that live live in him, who made the universe"]. He is the very Jeho-vahh which by his word made and brought forth all things that in heaven, earth, and hell have any being. He calleth *omnes stellas, omnem militiam celi nominibus suis* ["all the stars and all the hosts of heaven by their own names"]. This God hath revealed to man, the names of his creatures, so that by him man knoweth their force and strength, condition, and nature, order and policy, yea, the power and virtue of each thing both visible and invisible,[381] and thereof it cometh and proceedeth that man hath power and grace to invocate and call, to urge and compel, not only good angels, but also wicked spirits, first of the air, fire, water, and earth to come and appear, and appearing to do and fulfill the will of the caller and his request, and for that this shall not appear doubtful,[382] that angels should become succors, aiders, and helpers unto sinful and worldly creatures, I read that Raphael was appointed by God to young Tobias, *ut parentem sanaret, ex periculis liberat fillium,* ["that he should heal his father, and deliver his son from dangers"], and to bring him to his young wife *Ita Michael dei fortitudo, populum dei gubernat, Gabriel dei mitius missus fuit Danieli, Marie, Zacharie, Iohannis Baptistae patri,* ["So Michael, the 'strength of God,' governs the people of God; Gabriel, the 'messenger of God,' was sent to Daniel, Mary, and Zachariah the father of

---

380. (O God, author of all piety): From Véronèse, *L'Ars Notoria Au Moyen Âge,* 101 and LIH LXXXII.

381. This seems to be quoted from Arbatel: See Peterson, *Arbatel,* pp. 22–25.

382. In marg.: "w" glyph.

John the Baptist"], hereby we may be ascertained that these be given to us that ask
and they teach them that with heart and mind desire the true nature of things, but we
must use the ministration of them with fear, and trembling of the Creator, the Redeemer, and Sanctifier, the Father, the Son, and the Holy Ghost[383] now forasmuch as
our souls live forever, *per eum qui nos creavit*, ["by him who created us"], let us therefore call upon the Lord our God, *et ille soli servire* ["and may you serve him alone"],
God of us *requirit animum, ut honore filium, et filii verbum custodire* ["requires from
you a mind, in order to respect the Son, and keep the word of his Son"] in our hearts,
*hic sunt lex et propheta nemo potest sibi accippere quicquam nisi ei datum fuerit de
super well* ["here are (sic) the law, and no prophet can receive anything himself unless
it be given him from above"],[384] well *vivit deus* ["God lives"] and seeing we live by
him, let us pray only *pro fide constante, et deus* ["for a constant faith, and God"] shall
order no doubt all things *in tempore oportuno* ["in due season"],[385] for *omnia possi-
bilia sunt credenti et volenti, omnia impossibilia sunt incredulo et nolenti* ["all things
are possible to those who believe and are willing; everything is impossible to the unbelieving and unwilling"].[386] Let follow the counsel, nay, the commandment of our
Saviour etc. *Invoca in me in die tribulationis, et exaudiam te, et honorificabis me, omnis
autem ignorantia est tribulacio animi, Invoco ergo in ignorantia tua dominicum, et ex-
audeat te, et memento, ut honorem tribuas deo ac dicas cum psalmista non nobis domine
non nobis sed nomina tua da gloriam* ["'Call upon me in the day of trouble; I will deliver you, and you will honour me,'[387] the Lord says. All ignorance is but the tribulation of the mind, therefore call upon the Lord in your ignorance, and he will hear you
clearly. And remember, that you assign the honour to God, and say with the Psalmist:
'Not to us, O Lord, not to us but to your name be the glory'[388]"],[389] and be of a bold
heart and constant mind, and no doubt but the Lord shall defend you *tanquam pupil-
lam occuli sui* ["as the pupil of his eye"] deliver you from evil, fill your souls with
good,[390] and grant you your heart's desire, which God grant for his only and well-beloved son Christ Jesus's sake[391] which liveth and reigneth with thee and the Holy
Ghost, ever one God in glory eternally, world without end. Amen.

---

383. Also from Peterson, *Arbatel,* Aph. 13.

384. John 3:27. Peterson, *Arbatel,* Aph. 17.

385. Peterson, *Arbatel,* Aph. 18.

386. Peterson, *Arbatel,* Aph. 20.

387. Psalm 49:15 (KJV 50:15).

388. Psalm 113:9 (KJV 115:1).

389. Peterson, *Arbatel,* Aph. 7.

390. Peterson, *Arbatel,* Aph. 5, including quotes from Psalm 17:8 (Vulgate 16:8; also compare Deut.
32:10) and Matthew 6:13 (or Luke 11:4).

391. In marg. in pencil: "see page 20."

This done, let the master turn towards the east and say,

Angele qui meus es custos, pietate superna, me tibi commissum serva, defenda, guberna, benedicat me Imperialis Maiestas, foveat me regalis divinitas. custodiat me sempiterna deitas, protegat me ineffabilis bonitas, regat me potentia patris vivi[fi]cet me sapientia fillii, Illuminet me virtus spiritus sancti, Alpha et Omega + deus et homo sit isti invocatio mihi salus et protectio Amen.	O angel who is my guardian* through heavenly love we are brought together, serve, defend, and guard me. May the imperial Majesty bless me; may the royal Divinity favour me; may the eternal Deity guard me; may the glorious Unity protect me; may the infinite Trinity defend me; may the ineffable Goodness direct me; may the mighty Father rule over me; may the wise Son vivify me, may the virtuous Holy Ghost enlighten me, Alpha and Omega, God and Man. May I, your servant, the same one who is calling, have health and protection. Amen.†

* This is a variant of the popular prayer to the guardian angel.
† Compare parallel versions on Folger pp. 99 and 181.

Prayer to God which must be said within the circle, to the four parts of the world.[392]

Amorule, Taneha, Latisten, Rabur, Taneha, Latisten, Escha, Aladia, α et ω, Leiste, Oriston, Adonay, Clementissime Pater mi Celestis miserere mei, licet peccatoris clarifica in me hodierno die, licet indigno filio tuo tue potentie brachium, contra hos spiritus pertinacissimos: Vt ego, te volente, factus tuorum divinorum operum, contemplator, possim illustrari omni sapientia, et semper glorificare, et adorare nomen tuum. Suppliciter exoro te et invoco [+ut, tuo iudicio, hi spiritus, quos invoco,] convicti et constricti,	Amorule, Taneha, Latisten, Rabur, Taneha, Latisten, Escha, Aladia, Alpha and Omega, Leiste, Oriston, Adonay, most Merciful Father, show your heavenly mercy to me, although a sinner, reveal to me this day, although your unworthy child, the arm of your power against these most stubborn spirits, that I, through your will, may be made a prophet of your divine works, and may be illuminated with all wisdom, and always worship and glorify your name. I humbly implore and beseech you, [+ that

392. Compare Folger p. 20. Compare also H. and LIH, CXXXIII.33. In marg. in pencil: "Agripp. 84 / 565 Agrippa."

veniant vocati et dent vera responsa de quibus eos interrogavero: dentque et deferant nobis eaque per me vel nos precipietur eis non nocentes alicui creature, non ledentes, non frementes, nec me sociosque meos vel aliam creaturam ledentes et neminem terrentes, sed peticionibus meis in omnibus que precipiam eis sint obedientes.	these spirits which I call by your judgement,] may be bound and constrained to come, and give true and perfect answers to those things which I shall ask them, and that they may declare and show us those things which by me or us shall be commanded them, not hurting any creature, neither injuring nor terrifying me or my fellows, nor hurting any other creature, and affrighting none; but let them be obedient to my requests, in all these things which I command.

[102]

Then stand in the middle of the circle,[393] hold your hand towards the pentacle, and say,

Per pentaculum Salomonis advocavi dent mihi responsum verum. ["By the pentacle of Solomon I have called you; give me a true answer."]

Then say:

Baralanensis, Baldachiensis, Paumachie et Apologie seedes, per Reges potestates que magnanimas, ac principes prepotentes genio Liachide, ministri tartaree sedis, primac hic princeps sedis Apologie nona cohorte: ego vos invoco, et invocando vos coniuro atque superne Maiestatis munitus virtute potenter imperio, per eum qui dixit et factum est, et cui obediunt omnes creaturae, et per hoc nomen ineffabile + Tetragrammaton + Iehovah + in quo [est] plasmatum omne seculum, quo audito elementa corruunt aer concutitur, mare retrogradatur,	Beralanensis, Baldachiensis, Paumachia, and Apologia Sedes, through the most magnanimous kings and powers, and the mightiest princes, guardian spirit Liachidae, ministers of the Tartarean seat, chief prince of the seat of Apologia, in the ninth court. I invoke you, and by invocating, conjure you; and being armed with power from the supreme Majesty, I strongly command you, by Him who spoke and it was done, and to whom all creation obeys; and by this ineffable name, + Tetragrammaton + Jehovahh +, which being heard, the

---

393. In marg. in pencil: "See page 20 / Agrippa 565."

ignis extinguitur, terra tremuit, omnesque [+ exercitus] Celestium Terrestrium et Infernorum tremunt turbantur et corruunt, quatenus cito et sine mora et omni occasione remota, ab universis mundi partibus veniatis et rationabiliter de omnibus quacunque interrogavero respondeatis vos, et veniatis pacifice visibiles et affabiles, [+ nunc] et sine mora manifestantes quod cupimus, coniurati, per nomen eterni vivi et veri dei Helioren +, et mandata mea et nostra perfficientes persistentes semper usque ad finem et intencionem meam visibiles nobis et affabiles, clara voce nobis intelligibili et sine omni ambiguitate.

elements are overthrown, the air is shaken, the sea runs back, the fire is extinguished, the earth trembles, and all the heavenly, worldly, and infernal [+ hosts] tremble, are troubled, and are confounded. Wherefore, forthwith and without delay, come from all parts of the world, and make rational answers to all things I shall ask of you; and come [+ now] peaceably, visibly, and affably, without delay, manifesting what we desire, being conjured by the name of the living and true God, *Heliorem +, and fulfil our commands, and persist until the end, and according to our intentions, visibly and affably speaking to us with a clear voice, intelligibly, and without any ambiguity.

Begin this whereas [394] thou findest this mark.

First, before thou proceed any further, note that as soon as thou hast prepared thyself to begin this work, do as followeth before thou enter thy circle, being confessed to God requiring pardon and forgiveness of thy sins, praying unto him for his Son Christ Jesus's sake to show himself favourable unto thee and to pour his mercy on thee and to give unto thee the spirit of power and might and to send thee the comfort of his Holy Spirit and the aid and assistance of his holy, mighty, and blessed angels, this done with sincerity of mind and humbleness of heart, steadfastly believing to receive comfort in Christ Jesus. Go forward with this as followeth, with a steadfast faith unremovable. Make no doubt, for all things are possible with God, although impossible to man, wherefore give to God the glory and praise, for to him it belongeth, forward with a valiant courage in Christ Jesus to whom be all praise, might, majesty, and dominion for ever and ever. Amen.

---

394. Whereas: where. The matching marks referred to can be found on Folger p. 104.

The order of the circle work:

| Volens confiteri, dicat sacerdoti. | The priest says, be willing to confess. |

| Benedicite pater, sacer, dominus sit in corde tuo et in labiis tuis ad confitendum omnia peccata tua, In nomine patris et filii, et spiritus sancti Amen. | Father, let us bless.* (The priest responds) May the Lord be in your heart, and on your lips for confessing all your sins. In the name of the Father, Son, and Holy Ghost. Amen. |

* In left marg.: "w" glyph; in right marg.: "147."

| Tunc dicat peccata sua. | Then tell your sins. |

| Confiteor deo celi beate, Marie virginis et omnibus sanctis tuis O deus, et coram vera maiestate tua, quia peccavi nimis superbia in vana gloria, in extollencia occulorum et vestium ac fortitudine, In invidua et odio, Inavaricia tam honoris alterius quam peccunie, In Tristicia de bonis et honore alterius, In ira et Iracundia Inventris gule et comestionibus superfluis, In fabulis vanis et ebrietatibus gulosis, In osculi et amplexionibus et palpacionibus Immundis, et in multis aliis generibus sive actibus luxuriosus, In periuriis, furtis, et homicidiis, In exortacionibus parvis, et adulacionibus malignis, In deceptionibus proximorum, et oppressionibus pauperum, In iudicii temerariis falsis et Impiis, In mendaciis et iuramentis multi modis, In detractionibus et discordiis seminandis, inderisionibus et maledictionibus variis | I confess to God in heaven,* to the blessed Virgin Mary, and to all your saints, O God, and the presence of your true majesty, because I have sinned greatly in my pride, in haughtiness of eyes and clothes and firmness, in envy and hatred, in coveting the honours or money of another, in being sad about the good or honours of another, in anger and irritability, in gluttony and excessive consumption, in empty chatter, drunkenness, and gluttony, in impure kissing, embracing, and touching, and many other kinds or acts of wantonness, in perjury, theft, and homicide, in extortion by force, and spiteful flattery, in deceiving neighbours and oppressing the poor, in rash, false, and wicked testimony, in lying and many kinds of swearing, in slander and planting discord, in mocking and cursing the different vigils |

* Compare Folger p. 51.

vigiliis et ludis salutis anime mee contrariis, Intransgressionibus preceptorum tuorum, et odio proximi, Indando mala exempla mihi subditis, Innonvisitando infirmo et desalato. In malo observando solempnitatis sanctorum, gulose luxuriose in eis vivendo, in blasphemando alios, et in malum swadentibus consentiendo, In male redendo tibi deo creatori meo gracias et orationes de bonis et quas mihi concessisti.

and (instead) gaming, against the salvation of the soul, in violation of your teachings, in hatred of neighbours, being a bad example to my subordinates, in not visiting the sick and desolate, in living (with gluttons and wantons), in blaspheming others, and in urging others to do the same evil, in badly disregarding the gratitude and prayers owed to you, God the creator, and the good which you have granted me.

Confiteor tibi [o pate]r qui non solum peccavi in omnibus peccatis supradictis, sed in omnibus aliis quibus humana fragillitas cogitando, audiendo, videndo, loquendo, delectando, et concupiscendo peccare potest. Et ideo tibi domino meo Celi et terre Creatori potentissimo veniam de omnibus peccatis per me factis et commissis humiliter deposco ut non gaudeat super me Inimicus meus, et non glorietur adversum me in die Iuditii accusans mea peccata et stellera tacuisse et confessum non fuisse: sed sit gaudium de me in celo sic de aliis iustis et confessis, et me mundus et confessus de peccatis meis coram tua presentia altissime pater omnipotens per tuam clementiam da mihi ut obedire possum et cognoscere omnis spiritus quos invocare voluero, et concede mihi potestatem ut possim complere meam omni modam voluntatem per gloriosissimam maiestatem tuam in qua gloriosissime regnans et regnaturus es in secula seculorum, fiat fiat Amen.

I confess to you, O Father, not only because I have sinned in all the ways mentioned above, but also in all the ways of human frailty, in thinking, hearing, seeing, speaking, pleasure, lower passions, and all the ways that one can sin. And therefore I ask pardon from you, O my Lord, most powerful creator of the heavens and the earth, for all sins committed by me and brought about, I humbly beseech that my enemy may not rejoice over me, nor stand against me on the Day of Judgement, accusing my sins and crimes left unmentioned and unconfessed, but give me eternal joy in Heaven, with the other just and confessed, that I may face you in person, pure and confessed of all my sins, O most high Father, through your mercy, that I may be able to obey, and recognize all the spirits which I wish to invoke, and grant me the power to fulfill my will in all ways, by your most glorious majesty, whereby you reign most gloriously, and will reign forever and ever. Amen.

Tunc dicat sacer[dos].	Then the priest says:

Misereatur tui omnipotens deus, et dimittat tibi omnia peccata tua, liberat te ab omni malo, [concede te voluntatem et desiderium tuum] concervet et confirmet in bono et ad vitam perducat eternam Amen, et meritum passionis domini nostri Iesu Christi suffragia sancte Matris Ecclesie bona que qui fecisti, et quem per dei gratiam facies sint tibi in remissione peccatorum tuorum [+ Amen].	May almighty God have mercy on you,* forgive all your sins, and deliver you from all evil, grant you your desires and wishes, conserve and strengthen you in goodness and lead you to eternal life. Amen. By the merits of the passion of our Lord Jesus Christ, the prayers of our holy Mother Church, the good which you have done, and by the grace of God that you will do hereafter, be to you for the remission of your sins. [+ Amen].

* In marg.: "148."

And for special penance, say etc.[395]
Then he gives absolution.

Dominus noster Iesus Christus qui est sumus pontifex, per suam piissimam misericordiam te absolvat, et ego aucthoritate mihi concessa absolvo te primo a sentencia minoris excomunicationis si indigeas, deinde absolvo te ab omnibus peccatis tuis, In nomine patris et filii et spiritus sancti Amen.	Jesus Christ our Lord, who is the highest pontiff, by his most pious mercy, absolves you. I, by the authority granted me, absolve you first from the sentence of minor excommunication if you need it, and then from all your sins, in the name of the Father, and the Son, and the Holy Ghost. Amen.*

* See Folger p. 51.

This done, say the prayers afore going, devoutly praying unto God the prayers which is to be said before you begin your work.

After, say as follows:

[103]

Prayer before the circle

Then say after this prayer:

---

395. See Folger p. 51.

Veni Creator spiritus mentes tuorum visita Imple superna gratia que qui tu creasti pectora.	Come O Creator Spirit,* and visit your souls; fill the hearts which you have created with heavenly grace.

* "Veni Creator Spiritus" is a well-known ninth-century hymn invoking the Holy Spirit. It is normally sung at Pentecost.

Qui paraclitus diceris, donum dei altissimi, fons vivus Ignis Charitas et Spiritualis unctio.	You who are the Paraclete (Comforter), the gift of God most high, living source, fire, charity, and spiritual anointing.

Tu septiformis munere, dex[e]tre dei tu digitus, tu rite promissum [*promisso] patris, sermone dictans guttura.	You are the sevenfold gift, you are the finger of God's right hand, a gift duly promised by the Father, words which enrich the throat.

Accende lumine sentibus, infunde amorem, cordibus, Infirma nostri corporis, virtute firmans perpeti<m>.	Kindle in us the light, pour love into our hearts, continually strengthening our fragile bodies.

Hostem repellas longius, pacemque dones protinque [*protinus], ductore sic te previo, vitemus omne Noxium.	Drive the enemy far from us, quickly bring peace; thus leading us, we may avoid all harm.

Per te [+ sciamus] da patrem, Noscamus atque filium, te utriusque spiritum credamus omni tempore.	Through you [+ may we understand] the Father, and know the Son, and may we believe you, the spirit of each, for all time.

Sit laus patri cum filio, sancto simul paraclito, nobisque mittat fillius, carisima Sancti Spiritus. Amen.	Praise be to the Father, with the Son, likewise the holy Paraclete, and send to us the Son of the most dear Holy Ghost. Amen.

(Ver) Emitte spiritum tuum et creabuntur.	Send forth your spirit, and they shall be created.

| (Responsu) Et removabis faciem Terre. | (Response) And you shall renew the face of the earth. |

| Oremus | Let us pray. |

| Deus cui [*qui] omne corpatet, et omnis voluntas loquitur et que nullum seecretum latet, purifica per infucione Sancti spiritus cogitationes cordis nostri ut te perfecte deligere et digne laudare mereamur, per Christum dominum nostrum Amen. | O God, to whom all hearts are open,* and all desires known, and from whom no secrets† lie hidden, purify the thoughts of our hearts by the infusion of your Holy Ghost, that we may love you perfectly, and be properly worthy to praise you, through our Lord Jesus Christ. Amen. |

* In left marg.: "w"; in right marg.: "148."
† There is a "+" or perhaps "4" in brown ink above this word.

| Deus qui Tribus pueris mittigasti flammas ignium, concede propicius: ut nos famulos tuos non exurat flamma vicios. | O God, who delivered the three children from the flaming furnace, grant your favour, that the flames of sin may not burn me up. |

| Ure igne sancti spiritus renes nostros, et cor nostrum domine ut tibi casto corpore serviamus et mundo corde placeamus. | O Lord, enflame our reins and heart with the fire of your Holy Ghost: that we may serve you with a chaste body, and please you with a pure heart.* |

* "Enflame O Lord our reins, and heart, with the fire of thy Holy Spirit: to the end that we may serve thee, with a chaste body, and please thee with a clean heart." http://medievalist.net/hourstxt /litanies.htm.

| Acciones nostras quesumus domine aspirando preveni, et adiuvando prosequere, ut cuncta nostra [oratio et] operatio a te semper incipiat, et per te cepta finiatur. Amen. | Direct, we beg you, O Lord, our actions by your holy inspirations, and carry them on by your gracious assistance, that every prayer and work of ours may begin always with you, and through you be happily ended. Amen. |

Being towards the circle, say this *Dignare* ["Deem"] [396]

---

396. Under this in marg.: "G. t. f / G. S. t."

Dignare me domine die isto, sine peccatis costodire, dirige gressus et Actus meos hodie per semitas iustitie tue, sic tua iusticia ad esto fragilitati mee ut in nulla te recapitaliter offendam Amen.	Deem me worthy this day, O Lord, guard me from sin, direct my steps and my deeds this day, by the paths of your justice, thus your justice will be present in my fragility, so that I will in no mortal way offend you. Amen.*

| * In right marg.: "+" in brown ink, perhaps marking the end of the block of text similarly marked. ||

For opening the circle [397]

Domine deus noster Iesus Christus sis mihi salus et protectio, Attolite portas, Crux Crux Crux, dux, ban, Adonay, dominus dominantium qui frigisti claves inferni aperi mihi istam Circulum.	O Lord our God, Jesus Christ, be my salvation and defense, erect the gateway, O Cross, Cross, Cross, Dux, Ban, Adonay, Lord of Lords, who have broken the keys of hell, open to me this circle.

Next say *auffer* ["remove..."]:

Auffer a nobis domine quesimus, omnes Iniquitates nostris, ut ad hunc circulum puris mentibus mereamor introire, per Christum dominum nostrum. Amen.	Remove from us, we beg you, O Lord, all our iniquities, that we may be worthy to enter this circle with a pure mind, through Christ our Lord. Amen.

Entering into the circle

Make a cross in thy forehead and say, *In nomine patris et filii et spiritus sancti* Amen. ["in the name of the Father and the Son and the Holy Ghost. Amen."]

Then put into the circle thy right foot and say, standing still in that place,

---

397. "ad aperiendum Circulum" is repeated in the marg.

Benedicat me Imperialis Maiestas, protegat me regalis divinitas eius. Aufer a me domine queso, omnes Iniquitates meas, ut ad hunc Circulum puris mentibus merear Introire, per Christum Dominum nostrum Amen.	May the imperial Majesty bless me, may his royal Divinity protect me. Remove from me, I beg you, O Lord, all my iniquities, that I may be worthy to enter this circle with a pure mind, through Christ our Lord. Amen.

Being entered and standing in the midst of the circle.

Domine celi et terre omnium visibilum et Invisibilum, conditor et Creator: ego indignus, te iubente, te invoco, per fillium tuum, unigenitum dominum nostrum Iesu Christum, ut des mihi spiritum sanctum, qui me in veritate tua dirigat, ad omnem bonum tuum amen.	O Lord of Heaven and Earth, maker and creator of all that is visible and invisible; I though unworthy, call upon you and invoke you, through your only begotten son our Lord Jesus Christ, in order that you give your Holy Ghost to me, which may direct me in your truth, for the good of all. Amen.*
* From *Arbatel* Aph. 14.	

Deus pater omnipotens quia vero desiderio desidero artes huius vite et necessarias nobis perfecte cognoscere, que Immersae sunt tantis Tenebris et conspurcatae infinitis humanis opinionibus, ut ego videam me meis viribus nihill in iis assequturum te non docente, da mihi unum de spirittibus tuis N. qui me doceat ea, que vis nos discere et cognoscere, ad laudem et honorem tuam, et utillitatem proximi, da mihi etiam cor docile, ut que me docueris facile percipiam et in mente meam recondam inde	O God the Father almighty, because with true longing I desire to learn fully the skills of this life, and those things which are necessary for us, who are immersed in immense darkness and fouled with unending human beliefs, as I see that I can understand nothing through my own power, unless you teach me. Grant to me therefore one of your spirits N., who will teach me whatever you wish me to learn and understand, for your praise and honour, and the usefulness of our neighbors. Grant to me also a heart

| proferendam, tanquam de tuis in exhaustis Thesauris ad omnes usus Necessarios: et da mihi gratiam ut tantis donis tuis humillime cum metu et tremore utar, per dominum nostrum Iesum Christum cum sancto spiritu tuo Amen. | that is easily taught, so that I may easily retain in my mind what you have taught, and I will secure them there to be brought forth, as from your inexhaustible treasures, for all necessary uses. And grant to me your grace, that I may use these great gifts of yours only with humility, fear, and trembling, through our Lord Jesus Christ with your Holy Ghost. Amen.* |

* Also found on Folger p. 19, quoted from *Arbatel* Aph. 14.

Note that every one of the fellowship that entereth the circle, which reason requireth be two besides the master, shall say as is before from this mark and as order is prescribed.

[104]

Order of the circle

This done, all together *cum genu flectitur* ["with knees bent"] shall say *pater noster, Ave Maria, Credo in deum* ["The Lord's Prayer, Hail Mary, and the Creed 'I believe in God'"] etc. Then shall the two associates, one after another, unto the master say as followeth, kneeling upon their knees.

Benedicite pater ["Father, let us bless"],[398] to whom the master being a priest shall answer,

| Dominus sit in corde tuo et in labiis tuis, vere confitendum et declarandum omnia peccata tua In nomine patris et filii et Spiritus Sancti amen. | May the Lord be in your heart, and on your lips for confessing and declaring all your sins. In the name of the Father, and the Son, and the Holy Ghost. Amen. |

Then shall one say:

---

398. In marg.: "150."

Confiteor deo celi,* beate Marie virgine, et omnibus Sanctis eius, et tibi pater, quia ego miser peccator peccavi nimis Indictis, Infactis, Inverbis, Incogitacione et loqutione in dilectacione in pollucione, in concensu, intactu, auditus risus visus, verbo ore mente corde et opere participando, cum excomunicatis et in cunctis aliis vitiis mea, mala mea culpa, mea gravissima culpa, et ideo deprecor Sancta Maria et omnes Sanctos et Sanctas dei, et vos orare per me.	I confess to God in heaven and to the blessed Virgin Mary, and all the saints, and to you O Father, because I have sinned greatly against you, in thoughts and words and deeds and speech, in enjoyment, in pollution, in feeling, touching, hearing, laughter, seeing, word of mouth, with the mind, with the heart, and participating in the work with an excommunicated person, and with all my other sins, through my sin, my sin, my most grievous sin, and therefore I beg for Saint Mary, and all the saints of God—male and female—to intercede and pray for me.

* Compare parallel version of this confession on Folger p. 52.

Then the master shall answer and say:

Misereatur tui omnipotens deus et dimittat tibi omnia peccata tua, liberet te ab omni malo, conservet et confirmet in bono, et ad vitam per ducat te eternam Amen.	May almighty God have mercy on you, and dismiss all your sins, and deliver you from all evil, and preserve and strengthen you in goodness, and lead you to eternal life. Amen.

Then shall the master say, laying his right hand one the associate's head:

Dominus noster Iesus Christus qui est sumus pontifex, per suam misericordiam abso[l]vat te, et ego Auctoritate mihi concessa, absolvo te ab omni peccata tua In nomine Patris et filii et Spiritus sancti Amen.	Jesus Christ our Lord, who is the highest pontiff, by his mercy, absolves you; I, by the authority granted me, absolve you from all your sins. In the name of the Father, and the Son, and the Holy Ghost. Amen.*

* Compare with version on Folger p. 51.

This done, the other shall kneel down and say the same and the other arise, and say from this mark hither

Then all kneeling shall begin and say, in the middle of the circle eastward, shall say the Psalms where as this mark is made ——┼—— , the master beginning and saying one verse, they following, etc.

This being done, then begin where thou first findest this mark above and ——┼—— after thou hast done so, coming to the same mark / next before this, let pass and come to this as followeth, and let the master turn towards the east, but first cense the circle and place the associates and do as followeth.

Coniuro te N. per Iesum Christum et per Patrem eius et Spiritum Sanctum, et per gloriosam virginem Mariam et per prophetam Iohannem Baptiste, et Tabulas Moysy, et per virtutem Michaelis qui te de Celo expulsit, et per gloriosam Cyprianum Martiem qui te fecerit suis obedire mandatis, per tremendum diem Iudicii, per vulnus latere Iesu Christi, et per vulnera manum et pedum eius, per predicationem et mortem eius et resurrectionem eius. et ascentionem et Spiritus Sancti emisionem, ipsum ipsius quae patrem per sanctos gloriosos Apostolos, et per omnes virtutes Celorum, per beatam gloriosam Mariam Matrem domini nostri Iesu Christi, et per quinque eius	I conjure you,[*] O N., by Jesus Christ, and by his Father, and by the Holy Ghost, and by the glorious Virgin Mary, and by the prophet John the Baptist, and the tablets of Moses, and by the power of Michael who expelled you from Heaven, and by the glorious martyr Cyprian, who subjugated you with his command, and by the terrible Day of Judgment, and by the wound on the side of Jesus Christ, and by the wounds on his hands and feet, and by the proclaiming, and his death and resurrection, and ascension, and the sending out of the Holy Ghost, by its self and his Father, and by the saints and glorious Apostles and all the powers of heaven, by the blessed

[*] In left marg.: "w" glyph; in right marg.: "162."

gaudia, per assumptionem et coronationem eiusdem virginis et instantissime te N. Coniuro per illum super excelsum dei nomen + Tetragramaton + Ineffabile atque infinite virtutis quatenus in virtute omnium predictorum et specialiter virtute istius venerandi Nominis Iehovah + ut ad me Celeriter occurras et absque corustationibus tonitrius horribilibus et strepitu horribili appareret non Tardas, quatinus in te agnoscatur quam magnificentie est nomen suum, ut a quibuslibet adoretur tam celestibus celitus quam Terrenis et Infernalibus per virtutem dei patris omnipotentis suique benedicti filii ac Spiritus Sancti qui deus Trinus et unus viuit et regnat in secula seculorum amen.

glorious Mary, mother of our Lord Jesus Christ, and by her five joys, and by the assumption and coronation of the same glorious virgin, and I most urgently conjure you N., by that highest name of God + Tetragrammaton + ineffable and infinitely powerful, inasmuch as by the power of all the preceding, and specifically of that venerable name Jehovahh + that you come quickly to me, and without thunder, flashing, or terrible thunder, and without terrible noise, and that you appear without delay, inasmuch as you have recognised how vast is the greatness of that name of his, that is so honoured by heavenly, earthly, and infernal beings, and by the power of God, his almighty Father, who lives and reigns with the blessed Son and the Holy Ghost, one God and Trinity, forever and ever. Amen.

Coniuro te N per Angelos et Archangelos Thronos et Principatus potestates et per virtutes celorum, et per omnia mirabilia Iesu Christi ac per eiectionem demonem de hominibus et per flagellacionem eius, et per ingentissimum deffluentem sanguinem a latere et pedibus eius et manibus, et omnibus sui partibus, et per omnia terribilia in Celo et in Terra, et per Angelos bonos et malos, et ad huc Coniuro te N atque requiro in virtute crucifixit qui est Maior omnium, et per eius nomen + Tetragrammaton + quod est nomen honorabile et terribile ac etiam amabile cunctis Christianis, et

I conjure you,[*] O N., by the Angels and Archangels, Thrones and Principalities, Powers, and by the heavenly Virtues, and by all the miracles of Jesus Christ, and by the expulsion of demons from men, and by his whipping, and by that great flowing of blood from his side, and his feet and hands, and all the parts of his body, and by all the terrible things which are in Heaven and on Earth, and by the good and evil angels, and I conjure you and demand of you, O N. here, in the power of the crucified one who is greatest of all, and by his name + Tetragrammaton + which confers

* In marg.: "163."

terribile demonibus, quatinus omnia moram ac delatione exclusa mihi visibilliter appareas et absque simulacione fraude, vell versutia qualicunque mihi ad Interrogata fideliter respondeas, et meo iussu in omnibus obedeas per virtutem domini nostri Iesu Christi, qui vivit et regnat in secula seculorum amen.	honour and fear, but also inspires love in Christians, and fear in the demons. Therefore, appear to me visibly, without delay or postponement, and without pretence or fraud, or cunning of any kind, and faithfully respond to all that I ask, and obey all my orders, by the power of our Lord Jesus Christ, who lives and reigns forever and ever. Amen.

These being done, turn into the west, then into the north, and so into the south, into every of which parts, pronouncing the foresaid conjuration, but if then nothing be heard nor seen, repeat the same seven times over, as above, but note that most commonly he cometh at the third time. Note if thou hear any hissing as it were of adders or such like, etc., then say boldly + Boldly Tetragramaton + then read once again the conjuration, then rest by the space of the reading of the conjuration. Then if he come and stand still, then read this conjuration of obedience as follows.

[105]

Invocation

Coniuro te N * per istum Infinitum verbum quo cuncta creata sunt cum dixerit deus fiat et facta sunt. Coniuro et requiro et adiuro te spiritus N. qui ibi visibiliter extra circulum appareas per bonitatem qua deus hominen [sic] ad Imaginem suam plasmavit, et te per iustitiam suam et per vestram superbiam qui te damnavit et eiccit decelis, et per virginitatem et humillitatem beate Marie Genetricis domini nostri et ve[st]ri Iesu Christi, et per potenciam qua Inferum confregit et socios tuos plasmavit et crucitavit ut mihi de	I conjure you, O N., by that infinite word through which all things were created; when God spoke "let it be," and it was done. I conjure, demand, and adjure you, O spirit N., that you appear visibly through the goodness of God, who made people after his own image, and by the justice which has condemned you and expelled you from Heaven, and by the humble virginity of the blessed Mary, mother of our Lord and yours, Jesus Christ, and by the power which has plundered hell, and shaped and tormented your associates, that you faithfully respond

* In marg.: "163."

omnibus rebus fideliter dicas responsum et ut in quantum poteris obedientiam meis verbis faciatis, per dominum nostrum Iesum Christum qui venturus est Iudicare vivos et mortuos et seculum per ignem Amen.	to all that I ask, and obey my words and accomplish as much as you are able, by our Lord Jesus Christ, who will come to judge the living and the dead and the world by fire. Amen.

Now if he come, when the spirit appeareth in his proper form, 1.) let the Master turn himself towards him gently,[399] 2.) Then, by way of entreaty, enquire what is his name, and whether he have any other name, 3.) under what planet he is,[400] 4.) what is his office and dignity, and how many are under his subjection.[401]

5.) But if you see him stubborn or distrust him of lying, constrain him by a convenient conjuration, saying upon every question,

Coniuro te N. per <pal> Patrem et filium et spiritum sanctum, per Iesum Christum, ed per admirabilem dei Nomen + TETRAGRAMMATON + ut mihi vera respondeas de hac re.	I conjure you N., by the Father, and the Son, and the Holy Ghost, by Jesus Christ, and by the admirable name of God + TETRAGRAMMATON + that you answer me truly concerning this thing.

But note, the first time the spirit cometh, thou shalt not trouble him with any demand or question, neither yet the second time not passing on, but the first time thou shalt bind him and make him to swear to obedience, and to be ready to come at all times when thou shalt call him, and to fulfill thy will in all things, even to the uttermost of his office and dignity. In this manner shall ye swear him, that you may have a true and undoubted answer: stretch out your sword, and let him put his hand thereon, and swear this,

I, N., a spirit[402] of such element, east, west, north, or south, under such a planet viz. ♄♃♂☉♀☿ ☽ and of such an office, do protest, promise, and swear by the head and dignity of my prince, and as I hope at the terrible and dreadful day of judgment to be saved, to be ready at all times being called by N. N., the servant of the only true and everliving God + Jehovahh + and he, the said N. N., being the son of N. N.,

---

399. Gently: i.e., courteously. This paragraph is taken from Pseudo-Agrippa or a closely-related source.

400. Note: The assumption seems to be that every spirit is under a planet.

401. This section is repeated mostly verbatim on Folger p. 161.

402. In left marg.: "w"; in right marg.: "164."

whom I confess to have overcome me and made me by God's permission subject to
obedience, and that without hurting or harming of him or any living creature of
God's creation, and to give a true answer of all things that he shall demand or ask of
me, and to do most willingly, without deceit, craft, or cautell,[403] the uttermost of my
power and office and the whole and that to any part of my dignity appertaineth, and
for witness whereof to this book I have with mine own hand wrote my name set to
my character or seal, even the day of N. in *the year* 1583 etc.[404]

But if he come not at the reading of the conjuration before said, then read some
conjuration as thou shalt seem to be meet. Now if he come not, the same conjuration
being read, within one hour after, say:[405]

O Vrieus, Amaymon, Paymon, et Egin, qui estis quattuor reges potentissimi iuxta quattuor partes mundy et ceteris malis spiritibus praeestis.	O Urieus, Amaymon, Paymon, and Egin, who are the four mighty kings of the four parts of the earth, and in charge of the other evil spirits.

Nos facti ad Imaginem dei, dotati potentia dei, et eius facti voluntate per potentissimum et corrobaratum nomen dei + El + forte et admirabile vos exorcizamus spiritus N. et Imperamus per eum, qui dixit, et factum est et per omnia nomina dei et per nomen + Adonay + El Elohim + Elohe + Zebaoth + Elion + Escerchie + Iah + Tetragrammaton + Saday dominus deus excelsus exorcizamus vos atque potenter imperamus ut constringatis et coarctetis spiritum illum M pertinacissimum statim et sine ulla mora venire ante circulum hunc	We being made* in the image of God, endowed with power of God and made according to his will, do exorcise you N., by the most mighty and powerful name of God + El + strong and wonderful, and we command you by Him who spoke the word and it was done, and by all the names of God, and by the name + Adonai + El Elohim + Elohe + Zebaoth + Elion + Eserchie + Jah + Tetragrammaton + Saday, Lord God Most High. We exorcise you, and powerfully command you that you constrain and confine that stubborn spirit M. to immediately

* Compare H.: *exorcismus spirituum aereorum.*

403. Cautell: a cunning trick.
404. In brown ink in marg.: "1822/1583/----/239"; In pencil to the right (evidently later hand): "1642/../59."
405. Compare Folger p. 113. In left marg.: "[rea]de (?) fol. 65." This is evidently the contemporary foliation, corresponding with the more modern pagination 113, where this conjuration is repeated. In right marg.: "164."

in aspectum nostrum in pulchra forma pueri tres annos nati et implere voluntatem nostram, sine omni deformitate et tortuositate aliqua constringite et coarctate illum quia vos imperamus per nomen + Y et V + quod Adam audiuit et loqutus est: et per nomen dei + Agla + quod Loth audiuit, et factas salvus cum sua familia: et per nomen + Ioth + quod Iacob audiuit ab Angelo secum luctante, et liberatus est de manu fratris sui Esau: et per nomen + Anephexeton + quod Aaron audiuit, et loquens, et sapiens factus est: et per nomen + Zebaoth + quod Moyses nominavit, et omnia flumina et paludes de terra Egipti, verse fuerunt in sanguinem: et per nomen + Ecerchie Oriston + quod nominavit, et omnes fluvij ebullierunt ranas, et ascenderunt in domos Aegiptiorum, omnia destruentes et per nomen + Elyon + quod Moyses nominavit et fuit grando talis, qualis non fuit ab initio mundi: et per nomen + Adonay + quod Moyses nominavit et fuerunt Locustee, et apparuerunt super terram Egiptiorum, et [106] comederunt que residua erant grandini: et per nomen + Alpha + et Omega + quod daniell [+ nominavit], et destruxit bell, et draconis [*-nem] interfecit: et in nomine + Emanuell + quod tres pueri, Sidrach, Misach, et Abednago, in camino ignis ardentis cantaverunt et liberati fuerunt: et per [+ nomen] + hagios + et sedem + Adonay + et per + Otheos + Isckiros + Athanatos + Paracletus + et per hac tria secreeta nomina + Agla

come to us here before this circle in the fair shape of a three year old boy, to fulfill our wishes, without any deformity or tortuosity; constrain and confine him, because we command you by the name + Y and V +, which Adam heard and spoke; and by the name of God + Agla +, which Lot heard, and was saved with his family; and by the name + Joth + which Jacob heard from the angel wrestling with him, and was delivered from the hand of his brother Esau; and by the name + Anaphexeton +, which Aaron heard and spoke, and was made wise; and by the name + Zebaoth +, which Moses named, and all the rivers and swamps of Egypt were turned to blood; and by the name + Eserchie Oriston +, which he named, and all the rivers produced frogs in abundance, which climbed into the houses of the Egyptians, destroying all things; and by the name + Elion +, which Moses named, and there was great hail, such as had not been since the beginning of the world; and by the name + Adonai +, which Moses named, and locusts appeared upon the whole land of Egypt, and [106] devoured all that the hail had left; and by the name + Alpha and Omega +, which Daniel [+named], and destroyed Bel and slew the dragon; and in the name + Emmanuel +, which the three children, Sidrach, Misach, and Abednego, sung in the midst of the fiery furnace, and were delivered; and by [+the name] + Hagios +; and by the seat of + Adonai +; and by

+ On + Tetragrammaton + adiuro, contestor, et per hac nomina et per alia nomina domini nostri *Iesu Christi* dei omnipotentis, vivi et veri vos qui vestra culpa de ceeli eiecti fuistis usque ad infernum locum, exorcizamus et virilliter imperamus per eum qui dixit et factum est: cui omnes obediunt creature, et per illud tremendum dei iudicium, et per mare omnibus incertum, vitreum, quod est ante conspectum divine Maiestatis, gradiens et potentiale, et per [quattu]or divina animalia. .T. ante sedem divine Maiestatis gradientia, et occulos ante et retro habentia: et per ignem ante eius Tronum circumstantem, et per sanctos Angelos Celorum. T. et per eam que ecclesia dei nominatur: et per summam sapientiam omnipotentis dei viriliter exorcizamus ut *constringatis et coarctetis illum spiritum N*§ ante circulum *in aspectu nostrum venire cito ut sine omni mora* ad faciendam nostram voluntatem in omnibus, prout placuerit nobis: per sedem Baldachiae, et per hoc nomen + Primeumaton + quod Moyses nominavit, et in cavernis abissi fuerunt profundati vell absorpti, datan, Corah, et Abyrom,: et in virtute istius nominis + Primeumaton + tota celi milicia compellente, maledicimus vos, privamus vos

+ Otheos + Ischyros + Athanatos + Paracletos +; and by these three secret names, + Agla + On + Tetragrammaton +, I do adjure you, and appeal to God and by these names, and by all the other names our Lord Jesus Christ, God almighty, living and true, who found fault with you, and expelled you from Heaven to the infernal realm. I exorcise and powerfully command you, by Him who spoke the word and it was done, to whom all creatures are obedient; and by the dreadful judgment of God;* and by the uncertain sea of glass, which is before the divine Majesty, approaching (the throne) and powerful; and by the four† divine living creatures .T. before the throne, approaching the divine Majesty, and having eyes before and behind;‡ and by the fire round about his throne; and by the holy angels of Heaven .T., and by that which is named the Church of God, and by the most high wisdom of almighty God, we do powerfully exorcise you, that you constrain and confine that spirit N. to quickly come and appear to our sight before this circle, to fulfil our will in all things that will please us; by the seat of Baldachia, and by this name Primeumaton, which Moses named, and the earth opened and swallowed up

---

* So also H., but "*dei iudicium*" ["judgment of God"] is probably a typo for the more frequent "*die iudicium*" ["day of judgment"], which also occurs later in this paragraph.
† The MS has a blank to switch ink.
‡ Rev. 4:6.
§ Italics are JHP marking where Folger differs from H.

ab officio, loco et gaudeo vestro vsque in profundum abissy, et vsque; ad ultimum diem iudicii vos ponimus, et religamus in ignem eternum, et in stagnum ignis et sulphuris, nisi *constringatis et coarctetis spiritum illum N cito et sine omni mora venire* ante circulum *hunc in aspectu nostrum* ad faciendum voluntatem nostram in omnibus *prout placuerit nobis, i[n] omnibus constringite et coarctate illum N* per hac nomina Adonay + Zebaoth + Adonay + Amioram + *constringite, constringite, constringite, et illum,* imperat vobis + Adonay + Saday + Rex regum potentissimus et tremendissimus cuius vires nulla subterfugere potest creatura, vobis pertinacissimis futuris nisi obedieritis et *constringatus illum venire affabilem cito et sine mora* ante hunc circulum *in aspectum nostrum in pulchra forma pueri tres annos nati, et voluntatem nostram per implere,* tandem ruina flebilis miserabilisque et ignis in perpetuum inextinguibilis vos manet, *constringite ergo illum* in nomine + Adonay [+ Zebaoth + Adonay] + Amioram + *constringite, constringite illum N,* quid tardatis festinate, imperat vobis + Adonay + Saday + Rex Regum + El + Aty + Titeip + Azia + Hin + Ien + Minosell + Achadan + Vay + Vaa + Ey + Haa + Eye + Exe, *ael* + El + El + a + Hy + Hau + Hau + Hau + Va + Va + Va + Va +

Korah, Dathan, and Abiram;[*] and in the power of that name Primeumaton, commanding the whole host of heaven, we curse you, and deprive you of your office, joy, and place, and do bind you in the depth of the bottomless pit, there to remain until the dreadful day of the final judgment; and we bind you into eternal fire, and into the lake of fire and brimstone, unless you constrain and compel that spirit N. to come and appear to our sight before this circle, without delay, to do our will in all things that will please us. Constrain and compel that N., by these names, Adonai + Zebaoth + Adonay + Amioram +; constrain, constrain, constrain him, and he commands you, + Adonay + Saday + the most mighty and terrible King of Kings, whose power no creature is able to resist, this will be to you, most obstinate (spirit), unless you obey, and constrain that N. to come affably and without delay, to appear before this circle, in the form of a beautiful boy of three years, and fulfill our wishes, let doleful ruin and misery, and unquenchable fire remain with you; therefore constrain him, in the name of + Adonay [+ Zebaoth + Adonay] + Amioram +; constrain him, constrain that N., why do you delay? Hasten! He commands you + Adonay + Saday + the King of Kings + El + Aty + Titeip + Azia + Hin + Ien + Minosel + Achadan + Vay + Vaa + Ey + Haa + Eye + Exe + Ael + El + El + A + Hy + Hau + Hau + Hau + Va + Va + Va + Va+.[†]

---

[*] Psalm 106:17 recalling Num. 16:30.
[†] In left marg.: "w" glyph; in right marg.: "165"; below it "166."

This being done, read the strong conjuration, which being done and nonappearance be had, then call upon the seven senators, without whose licence scarcely will appear any spirit or angel come to fulfill your desire. These be they:

1 Ormell 2 Teygra 3 Danall 4 Salerica 5 Asmoe 6 Pascari 7 Boell

These are to be called on this wise:

O noble and most renowned Senators, you are to be regarded with a good aspect, therefore I N. now pray you to have N., a spirit that shall serve me and fulfill my request and desire, and that he may be obedient unto me and to my call, O noble and magnificent Senators, grant me to have such a one, whom I shall call or name to come unto me, and that this be done, I most humbly beseech you, by the obedience you bear to the Immaculate Lamb which sitteth on the seat, before whom continually you sing without ceasing songs of great and unspeakable joy. So be it.

Note: in every hour you call, you shall cense the book, and all about the circle, saying:

O thou angel which art my keeper, now save, defend, and guide me, committed unto thee by grace from above, O thou sweet angel which remaineth with me, albeit notwithstanding thou speak not personally with me: yet I beseech thee now to preserve me both in soul and body, and especially to this office to the which thou art appointed. O blessed angel, messenger of God, prosper and direct these my doings, and that to the pleasure of the most highest.

Then say towards the east:

O God, which grantest some of thy holy angels gently to assist thee, and commandest some to serve men and that here on Earth, favourably and mercifully grant thy angel committed to me [406] for the custody of my soul, now to direct me in all godliness, and to stir me up daily to virtuousness, and chiefly to rid me from the whirlpit [407] of sin and wickedness, that in thy rigorous and just judgment, when there shall be one fold of men and angels, that I may here in this shadow of life, or rather slippery passage unto death, so behave myself, that I may merit and deserve amongst the sheep of thy flock, and through Jesus Christ our Lord, who liveth and reigneth with thee in unity of the Holy Ghost, God for ever and ever, *nunc et in eternum* ["now and forever"], so be it.

Note that the associates must say this prayer also, and that in every of the three quarters, viz. west, north, and south.

---

406. A guardian angel.

407. Whirlpit: whirlpool.

[107]

The consecration and fumigation of the circle

This done, read the proper conjuration belonging to the spirit, if there be any, or else some other perfect one, during the which reading, continually must the master look on his book, and let the seer be circumspect in the view and tell what he seeth, otherwise all is in vain.

Fumigations that rejoiceth spirits [408]

Here, as at all other times, forget not to make such fumigations that delighteth the spirit, and that will urge him a body.

Amber, lignum aloes, costus, musk, crocus, the blood of a lapwing, and frankincense.[409] These be meat, drink, and gladness to the spirits of the air and gathereth them together and urgeth them to appear as sayeth Hermes.

Greek incense, mastic, sandalwood, galbanum, *muscha lazerat*, myrrh, and amber. These are collectors of spirits and placaters of them.

Now, when[410] the spirit cometh, [one] of the fellows must heave up the covering of the pentacle, which the master must have on his breast covered with a silk cloth, and show it to the spirit, which will move him to his circle, and then will he obey and grant thee thy desire.

Note, so oft as the master doth show the scepter with the lamina unto the spirit, or touch the lamina, you must do it with great reverence and obedience to God.

After this, if he does not appear, say this:

Hec sunt signa et nomina seecreta secretorum et quisquis erit eis contradicens et rebellis signis et nominibus triumphatoris qui totum regit et gubernat mundum rebellis erit venias ergo [space]	These are the signs* and names, the secret of secrets and who dares to speak against and rebel against the signs and names of the conqueror who rules and guides the whole world. Come therefore
* In marg.: "167." Compare Sloane 3847, fol. 13v; Additional MS. 36674, 6v.	

---

408. This section is repeated on Folger p. 63.

409. Compare Raziel, e.g., Sloane 3846, 140r: "Hermes said there is not such suffumigacions for to inclepe Spirits as Ambra & lignum aloes, costus, mustus, crocus & bloud of a lapwinge with thimiamate." Agrippa quotes this in OP book 1 chapter 43.

410. In marg.: "166."

hic coram nobis in quacunque parte mundi sis, et in aliqua parte mundi non tardetis, venite venite venite ad videndum seecretissima secretarum et ineffabile signa et non respuas respondere.	[space] here before us, from whatever part of the world you may be. Do not delay. Come, come, come and behold these most secret of all secrets and ineffable signs, and do not turn away from answering.

If he still doesn't appear, the master should raise his voice, and expel a magic hissing (or whistle), which flogs the air everywhere, and in a very firm voice, say:[411]

Coniuro te N per corroboratum nomine dei El + forte et admirabile virtuosam et amiabile tibi impero ut nulla mora facias et sine strepitu et omnia fallatia et absque omni deformitate in forma pueri tres annos nati venias, O N te exorcizo et potenter tibi impero per eum qui dixit et factum est, et per omnia nomina ipsius + Pneumaton + Adepleniton + Adonay + Zebaoth + Amioram + Comiceron + Sedalay + Tohomos + Zofyn + Agata + Bycol + Ycos + ut mihi alicui socioram meorum aliquod malifacias sed omnia perfeceris per inde ac nos iusserimus vel aliquis nostrum Iusserit alioquin a dignitatibus vestris te privabimus et in stagnum Ignis et sulphuris te precipitabimus eternaliter comburendum O N. in quacunque parte mundi sis. veni ergo et vide nomina et signa consecrata summum triumphatrem	I conjure you, O N., by the strengthening name of God EL + strong and wonderful, virtuous and adored by you, I command that you come with no further delay and without noise, and without any deceit, and without any deformity, in the form of a child three years old. O N., I exorcise and powerfully command you, by He who spoke and it was done, and by all his names + Pneumaton + Adepleniton + Adonay + Zebaoth + Amioram + Comiceron + Sedalay + Tohomos + Zofyn + Agata + Bycol + Ycos* + that you do [+ no] wrong to me or any of my associates, but complete all that we have ordered, otherwise we will deprive you of all your dignities, and cast you into the pit of fire and brimstone, forever burning. O N., come therefore from whichever part of the world you may be, and behold the names

* These last seven names appear on Folger p. 61, and also in the last paragraph of Sepher Raziel liber Salomonis (Sloane 3846).

---

411. Compare Sloane 3847, 13v: "... *et cum non apparuerint exaltet vocem suam sibil[??] magnum exeat cum magna impetu (?) quasi aerem verberans undique socios iterum iteratur et voce firmissima dicat* ..." It is tempting to connect this to the magic whistle.

[*summi triumphatorem] et per virtu-tem eorum nobis obedire tenearis sint que verba que de ore nostro [*meo] ex-ierunt tibi ignis ferventissimus que te comburent in eternum.	and consecrated signs of the most high conqueror, and by that power you are compelled to obey us, which words from my mouth are a burning fire to you, which will burn you eternally.*
* Compare Sloane 3847, 17r.	

If he has not appeared, the master should rise and strongly reassure his associates, and then slash the air with the sword, towards each of the four quarters of the world, saying these words, first towards the East:

Ubi es N spiritus veni, veni, veni, e vide celestia signa ineffabilia singularia nomina, et nomina creatoris, et nomina angelos qui socii tui extiterunt, iterum atque iterum te exorcizo atque impero per potentissimum atque coroboratum nomen + El + forte et admirabile ut nulla mora facias, et sine strepitu et omni deformitate venias informa pueri tres annos nati, et nobis ad interogata re-spondeas.	Where are you, O spirit N.? Come, come, come and behold the celestial signs and ineffable singular names, and the names of the creator, and the names of the angels whereby your associates have come forth.* Again and again I ex-orcize you and command you by the most powerful and strengthening name + El + strong and wonderful, that you make no further delay, and come with-out loud noise or any kind of deformity, in the form of a child three years old, and respond to our questioning.†
* Compare Michael 276, *Key of Solomon* II, 33: *uenite et uidete celestia signa et sitis testes coram altissimo inobedientie horum spirituum qui uestri socii extiterunt.* ["Come and behold the heavenly signs and bear witness before the Most High of the disobedience of these spirits, whereby your associates have stood out."] Similarly Mathers, *Key of Solomon* I, chap. 6; Aubrey 24, 81v; Sloane 3847, 17v.	
† Compare Sloane 3847, 17v.	

This say in the four parts

If he does not appear, the master should reform the circle and project the whistle towards the four quarters of the world, and in all adjoining, and bending his knees towards the North he should say:

In Nomine + Adonay + Eloe + Sabaoth + Saday + qui est dominus deus excelsis omnipotens Rex Israell N. sis nobis obediens in omnibus.	In the name of + Adonay + Eloe + Sabaoth + Saday + who is the Lord God on high, almighty king of Israel. O N., may you be with us, obeying in all things.

Then the master may rise and spread out his arms, as if to embrace the air towards the four quarters of the world. [412]

Coniuro te N in quacunque parte mundi sis per potentissimum et coroboratissimum nomen + dei El + forte et admirabile, et Adonay + sigillo Solis et Lune O N Te constringo et ligo [???]tibi precipio te coniuro et terribiliter, coniuro et exorsizo ut ad nos sine terrore et absque omne metu et sine omni deformitate de quovis loco ubicunque vis sis occurras ante circulum hunc ad faciendum totam nostram voluntatem supplex et mansuetus, et cum omni discretione discretus, quod si tardaveris et creatori nostro rebellis fueris tu in turpissimam lepram cades et in turpissima morte morieris et in igne quite vret et devestabit ex ipsa dei presentia coniiceris et in flamam ignis in flatus eris nomen tuum rescribam et in igne sulphuris et eorum periiciam, ita ut in eternum affligare, Iterum Coniuro te N et exorsizo te per nomen + Ia + Ia + Ia + quod interpretatur deus deus deus et per nomen + Tetragramaton + et per nomen ineffabile quod es + Iah + hee + he + vau + et	I conjure you, O N.,[*] in whatever part of the world you may be, by the most powerful and strengthening name + of God EL + strong and wonderful, and Adonay + with the sigil of the Sun and the Moon. O N., I constrain and bind you [???],[†] I order you, I conjure you, and terribly conjure and exorcize you, that (you come) to us without terror or any fear or ugliness, from whatever place you are, to come before this circle to do our will in all things, humbly and agreeably, and discreetly with all discretion, but if you are slow and rebel against our Creator, you will fall into the most foul leprosy, and die a most foul death, and in fire which will burn and lay waste to you, and cast you from the presence of God, and your name will be blown into burning flames; I will rewrite your name, and throw it down in flames of brimstone, just as you will be eternally afflicted. Again I conjure you N., and exorcise you by the name + Ia + Ia + Ia + which means "God, God, God" and
* In marg.: "167." † There is a blank space here.	

---

412. Compare Sloane 3847, 18r.

per nomen vell in nomine ignis qui potentissimum regnat et super omnem ignem dominantur ut ad nos venias cum celestia veritate et non cum aliqua falcitate.	by this name + Tetragrammon + and by the ineffable name, which is + Iah + Hee + He + Vau + and by the name or in the name of the fire which reigns most powerfully, and has dominion over all fires, that you come to us with heavenly truth, and without any deception.

[108]

How to call

Now when he is come, show him the exorcised pentacles which are on your chest, which, when he seeth, he will bow the knee and say, "What do you want, or why have you brought me here?"[413]

Then the exorcist, with an air of indignation, should command him to calm down, and be peaceable and silent. Then the master should make a fragrant odour, and he should cover the pentacle, the silence given. You may ask for whatever you wish.

Now when you have your desire, let the master say, *Vade in pace in locum tuum, et pax sit inter nos et te, In nomine patris filius et spiritus sanctus amen.* ["go in peace, and let there be peace between you and us, in the name of the Father, Son, and Holy Ghost. Amen."] [414]

Afterwards, recite the Gospel of John, "In the beginning was the Word, and the Word was with God" etc., "I believe in God" etc. (Apostles' Creed); for undermining (?) in love, say "Whoever will be saved" etc. (Athanasian Creed), etc.

Then they may leave the circle,[415] one after another, and wash their faces with water and hyssop, and they may return to their other clothes and business,[416] etc.

And note, because he might be bound with chains of iron or fire, no spirit will dare to make any delay.

And if he might be in any part of the world, you should add to the conjuration that he should at least send a messenger to declare how they are occupied.

---

413. In marg: "168."

414. JHP believes this is adapted from the standard closing words of the mass.

415. Compare Mathers, *Key of Solomon,* Book 1 and of chapter 7.

416. The last part of the sentence seems to be corrupt, but so the parallel texts in various *Clavicula* manuscripts.

And if he is rebellious against the exorcist and is unwilling to come, then write his name on paper, and soil it with mud, and a fire should be kindled with sulfur, pitch, horn, and other foul smelling things, and say the exorcism.

Coniuro te ignis per illum qui orbem contremere facitt quatinus spiritum illum N. callefacias et comburas ita quod in sua persona sentiat eternaliter.	I conjure you O fire* by him who makes the world tremble, that you heat and burn up this spirit N. and thus he will feel it forever.
* In marg.: "These maled. is set downe fol. 35 p. 2."	

And then throw the paper into the fire and say:

Maledictus et blasphematus sis N perpetualiter et in pena eternaliter et nulla requies sit in te in aliqua hora nec die nec nocte, si statim non eris obediens verbis que dicuntur de illo qui cremere facit orbem, et per hac nomina istorum nominum quibus omnia creatura humiliter obedit et pavere ac timore omnis eorum creatura contremiscit et in eis tonitrua et fulgura sunt creata que te et tuo subditos destruant: que sunt hec Adepleniton, Perasac, patir, fome, lameth, mem, menene, sameth, ay, ey, ffy, asode, Costin, vod, per ista nomina te N maledicimus et privamus ab omnibus graciis et priorum virtutem in stagnum ignis et sulphuris ut hostem [*usque]† in profundum abissi te religamus eternaliter nunc et in eternum.	May you be perpetually cursed and blasphemed, O N., and in eternal punishment, and may you have no respite at any time by day or night, if you do not immediately obey the words which are spoken by him who made the world tremble, and by these names of his, whom all creatures humbly obey, and tremble with fear and dread, which can subdue the thunder and lightning, these names of him who created you and who can destroy you; these names which are Adepleniton, Perasac, Patir, Fome, Lameth, Mem, Menene, Sameth, Ay, Ey, Ffy, Asode, Costin, Vod.* By these names I curse you, O N., and deprive you of all grace and prior powers, and relegate you to the lake of fire and sulphur, and into the deepest abyss, now and forever.
* In this *Clavicula* prototype this is the list of letters of the Hebrew alphabet, namely: Aleph, Beth, Gimel, Daleth, He, Vau, Zayin, Cheth, Teth, Yod, Kaph, Lamed, Mem, Nun, Samekh, Ayin, Pe, Tzaddi, Qoph, Resh, Shin, Tau. † So Aubrey 24, 83v; Michael 276, 56; and Additional MS. 10862, 49v.	

Orders for the excommunication [417]

Write the spirit's name, etc., and grave[418] or in paper make his picture, and while the malediction is reading, hold them over the fume, and at last throw them into the fire maledicted, and there let them burn. Note that the fire must be made with coals not consecrated, wherein must be put brimstone, hore,[419] cat's turds, leather, rags, asafoetida, pitch, etc.

Then without delay they will come to you from everywhere, saying "O Lord and prince, deliver us from this punishment." Then rewrite their names, and make a fragrant fire, and perfume it with fragrant spices, reveal the pentacle, and ask for your desires, and you will have them granted.

Know thou, whoever thou be, that shalt be master in this work, high, secret, and profound, that all is before said may be most perfectly done, and yet the spirit not come, nor be made subject, and the reason may be, for that something may be polluted, it may be the first month that he was called, or the first time he was called by the book, but therefore dismay not thyself, but put thy trust in God, observe the observations, be sure to have all needful necessaries, a fit place, convenient time, an intent to persevere and not to give over until thou have thy purpose, and then no doubt, but thou shalt prevail, and at length obtain thy purpose, but and if the spirit do, understand that thou once faint and mean to give over, if thou speed not at the first or second time, then will he be obstinate and delay his coming to the end to put thee from thy purpose, wherefore, once beginning, prosecute and persevere.

The spirit being excommunicated, as before is said, let him so continue by the space of twelve hours, which term being expired, read the invocation or conjuration for the four kings:

O Urieus, Amaymon, Paymon et Egine, etc. Which being done and yet the spirit not come, write their names, make their pictures, etc., doing with them in every respect as was done with the spirits, saying over the fire this:

Coniuro te ignis et exorciso te per illum qui orbem contremere facit ["I conjure and exorcise you, O fire, through him who makes the universe tremble"] and by him whose presence made the infernal powers to quake, that thou, O fire and angel of the most high God be now and from henceforth and that forever maledicted and accursed, and in as much as in thee lieth, grieve, torment, waste, and burn these names and pictures of these obstinate, stubborn, rebellious, and disobedient spirits, wicked kings, and unbelieving mates of that great and unhappy prince Luciffer, Oriens,

---

417. In marg.: "w" glyph.

418. Grave: engrave.

419. Hore: dirt, filth.

Amaymon, Paymon and Egine, so that even as thou, O fire, dost grieve and vex their names, or at least burn and consume them, so their proper persons, forms, and shapes most cursed may be afflicted, [109] and that most acerbitly,[420] in the bottomless pit, deep dungeon, and odious lake, which continually and without ceasing leaveth not off to burn with unquenchable fire mixed with sulfur, pitch, and other matter increasers of those flashing flames, being just plagues and punishments of God ordained, and for their merits Vriens, Paymon, Amaymon, and Egine etc., most justly provided. O fire, the Father curse thee, the Son curse thee, the Holy Ghost curse thee, all Angels, Archangels, Cherubim, Seraphim, Powers, Potestates, Principates, and Dominations curse thee, all holy patriarchs, prophets, apostles, martyrs, confessors, and virgins curse thee, O fire. All the powers of heaven, and elects of God curse thee, the licences, conjurations, threats, and indignations of God curse thee, and I now by the power and authority of my own priesthood, and by the virtue of all other priests that have been, are, and shall be in the church of God, in all countries, in all ages, and in all times now and forever, curse thee, the curse wherewith Cain, the whole world, and Judas were cursed, curse thee, all benedictions and blessings of God the Father, the Son, and the Holy Ghost curse thee, and curse thee again, and make thee of such power that thou mayest persecute, vex, waste, burn, and consume so the names of these rebellious and wicked kingly spirits, Oriens, Paymon, Amaymon, and Egine, that they may be urged thereby to come running and appealing to me for help, and requiring to be released of their anguish, sorrow, and unspeakable punishments, and that by the power and virtue of our Lord Jesus Christ who is the fire and light of all mankind, so be it. Fiat, fiat, fiat.

After [421] you have this done, throw into this maledicted fire, being mixed with the odours before spoken of, the names and pictures of these four kings, suffering the same to consume and burn, and then rest by the space of six hours, during which time if they come any one of them, or any others sent from them, then burn fragrant savours, and therein cast their names and pictures being newly written in paper or parchment.

But if they nor none from them come not after the twelve hours being expired from the excommunicating of the spirit as before, then anew write his name and picture, and a fair new fire being made with sweet savours. Cast the same in and say in the four quarters, having the sword and scepter in thy hands:

---

420. Acerbitly: harshly.

421. In left marg.: "w"; and in right marg.: "170."

Quid tardas? moraris? quid faci[ti]s O N preparate ipsum et obedias preceptorie tui, in nomine + domini Bachat + vel Vachat + Snyer [*super] + Abrac + Ruens + super vivens + Abeor + sny [*super] + Aberer +	Why do you delay?* What is making you late? O N., prepare yourself to obey your master, in the name + of the Lord Bachat + or Vachat + rushing upon + Abrac + surviving + Abeor + over + Aberer +
* Compare H., 124–125; LIH CXXXIII.56; and Folger p. 24, which is closer to H. and LIH..	

O N in nomine + Adonay + Eloy + Sabaoth + Sadaym + qui est dominus deus excelsus, Rex Israel sis nobis obediens in omnibus.	O N., in the name + Adonay + Eloy + Sabaoth + Sadaym + who is the Lord God on high, King of Israel may you be with us, obeying in all things.

Ubi es N. spiritus veni veni veni,	Where are you, O spirit N.? Come, come, come.

Then show the pentacle, and say:

Ecce conclusionem vestram nolite fieri inobedientes	Behold your conclusion if you are disobedient.

This done, here begins the bonds over the four elements which must be read for all experiments.

O vos Elementa quattuor viz Ignis, Aer, Aqua et terra, vos exorcizo per hac quattuor nomina dei quorum virtute vos dampnum, + didragramay vel dydagamay + Saday + Ya + Yoth + et per hec sex nomina quorum virtute sit celorum et Infernus sex diebus + dodrast + gimel + ditro + Alpha + Congor + Coron + , et per sx Ignis ante conspectum dei comburentes, quorum virtute stelle lunem capiunt, viz + Nodgor + Romathi + Laromathi + dimider + gridorio + piri + et per sex Angelos ante	O you four elements, namely fire, air, water, and earth, I exorcise you by these four names of God by the power of which you were damned, + didragramay (or dydagamay) + Saday + Ya + Yoth + and by these six names by the power of which he [+created] Heaven and Hell in six days:* + Dodrast + Gimel + Ditro + Alpha + Congor + Coron +, and by the six fires which burn before the face of God, by the power of which the Moon and stars are captured, namely + Nodgor + Romathi + Laromathi + Dimider +
* Reading "creavit caelum et infernum in sex dies." Folger: "sit celorum et Infernus sex diebus."	

Tronum dei cantantes cantica nova quibus totus mundus salvificabitur + Uriel + Asturco + Ronos + Perth + Pariel + Cutro + et per sex animalia ante deum gradiencia occulos ante et retro habencia, quorum virtute visum capiunt occuli generacionis continantur moventer mare et ayer, + parcoth + Vstiron + Nossor + Surth + detriell + Arro +, per primum dei adventum, etiam per smargeon + cuius virtute Adam factus loquebatur carnationem, et per Baptismum quod accepit in flumine Iordanis ostendens exemplum Christianitatis, et per suam circumcicionem, per ieiunium suum, et per passiones suas, et per resurrectionem suam, et crucem suam in qua mortem accepit, per salute humani generis, et per gloriosam resurrectionem suam, et per hac sanctissima nomina + dupo + Sulon + Nocdi + Rimeloth + e per admirabilem assencionem suam, et per tronum ubi sedet Aymaelion + per eum qui facit Angelos suos spiritus et ministros suos ignem comburentem qui virtutem capit altitudinis + Noscor + Retulo + qui venturus est iudicare vivos et mortuos, Invirtute + Breri + Mylmo + et nomina dei + Reggo + Miso vel dusperha + Palusper + Noroth + Tetragrammaton + Vilgo + Nycetus + Lillo + quorum potestate continentur universalis ecclesia, et per omnia que que de nobis, invirtute Stelco + et suo potencia et per excellenciam

Gridorio + Piri + and by the six angels singing new songs before the throne of God with which the whole world will be saved [*] + Uriel + Asturco + Ronos + Perth + Pariel + Cutro + and by the six living creatures walking before God, having eyes in front and back,[†] by the power of which the eyes capture the vision of the generation they encounter, the sea and the air are moved,[‡] + Parcoth + Vstiron + Nossor + Surth + Detriell + Arro +, by the first advent of God, also by Smargeon + with the power of which speaking Adam became flesh, and by his baptism which was taken in the river Jordan, showing the precedent of Christianity, and by his circumcision, by his fasting, and by his passion, and by his resurrection, and by his cross, where he accepted death, (and) by the salvation of the human race, and by his glorious resurrection, and by these most sacred names + Dupo + Sulon + Nocdi + Rimeloth + and by his admirable ascension, and by the throne where he sits Aymaelion + and by Him who makes his angels, spirits, and his ministers a burning fire which captures the power of the height + Noscor + Retulo + who will soon come to judge the living and the dead, with the power of + Breri + Mylmo + and the names of God + Reggo + Miso vel dusperha + Palusper + Noroth + Tetragrammaton + Vilgo +

---

[*] Compare Revelations 14:3.
[†] Compare Revelations 4:6.
[‡] Meaning unclear.

et maiestatem et dignitatem quas scimus servare invirtute + polio + dydagramay + ditro + Northi + Paldo + Palloqui + et per Sancta Cherubine et Seraphin quem scimus regnare cum novem nominibus et ordinibus + Angelorum + serph + Velco pitros + vertes + velio + verlery + Nogel + Anero + Nisanl + per virginitatem beate Marie cuius castitas est Innortho + et ditroel + Nondoel + Nemper + quorum [110] virtute nascitur deus de Maria virgine, et per Gulprul + cuius virtute veniant et integra et pura corpor a nobis accipiant et visibiliter appareant mihi iste spiritus N cum omnibus sociis potestatibus et virtutibus ad obediendes mihi Ita quod in vobis nullam inveniam defectum quin visibilliter et humiliter veniat in forma humana facturus quicunque illis precipiam invirtute dei omnipotentis sine dolo et sine mendacio, et sine omne lesione mei corporis et anime mee Amen.

Nycetus + Lillo + which hold the power of the Universal Church, and all which is from us, with the power of Stelco + and with its might and by the excellence and greatness and dignity, which we know to protect with the power + Polio + Dydagramay + Ditro + Northi + Paldo + Palloqui + and by the sacred Cherubim and Seraphin which we know to reign with the nine names and orders of + Angels + serph + Velco Pitros + Vertes + Velio + Verlery + Nogel + Anero + Nisanl + by the virginity of the blessed Mary whose chastity is Innortho + and Ditroel + Nondoel + Nemper + by the power of which *[110]* God was born from the Virgin Mary, and by Gulprul + by the power of which may they come and take whole and pure bodies, and may this spirit N. appear visibly before us with all associates, powers, and virtues, obedient to me. Therefore because I will discover no defect in you unless he may come visibly and humbly in human form accomplishing whatever things I will order, by the power of almighty God without trickery or deceit, and without any injury to my body or soul. Amen.

And if you invoke more spirits include this:

... quatinus vestram virtute veniant et integrum et purum corpus a nobis accipiant et visibilliter mihi appareant istus spiritus et reges cum omnibus eorum ministris principibus, ducibus

... as far as your power may they come and take whole and pure bodies, and may those spirits and kings appear visibly to me, with all their ministers, princes, dukes, domestic powers.

potestatibus familiaribus ita quod in vobis nullam inveniam defectum qui visibiliter et humiliter et non terrebiliter pacifice quiete et honeste veniat in forma humana facturi quicquid illis precipiam lesione omni mei corpus et anime mee etc.	Therefore because I will discover no fault in you unless they come visibly, with humility and not terror, peacefully, quietly, and honourably, in human form, quickly doing whatever I will order, and [+ without] any harm to my body or soul, etc.

The necessaries for this art of Necromancy

First have faith[422] in God, acknowledge him to be almighty, call for his help, lean upon his sufferance, do work of charity, use abstinence, confess thy sins, repent truly, and transport thyself to a better kind or shape, and fulfill enerirnell,[423] and keep observations.

Then provide an honest consecrated priest, three honest associates, books, vellum, standish,[424] circle, palm crosses, sticks, a knife with a white haft, a black goat's horn, a sword, a scepter, two rings, one of copper, another of silver gilt, in the one must be written Tetragrammaton, in the other words to please the spirit, a rod of correction, the lamina, the principal's crown, a crown of virgin parchment for every of the associates, ink to write orderly prepared, Solomon's pentacle, Solomon's seals, seven planets, and their characters, oils, powders, blood, chalk, pens, suffumigations, a copper needle, vestment, albs, stole, fannell,[425] glove, garments white, candles, coals, censer, holy water bucket, sprinkle,[426] water, salt, tewisons,[427] defensatives viz. or protections, silk to cover the lamina, *sede maiestatis dei* ["the seat of the majesty of god"], and a cover for the same, a cover for every one of the seven planets, spices or odors for the same, a table, a tablecloth, a chair for the master, stoles for the associates, two white candlesticks, four evangelists, ashes made of a palm stick hallowed on Palm Sunday, the plate of copper having thereon pictured the spirits, suffumigations for the angels,

---

422. In right marg.: "140."
423. Unknown meaning.
424. Standish: an inkstand.
425. Fannell: a band worn on the priest's left wrist.
426. Sprinkle: a sprinkler for holy water.
427. Unknown.

suffumigations to please the spirit, suffumigations to urge the spirit a body, ordures for the excommunication, etc.

The Beginning of Circle Work

First the master and all the associates must bleed a little. They must use abstinence, and with a true believing heart on the first Wednesday of the new Moon, and in the hour of Mercury, let the master confess himself unto God, and the same day at night let there be a bath provided of fair running water, mixed with bay leaves and lavender, etc. which must be of the priest hallowed as holy water is, and of the same being naked, let him take and put upon his head that it may run down to his feet, and say, "I christen or baptize me, N., in the name of the Father, and of the Son, and of the Holy Ghost. Amen." Then let him say:

O Lord Jesus Christ that madest me, an unworthy and wretched sinner, unto thy similitude, O Jesu, now vouchsafe to bless, sanctify, and hallow this element of water, that it may be a cleansing unto me now both in body and soul, and that no illusions nor deceit overcome and vanquish me, and thou almighty Father that gavest thy only begotten son to be baptised in the flood Jordan and that of John Baptist. I most entirely pray and beseech thee, that thou wilt grant me that this water here present may be to me instead of baptism, so that now thereby I N. may be renewed, cleansed, and made free from all manner of uncleanness, wherewith, O God, I confess it is inflicted and that by the infection of the old man, and crafty assaults of Satan, and that I may be made pure from all [???]429 and all manner of sins viz. past, present, and to come, and that by the virtue of our Lord Jesus Christ, thy holy, true, and only son, which liveth and reigneth with thee and thy Holy Spirit now and forever, one God, world without end. Amen.

Then wash all thy body in that water, which being done, christen all thy fellows as is above said, and put on them their white vestments, clean and well smelling, and having used abstinence three days at the least during which time orisons have been

---

428. In marg.: "w" glyph.

429. A word seems to be omitted here.

used. Then let them demean themselves towards the circle, the master having the sword in his left hand, the ring upon his little finger of the same hand and the scepter in his right hand. Let the associates bear the charact[er]s, censer, suffumigations, etc., saying, *Si deus nobiscum quis contra nos.* ["if God is with us, who can stand against us?"], etc....

In dei nomine amen ["in the name of God. Amen."].

I shall show you the way of operation after the mind of some who were herein expert.

[111]

1. First you[430] shall understand that this art is divided into three manner of things viz. in the disposition of working of it.

2. The second in the constraining of them that shall answer thee.

3. The third in fulfilling of your purpose.

In disposition of works, there is to be required clemence[431] of soul, for thou must be clean, confessed of thy sins, contrite and penitent for the same fully purposed of amendment,[432] and receive the benefit of absolution, even as though thou shouldest depart out of this wretched state of life presently.

Also thou must have cleanness of body, for thou must be newly changed as in bathing, shaving, washing, and scouring, and made clean from sweat and all other corruptions of body.

Then thou[433] must have cleanness of clothing, for all thy clothing must be sweet smelling, and of good savour, for spirits therein delight exceedingly. Wherefore thou shalt know for certainly that if thou have any spot of sin or other filth or corruption in thy clothes, or deadly sin in thy soul, the spirits will not obey thee, for they think thee unworthy to call, constrain, bind, or compel them, for that thou art unclean, either bodily or ghostly.

Rules

Hope thou must also as this, thou mayest not come to this work neither contemptuously or temptingly, as who would say presuming to attempt to assay and prove

---

430. In right marg.: "140."

431. Clemence: mildness.

432. I.e., completely committed to correcting your faults.

433. In left marg.: "w"; in right marg.: "141."

whether your experiment be true or false as one that is foolhardy. Nor thou mayest not come to this work heedely [434] or over boldly, but must have thy necessaries required in this noble craft or science of magic, thy book, thy confession fair written, thy instruments and other necessaries, for thou must not trust in thine own strength, but thou must wholly trust and depend in the might and power of God, wherefore thou must know for certain, that if thou go to this work unadvisedly, temptingly, or scoffingly, thy operation shall be fearful, thy answer none at all, or very subtle and false. Also thou must go to this operation as sadly, devoutly, and holy as thou shouldest go to receive the blessed sacrament of our Lord's body and blood, trusting undoubtedly that, by the merits of Christ's passion of thy unfeigned faith of thy clean life and great devotion, that thou shalt have grace to constrain, to compel, and subdue to thy commandment all manner of spirits, both of good and evil.

The day [435] that thou goest to this work, thou shouldest hear three masses even to the end. One must be of the Trinity, one of our Lady, and one of Saint Cyprian, and at every of them, offer one penny. When thou enterest thy work, thou must of necessity be fasting and so must continue thy work in abstinence. Until thou have done, thou must demean thyself as honestly as possible thou canst, and let thy meat be white meat as small [436] etc.

Preparing days

Note: During the preparing days before thou work, it behooveth thee to say these Psalms:

"*Deus in nomine tuo*" ["Save me, O God, by your name"], Psalm 53; "*Deus misereatur nostri*" ["May God have mercy on us"], Psalm 66; "*Mittere mei deus*" ["Be merciful to me, O God"], Psalm 50; "*Benedicite omnia opera domini*," ["O all works of the Lord, bless ye"], Psalm [???][437]; "*Laudate domini de celis*" ["Praise the Lord from the heavens"], Psalm 148; "*Nunc dimittis servum tuum domine*" ["Now you dismiss your servant, O Lord"], Psalm,[438] and ever praise God of his infinite mercy to grant thee grace to make a perfect conclusion, and that thou mayest have thine intent, for without his grace and succours thy labour is but in vain, time lost, charges cast away, and thou in great danger, and thou must devoutly pray to the angels and to all saints to extend to thee their help and to further thy work, thou must have also perseverance viz., though thou have no

---

434. Heedely: giving attention (probably a mistake.)

435. In marg.: "141."

436. Small: from a small animal

437. There is a blank space in the manuscript. This is Daniel 3:57 (KJV Daniel 34 ff).

438. Luke 2:29–32.

appearance or sight by calling one hour, 2, etc., one day, 2, etc., one week, 2, etc., one month, 2., etc., thou must neither faint, nor mistrust thy work to be unperfect or false, and so of good hap[439] to despair, but determine thyself to persevere and not to give him over etc. For it may be so that time or place is not convenient nor according to the experiment or conclusion, or it may fortune that the spirits that thou callest be occupied with some others that hath by constraint them bound unto him, and so by that means may defer their coming for a time. Further know thou that spirits be very loath to be brought to subjection, and that is the cause sometimes that they come not at the first, second, third, etc. calls. But their nature is to prolong their coming as long a time as possible. They may and as much as in them lieth, will minister cause to urge you to infringe your work and to give over your purpose, but dismay not thyself. Therefore be constant and bold, have faith, hope to do well, continue thy purpose, and have a desire to see the end, and doubt not of good[440] and happy success, for having once constrained and bound them, ever after of force they must needs be pressed to come and obey thy commandment and will, and that upon the reading of their proper invocation to the which they be sworn, or to some other strong vincle[441] orderly done, etc., and above all thou must work so secretly, that none know thy intent nor purpose other than such as are sworn and present at the work.

Note: whatsoever is practiced in the said work or done by the workmen, whatsoever is seen or heard, by the spirits' illusions or otherwise, it must not be discovered to any other earthly creature, nor the spirit to be called once in vain named, but the society may talk of all secrets among themselves and impart the same to the ghostly father which must ever be but one priest, for if ever they discover the secrets thereof to any others, though shalt either never or very hardily have thy intent performed, and to be short, if counsel of all hands be not kept, it may turn to your own destruction sundry ways.

[112]

Place, time, person, method

The third part is to call and constrain any spirit, etc., to make answer and to perform thy intent. This is divided into four parts, viz., where thou shalt call, when, whom, and how. First thou shalt call in a fair chamber quadrant and twenty or twenty-four at the most in broad in every part, a window a cubit wide or a little more, east, west, north, and south. The floor of the chamber must be paved, border or plas-

---

439. Hap: fortune.
440. In right marg.: "141."
441. Vincle: bond.

tered very plain and close so that thou mayest make thy circle thereon, with chalk or coal, that it may be perfectly seen. This house or chamber must be in a void place, and not near the course of men, for the opinion of some expert men in this art, is that spirits are more willing to appear in some waste place, as in woods, heath, fens, moors, downs, or in any place where is no great resort, nor where none of the seven sacraments have been ministered, for they hold opinion the place is holy where such is practiced. Be warned.

Also thou[442] must understand that all times are not convenient for to work in, for after the opinion of some from the change of the Moon unto the opposition, thou mayest work, but Solomon sayeth the most best times be the even days betwixt the change and the full, as 2, 4, 6, 8, 10, 12, 14, which being ended, look thou work no more until the next change. This rule is the most profitest[443] of others. Also some necromancers say they have begun in the new of the Moon, and it hath been thirty days' labour before they could have any appearance or answer, therefore let not this work seem tedious, nor think for one day 2, 3, 4, etc. being spent therein, and no good done, that all is in vain, seeing great clerks and expert herein have traveled many days as namely three, and that after they have once had appearance, or ever they could have any sight or appearance. Also every hour is not necessary nor expedient to thine operation, for every spirit is subject to one of the seven planets, and he will not lightly obey, nor come in none other hour, but in the hour of his own planet, and when his own planet reigneth, and in that he must needs obey, etc. Wherefore thou must know under what planet thy spirit is or else thou must prove every hour until thou find that is necessary and expedient, etc., which mark.

Also thou must note that all weathers are not good to enter thy work. Wherefore when thou wilt begin thy work, see that the air be clear, and if it be in the day that the Sun shine, if in the night that the Moon shine, or the skies full of stars, but take heed of foul weather, or close weather, for in that the spirit may not come, and why? Because he cannot receive bodily form or shape. Wherefore select fair weather for the spirit much delighteth therein.

Now I have shewed thee place and time, thou oughtest to work in, whom thou shalt call, and how, now thou shalt understand that thou mayest call unto the circle spirits good and bad, first celestial angels, spirits of the air, and devils of hell, etc., and that in this manner. First when thou art well-disposed as is before said, choose a good time and weather according with a planet congruent to thy operation, and look that

---

442. In marg.: "162."

443. Profitest: profitable.

thy circle hallowed with all thy instruments necessary, and thy fellows virtuously disposed, and being in the circle, deliver him that shall hold it the sword, saying,

Frater per virtutem sanguinis domini nostri Iesu Christi, do tibi potestatem ut hunc gladium benedictum tangere, tenere, gubernare valeas, cum quo per ignem nominis, fraudilosae malignorum ipsum portas compestas, per eum qui venturus est iudicare vivos et mortuos et seculum per ignem Amen.	O brother, by the power of the blood of our Lord Jesus Christ, I give to you the power, that this sword may be strong to touch, hold, control, with which, through the fire of the name,* you will compel the gates† of the fraudulent and evil spirits. Through Him who will come to judge the living and the dead and the world by fire. Amen.‡

* Instead of "*cum quo per ignem nominis, fraudulosae...*" Sloane 3849 reads *cum quo et per quem omnis* ["with which and by which, all fraudulent..."].
† Sloane 3849: *potestas* ["the power"].
‡ Compare Sloane 3849, 24r.

Having the sword, then must he sit down, turning his face unto thee, being the master, and hold the sword as upright as is possible, then the master must put the ring with great devotion upon his little finger of the left hand, and take the scepter in the right hand, and turn towards the place where the spirit inhabiteth, saying devoutly and with a heavenly faith this invocation following:

O thou[444] spirit N., or whatsoever name thou will call, wherever thou be, etc. I thee call in the name of the eternal God. I conjure thee by the might of him that is almighty. I bid and command thee by him that is most holy. I charge thee by the might of the Father omnipotent, by the wisdom of the Son most loving, by the Holy Ghost the comforter, by the holy and undivided Trinity, and by all the holy names of God, and especially by the virtue and might of these most holy names + Tetragrammaton + Iesu + Alpha + and Omega + Agyos + Emanuell + Agla + Usyon + basyem + Christus + Sabaoth + Adonay + panton + Craton + Ysus + Messias + Medekym + Halvecia + Hekesy + Heban + Medan + Trabema + zarohaday + flioboy + Obba + Alba + Senaphenas + and by all other names of God by the which thou art commanded, constrained, and bound, I constrain, conjure, and command thee by all miracles and deeds of our lord Jesu Christ, and by all pains and passions that he suffered in his glorious body, and by his marvelous nativity, by his annunciation, by his circumcision, by his tribulation, by his scourging, by his beating, and by his most precious death the which he meekly and graciously suffered to redeem mankind, by his

444. In marg.: "142."

descension to hell, whither he brought Lucifer and bound him and brought his well-beloved children, out of those most painful and lamentable hellish torments, to the joys of the heavenly paradise, by his wonderful resurrection and marvelous ascension, and by the might and virtue of him when he shall come in the end of the world to judge both the [113] quick and dead, etc.

Well now[445] I have taught thee the manner of calling: first where, when, whom, and how. Now shall I show the last part, viz., to fulfill thy purpose wherein there is no more, but when thou hast them before thy presence, make thy conclusion, incense them with incense and sweet savour till they have fulfilled thy purpose, and when thou hast thy intent, licence them to depart in this manner,[446] that as at this time ye depart and go to your place where God hath ordained you to abide without any great noise or storms, so at all times when I call or shall call you again, without any manner of tarrying that you come unto me and fulfill my intent,

| Discedite nunc discedite nunc discedite nunc per virtutem istorum nomina dei + Agla + Agla + Agla + Tetragramaton + et per virtutem omnium sanctorum nomine dei, et per virtutem domini nostri Iesu Christi qui venturus est iudicare vivos et mortuos et seculum per ignem Amen Ite in pace pax domini nostri Iesu Christi sit inter nos et vos. In nomine patris et filii et Spiritus Sancti Amen. | Depart now, depart now, depart now, by the virtue of these names of God + AGLA + AGLA + AGLA + Tetragrammaton + and by the virtue of all the holy names of God, and by the virtue of our Lord Jesus Christ, who will come to judge the living and the dead and the ages by fire. Amen. Depart in peace. The peace of Our Lord Jesus Christ be between you and us. In the name of the Father and the Son and the Holy Ghost. Amen. |

An invocation unto the four kings to urge and constrain a spirit

| O Oriens, Amaymon, Paymon et Egin, qui estis 4or reges potentissimi iuxta 4or partes mundi et ceteris malis speritibus praeestis, nos factiad Imaginem | O Oriens, Amaymon,* Paymon, and Egin, who are the four mighty kings of the four parts of the universe, and who are in charge of the other evil spirits; we |
| * In left marg. in pencil: "See page 105." Further down in brown ink is "108" and "w" glyph. In right marg.: "83. a." | |

---

445. In marg.: "143." Several pages of Sloane 3849 don't seem to be represented, but the next part corresponds with fol. 28v.

446. In marg.: "Licens."

dei, dotati potentia dei et eius facti voluntate per potentissimum, et coroboratum nomen dei, + El + forte et admirabile vos exorcisamus et Imperamus per eum qui dixit et factum est, et per omnia nomina dei, et per nomen + Adonay + Ely + Elohim + Elohe + Zebaoth + Elyon + Escherchiae + Iah + Tetragramaton + Saday + domi[n]us deus excelsus, exorcizo vos atque potenter imperamus vos Oryens, Amaymon, paymon, et Egin, ut constringatis et coerctetis spiritum illum Oberion pertinacissimum statim et sine ulla mora venire ante circulum hoc in aspectu nostrum in pulchra forma, viz pueri tres annos nati, et [+implere voluntatem nostram,] sine deformitate et tortuositate aliqua, constringite et coarctate, [illum] quia vos imperamus per nomen + Y + et V + quod Adam audiuit, et loqutus est, et per nomen dei + Agla + quod Loth audiuit et factus salvus cum familia sua, et per nomen Ioth + quod Iacob audiuit ab Angelo secum luctante et liberatus est de manu fratris sui Esau, et per nomen + Anephexeton + quod Aaron audiuit et loquens et sapiens factus et est et per nomen + Zebaoth + quod Moyses nominavit et omnia flumina et paludes de terra egipti verse fuerunt in sanguinem, et per nomen + Ecerchie + Oriston + quod nominavit et omnes fluvij ebulierunt ranas, et ascenderunt in domos egiptios omnia destruentes, et per nomen + Elion + [+quod]

being made* in the image of God, endowed with power from God and made according to his will; we exorcize you by the most powerful and strengthening name of God, + El + strong and wonderful, and we command you by him who spoke the word and it was done, and by all the names of God, and by the name + Adonay + Ely + Elohim + Elohe + Zebaoth + Elyon + Escherchie + Iah + Tetragrammaton + Saday + Lord God Most High: we exorcise you, and powerfully command you Oriens, Amaymon, Paymon, and Egin, that you constrain and confine that most stubborn spirit Oberion to come immediately and appear to our sight without any delay before this circle in an agreeable form, namely that of a three-year-old boy, and [+to satisfy our wishes,] without any ugliness or deformity, constrained and bound, because I command this by the name + Y and V + which Adam heard and spoke; and by the name of God, + Agla +, which Lot heard, and was saved with his family; and by the name Joth + which Jacob heard from the angel wrestling with him, and was delivered from the hand of his brother Esau; and by the name + Anaphexeton +, which Aaron heard and spoke, and was made wise; and by the name + Zebaoth +, which Moses named, and all the rivers were turned into blood; and by the name + Eserchie + Oriston +, which Moses named, and all

* Compare H.: *exorcismus spirituum aereorum.*

Moyses nominavit et fuit grando talis, qualis non fuit ab initio mundi, et per nomen + Adonay + quod Moyses nominavit et fuerunt locustae, et apparuerunt super terram Egiptios, et comederunt qui residua erant grandini, et per nomen + Alpha et Omega + quod daniel nominavit et destruxit bel et draconem interfecit, et per nomen + Emanuell + quod trees pueri Sidrach, Misach, et Abednago in camino ignis [+ardentis] cantaverunt, et liberati fuerunt, et per [+nomen] + hagios + et sedem + Adonay + et per + Otheos + Iskiros + Athanatos + Paracletus + et per hac tria seecreta nomina + Agla + On + Tetragramaton + adiuro et contestor, et per hac nomina et per alia nomina domini nostri dei omnipotentis vivi et veri, te Oberion quia tua culpa de Celo eiectus eras, usque ad internum locum exorsizamus et viriliter imperamus vos Oriens, Amaymon, Paymon, et egine per eum qui dixit et factum est, cui omnes obediunt creature, et per illud tremendum dei iudicium, et per mare omnibus incertum, vitreum, quod est ante conspectum divine, maiestatis grandiens et potentiale, et per 4or divina animalia T ante sedem divine maiestatis gradientia, et occulos antea et rete habentia, et per ignem ante eius Thronum circumstante, et per sanctos Angelos Celorum, T et per eam qui Ecclesia dei nominatur, et per summam sapientiam omnipotentis dei viriliter exorsizamus

the rivers brought forth frogs, and they ascended into the homes of the Egyptians, destroying every thing; and by the name + Elion +, [+which] Moses named, and there was great hail, such as had not been from the beginning of the world; and by the name + Adonai +, which Moses named, and locusts came, which appeared throughout the whole land of Egypt, devouring all that the hail had left; [+and by the name + Schema Amathia +, which Joshua called upon, and the sun stayed his course;]* and by the name + Alpha and Omega +, which Daniel named, and destroyed Bel and slew the dragon; and by the name + Emmanuel +, which the three children, Sidrach, Misach, and Abednego, sung in the midst of the [+fiery] furnace, and were delivered; and by the [+name] + Hagios +; and by the seat of + Adonai +; and by + Otheos + Ischyros + Athanatos + Paracletos +; and by these three secret names, + Agla + On + Tetragrammaton +, I do adjure and call you to witness, and by these names, and by all the other names of our Lord, God almighty, living and true, you, Oberion, because of your crime you were expelled from Heaven, all the way to hell. We exorcize and powerfully command you, Oriens, Amaymon, Paymon, and Egin, by Him who spoke and it was done, whom all creatures obey, and by the dreadful day of judgment, and by the uncertain sea of

* So H., probably omitted by mistake.

vos Oriens, Amaymon, Paymon, et Egine, ut constringatis et coerctetis illum spiritum Oberion ut nobis hic ante hunc circulum in aspectu nostrum venire cito et sine omni mora ad faciendam nostram voluntatem in omnibus prout placuerit nobis per sedem + Baldachie + et per hoc nomen + Primeumaton + quod Moyses nominavit, et in cavernis abyssi fuerunt profundati vell absorpti, Datan + Corah & Abiron, et in virtute istius nominis + Primeumaton + tota Celi militia compellente, maledicimus vos, privamus vos Oriens, Amaymon, Paymon, et Egine ab omni officio, loco, et gaudio vestro usque in profundum abyssi, et usque in ultimum diem Iudicii vos pono, et religo in ignum eternum, et in stagnum ignis et sulphuris, nisi statim constringatis et coarctetis spiritum illum Oberione cito et sine omni mora venire ante circulum, hunc in aspectum nostrum ad faciendam voluntatem nostram prout placirit [*placuerit] nobis, Oriens, Amaymon, Paymon, et Egin, in omnibus constringite, et coarctate illum Oberione, per hec nomina + Adonay + Zebaoth + Adonay + Amioram + constringite et coarctate Oberione, imperat vos + Adonay + Saday + Rex regum per potentissimus et tremendissimus, cuius vires nulla subterfugere potest creatura, vobis pertinacissimis futuris nisi obedieritis et constringatis illum Oberione venire affabilem cito et sine mora ante hunc circulum in aspectum nostrum

glass, which is before the face of the Divine Majesty, making great* and possessing power, and by the four divine creatures T going before the seat of the Divine Majesty, having eyes in front and behind, and by the fire which is on both sides of his throne, and by the holy angels of Heaven, T and by that which is called the Church of God, and by the most high wisdom of almighty God we powerfully exorcise you Oriens, Amaymon, Paymon, and Egin, that you constrain and confine that spirit Oberion to come immediately and appear to our sight without delay before this circle to accomplish our will in all things, by the seat of + Baldachia + and by this name + Primeumaton +, which Moses named, and the earth opened up and swallowed up Corah, Dathan, and Abiram, and by the power of this name + Primeumaton + commanding the whole host of Heaven: we curse you, and deprive you of your office, joy, and place, O Oriens, Amaymon, Paymon, and Egin and I send you to the abyss of abysses until the final judgment day, and bind you fast into the eternal fires and into the pool of fire and brimstone, unless you immediately constrain and confine that spirit Oberion and come before this circle without any delay, to appear to our sight and fulfilling our will, Oriens, Amaymon, Paymon, and Egin, constrain him in all things, and compel that Oberion, by these names + Adonay + Zebaoth +

---

* H. had *gradiens* ["going"], echoing the subsequent phrase.

pulchra forma pueri tres annos nati et voluntatem nostram perimplere, Tandem ruina flebilis miserabilisque et ignis in perpetuum [in]extinguibilis vos manet, constringite ergo illum Oberione in nomine + Adonay + Zebaoth + Adonay + Amioram + constringite, constringite, constri[n]gite illum Oberionem, quid tardatis quid tardatis, festinate, imperat vobis Oriens, Amaymon, Paymon, et Egine + Adonay + Saday + Rex regum + El [+] aty + Titeip + Azia + Hyn + Ien + Minosel + Acadan + Vay + Vaa + Ey + Haa + Eie + Exe +A + El + El + El + A + hy + hau + hau + hau + Va + Va + Va + Va +

Adonay + Amioram + constrain and compel Oberion. He commands you, + Adonay + Saday + King of the kings, the most powerful and most terrible, whose strength no creature can evade; yours will be the most unyielding existence unless you obey and constrain that Oberion to come immediately and appear to our sight before this circle in an agreeable form, namely that of a three-year-old boy, and fulfill our will, otherwise you will remain in miserable ruin and unquenchable fire forever, unless you constrain that Oberion in the name + Adonay + Zebaoth + Adonay + Amioram + constrain him!, constrain him!, constrain that Oberion, why do you delay? why do you delay? hasten!, he commands you, O Oriens, Amaymon, Paymon, and Egin, + Adonay | Saday | King of Kings + El [+] aty + Titeip + Azia + Hyn + Ien + Minosel + Acadan + Vay + Vaa + Ey + Haa + Eie + Exe +A + El + El + El + A + hy + hau + hau + hau + Va + Va + Va + Va +.

[114]

An Invocation / last

O thou Emperor and most magnificent ruler of all spirits, and thou thyself being a spirit known and called by the name and title of Tantavalerion *vel* ["or"] Golgathell, I command, exorcise, and charge thee by the mighty power and virtue of the true and living God, mine and thy Creator, by the mercy, pity, and compassion of Jesus Christ, his only son and the world's Saviour, and by the inestimable grace and goodness of the Holy Ghost, of all creatures the sanctifier, that thou bid and command N., that rebellious, stubborn, disobedient, cursed, and wicked king and spirit and an inferior vassal of thine, to come even now unto me and that without any tarrying or delay or hurt to me or my fellows or any other Christian or living creature, and that he do and fulfill my will even to the uttermost of his power in such sort, order, and manner as I have commanded him.

O you seven Senators,[447] Orymell, Tygra[,]danell, Salaryca, Asmo, Pascary, and Boell, I conjure you by the promise that God made to Adam of his son, Jesus Christ, that in the fullness of time he should come and break the serpent's head, to destroy all the rigor and cruelty of Satan, by the same faithful promise and by the coming to judgment of the same seed promised at the last day, called the terrible and dreadful day of doom, as when Michael the Archangel shall blow with his trump[448] unto wicked and disobedient spirits, a most fearful and hideous voice, "*Surgite mortui venite ad Iudicium*," ["arise, O dead, and come to judgement"], even as you, O noble and puissant senators, do trust and certainly believe as then and at the same day to be saved, and again to possess and enjoy your former rooms and place from which with the great prince Lucifer for your pride and disobedience you were cast forth, that you do your best, and be not slack therein, to cause and procure that obstinate and stubborn spirit [???][449] to come speedily unto me, and to fulfill my will and desire in all things, even as oft times I have before this time required him thereunto and that without molestation of the air, without thunderings, lightnings, blustering, or lofty winds, or tempests, either by sea or land, or hurting of me or any creature that ever God made other than to him by me for his good service shall be appointed him. And you four kings, viz., Orience, King of the East, Paymon, King of the West, Amaymon, King of the South, and Egine, King of the North, and thou Fenell, Alphasis, Emlon, and thou O Rodybell, Sylquam, Malcranus, Maltrans, and Rasyel, Rasinet, I conjure and straightly command you by the power and authority of the most high God the Father + Alpha + and + Omega +[450] the first and the last, the beginning and ending, and by him that all creatures obey, and by him the which all the company of Heaven and angels and all the powers of hell and you spirits of the air, water, earth, and fire do fear and reverence, and by all his great and wonderful names effable and ineffable within this book contained, or written in any tongue, speech, or language elsewhere, and namely by this great name, and name of excellent Majesty + Tetragramaton + and by all his power and might, by his son Jesus Christ's nativity, baptism, circumcision, fasting, praying, and temptation, by his preaching, miracles and holy supper, by his cross, death, and passion, by his burial, descension,[451] and glorious resurrection,

---

447. In marg. in pencil: "See 106."

448. Trump: trumpet.

449. There is a blank space in the Folger MS.

450. In marg.: "w" glyph.

451. Descension: descent.

and by his appearing to Mary Magdalene and his Apostles, and wonderful ascension, and by his sitting at the right hand of his father always for us miserable and sinful wretches making intercession, and by his glorious, triumphant, and most fearful coming to judgment in the last day, as when all flesh and all you spirits whose aid I now require, shall stand naked and bare, quivering and quaking before his tribunal seat and seat of singular brightness, to hear the sentence, that then and there shall proceed and go forth of his mouth compared to a two-edged sword which divideth in sunder[452] and entereth in through the reins[453] and marrow by these words and by these great names of God + Indros + Adros + Edros + Esaram + Agla + El + Adonay + Sabaoth + and by all other his holy and most virtuous names, I now here incite and charge you and every one of you, by your several names and offices, and that by the authority of our Lord Jesus Christ and of the Blessed Virgin Mary his Mother, who was *virgo ante partum, et post partum* ["a virgin before birth, and after birth"] a virgin when she conceived, and a virgin all her life continued by all other virgins and godly matrons, twelve Apostles, patriarchs, martyrs, confessors, and virgins, and by Saint Cyprian and by all other saints of God whose prayers, merits, and desserts I now at this time require to the furnishing of my request and desire in manner and form as is before said, or hereafter to be said, excogitated,[454] or meant, that now we may be safe from all perils of wicked and malicious spirits whom daily wait and lie in ambush to overthrow the prosperous and most happy estate of man, and further that all you, or some one of you or me, bring or send or cause to be brought or sent the spirit N., and that he coming may as well answer make for his contempt against God and me calling him by the power and might of his name and names, as also to enter the circle prepared for him with his name written therein and there still to remain and not to depart thence, till I have my desire and request in each point fulfilled, and licence, or give leave to him to depart to the place appointed him by God.

[115]

Wherefore, O ye noble and royal spirits, why tarry ye: why send ye him not? Why doth he not come hither and appear before me in a fair human form, *quasi puer tres annos nati* ["like a child of three years"], and that without tarrying, and to bring with him and to show and deliver me, here within this circle, the sum of gold or money, which by invocation and calling on I have and do desire, and still shall, till I obtain of him N.

---

452. In sunder: separated.

453. Reins: kidneys.

454. Excogitated: thought up.

Note: The spirit's [455] name must be written in virgin parchment, and say to that name, "O N., come quickly to the place here *iuxta nos posita et pro te facta* ["placed near us and made on your behalf"], O N., and that in the likeness of a child of three years of age, and now because thou hast been lawfully cited, invocated, conjured, and called, and that for thy stubbornness, disobedience, and contempt, thou hast neglected to come and appear and do my will, therefore and in consideration thereof, and that by the power of God *et auctoritatem mihi concessa* ["and permitted by my authority"], I do charge and bind thee upon pain of eternal death, continual horror, and everlasting torments and damnation, O thou spirit N., that thou leave off thy delays and speedily come and that presently."

Then hold the spirit's name and the picture of him, the cat's turds, etc., and the rest of the ordures for excommunicating in thy hand over the fire and say:

[+ Malediction]

I conjure thee, thou spirit, and that by him that did make the world to shake, and by him that made the stones rent, the graves open, and dead bodies to rise up, and by him that entered the lowest parts and dispossessed devils forth of men, that this fire of hell may burn thee, that thou may now feel thyself to burn and be pained, and that in thine own person, eternally.

[No]w if he come not

O thou spirit [456] N., the which hath not obeyed the precepts and commandments of God, nor yet hast obeyed me, and yet I am and will be the true and faithful servant of the everlasting and eternal God. I command thee here to appear or ever that I do fully and effectually excommunicate or curse thee, and for thy contumacy if thou do not come, and appear here forthwith, that then, O thou spirit N., I do here excommunicate, maledict, and curse thee by the name of N., and thy name here written, and that by the great sentence and curse of our holy church of God, and that by the whole authority of our Lord Jesus Christ and of all his angels and saints, that now thou be excommunicated and cursed, and thy name that here is written, and that here to burn in this material, fire, and stink, and that under the smoke. [457]

Then cast the name and the picture into the fire and say,

---

455. In marg.: "106. a."

456. In marg.: "107. a."

457. In marg.: "w" glyph.

So thou spirit, be thou cast into the deepest and bottomless pit of hellfire, and that there to burn in brimstone, pitch, and fire, and that by the virtue of God, and there to remain until the terrible and most dreadful day of judgment, and that from henceforth never any remembrance to be made of thee, before the face of the great true and living God, the which shall come to judge the world the quick and dead and consume the same by fire, and here I cite and excommunicate thee, yea, and I curse and maledict thee, thou spirit N., that thou by the sentence and curse pronounced by God against Lucifer, sometime an angel of brightness, as thou right well knowest. I do cite thee here to appear now at these my words and speeches, and that upon pain of endless damnation, and N., I charge thee make no tarrying, and that by the might of the word that Saint Margaret spake when she bound the fiend with, the which being sent of Olybrius,[458] would have destroyed her, and here I cite and curse thee, and that by all God's words and works, and by his great Godhead that thou N. now to tarry no longer, but as faithfully as I do believe in the articles of the Apostles, Athanasius, and Nicene Creeds. So faithfully do I believe that thou N. hast no more power ne stay to abide in the same place in the which thou now art, and so to hear these words named which I have already recited, and yet I charge thee N. by the virtue of my *pater noster*, that thou now here, and that openly in my sight, here to appear and that before me and my fellows here present with me, or that now I do say my belief, and that by the great power and might of God, O N., I do conjure and exorcise thee by the crown of thorn, and by the nails and spear that did pier[c]e that blessed head, hands, feet, and side of our Lord Jesus Christ, and by all his whole passion and shedding of blood, and by the great curse of God, and by the curse that God pronounced to Cain and to all other cursed things, and now by the virtue, strength, and authority of God, I now yet once again do curse thee, and that into the foulest and deepest pit of all the infernal powers, and that thou forthwith come not to me here etc., the great curse of God the Father, God the Son, and God the Holy Ghost, all three curses being joined in one curse, now be upon thee, descend upon thee, light upon thee, and continually rest and abide upon thee, thou evil, wicked and rebellious, obstinate and contentious spirit, and that by the name of God omnipotent. Now I thrust thee, N., from thy power, authority, and office, and now I cast thee into the bottomless pit and hellish lake which continually burneth with *ignem inestinguibile* ["unquenchable fire"], and that from this time forward for ever and ever, there thou to abide in everlasting pains, so be it. *Fiat, fiat, fiat.* Amen.

---

458. Olybrius was a government official in Antioch who imprisoned Saint Margaret and caused her to be eaten by a dragon.

[116]

Yet in the name[459] of the great and everliving God + Tetragramaton + I conjure thee, spirit N., and by the Sun and by the Moon, by the seven planets, by all stars, and by all their virtues, and by Heaven and Earth, and by all that in them is, and by all creatures that beareth name, and that most high and blessed virgin of all virgins, Mary Mother of our Lord Jesus Christ, and by the merits of Saint John the Baptist, and by the merits of Saint John the Evangelist, and by the nine orders of Angels, Archangels, Cherubim, Seraphim, Thrones, Dominations, Principates, and Potestates, which cease not but continually cry and laud and praise God, and that before the Throne of God, saying, "*Sanctus, Sanctus, Sanctus dominus deus Sabaoth +*" ["Holy, holy, holy, Lord God of Hosts +"] and I conjure thee, spirit N., and by the gifts of the Holy Ghost, and by the eight beatitudes, and by the two Tables of Moses, by his five books, by his rod and pot of manna, and by the Ark of God, and by the old law and new law, by Urim and Thummin, and by all those good documents that God taught Moses in the Mount Sinai, and by the twelve small prophets, and by Esau, Jeremiah, and Ezekiel, and by the four Evangelists, Matthew, Mark, Luke, and John, and by the twelve apostles and all other disciples and servants of our Lord Jesus Christ I now conjure thee, spirit N. before named, and by Saint Katherine, Saint Lawrence, and Saint Steven, and by all the merits of all other martyrs, confessors, and virgins. O N., I conjure thee by all holy men and women that be of the number of Christ's Church, and by all holy, sacred, and anointed priests, canons, hermits, deacons, subdeacons, collects,[460] door openers, carriers of the holy books, and other necessaries as oil, incense, wine, water, copes, vestments, albs, fannells,[461] stools, amice,[462] chalice, and corporas[463] with such like, and namely by virtue of mine own holy priesthood, which I have received by authority from above given unto me and by all the elect of God, and I do conjure thee, O N., thou spirit before named, and by all the goodness that hath been done, is or may be done, and that in all the world and in all ages, even to this moment, that thou come speedily, and deliver thyself from acerbit[464] banes, torments, and griefs, and yet I conjure thee, O spirit N., and that by all the doctrine and by all the faith that hath been and is in Christendom that God hath instituted, and by the righteous company the which hath follow the Immaculate Lamb's steps, and by the

---

459. In marg.: "108. [a.]"

460. Collects: a shortened form of "acolytes."

461. Fannell: a band worn on the priest's left wrist.

462. Amice: hat or hood worn in religious orders.

463. Corporas: the cloth on which the Mass is conducted and used to cover the sacred items afterward.

464. Acerbit: bitter, sharp.

seven stars fixed in the tegument, O moon's globe,[465] betokening the seven spirits *Sapientia, Prudentia, Iustitia, Temporantia, Fortitudo, Timora, et Amor* ["Wisdom, Prudence, Justice, Temperance, Strength, Fear, and Love"],[466] and I conjure thee, N., and that by the annunciation of Christ by his bapti[s]m and circumcision, etc., and by the bread that he brake and gave to his disciples in his holy Maundy,[467] saying to them, "Take, eat all of this, for this is my body which shall be broke for you," and by the wine which he gave thus in like manner, saying, "Take and drink ye all of this, for this is my blood of the new testament which is shed for many for remission of sins;" and by the rac[k?] and manger that our Lord and Saviour Jesus Christ was laid in at the time of his birth, and by all the joys of his blessed, righteous, and most clean Mother and Virgin, and by all the marvels and miracles of God. I do conjure thee, N., a spirit oftentimes before named by virtue of all and every word, character, herb, fruit, and stone, and I conjure thee, N., and that by the ring and seal of Solomon, and by the nine celestial lights, the which were showed, and that from the most highest of all, and by the bodies and souls that God hath taken mercy on, and that from the beginning of times until now. I conjure thee, spirit N. before said, and that by the twenty-four Seniors, and by the four thousand elect, the which are mentioned in the book of life, and therein to dwell and abide, and to have everlasting and true light. I now conjure thee, spirit N., so often here rehearsed, and that by the earth, dews, hails, and storms, and by the four winds that blow in the four parts of the world, and by all that is in Heaven, and heavens, earth, waters, seas, and floods, or in the air, and by all things that God hath created in the land of his holy name, and his high majesty, and by the firmament of his power and their virtues.

Here endeth the malediction of the special spirit.

Here beginneth the conjuration of the others

I conjure you[468] and I exorcize you, O repugnant spirits, yea, I admonish and here now constrain and command you, Tantavalerion, vel Golgathell, Emperor of all spirits, and you seven Senators, Orymell, Tygra, Danall, Salarica, Asmoo, Pastarie, and Boell, and you four kings, Orience, Paymon, Amaymon, and Egine, and you, Temell or Semell, Alphassis,[469] Emlon Rodobell, and all others, and I conjure you and every

---

465. In marg.: "109 [a]."

466. In marg.: "w" glyph.

467. Maundy: the Last Supper.

468. In marg.: "11[0 a]."

469. There is a "-" above the a.

of you, and that by the most mightiest names, and the most dreadful name of God +
El and + Tetragrammaton[470] + and by the glorification and laud that he hath in
heaven and earth, and by the marvelous battle that was between the orders of holy
angels and Lucifer and his adherents, and by their great holiness, righteousness, and
fearfulness. I do conjure you and straightly command you, that you do make no more
tarrying, but that you or someone of you send or cause to be sent to me in manner
and form as is before said and to fulfill my petition or desire that he bring to me in
good and perfect gold and silver from some region, the sum of one 100,000 pounds,
and that in lawful coin, presently, without any longer tarrying, and I conjure you and
all you spirits aforenamed and here written, and that by the Father, the Son, etc., and
by all that live under his power and obedience, and by all mankind and virtues that
mankind hath, and by the virtue that God hath given to me, most vile wretch, [117]
and his unworthy servant, yet nevertheless believing in his name, and by all the virtues that God himself hath, now shortly and that without any tarrying you cast lots
amongst you, I mean, of as many of you that are of more power than this N., and that
he the said N. may be enforced to come and to speak to me, and to bring either
100,000 as afore is said of good treasure, or else the uttermost farthing of his office if
it be not so much, and that without any deceit or craft, and further that here he give
me a just and true answer of every thing or things, the which here I shall now demand
of him require and by the virtue of all these holy names of God + Adonay + Eloy +
Sada + Sabaoth + Saday + the which the most high Lord God almighty and great
King of Israel made. I conjure thee and you spirits that be afore named, and that by
all these aforesaid names and words, all sacraments of the Church, and by all the
world which was made to the laud and praise of God and our Lord Jesus Christ, that
now you spirits may send N. to me, and that in the shape of a child of three years of
age and in a fair proportion, here to fulfill my will etc., the sum of 100,000 etc., and
that in the name of the everlasting and living God so be it. To me now, by the whole
power and strength of our Lord Jesus Christ, God's son, and the Holy Trinity, and by
the whole power and strength and authority of God the Father, the Son, and the Holy
Ghost, I conjure you Tantavalerion and all the rest afore lately remembered, with all
other that be your messengers and ministers that you send [blank space] that he may
come to my presence openly unto my sight in form aforesaid, bringing with him his
burden of 100,000 etc., and that he enter the circle *iuxta nos propter illum factum*
["near us made for that purpose"], and not thence to depart until he shall be by me
licenced so to do, and that by the virtue and power of the first word of my belief or
credo, and all the rest of the words of the same, with the twelve Apostles and followers

---

470. Folger: Tetrgramaton.

of yours and my Saviour Jesus Christ after his ascension made, that now you procure Oberion here to appear. I say N., come and appear, appear, appear, in the blessed name of Jesu come, come, come, or else be now unto you all the pain of everlasting damnation. O you forenamed spirits, I conjure you in the name of Jesus of Nazareth and King of the Jews, that you cause N. to come and fulfill my desire, or if he be otherwise busied and cannot, that then either his or your messenger come and show me the cause of his absence. O thou Beliall, O thou Maleus, O thou Malcranus, who keepeth the gates of hell, I now conjure you and every one of you, that you do nothing against my will herein, nor to your power suffer none other to do any thing that may hinder my will and purpose, but grant me now your aid that N. may come unto me etc.[471] O thou Lucifer and all thy whole company, I now conjure you all together, and that by the virtue of the bread and wine, by water, air, fire, and earth, and by the Father, the Son, etc., and by all things that ever God made and created. Yea, I conjure you, Lucifer, by the Sun and Moon, planets, stars, and constellations fixed in the concave or cope of heaven, that now forthwith, if the spirit N. be with you, that now forthwith and that without any tarrying you will suffer him to depart from you, and send him unto me to fulfill my will and pleasure. O you Prince Lucifer and all you spirits infernal, and all other spirits, I conjure you by all the goods of the earth the which are laid up, or for to be laid up, and as well past [as?] present, as for to come, that now forthwith and without any delay you come together and so do that I may have your succours that Oberion may come and speak with me and that by the great name of God + Tetragramaton + and by all the grammarians, logicians, astrologians, magicians, and mathematicians invisible and intelligible, that now you send to me the spirit N., after whom I have so sore longed, together with one other spirit and one of the best learnedst or most skillful spirits and an expert messenger,[472] having knowledge in every art or science, and such a one that is meet and able to serve my purpose and especially to aid and help N. if he have any need, for the sum of 100,000 pounds in gold and silver, or gold or silver to the same sum, and further that the said N. answer me truly of all such things as I shall demand of him, and that he may be a subject unto me for a time till I shall licence him to depart, and that on your behalf, and ready to obey God, the which God hath power to fulfill this my desire, and that in a fair form etc. Come, N., come, come, come quickly now, and that with all speed that may be thought or done. O you spirits afore named, come out of all four quarters and make diligent search and inquiry for this spirit or king N. and urge him to come unto me, and that by God and his blessed mother Mary Maid and Wife, and by her blessed

---

471. In marg.: "w" glyph.

472. Three spirits summoned at once.

virginity, of Saint John Evangelist and by all his holy life. I charge you to bring or send him, the said N., unto me etc., and that by the virtue of Saint John when he said, "*Vade et mitte hanc tunicam super corpora defunctorum,*" ["Go and throw this tunic over the bodies of the dead"][473] and thereby the dead bodies revived to life again. O N., I say unto thee come. Why tarriest thou? Come quickly, and that by the power and virtue of him that made this conjuration, and to the end to bind and constrain spirits, and that now by the sufferance of my Lord God. O N., thou wilt appear and come to me as certainly and as quickly as the dead bodies did appear in the holy city to diverse, as when the word or second person in Trinity did yield up to his father the life of his manhood. I charge you, spirits of the air, of the earth, fire, and water, that now you incontinent gather yourselves together and send to me N. the spirit, and by the virtue of [118] these words that our Lord Jesus Christ spake, "*Die dominica convenit ad Iohannem universa multitudo populi.*" ["The Lord's Day (Sunday), the whole multitude of the people come together to John."] I conjure thee, O N. afore named, that by the dreadful sentence that Saint John gave out against all those spirits that came not but disobeyed, to be at the correction of these words,[474] and book, and to me, thereupon, O N., I charge thee, and yet I charge thee again, that thou come and make no more tarrying, but that by the space of saying these blessed words and reverend names of God + Salvator + Unigenitus + Adonay + El + Tetragrammaton + Alpha + and Omega + dybbatary + Martina + Iones + Artike + Marta + Fenibie + Lomna + Ballerake + Fasmena +Totes + Feyereth + fiat, fiat, fiat + come now and obey to me and, O most noble N., yield to me as now thy service, do thy office and bring to me even to this present place, and that even by and by, the sum of one 100,000 of good and perfect gold and silver, from what place that to you shall seem best, and through it into this circle, and there leave it and so depart and go into the circle appointed for thee. O N., I pray thee this do for me, and I promise upon my credit and truth to do for thee, and thereupon come, come, come quickly, and that upon pain of the great curse of [God] [475] to be pronounced both against thee and the rest I have before named.

Now if he nor none for him come not, then repeat the same conjuration three or four times, and within that space undoubtedly he will appear.

Quid vis quid petis ["What do you wish? What do you desire?"],[476] then say, "O thou, etc., which now cometh, I now in the name of the Father + the Son + and the

473. *Breviarium Ad Usum Insignis Ecclesiae Sarum*, p. ccix.

474. In marg.: "113 [a.]"

475. There is a short space in Folger presumably to switch ink.

476. Compare below, Folger p. 167.

Holy Ghost + I conjure thee etc., and that by the chiefest virtue of God, Jesus Christ, the Holy Spirit and invisible and blessed Trinity, and by the dignity of the blessed and immaculate lamb, and by the pure and undefiled Virgin Mary, and by the virtue of all the words and names of God, seals, signs, and characters of Solomon, and by Jesus Christ, whose power thou and all other spirits are made subject to man and namely to me, and by the virtue of him that hath made thee, Oberion, to come now here to answer to me, and that now that thou N. thereupon to go and without any tarrying to fetch to me now forthwith the whole of my request and desire, that is to fetch and bring me hither the sum of 100,000 of good and true lasting[477] gold or silver, and that it to be done I charge thee without all craft, or disobedience, and that is to be done. I charge thee by the almighty, which liveth and reigneth ever one God, world without end. Amen. Amen."

Then say to him when he appeareth

Take thou to me,[478] and give to me as this writing doth make mention, which is the sum of 100,000 in gold or silver or both, and that good and perfect, and to be brought me and that forthwith, and without all craft or any deceit, so that it may be to the laud and praise of God and to the relief and comfort of me and of my family, and to the succour of the needy and helpless poor, so be it. *Fiat, fiat, fiat.* Amen.

But and if he come not and appear

Take thou the fire maledicted and the picture with his name, and the pictures and names of all those spirits thou calledst written in paper, and cat's turds, pitch, leather, brimstone, asafoetida, old rags, and feathers, and hold those names and picture over the fire and say this curse and malediction upon them.[479]

Now by God the Father almighty + and by God the Son almighty + and by God the Holy Ghost almighty, three persons and one God in Trinity, and by all the virtues and powers of heaven, earth, air, and hell, now all these maledict and curse you and every of you, and utterly I do excommunicate you, Tantavalerion or Golgathell, Orymell, Tygra, Danall, Salarica, Asmoo, Pastary, Boell, and you Orience, Paymon, Amaymon, and Egyne, and you Sylquam, Maleranis, Rasynet, and you Temell, Alphasis, Emlon, Rodybell, and all the rest of you upon whom I have called, whose succours

---

477. The concern was that the riches would transfer into nothing upon the spirit's departure.

478. In marg.: "114 [a]."

479. In marg.: "w" glyph.

I have required, and whose names I have recited and named, and yet once again in especial, all you whose names, behold, I have here in my hand written, God and all his mighty virtues names maledict and curse you, and every of you, deprive you of your offices and royal estates, remove you out of your places, and for your contumacy throw you into the eternal pain and that of all pains where I, by mine authority, given me of God, will you shall remain, and that in great tribulation, horror, stench, and continual flashing flames. All angels and saints, patriarchs, prophets, martyrs, confessors, and virgins, the twelve Apostles with all godly and chaste matrons, the Blessed Virgin Mary with Ursula and her companions, Saint Ann, Elizabeth, Katherine, and Margaret, and all other creatures, Solomon, Saint Cyprian, and all professors of this high science called secret of secrets, do curse and maledict you, O you wicked and froward[480] spirits, and I N., the son of N., do excommunicate you and all you and do throw upon you the great and fearful curse of the great and ever living God, the omnipotent Father, and by the power of his most bitter death and passion of his only son, Jesus Christ, I do yet once more excommunicate and curse you and every of you spirits most disobedient, and the ineffable name of Jesus Christ, which is both God and Man, and Son of the most highest God, do now excommunicate and curse you and all you, and the high name of God + Tetragramaton + and the twelve excellent names of God, the which O thou N. [119] and all the rest of you do know very well, all and every of those names do curse you, and all you spirits afore named, and now do I, by the power and grace of the very fountain and wellspring of all virtues, do condemn you and separate you from all the rest of your company, and do clean deprive you of all homage, fewte,[481] or service that any of your inferiors or ministers owe unto you, and I do now, even as I throw this paper into this fire, throw you into the bottomless pit of hell, or continual burning lake, where there is pains unspeakable, where there is darkness without any light where the seely[482] damned wretches cry night and day without knowledge of time, "*Ve Ve Ve quante sunt hii Tenebre*" ["Alas! Alas! Alas! how great is this darkness?"], and now, O wicked devils and obstinate spirits, that most excellent and reverent name of + Jesus + unto which name all knees do bow as well things in heaven as in earth and hell do bow to and obey, do now maledict and excommunicate you and every of you, some and all, jointly and severally, superior and inferior, whose names I have here written and hold in my hand, except that you, or one of you or some other for you, do come here to me and that by and by, and bring with you the spirit N. whom I have called and will not cease

---

480. Froward: difficult to handle.
481. Fewte: fealty.
482. Seely: pitiable.

to call until he come, and also the money or treasure I desire to have, viz. 100,000 pounds, and that in good and true lasting gold the which now is my petition and desire, which if it be not done, and that forthwith, thou in the name of the Holy Trinity, and by the sufferance of God's divine Majesty, and by the virtue of all the holy words, names, and ch[aracter]s of God, I myself now here do curse and excommunicate all and every one of you spirits aforenamed, and cast you and curse you into *ignem inestinguibilis ubi est fletus et scridor dentium* ["unquenchable fire where there is weeping and gnashing of teeth"], where the fire never goeth forth nor the worms leave off gnawing, a place wherein is always crying alas and woe, pain of pains, grief of griefs, and sorrow of all sorrows, a place where is trouble and anguish, the wrath and hatred of God, and yet by the authority of this name Jesus, I now, to augment your pain and smart, cast you into the great furnace of horrible and ever-burning sulfur where there is the punishment and vengeance of God daily and hourly without ceasing practised, and that now, by the might of the Trinity, I do curse you into that cursed prison and dungeon of eternal death and damnation, where no order is, but all disorder, everlasting dissension, pain, and woe, thither, thou spirit N., and all you spirits before named, whose names behold these are, go ye and there still inhabit and dwell, and never come to your former roams,[483] unless that it be let, and that by the virtue of the omnipotent God. And now by all these maledictions and curses, and cursedness of all these afore written and named pains, griefs, and woes,[484] may be now multiplied and that upon and all you wicked aforenamed, and that now and ever to be multiplied, and that so plentifully, as that there be gravels or sands on the seashore, stars in the skies, or grasses upon the face of the earth, and this by the presence of our mother holy Church, and now by all these aforesaid sentences, words and names, signs, seals, and characters, now to stand and be in full power, authority, and strength, and that now by the power of God the Father, God the Son, and by the power of God the Holy Ghost, and by the power of all these three persons, and yet but one God in Trinity, now to grant it so to be on you, N., and on all you N., rebellious spirit whose names these be, this God grant now and forever. Amen.

Then cast[485] their pictures into the fire and that of Sylquam, Malcranis, and Rasynet, and the cat's turds, etc., and burn them as above, saying,

---

483. Roam: space where one's roaming occurs; roughly, territory.

484. In marg.: "w" glyph.

485. In marg.: "117."

A malediction

*Maledictio dei patris **omnipotentis**, eius filii et Spiritus Sancti* ["The curse of God the almighty Father, his Son, and the Holy Ghost"], be upon you, and remain upon you, deprive you of all your power and authority, and cast you into the bottomless pit and stinking dungeon of fire and brimstone, and there to detain you in the place of endless and uns[p]eakable[486] pains forever and ever, fiat, fiat, fiat, unless you now come and speedily appear unto me and cause N. to come and fulfill my desire and bring with him the aforesaid money or treasure to the sum of 100,000 pounds in true, lasting, and good gold or silver.

This done, he or they will come running, and say unto thee, "Help me out of this pain," and speak and bid them fulfill thy desire, and it shall be done.

A licence if he do appear and fulfill, then licence him to depart, saying:

I conjure thee, spirit or spirits, and that now by the virtue of our Lord Jesus Christ, the which was put upon the Cross for you and all you spirits,[487] that you and every of you do return into your proper places, and by the virtue of the high God, and that you do not noy[488] ne hurt me, nor yet none other creature, but that now forthwith you do return unto your proper places, and that when I shall call you, or any of you, to answer unto me again or to give me that that I shall require and desire, and that you do it quickly and that with all obedience, to be ready to come and fulfill my request and commandment, *rede, rede, rede in pace* ["return, return, return in peace"], and the peace of Jesus Christ be now between you and me and that in the name of the Father + and of the + Son + and of the + Holy Ghost. Amen. Three persons in Trinity and one God in unity be rendered all laud, praise, and dominion, both now and forever, world without end. Amen.

After you have done

Tarry in the circle two or three hours, and say the Gospel of Saint John, "*In principium erat verbum*" ["In the beginning was the word"], etc., the Lord's Prayer, the salutation of the Virgin Mary, the Creed, and if you doubt, "*Quicunque vult*" ["Whoever will (be saved)"] etc.,[489] and one after another go out of the circle, and go to your

---

486. There is a large * in pencil in the left marg.

487. Another example of a sort of Tikkun doctrine, in which spirits might be redeemed.

488. Noy: annoy.

489. The Athanasian Creed.

house or chamber another way than that you came, and wash your faces with water and hyssop, and say your prayers with great devotion. This done they will come at all times, although they were bound with chains, and remember still [120] and if they come not themselves to send then their messengers, and if they come not, then write their names and pictures in paper and burn them in the fire with orders as above and pronounce very angrily. etc.

A good constriction for a spirit

I conjure thee, spirit[490] etc., which art here before me, by the Father, the Son, and the Holy Ghost, and by these names of God + Saday + Tetragramaton + Tetragramay + Adday + Algramay + and by all the names of God, that thou have no power to hurt nor resist us neither in our heart, soul, nor body, neither to disobey us nor to depart from our sight, until you give us an answer to all our interrogatories, without any lying, deceit, craft, or falsehood, and I conjure thee, spirit, in the name of Saint Mary the Virgin Mother of Jesus Christ, by the head of your prince, by my Christianity, and by the mighty government that our Lord Jesus Christ hath over us, that you nor none for you have power to hinder my sight, but that I may see and know you in the fair form of a child of three years of age, so that thou mayest have no power to depart from my sight, until thou be licenced by me, in the name of the Father, and of the Son, and of the Holy Ghost. Amen. *Finis.*

For the ground

In the name[491] of our Lord Jesus Christ and by his licence, I conjure thee, wicked spirit and all thy fellows, if any more be with thee, by the virtue and power of the Father, the Son, and the Holy Ghost, three persons and one God, and by the virtue of our blessed Lady the Virgin, and all other saints and virgins, and by the nine orders of angels which are ministers unto the majesty of our Lord Jesus Christ, viz. Michael, Gabriel, and Raphael, Cherubim and Seraphim, Thrones, Dominations, Principates, Potestates, with all their fellowship, and by all the virtues and mighty powers of heaven and earth, and by the virtue and power of the sea, and all that therein is, and by the virtue of all virtues (?)[492] and by the virginity of Saint Katherine, Saint Margaret, Saint Barbara, and of all the rest holy and unpolluted virgins and saints, and by the virtue of the dreadful day of judgment, and by the virtue of all patriarchs, prophets, apostles,

---

490. In marg.: "118." Compare Sloane 3853, fol. 20r.

491. In marg.: "214 (?)."

492. *Sec. man.*

martyrs, confessors, and by the virtue of the four evangelists Matthew, Mark, Luke, and John, I bind you, spirit or spirits, by these and all powers in heaven, earth, sea, and hell, and all deep places. I bind you, spirit or spirits, by all holy ways that the Apostles followed our Lord Jesus Christ, and I conjure you, spirit or spirits, if any be here within this ground or within a hundred foot especially, by these holy and high names of our Lord Jesus Christ + Agios + Otheos + Yskyros + Athanatos + Panton + Craton + et Ysus + Emanuell + Tetragramaton +[493] and by the virtue of the blessed sacrament of the altar, and by the virtue of the seven sacraments, and by the virtue of all holy prayers and words that ever the great priest Aaron or any other priest of his order said or spake, that you spirit or spirits obey this my adjurement and conjuration, and immediately fly from hence, and being departed, to come hither until fifteen days from this present hour be fully completed and ended,[494] and that thou or you spirits go and depart hence from this ground so far off that thou spirit or spirits neither see us nor hear us, and that to a place where God will that you be agreeable to his good pleasure and our salvation, and also that during the time of our working here now at any other time and in any other place no trouble nor molestation happen or chance either to me or any of my fellows now present, and thereto I conjure thee, spirit or spirits, by the virtue of the holy name + Ebrea + Stulpha + Alpha + Draco + and by the virtue of the blessed passion of our Lord Jesus Christ, and by the virtue of his blessed blood that he bled in the said his holy passion, and namely by the great virtue of the water and blood that came and issued from his heart, and by the virtue of the spear that piercing his side it made the same wound, also I conjure thee or you spirits by the virtue of the crown wherewith he was crowned, and by the virtue of the three nails wherewith his hands and feet were to the Cross fastened, and by the virtues of the scourges that his tender and blessed body was scourged with, and by the blessed and sacred words that he spake on the Cross, + Heloy Heloy + Lamazabathani + *deus meus deus meus ut quid derelequisti me* ["my God, my God, why have you forsaken me?"]. Also I conjure thee spirit or you spirits by our Lord Jesus Christ's glorious resurrection, and by the steps he took when he harrowed hell, and by the virtue of his wonderful ascension into Heaven, and by his sitting on the right hand of his Father, and by his coming at the last day to judgment wherein all shall rise as well the good as bad, the happy as unhappy, the saved as damned, and by the mercy shewed to Mary Magdalene, and by the virtue of the Holy Ghost that he sent down to his Apostles, and by the virtue of the assumption of our Lady Saint Mary and by all her virtues, and by all that God made, and by the virtue that God gave to words, herbs, and stones, and each other thing as well in Heaven as in earth, as in the sea, as

---

493. In marg.: "w" glyph.

494. Wellcome MS. 110, fol. 32v ff, has a similar operation "to drive spirits out of the ground" for at least thirty feet downward and forty feet across, and fifteen days; the wording is different however.

without the sea. *Iterum* ["again"] I conjure thee spirit or you spirits in the name of our Lord God which Moses bare in his forehead, and Aaron on his breast. Also I conjure thee spirit or spirits, [121] what kind[495] so ever ye be, of fire, water, earth, or air, malignant or infernal, by all the conjurations, invocations, vincles,[496] and licences that ever Cyprian, Solomon, Alexander, Aristotle, Bacon, Bungi, Lumbarte, Wale Cornelius, or any other spake or wrote, and by the dread that thou spirit or you spirits have in thine or your lord, and by the virtue of the four kings of the air and their four princes under them, and by the love and dread that thou and you have in our Lord Jesus Christ, to whom all knees do bow. I conjure thee spirit or you spirits, by the virtue of this conjuration and all others in this book contained,[497] and by the virtue of all the conjurations that ever were made, are made, or shall be made, that thou spirit or you spirits which be keepers of this treasure here hidden or laid, that you obey me and my conjuration, and that by the virtue and power of our Lord Jesus Christ, and that you neither trouble nor molest me nor my fellows, nor hurt me nor them, neither in body nor in soul, but as verily as our Lord Jesus Christ said to his disciples, *pax vobis* ["peace be with you"], so verily peace be between thee spirit and thy fellows, if there be any, and peace be between thee, thy fellows, and us, and I charge thee, thy fellows, and us that thou or ye flee from this ground, and from the treasure hid or laid in this ground, and that you do not draw it nor move it now away out of the place where now it is, nor alter nor change it by no delusion nor craft, and that in the pain of endless damnation, and the pain of the great curse that God shall give at the great day of doom. *Iterum* ["again"] I conjure thee or you spirits that you trouble nor vex me nor my fellows in the time of our working and that by all the holy words before rehearsed, that thou spirit or spirits from hence peaceably in all haste depart and go, and for the space and time of fifteen days and fifteen nights even from this selfsame hour, thou or ye do exempt yourselves and go and remain in the place whereunto God hath and shall appoint you, and without returning during the said time to trouble, molest, or grieve me or us or any of us with word, fantasy, vision, or illusion, either with fire, water, wind, or blassing,[498] but to suffer us to take it and carry it away and apply it to what use we shall think it most meet without your molestation, either waking or sleeping, eating or drinking, resting or walking, now present or in time to come,[499] whereunto I conjure thee or you spirits by the virtue of all the words that ever Christ spake or man wrote, in this conjuration rehearsed or hereafter may be rehearsed. I charge and command you, O thou spirit or you spirits, and that

---

495. In marg.: "216."

496. Vincles: bonds.

497. Given the nature of the work as a miscellany, this statement is likely from another source that was compiled with the rest without change.

498. Blassing: blasting?

499. In marg.: "w" glyph.

by the virtue, power, and might of God the Father, his word, and Holy Spirit, and as certainly as the promised seed, and brake the serpent's head, and as Mary the Virgin bare the seed, and as Eline,[500] the most Christian Queen, found the Holy Cross, even so certainly we may find that we seek for, here hid or laid and the same process and enjoy, even to the good pleasure of God, the profit of the poor, and to the salvation of our own souls, whereunto I say. Amen. *Fiat, fiat, fiat.*

This must be laid in the earth to urge a late dead man to appear and speak[501]

---

500. According to the popular medieval text *The Golden Legend* (Volume 3, London: J. M. Dent and Co., 1900, p. 171), the Holy Cross was discovered by Helena, mother of Constantine.

501. In marg.: "218."

[122]

These letters before passed must be laid in the earth to urge a late dead man to speak.

For hidden treasure

First of all you must [502] believe that this work is and hath been approved most true. Secondly, you must take heed when the Moon changeth, and in the night following, go unto the place where the treasure is hid, and in that place take a clot of earth, and carry it home with thee, [503] to the privy place where you will work. There make a circle in the which the spirit may appear, and another for thee and thy fellows, distant from the spirit's circle three, five, or nine foot, and put the clot of earth in the spirit's circle, and then kneel down towards the east, saying devoutly this orison or prayer, "In the name of the most merciful God, *deus fortis et patiens*" ["God, strong and patient"] etc. This done, arise and say this conjuration as followeth. [504]

I conjure thee or you spirits, to whomsoever you are subject, in what place of the earth ye do abide, which do keep this treasure, and have any power over it, or any others now remaining in the earth, by the space of twenty-four foot round, in breadth, height, or deepness from whence this clot or part of earth was taken and now presently lieth in the circle for thee or you prepared, whether you be one or moo, [505] that you come quickly without delay or noise, and that without hurting of me or any of my company or other living creature.

I conjure you that you arise even now, and appear visibly unto us in the circle for you prepared, being distant [...] [506] foot from this circle wherein we now stand, and that in a fair form and likeness of a man, bringing with you manifestly to our sight the treasure or any other good being hid there from whence I took this piece of earth, or within twenty-four foot of it round about, as well in deepness as breadth, height, or length, without deceit or craft, without changing or diminishing thereof, and that you lay it upon the ground, the which is between your circle and ours, and that to our use so that we may have and enjoy the commodity thereof, as things wholly and appertaining and belonging to us, to that place that I shall appoint you to, and that by the virtue of the passion of our Lord Jesus Christ, and by all his holy and blessed names which shall be here said to his praise, and to bind and constrain you. I conjure

---

502. In marg.: "2[19.]"

503. Compare Kelley's collecting earth from treasure locations in *John Dee's Five Books of Mystery*, 410–412. He probably had instructions similar to these.

504. In marg.: "w" glyph.

505. Moo: more.

506. There is a blank space in the Folger MS.

thee or you spirits again with all your powers, by heaven, by earth, by sea, and by hell, and by all things contained in them, and by all the words that God spake [Margin: 1] in the creation of the world,[507] and of all creatures by the first word that he said, when he made light, "Let light be made," and it was made, the second when he did create the [Margin: 2] firmament, in the midst of the waters that it might separate one water from another.

[Margin: 3] The third word, in gathering together the waters which were under heaven, saying, "Let the waters be gathered together, which are under heaven, and let them be dry."

[Margin: 4] The fourth word was when he made trees and herbs to grow, saying, "Let the earth bring forth green grass, and fruit, and their trees in the kind bring forth fruit, whose fruit is within themselves upon earth."

[Margin: 5] The fifth word was when he made the Sun, the Moon, and stars, saying, "Let light be made in the firmament of heaven, that they may divide the day from the night, and let the days and years be tokens that they may shine in the firmament and lighten the earth."

[Margin: 6] The sixth word was, when he made fish and fowl, saying, "Let the waters bring forth all creeping things that have life, and that can fly upon the earth under the firmament of heaven."

[Margin: 7] The seventh word was when he blessed them, saying, "Increase and multiply upon earth, and fill the earth, the waters, and the sea."

[Margin: 8] The eighth word was when he made beasts, worms, and serpents, saying, "Let the earth bring forth all living things, and beasts in their kind."

[Margin: 9] The ninth word was when he made man, saying, "Let us make man unto our own likeness, and let him be head over all the fishes in the sea, birds of the air, and beasts of the field, and all creatures that live in the earth."

[123]

[The] tenth word was, when he created man and woman, and did bless them, saying, "Increase and multiply, and fill the earth, and let all living things be under them." O you spirit or spirits, I conjure you by all the words which God spake to Moses, and to all other prophets, and by the four elements, and by all the virtues of heaven, and by all the names of God, by the Incarnation of Christ, by his nativity, baptism, circumcision, and passion, and by the shedding of his most precious blood, and by his sepulcher, by his resurrection and ascension, and by the coming of the Holy Ghost, by the dreadful day of judgment, wherein he shall come and judge you and all mankind.

---

507. Compare below, Folger p. 129.

O thou spirit or spirits with all your company, if you have any, I do conjure you by the head of Saint John Baptist, and by all patriarchs, prophets, and apostles, martyrs, confessors, and virgins, and under and upon pain of eternal or everlasting damnation, that you or thou dost appear incontinently visibly before me and my company, in the circle which is made for you, in fair human form and shape, etc. I conjure thee or you, O spirit or spirits, by the head of your prince, and by the virginity of our blessed lady, virgin and wife, and yet Mother of our saviour Christ, and I adjure thee or you, with all your fellows, under the pain of everlasting torments and the malediction of all Holy Church, and under your continual remaining in hell until the day of judgment, that you or thou arise and appear quickly in the form and shape of a man, and fulfill my desire in each point, and that by him which shall come most fearfully to judge the quick and the dead and the world by fire. Arise, O thou or you spirits, with all your company, I say arise, and that by the power and strength of the holy and indivisible Trinity, the Father etc., three persons and one God, Arise, O thou or you spirits with all your company, I the great power, strength, and fear of almighty God and most holy father of Heaven, Earth, and Hell, and by the virtue of all his works and miracles of his Son, that Immaculate Lamb without spot Jesus Christ and by his wonders and words, I say, O thou spirit, arise, by him to whom all honour and glory is given in Heaven and Earth, and whom you spirits fear and obey. I conjure[508] you by the virtue of him, at the hearing of whose most high, reverend, and glorious names, all devils and you spirits do tremble and quake, Jesus Christ, the son and only wisdom of God his Father, Creator of the world, Saviour of mankind, judge of quick and dead and confounder of all disobedient and malign spirits, which is called holy king and Lord of Glory. Yea, I conjure you by the virtue of his most bitter passion, love, meekness, and great goodness, and by the virtue of all his godliness and pureness, by his pity, mercy, and sweetness, and by his continual and everlasting reign with his father in his kingdom of everlasting glory most triumphantly to judge the world, as well the quick as dead as devils, spirits, airy, fiery, earthy, and watery, as also all elves or elfins[509] and other incorporate or inhuman creatures, Arise, o you wicked spirits, etc., by Jesus Christ, the son of the pure Virgin Mary, and that upon the earth in the circle for you prepared visibly to our sight, and that in the likeness of a fair man, without thunder, lightning, or tempest, without hurting, harming, or fearing of me or any of my fellows, or any other living or Christian creature, and give me a true and direct answer of all things that shall demand or ask of you. I conjure and warn you, O spirits, to arise in the virtue of the Holy Ghost and by his Godhead, which he hath reigning

---

508. In left marg.: "w"; in right marg.: "266."

509. Elfin: another term for elves.

with God the Father and the Son in eternal and everlasting glory. Arise thou or you spirits, by the virtuous power of God, and by the virtuous grace of God, and by the virtuous virtue of all creatures praising and lauding God, by the virtue of God and of all things that are alive or dead, moveable and unmovable, that in heaven or earth have any being. Arise ye or thou spirits, in the strength, and by the strength, of the death and passion of Christ, and by his most sweet face, which was covered with blood, in his Holy Sudary[510] carrying huge and great cross. Arise thou or you spirits, by the virtue of the right hand of the same Jesus Christ which was nailed upon the Cross and with a second nail pierced through, so if you will not arise and appear, be you or thou spirit or spirits stricken with the pains and torments of hell, and that by the virtue of his said pain, and as he was handled with cords on the Cross, and his left hand nailed thereon, so be thou or ye spirits nailed and handled with the most strong pains of the infernal lake, and be bound with fiery chains until you do come and appear visibly to me and my fellows, and that by the virtue of the pains which Christ did suffer upon earth as well upon the cross as elsewhere, so be thou or ye spirits nailed and thrust through with the pain of everlasting damnation in hell, by the virtue of the pains that Christ did suffer in his left foot upon the Cross, so be ye spirits or spirit punished with pains of fire, which shall continually burn, except ye appear and come quickly, etc. That spear which did pierce and open the side of our Saviour Christ Jesus, O spirit or spirits, for your contumacy and disobedience pierce thee or you, and that with most strong strokes of flames of fire and thunder and withal, and all manner of hellish torments of that damnable pit. O thou spirit or you spirits, the pains of hell, devils, and damned souls light upon you and every of you, unless or except you come quickly and appear visible to my sight. Arise therefore, ye or you spirits, I conjure you by the most sharp and bitter passion of our Lord Jesus Christ and by the virtue of his most precious blood and water which issued out of his most blessed side, in time of his said passion, by his salt tears distilling from his pitiful eye, as when he wept languishing upon the cross and cried to his father + Heloy + Heloy + Heloy + Lamasabathani and by that word that he said unto the thief (?) [124] hanging on the cross, by these and all others pertaining to his holy Incarnation, nativity, baptism, fasting, and temptation, by his crucifying on the Cross, death, and passion, by his descending and ascension, by his glorious resurrection, and by the coming of the Holy Ghost on the twelve Apostles, by the virtue and power of all these aforesaid do I charge and command you to come and presently yield unto me your obedience. If you refuse this to do, by the virtue and power of all these be horrors and terrors upon you binding and chaining you, pressing you and rending you by omnipotent power

---

510. Sudary: Christ's winding sheet.

for your disobedience shewed unto me, and never have you a moment of joy, lisse,[511] or ease, but every twinkling of an eye be your horror and unspeakable anguishes upon you for your disobedience. Grant this, O Lord God, for thy Son, Christ Jesus's sake, which liveth and reigneth with thee and the Holy Ghost ever one God to whom be rendered all laud, praise, might, majesty, and dominion, both now and forever. Amen.

For a keeper of treasure

O thou,[512] spirit N., with thy fellows, if thou have any, know[513] thou that Christ + doth overcome, + Christ doth reign + Christ doth command in heaven, the air, earth, seas, and hell, what place or habitation is where the power of the Lord is not seen, the look up to the air, etc. O thou spirit N., arise, come thou, and enter into this mirror visibly and in a fair form and comely shape.

Let this be said thrice, and then let the master stand on his feet and say,

O thou, spirit N., be thou ready to my will. I conjure thee by the power of the omnipotent God the Father, etc., and by the incarnation, circumcision, and passion of our Lord Jesus Christ, and by his resurrection and ascension, and by his coming most gloriously to judgment at the last day. I conjure thee, N., by the holy Virgin Mary and by her virginity, and by the merits of all saints, angels, archangels, patriarchs, prophets, apostles, martyrs, confessors, and virgins, and by the head of your prince, that thou be quickly and incontinently obedient unto me, and that thou dost not tarry by no means, but by and by all occasions, excuses, and delays set apart, that thou dost arise and enter visibly into this [mirror] plainly appearing unto me and to my sight, showing and perfectly speaking unto me, and unto all men here standing about thee, the truth of all things that shall be asked or demanded of thee, but true and truly according to my meaning speedily and unfeignedly to fulfill my request to the uttermost of thy power, without craft, guile, or any dissimulation, but in all things to arise, come, and give a true answer. *Fiat, fiat, fiat.* Amen.

---

511. Lisse: happiness.

512. In marg.: "269."

513. Know: understand.

Say three times, if he come not, then say this:[514]

I conjure thee, spirit N., which I do call by the Father etc., and by the faith which you do owe unto your private lord, and by the virtue of the true and living God, and by the angel that shall blow with the trumpet that most terrible and fearful blast *surgite mortui venite ad iudicium* ["arise, ye dead, come to judgment"]. I conjure thee, N., as thou trustest as then to be saved, so now by that salvation the which the blessed shall have, and by that glory the which they shall possess, I charge thee, N., arise and come, and that in a visible shape, and answer me to all such things as I shall demand. I conjure thee, N., by all the torments, pains, and griefs that Christ God and Man suffered in the time of his passion, that thou N. do appear unto me in this same N. [mirror] appointed for thee, visible and in a fair colour, form, and shape, without any hurt or harm doing to me or to any other living creature upon earth, and that thou dost shew unto me all things which I shall demand of thee quickly, without any deceit, fraud, craft, or long delay, but except thou dost come and personally appear in this same N. [mirror] etc., perpetual damnation descend upon thee and be multiplied, and, for thy iniquity and contempt, eternal pains, judgment, and fiery chains, vex and trouble thee, and that forever thou mayest sustain pains and torments in the furnace unquenchable, and also that thou be deprived of thy power, office, and dignity, and suddenly fall from the place where thou now art, except thou arise and come speedily. *Fiat, fiat, fiat.* Amen.

When he is come, bind him

I conjure thee, N., by the obedience which thou owest unto thy private lord, and by the power and virtue of this most holy high and reverend name of God + Tetragramaton + and by Saint Michael the Archangel, which did cast out infernal spirits, and by the Annunciation of the Blessed Virgin Mary, Mother of our Lord Jesus Christ, and by his nativity, circumcision, passion, death, resurrection, and ascension, and by the continual weeping of the same our blessed lady and virgin for her son, and by the darkening of the Sun in his death, and by all things that ever was done in heaven, earth, and hell. I charge thee that thou dost show unto me the truth of all things the which I shall ask or demand of thee, without fraud, deceit, or lie invented, but true and truly according to thy knowledge and my intent and meaning, and that speedily and unfeignedly to fulfill my request to the uttermost of thy power, and that thou dost not go nor vanish away out of my sight, nor out of this M[irror], until I be answered of the very truth of all things that I shall ask of thee or of thee shall be de-

---

514. In marg.: "w" glyph.

manded, required, or enquired, by me or any others, so that I may give unto God the Father etc., laud and praise which is and shall be one God in trinity for ever and ever, world without end. Amen. *Finis.*

[125]

To bind the ground, the spirit that keepeth any treasure

In the name[515] of the Father, and of the Son, and of the Holy Ghost. Amen. I bind you spirits to avoid out of this ground wherein I now stand, and that with all festination[516] and speed possible, by the space of a hundred foot and more. I bind you to avoid and no longer to tarry by all the merits of our Saviour Christ's passion, death and burial, glorious resurrection, and wonderful ascension, and by the coming of the Holy Ghost. I command you to avoid out of this ground upon pain of everlasting damnation. The malediction and curse of God the Father fall upon you spirits, keepers of this treasure, here or within thirty foot of this place by me marked, unless you remove hence and avoid, O spirits, keepers of this treasure. I bind you and every of you one or more by the unspeakable power of the almighty God, and by the power and virtue of all saints, that you depart and go from this treasure, and that you be not so hardy to come near it, to remove or translate it, nor to change nor transport it by your devilish or hellish power. I charge and bind you, O spirits some and all, by the power of the almighty and everliving God, and by all his virtues. I bind you by his Holy Circumcision. I bind you by his fasting and temptation. I adjure you by his most bitter passion, which he suffered in his manhood here upon Earth, wherein he was most painfully tormented, scourged, and beaten. I bind you by his dolorous grief and pain when he was mocked and despitefully entreated. I bind you by his great pain he suffered when he was crowned with sharp thorns. I bind you by his most blessed wounds five, and namely by that most deep and wide wound made in his most tender side and pitiful heart. I bind and charge you by his most precious blood, which he shed in the time of his said passion. I bind you by those most holy words which he spake hanging upon the cross of tree.[517] I bind you by the great pity and compassion that his blessed mother, Saint Mary, that holy virgin, had in the time of that most dolorous and grievous passion. I charge and command you spirits that keep here any treasure of gold, silver, or precious stone, yea, I command you, O spirits present or that are to come, that you remove not this treasure nor no part thereof from us, but

---

515. Compare Sloane 1727, 19r. In marg.: "270."

516. Festination: speed.

517. In marg.: "w" glyph.

suffer it to remain and be there where it now is, and that you peaceably go and quietly depart away from the same by one hundred foot, and not to return again to the same place before we have our desire and request thereof. O spirits, I charge and bind you, that you shew no visions or illusions whereby we may be let or hindered from our purpose and intent, and thereby you still suffered to keep and detain the same. I charge you, etc., that you in no manner of wise neither harm nor hurt us, neither bodily nor ghostly, but that ye permit and suffer us peaceably and quietly to take and detain this treasure. I charge and bind you, O spirits, by all patriarchs, prophets, martyrs, confessors, and virgins, by all the evangelists, doctors, widows, holy matrons, and innocents, that ye be not disobedient unto me, but obey me in all things before spoken and rehearsed, and I charge, bid, and command you that none of you by any craft or subtlety in any respect make against us, but also grant and give us your aids and succours, even to the uttermost of your powers and that to your office appertaineth. To this I do bind you and every one of you, one and all, how many soever you be, by the mighty power of God the Father, the Son, and the Holy Ghost, by the meekness of the Blessed Virgin Marie, and the holiness of angels, all these urge you to obey, destroy your power, make vain your craft and subtlety, and forever cause you to come unto me, being by name called or invocated. That this be done, I charge you by the most mighty excellent and unspeakable name of God + Tetragramaton + and that even now most speedily ye depart and go hence from this treasure, and leave it in the self [518] place where it was first laid, and, being departed, ye come no more unto it before such time we have our wills thereof. Depart, I say, O ye malignant and wicked spirits, and come no more thereat by no kind of means nor ways. Hereunto I bind, charge, exorcise, and command you, and that none of you by your devilish might or power do neither hurt nor harm me, nor none of my fellows, nor no other living creature of God's creation, by neither voice, sound, noise, sight, sign, or token, but most quietly and peaceably to depart from it and the place wherein I now stand by the space of a hundred foot, and that under the pain of everlasting death and damnation. Amen.

This [done], dig a certain breadth and a certain depth, and if ye cannot see it, then read this invocation aforesaid again, and also this hereafter, both with devotion and solemnity, pronouncing every word plainly and distinctly.

[126]

I conjure you, spirits, by the Father, the Son, and the Holy Ghost, which is + *Alpha et Omega* + *primus et novissimus, initium et finis* ["Alpha and Omega +, first and last,

---

518. Self: same.

beginning and end"], and by the most terrible and dreadful day of judgment, and by the faith and obedience that you owe unto the everlasting true and most great God, that ye by no means nor no ways remove not this treasure of gold, silver, or others, but that depart therefrom, and in departing ye leave it in the same place where as it was first laid or put in the same manner and form, and in the self similitude and likeness, without altering, changing, or diminishing the same or any part thereof.

I conjure[519] you, O spirits, by the Father of might, and by his infinite power, and by Jesus Christ his Son, full of all grace and mercy, and by the Holy Ghost, God proceeding from them both, and by his unspeakable virtue and clemency. O spirits, I conjure you by this most holy blessed and glorious Trinity, three persons and one very and true God without beginning and without ending, and by the Sacrament of Christ's most precious body and blood, by the virtue of his substance, by his holy name, by his strength and virtue, of the air, fire, sea, and land, and all things therein contained and have any being, that ye minish not nor change this treasure here hid or laid or within [100] foot of this place wherein I now stand, but depart and avoid therefrom, and suffer us to take, enjoy, and possess the same after our wills. Hereunto I bind and most earnestly command you, O you spirits, by all Angels, Archangels, Cherubim, and Seraphin, Dominations, Principalities, and Powers, and by the virtue, strength, and efficacy of every of their dignities and offices, and by the virtues of the heavens and powers therein, that ye spirits go even now, without any more delays, from this treasure, and leave it within the compass of this circle, so that we may peaceably have it, and this I charge you under the pain of eternal death and everlasting damnation.

Then begin again and dig, etc., then say:

I conjure you, O spirits that be keepers of this treasure here hid, by the Sun and Moon, and by the virtue of the seven planets, and by all other stars fixed in the tegument,[520] concave,[521] or cope of heaven,[522] and by the most mighty power of God the Creator of them and all creatures, and by all the works that ever God wrought, ordained, or made in his own name and by his virtue, when he made man to his own image, similitude, and likeness, and by the virtue of God when he gave water out of the hard and stony rock of flint, and by the righteous sentence of judgment that God

---

519. In marg.: "274."

520. Tegument: a cover.

521. Concave: the vault of the sky.

522. Cope of heaven: as above.

gave upon you for your transgression and fall,[523] and by the great mercy and pity that he had upon those penitents Peter, Paul, and Magdalene, and by all the virtues of his passion most bitter, his resurrection most glorious, and his ascension most wonderful. I bind and charge you that you go and depart from this treasure, and that you come no more nigh it by 100 foot, but let it be and remain within the compass of this circle, to the end we may quietly and peaceably come by it. This I charge you by all the holy words rehearsed and spoken, yea, I conjure you spirits by all patriarchs and prophets and their estates, and by the inestimable estate and dignity of the mighty Godhead, and by the golden altar before the Throne of God, and by the seven lamps continually burning before the same, and by the golden censers and most sweet savour and smell that is forever offered by the angel in the sight of the Deity, and by the painful death and passion of all holy martyrs, and the devotion of all the blessed confessors, and by the immaculate virginity of the most pure and undefiled Mother of God, Saint Mary, Mother of all virgins, and by the virtue of all things that God would have worshipped and praised, and by the virtue and strength of all holy and clean things, that you obey to all things foresaid which I have bound you unto, and that in every thing without craft, cautel,[524] or guile. Also I conjure you spirits by our Son[525] Jesus Christ, both God and man, and by all his holy names written in Hebrew, Greek, Latin, or English, to you known and unknown, that you obey this my will and commandment, and that in each point ye fulfill the same as truly as God shall judge you at the last day in the great judgment, and also I charge you by the might and power that he had when he arose from death to life the third day, and by the virtue, strength, and power whereby he descended into hell and from thence fett[526] out Adam and the rest of the holy and believing Fathers that aspected[527] his coming in the flesh. By all these, O spirits most ungracious, I charge and command you to obey my will and bidding, and that as meekly as Jesus Christ, the only Messias and mediator betwixt God and man, did fulfill and obey the will and pleasure of God his Father, so likewise I charge you to depart and go from this treasure, that we may safely have and enjoy it without any fear, hurt, or harm doing to me or to any living creature, as ye will answer at the great day of doom before that most dreadful and just Judge. Also I conjure you by Christ's birth and nativity, by his circumcision, by his [127] fasting and temptation, and by his pure, holy, mighty, and renowned name + Tetragrammaton + by his agony, death, resurrection, and ascension, and by the great meekness that he

---

523. In marg.: "w" glyph.

524. Cautel: trick.

525. Son: should be "Lord."

526. Fett: fetched.

527. Aspected: looked for.

shewed when he washed the feet of his disciples, and by the crown of thorn wherewith he was crowned, and by all the pains and pangs of his dolorous passion, as
mockings, spittings, and buffetings, by his precious body and blood, and by the great
heaviness and sorrow that his blessed Mother had when she saw him, her dear son,
hang upon the + and by the unspeakable joy that she had when he rose from death to
life the third day. By these and all other aforesaid, I charge and bind you spirits that
you be no longer obstinate nor disobeying, but obedient and willing to depart and go
hence quickly and quietly from this treasure, and that by and by, and without any tarrying or longer delays,[528] and that you remove it not from the place where it was first
laid, and that you alter nor change the nature nor shape thereof. I conjure you and
charge you spirits, by the strength, might, and virtue of all the holy words that God
spake in and at the Creation of the world, and by the virtue, might, power, and
strength, that God had when he commanded Lucifer, your prince, with all his adherents and companions to fly from their place of joy and felicity, and by the virtues of
all the Sacraments, all prayers, fastings, just deeds, and watchings, at any time or times
practised within the whole and universal Church militant and by all holy characters,
signs, and seals that King Solomon used, by these and by all the whole virtue, strength,
might, power, and brightness of the glorious Trinity, I charge and command you spirits to depart and avoid from this treasure.

An expediment for the ground

First the master of the work must hear a Mass of the Holy Ghost [and] a memory[529] of the holy + and he must be in clean life and in steadfast faith and trust, this
for to be true, for it hath been proved many times,[530] and the first 2–3 nights are best,
when the Moon is new and the first is best. In the first place, the master of the work
must go with his fellows there as the treasure is, with a clerk with him to help to say
the prayers that belong thereto with good devotion, and when they come there as it is
prick down a wand of hazel[531] of one year's growth, and go there from thirty foot,
and kneel down, and first say this Psalm:

*Deus in nomine tuo sal me face: Et deus misereator nostri: misere et nun dimittis:
laudate domini omnes gentes magnificat anima: Deus deus meus respice*: ["O God, save

---

528. In right marg.: "272."

529. Memory: a commemorative act. In left marg.: "w" glyph; in right marg.: "256."

530. In marg.: "Probatim est."

531. Scot, *Discouerie of Witchcraft*, book 10, chapter 7.

me by thy name";[532] and "O God, be merciful to us";[533] "Have mercy";[534] and "Now you dismiss";[535] "Praise the Lord, O all you nations";[536] "My soul magnifies";[537] "O God my God, look upon me"[538]].

Then the master of the craft shall say this that followeth with a faithful and merry spirit:

Thou, N., that keepest this treasure that we have marked, or within the space of thirty foot or more, I charge thee by the virtue and sufferance of almighty God that thou spirit arise and appear, through the virtue of his passion that here shall be rehearsed on this manner as followeth, in the worship of God and constraining of thee or you:

Ego Coniuro te vel vos speritus per Patrem et Filium et Spiritum Sanctum, et aerium et terram et mare et inferniem et omnia que qui in eis sunt et per omnia verba que qui dominus dixit in creacione mundye et omnium creaturarum et per omnia verba qui deus dixit ad Moise et omnibus alliis Sanctis prophetis et per 4or elementa et per omnes virtutes Celorum et per omnia nomina dei effabilia et ineffabilia et per incarnationem nativitatem et pacioneem et effucionem [+sanguinis] eius et per omnes vulneras de Iesu Christi: Coniuro te N vel vos spiritus per ignem et per aquam et per principes vestrem vel vestrim et per virginitate beate Marie virginis et Matris dei et per capud Sancti Iohannis Baptiste et per	I conjure you,[*] O spirit or spirits, through the Father, and the Son, and the Holy Ghost, and the air, the earth, the sea, and hell, and all that are in them, and by all the words which the Lord spoke at the creation of the world and all its creatures, and by all the words which God spoke to Moses and all other holy prophets, and by the four elements and by all the powers of Heaven, and by all the names of God, effable and ineffable, and by his incarnation, nativity, and passion, and by the outpouring of his [+ blood], and by all the wounds of Jesus Christ. I conjure you, O N. (or "you spirits"), by the fire and by the water, and by all your princes, and by the virginity of the blessed Mary, virgin and mother of

* Compare below, Folger p. 129.

---

532. Psalm 53 (KJV 54).

533. Psalm 66 (KJV 67).

534. Psalm 50 (KJV 51)? Psalm 55 and 56 (KJV 56 and 57) also start with this word.

535. Luke 2:29–32. Not a Psalm, but often used as the final song of a religious service.

536. Psalm 116 (KJV 117).

537. Luke 1:46–55.

538. Psalm 21 (KJV 22).

omnes patriarchas Appostolos Martires Confessores et Virginis et per tormenta Inferni ad huc Ego coniuro te vel vos spiritus sub pena maledicciones ecclesie Sancti et ego ad monio te vel vos spiritus sub pena inclucionis usque ad diem Iudicii ut cito et aperte aperias vel aperiats mihi et socios meos sine lecione et falcione creature dei et respondeatis veraciter ad interrogacionem meam, Amen.	God, and by the head of Saint John the Baptist, and by all the patriarchs, apostles, martyrs, confessors, and virgins, and by all your torments in hell. I conjure you, spirit or spirits, under penalty of the holy Church's curse, and I warn you, spirit or spirits, under penalty of imprisonment until the Day of Judgment, that you come quickly and appear openly to me and my associate (or associates), without malice or deceiving the creatures of God, and respond truthfully to my questioning. Amen.

And then say the Fifteen O's,[539] then say this, "*O domine Iesu Christie eterna dulcedo*" ["O Lord Jesus Christ, eternal delight...."],[540] etc.

Then must the master and the clerk stand on their feet and say the Psalms of the passion of our Lord Jesus Christ, and the master must say as followeth with a faithful and merry spirit.

O thou, N., that keepest this treasure where we have marked about this wand[541] by the space of thirty foot or more, I charge thee by the virtue of God and of his passion that here shall be rehearsed, that by and by thou arise *cum socios* ["with your associates"] in the likeness of a child of the age of ten years in the pain of endless damnation, and by the virtue of all the holy words that followeth:

O tu N vel vos spiritus qui hic custodis thesauris vel custodit aliquid thesaurum vel aliud bonum habet vel habetis hic aliquam potestatem et dominationem [128] ubi sint vel fueritis veni venite et aperire super terram istam et super thesaurum aperte in forma puerum	O you N., (or "you spirits") who guards this treasure, or guards any treasure, or has other goods, or any power and dominion [128] here or wherever these goods may be or where you will have been, come now and reveal this earth, and appear over this treasure in

---

539. The XV O's of the Crucifixion are fifteen prayers attributed to St. Bridget of Sweden, but now thought to have originated in England. See http://www.umilta.net/xvosyon1.html.

540. Ibidem.

541. In right marg.: "256."

decem Annorum visu mei et sociorum meorum obediuntur respondeas vel respondeatis in omnibus rebus de quibus interrogabo te vel vos per alteriam fortetudinem et potestatem Sanctem dei Trinitate:	the form of a child ten years old, to my sight, and to the sight of my associates, obediently answering to all things which I will ask you, through the one strength and power of the holy Trinity of God.
Surge o tu spiritus com sociis tuis et aperire vel aperiatis mihi coniuro te vel vos [+ per] alteriam fortitudinem et timore altisime dei patris in Celo et per virtutem magnam veritatis et per beatitudinem divnitatem altisimi patris in Celo et per virtutem omnium Miraculorum et mirabillium per omnia sancta nomina dei et verba dei sancte quem in Celo et in terra surge o tu spiritus com sociis tuis qui est custodis vel custodies in hac terra aliquius thesaurie vel aliquius rei infra spaciem tregente pedum in latitudinem et in longitudinem et profunditatem:	Arise, O you spirit, with your associates, and appear to me. I conjure you [+ by] the one strength and by the fear of the highest God the Father in Heaven, and by the great power of truth, and by the blessed divinity of the highest Father in Heaven, and by the power of all miracles and wonders, and by all the holy names of God, and by all the holy words of God in Heaven and Earth. Arise, O you spirit with your associates who guard or will guard any treasures in this earth, or any things within thirty feet in width, length, and depth.
Coniuro te vel vos per allteriam potenciam et fortitudinem Iesu Christi Regis bonitatis, et per virtutem omnes potestates et mundicia, et per virtutem m[ag]nie (?) generositatis Iesu Christi Regis bonitatis, et per virtutem amoris Iesu Christi comfortacionis et leticie Iesu Christo dei Celi, et per virtutem claritatis et bonitatis ipsius, et per virtutem veri Christi fili dei et altitudinem	I conjure you* by the one force and power of Jesus Christ, king of goodness, and by the strength of all power and purity, and by the power of the great generosity of Jesus Christ, king of goodness, and by the power of the love of Jesus Christ, the comfort and joy of Jesus Christ, God of Heaven, and by the power of his brightness and goodness, and by the true power of Christ, son of God and

* This was evidently composed by someone with a poor command of Latin, as evidenced by such forms as "omnie" and "saluacioneorum" (corrected).

dei, qui veraciter regnat in eternam, gl[ori]am (?) cum prie maiestattis fortis et per tremendum diem Iudicii eius, dein dicabit omnem (?) genus humanum tam vivam quam mortuum et demones et elphus (?) et omnes malos spiritus in eodem tam vinam quam mortuam et eum cuie omnie genus flectite Iesu filio salvationum fratri omnium bonorum filiorum:	height of God, who truly reigns in eternal glory with the Father of strong majesty, and by his terrible Day of Judgment. Thereafter he will judge all the human race—the living and the dead, and the demons, and elves, and all evil spirits, at the same time the living and the dead, and all knees will bend to him—to Jesus the son of salvation, the brother of all good children.

Surge o tu spiritus com socciis tuus si habes aliquos tecum: aliter, surge super thesauorum aperte visu mei sosiis meis qui hic mecum in simillitudinem pueri decem annorum et loquere mi, et des mi vera responsa de omnibus rebus quibus te interrogavero: Surge o tu spiritus et ego coniuro te et admoneo te in virtute spiritus sancti et per virtute omnes filii [*consilii?] spiritus sancti et per virtutem et divinitatem omnes sapientie spiritus sancti, et intellectus pietatis spiritus sancti, et per virtutem siencie spiritus sancti, et per virtutem timoris immundio [*domini (?)] spiritus sancti, et per virtutem omnium nomine dei graciam spiritus sancti:	Arise, O you spirit, with your associates if you have any with you. Otherwise arise over the treasure, plainly to my sight, and to my associates, in the form of a child ten years old, and speak to me and give me true answers to everything that I will ask. Arise, O you spirit. I conjure you and I admonish you by the power of the Holy Ghost, and by the power of all children [*counsel] of the Holy Ghost, and by the power and divinity of all wisdom of the Holy Ghost, and the understanding [and] of the piety of the Holy Ghost, and by the power of the knowledge of the Holy Ghost, and by* the power of the fear of the Lord of the Holy Ghost,† and by the power of all the names of God, the grace of the Holy Ghost.

* In left marg.: "w" glyph; in right marg.: "257."
† Compare this list with the well-known "seven gifts of the Holy Ghost:" *sapientia, intellectus, consilium, fortitudo, scientia, pietas, timor Domini* ["wisdom, understanding, counsel, fortitude, knowledge, piety, fear of the Lord"]. See Isaiah 11:2–3.

Surge o tu spiritus coniuro te per magnam potenciam et fortitudinem et divinitatem q[ue]m ipse habebit regnas potestatem, et filio in unitatem Trinus et unus deus omnipotentis dei, Surge o tu spiritus per virtuosam m[aiestate]m (?) dei surge o tu spiritus et coniuro te per magnam fortitudinem omnipotente dei o tu spiritus, surge [+ per] virtuosam graciam dei, surge o tu spiritus per virtuosam victoriam dei: surge o tu spiritu[s], coniuro te spiritus per virtutem omni Coelos et Ecclestium omnium creaturarum adorant cuam deum omnipotente:

Surge o tu spiritus per virtutem dei omni Rerum et mortuorum et mobilum adorantium dei surge o tu spiritus com sociis tuis si aliquos habeas tecum alliter: surge o tu spiritus per virtutem et fortitudinem sancti passionis Iesu Christi et per virtutem dulsis facie dei Christi qui fuit dedicate rubio sanguinem in sua sancta passionem: surge o tu spiritus per virtutem dextera manus Christi qui fuit clavatus ligno crucis perforatus, sic tu spiritus sic percussus / cum pena Inferna surge o tu spiritus per fortitudinem et per virtutem illis, vulneris qui fuit in latere: Christi et sicut ipse fuit tractum cum cordis lignum fixus com clavatos et tractis com fortissimis penis inferni et com corde Igneis nisi venias et appares ante aperte per virtutem illius pene quam Christus sustinuit super dexteriam pedem clavatam sic tu ligno crux sic tu sis com sociis tuis clavatus

Arise, O you spirit. I conjure you by the great force and strength and divinity which itself will have you reign, the power, and the Son in three-fold unity, and one God, of almighty God.* Arise, O you spirit, by the virtuous majesty of God. Arise, O you spirit. I conjure you by the great power of almighty God. O you spirit, arise by the powerful grace of God. Arise, O you spirit, by the powerful victory of God. Arise, O you spirit; I conjure you, O spirit, by the power of all the heavens, and ecclesiastics, and all creatures who honour almighty God.

Arise, O you spirit, by the power of God, of all things, both dead and moving, honouring God. Arise, O you spirit, by the power and strength of the sacred passion of Jesus Christ, and by the power of the sweet face of God Christ who has consecrated his red blood in his sacred passion. Arise, O you spirit, by the power of the right hand of Christ, which was pierced and nailed to the wood of the cross, thus you, O spirit, will be beaten with infernal punishment.

Arise, O you spirit, by the power and strength of that one whose side was pierced: Christ, and as he himself was dragged with ropes, fasten to wood with nails, and so you will be dragged with the strongest penalties of hell, and with cords of fire, unless you come and appear before us openly, by the power of that pain which Christ endured when his right foot was nailed, so you will suffer being nailed to a wooden cross, along

---

* Perhaps the scribe missed a line, resulting in this awkward text.

passiones et perforatiam com pena inferni, surge o tu spiritus per virtutem illius passiones in veneris cito pena quam Christus sustinuit in sinestra peda puneat te et clavat te com penis igneis que semper ardebunt et desendat super te vel vos cum fortissimis ictibus tonitrus et fullminis et cum fortissimis igneis Inferni et gladio mortis terrorum et pauores et omnium tormentum omnim demonum Inferni omnis penis dessendunt super te vel vos nisi veneris sito appereas mihi aperte visui meo,

Surge o tu spiritus coniuro te vel vos per fortem passionis Christi fili dei surge o tu spiritus conioro [sic] te vel vos et admonio te vel vos per virtutem illius presiosi sanguinis et aque quos Christus in cruce effundebat forte [*de latere] sua et Acerba passione et Aque et pauores et per salsas lachriimas quas Beatie Marie sua dulsissima Mater ploravit in tempore passionis sue: surge o tu spiritus per virtutem omni Sanctos verborum que ipse Iesus loquebatur in sua passione videlicet qum audo [*deo] oravit per crucifigentibus sic dicens patri ignossi illis quia nessiunt quid faciunt et per verba qui ipse dixit mulier ecce fillius tuis et addissipulum ecce mater tua, et per illud verbum sacrum sitio et per illa verba Eloy Eloy Lamazabathany quod est deus meus deus meus ut quid de relinquisti me et per illa verba sacrum consumatum est, et per illa | sacra verba pater in manus tuas <domine> [+ commendo spiritum meum], et per virtutem

with your associates, will be pierced with the punishment of hell.

Arise, O you spirit, by the power of that pain which will come quickly, which Christ endured when his left foot was nailed, so you will suffer with the punishment of ever-burning fire, which will descend onto you with the most mighty blows of thunder and lightning, and with the strongest fire of hell, and with the sword of death, of terror, and of fear, and all the torments of all the demons of hell will descend onto you, unless you quickly come and appear openly to my sight.

Arise, O you spirit. I conjure you by the strong suffering of Christ, the son of God. Arise, O you spirit. I conjure you and warn you by the power of that precious blood and water which flowed from Christ's side while on the Cross, and by the harsh suffering and fears, and by the salty tears which his blessed mother Mary wept for him at the time of his suffering.

Arise, O you spirit, by the power of all the holy words which Jesus himself spoke at the time of his passion, namely, when he prayed to God while being crucified, saying "forgive them father, for they know not what they do;" and by the words which he said to his mother when he said, "woman, behold your son," and to his disciples "behold your mother;" and by the sacred words "I am thirsty," and by those words "Eloy Eloy Lamazabathany," which is interpreted, "My God,

sancte Marie que portavit Iesum Christum et per virtutem sancte Crucis quam
Christus portavit passioni sue surge o tu
spiritus et aperire aperte visui meo et sosiis meis in forma predicta com sosiis
tuis, si habes aliquos et alliter, coniuro te
per Iesu Christi et per virtutem omnium
vulnerum que Christus habuit et efudit
in sua passionem et per virtutem resurrectionem et ascentionem suam et per
tremendum diem Iudicii domini nostri
Iesu Christi vivi

Surge spiritus et aperire aperte et respondeas mihi in omnibus rebus de quibus intterogabo te nisi cito venies sine
mora <omnipotente: deus pat[e]r sancte
celi et terre> excommunico excommunico te vel vos com sosiis tuis et per ie-
iiciat te vel vos spiritus in Ignem eternum, et unicum filius dei Iesus Christus
maladicat te vell vos spiritus com cathenis mutvum et surdum vel mutuos et
surdos in fortissima pena inferni, o tu
spiritus ego excommunico te vel [129]
vos per Ecclesia dei, et cum omnibus
Sanctis sacramentis et Sancta Trinitas et
omnie [*omnes] Sancte [*sanctos] dei,
et sanctam puerum et Matrum eius te
vel vos spiritus com dolore et tristicia et
omnie tormentum eiiciat super te vel
vos et cadat super te vel vos miserie perducat te vel vos *rebelling spirits if you do
not come quicky and stand before us without let and answer me* fiat fiat Amen.

my God, why hast thou forsaken me?"
and by those holy words "it is finished"
and by those holy words "Father, into
your hands [+ I commend my spirit]",
and by the power of Saint Mary, who
carried Jesus Christ, and by the power of
the holy cross, which carried Christ during his passion.

Arise, O you spirit, and appear
plainly to my sight and that of my associates, in the form specified before, along
with your associates, if you have any, and
otherwise, I conjure you alone, by Jesus
Christ, and by the power of all the
wounds which Christ had and poured
out in his suffering, and by the power of
his resurrection and ascension, and by
the terrible Day of Judgment of our living Lord Jesus Christ.

Arise, O spirit, and reveal everything
plainly, and respond to me in all things
which I will ask you. Unless you come
quickly, without delay, <almighty God,
holy father of Heaven and Earth> I will
excommunicate you with your associates, and expel you into eternal fire, and
the only son of God, Jesus Christ will
curse you, O spirit, with chains, mute
and deaf, in the strongest punishment of
hell. O you spirit or spirits, I excommunicate you *[129]* by the church of God,
and by all the sacred sacraments, and by
the holy Trinity, and by all the saints of
God, and by the holy child and his

	mother, O you spirit or spirits, with pain and sadness and all torments will fall upon you, and misery will overcome you rebelling spirits, if you do not come quickly and stand before us without let,* and answer me. Fiat, fiat. Amen.
* Let: permission, leave.	

And charge him that he appear by the virtue of all the holy words that our Lord God spake in the creation of the world and all creatures visible and invisible.

I conjure and charge thee that thou appear by the virtue of the words that are written hereafter:[542] I charge thee that thou arise and appear to us by the virtue of the first word that our Lord spake in the creation of the world,[543] when he made light to spring, he said, "*Fiat lux et facta est lux*" ["let there be light, and there was light"];[544] and by the virtue of the second word that he said when he made the firmament, "*Fiat firmamentum in medio aquarum et deuidat Aquas ab Aquis*" ["let there be a firmament in the midst of the waters, and let it divide the waters from the waters"]; and by the third word when he made the firmament, he gathered all the waters that were under Heaven into one place, he said, "*Congregentor Aqueque sub Celo sunt [in locum unum] et appariam arida*" ["let the waters which are under the heavens be gathered together in one place, and let the dry land appear"]; and by the virtue of the fourth word when he made to spring trees and herbs, he said, "*Germinet terra herbam virentem, et facientem semen, et lignum pomiferum faciens fructum juxta genus suum, cujus semen in semetipso sit super terram*" ["let the earth sprout forth green herbs, and those producing seeds, and trees bearing fruit in which is seed of its kind, over the earth"]; and by the virtue of the fifth word when he made the Sun and the Moon and the stars, he said, "*Fiant luminaria magna in firmamento Celi et dividant diem ac noctem et sint signa et tempora et dies et Annos ut luceant in firmamento Celi ut illuminent terram*" ["let there be lights in the firmament of heaven, and may they divide the day and the night, and may they be for signs and seasons, days, and years, to shine in the firmament of heaven, and light up the land"]; and by the virtue of the sixth word, when he made fishes and birds, he said, "*Producant aque reptile anime viventis et volatile super terram sub firmamento Celi*" ["let the waters bring forth the creeping things

---

542. In right marg.: "257."

543. Compare parallel versions of this text on Folger pp. 122, 132, and 217. In marg.: "*Verbum primum creationis.*"

544. The passages that follow are from the Vulgate Bible.

with living souls, and those that fly over the earth under the firmament of heaven"];
and by the virtue of the seventh word when he blessed them, he said, "*Crescite et multiplicamini et repletae aquas maris aves multiplicentur super terram*" ["Go forth and multiply and fill up the waters of the sea, and let the birds be multiplied upon the earth"];
and by the virtue of the eighth word when he made beasts, worms, and serpents, he
said, "*Producat terram aliam in genero suo iumenta et reptilia secundum species suas*"
["Let the earth bring forth living creatures and beasts of burden and creeping things
according to their own kinds"]; and by the virtue of the ninth word, when he made
man, he said, "*Faciamus hominem ad Imaginem et similitudinem nostram et presit pissibus et volatilibus Celi et bestias terre et universi creature qui reptile quem mouentur in
terra*" ["Let us make man in our own image and likeness, and let him preside over the
fishes of the sea, and flying creatures of the heavens, and the beasts of the earth, and
all creatures which move or crawl upon the earth"];[545] and by the virtue of the tenth
word, when he put Adam and Eve into paradise, he said, "*Crescite et multiplicamini et
replete terram subiugate eam et dimitte vivi pissibus maris et volatilibus Celi et bestias
terre et uniuersis animantibus quem moventus super terram*" ["Increase and multiply
and fill the earth, and subdue it, and be master of the fishes of the sea, and the flying
things in the heavens, and the beasts of the earth, and all creatures which move upon
the earth"]; *et per hac verba que dominus dixit ad Moyse et omnibus Aliis Sanctis prophets, et per 4or Elementa et pulcritudine Celorum et omnia dei ineffabilia et per incarnationem domini nostri Iesu Christi et per sepultum eius, et per passionem eius, et per ef-
fucionem preciosi sanguinis domini nostri Iesu Christi et per gloriosum resurrectionem
eius et per admirabilem assentionem eius, et per admentum [*admonitum?] domini
diem iudicii quia iudicabit vivos et mortuos et seculum per ignem, Surge o tu spiritus ego
te coniuro te vel vos spiritus per ignem et aquam et per capud vestri prenceps et per vir-
ginitate Beate Marie virginis Matris dei et per capud Sancti Iohannes Baptistie et per
omnes patriarchas prophetas Apostolos Martires confessores et virgines, et per tormenta
inferni ad huc que te subpena maladictiones Ecclesie et ego admonio te vel vos spiritus
subpena incluciones usque diem iudicii ut citum aperte appareas mihi et sosiis meis sine
fallacia et lecione ad mei vell socios meorum vel allicuius rei vel creature dei et veraciter
respondeas ad omnia interrogata fiat fiat fiat Amen.* ["And by these words which the
Lord spoke to Moses and other holy prophets, and by the four elements, and the
beauty of the heavens, and all the ineffable (things)[546] of God, and by the incarnation
of our Lord Jesus Christ, and by his burial, and by his passion, and by the shedding of
the precious blood of our Lord Jesus Christ, and by his glorious resurrection, and by

---

545. In marg.: "w" glyph.
546. Perhaps *nomina* ["names"] omitted by mistake.

his admirable ascension, and by the command (?) of the Lord on the Day of Judgment, for he will judge the living and the dead and the world by fire, (saying): Rise up, O you spirit. I conjure you, O spirit or spirits, by fire and water, and by the head of your prince, and by the virginity of the blessed Virgin Mary, mother of God, and by the head of Saint John the Baptist, and by all the patriarchs, prophets, apostles, martyrs, confessors, and virgins, and by the torture of hell which will be the penalty of the Church's curse on you. I warn you, O spirit or spirits, under penalty of imprisonment until the day of Judgement, that you quickly and openly appear to me and my associates, without deceit or harm to me or my associates or any thing or creature of God, and answer truthfully to everything that is asked. Let it be so! Let it be so! Let it be so! Amen."]

And when he is risen[547] or appeareth, speak to him in the mother tongue what he doth there and what he keepeth there, other gold or silver or any other treasure, or by what means ye may come to it best, and what time, and then beware how you do examine him to fare forth, for some will speak and some will not, and if he speak, then ask him how ye may best come to it, and charge him to be ready when ye call him again, and then set him to keep a stake or a wand of hazel of one year's growing and cast it out aside, and if he be well bound, he will take it upon him by the same bond aforesaid and shall bring it to you. Then charge him that he go to the place that he was assigned to and thereto abide the doom of God the Father, the Son, and the Holy Ghost, and if he be obstinate to tell you, then charge him by all the words abovesaid, upon the pain of everlasting damnation, that he set it up before you, but then he will ask something for his labour, but give him nothing but charge him that he go into the place that he was assigned to and there to abide the doom of God our Lord Jesus Christ the Father, [the Son,] and the Holy Ghost, three persons and one God in Trinity.

The end. Proven, and for certain.

---

547. In right marg.: "158."

[130]

548

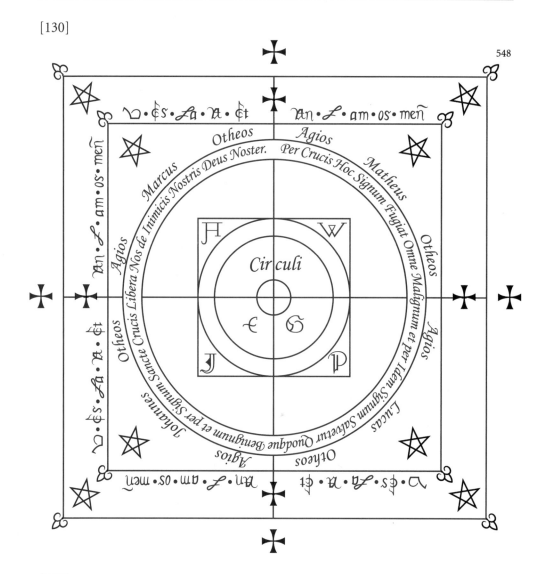

[131]

The spirit of the North, who is called King Egin. It is proven.

I Conjure thee, Egin, King[549] of the North, and also charge thee that thou appear before me, before this circle, by the sufferance of almighty God, and by the virtue of his passion that here shall be rehearsed on this manner that follows to the worshipping of God and the constraining of thee, I conjure thee, spirit Egin, by the Father, the

---

548. Text reads: *Per crucis hoc signum fugiat omne malignum et per idem signum salvetur quodque benignum [et] per signum sancte crucis libera nos de inimicis nostris deus noster* ["By this sign of the cross, may all evil flee, by the same sign may all good be preserved, and by the sign of this holy cross deliver us from our enemies, O our God."]: The other phrase reads "V. os. la. A. Et. An. l. am. os. Meñ", which is obscure. In marg.: "w" glyph.

549. In right marg.: "259."

Son, and the Holy Ghost, and by the heavens, the air, the earth, and the sea, and by hell and by all that therein is contained, that thou come shortly and appear to me and my fellows, not terrible nor fearful. Also I conjure thee, thou sp[i]rit Egin, by all the holy words that God spake in the creation of the world, and of all creatures visible and invisible, and by the four elements, and by all the virtue of heaven, and by all the holy words that God spake unto Moses and to all other prophets, and by the incarnation of Jesus Christ, and by his nativity, and by his passion, and by the shedding of his precious blood, and by his taking down off the cross, and by [his] burying. I conjure thee, Egin, by his glorious resurrection, and by his mighty ascension, and by the coming of the Holy Ghost. I conjure thee, Egin, by all the bitter wounds of our Lord Jesus Christ, and by the dreadful day of judgment of our Lord Jesus Christ. I conjure thee, Egin, that thou appear before me, by the virtue of the Blessed Virgin Mary, Mother of God. I conjure thee, Egin, by the virtue of Saint John Baptist and Saint John the Evangelist. I conjure thee, thou spirit Egin, by the virtue of all patriarchs, prophets, confessors, martyrs, and virgins, and by all the powers of heaven, and by all the pains of hell. I conjure thee, thou spirit Egin, under the pain of condemnation unto the great day of judgment. I conjure thee, thou spirit Egin, by the great curse of God and all holy church, that by and by thou appear to me and to my fellows without deceit, fraud, craft, or illusion, and that thou hurt not me or any Christian creature, and that thou go not away without licence of me. Also I conjure thee, Egin, by all the high names of God, and by all the holy words of God that is in heaven and earth. I conjure thee, Egin, by the high power and strength of our Lord Jesus Christ, the son of God, the heavenly king of glory, and I conjure thee, thou spirit Egin Mosacus,[550] in what place of the world soever thou art in, or to whom soever thou art bound, that thou come and appear before me in the likeness of a child under the age of ten years, and that thou go not away without licence of me. I conjure thee by the virtue and blessed passion, and by the virtue of all charity and love of the Holy Ghost, and by the love of Jesus Christ that he bare to all creatures visible and invisible.[551] I conjure thee, Egin, by the great comfort and sweetness of Jesus Christ, and by all the virtue and gladness of Jesus Christ. I conjure thee, Egin, by the high power and virtue of Jesus Christ, Son of God, and the most mercifullest God, and by his only begotten son, Jesus C[hrist], which livest and reignest with his Father in his majesty, and by the dreadful day of judgment where he shall come to judge the quick and the dead, by whose power all heaven, earth, and hell do bow. I conjure thee, Egin, by the same Jesu, the son of David, the son of the Blessed Virgin Mary, and son of salvation of all the elect children of God. I conjure thee, Egin, by the virtue of the Holy Ghost, and by the wisdom

550. Possibly indicating the incantation can be used for multiple spirits.

551. In marg.: "w" glyph.

and understanding of the Holy Ghost, and by the meek counsel of the Holy Ghost. I conjure thee, Egin, by the wisdom and sapience of the Holy Ghost. I conjure thee, Egin, by all the mercy and grace of God, and by the great power and strength of God, and by the glorious mercy of God, and by all the creatures of heaven that do worship in the sight of God, and by all the creatures in earth that do worship him. I conjure thee, spirit Egin, that thou arise and appear, O thou spirit Egin, by all the spirits, quick and dead, that do worship in the sight of God. I conjure thee, spirit Egin, that thou appear before me, by the hands and feet of Jesu that were fast nailed unto a tree of the cross for my redemption and thy great confusion. Such great pain light upon thee, with the great uncomfortable pains of hell may light upon thee, thou spirit Egin, ever without hope of salvation, except thou dost come and appear before me. I conjure and call thee, thou spirit Egin, by the virtue of his blessed passion, and by the shedding of his most precious blood. I do accite[552] and lay upon thee, by the power of God, such great pains for to light upon thee with the flame of fire, of sulphur, and of thunder and lightning, with the sword of sorrow and all the pains that all devils suffer, with the horrible pains of hell, may light upon thee, except thou dost appear to me, incontinent, without hurt doing to me or to any living creature. Also I conjure thee, thou spirit Egin, that thou appear visible to me and to my fellows, by the sharp and strong passion of our Lord Jesus Christ, the son of the true and living God, who is the saviour of all the world, and by his precious blood and water that ran out of all parts of his blessed body, that in what parts of the world soever thou art or be in, or whosoever hath the government of thee, thou spirit, that thou dost come and appear to me and to my fellows and to answer me, true and truly, according to my meaning, speedily and unfeignedly, to fulfill all my requests and demands. I conjure thee, O thou spirit Egin, and call thee by the bitter weeping that the Blessed Virgin Mary wept in the time of her son's bitter passion. I conjure thee, by the virtue of all the words that our Lord spake as he hanged upon the Cross,[553] which was when he prayed devoutly to his father for his enemies, saying, "Father, forgive them, for they know not what they do." I conjure thee, Egin, by the virtue of the [132] second word, when to his sorrowful Mother, he said, "Woman, behold thy son." I conjure thee, Egin, by the virtue of the third word, when he said to his disciple John, "Behold thy mother." I conjure thee, Egin, by the virtue of the fourth word, when he said, "I thirst." I conjure thee, thou spirit Egin, and call thee by the virtue of the fifth word, when he said, "Heloy, heloy, lama zabathanie." I conjure thee, Egin, by the virtue of the sixth word, when he said, "*In manus tuas domine commendum spiritum meum redemisti me domine deus veritates.*" ["Into your hands, O Lord, I commend my spirit; you have re-

---

552. Accite: summon.

553. Compare Folger p. 20. Compare also Additional MS. 36674, fol. 97r.

deemed me, O Lord God of truth."] I conjure thee, thou spirit Egin, and call thee, by the virtue of the seventh word, when he said, "*Consumatum est.*" ["It is finished."] I conjure thee, O thou spirit Egin, and call thee, by the virtue of that heavy + that Christ bare unto the [place?] of his passion, where he suffered the most shamefullest death that could be devised or thought. I accite and cast, by the sufferance of God, such heavy burden and pain to light upon thee, except thou meekly here appear to me and to my fellows, visible and in fair form, of a child under the age of ten years. I conjure thee, by all the virtues of the Blessed Virgin Mary and Mother that bare Christ in this world. I conjure thee, Egin, and call thee by and in the pain of thy utter and everlasting damnation, that thou appear before me openly, in human form, without hurt doing to me or to my fellows, or to any thing that ever God created. I conjure thee, Egin, and call thee by the virtue of Christ's death, resurrection, and mighty ascension, and by the coming of the Holy Ghost. I conjure thee, Egin, and call thee by the dreadful day of judgment, that thou never rest nor stay in any place, but that thou appear before me, and if thou be bound to any man before this time, I charge thee and conjure thee, by the virtue of the words that I have before spoken or rehearsed, that thou send one of thy legion next under thee that is out of bondage to answer me truly to all my demands and to obey me upon the pain of utter and everlasting damnation, and upon the pain of the great curse of God that here shall be rehearsed, that thou, Egin, with all thy legions, dost come and appear meekly and in fair form, *Omnipotens deus pater sancti Celi et terre excommuniat te et progeciat te in Ignem inferni et unicus Iesus Christus filius dei maledicat te com cathenis et com dolore et tristicia et omnem tormentum Inferni percusiat te et cadat super te miserie et perducat te horribellum [*rebellem]* [554] *spiritus si, non veneris statim sine mora et respondeatis mihi in omnibus questionibus mei ita fiat fiat fiat Amen* ["Almighty God, the father of the holy heaven and earth, excommunicates you and throws you into the fires of hell, and the only son of God Jesus Christ curses you with chains and pains and sorrow and all the tortures of hell will beat you and misery will overcome you, O rebellious spirit, if you do not come immediately and respond to all my questions; thus, let it be so, let it be so, let it be so. Amen."]

Iterum atque iterum ["Again and again"] I charge thee, and also conjure thee, thou spirit Egin, King of the North, in what parts or part of the world soever thou art in, to appear before me, and if thou be bound to any man before this time, then by the same bond and virtue, I charge thee to appear before me, or to send one next unto thee of power, to answer me to all my demands, by the virtue of all the words that God spake in the creation of the world, and of all creatures. I conjure thee by the virtue of the first

---

554. Following parallel passage on Folger p. 129.

word[555] when he made the light; he said, "Let the light be made," and it was made. I conjure thee, Egin, by the virtue of the second word when he made the firmament, and said, "*Fiat firmamentum in medio Aquarum et deuidat Aquas ab Aquis.*" ["Let there be a firmament in the midst of the waters, and let it divide the waters from the waters."] I conjure thee,[556] Egin, King of the North, and call thee by the virtue of the third word; when he had made firmament, he gathered all the waters under heaven into one place, then he said, "Gather all ye waters together under heaven, that the dry land may be seen." I conjure thee, Egin, and call thee that thou appear before me and my fellows in the form of a child under the age of ten years, by the virtue of the fourth word, when he made trees and herbs to spring; he said, "*Germinat terram arbam verentem facientem in semet ipso sit super terram.*" ["Let the earth sprout forth green herbs, and those producing seeds, and trees bearing fruit in which is seed of its kind, over the earth."] I conjure thee, Egin, King of the North, by the virtue of the fifth word, when he made the Sun and the Moon and the stars; he said, "Let great lights be made in the firmament of heaven, to divide the day from the night, and let them be into signs and times and unto days and years, and let them be in the firmament, that they may shew light on the earth." I conjure thee, Egin, by the virtue of the sixth word when he made fishes; he said, "Replenish the waters and the earth with living fowls under the firmament of heaven." I conjure thee, thou spirit Egin, and call thee by the virtue of the seventh word, when he blessed them; he said, "Multiply, and increase, and fill full the <the> waters of the sea and the birds; multiply upon the land." I conjure thee, King Egin, and call thee by the virtue of the eighth word, when he made beasts and worms; he said, "Multiply, ye one, the earth after your kind." I conjure thee, Egin, by the virtue of the ninth word, when he made man; he said, "Make man after our own likeness, that he may rule the beasts on the earth, and fishes of the sea, and birds of the air under Heaven, and all the universal creatures of the air, earth, and water." I conjure thee, thou spirit Egin, by the virtue of the tenth word, when he made Adam and Eve and put them into paradise; he said, "*Cresite et multiplicamini et replete terram.*" ["Go forth and multiply and fill up the earth."] I conjure thee, Egin, and call thee and constrain thee to come and appear before me and my fellows, by and by, by the virtue of all the holy words that God spake unto Moses and all other holy prophets. I conjure thee, Egin, and call thee by the four elements, and by all the glory of heaven. I conjure thee, Egin, and call and constrain thee to come and appear unto me and my fellows, by these names, + Heeb + yreos + Iesus + fortis + fons + salvator + Eloy + Theos + Deus + Christus + Iiectata + Sabaoth + Degramonis + Agie + virtus + lotis + helium + histerium + Adonay + risus + laabatonis +

---

555. Compare above.

556. In marg.: "w" glyph.

Tetragramaton + Semeton + Graton + Maton + lection + Messias + [133] lactea + Abite + Aponas + heleos + helebe + Agie + Agee + Paton + Regum + Abraca + Bata + legita + Yreos + Victor + Osanna + hebonibatica + Helsell + Nazarenus + helemon + Vita + Victor + Theos + Thea + Thanatos + Thesion + Perceveratori + Lam + Gesa + Emanuell, that thou, Egin, dost appear before me and my fellows at this present time without any delay, fallacy, or fraud, and not to depart without licence of me. Also I conjure thee, Egin, and call thee by all these other names of God Scra + Crasme + Varios + dominus + Leta + Apres + Elon + Vrsta + Gloriosus + Bonus + On + Vnigenitus + via + vita + Manus + homo + vsion + principium + primogenitus + Sapientia + Virtus + Alpha + et Omega + Capud + et finis + Origo + Paracletus + petra + lapis + Angularis + Pastor + propheta + Sacerdos + Athanatos + Kerios + et Isus + hogeron + Allaluia + Abednago + heretis + hesben + Geroti + Covit + Absia + Sminina (?) + *et ista + predicta* ["and with this preceding"] [557] + I conjure thee, thou spirit Egin, King of the North, and I call thee and charge thee to appear by all the holy names aforesaid, that you come meekly without any troubles or commotions of any of the four elements, as thou art called by that salvations that thou thinks to have of our Lord God and of his son, Jesus Christ, to whom with God the Holy Ghost be all honour and glory, might, majesty, and dominion rendered, both now and forever, world without end. Amen.

It is proven and certain without doubt.[558]

---

557. Scra + Crasme: perhaps *sacratissime* ["most holy"]; *Varios* ["different"]; *dominus* ["Lord"] + *Leta* ["joyful"]; Apres + Elon + Vrsta + *Gloriosus* ["glorious"]; *Bonus* ["good"] + On + *Vnigenitus* ["only begotten"]; *via* ["the way"]; *vita* ["the life"]; *manus* ["hand"]; *homo + usion* ["of one substance (with the Father)"]; *principium* ["the first"]; *primogenitus* ["first begotten"]; *Sapientia* ["wisdom"]; *Virtus* ["virtua"]; Alpha and Omega; *Capud* ["the head"]; *et finis* ["and the end"]; *Origo* ["the origin"]; *Paracletus* ["Paraclete"]; *petra* ["the rock"]; *lapis angularis* ["the cornerstone"]; *Pastor* ["shepherd"]; *propheta* ["prophet"]; *Sacerdos;* ["priest"]; *Athanatos* ["immortal" (Gk)]; *Kerios* ["Lord" (Gk)]; and Isus + hogeron + Allaluia + Abednago + heretis + hesben + Geroti + Covit + Absia + Sminina (?) + et ista + predicta

558. In left marg.: "w" glyph. In right marg.: "261 b." Beneath in pencil: "See this page 48 MS Palimis." An abbreviated version of this rite may be found in Raphael, *The Astrologer of the Nineteenth Century*, 214–20.

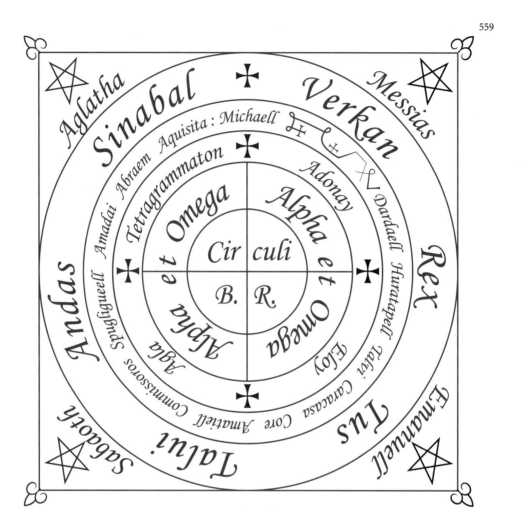

[134]

[+ Conjuration of Baron]

This experiment [560] can be done in the house or outside, in any secret place or time, during the day or night, in whichever you prefer to operate.

---

559. Magic Circle. This is a version of the magic circle from de Abano's H.: Compare http://esotericarchives.com/gifs/heptam2l.gif. According to that text, the names should be varied according to the time the operation is conducted. Text in upper left corner reads: "Aglaitha" (i.e., Aglatha). Text in circle: "+ Ver-kan Rex, Tus, Talui, An-das, Sina-bal / Michael [sigil of Michael] Dardael, Huratapell, Talvi, Cara[ca]sa, Core, Amatiell, Commissoros, Spugligueell, Amadai, Abraem, Aqusita:" / "+ Ado-nay + Elo-y + A-Gla + Tetragrammaton"; (inside:) "+ Al-pha et ω +Al-pha et ω" / (center:) "Cir-culi B. R." ["the circle of B.R."].

560. Compare Folger pp. 40 and 175.

Here begins the conjuration of Baron, first northern spirit, with circle and sceptre, with his characters written in his circle, with two types of sword, and these characters of his as following below, and make similar ones in the circle.

But when you wish to operate, hold the preceding characters in your right hand, and say three times in a row the Psalm "Have mercy upon me, O God," then say this Psalm: "Judge, O Lord, those who wrong me"[561] and then:

Adiuro te spiritus Baron per virtutem domini nostri Iesu Christi fili dei viui et veri pueri [*dei] miserecordissime et per illum Angelum qui in tuba canet in die Iudicii dicet venite: coniuro te Baron per penas domini nostri Iesu Christi filii dei viui veri et miserecordissime et per illum patibulum crusis in qua suspensus est deus et homo et per *danos quibus affectus qui hic demonstra* et per lapidem angulariem et per virtutem qua ☉ll Obscuratus est et tenebre facta sunt et multa corpora Sanctorum que dormierunt et surrexerunt et per virgam Aaron et Archam federis Christi nostri domini et per thuribilium aureum: <I> (!) coniuro te spiritus Baron gloriosam virgenem Maria Matriem domini nostri Iesu Christi qui filium dei portavit in utere et per eius Sanctum nomen et per dulsisemum lac eiusdem	I adjure you, O spirit Baron, by the power of our Lord Jesus Christ, son of the living and true God, most merciful God, and by that angel who will blow the trumpet on Judgement Day and say "Come": I conjure you, O Baron, by the punishment of our Lord Jesus Christ, son of the living and true God, and most merciful, and by that gibbet of the Cross on which was suspended God and man, and by … (?), which you demonstrate here, and by the cornerstone, and by the power which obscured the Sun and brought darkness, and caused the bodies of many saints who had slept to rise up,* and by the staff of Aaron, and the Ark of the Covenant of our Lord Christ, and by the golden censer. I conjure you, O spirit Baron, by the glorious virgin Mary, mother of our lord Jesus Christ, who carried the son of God in her womb, and by his holy name, and by the sweetest milk of the same Virgin
* Matthew 27:51.	

561. Psalms 50 and 34 (KJV 51 and 35).

virginis Marie et per verba eius et per nomen / sanctum dei Adonay quod dominus faciat omnes lapides terre et edificia et dicent tunc viuentes montibus cooperite nos a facia sedentes super thronum et per hec ineffabilia [+ nomen Ya]:

Coniuro te Baron et exorciso te ut sis spiritus benignes et humilis rebus mihi in omnibus faciunt et sosiis tuis per benedictionem in formando [*firmamento] celi et per laudabilem et admirabilem ascentionem [+ eius] et [+ per] gloriosam formidabilem iudicium in secula seculorum:

Coniuro te Baron per Angelos et Archangelos Martires Confessores et virgines et per Trones Potestates per virtutem omnes spiritus virtutes et omnes Celos dei: Coniuro te Baron per aquas que que super Celi sunt et per omnes virtutes dei per lunam et solem et imbrem et omnes spiritus dei Coniuro te Baron per ignem et estum frigus et estatem [+ et] glaces per omnes noctes et dies per Nubes et fulgura Coniuro te Baron per terram et per quattuor Elementa: Coniuro te Baron per omnes volucres Celi et per omnes bestias terre et per omnes filios hominum.

Mary, and by his words, and by the holy name of God Adonay, because the Lord made all stones of the earth, and buildings, "and then the living will say to the mountains, cover us from the face of him that sits on the throne"[*] and by this ineffable [name Ya].[†]

I conjure and exorcise you, O spirit Baron, that you and your associates may be kind and humble to me in all things that they do, by the blessed (Lord who is) in the firmament of Heaven,[‡] and by his praiseworthy and admirable ascent, and by the glorious, terrifying judgement forever.

I conjure you, O Baron, by the angels[§] and archangels, by the martyrs, confessors, and virgins, by the Thrones and Powers, by the power of all spirits, powers, and all heavenly beings of God. I conjure you, O Baron, by the waters which are above the heavens, and by all the powers of God, and by the Moon and the Sun, and rain, and all spirits of God. I conjure you, O Baron, by the fire and heat, winter and summer, and ice, and by all the nights and days, by the clouds and the lightning. I conjure you, O Baron, by the earth and by the four elements. I conjure you, O Baron, by all the birds in the sky, and all the beasts on the earth, and by all the children of mankind.

---

* Revelations 6:16. Compare Folger pp. 41 and 175. See also Luke 23:30.
† So Folger pp. 41 and 175 as well as Wellcome MS. 110, 37r, and Sloane 3853, 216r.
‡ Following Sloane 3853: "*per benedictum dominum qui est in firmamento celi.*"
§ The general outline for this section seems to be based on the Song of the Three Children (Anania, Azaria, and Misael), i.e., Daniel 3:56–88.

Coniuro te Baron per Israelem et omnes Sacerdotes et servos dei et per omnes spiritus et animas iustorum Coniuro te Baron per omnes Sanctos Appostolorum dei Iacobum et Iohannem per queram Ecclesie edificatione ista facio invocationem et per omnes Sanctos et humiles corda Coniuro te Baron eterñn [*etenim] per Ananiam Azariam [+ et Misaelem]	I conjure you, O Baron, by Israel, and by all priests and servants of God, and by all spirits and souls of the just. I conjure you, O Baron, by all saints and apostles of God, by Jacob and John, by the members of the church I make this invocation, and by all saints and those of humble heart. I conjure you indeed, O Baron,* by Ananias, Azarias, [and Misael].
Coniuro te Baron per pulmonem et iepre [*hepar] domini nostri et per omnes membra dei et per quinqua vulnera dei principalia, et per septem sacramenta ecclesia ut venias hunc coram me et facie mee in forma humana et non noceas mihi vel da mihi miseras mihi vel sosiis mei sed pacifice et quiduis facias et compleas omnia quicunque vel principio tibi.	I conjure you, O Baron, by the lungs and liver of our Lord, and all members of God, and by the five principal wounds of God, and by the seven sacraments of the church, that you come to me here personally, and appear to my face in human form, and not harm me or my associates, nor make us unhappy, but peacefully accomplish everything I will ask you.

* (?) Parallel version on Folger p. 176 has *animam* ["the soul"], which doesn't make sense if it is talking about the children (plural). Wellcome MS. 110 and Sloane 3853 don't have any extra words here.

[In margin:] Then he will appear in the form of a man, and then thou may ask whatsoever thou wilt. Then say,[562]

I charge thee, thou spirit Baron, as thou appearest unto me by this conjuration and invocation, that thou show what is thy property to do, without any dissimulation, and whether thou be bound to any man, or not before this time, and I charge thee to tell me if such a spirit N. be bound to any man or not before this time, and also I charge thee, thou prince Baron, which appearest unto me before this circle, by the virtue of the most holy and dreadful names of God, all which are graven in this scepter pentacle, representing the strong pentacles of Solomon containing in it the foresaid dreadful names of God + El + Eochye + Elan + helt + Agla + Yonthachy + Theanothe[563] + Nalta + by the which he subdued and included all spirits in a vessel of

562. In right marg.: "2[62.] (?)"

563. The last letter may have been struck out.

brass or glass. Also I charge thee, Baron, by the virtue of the excellent name of God +
Tetragramaton + that I hold in my ring on my left finger, that thou go to such a place
and bring with thee the treasure that there lieth, and, if there be none, I charge thee to
go to the sea or some other place where thou knowest any hid from the use of man,
and bring with thee to the value of 6,000, and safely deliver it to me by the virtue of
the superial [supernal?] majesty of the blessed Trinity, which is signified in the crown
imperial standing in the top of my scepter, and by the mystical scripture of the same,
and by the conjuration aforesaid, and by the virtue of the Holy names and mysteries
aforesaid, that thou bring with thee to the value of 6,000 pounds, and that thou suffer
me and my fellows to have and to carry away the same without any interruption or
letting of thee or any other spirit; and unto this I charge thee, thou spirit Baron, by
the virtue of the blessed Passion of Jesu Christ and by the virtue of his five principal
wounds, and by the dispersing of his precious blood, that thou go without tarrying or
any hurt doing to me or any earthly creature. *Fiat, fiat.*

[135]

Precipio tibi per virtute domini nostri Iesu Christi et per passionem eius quod mihi reuenias et respondatis vel respondias mihi de omnibus de te interrogavero in quacunque die vel in quocunque nocte et quocienscomque et interrogavero et respondeas mihi deinceps obidientis et humilis sitt et ut sumsecurus.	I command you by the power of our Lord Jesus Christ, and by his passion, that you return to me and answer all things which I have asked in whatever day or night, and however often, and respond to me thereafter, obedient and humble, and such that I am safe.

Precipio tibi Baron per coniurem et invocationem predictum ut postquam te in trinitur [*iterum?] invocavero intres lapidem Anepestem [anepostem?] In argenta pilla hac inclusum inque inde exituris nisi A me licentiatus confueris per virtutem domini nostri Iesu Christi dei vivi misserecordissime. Amen. fiat fiat fiat Amen Amen	I warn you, O Baron, by the preceding conjuration and invocation, that hereafter you …(?) I will have called you into the stone … (?) enclosed in this silver ball, and not leaving until I have given you licence, by the power of our Lord Jesus Christ, the living and most merciful God. Amen. May it be so, may it be so, may it be so. Amen.

| Et Iam vade In Pace et Recede per Passionem domini nostri Iesu Christi In nomine patris et filii et spiritus sancti Amen fiat. | And so go now in peace and depart by the passion of our Lord Jesus Christ, in the name of the Father, and the Son, and the Holy Ghost. Amen. Let it be so. |

The End. It is proven without doubt.

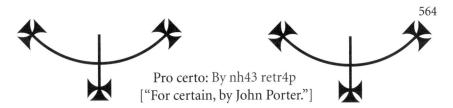

564

Pro certo: By nh43 retr4p
["For certain, by John Porter."]

An experiment of Rome [565]

An experiment[566] of the secrets of Rome, whereby the Romans know all things present, and of things past, and things to come by a spirit that is called Sathan and was invented by William Bacon, Greyfriar. That spirit will appear in a basin of water, and the master needeth not to have no child in this experiment.[567] He may do this every day, except holy days, and first be well ware that thou be not polluted with any lechery, but fast, and work fasting, and be steadfast in faith, and have a fair chamber and have a one clean basin full of water and clear, and have with thee a sword or a knife to make a circle, and thou must have four candles of virgin wax, and write on every candle: "Moyses • Aaron • Iacobe • Usion • Tetragramaton + mei Ratoim," and then fasten the candles on their brim of the basin as ye shall see the form hereafter. Then sit in the midst of the circle, looking toward the south, putting the basin without the circle and first anoint and fumigate the basin, with mastic and lignum aloes, and saying, "*In principio erat verbum*" ["In the beginning was the Word"], unto the end, and bless thyself with the sign of the cross, saying:

"*Per crucis hoc signum fugiat procull omne malignum et per idem signum salvetur quodque benignum et per signum sancta crucis de Inimicis nostris libera nos deus noster.*" ["By this sign of the cross, may all evil flee away, by the same sign may all good be preserved, and by the sign of this holy cross deliver us from our enemies, O our God."]

---

564. Decoded in pencil thus: "John Porter. See p. 143 John Weston."

565. The word ends with a curious flourish.

566. In right marg.: "263 b."

567. Although the use of a child medium was common in divination, the author seems to have shied away from such rituals.

Then begin the conjuration as followeth, so loud that thou mayest be heard:

Coniuro te Satanni* per patrem et filium et Spiritum Sanctum et per Sancta Maria Matrem domini nostri Iesu Christi et per omnes Apostolos dei, et per omnes virgines et viduas dei et per faciem dei, et per capud dei, et per coronam dei, et per nasum dei, et per dentibus dei et per occulos dei, et per linguam dei, et per aere dei, et per ungues dei, et per polices dei, et per venas dei, et per tiberias dei, et per plantas dei, et per quinque vulnera dei, et per omnia tormenta dei, et per omnium sanctorum eius et per nativitatem dei, et per passionem dei, et per merita dei, et per mortem dei, et per crucem dei, et per diem Iuditii Incoqumes Christiana et humana erit in statum trigintem annorum, et per 4or animalia ante Tronum sedem dei habens occulos ante e retro, et per sapientiam Salamonis, coniuro te Satanum per virtutem horum verborum predictorum, ut statim venias et aparias in hac pelui [+ in forma] Albi monachi et integram veritatem illius rei dicens de qua interrogabo te sine aliqua falcitate vell fallatia.	I conjure you, O Satan, by the Father, and the Son, and the Holy Ghost, and by holy Mary, mother of our Lord Jesus Christ, and by all apostles of God, and by all virgins and widows of God, and by the face of God, and by the head of God, and by the crown of God, and by the nose of God, and by the teeth of God, and by the eyes of God, and by the tongue of God, and by the air (?) of God, and by the nails of God, and by the thumbs of God, and by the veins of God, and by the legs (?)[†] of God, and by the feet (?) of God, and by the five wounds of God, and by all the tortures suffered by God, and by all his saints, and by the birth of God, and by the passion of God, and by the merits of God, and by the death of God, and by the cross of God, and by the Day of Judgment, *Incoqumes* (?) who will be Christian and human, appointed for thirty years, and by the four living creatures who are before the throne of God, having eyes before and behind,[‡] and by the wisdom of Solomon. I conjure you, O Satan, by the power of the preceding words, that you immediately come and appear in this basin [+ in the form][§] of a white monk, and speak the whole truth to all things which I will ask, without falsehood or deceit.
* There is ~ above the "nn" in "Satanni." † ? reading *tibiis.* ‡ Revelations 4.6. § See next paragraph and further passages below.	

Then put out the candle, standing in the part before thee, then fumigate as you did before, saying, "In the beginning was the word" etc.[568] Then say,

Coniuro te Sathan per ista nomina dei arceret, feodem, funcigor, fea, filet, gonca, gara, Masi, Mortha, Morarie, Mobonum, Magon, Alba, Azaray, Abba, Adonay, Sabaoth, Messias, Sother, Saba, Agla, Sponsus, Isus Acme didatur et Sancta corpora Sanctos Mortuos, et per Sigillum dei vivi: Coniuro te Sathan ut mihi aparias in istud vas in forma albi monachie et dicence ac demonstres mihi veritatem de omnibus questionibus sine fraude et falacia et dolo:	I conjure you, O Satan, by these names of God, Arceret, Feodem, Funcigor, Fea, Filet, Gonca, Gara, Masi, Mortha, Morarie, Mobonum, Magon, Alba, Azaray, Abba, Adonay, Sabaoth, Messias, Sother, Saba, Agla, Sponsus ["bridegroom"], Isus Acme, and by the holy bodies of the dead saints, and by the sigil of the living God. I conjure you, O Satan, that you appear to me in this vessel in the form of a white monk, and speak and explain to me the truth to all questions without fraud, falsehood, and deceit.

Then put out the candle that standeth in the part, and turn thee toward the north, with the basin fumigated as ye did before, saying, "In the beginning was the word," etc.[569] And then say:

Coniuro te Sathan per virgam Moysi et per nona candelaria Celestiam et per tres principium figura et per danielem prophetam et per Sanctam Petrum et Paulum et per ista nomina dei + Agla + Marra + Mandra + Natha + Matha + Morarimionbon + Moncray + Nazay + Nazay + Matray + Mataliza + et per clavos Christi Crucifixi et per Orientem Meridiem Occidentem et Borialem et per 7em planeta et per 4or Elementa fire Ignem Areum Aquam et terram et per	I conjure you, O Satan, by the staff of Moses, and by the nine heavenly candles, and by the three principal figures, and by the prophet Daniel, and by saints Peter and Paul, and by these names of God + Agla + Marra + Mandra + Natha + Matha + Morarimionbon + Moncray + Nazay + Nazay + Matray + Mataliza + and by the nails of Christ's crucifixion, and by east, south, west, and north, and by the seven planets, and by the four elements—firc [sic], air, water, and earth—

568. John chapter 1.
569. John chapter 1.

duodecim firmamenti ut sine aliqua fallatia dicas mihi non figendo non menciendo	and by the twelve firmaments, that without any deceit you will speak to me without fastening (?)* and without lying.

* *Figendo*: JHP would expect another synonym of deceit, or possibly "delay."

Then put out the third candle, and turn thee toward the east, and fumigate the basin as ye did before, saying, "In the Beginning was the word" etc. Then say:

Coniuro te Sathan per vincula Salamonis et per sigillum virgilii et per sig[i]llum Wilhelmi Bacon et Ramundi desitur catenalentis, et per Sanctum Michaelem et per illam Sanctam [136] Salutacionem qua Sanctas Gabriell sallutavit Sancta Maria dicens: Ave Maria gratia plena dominus tecum et per omnia bona qui possunt esse In Celo et in Terre et per omnes Celos et per omnia qui in eis continentur et per Librum Vite et per Spiritum Sanctum qua deus Misit in cruce emitte Spiritum et illa sanctam verba qui dicebat in Cruce pendens dicendo Consumatum est et per omnia alia verba qui possunt et qui sunt Ineffabilem:	I conjure you, O Satan, by the chains of Solomon, and by the sigil of Virgil, and by the sigil of William Bacon, and the binding chains that Raymond taught (?), and by Saint Michael, and by that holy [136] greeting by which Saint Gabriel greeted Saint Mary, saying, "Hail Mary, full of grace, the Lord is with you," and by all good which is possible in Heaven and Earth, and by all the heavens, and all that they contain, and by the Book of Life, and by the Holy Ghost which God expelled at the cross, and these holy words which he spoke while suspended from the cross, when he said, "it is finished," and by all other words which may be, and which are ineffable.
Coniuro te Sathat (!?) ut aparias mihi in forma albi Monachi sine fallacia: et vellem meam per feciendo et tu volueris precepta mea facere et dissolvo te ab offecio tuo et pone te in abissum Aquarum usque ad diem Iuditii fiat fiat fiat Amen:	I conjure you, O Sathat (sic),* that you appear to me in the form of a white monk, without deceit, and willing to accomplish my will, or I will strip you of all offices and send you into the abyss of water until the Day of Judgment. May it be so, may it be so, may it be so. Amen.

* This seems to be a simple typo for Satan.

Then the spirit will appear in manner aforesaid, and when he hath fullfilled your desire, then licence him to go from whence he came.

The end. It is proven for certain.[570]

571

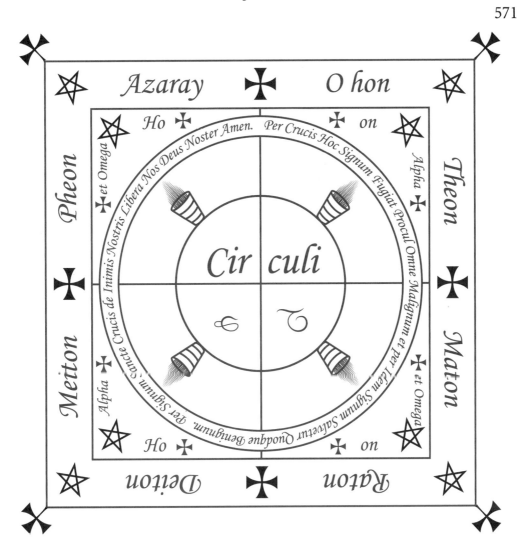

570. In left marg.: "w" glyph; in right marg.: "264."

571. Magic circle, surrounded by four incense burners (or shafts of wheat?). Compare with figure on Folger p. 130. The phrase in the circle reads: *per crucis hoc signum fugiat procul omne malignum et per idem signum salvetur quodque benignum. Per signum sancte crucis de inimicis nostris libera nos Deus noster Amen* ["Through this sign of the cross may all evil flee, and through the same sign let everything that is kind and good be preserved. Through this sign of the cross free us from our enemies, O our God. Amen."]
Outside circle, starting at top: "Ho + +on / Alpha + & o / Ho + + on / Alpha + + Et (!) & o."
Outer square, starting at top: "Azaray + O hon / Theon + Maton / RATON + Deiton / Meiton + Pheon."
The word (or name) Azaray occurs in the conjuration on Folger p. 135, but the rest don't seem to appear elsewhere.

[137]

In order to know about things lost, or accumulated, or hidden in the earth, make this figure in the courtyard of the house, in the following specific form as shown, and afterwards say:

O tu Kerythe, ego te adiuro cum omnibus sociis tuis per patrem et fillium et Spiritum Sanctum, et per tremendum diem Iudicii, per omnes ordines Angelorum et per centum quin[qua]ginta [*quadraginta] quatuor millia Innocentium, qui per Christi nomen passi sunt mortem, et per Angelos, et Archangelos Thrones, et dominations, principatus, potestates, Cherubine et Seraphine, et Virtutes, Coniuro vos omnes per beatissimam virginem Mariam Matrem domini nostri Iesu Christi, et per duodecem Apostolos, et per omnes Sanctos Martires Confessores et Virgines, et per omnes Sanctos et electos dei, Item adiuro et Coniuro vos per Ceelum et per mare, et omnia que in ea sunt, et per summam sapientiam Salomonis, et per annulum eius, et per sigillum eius, et per vinculum eius et per omnia vocabula in eodem vinculo, et significatio vocabulorum, in hoc Tetragono nocte ista detis de redubitabili et quesita.

O you Keryth, I adjure you along with all your associates, by the Father and the Son and the Holy Ghost, and by the terrible Day of Judgment, by all the orders of angels, and by the one hundred fifty-four thousand innocents,* who, by the name of Christ have suffered death, and by the Angels, Archangels, Thrones, Dominations, Principalities, Powers, Cherubim, Seraphim, and Virtues. I conjure you all by the most blessed Virgin Mary, mother of our Lord Jesus Christ, and by the twelve Apostles, and by all the holy martyrs, confessors, and virgins, and by all the saints and elect of God. Again I adjure and conjure you, by the heavens and the sea, and all that are in them, and by the great wisdom of Solomon, and by his ring, and by his sigil, and by his bonds, and by all the names in those same† bonds, and the meaning of the names, in this quarter of the night‡ may you give [+ knowledge?] concerning the thing in doubt and sought.

* Probably meaning the 144,000 innocents of Revelations 14:3–5.
† In right marg.: "219."
‡ See below.

Then write your petition on some piece of paper, and place the paper in the middle of the said figure with tweezers, and return to the same place in the morning before daybreak, and you will discover what you asked for, written in such idiom as though you have written on the paper previously.

You should always perform this work in the first quarter of the night.

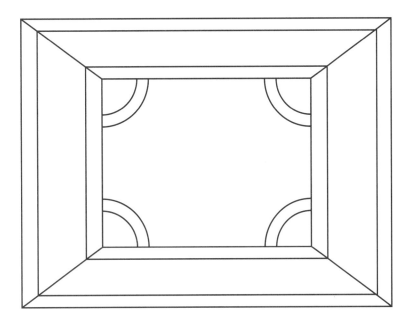

Beginning of the treatise on the experiment for a theft

Take silver foil, and temper it with glier,[572] and they ground together. Take a stick of cypress and paint upon a wall an eye with the one end of the same stick, and write with the other end about the eye with the matter aforesaid these four names Malkeo, Nabbasr, Colkeranon, Battenayer, and then get a nail of clean copper, and touch the eye in the black with the nail's sharp end, and say these words, "Malkes Nabbas Colkeran and Battenaye, *Coniuro vos spiritus ut faciatis furem apparere, et appereries os suum et recognoscere furum quod querimus* ["I conjure you, O spirit, that you make the thief appear who we are seeking, and make his face be shown and recognized"]." Then rehearse his name that thou dost suspect, and if it be he, *statim clamabit* ["he will immediately acknowledge"]. Grind thy foil and glier, upon a marble stone, and therewith make the eye, and the names as here followeth.[573]

---

572. Glier: likely gleir, or a substance made from egg whites.
573. In right marg.: "219b."

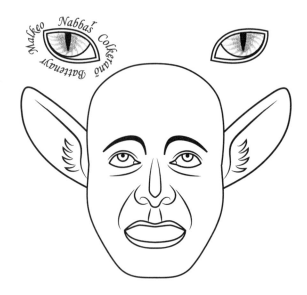

[138]

To make an oil which is precious most rare and excellent of all others, for seeing spirits from the air, as followeth [574]

Take the white howlet in the day and hour of Mercury. Kill him under the right wing, saying these words: Iuuan, handavmusdah, Faon, Dyiaga, Sumiellam Rostafala-gath. This fowl I kill in the name of you all, commanding you by this name, Rufan-goll, your superior, by whom you do all secrets in earth amongst men, and by Heme-olon, your prince. I adjure you, that you do your humble obedience unto me, J. B., at all times henceforth, and, with your power unknown, give virtue and strength to this my purpose, constraining all inferiors under you to serve me at all times, days, hours, and minutes, at all times and in all places, without hurting of me, my body or soul, or any other living creature.

Then reserve his blood in a clean vessel, and of his fat in another clean vessel. Then in the day of Jupiter consequently following and in the hour of Mercury.[575]

Take a lapwing and kill him as you did the howlet, under the right wing, saying these words: Dala, Dangolath, Emenguilla Saluagan, Arsdortho Sedaon, Pandlath. This fowl I kill in the name of you all, commanding you by this name, Rufangoll, your superior, by whom you do all secrets in earth amongst men, and by Hemeolon, your prince, I adjure you that you do your humble obedience unto me at all times hence-forth and, with your power unknown, give virtue and strength to this my purpose,

---

574. In marg.: "1 on Wednesday ☿ / 1 A howlet."
575. In marg.: "2 on Thursday ♃ / 2 A lapwing."

constraining all inferiors under you to serve me at all times, days, hours, and minutes, at all times and in all places, without hurting of me, my body and soul, or any other living creature.

Then reserve his blood in a clean vessel, and of his fat in another vessel. Then, in the day of Venus and in the hour of Mercury ensuing.[576]

Take a black hen and kill her as you did the lapwing against the heart, saying these words: Eloofe, Pandugell, Etheluill, Euantr Dirathon Riamiuta, Edlodell. This fowl I kill in the name of you all, commanding you by this name, Rufangoll, your superior, by whom you do all secrets in earth amongst men, and by Hemeolon, your prince, I adjure you that you do your humble obedience unto me, at all times henceforth, and, with your power unknown, give virtue and strength to this my purpose, constraining all inferiors under you to serve me at all times, days, hours, and minutes, at all times and in all places, without the hurting of me, my body or soul, or any other living creature.

Then reserve the blood in a clean vessel, and of the fat in another vessel. Then, in the day of Saturn and the hour of Mercury next following.[577]

Take a black cat and kill her under the right side against the heart, saying these words: Fellofell, Gariguanim, Samionim Elogamillo Reumdatha Iesoraell, Hermadafinuni. This beast I kill in the name of you all, commanding you all by this name, Rufangoll, your superior, by whom you do all secrets in earth amongst men, and by Hemeolon, your prince. I adjure you that you do your humble obedience unto me at all times henceforth, and, with your powers unknown, give virtue and strength to this my purpose, constraining all inferiors under you to serve me at all times, and in all places, without hurting of me, my body or soul, or any other living creature.

Then reserve the blood in a clean vessel, and of the fat in another vessel. Then, in the day of the Sun and in the hour of Mercury ensuing.[578]

Take a want or mowld.[579] Kill her under the right side, saying these words: Odauan Opathan, deothan, hermyadell, fervolam, ganyhaon, flodalath. This beast I kill in the name of you all, commanding you all by this name, Rufangoll, your superior, by whom you do all secrets in earth amongst men, and by Hemeolon, your prince, I adjure you that you do your humble obedience, unto me, at all times henceforth, and with your powers unknown, give virtue and strength to this my purpose, constraining all inferiors under you to serve me at all times, days, hours, and minutes, at all

---

576. In marg.: "3 on Friday ♀/ 3 a black hen." Below it in marg.: "w" glyph.

577. In marg.: "4 on Saturday ♄ / 4 A black cat."

578. In marg.: "5 on Sunday ☉ / 5 a mowld."

579. Want or mowld: a mole.

times [sic] and in all places, without hurting of me, my body or soul, or any other living creature.

Then reserve his blood in a clean vessel, and of his fat in another vessel. Then, in the day of the Moon and in the hour of Mercury ensuing.[580]

Take a bat and kill her under the right wing, saying these words: Ramasaell, Kaelldath, Riarufa, Exoniloelli Iesaloeella Reralath, Dupanfalo. This fowl I kill in the name of you all, commanding you all by this name, Rufangoll, your superior, by whom you do all secrets in earth amongst men, and by Hemeolon, your prince. I adjure you that you do your humble obedience unto me at all times henceforth, [139] and with your powers unknown, give virtue and strength to this my purpose, constraining all inferiors under you to serve me at all times, days, hours, and minutes, at all times [sic] and in all places, without hurting of me, my body or soul, or any other living creature.

Then reserve his blood in a clean vessel and of his fat in another vessel. Then in the day of Mars and in the hour of Mercury ensuing.[581]

Take a raven and kill her under the right wing, saying these words: Ohorma, Sede llpha, Oremaelle Saquidaell, Myiasaleti Rendos, Lymaxillō. This fowl I kill in the name of you all, commanding you all by this name, Rufangoll, your superior, by whom you do all secrets in earth amongst men, and by Hemeolen [sic], your prince, I adjure you all, that you do your humble obedience unto me at all times henceforth, and with your powers unknown, give virtue and strength to this my purpose, constraining all inferiors under you to serve me at all times, days, hours, and minutes, at all times and in all places, without hurting me, my body or soul, or any other living creature.

Then reserve his blood in a clean vessel, and of the fat in another vessel, the mixture of all these as followeth.

Take the fat of all these foresaid fowls and beasts. Of each of them, seven drams; mix all well together with a slice of a bay tree. Upon the palm of your hand, clean washed with rose water, saying in tempering of it these seven words or names:[582] Iulia • Hodelfa • Iuafula • Sedamylia • Roauian Segamexe Delforia • Inferiors and servants to the Empress and princes of all fairies, Sibilis, and all amiable creatures delighting in the company of human people, Lady Delforia, as you be present amongst men invisible at all times, as soon as I shall anoint mine eyes with this commixture, and that you be as familiar with me as you were with King Solomon, that mighty prince, and

---

580. In marg.: "6 on Monday ☽ / 6 A bat."

581. In marg.: "7 on Tuesday ♂ / 7 A raven."

582. In marg.: "w" glyph.

as you were with Prince Arthur,[583] that valiant prince, and as you opened and showed to King Solomon the hidden natures, properties, and virtues of metals, precious stones, trees, and herbs, and the secrets of all sciences underneath heaven, even so I command, require, and adjure you, Iulia • hodellfa: Iuafula: Sedamilia • Roavian • Segamexe, with the Empress Delforia, to do the like to me at all times, without disdainfulness, by these names whereby I do bind you: + Gath + Vasgath + Vlagar + Ieramila + Roboracath + Redath + Segath + even as you fear the just judgment of Readufan, upon pain of hellfire and everlasting damnation.

This done at the conjunction of the Moon in the hour of Mercury, put the ointment in a vessel, into the midst of the fairy throne,[584] but first take two or three drams of each blood and write these seven names in virgin parchment: Iulia • Hodelfa • Iuafula • Sedamilia • Roavia[n], • Segamexe and Delforia: all these names written seven times, three times with a pen made of the third feather of the lapwing of the left wing, four times with the feather of a raven made of the fifth feather of the right wing with

these characters.

Then lap it about the vessel, and seal it fast with virgin wax, repeating these seven names: Iulia • Hodellfa • Iuafula • Sedamilia • Roavian • Segamexe and Dellforia. In sealing of it, the seal must be made in figure following of copper.

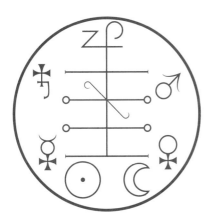

But first, or [ere] thou do put this into the fairy throne, provide four hazel rods of one year's growth. Cut them in the day and hour of Mercury, the Moon increasing, shave them white, then write upon every one of them these seven names in the hour of Mercury: Iulia etc. Put these four wands in the four quarters, east, west, north, and south of the fairy throne in the hour of Mercury and put the vessel in midst of the fairy throne, repeating these seven names: Iulia: Hodelfa: etc. These seven names, three times at every wand, first to the east,

west, south, north, saying these seven names:

583. King Arthur, or Prince Arthur, the Prince of Wales (1486–1502). Note link to Sibilla, who appears in Scot, *Discouerie of Witchcraft*.

584. Compare Bodleian MS. Ashmole 1406 (circa 1600). Briggs quotes a passage that describes the mechanics of a rite for conversing with fairies and the use of hazel rods and the curious phrase "fairy throne."

Iulia: Hodellfa: Ivafula: Sedamilia: Roavian: Segamexe with Delforia, the empress of all fairies, Sibbells, and all other amiable creatures delighting with the company of Christian people, hear me. I call you, every one, by the name N. Iulia, etc., and by the mighty names of ligation where with Solomon did include[585] you into a ball of glass + Pannath + Davion + Segamilion + Svgamyell + darvfa + Ierasami + Ariamilath + that you come at this present, and make perfect this ointment, that as often as I shall anoint my eyes therewith, I may see you in your perfect being, without fraud or collusion, truly shewing to me all secrets of herbs, trees, stones, metals, and privy talks of people, even as you fear the just judgment of God upon pain of hellfire and everlasting damnation, whose names here included sealed with the seal of King Solomon, the mighty prince, with which seal here sealed the vessel wherein he bound you. *Fiat, fiat, fiat.*

[140]

Making this pentacle [586] over the vessel upon the ground within the fairy throne with a hazel rod of one year. This do three days, three times a day, every day. This done or ended, take it up and put it into a secret dark place three other days. The three days ended, put it into the Sun to rectify five other days. Secretly turn thy vessel three times every day. Five other days let it remain not moved, but first before thou anoint, or presume to anoint, thine eyes therewith, be in clean life the space of seven days. Then anoint therewith and look towards the east, then thou shalt see diverse creatures most beautiful to be behold in garments of diverse colours. Then speak to one of them which thou likest best beckoning thy head towards her with saying:

O thou beautiful creature and gentle virgin, by what name soever thou art called, and of what order soever thou art, to what use soever thou art created, by God the Father I call thee, by God the Son I command thee, by God the Holy Ghost I choose thee, and by the obedience thou owest to thy Lord God, I adjure thee to be obedient to me forever henceforth, as thou dost hope to be saved at the dreadful day of judgment, in which he shall say, "Come ye blessed, and inherit my Father's kingdom, and go, ye cursed, into everlasting damnation in hellfire to burn forever," even as thou dost fear the just judgment of God upon pain of hellfire and everlasting damnation. Give me true answer of all such things as I shall ask and demand of thee. To this I swear thee, by God the Father, the Son, and the Holy Ghost,[587] to be true to me at all times, even as thou wilt avoid the heavy wrath of God sitting in his high throne to judge everyone according to right, and also I command ye by all power that God hath over all creatures in heaven, in earth, and in hell, hereafter to meet with me at all

---

585. Include: enclose.

586. Compare Sloane 3851; *Grimoire of Arthur Gauntlet*, 293–4, which only shows a hexagram with "T" in center.

587. In marg.: "w" glyph.

times, thyself alone quietly, whereupon depart at this time and the peace of God be between thee and me, now and forever. Amen.

Then at all times she will meet with thee at what time thou anointest thy eyes. Of this assure thyself to be most true, but when thou talkest with her, talk not long, neither yet demand her name, her parentage, nor yet her kindred, or for what she is, for fear of indignation, neither yet whether she be a spirit or woman. Let that talk go, but demand things necessary for thy purpose. Beware you offer her no discourtesy at any time of polluting thyself. When thou hast talked enough with her, wash thine eyes with rose water, or some other sweet water, and when she doth depart, say these words:

Now go in peace, thou beautiful creature of God, to the place appointed of God, signing thyself with the sign of the cross.

Finis.

An experiment of two hazel rods of one year's growing

Note that[588] the rods be but of one year's growth and not above, because that if they be there will be a fault in the operation. When thou wilt gather them, let it be upon the first Friday of the Moon before the Sun rising, in saying, "In the name of the Father, I have sought thee. In the name of the Son, I have found thee. In the name of the Holy Ghost, I do cut thee," either of them at four strokes, and that being done, say, "*In principio erat verbum*, etc.," which being said, say three *Pater Nosters*, in the honour of the Trinity, seven *Ave Marias*, in the honour of the seven joys of Mary the Virgin. Then say, "O Lord by whose providence mankind is increased, and all things have their being, humbly we beseech thee to put away from us all hurtful things, and that thou wilt grant to us that all things may be brought to good pass that we take in hand, through Jesus Christ our Lord. Amen."

In Nomine Patris, Filii, et Spiritus Sancti ["In the name of the Father, Son, and Holy Ghost"]. Amen. Lord, hear my prayer and let my cry come unto thee. Let us pray. O Lord, by whose providence the earth and all therein was created, grant grace to these, thy creatures, that they may be unto me aiding, both now and at all other times as when I shall have cause to use them, so that the rather by them I may come to the knowledge of that thing I desire. This grant, good lord, I do beseech thee for thy dear Son Jesus Christ's sake. Amen.

This being said, say:

I conjure you, hazel rods of one year growing this day, by the ineffable names of God + Hely + Helyson + Orca + Tetragrammaton + that you bring me without all manner of deceit and craft unto the place where any treasure is hidden, or any other thing, and that by the virtue of the holy name of God written in you. I command you

---

588. In right marg.: "220 (?)."

that you do not rule in vain. I adjure you, O hazels of one year's growth, by the three kings of Cullen, Jasper, Melchior, and Balthazar, that, as they being wise and prudent men, were conducted and led by a star where as they found Christ, that so you may bring me into the certain and sure place where any treasure is or metal is hid or hath any being, and that this be done. I bid and command you by the power of God the Father, who hath made you, by God the Son, who hath redeemed me, and by the Holy Spirit who hath sanctified me and all creatures. Amen. Amen.

In the first rod, write arifax + Agla + three times. In the other, write + Adonay + three Raavarax times.

[141]

This is the office of angels, spirits, and devils, and by God's permission, grace, and sufferance, how to see them and overcome them

First, look[589] that the Sun do enter into Aries or Taurus, which is the most fittest time, for in the month of March, you may take the adder's skin, being cast voluntarily, and make powder thereof. Then take the powder of Carpobalsamax [590] 2 or 3 oz., and of the earth of a grave in the churchyard four spoonfuls, and the like quantity of the oil of Carpobalsamax. Then take 5 or 6 oz. of the powder of the root of Mandragoras, and take 6 oz. of the oil of juice of the leaves of Mandragoras, and for want of this oil of Carpobalsamax, you may take oil olive. All these being mixed well together, put them into a silver vessel, and look when the Sun is four or five degrees in Aries or Taurus,[591] make thee a circle of as hereafter appeareth, and make it in a house or fair chamber, and set the vessel of oil in the midst of the circle, so that it may stand between thy legs, and cover it with a cloth, and remember there be so much of the earth of the churchyard where one was buried be well mixed with the foresaid oil. This mixture is best to be made when the

---

589. In right marg.: "192."

590. According to Robley Dunglison, *A Dictionary of Medical Science* (Philadelphia; New York: Lea Bros. & Co., 1903), *Carpobalsamum* corresponds to Amyris Opobalsamum and Balsam of Gilead.

591. Corrected thus in marg.

Sun is in the opposition of 11ᵗʰ degree of Mercury Mars, and to make the circle also in the same Saturn and the[592] degrees when the Moon is new and increasing, in the circle thou mayest stand or sit, but thou must use abstinence only with bread and water for three[593] days.

And during that time, continuing in prayer, and refrain from venery, etc., then take the sword, crown and scepter, ring, and other necessaries. Enter and turn towards the east, and then into the other parts of the world, lifting up thy scepter, devoutly saying this prayer, "*Domine ante pr* etc.,"[594] and hear three masses before thou enter: one of the Trinity, one of our Lady, and one of Saint Cyprian, and offer at every one a penny, and look thou be confessed, and thy garments clean. Now being in thy circle, place the sword and other necessaries near to the oil, but beware the place or lamina touch not the earth at no time, and let thy ring be always on thy little finger, and note that the first night after thou hast entered thy circle, thou mayest lie in a clean bed alone, which bed must be near to the circle, and not within the circle, and without doubt about midnight, thou shalt hear a sound, which is of spirits coming to the circle to bless and consecrate it, and the oil,[595] I find that it is written there shall come a thousand angels to bless the oil or mixture, and that about midnight, who shall pronounce words the sound whereof thou mayest hear, but the words thou shalt not understand, but if thou look well and be vigilant, thou shalt see the scepter lifted up In the circle, and likewise the sword, and yet thou shalt not perceive what they be that do it, and the vessel shall be opened which thou didst cover, but in any wise look thou be clean when thou touchest it, for fear of polluting it. Note that it were of much greater virtue, that a consecrated priest should both mix it and handle it. Look thou keep the oil in the vessel still, and robe it in some fair cloth or silk, and hang it about thy neck, and bear it on thee, during all which time have good regard to thyself, and look thou be clean in all respects, upon peril that may fall thereon. And then when you will you may anoint your eyes with the oil, and look out at the east window, or in any part you will into the air, and you shall see the spirits standing in their order, and some with their legions as appeareth in the book of pictures[596] etc., and when thou seest them, thou mayest call one of them to come unto thee, and he will come immediately, of whom thou mayest demand his name, office, superintendents, constellation, and planet, and no doubt but he will tell thee, and if he be not for thy purpose,

---

592. These three words are crowded to the left of the text, and may be misplaced.

593. Originally written "30" in red ink, but the "0" is crossed out in black ink.

594. Perhaps the preliminary communion prayer "Domine sancte Pater omnipotens"? See http://www.preces-latinae.org/thesaurus/Pater/DomineS.html.

595. In marg.: "w" glyph.

596. Unknown significance—possibly a reference to the pictures later in the book.

then command him to depart and to set [fett[ch]?] one that is, and whose office is to do that thou requirest and to bring him with all speed possible. If thou wilt have any to bring thee money, to teach thee the art of necromancy, or any other science, to tell the truth of all questions and doubts, to declare the very way to make gold and silver by the art or science of alchemy, and to make the Philosopher's Stone, and that as speedily as is possible.

[142]

To see spirits in the air or elsewhere

To have[597] the sight of spirits, take a lapwing two or three and kill them, and save the blood in a vessel as above that is very close,[598] and so keep it ten or twelve days, that no air come in nor go out, and at the end of the same days, it will be turned into worms, and within another ten or twelve days, it will be turned into one worm. Then make paste of walnuts or almonds beat small, etc., and put the worm therein, and cover it close with a cover of the same stuff, and look that there be room enough for it to increase therein, and let it lie therein another ten or twelve days, or more if need be, and then that worm will be turned into a lapwing. Note: you may look unto it after ten days, now if it be not fully grown, to a lapwing again. Now when the same is ready in proportion, then take her out, and let her blood under the right wing, and save the blood as is before said, and when thou wilt see the spirits, anoint thy eyes with the blood, and look forth at the east window, etc., or eastward, and sooth thou shalt see the spirits of the air, of which thou mayest call on, etc., and having thy purpose, discharging him say, "*vade pax sit inter te et me, in nomine patris et filii et spiritus Sancti + Amen.*" ["Go, let there be peace between thee and me, in the name of the Father, the Son, and the Holy Ghost + Amen."] Note in March, April, May, June, and July, the weather being fair and warm, is best working this work of the lapwing, and in the hour of Saturn and Mars being in opposition and triangle of them.

The oil[599] or mixture aforesaid is called the oil of the choleric, or the anointment to see spirits, etc. The great living God is he that hath given the gift and the knowledge to the learned, and also freely doth permit and suffer us to speak of this most precious oil or ointment, which I myself saw it once made of a learned Turk, the which was sometime a companion of one Mr. W. On a time the same Turk, because he would not reveal or declare the manner of making this precious and most secret

---

597. In right marg.: "193."

598. Very close: i.e., a vessel that seals tightly.

599. In left marg.: "w" glyph; in right marg.: "194."

ointment, and that to the Soldan[600] then being in Alexandria by the Soldan, the Turk was commanded to be slain, and as the Turk was led towards the place of execution, the Turk desired that he might talk with the said Mr. W., or that he suffered, which was granted him and so we [601] conferred together, and at my departing from him, I kissed the Turk, and as I was kissing him, he gave me, the said W., a ring wherewith I might go invisible, and so I did. And when that I did perceive myself to be invisible, then secretly I did deliver the ring to the Turk again, and thereby forthwith the Turk escaped the danger he was in by the means of invisibility and so fled from them, and thereupon they apprehended me, and brought me before the Soldan, and charged me, as they supposed that I had delivered the Turk by the virtue of my kiss. And as they were a leading of me towards the Soldan, the Turk came to me invisibly, but I saw him not, then forthwith he anointed mine eyes with this aforesaid choleric or ointment, and forthwith I saw him and an infinite number of spirits, and then I spake to them, and forthwith commanded them and charged them that they should minister to me their help and deliver me from that peril I was in. And suddenly there happened a great tempest, and so great thunder and lightning that the Saracens which led me fled and were so dispersed, that they left me alone, and I seeing them in such fear that they ran away, and as men dismayed fled, then I fled to my fellow the Turk, and so he and I went to his house both speedily and quietly, from whence the same night we fled secretly and went towards Jerusalem and Lombardy, and leaving our goods behind us, the which goods were brought unto us afterwards by the spirits with much more. And this choleric or ointment I have used many times sithens,[602] and I dare be bold to say, that at that time in all the world, there was not above three persons that could make that ointment, of which three my fellow the Turk was one, and J. W. was another, but the Turk was the most excellentest in all the world thereat, and his name was Joseph, who was both a great philosopher and very rich. He taught me and gave me this copy etc., to the end I should not forget it, and here I do write the same for learned men to solace themselves withal, and, that as occasion is offered, they might put it in practise, lest I should be accompted [603] with the unprofitable servant, who hid this talent in the earth. I, John Weston, Gent', being in Henowaye, in a city there called Dowway,[604] and in the company of a canon, a very honest and godly man, who,

---

600. Soldan: a great Muslim leader, especially of Egypt.

601. Note the change in person in this story, indicating a clumsy effort to integrate a narrative from another source into the text.

602. Sithens: afterward.

603. Accompted: accounted.

604. Dowway: Douai, a city in France that served as a refuge for English Catholics when Elizabeth took the throne. It was the site of the English College founded in 1561.

joining with me and others, we entered in league and attempted a secret work for the Prince of Pavoye [605] and for one Monsieur Brettencort, who was one of Arasey and was lieutenant to the said prince of Pavoy, and this canon did so favour me that he told me how he came by this ointment, etc., and how he came by it. For the goodwill he bare me, he gave it unto me, and anointed mine eyes therewith, and I saw a heavenly sight, and I gave him a great thanks.

[143]

This, if thou [606] regardest that which is before said and do all accordingly as is prescribed, thou mayest be rich in substance, and do many strange and wonderful things to God's honour and comfort of the poor. For hereby thou mayest call the great and mighty power of spirits as emperors, kings, princes, dukes, etc., every one in his degree, etc.

The secretness of secrets hid ☿

Take a lapwing [607] and slay it on the Wednesday in the hour of Mercury with a knife steel and made of brass, and let the blood run into a vessel made of baaye, [608] and beware you shed no blood, but that all run into the vessel, and keep it therein well covered, and put it in a privy place, where no man cometh but yourself, and look that no man see the same vessel, but yourself, nor as near as you can come there nigh, and provided always that you yourself shall not see the same in nine days as when you may look thereinto, and then you shall see the blood full of worms. Then cover the vessel again, and so let it rest another nine days, as when you may look therein again, and you shall see but one worm. Then take the meat of dates and kernels of walnuts, small nuts, and of almonds and figs, and bruise them all together, and make a paste thereof round as a ball, and make in the midst thereof a hole, and cover the vessel therewith, so that no air come thereto more than cometh in at the hole in the cover, and set it up again, and so let it stand ninety days. Then uncover the vessel, and you shall see a chicken, in the likeness of a lapwing. Slay it and put it on a spit and roast it, and make the fire with date stones and shells of walnuts, and as it roasteth keep the grease that droppeth therefrom, and when you will work any work of philosophy,

---

605. Savoy?

606. In right marg.: "198 (-?)."

607. In left marg.: "w" glyph; in right marg.: "220."

608. Baaye: possibly either boxwood or bay.

anoint thy face and thy eyes with the grease, and you shall see spirits face-to-face, what they do, and they shall not be able to hide their doings from you, and they shall seem to you as though they were men and your fellows, and you shall hear them, and speak with them, and ask of them what you will, and they shall tell you, and they shall hide nothing from your presence, and you need not to be afraid of them, for by this means was our science found out. But thou must first do as thou shalt find in folio 97, or else if thou neglect or omittest one thing, thy labour is lost.

Now when you will no longer see them, wash your eyes and face with water that swallows were sodden[609] in, but secretly. Note that the vessel must be made on the Wednesday under Mercury and the Sun, also the knife of brass steel, and that this experiment must be done under Mercury and the Sun and on the Wednesday at the hour of Sun, or else thou canst not do. Look in the previous folio, and there thou shalt find thy chiefest substance, without the which it may not be done.[610]

---

609. Sodden: soaked.

610. At the bottom in pencil is written: "John Weston / See folio 135 John Porter."

[144]

[+ A collection of talismans]

611

This seal gives love
of men and women.

Carry this seal with you,
and everyone will be joyful to you.

Carry this seal with you,
and foes and evil will be slowed.

Carry this seal with you,
and nobody will have hatred towards you,
but you will be pleasing to everyone.

Against visible and invisible enemies,
and against demons and ambushes.

---

611. Seven talismans. First one "gives love" and has the words *sana* ["healthy"], *fama* ["reputation"], *fanna da rea* ["you give sanctuaries to the defendant"], *ave maria* ["hail Mary"], *Anarathrra & lorabonus / homo* ["man"], "i." The sixth has the words: *Mentem – sanctam – spotaneam – honorendeo – et preces ei – veracionem* ["Mind – holy – ? –? – and prayers to him –?"]

[145]

612

That you may not fear an enemy,
but only fear God.

This is the infallible name of God,
which Aaron brought against all dangers.

Carry this seal with you and all
aeriel and infernal powers will obey you.

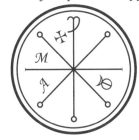

Behold the cross of the Lord!
Flee ye adversaries!
And obey terrestrial and infernal.

This seal is powerful against all danger,
and will make a man agreeable.

Carry this seal with you
and you will fear no evil,
injury, serpent, nor demon.

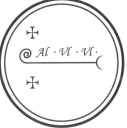

This seal will soften the tongues
of the wicked, and reveals love.

---

612. Seven talismans. The second one has the words *Con Dio* [=condio "I preserve"?]. *Eloe – Agla – Semaphoras – Tetragra-maton / EL – On – El – On – El – On – [Venus] / a a g l a.* Semaphoras is a corruption of Shem Ha-Mephorash (שם המפורש) ("the explicit Name [of God]"). The fifth has the words and names "Primellus" – *panton craton* (Greek "Ruler of all") – *Chaie assera* – *Sabbte*~ (?) / *homo-usyon* (Greek "of one substance") / *fortu Christus aem*.

[146]

This sign no evil can prevail against you.

By this seal all powers and 613
infernal spirits will obey.

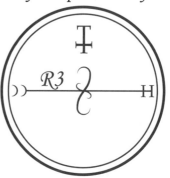

Whichever day you shall have seen this seal,
you will be delivered from all evil.

By this seal all infernal
spirits and powers will obey.

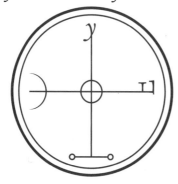

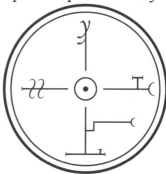

Carry this seal with you in war,
and you will not fear your enemy.

Carry this seal with you,
and you will be delivered from all fear,
and against shot to be further off.

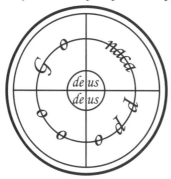

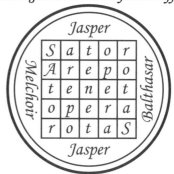

---

613. Six talismans. The last one has the traditional names of the three Magi: Jaspar, Melchior, and
Balthazar. Also in center is famous "SATOR AREPO TENET OPERA ROTAS" square.

[147]

614

Against all married women and mothers

Sigil of the earth

Sigil of the seven planets

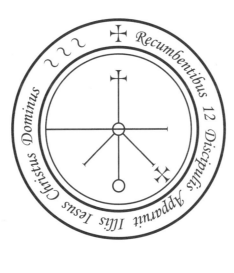

614. Four talismans. The last one includes the words: *Recumbentibus 12 discipulis apparuit illis* ["He appeared to the twelve disciples as they were at table"]. Compare Mark 16:14, where the number of Apostles mentioned is eleven. And *Iesus Christus Dominus* ["Jesus Christ the Lord"].

[148]

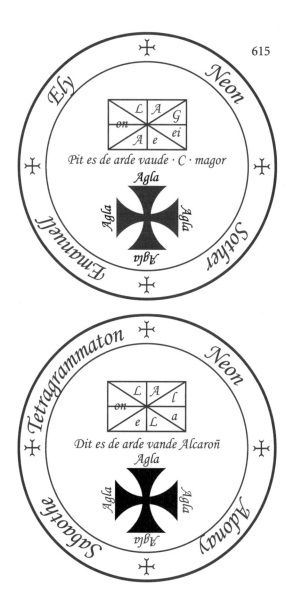

615

615. The next seven figures appear to be a set. Analogues can also be found in Sloane 1727 and
Sloane 3824, where they are described as circles for calling forth a series of spirit kings. In Sloane
1727, 11r-17r, they are named Magoth, Acharon, Ysquisy, Macharioth, Ysus, Jennathan, and
Achachardus. Sloane 3824 describes them as "the Seaven Regall Spirits" and gives the names as
Macharioth, Isus, Jenathon, Acharon (or Acheron), Maguth, Achachardus, and Ysquy; it describes
their purpose as follows: "These following serveth the Invocant to stand in, when he calleth any of
the aforesaid Kings."
The first on this page includes the words *Sother* (Gr. "Saviour"); "Eman[u]ell, Ely, + Neon" …
A G l a On – e l." and "Pit es de arde vande C. magor." The latter is probably a corruption for
something like "this is the circle for the spirit Magor/Magoth," perhaps in some Dutch dialect.
In Sloane 1727, the circle for Magoth has the words "NEON: OST: THEON | SOTHER: OST:
MOTHER | EMANVEL | NEON: SABAOTH." The second talisman has the text "Tetra[gra]
mmaton + Neon + Adonay + Sabaothe +" inside: "Dit es de arde vande Alcaroñ" (*this is the
circle for the spirit Alcaron/Acharon).

[149]

616

616. First circle text: "Messias + Neon + Agios + Agla +" inside "Dit es de~ Arcle~ vande~ ysus" (*this is the circle for the spirit Ysus). Second circle text: "Sabaoth + Neon + Dominus + Agla +" and "Dic es de circle vanden com~c isquier" (*this is the circle for the spirit Isquier).

[150]

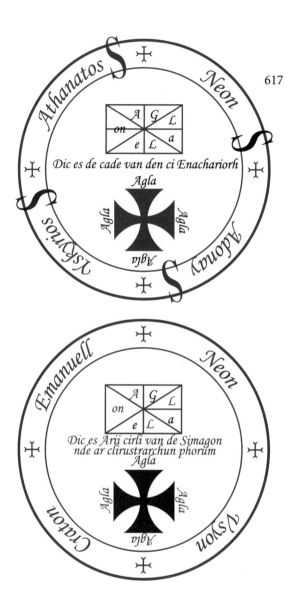

617

[151]

617. First circle text: "+ Neon + ADONAY + Yskyrios + Athanatos" and "Dic es den caclen van den ci enachariorh" (*this is the circle for the spirit Enachariorh/Macharioth). Second circle text: "NEON + VSYON + CRATON + EMANVELL" and "Dic es Arii cirli van de Simagon Inde ar clirustrarchun phorum" (*this is the circle for Simagon / ....?) Following the pattern in Sloane 1727, JHP would expect this to be the circle for king Jennathan.

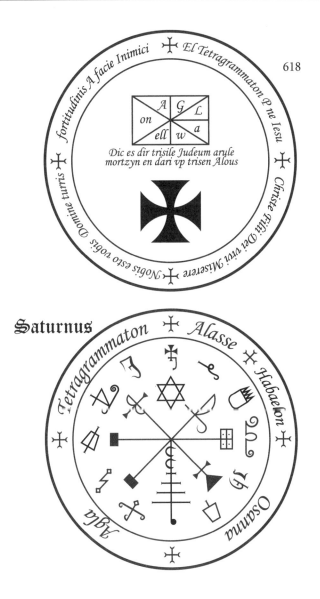

618

Saturnus

618. Large circle and Saturn talismans. The first figure completes the series of seven circles with the characteristic "AGLA" box inside. The text reads + *El Tetragrammaton P ne Iesu Christe* + *filii Dei vivi Miserere* + *Nobis esto vobis Domine turris* + *fortitudinis A facie Inimici* ["El, Tetragrammaton … Jesus Christ + Son of the living God have mercy. + Be a tower of strength to us in the face of our enemies."] Inside: *Dic es dir trisile Judeum arule mortzyn en dari vp trisen Alous* [*this is the …?] Following the pattern in Sloane 1727, I would expect this to be the circle for king Achachardus.

The second figure starts a series of eight planetary talismans (there are two for Jupiter). The first (labeled "Saturnus") includes the words: "+ Alasse + Habaelon + Osanna + Agla + Tetragrammaton."

[152]

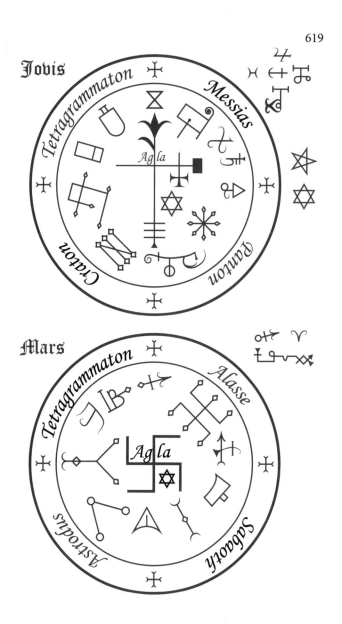

619. The Jupiter talisman has "Messias + PANTON + CRATON + Tetragrammaton: +." Messias being Greek for "Messiah," and Panton Craton Greek for "Ruler of all." The original drawing in the manuscript has a note saying "this is false, but it follows hereafter parfitt (=perfect)" and this corrected version is provided on Folger p. 155. In marg.: "w" glyph. The second talisman is of Mars, and includes the words "+ Alasse + Sabaoth + Astrodus + TETRAGRAMMATON.

[153]

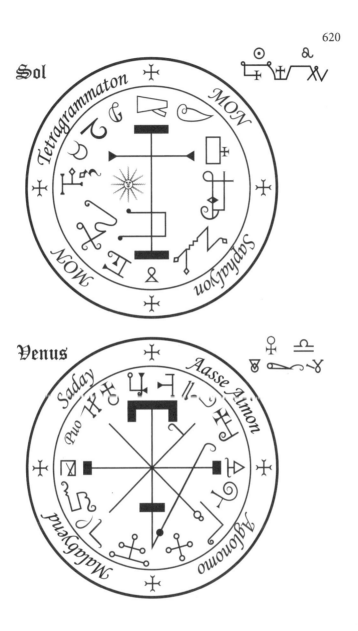

620. Sun has "MON + Saphalyon + MON + Tetragrammaton +" and Venus has "Aasse Almon + Aglonomo + Malabyend + SADAY +."

[154]

621

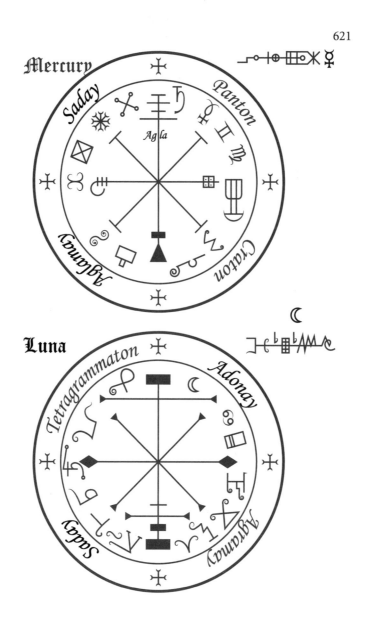

[155] [622]

---

621. Mercury and Luna talismans. Mercury has "Panton + Craton + Aglamay + Saday +"; Luna (the Moon) has "ADONAY + AGRAMAY + SADAY + TETRAGRAMMATON +."

622. This page of the manuscript has a corrected version of the Jupiter talisman; see Folger p. 152.

[156]

Characters of the planets.

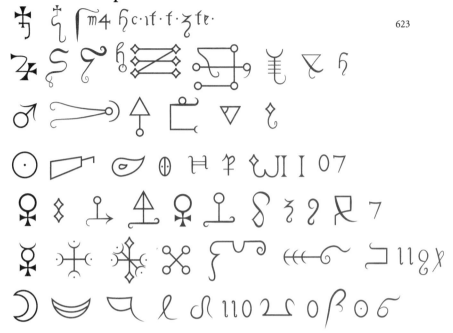

623

The sigil of the planets of the pentacles of Solomon.

623. Characters of the planets. The closest analogues I have seen are in Sloane 3850, 121v–122r, and Sloane 3885, 32r.

The ten most sacred names of God, from Agrippa book 3 chapter 10.

Eheie	יה Iah
Iod	אל El
Tetragrammaton Elohim	עליון Elion
El	אלהים Elohim
Elohim Gibor	יהשוה Ihesuh
Eloha	הוד Hod
Tetragrammaton Sabaoth	יוד הא ואו הא Tetragrammaton*
Adonay Sabaoth	אדני Adonay
Saday	יהוה צבאות Tetragramaton Sabaoth
Adonay Meleh	אלהים גיבר Elohim gibor

* I.e., "The Name Jehovahh of ten letters Extended." See OP Book 2 chapter 13.

[+ Hebrew for the planets]

שבתאי	צדק	מאדים	שמש	נוגה	כוכב	לבנה
Saturn	Jupiter	Mars	Sun	Venus	Mercury	Moon

[157]

Seals without characters of the seven planets[624]

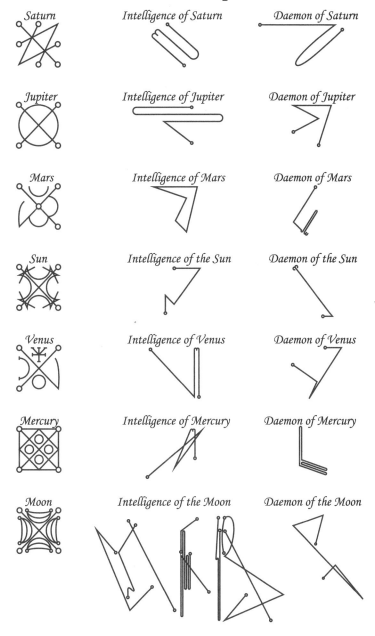

---

624. At the top are planetary Kamea Seals and Signs, from OP Book 2 chapter 22. At the bottom are the geomantic characters of the Moon from OP Book 2 chapter 51. These have been corrected according to Agrippa. In marg.: "w" glyph. There appears to be something in brown ink smudged out at the top (Tetr?). In right marg.: "294.

[158]

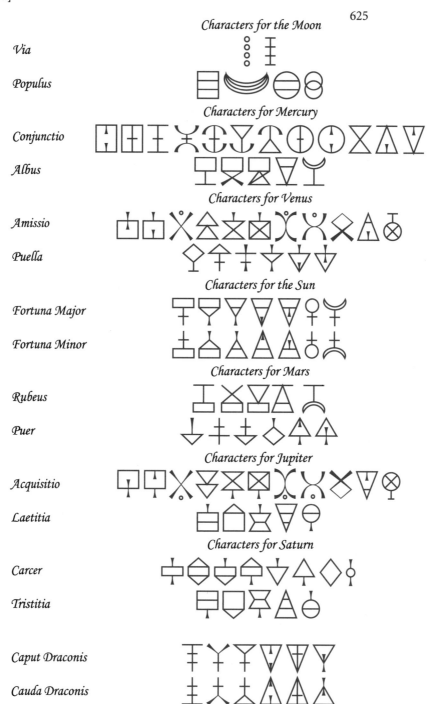

Characters for the Moon   625

Via

Populus

Characters for Mercury

Conjunctio

Albus

Characters for Venus

Amissio

Puella

Characters for the Sun

Fortuna Major

Fortuna Minor

Characters for Mars

Rubeus

Puer

Characters for Jupiter

Acquisitio

Laetitia

Characters for Saturn

Carcer

Tristitia

Caput Draconis

Cauda Draconis

---

625. Geomantic characters of the planets and labels from OP Book 2 chapter 51. In marg.: "w" glyph.
Note the characters of the Sun are missing.

From Petrus de Abano [+ fumigations]

The fumigation of Sunday: Red sandalwood

The fumigation of Monday: Aloe

The fumigation of Tuesday: Pepper

The fumigation of Wednesday: Mastic

The fumigation of Thursday: Crocus

The fumigation of Friday: Costus

The fumigation of Saturday: Sulfur

Agrippa, book 1, chapter 43 [+ fumigations]

There are fumigations made under favourable influxes of the stars that cause spectres of the daemons to appear immediately in the air or elsewhere. Thus they say[626] if a fumigation is made out of coriander and parsley or henbane, with hemlock, the daemons will immediately be congregated. Hence they call those the herbs of the spirits.

[159]

Brief notes concerning the course of the Moon[627]

The 1st, 2nd, and 3rd days, the Moon hath her course in Aries. In the first house, the Angell Samiell; in the 2nd, Emediell; in the 3rd, Agnix.

The first day, available to[628] journey, and breed discor[d]. The second day available to find treasure, and to retain captives. The third day available for sailors on the sea, for hunters and alchemists.

257 the first day, good to obtain audacity, fortitude, and unshamefastness;[629] the 2nd, to get nobility and power in dominion; the 3rd, to get wisdom, courtesy, [??]e and beauty 264

The 4th and 5th in Taurus. In the 4th house, Ayeariel hath dominion; in the 5th, Cakiel.

---

626. Agrippa based this on Raziel 2:3, 27v ff; see V. Perrone Compagni in his edition of Agrippa, *De Occulta Philosophia Libri Tres* (New York: E.J. Brill, 1992), 166 n.

627. Compare OP Book 2 chapter 33, based in David Edwin Pingree, *Picatrix: The Latin Version of the Ghiyat alhakim* (London: Warburg Institute, 1986), 1:4. There are again twenty-eight angels, which rule in the twenty-eight mansions of the Moon, whose names in order are these: *Geniel, Enediel, Amixiel, Azariel, Gabiel, Dirachiel, Seheliel, Amnediel, Barbiel, Ardefiel, Neciel, Abdizuel, Jazeriel, Ergediel, Ataliel, Azeruel, Adriel, Egibiel, Amutiel, Kyriel, Bethnael, Geliel, Requiel, Abrinael, Aziel, Tagriel, Alheniel, Amnixiel.*

628. Available to: efficacious for.

629. Unshamefastness: indecency, immodesty.

The fourth day is available to destroy and to hinder buildings, fountains, wells, and gold mines, to drive away creeping beasts and to engender discord. The fifth day is available to return from a journey, to instruct scholars, to raise buildings, to give health and benevolence; the Moon being in Taurus, it is good for the obtaining of wealth.[630]

The sixth and seventh day, in Gemini and thus is completed the first quarter of the sky, in which the Moon is hot and moist 2 5 6. In the 6th house Birachiel hath dominion; in the 7th, Scholiel:

The sixth day is available to hunt, to besiege cities, for the revenge of princes, to destroy corn and fruit, to hinder the endeavor of physicians. The seventh day is available to obtain wealth and friendship for lovers, to drive away fleas, and to destroy offices.

The eighth day in Cancer. In the 8th house, Amediell hath dominion.

The eighth day is available for love, friendship, and for the society of those that journey by the way, to drive away mice to afflict prisoners, and to confirm the prison. The Moon being in Cancer, it is good to get riches.

The 9th, 10th, 11th, 12th day in Leo. In the 9th house, Barbiel hath dominion; in the 10th house, Ardosiel; in the 11th, Neael: in the 12th, Abdizenel.

The ninth day is hurtful to harvest and to those that labour in a journey, and good to breed discord among men. The tenth day, good to build, to obtain love and benevolence against enemies. The eleventh day available for those that journey, to obtain gain by traffic, to redeem captives. The twelfth day, prosperous for corn and plants, hurtful for sailors, good to better the estate of servants and captives.

The 13th, 14th day in Virgo and thus the second quarter of the sky is completed, in which the Moon is warm and dry.[631] In the 13th house, Cazariel hath dominion; in the 14th, Engadiol.

The thirteenth day is available to obtain benevolence, wealth to enter a journey, for corn, for the delivery of captives. The fourteenth day is available to increase the love of married folk, to heal the sick, profitable for sailors, but hurtful for those that journey on the land. The Moon being in Virgo, it is very available to gather riches, 26

In June is one day for preparing truly destructive, namely the seventh, according to Bacon.

---

630. In right marg.: "264."

631. OP Book 2 chapter 32: "for in the first quarter, as the Peripatetics deliver, it is hot and moist; in the second hot and dry; in the third, cold and dry; in the fourth cold and moist; and although it is the lowest of the stars, yet it bringeth forth all the conceptions of the superiors; for from it in the heavenly bodies beginneth that series of things which Plato calls the Golden Chain."

It behooveth that the worker of magic be of a constant credulic[632] and confident, and that he do in no wise doubt neither stagger in his mind for the obtaining of his purpose for as a firm and steadfast credulic doth work marvelous things, so a distrust and doubt destroyeth the virtue of worker's mind, and defraudeth him from his desired effect.

The spirits of the planets

The spirit of Saturn[633] is called Sabathiel: the Spirit of Jupiter, Zedekiel: the spirit of Mars, Madimiel: the Spirit of the Sun, Semeliel, or Semeschia; the Spirit of Venus, Nogahel; [+ the spirit of Mercury, Cochabiah, or Cochabiel;] the Spirit of the Moon, Jareahel, or Levanael.

[160]
The spirits of the signs at the circle[634]

Aries is presided over by Teletiel, Taurus by Suriel, Gemini by Tamimiel [*Tomimiel], Cancer by Sartamiel, Leo by Ariel, Virgo by Betuliel, Libra by Magniel [*Masniel], Scorpio by Acrabiel, Sagittarius by Chesetiel, Capricorn by Godiell [*Gediel, Aquarius by Doliol [*Deliel], and Pisces by Dagymiel.

---

632. Credulic: credulity?

633. OP Book 3 chapter 28. In left marg.: "w" glyph; in right marg.: "289."

634. Ibid. Signarum: i.e., signs of the Zodiac.

Before beginning you should say:

psal 9: psal 18: psal 24: usque ad versum 8: psal 32: psal 35: a\<d\> versum 5: usque ad finem. psal: 50: psal 135 psal 148	(KJV:) Psalms 9,* 19, 25:1–8; 33, 36:5–13; 51, 136, 148
* In right marg.: "290."	

Benedicitus dominus deus Israel, a seculo et usque in seculorum fiat fiat psal 40: 14 ver	Psalm 41:14: "Blessed by the Lord the God of Israel from eternity to eternity. So be it. So be it."

When we enter the circle:

psal 17: usque ad ver 5: psal 116: 1	(KJV) Psalm 18:1–5; Psalm 117:1 ("O praise the Lord, all ye nations: praise him, all ye people.")

Domini est Terra et plenitudo eius, orbis terrarum, et universi qui habitavit in eo. Quia ipse super Maria fundavit eum et super flumina preparavit eum psal 23: ver 1[-]2	(KJV) Psalm 24:1–2: "The earth is the Lord's and the fullness thereof, the world, and all those who dwell therein. For he has founded it upon the seas, and has prepared it upon the rivers."

Domine abscondes nos in abscondito faciri tuae, a conturbatione inimicarum. Proteges nos in tabernaculo tuo, a contradictione linguarum psal 30 ver 21:	(KJV) Psalm 31:21 (paraphrased): "O Lord, you shall hide them in the secret of your face, from the disturbance of *enemies*. You shall protect them in your tabernacle from the contradiction of tongues."

Domine custodi nos, protectio tua, descendat super nos: custodi nos domine ab omni malo custodi anima nostras domine domine custode Introitam nostrum, et exitum nostrum, ex hoc nunc, et usque in seculum.	Guard us, O Lord; may your protection descend over us. Guard us, O Lord from all evil; guard our souls, O Lord. O Lord, guard our entrance and our exit, from now until eternity.

Before the invocations:

psal 8: psal 27: psal 74 75 psal 85 psal 90:	(KJV) Psalm 8, 28, 75, 76 (?), 86, 91

Domine, ne memineris iniquitatem nostrarum antiquarum cito anticipent nos miserecordiae, tuae quia pauperes facti sumus nimis. Adiuva nos deus salutaris noster, et propter gloriam nominis tui audiuua nos et propitius esto peccatis nostris, propter nomen tuum. psal 78: ver 8[:]9:	(KJV) Psalm 79:8–9: "O Lord, remember not our former iniquities: let your mercies speedily go before, for we have become exceeding poor. Help us, O God, our saviour: and for the glory of your name. O Lord, deliver us, and forgive us our sins for your name's sake."

Respice in nos servos tuas [*tuos], et [in] opera nostra et dirige [nos] sit splendor tuas super nos, et propitius esto peccatis nostris dirrige psal 89: ver 16:17:	Psalm 90:16–17: "Look upon us, your servants, and upon our work, and direct (us), and may your brilliance be upon us, and be favourably inclined to correct our wrong doings." *
* Adapted from Psalm 89:16–17 (KJV 90).	

Adiutorum nostrum in nomine dommini qui fecit celum et terram psal 123: verse 8:	(KJV) Psalm 124:8: "Our help is in the name of the Lord, who made heaven and earth."

At the time of the invocations:

psal: 2: psal: 12: psal: 19: psal: 171: psal: 43:	(KJV) Psalm 2, 13, 20, 171 (?),* 44.
* There is no Psalm 171.	

Deus Iudex Iustus, fortis et patiens nunquid Irascitur per singulos dies. Nisi conuersi fueritis, gladium suum vibrabit, arcum suum te tendit, et ponaouit illum: psal: 7: ver: 12: 13:	Psalm 7:12–13: "God is a just judge, strong and patient; is he angry every day? Unless you will have been converted, he will brandish his sword; he has bent his bow and made it ready."*
* In marg. in pencil is small figure.	

Exurge domine deus, exaltetur manus tua, ne obliviscaris pauperum: psal: 10 ver 12.	(KJV) Psalm 9:32: "Arise, O Lord God, let your hand be exalted; forget not the poor."

Respice in me domine, et miserere mei quia unicus et pauper sum ego. Tribulationis cordis mei multiplicatae sunt de neacessitatibus meis erue me psal: 24: ver: 16: 17:	(KJV) Psalm 25:16–17: "Look upon me, O Lord, and have mercy on me; for I am alone and poor. The troubles of my heart are multiplied: deliver me from my necessities."

In deo faciemus virtutem, et ipse ad Nihilum deducet tribulantes nos psal: 59: ver: 14:	(KJV) 60:14: "Through God we shall do mightily: and he shall bring to nothing them that afflict us."

Deus confringet capita Inimicarum suarum verticem capilli perambulantium in delictis suis psal: 67 ver 22 et lege psal: 43: ver: 22: usque ad finem.	(KJV) 68:22: "God shall break the heads of his enemies; the hairy crown of them that walk on in their sins." And read Psalm 44 verse 22 all the way to the end.

Between the invocations:

Psal: 2: psal: 5: psal: 12: psal: 46: psal: 65 et 66: psal: 73: psal: 76: psal: 79: psal: 82: psal: 84: psal: 90: psal: 146: psal: 85:	(KJV) Psalms 2, 5, 13, 47, 66, 67, 74, 77, 80, 83, 85, 91, 147, and 86.

For expelling fear:

Psal: 6: non timebo millia populi circumdantis me exurge domine salvam me fac deus meus psal: 3: ver 7:	Psalm 6,* and Psalm 3:7: "I will not fear thousands of the people, surrounding me: arise, O Lord; save me, O my God."
* In right marg.: "291."	

Tu domine servabis nos et custodies nos a generatione hac in eternam spal 11 ver 8:	(KJV) Psalm 12:8: "You, O Lord, will preserve us and keep us from this generation for ever."

| Conserva me domine quoniam spe- ravi in te dixi domino deus meus es tu quoniam bonorum mearum non eges spal: 15: ver: 1: | (KJV) Psalm 16:1: "Preserve me, O Lord, for I have put trust in you. O my soul, you have said to the Lord: you are my God, my goods are nothing to you." |

| A resistentibus dextrae tuae, custodi me ut pupillum oculi sub umbra alarum tuarum protege me psal: 16: ver: 8: et si ambulavero in medio umbrae mortis, non timebo mala quoniam tu mecum es domine.

Virga tua et a baculus tuus ipsa me consolata sunt psal 22 ver 4: | (KJV) Psalm 17:8: "From them that resist your right hand keep me, as the apple of your eye. Protect me under the shadow of your wings."

Psalm 23:4: "For though I should walk in the midst of the shadow of death, I will fear no evils, for you are with me, Lord. Your rod and your staff, they have comforted me." |

[161]

Circle work[635]

| Conuertat te Deus In Infernum psa: 9: ver 18 pluat deus super te laqueas ignis, [et] sulphur, et [spiritus] procellas psa: 10 ver: 6: verberet te deus virga ferrea et tanquam vas figuli confringat te psa: 2: ver: 9: confundat te deus psa: 24: ver: 3 veniat morse super te et descendat in Infernum vivens psa: 54: ver: 16: deducat te deus in puteum Intaritus ibidem ver: 24: Confringat deus caput tuum et verticem capilli tui [+ perambulantium] in delictu tuis, psa: 67 ver: 22 obscurentur occuli tui ne videas et dorsum tuum in curvetur semper, Effundat deus super te Iram suam, et furam eius te comprehendat percutiet te deus et persequater | O N,, God will return you to hell (Psalm 9:18). God shall rain snares upon you, fire, brimstone, and storms, O N., (Psalm 10:7). O N., God shall flog you with an iron rod, and shall break you into pieces like a potter's vessel (Psalm 2:9). O N., God shall confound you (Psalm 24:3). Death will come to you, and you will descend alive into hell (Psalm 54:16). God shall bring you down into the pit of destruction (Psalm 54:24). God shall shatter your head, the hairy crown of you who walk in sin (Psalm 67:22). Your eyes will be darkened that you see not, and your back will always be bent (Psalm 68:24). God will |

---

635. In marg.: "With penalty inflicted." Another version of this curse can be found on Folger p. 62.

te et super dolorem vulnerum tuorum addat psa: 68: ver: 24 avertat te deus retrorsum et erubescas psa: 69: ver 41 [*4]: ponat te deus ut rotam, et ut stipulam ante faciem venti, sicut ignis qui comburit siluam et sicut flamma comburens montes persequatur te deus in tempestate sua et in Ira sua turbet te Impleat deus faciem tuam ignominia ut obedias nomini illius conturbet te ut pereas in seculum [+ seculi. Transeat te in ira domini, et] terrores eius te conturbent ps: 87: ver: 17: visitet te deus in virga, Iniquitates tuas, et in verberibus peccata tua psa: 88: ver 33: Ira dei exardescat in te tanquam Ignis Ibidem ver: 47: ignis ante deum praecedat et in circuitu Inflammet te psa: 96: ver: 3: cadant super te carbones in ignem deiiciare, in miseriis non subsistas psa: 139: ver: 11:	pour out his anger upon you, and his wrath will seize you (Psalm 68:25) God will strike you and persecute you, and add grief to your wounds (Psalm 68:27). God will turn you backwards, and you will blush in shame (Psalm 69:4). God will place you like a wheel, and like straw before the face of the wind (Psalm 82:14), a like fire which burns wood, and like a flame burning mountains (Psalm 82:15). God will take vengeance on you in his tempest, and shall trouble you in his wrath (Psalm 82:16). God will fill your face with shame, that you will obey his name (Psalm 82:17). O N., he will confound you, so that you will perish forever (Psalm 82:18). The wrath of the Lord has come upon you, and his terrors have troubled you (Psalm 87:17). God will visit you in your iniquity with a rod, and your sins with lashes (Psalm 88:33). God's anger will flare up against you like fire (Psalm 88:47). A fire shall go before God, and shall burn you (Psalm 96:3). Burning coals will fall upon you; in misery you will not be able to stand (Psalm 139:11).

After the licence

Psalm 58 ("Unto the end, destroy not"), Psalm 67 ("Let God arise and let his enemies be scattered").

Observations, after the spirit has appeared

1 If he appear in his proper form, turn yourself towards him, receive him gently, etc.

2 Then, by way of entreaty, enquire what is his name and whether he have any other name.

3 Under what planet he is.

4 What is his office and dignity, and how many are under his subjection.

5 But if you see him stubborn, or distrust him of lying, etc., constrain him by a convenient conjuration, saying upon every question, "*Coniuro te, N., per patrem et filium et spiritum sanctum, per Iesum Christum et per admirabilem dei nomen Tetragramaton + ut mihi vera respondeas de hac re,* ["I conjure you N., by the Father, and the Son, and the Holy Ghost, by Jesus Christ, and by the admirable name of God + Tetragrammaton + that you answer me truly concerning this thing."] [space] or I conjure thee, N., as thou hopest to be saved etc. [space] or *coniuro te, N., subpena damnationis* ["I conjure you, N., under penalty of damnation"] etc.

But if you will be sure of a true answer, stretch out your sword, and let him put his hand thereon, and swear.

Our general request

That you bring or cause to be brought unto me speedily, either from the parts of this realm, N., or from the parts of some other nation, treasure to the value of [omitted], and that you cast it without delay or lingering, covin,[636] guile, or fraud into the midst of this circle, wherein I am, without hurt or damage either to me or to any one of my fellows, and without hurting, bruising, or impairing of the treasure or any part thereof.

That you tell me truly what treasure is hidden in this house called, and in what house is treasure, how much, and where it lieth, and by what means I may come by it and whether there be any keepers thereof or no, and what be their names and offices and whom be they under.

At the entering of the circle

O everlasting God, maker of mankind, which willed not the death of a sinner, but rather that he be converted and live, I beseech thee that thou wilt save and preserve us, thy unworthy servants, tempting thee in divine and secret matters, and that thou wilt defend us with the right hand of thy deity and bring us to the fulfilling of thy commandments and grant us our desire by Christ our Lord. Amen.

---

636. Covin: trickery.

| Munda me domine ab omni in-quinamento mentis et corporis ut possim mundus Implere hoc opus sanctum. | Cleanse me, O Lord, from all impurity of mind and body, that I may be clean for completing this holy work.* |

* From the Mass—order of communion.

| In spritu humilitatis et in animo contrito suscipiamur domine a te: et sic fiat factum nostrum in conspectu tuo ate suscipiatur hodie et placeat tibi: domine deus. | Accept us, O Lord, in the spirit of humility, and contrite heart, and grant that the act which we offer today in your sight may be pleasing to you, O Lord God.* |

* Also from the communion, where it reads *sacrificium* ["sacrifice"] instead of *factum* ["act"].

| Da pacem domine in diebus nostris quia non est alius qui pugnat pro nobis nisi tu deus noster. | Give us peace in our time, O Lord, for there is no one else who will fight for us, if not for you, our God. |

| Tua est potentia tuum est refugium domine, tue es super omnes gentes da pacem domine in diebus nostris. | Thine is the power. Your power is a refuge, O Lord. You are above all nations. O Lord, give peace in our days. |

| Exaudiat dominus orationes nostras: et reconcellietur nobis, nec nos deserat in tempore malo. domine deus | May the Lord hear our prayers, and restore us, and not abandon us in evil times.* |

* 2 Mac. 1:5

| Ne derelinquas me domine pater e[t] dominator vite mee: ut non cor[r]uam in conspectu adversariorum meorum, ne gaudeat de<e> me inimicus meus[,] apprehende arma et stutum: et exurge in adiutorum mihi. | Do not abandon me, O Lord and father, and ruler of my life, that I may not be humbled in the sight of my adversaries, not that my enemies may triumph over me. Therefore come to my help. |

[162]

After you have made the invocation at the circle

Libera nos quesumus domine ab omnibus malis preteritis presentibus et futuris, et da pacem in diebus nostris ut opere miserecordie tue domine (?) adiuti: et ab ira et malignatia diaboli simus semper liberi, et ab omni [per] turbacione securi.	Deliver us,* O Lord, we pray, from every evil, past, present, and future, and grant us peace in our days, that with the help of your mercy, we may always be free from anger and † the malice of the devil, and safe from all distress.‡

* In right marg.: "281."
† This word is underlined, and has "o" over it
‡ This paragraph is largely based on the so-called embolism of the Mass.

Deus pater fons origo totius bonitatis, qui ductus misericordia unigenitum tum pro nobis ad infimandi descendere et carnem voluisti, te adoro te glorifico, tetota mentis ac cordis intencione laudo et precor: ut nos famulos tuos non deocroo, ood adiuva nos, et petam nostram dimittas et concede cum puro corde et casto corpore te servire valeamus per Christum dominum nostrum	O God the Father, source and origin of all goodness, who, moved by your mercy, willed your only-begotten son to descend for us to this base world and [take] flesh: I worship you, I glorify you, I praise you with the whole attention of my mind and my heart, and beseech you not to forsake your servants, but help us, and forgive our sins, and grant that with a pure heart and chaste body we may prevail, through Christ our Lord.

Domine deus virtutum converte nos, et ostende faciam tuam et salvi erimus.	O Lord God of power, restore us, and show us your face, and we shall be saved.

Dominem exaudi orationem meam, et clamor meus ad te veniate	O Lord hear my prayer, and let my cry come to you.*

* Psalm 101 (KJV 102).

Veni Sancte Spiritus corda fidelium: et in amoris in eis ignem accende. Sancti Spiritus assit nobis gratiam, qui cordam, nostram sibi faciat habitacula, Acciones nostras quesimus domine asperando preveni et adiuvando prosequere ut cuncta nostra operatio a te semper Incipiat et per te incepta finiatur: Amen.	Come, O Holy Ghost, fill the hearts of your faithful, and enkindle the fire of your love in them. May the grace of the Holy Ghost be with us, and make a home in our hearts. Direct, we beg you, O Lord, our actions by your holy inspirations, and carry them on by your gracious assistance, that every prayer and work of ours may begin always with you, and through you be happily ended. Amen.[*]

* This prayer appears in the *Book of Hours* and other medieval collections of prayers, including Church of England, *Liturgical Services Liturgies and Occasional Forms of Prayer Set Forth in the Reign of Queen Elizabeth* (Cambridge: University Press, 1847), 398. It is also the first prayer in LIH (ch. vi).

Aufer a nobis quesumus domine omnes iniquitates nostras, ut ad hunc circulum, puris mentibus mereamr Introire, per Christum Dominum nostrum Amen.	Remove from us, we beg you, O Lord, all our iniquity, that we may be worthy to enter this circle with pure minds, through Christ our Lord. Amen.

Veni Creator spiritus mentes tuorum visita: Imple superna gratiae qui tu creasti pectora.	Come, O Creator Spirit,[*] and visit your souls; fill the hearts which you have created with heavenly grace.

* This is "one of the most widely used hymns in the church." http://www.preces-latinae.org /thesaurus/Hymni/VeniCreator.html.

Qui paraclitus diceris donum dei altissimi, fons vivus ignis charitas et spiritalis unctio.	You who are the Paraclete (Comforter), the gift of God most high, living source, fire, charity, and spiritual anointing.

Tu Septiformis munere dextre dei tu digitus, tu rite promis<e>sum patris sermone ditans guttura.	You are the sevenfold gift, you are the finger of God's right hand, a gift duly promised by the Father, words which enrich the throat.

Accende lumen sensibus infunde amorem cordibus, infirma nostri corporis virtute firmans perpetim.	Kindle in us the light, pour love into our hearts, continually strengthening our fragile bodies.

Hostem repellas longuis pacemque dones protinus, ductore sic te praevio vitemus omne noxium.	Drive the enemy far from us, quickly bring peace; thus leading us, we may avoid all harm.

Per te sciamus da Patrem noscamus atque filium teque utriusque Spiritum credamus omni tempore.	Through you may we understand the Father, and know the Son, and may we believe you, the spirit of each, for all time.

Sit laus Patri cum filio sancto simull Paraclito nobisque mittat filius carissma Sancti Spiritus. Amen.	Praise be to the Father, with the Son, likewise the holy Paraclete, and send to us the Son of the most dear Holy Ghost. Amen.

Emitte spiritum tuum et creabuntur et ren[o]vabis faciem terre. Oremus	Send forth your spirit, and they shall be created, and you shall renew the face of the earth. Let us pray.

Deus cui omne cor patet et omnis voluntas loquitur et quem nullum latet secretum: purifica per infucionem spiritus sancti cogitaciones cordis nostri ut te perfecte dilligere et digne laudare meream[u]r per dominum nostrum Iesum Christum etc.	O God, to whom all hearts are open, and all desires known, and from whom no secrets lie hidden, purify the thoughts of our hearts by the infusion of your Holy Ghost, that we may love you perfectly, and be properly worthy to praise you, through Jesus Christ, etc.*
* Who lives and reigns with you in unity with the same Holy Spirit, forever and ever. Amen.	

Da pacem in diebus nostris ut opere misericordie tue adiuti: et a peccato simus [*sumus] semper liberi, et ab omni per turbacione securi. Amen.	Grant peace in our days, that being assisted by the help of your mercy, we may always be delivered from sin, and secure from all turmoil. Amen.

[163]

[+ Instruments of the Art]

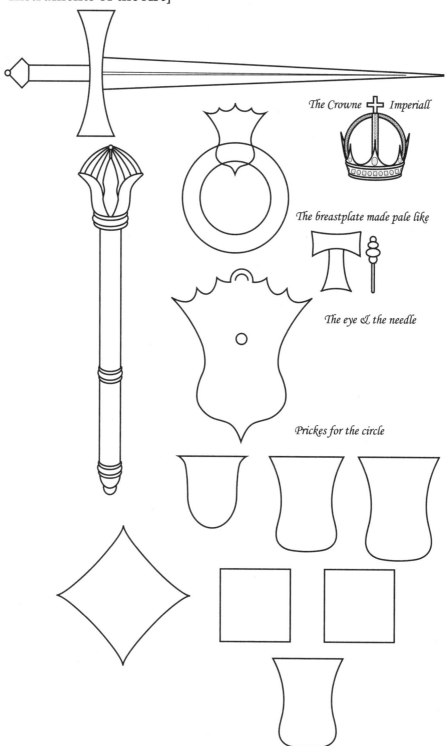

The Crowne Imperiall

The breastplate made pale like

The eye & the needle

Prickes for the circle

[164]

An experiment approved by Friar Bacon to have a spirit appear in a circle to make answer to any question to be demanded.

637

First you must make two circles, the one for yourself, and the other for the spirit, on this sort as followeth.

These circles must be made with a knife having a white haft in the 2nd, 4th, 6th, 10th, or 12th day of the month,[638] the air being clear.

639

---

638. Also found in Sibley, *The Clavis or Key to the Magic of Solomon* (2009) and known from many manuscript sources.

638. Month: from the context, this would seem to mean the lunar month, instead of the calendrical month.

639. The text in circles read "Othe Orno Thou Ches / Birto" and "Alpha & Omega + Seme-phoras +." The second circle is often labeled as "Magister." In marg.: "w" glyph.

Then, thou sitting in thy circle upon thy knees towards the east, say this conjuration:

O Lord holy father almighty and everliving God, I pray and beseech thee by the virtue of thy holy +, and by thy power that you suffer me, thy servant N., who thou hast made to thy own image and likeness not to be oppressed with the deceit of enemies, neither with adversity or need, by Jesus Christ our Lord the Redeemer and saviour of the World and king of glory. Amen. Christ + overcometh + Christ commandeth + Christ + vouchsafe to command me to be a triumpher over all my enemies bodily and ghostly, visible and invisible. Amen.

Psalm 54, "*deus innocent, tuo salvum me fac*," then say the Psalm as is before said.

Then say this conjuration:

I conjure thee, O spirit which art called Birto, by the dignity of thy prince Ornothochos and Booth and the Father, the Son, and the Holy Ghost, Alpha and Omega, one God for evermore, that thou do here appear in the circle assigned for thee in a fair shape of a man, and that thou tell me the truth without any falsehood or craft, of all such things that I shall ask or demand of thee, by him to whom be all honour and glory, power and dominion, for ever and ever. Amen.

Then demand of him what thou wilt and he will openly declare to thee thy desire, but note thou must say these conjurations and Psalm three times before thou demand any question.

Then when thou hast ended thy work and hast thy desire, licence him on this wise to depart.

O Birto, by all the words that I have spoken, and by the same virtue that thou didst come hither at this presence unto me, I command and charge thee to depart in peace, and rest with thy God, and be ready to come unto me another time when I shall call thee by the virtue of our Lord Jesus Christ, to whom be all honour, power, and glory, for ever and ever. Amen.

This experiment of Birto was proved at the instant request of Edward the 4th, King of England, and therefore keep it safely. Finis.

[165]
Bilgall [640] [+ Conjuration of the Spirit]

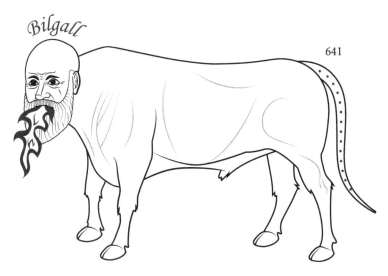

641

Ego exhorter te Bylgall per deum qui te est creator ceeli et terre maris et omnium que que in eis sunt, per quattuor Elementa viz aerem, ignem, aquam et terram, per omnem potestatem celi, per virtutem lapidum et prophetarum, et per virtutem omnium verborum. ego coniuro te Bylgall per verum deum per sanctum deum, et per obedientiam quam tu debes deo omnipotenti quod statim in isto christallo visibilliter in pulcra forma humana apereas et facies istum lapidem crescere in longitudinem et latitudinem in visione istius pueri N et nominando illum.	I[*] exhort you, O Bylgall, by the God who is the creator of Heaven and Earth, the sea, and all which is in them, by the four elements, namely air, fire, water, and earth, and by all the powers of Heaven, by the virtue of the stones and the prophets, and by the virtue of all the words. I conjure you, O Bylgall, the true God, by the holy God, and by the obedience which you owe to almighty God, that you immediately appear visibly in this crystal, in a fair human form, and make this stone grow in length and width in the sight of this child N. (naming him).

* In marg: "w."

---

640. Compare Sloane 3826, fol. 99v ff, and Sloane 3846, fol. 109r. There is a "G" at the top of the page, and "189" in the right marg.

641. This figure seems to have been inspired by Boaistuau and Fenton, *Certaine secrete wonders of nature* (1569), 144, which describes it as follows: "This as you see (resembling most a Calfe) hath the head of a man, bearing a beard, with a brest like to a man, and two dugges well formed." The section describes deformities at birth. Fenton's text in turn was based on Pierre Boaistuau, *Histoires Prodigieuses* (London: 1569). The original manuscript of the latter is fully digitized on Wellcome's website, with colour illustrations. http://blog.wellcomelibrary.org/2012/12/a-book -fit-for-a-queen/.

Afterwards the boy or man should say as follows:

Ego exhortor te Bylgall per ista nomina per qua exhortatus a magistro meo es, et per meam castitatem fructum meum, et per illum casum per quem cadebas a throno celi, et per illam nomina per quem maledictus es, Primeumaton, quod te iam manifestes in isto lapidem in pulcra forma humana, et facias te crescere visibilliter, et non recedas ex eo sine licentia mea et magistri mei, et hoc precipio tibi per omnipotentum deum omni creatorem, qui vivit benedictus eternaliter et Regnat benedictus eternaliter. Amen.	I exhort you, O Bylgall, by those names by which you were exhorted by my master, and by my chastity, and by that event by which you fell from the throne of Heaven, and by that name through which you were cursed, Primeumaton, that you now manifest in this crystal in a fair human form, and make you arise visibly, and not depart from it until my licence, and that of my master, and this I order you by almighty God, creator of all, who lives blessed forever, and reigns blessed forever. Amen.

quando compareat dic ut sequitur	**When he appears, he should say as follows:**

Ego N fillius N precipio et ligo te Bilgall in isto lapidem christalli, per virtutem illorum verborum per qui Michaellem Archangellum Angeli Terrenus ligavit Luciferum draconem Infernalem sz portisan, fortisan, Alingon, per ista nomina intelligas, hoc quod non recedas ab isto lapidem per mi~quitalem (iniquitalem?) adiuratus sine licentia mea et magistri mei, quoniam prius facias ac compleas omnia que tibi precipiam et a te invirtute demonstrari desiderabo, fiat, fiat, fiat.	I N., the child of N., order and bind you Bilgall in this crystal stone, by the power of those words through which the Archangel Michael bound the earthly angels, Lucifer the infernal dragon, namely Portisan, Fortisan, Alingon, by these names you understand, that you not depart from this stone charged by Minquitalem without my licence and that of my master, because you must first do and accomplish all that I will order you, and explain by perfect demonstration what I desire. *Fiat, fiat, fiat.*

The licence of Bilgall

Per illam virtutem per quam domi- nus ligauit te et per sua sancta nomina precipio quod tu recedas ab isto lapidem sine nostro tedio aut nocumento aut le- sione alicuique creature humane, cum alias te Invocavero iterum sis paratus mihi et obediens per nomen domini nostri J Christi fiat fiat fiat.	By that power through which the Lord bound you, and by his holy names, I command that you depart from this stone, without any weariness, harm, or malice to us or to any human creature, and be prepared to return when I invoke you again, and obey by the name of our Lord Jesus Christ. *Fiat, fiat, fiat.*

Do this these three days only: The days of the Moon, Mercury, Venus

For enclosing a spirit in a ring[642]

But I now digress and note for you a means of enclosing [+ a spirit], which I have tested the truth of beyond doubt a hundred times, which I received from my associate, a Turk, who had himself learned the method from the spirit Seraphius, since[643] he had been recently baptised.

First, therefore, make the following circle in the hour of Mercury, and your garments and all things should be clean, then enter the circle with the instruments and censer, and you should also have whatever you wish to enclose them in, but most often I have tested this in the hollow of a golden ring, and this they have greatly preferred because the metal is so precious.[644] You should work in the day of Mercury and it is better if the whole is done in the hour of Mercury[645] but if well prepared, and the ring completely sealed up and pure,[646] and carry it with you [+ into the circle, and place it in the western part of the circle in a very pure][647] veil or covering. But know that you should make the ring with a small door over the opening through which something can enter, and thence enclose it in the inner part of the ring.

---

642. In right mar: "169." Compare Sloane 3853, 42r; Wellcome MS. 110, 85r; and Mun. A.4.98, 121.

643. Wellcome MS. 110: idem.

644. Following Wellcome MS. 110, 85r: "*et hoc multum affectant ut mihi retulerunt spiritus propter pretiositatem metalli.*" Sloane 3853, 42r, is similar: "*hoc multum affectant propter preconsitatem auri quod est metallum preciossissimum ut mihi retulerunt s.*"

645. Sloane 3853 and Wellcome MS. 110: die mercurii.

646. Instead of *obturatus anulus et purus* ["the ring sealed up and pure"], Sloane 3854 and Wellcome MS. 110 read *anulo totaliter obrizato et puro* ["the ring highly refined and pure"].

647. So Sloane 3854 and Wellcome MS. 110; without which the meaning is obscure.

[166]

With the ring thus hidden, begin the following conjuration

Coniuro te o princeps Alastiell et omnes spiritus tibi subditos per illud Infinitum dei verbum quo cun[c]ta creavit. Coniuro vos omnes et requiro per bonitatem dei qua deus hominem ad ymaginem suam creavit, et vos per iusticiam per vestra superbia dampnavit et eiecit de caelis, et per quam Iusticiam primos parentes nostros damnavit ad tempus et per Infinitam bonitatem qua eosdem sanguine redemit, et per virginitatem humilitatem et fecunditatem sacratissime virginis Marie Mater domini Iesu Christi, per potestatem qua Infernum spoliavit et demones cruciavit, et per tremendum diem Iuditii, et omnem celi miliciam, et Angelos et Archangelos, per prophetas patriarchas Martires et confessores et omnes virgines et per omnia dei nomina et eius fillii domini nostri Iesu Christi passionem mirificam conversacionem in terris, et per hac Iudicabile nomen dei + Tetragrammaton + quod erat in fronte Moysy et in hoc sceptro consecrato, et in anulo mirifice extitit insignitum quia inter vos tu princeps Alastiel in unum veracem assignes spiritum non Inferiorum sed supreme scientie qui mihi poterit ad terminum vite mee fideliter respondere de	I conjure you, O prince Alastiel,* and all your subordinate spirits, by that infinite God who has created all things with a word. I conjure and demand of you by the goodness of God, which God created mankind in his own image, and by the justice which has condemned you and expelled you from Heaven because of your arrogance, and by the justice which condemned our first parents (Adam and Eve) at the time and by the infinite goodness which has redeemed the same sin with blood, and by the humble virginity and fertility of the most holy virgin Mary, mother of the Lord Jesus Christ, and by the power which has plundered hell and tormented the demons, and by the terrible Day of Judgement, and by all the hosts of Heaven, and the Angels and Archangels, by the Prophets, Patriarchs, Martyrs, and Confessors, and all virgins and by all the names of God and the passion of his Son our Lord Jesus Christ and his wonderful way of life on earth (?),† and by this declarable name of God + Tetragrammaton + which was on the front of Moses [*breastplate of Aaron]‡ and on this consecrated sceptre, and wonderfully displayed on the ring, that among

* Compare Sloane 3853, fol. 43r ff, and Wellcome MS. 110, 85r.
† Wellcome MS. 110 and Mun. A.4.98, 122, also read *in terris* ["on the earth"], whereas Sloane 3853 reads *eius matris* ["of his mother"].
‡ Wellcome MS. 110 and Sloane 3853 both read "Aaron" which is probably more correct.

quisitis non menciendo, non simulando, nec fraudem faciendo sed veraciter mihi de quesitis et interrogatus abeo fideliter respondendo, hunc ergo coarctam per tuis viribus ut quamdiu Anulus Induraverit illi eum ingrediendo numquam exeat nisiame ad hoc licentiatus fuerit et hoc tibi precipio virtute huius thurificacionis et sacrificii per omnia verba realiter supradicta per eum qui v. e. I. v. e. m. e. S. per ignem Amen.

you, O Prince Alastiel, you may assign to me one truthful spirit, not inferior but of highest knowledge, who will be able to faithfully answer my questions, until the end of my life, without deceit, dissimulation, or fraud but responding truly to any questions I ask. Therefore may you constrain (one) by your strength, and as long as the ring will endure, may he never emerging from it or depart from me unless I authorize it, and this I command by the power of this incense and offering, and by all the words mentioned above, though him who will come to judge the living and the dead and the world by fire. Amen.

But it is necessary for you to say this conjuration three times, because otherwise he will be unwilling. Then take the ring and throw it outside the circle towards them, and then you will see all the spirits gather together and consult amongst themselves, and they will assign one of themselves who they will close up. When this is done and the spirit assigned, they will put the ring back next to the circle. Take it into the room with you. Which done, all the spirits will remain in the window, in order to hear your words. And then say this conjuration:

Coniuro te spiritus inclusus per summam dei potentiam, et per verba tua in operacione astringencia, et per mirabilia Iesu Christi, et per illud Ineffabilem nomen dei + Tetragrammaton +, quod hic in Annulo et sceptra meo inscriptum est quatenus hunc locum quem ingressus es et virtutem tui principis et mee coniurationis nunquam exeas nisi a me primus licentiatus fueris mihi qui diligentur de quesitis quacunque Interrogavero sine fraude et fallacia ut alia

I conjure you, O spirit, enclosed by the utmost power of God, and by all the words used in your binding operation, and by all the miracles of our Lord Jesus Christ, and by that name of God + Tetragrammaton + which is engraved here on my ring and sceptre, that as long as you remain in this place which you have entered, by the power of your prince and my conjuration, that at no time may you emerge, unless authorized beforehand by me, but faithfully respond to whatever

| aliqua simulacione respondeas et sic In-clusus non plauees et mihi de quesitis non deferas veritatem refferre, per eum deum domini Iesu Christum qui v. e. I. v. e. M. e. S. per ignem. † Amen. | I ask without fraud, deceit, or any other dissimulation, and thus confined you will not hesitate* to reveal the truth to my questions, through him, God, our Lord Jesus Christ, who will come to judge the living and the dead and the world by fire. Amen. |

* Reading *pigres*; Folger: *plauees* (?).Wellcome MS. 110 and Sloane 3853: *planges* ["strike" or "lament"].

† Qui v. e. I. v. e. M. e. S. per ignem: qui venturus est ludicare viuos et mortuos et seculum per ignem. In right marg.: "190."

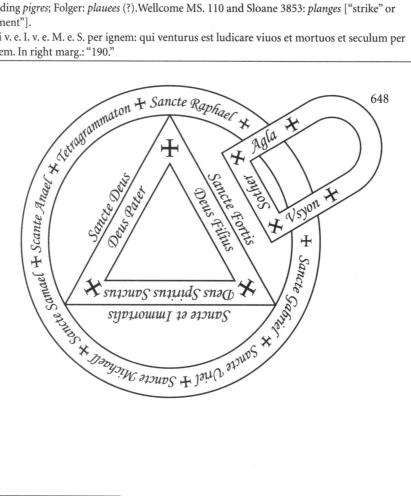

648. Circle, triangle, and mirror (?). Analogue in Wellcome MS. 110, 98r. Text reads: + *Tetragrammaton* + *Sancte Raphael* + – + *Sancte Gabriel* + *Sancte Uriel* + *Sancte Michaell* + *Sancte Samael* + *Sancte Anael* ["Tetragrammaton + O holy Raphael" etc.] Inside: *Sancte fortis, Sancte et immortalis, Sancte Deus* ["O holy power, O holy and immortal, O holy God", and inside triangle: + *Deus pater* + *Deus filius* + *Deus Spiritus Sanctus* ["+O God the father + God the Son + God the Holy Ghost"]. To the right is a shape that might be a path into or out of the circle, which is a common enough feature, or possibly a mirror, with the words + *Sother* + *Agla* + + *Usyon* [Gk. "Saviour + AGLA + of (one) substance"].

[167]

For having whatever you may covet. Lapwing.[649]

Whoever wishes to obtain for themselves something desired should examine this chapter of the work, and see how easily it can be fulfilled. Beforehand you must obtain a lapwing, and when you wish to operate, you should extract its blood and carefully preserve it in a glass vessel, closing it so that no air or impurities can enter. And when you wish to operate, go to a secret wood with a bright sword in your right hand, and when entering you should remember, you should arrive (?),[650] begin to write on virgin parchment with the above-mentioned blood: Bethala / inus (?) / suspensu suspensus in ethera super ea enpeogidum pamelon anguis norius Egrippusi fons florisses de sede Baldachison saporisi Araarastano.

These are names of the necromantic art.

Afterwards rise to your feet, and make a squared circle as shown below, with the same sword held in your hand, and standing in the middle of the circle, say the words you have written two or three or four times, toward the east, as the time of the Moon might require. When that has been spoken, you will immediately see a fair soldier sitting on a horse, carrying a hawk on his hand. And he will say to you, *quid vis quid petis, cur vocastii me paratus ad omnia respondere et voluntatem tuum ad implere* ["What do you wish? What do you desire? Why have you called me? I am ready to answer all things and fulfil your wishes."]

But avert your eyes from him, as though with indignation, and say nothing to him, and then he will immediately depart. You should rest for a little while in the middle of the circle, while he is departing.

Then rise again to your feet and face the north, and recite Bethalani etc. as before. And immediately a second soldier will appear to you, even more fair than the first, and more distinguished, on a horse, carrying a hawk like the first, and he will also

---

649. Compare Sloane 1727, 18 as transcribed in Brian P. Levack, *The Literature of Witchcraft* (New York: Garland, 1992), 242. Compare also LIH, CXXXIII.18: "Bethala suspensus in ethera, payga. permyga. percuretaih. perrenay. atariron. aboaga. convenite et concurrite ab omnibus mundi partibus, (19) ara. aray. pangula. iamtarpa..." Compare also Honorius, *Grimoire of Honorius*, Conjuration du roi du Septentrion: "Balandier, *suspensus, iracundus, Origratiumgu, Partus, Olemdemis et Bantatis*, N. je t'exorcise..."

650. Sloane 1727, 18r: "when you would worke: goe p[rivi]lly. to a woode, and first hold a bright sword in thy hand and say these words (which must be written in an Abortive) with the same blood. And in the entring into the wood begin and say thus Betha suspensus in Ethera super Ea Enpion, Emprogudum, pamelion anguis Marius Egripus fons floriseme de sede baldithe sapors ana vel arca siras: but these are truer: beltha suspensus Mathexa Superea Implex pamilion auanrius fons floris Tresdosed Baldachia sarins Mars."

speak like the first, but do not speak to him, but do everything as you did with the first. And he too will soon depart.

For a third time, rise to your feet and say as before, Bethalani etc. facing west, and soon a third soldier will appear to you, more noble and fair that the previous two, on a horse, carrying a hawk on his hand, crowned with a golden diadem. And he will say, *ecce ad sum tota die fatigatus, et dicet, quid vis* ["Behold, I am here the whole day, wearied" And he will say, "What do you wish?"] etc.

Then you may speak with him and examine him without fear, and petition him for what [+ you wish], and he will calmly respond, and will ask, *vis societatem meam* ["do you wish my fellowship?"] But you should respond with discretion, and defer that possibility to another day. When he hears this he will immediately depart. Nevertheless, in the morning you will discover what you desired.[651] I have proven this many times. [652]

Experiment of Solomon for what you wish[653]

654

Finis

---

651. Folger adds *falcitate exuleque nil* ["with falseness and exile nothing"], which JHP is unable to make sense of. Sloane 1727: "and soe leave untill the next day: and the next day *come againe* and thou shalt find what thou desirest: Approved."

652. In marg: "191."

653. These words are in the marg., and are the label of the figure.

654. Words read *ista pars versus occidentem* ["this part faces west"].

[168]
Annobathe
Annabath

Annabath[655]

This spirit is under Egin, King of the North, and is one of the twelve noblest of his number. His office is to make one marvelous cunning in necromancy and to shew hid treasure and to tell who are the keepers, and if he or they be of the north, he can drive them away. He can tell of diverse strange things and appeareth like an armed knight.

---

655. In left marg.: "w" glyph; in right marg: "126."

[169]

[+ Conjuration of Ascariell][656]

Ascariell

657

[+ First Conjuration]

Coniuro te Ascariell per deum patrem omnipotentem, et per Jesum Christum filium eius et per spiritum sanctum, et per sanctam Trinitatem, personam (?) et verbum et spiritum sanctum et per veritatem eius, et per provedentiam quam deus in mente sua habuit ante quam passus fuerit, et ipsam bonitatem	I conjure you, Ascariell, by God the almighty Father, and by Jesus Christ his Son, and by the Holy Ghost, and by the holy Trinity, the Person, and the word, and the Holy Ghost, and by his truth, and by the foresight which God has had in his mind before it has been allowed,* and by the goodness through which he

* Black, "Notes on a Silver-Mounted Charm-Stone…" (1894) reads: *antea qua mundum fecit* ["before he made the world."]

---

656. This text can be traced back to Sloane 3849. Compare George F. Black, "Notes on a Silver-Mounted Charm-Stone," *Proceedings of the Society of Antiquaries of Scotland* 39 (May 1894): 445 ff. Compare also C. J. S. Thompson, *The Mysteries and Secrets of Magic* (New York: Causeway Books, 1973), 267. Sloane 3851, 93b, mentions Askariel, as does Sloane 3853, fol. 142r.

657. Perhaps inspired by Boaistuau and Fenton, *Certaine secrete wonders of nature* (1569), 38, at the beginning of "A wonderfull discourse of precious stones."

per quam omnia fecit, et per sapientiam deus caelos collocavit, et per terram seorsum fundavit, et per Mare et omnia qui in eis sunt, et per profunditatem abissi, et per mundum quatuor elementa, et per virtutem elementis confucione imisit superius (?spus) misericordie, et per iussionem quam lucem creavit, et per sapientiam quam deus diem et noctem ordinavit, et per Angelos et Archangelos et Tronos, dominaciones principats et potestates virtutes cherubine et seraphine et per eorum officia, et eorum coniurationes, et per eos qui praesunt aliis, et per eos qui sub ipsius positi sunt, et per ea qui deus creavit ad lawdem et honorem nominis suo maiestatis, et per firmamentum celi, et per omnia ea qui sub firmamento sunt, et per omnes celos et omnes virtutis eorum celorum, et per omnia que in celo et sub celo sunt, ut ad me venias et omnia interogata veraciter mihi respondeas, et quod semper et sine mora cum Invocavero ad visionem meam ac preceptum meum venias in omnibus horis Amen.	made all things, and through the wisdom by God has arranged the heavens, and by the earth separately established, and by the seas and everything which is in them, and by the depths of the abyss, and by the four pure elements, and by the power he mingled with the elements, [and by works] of mercy, and by the command whereby He created the light, and by the wisdom which God arranged the day and the night, and by the Angels and Archangels, Thrones and Dominations, Principalities and Powers, Virtues, Cherubim, and Seraphim, and by their offices, and by the conjurations of them, and by those who preside over the others, and by those who have been placed under them, and by those who God created for the praise and honour of his greatness of his name, and by the firmament of Heaven, and by all that is under the firmament, and by all the heavens, and by all the powers of those heavens, and by all which is in heaven and under heaven, that you come to me and answer all my questions truthfully, and that you always come without delay when invoked, at all hours, visible to my perception. Amen.

Second Conjuration[658]

Coniuro te Askariell per virtutem dei quo creavit deus caelum et terram et herbam viventem, et per omnem semen quodcuque est, et per omnia alia	I conjure you, O Askariell, by the power of God who created heaven and earth, and the living plants, and by all that has seeds, and by all the life which

---

658. In marg.: "w" glyph.

viventia in germina eorum, et per terras et o[mn]es creaturas, et per omnia que in eis sunt, et per aquas quas deus produxit, de petra, et per omnia reptilia terre, et per volatilia celi, et per omnia que sub celo sunt, et per ea qui sub firmamento sunt, et sub terrae, et sub mare, et per infernum, et per omnia que in inferno sunt, et per preceptum dei qui creavit celum solem et lunam et omnes stellas et eorum officia, et per eorum Temporalia signam, et per bonitatem quod deus habet ad Imaginem suam creavit, et per Iustitiam illam qua deus damnavit malos spiritus et misericordiam suam qua deus bonos spiritus redemit et salvabit, et per omnia qua deus imperio hominis subiecit.

they sprout forth, and by the earth, and by all its creatures, and by the waters which God produced, and the rocks, and all the creeping things of the earth, and by the flying creatures of the sky, and by all that is under the heavens, and by that which is beneath the firmament, and under the earth, and under the sea, and by hell, and everything which is in hell, and by the perception of God, who created Heaven, the Sun and Moon, and all stars and their offices, and by their temporal signs, and by the goodness which God has for the image which he created, and by that justice by which God condemned the evil spirits, and by his mercy by which God redeemed and saved the good spirits, and by all the commands of God which man is subject to.

Third Conjuration

Coniuro te Askariell per duodecem prophetas, et per duodecem patriarchas et per eorum preconia, et per xii Appostolos, et per eorum iudicium, et per 24 seniores et eorum coronas, et per eorum stellas, et per eorum palmas, et eorum sedillia, et per sedem Maiestatis dei, et per Altare aurum quod est ante occulos dei, et per terribilia auria et per fulgura, et per voces egrediuntur e Trono dei, et per passiones Martirum, et confessorium, et per o[mn]es sanctos et sanctas dei, et per sanctos sacerdotes et per omnia que deum laudante et adorant Amen, Amen.

I conjure you, Askariell, through the twelve prophets, and through the twelve patriarchs, and through their praises, and through the twelve apostles, and through their judgement, and through the twenty-four elders and their crowns, and through their stars, and through their palms, and through their seats, and through the seat of God's majesty, and through the altar of gold which is before the eyes of God, and through the terrible breeze (?) and by the lightning, and by the voices which emerge from the throne of God, and by the passion of the martyrs and confessors, and by all the saints of God—male and female, and by all the holy priests, and by all who praise and honour God. Amen, Amen.

Fourth Conjuration

Coniuro te Askariell per eum qui est + Alpha et Omega + initium et finis et ista sancta nomina dei que sunt hec + Eli + El + Erros + Jesus + fortis + fontis + salvator + Eloy + Theos + deus + omnipotentes + hiceteca + sabatho + Agramo~ + virtus + loth + ho~le~ (?) + histerion + Adonay + risus + Beabaco + Tetragramaton + Ageos + feneton + craton + saton + lexaon + messias + lactea + Alte + Appanas + heles + helibe + Tocipaton + Oratos + holos + Age + pate + regum + Abraca + brata + legota + Ely + Victor + Osanna + conhibenebaceta (?-) + Elfel + Nazarduus + heleno + Vita + Abycor + Thalim + Thabin + Thea + Ancior + Leo + Thanatos + La + On + gesa + Emanuell + et per omnia nomina dei sanctissima quatinus tu Askariell in ista gemmam christalli intres etc. ut supra sine mora certissime venias in persona tua propria veraciter in pulcra forma et certum in capito tuo portas te visibiliter mihi demonstres et omnibus circumstancius cito apparias et tuas socios mihi adducas ut te et illos aptissime videre possimus [170] per sentum [*preceptum] meum et coniurationem meam, et per omnia que tibi iussero: et si hec non feceris ego te in virtute et per virtutem dei et per potestatem sanctorum nominum suorum condemno te Askariel in infernum et in ignem eternum usque ad ultimum diem Iudicii fiat fiat fiat.	I conjure you, Askariel, through him who is + Alpha and Omega + the beginning and the end, and through these sacred names of God which are: + Eli + El + Erros + Jesus + fortis + fontis + Salvator + Eloy + Theos + deus + omnipotentes + hiceteca + sabatho + Agramo~ + virtus + loth + ho~le~ (?) + histerion + Adonay + risus + Beabaco + Tetragramaton + Ageos + feneton + craton + saton + lexaon + messias + lactea + Alte + Appanas + heles + helibe + Tocipaton + Oratos + holos + Age + pate + regum + Abraca + brata + legota + Ely + Victor + Osanna + conhibenebaceta (?-) + Elfel + Nazarduus + heleno + Vita + Abycor + Thalim + Thabin + Thea + Ancior + Leo + Thanatos + La + On + gesa + Emanuell + and through all the most holy names of God, that you enter this crystalline gem etc. (as above) come quickly, without delay, truly in person, in a fair form, wearing a garland on your head, and visibly explain to me with all details, and may you appear quickly, and may you lead your associates to me, so that it will be possible to see you and them clearly, by my [170] order* and my conjuration, and by all which I have ordered of you: And if you do not act on these, in the power and by the power of God and by the power of his holy names I will condemn you, O Askariel, into hell and into the eternal fire until the day of Final Judgement.

* Original wording "sentum." Corrected per the similarly worded passage below.

Et condempno te Askariell per virtutem omnium creaturarum qui sunt in celis et in terris et Infernis, ego N. N. aplico tuas penas nisi veraciter compleas desiderium meum ergo maledicti te Askariel Recognosce sentenciam tuam per virtutem domini nostri Iesu Christi Amen, Amen, Amen.	And I condemn you, O Askariel, through the virtue of all creatures which are in the heavens, on the earth, or in hell. I N. N. impose punishment on you unless you truly fulfill my desires. Therefore, being cursed, O Askariel, acknowledge your sentence through the power of our Lord Jesus Christ. Amen, Amen, Amen.
Citius accedas et ad me venias et omnia interrogata veraciter mihi respondeas et quod semper et sine mora cum invocavero ad viscionem meam ac preceptum meum venias in omnibus horis Amen. Amen. Amen.	May you quickly approach and come to me, responding honestly to all questions, and do so always without delay when I call, appearing at all times to my vision and perception. Amen. Amen. Amen.

Fifth Conjuration

Ad huc Coniuro te Askariel per alia nomina dei sancta que sunt reverendissimo, vero + dominus + Leto [*Leta?] + Apnes [*Apres?] + Eloy + Vstra + gloriosus + bonus + on + Vnigenitus + via + vita + manus + homo + ysion + principium + finis + fons + et Origo + paraclitus + splendor + sol + gloria + Lux + Imago + panis + flos + vitis mons Ianua + petra + lapis Angnilaris [*Angularis] + pastor + propheta + sacerdos + Athanatos + Kiros + Theon + panton + ysus + Agerion + Vlla + Abbimagothereth + Iheun + Eros + conhapea (?) + Sannagh (?) + ut in ista gemmam cristalli intres etc Sicum ut supra.	From here I conjure you, O Askariel, through the other holy names of God, which are most awe-inspiring, True + Lord + *Leta + Apnes [Apres]* + Eloy + Ustra + Glorious + Good + On + Onlybegotten + The Way + The Life + The Hand + Man + Ysion + The Beginning + The End + The Fountain + and The Source + Paraclete + The Brilliance + The Sun + The Glory + The Light + The Image + The Bread + The Flower + The Vine + The Mountain + The Gateway + The Rock + The Cornerstone + Shepherd + Prophet + Priest + Athanatos + Kiros + Theon + Panton + Ysus + Agerion + Vlla + Abbimagothereth + Iheun + Eros + Conhapea (?) + Sannagh + so that you will enter into this crystal gemstone as said before.

* Compare Folger p. 133.

Sixth Conjuration

Ad huc Coniuro te Askariell et con-stringo et adiuro te per bonitatem dei et per ieiunium dei, et per circumcitionem Christi, et per hoc nomen Ineffabile + Tetragrammaton + et per patientiam Christi, qua mortuus est sustitatus, et per humilitatem qua deus pedes suorum dissipulorum lavit, et per spineam coro-nam quam deus in capite suo habuit, et per passionem Christi, et per clavos qui-bus manus et pedes Christi perforati fuerunt et per crucem Christi, et per mortem Christi et per lanceam qua latus Christi perforatum fuerit in cruce et per acetam quod potavit, et per sanguinem et aquam que de Christo latere emana-vit, et per Invocationem dulcissimam quae ante deum patrem omnipotentem invocavit, et per figuram [*scissuram] templi et virtutem qua obscuratus est soll et tenebras facti sunt, et per sepul-crum in quo positum est Jesu Christi, et per hac nomina supradicta,

Coniuro te Askariell et tibi precipio qua tenus in ista gemmam cristalli in hac hora statim sine mora certissime venias et persona tua propria veraciter in pul-cra forma et fertum in capite tuo por-tans et te visibilliter mihi demonstres et omnibus circumstantibus cito apparias in ista gemma cristalli in hac hora statim et sine mora ut intres tu Askariel in ista gemma christalli sine mora certissime venias in persona tua propria veraciter in pulchra forma et certum in capite

I conjure you again, O Askariell, and constrain and adjure you by the good-ness of God, and by God's (Christ's) fasting, and by Christ's circumcision, and by this ineffable name + Tetragram-maton + and by Christ's suffering, who died and rose again, and by the humility with which God washed the feet of his disciples, and by the crown of thorns which God had on his head, and by Christ's suffering, and by the nails which pierced Christ's hands and feet, and by the cross of Christ, and by Christ's death, and by the lance which pierced Christ's side on the Cross, and by the vinegar which he drank, and by the blood and water which came from Christ's side, and by the most sweet invocation which he made before God the almighty Fa-ther, and by the *tearing of the veil in the temple, and by the power which hid the Sun and made it dark, and by the tomb in which Jesus Christ was placed, and by those names mentioned above.

I conjure you, O Askariell, and order that you enter this crystalline gem in this hour, come quickly, without delay, truly in person, in a fair form, with a garland on your head, and visibly explain to me in all details, and may you appear quickly in this crystal, in this hour, quickly and without delay, and enter into this crystal gem, O Askariel, and may you lead your associates to me, so that it will be possible to see you and

tuo portans ut te vissibilliter mihi demonstres et omnibus circumstantibus cito apparias et tuos socios tecum adducas sicut et illos apertissime videre possimus per preceptum meum et coniurationem meam, et per omnia que tibi Iussero, et si hec non feceris ego te in virtute et per virtutem dei et potestatem sanctorum nomen suos condempno te Askariel in infernum et in ignem eternum usque ad ultimum diem Iuditii fiat fiat fiat Amen nisi citius accedas et ad me venias et ad meam Interrogatam vera respondeas et quod semper et sine mora cum te vocavero voluntatem meam et preceptum meum venias in omnibus horis fiat fiat fiat Amen Amen Amen.

them clearly, by my order and my conjuration, and by all which I have ordered of you: And if you do not act on these, in the power and by the power of God and by the power of his holy names I will condemn you, O Askariel, into hell and into the eternal fire until the day of Final Judgement. Fiat, fiat, fiat. Amen. Amen. Amen. Unless you quickly come to me and answer truthfully my questions, and that you always come without delay when called, obeying my wishes and orders at any time. Fiat, fiat, fiat. Amen. Amen. Amen.

For making a stolen item return again

Fast for one day, and when you go to sleep, or to your bedroom, put a burning candle next to you, and have these names written on your right hand: Acherim, Charitates, and Melchor, and you will dream truly of the things that were stolen.

An experiment to see in thy sleep whatsoever thou shalt desire. Psalm 4

First say the Psalm, "*Cum Invocarem exaudivit me deus*" ["Answer me when I call to you, O God"],[659] and thou shalt come to this verse, "*Irascimini et nolite peccare*" ["tremble and do not sin" (verse 5)], and say it three times, in the end of the Psalm say, "*Kyrie leizon Christe eleyzon, kyrie eleyzon: pater noster Ave Maria et creedo in deum*" ["Lord have mercy; Christ have mercy; Lord have mercy; Our Father.... Hail Mary.... I believe in God...."]. Then write these Greek names or words in virgin parchment: + Agla + Leta + Yskyros + Mediator + Eleyson + Panton + Craton + In the name of our Lord Jesus Christ life everlasting. Wrap it in virgin wax, and put it under your head and sleep upon it, and thou shalt see in thy sleep what thou wilt desire.

---

659. Psalm 4.

[171]

To know whether one suspect be the thief or no

Write the names [660] of these whom thou hast in suspicion in virgin parchment, and our Lord's name also + Alpha + and Omega + and put everyone in a ball of clay by himself, then make a circle of this fashion following, and set a basin of water in the midst of it, and put all the balls therein. Then say this Psalm three times, "*quicunque vult salvus esse*" ["Whoever will be saved"],[661] kneeling once, standing once, lying once, and then shall his name that is guilty rise. If there be none guilty, the Lord's name will rise. Bero + Barto + Bartoras + quinquiel, consuratur est:

This must be done on a Wednesday and under Mercury.[662]

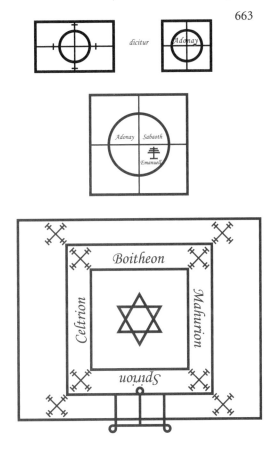

---

660. Compare Sloane 3846, 43r and 71v.

661. The Athanasian Creed.

662. In marg: "223"; below that in left marg: "w"; in right marg: "222 – 6 (?)."

663. First includes the word *dicitur* ["it is said"], perhaps indicating a second variant. The third square has "Boitheon, Mahurion, Spirion, Celtrion." Compare Folger p. 68, where the four kings' names are spelled "Theltrion, Speryon, Boytheon, and Mayeryon or Maorys." Another analogue in Wellcome MS. 110, 94v, reads "Boicheon + Machniron + Spirion + Celtrion +." Also Rawlinson D. 252, 103r: "Theltrion, Spirion, Botheon, Mahyrion (or Mahireon)." Also Sloane 3853, 91r: "Teltrion + Sireon vel Spirion vel Spirdon + Bethereon vel Betheron + Mahireon vel Mahereon."

Whoever has this sign in their house, nothing can be removed from the house, but it will always be bound until the owner returns.

[172]

Satan [+Conjuration of the Spirit][664]

665

If you wish to invoke the spirit Satan, make a circle with the polished sword, and also make it with clay or with quicklime, because I have tested this. But beware that you make nothing unless it can be completed in one hour, in whatever hour you wish, around the middle of the hour, and you should be clean on account of the holiness of the names. Here is that invocation with which you can compel the demon, so that he will immediately provide a true answer, when you wish to know the truth. From the invocation Solomon congregated the names.

But first, before making the invocation, you must fast for three days on bread and water in honour of our Lord Jesus Christ, and of the sacred names whose power you do this with.

On the fourth day, when you wish to operate, make a circle as shown below, and say the following while making the circle:

+ orion + Musion + Tetragramma-ton + יהוה + fons + virtus + sapientia + deus +	+ Orion + Musion + Tetragramma-ton + יהוה + the Spring + the Virtue + the Wisdom + God +

---

664. In right marg: "243."

665. Seems to have been inspired by Boaistuau and Fenton, *Certaine secrete wonders of nature* (1569), 110, depicting "a Monster, having the shape of the face of a man, who was taken in the forrest of Haneberg, in the yere. 1531."

And when you have done this, stand in the middle of the circle and say:[666]

Deus qui hominem ad Imaginem tuam formasti, et post ea eum in paradizo constituisti, et Evam ei ad societatem tradidisti, propter eos Adam et Evam in mundo venisti, et ut peccata nostra Redimeris a sede Maiestatis patris tui in uterum virginis descendisti, circum cidi, et baptizari, et mortem pati, deinde resurgens a mortuis, ad celos ascendisti, post spiritum sanctum tuum Apostolis tuis mirabiliter transmicisti.	O God who formed man after your own likeness, and then placed him in Paradise, and gave him Eve to keep him company, because of them, Adam and Eve, you came into the world from the seat of your Father's majesty, in order to redeem us from our sins you descended into the womb of a virgin, were circumcised and baptized, endured death, and were reborn from the dead, ascended into Heaven, after you miraculously transmitted your Holy Ghost was to your Apostles.
Te exoro clementissime deus ut me ab omnibus Insidiis diaboli, et a malis conserva digneris, qui vivis et regnas deus per omnia secula seculorum Amen.	I beg, O most merciful God, that you deign to preserve me from all snares and malice of the Devil, through you who lives and reigns, God forever and ever. Amen.

O Almon + caron + Staron + Deyron + rex fortis qui dominaris in omnibus qui omnia ex nichillo fecisti, qui Lucifferum de celo eiecisti, et Angelos in eo credentes cum eo. te exoro clementissime deus per sanctissime nomina que superioris nominari, et per hoc nomen maximam + Iskiros + et per hoc nomen + Agla + ut valeam Satan ad meam voluntatem Coniurare coram compellere, ut in pulcra forma veniat et appareat vel servum suum per se mittat qui super ea que abs ea Interrogavero verum Responsum exibeat et faciat ea que ei precipero.	O Almon + caron + Staron + Deyron + mighty King who is the master of all things, who made all things from nothing, who expelled Lucifer from Heaven, along with those angels who believed in him, I beg O most merciful God, by the most holy names which are the greatest to be names, and by this greatest name + Iskiros +, and by this name + AGLA + that I have the strength to conjure Satan's presence according to my will, that he comes and appears in a fair form, or else sends his servant, to furnish a true answer, and he and they may do as I have ordered.

---

666. In marg.: "w" glyph.

The prayer completed, say: [667]

O Satan qui temptatisti dominum mundi, te per eum diem (?) dominum, Coniuro et Impero, ut tu ipsem venias vel unum de fatellibus tuis, qui mihi super ea que te vel ipsum Interrogavero verum responsum exibeas. O Satan Coniuro te per excellentissima nomina dei vivi, quod sunt hac + Almagros + Ismagros + Achiriachim + Almatrolos + quibus non potest recistere aliquis malignus spiritus quin ut venias vel servum tuum pro te transmittas qui mihi super hiis, que ab eo interrogavero verum responsum exibeat + Agios + Otheos + Agios + Iskiros + Agios + Athanatos + Agla + Erigerio + deus meus [+turris fortitudinis] a facie Inimici mei.	O Satan, who tempted the Lord of the world, I conjure and command you by the same Lord, that you come yourself, or one of your attendants, and moreover to provide true answers to my questions. O Satan, I conjure you by the most excellent names of the living God, which are these: + Almagros + Ismagros + Achiriachim + Almatrolos + which no evil spirit is able to resist, that you come, or send your servant on your behalf, to provide true answers to my questions + Agios + Otheos + Agios + Iskiros + Agios + Athanatos + Agla + Engerio + O my God, [+ be a tower of strength] in the face of my enemies.

Then say:

In manus tuus domine, commendo spiritum meum Redemisti me domine deus veritatis Amen.	Into your hands, O Lord, I commend my spirit. You have redeemed me, O Lord God of truth. Amen.

O Satan qui temptatisti dominum mundi, te per eum diem (?) dominum, Coniuro et Impero, ut tu ipsem venias vel unum de fatellibus tuis, qui mihi super ea que te vel ipsum Interrogavero verum responsum exibeas. O Satan Coniuro te per excellentissima nomina dei vivi, quod sunt hac + Almagros + Ismagros + Achiriachim + Almatrolos + quibus non potest recistere aliquis malignus spiritus quin ut venias vel servum	O Satan, who tempted the Lord of the world, I conjure and command you by the same Lord, that you come yourself, or one of your attendants, and moreover to provide true answers to my questions. O Satan, I conjure you by the most excellent names of the living God, which are these: + Almagros + Ismagros + Achiriachim + Almatrolos + which no evil spirit is able to resist, that you come, or send your servant on your behalf,

---

667. In marg: "244."

tuum pro te transmittas qui mihi super hiis, que ab eo interrogavero verum responsum exibeat + Agios + Otheos + Agios + Iskiros + Agios + Athanatos + Agla + Erigerio + deus meus [+turris fortitudinis] a [+facie] Inimici mei.	to provide true answers to my questions + Agios + Otheos + Agios + Iskiros + Agios + Athanatos + Agla + Engerio + O my God, [+ be a tower of strength] in the face of my enemies.

Then say:

In manus tuus domine, commendo spiritum meum. Redemisti me domine deus veritatis Amen.	Into your hands, O Lord, I commend my spirit. You have redeemed me, O Lord God of truth. Amen.

[173]

Then:

Coniuro te Satan per nomina maxima + Yskiros + et Ala + et hac nomina Sancta + Athanatos + Engelat + Almarios + Archiriachim + Almatillos + On + Tetragramaton + יהוה + α + et ω + ut mittare (?) michi prendam (?) ex Angelos eius quos superius nominavi veritatem demonstre.	I conjure you, O Satan, by the greatest name + Yskiros + and Ala + and these holy names: + Athanatos + Engelat + Almarios + Archiriachim + Almatillos + On + Tetragramaton + יהוה + Alpha + and Omega + to send me one of his angels whom I have named above, to disclose the truth.

O Almon + Caron + Staron + Deyron + rex fortis, qui dominaris in omnibus qui cuncta ex nihil fecisti, qui Lucifferum propter superbia eiecisti, et cum Angelos in eo credentes, te exoro clementissime deus, per sanctiissima nomina qui superius nominavi, et per hoc nomen maximum + Iskiros + et per hoc nomen + Agla + ut valeam Satan ad meam voluntatem, Coniurare et coram me compellere ut in pulcra forma compareatur, vel compareant, vel Servum suum per se mittat, qui super ea que eum Interrogavero verum responsum exibeat et faciat que ei precepero, quia	O Almon + Caron + Staron + Deyron + mighty king, who is the master of all things, who made all things from nothing, who expelled Lucifer from Heaven, along with those angels who believed in him, I beg, O most merciful God, by the most holy names which are the greatest to be names, and by this greatest name + Iskiros +, and by this name + AGLA + that I have the strength to conjure Satan's presence according to my will, that he comes and appears in a fair form, or else sends his servant, to furnish a true answer, and he and they may do as I have ordered. Because I am

ego nonsum tanti momenti aut meriti, ut Angelum Luces Andeam Rogare in hiis rebus et eo obcansam peto Angelum Tenebrarum qui mihi de re dubia certitudinem dicet nec me terreat, neque alicui creature noceat, sed in pulcra forma coram me compareat et super eaque eum Interrogavero, veritatem demonstret.	not of great importance or merit, that I would dare to ask an angel of light for these things, therefore I ask an angel of darkness to declare the truth regarding these uncertain things, and may he not frighten me, nor harm any creature, but may he appear before me in a fair form, and moreover may he reveal the truth concerning all that I will ask.
O domine Iesu Christe que semper es propicius peccatorem rogantem bono in animo exaudi et costodi corpus meum et Animam meam, ab omni periculo et mecum sis nunc et semper Amen.	O Lord Jesus Christ, who always kindly hears a sinner seeking goodness in his heart, hear and guard my body and soul from all danger, now and forever. Amen.

After praying, say:[668]

Coniuro te Satan per omnes virtutes celorum per Angelos et Archangelos, per Tronos et dominationes, per principatus et potestates, per Cherubine et Seraphine et per Asistentes Angelos ante Tronum dei, qui assidue cantat, gloriam in excelsis deo et per Infinita seculorum secula Amen.	I conjure you, O Satan, by all the powers of Heaven—by the Angels and Archangels, by the Thrones and Dominations, by the Principalities and Powers, by the Cherubim and Seraphin, and by all the angels standing before the throne of God, who continually sing "glory to God on high," and by the infinite ages of ages. Amen.
Coniuro te Satan per beatem virginem Mariam Matrem domini nostri Iesu Christi quem virgo concepit, virgo peperit, et virgo fuit ante partum, et post partum, virgo per mansit, coniuro te Satan per sancta Iohanem Baptistam et per omnes baptizatos in nomine patris et filii et spiritus sancti Amen.	I conjure you, O Satan, by the blessed Virgin Mary, mother of our Lord Jesus Christ, who was conceived by a virgin, born of a virgin, and remained a virgin before giving birth and after giving birth. I conjure you, O Satan, by Saint John the Baptist, and by all the baptized, in the name of the Father, and the Son, and the Holy Ghost. Amen.

---

668. In marg.: "245."

Coniuro te Satan **per** sanctam Johanem Evangelistam et **per** omnes Evangelistes, Matheum Marcum, et Lucam, et **per** omnes Martires et Confessores dei, ut ad me venias aut velociter mittas ad me Servuum tuum per te et in nomine tuo, qui super ea qui eam Interrogavero verum responsum exhibeat et faciat quod ei precepero.	I conjure **you**, O Satan, by Saint John the Evangelist, and by the other evangelists—Matthew, Mark, and Luke, and by all martyrs and confessors of God, that you come to me quickly, or else send one of your servants in your name, who will answer my questions truly, and accomplish whatever I order.

Coniuro te Satan **per** omnes patriarches, et **per** Sanctam Moysem, et **per** omnes prophetas, et **per** Sanctum petrum et per omnes Apostolos, et per centum quadraginta quatuor milia signatos et beatos in conspectu dei et Agni, ut ipse venias vel servum tuum ad me mittas ut super ea que eum Interrogavero verum responsum exibeat.	I conjure **you**, O Satan, by all patriarchs, and by Moses the saint, and by all prophets, and by Saint Peter, and by all the Apostles, and by the one hundred forty-four thousand sealed and blessed in the sight of God, and of the Lamb,* that you come yourself, or send one of your servants, to give true answers to my questions.
* Revelations 7.	

Iterum coniuro te Satan **per** hac nomina dei + Algramay + Saday + Diagramay + ut ad me venias vel servum tuum per te mittas et statim cum voluero, et cum precipiam recedas, et super hijs abs te Interrogavero verum responsum exibeas.	I **again** conjure **you**, Satan, by this name of God + Algramay + Saday + Diagramay + that you come to me or send your servant, and immediately at my wish, and leave when I order you to leave, and moreover give a true answer to whatever I will ask.

Iterum coniuro te Satan **per** omnia potentiam dei, et **per** eius virtutem et **per** coronam dei, et **per** capitum suum, et **per** omnia membra dei, et **per** omnia que sub deo sunt, et **per** celum et terram mare et omnia que in eis sunt, **per** tonitruum altito nantes [*intonantes?], et **per**	Again I conjure **you**, O Satan, by all the power of God, and by his virtue, and by the crown of God, and by his head, and by all of God's limbs, and by everything that is beneath God, and by the sky, the earth, the sea, and everything that they contain, by the *resounding

| omnia celestia terrestria et Infernalia, ut velociter ad me venias vel servum tuum ad me mittas qui super ea que eum interrogavero, verum responsum exhibeat et faciat quod ei precepero. | thunder, and by all celestial, terrestrial, and infernal creatures, that you quickly come to me, or send your servant who will answer my questions truly, and accomplish whatever I order. |

| Iterum coniuro te Satan per tremendum diem Iudicii adiuro te ut in quantum poteris adveniendum festines ad voluntatem meam perficias astrictus et constrictus per eum qui vivit et regnat per omnia secula seculorum Amen. | Again I conjure you, O Satan, by the terrible Day of Judgment, I adjure you that as much as you are able, that you come quickly and fulfill my will, constrained and bound, through Him who lives and reigns forever and ever. Amen. |

When the large circle N. has been made, make a small circle in this fashion, as shown below, with ʒo ∆∆ −∧⅃, +o ⅄⅄ ɔ,, in which the spirit will appear ⫙ X. At the entrance of the circle you must write: *Iesus Christus + Agla + Adonay +* ["Jesus Christ + AGLA + Adonay +"], and after you have entered, as shown in the following circle, observing that he must write: *mihi domine* ["to me O Lord"] in the farthest circle, as the lower part.

[174]

Here follows the circle for the spirit called Satan.[669]

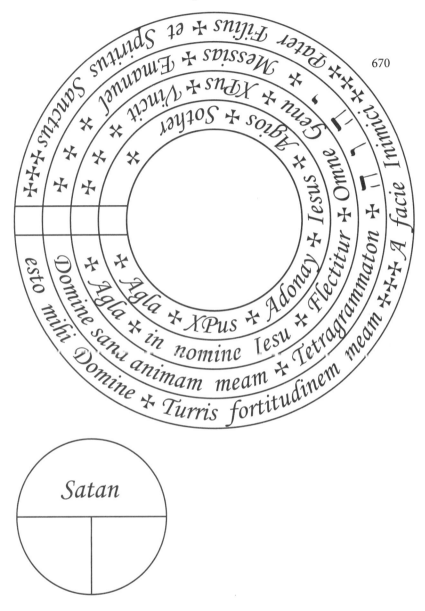

---

669. In right marg: "245."

670. The text reads: *esto mihi domine turris fortitudinem meam a facie inimici* ["you shall be to me, O Lord, a tower of my strength, in the face of enemies"]. The "domine" is abbreviated "dne" with a tilde above the n.
Next line reads: *D[omi]ne [sana] animam meam* ["O Lord, [heal] my soul"], etc.
Third line: + *Agla* + *in nomine Iesu* + *flectitur* + *omne genu* + χρus *VINCIT* + + + ["+Agla + in the name of Jesus + all knees + bend + Christ conquers +++"].
Next line: *Agla* +χρus + *Adonay* + *Iesus* + *Agios* + *Sother* +

[175]

Concerning all days and hours.

Experiment concerning the spirit called Baron, Baaran, Bareth, or Baryth

This experiment can be done at any time or any respectable place, whether an open place or a room, with a seat (?) and country house if necessary.[671]

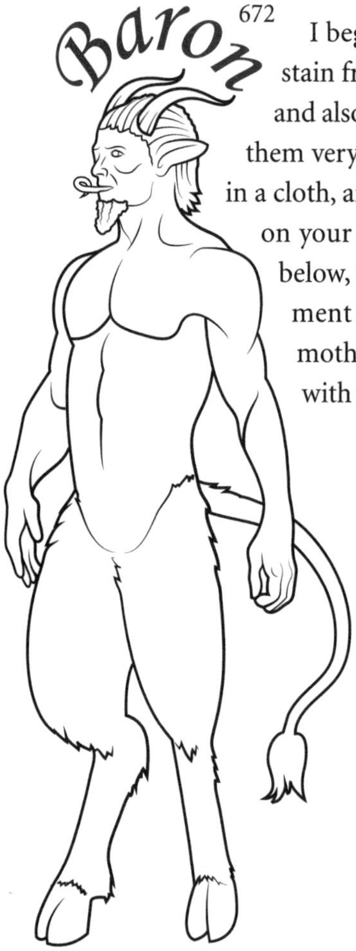

Baron[672] I begin a time-honoured experiment. For three days abstain from sexual gratification, and fast on bread and water, and also wash your whole body, and clip your nails and make them very clean—hands and feet, and you should guard them in a cloth, and when you wish to begin the work, you should put on your linen shirt. Then draw the circle in earth as shown below, with the consecrated sword. Then take virgin parchment from a small dog which has not sucked from its mother's breasts, and write on it the following characters with the blood of a lapwing or a mole.[673]

---

671. Wellcome MS. 110: *sive in domo, sive in agro, sive extra domum, sive in villa sive extra* ["whether in a house or field, or outside the house, or in a country house or outside it"].

672. Perhaps inspired by Boaistuau and Fenton, *Certaine secrete wonders of nature* (1569), 30, showing the conversation between St. Anthony and a satyr.

673. The Latin reads *upupa*, but see note on Folger p. 40. Again, the editors strongly condemn mistreating any animals.

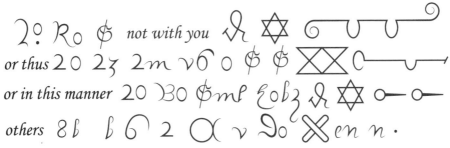

or thus

or in this manner

others

And when you wish to try the experiment, take the sheet of paper in your right hand, and say three times in a row Psalm 51 *"miserere mei deus"* ["Have mercy on me, O God"],[674] standing in the middle of the circle after you have spoken, afterwards say the following conjuration until the spirit appears.

Conjuration

Coniuro te spiritum nomine Baron per fidem quam debes socio tuo dno [*demoni] privato, per virtutem et veritatem dei veri et viui et miserecordissime, et per illum [+ angelum] qui tuba canit in die Iudicii et dicet venite venite venite, et per omnes Angelos, Archangelos, Tronos, dominationes, principatus, potestates, cherubin et Seraphin, Adiuro te Baron per penas domini nostri Iesu Christi, per patibulum crucis in quo suspensus est, per clavos quibus confixus est, per lanceam quam perforavit latus	I conjure you, O spirit named Baron, by the loyalty which you owe to your private servant demon,* by the power and truth of God, living and true and most merciful, and by that angel who will blow the trumpet on the Day of Judgment and say "come, come, come," and by all Angels, Archangels, Thrones, Dominations, Principalities, Powers, Cherubin, and Seraphim. I adjure you, O Baron, by the punishment of our Lord Jesus Christ, and by the gibbet of the Cross on which he was suspended, and

* Following parallel version of this text on Folger p. 179 and Wellcome MS. 110, 42v; Folger: dnō, but a reading of *domino* ["to the lord/master"] wouldn't fit as well. Elsewhere, "your private demon" or "your private associate/servant."

---

674. Psalm 50 (KJV 51)

eius, per spineam coronam quam in capite suo portavit, per mortem eius, per resurrectionem eius, per ascentionem eius, per septiformam Sancti spiritus gratiam, per sigillum Salomonis, per lapidem Angularem, et per virtutem qua sol absturatus est et petrae scissae sunt, et monumenta aperta sunt, et multa corpora que diu dormierunt resurrexerunt, per virgam quod Mare aparuit et per virgam Aaron, per thronum dei, per Thuribelum aureum, per candelebrum aurem, per archam federis, et per Altare aurem quod est ante occulus eius, per mensus pro positionum et per Sanctos et Sanctas.

by the nails which fastened him, and by the lance which pierced his side, and by the crown of thorns which he wore on his head, and by his death, and by his resurrection, and by his ascension, and by the seven-fold grace of the Holy Ghost, by the Seal of Solomon, by the power which obscured the sun and crumbled the stones, and opened the tombs, and resurrected the bodies of many saints who slept,[*] and by the staff which parted the sea, by the staff of Aaron, by the throne of God, by the golden censer, by the golden candelabra, by the Ark of the Covenant, and by the golden altar which is before his eyes, by the weighing of the facts, and by all saints—male and female.[†]

---

[*] Matthew 27:51–52.

[†] Compare Folger p. 40. Wellcome MS. 110 and Sloane 3853 read *per omnes missas prophetarum* ["by all the Masses of the prophets"]. Since this is evidently structured on Revelations 8:3, it originally probably read something like *per omnes preces sanctorum et sanctarum* ["by all the prayers of the saints"].

Coniuro te spiritus qui vocaris Baron, per gloriosam virginem Mariam Matrem domini nostri Iesum Christi que filium dei portavit, et per sanctissimum lac eius quod gloriosus deus per os suum suscepit vocatus Athanatos, Lux, Eloy, Vasaday, Emanuell, Arsetice et per sanctum Semiphoras, et per nomen Adonay quo dominus media nocte clamavit, ad quam vocem omnes mortui boni ac mali in ictu occuli resurgent, et per nomen Sother + in quo dominus frangit omnes lapides terrae et omnia

I conjure you, O spirit who is called Baron, by the glorious Virgin Mary, mother of our Lord Jesus Christ, who carried the son of God, and by her most holy milk which the glorious God accepted into his mouth. He is called Athanatos, Light, Eloy, Vasaday, Emanuel, Arsetice, and by the holy Semiphoras, and by the name Adonay, which the Lord proclaimed in the middle of the night, which being called all the dead—good and evil—will be raised up in the blink of an eye, and by the name Sother

edificia in uno die adversus distruere et debellare et tunc dicet montibus cadete super nos, et collibus Apere nos, et per Inestimabile nomen + yay + in quo dominus Iesus peracto Iudicio diabolum cum se peresis et cum omnibus suis Impiis in carcerem i.e. in stagnum ignis triumphali gloria in celestem patrem revertetur.

Coniuro te Baron et exorcizor te ut spiritus humile sis cum omnibus tuis sociis, per benedictum nomen dei in firmamento caeli et per laudibile virtuosum admirabilem creatorem mundi A sanctis sanctorum.

Coniuro te iterum Baron, per Angelos domini et ceelos dei, per solem et lunam et per stellas celi, et per imbrem et rorem et omnes spiritus dei, coniuro te per ignem et aestum frigus et estatem, per glacies et nives noctes et dies, per lucem et tenebras, per fulgura et nubes, coniuro te N per terram et omnia elementa, per montes et colles, per omnia germinantia in terris, per fontes et maria flumina et omnia que moventur in aquis, per omnes volucres celi, per omnes bestias et peccora, et per omnes filios hominum et Israelis. Per sacerdotes et omnes Servos dei, [176] et per omnes

+ by which the Lord crumbles* all stones of the earth and all buildings in a single day, demolishes and vanquishes opponents, "and then the living will say to the mountains, fall upon us, and to the hills: cover us",[†] and by the inestimable name + Yay + by which Jesus the Lord will be returned to carry out judgment against the Devil with all his wicked, who will be consumed in the lake of fire,[‡] and the triumphant glory of the Heavenly Father will be restored.

I conjure you, O Baron, and exorcize you, that you be humble, along with all your associates, by the blessed name of God in the firmament of Heaven, praiseworthy, virtuous, admirable creator of the universe from the Holy of Holies.[§]

I again conjure you, O Baron, by the angels of the Lord, and by the heavens of God, and by the Sun and Moon, and by the stars in the heavens, and by the rain and the dew and all the spirits of God, I conjure you by the fire and the raging heat, by the winter and the summer, by the ice and snows, by night and day, by light and darkness, by the lightning and the clouds. I conjure you, O N.[¶] by the earth and all the elements, by the mountains and hills, and all that sprouts forth

---

* Folger p. 134 and Wellcome MS. 110: *faciat* ["made"].
† Luke 23:30.
‡ Revelations 20:9.
§ Instead of a *sanctis sanctorum* the parallel texts read in *secula seculorum* ["forever and ever"].
¶ It is interesting to see the generic "N." here instead of "Baron" or "Barachin" in the parallel texts. Maybe an indication of an earlier archetype?

spiritus et Animas Iustorum dei, et per omnes humiles corde et per Ananiam Azaariam et misaell, et per pulmonem hepar domini, et per omnia interiora membra eius ut cito venias ad me et facias et compleas quecunque tibi dixero etc.	on the earth, and by the springs and seas and rivers, and all that moves in the waters, by all the birds in the skies, and by all the beasts and cattle, and by all the children of mankind and Israel. By all the priests and servants of God, *[176]* and by all the spirits and souls of the just of God, and by all those of humble heart, and by Anania. Azaria, and Misael,* and by the Lord's lungs and liver, and all his internal organs, that you come to me quickly and accomplish whatever I ask you.

* Or Hanani'ah, Azari'ah, and Mish'ael from the Benedicite, i.e., Daniel 3:66.

Then immediately Baron himself will come to you in the form of a man, and tell you whatever you wish, and then you may make your petition and he will answer, and if you wish he will transport whatever you desire, and will carry it to wherever pleases you, and after he has fulfilled everything he will say to you, give me leave to depart, and then give him his freedom, and order him to return whenever you call by conjuration. Then say three times:

Recede in pace.	Depart in peace.

675

Circulus Baron

Order what you wish, and it will be done, then licence him thus:

In nomine patris et filii et spiritus sancti ite in pace ad loca vestra et pax sit inter nos et vos, parati sitis venire vocati.	In the name of the Father and the Son and the Holy Ghost, depart in peace to your place, and peace be between you and us, and be ready to come again when called.

Then, if he be stubborn and do not appear, then pronounce this, which is Solomon's bond:

O N., by the virtue, might, and power of this most great and unspeakable name of God + Tetragrammaton + and in the virtue and power of this name + Tetragrammaton + which was written in a plate of gold in the forehead of Aaron the high priest, I conjure thee into the depth infernal and bottomless pit of hell, there to be tormented with extreme torments until the last and dreadful day of doom, except thou come and fulfill my will and commandments, O N. This if thou deny to do, then God the Father, the Son, and the Holy Ghost curse and condemn thee from this same hour forever and ever in the fiery lake of hell, and make thee partaker of some and all of those hellish and horrible torments, O N., except thou come and fulfill my will and obey my precept and commandments. Heaven and earth curse thee and condemn thee unless thou speedily come and appear visibly unto me, and fulfill my commandments truly and unfeignedly, without fraud or guile. This, if thou do not, then all the members of the blessed be unto thee everlasting torments, O N., thou most wicked

---

675. Text reads + *IHS* + *Messias* + *Emanuell* + *Sother* + *Eloy* + *Agla* + *IHS* + *Nazarenus* + *Rex* + *Iudeorum* ["Jesus, Messiah, Emanuel + Saviour + Eloy + Agla + Jesus + of Nazareth + King + of the Jews"]. Inside: *Circulus Baron[is]* ["Circle of Baron"].

and obstinate spirit, except thou come and fulfill my will and commandments, then like as this M. doth consume in this noisome stink, so by the virtue, power and strength and force of this holy name of God + Tetragramaton + I condemn thee into the most terrible pains and punishments forever, this grant O Lord Jesus Christ which in the unity of the Trinity liveth and reigneth with God the Father, for ever and ever. Amen.

[+ Saint] George

Whoever wishes to know the abundant truth concerning anything stolen, veiled, or suspected, first select a virgin and proper person, and make a circle in a secret location, the Sun being very clear, and make the first seat inside, then scrape[676] the thumbnail of the right hand, then anoint it carefully with olive oil, while saying the following words:

O sancte Georgi mile Christi Coniuro te per dominum nostrum Iesum Christum per sanctissimam virginitatem gloriosissime virginis Marie Matris eius et per virginitatem lactis quod ipse succit ab uberibus Matris sue, et per virginitatem gloriosissi matrium (?) virginum, Innocentium martirum et per totum posse quod deus habent in terra et aqua and in aere in igne et in celo et in sede sua, et per sanctissima resurrectionem, suam quod vos in ungula pollicis dextre manus istius pueri in tua cathedra	O Saint George, soldier of Christ, I conjure you by our Lord Jesus Christ, by the most holy virginity of the most glorious Virgin Mary, his mother, and by the virgin milk which he sucked from the breasts of his mother, and by the virginity of the most glorious virgin mother, the innocents, martyrs, and by the whole capacity which they have, O God, in the land and water, in the air, fire, and sky, and in his seat, and by his most sacred resurrection, that you appear in the nail of your right thumb of the whole

---

676. Compare Thomas Hearne, *Remarks and Collections of Thomas Hearne. 3, May 25, 1710–December 14, 1712* (Oxford: Clarendon Press, 1889), 365, which quotes from a text attributed to one Master John de Belton circa 1391. In de Belton's text, the thumbnail is scraped with a new knife with a white handle. Jean-Patrice Boudet, *Entre Science et Nigromance: Astrologie, Divination et Magie Dans L'occident Médiéval, XIIe-XVe Siècle* (Paris: Publications de la Sorbonne, 2006), 398–399, also mentions an onychomancy exsperiment attributed to John de Belton in a fifteenth-century manuscript.

cathedra sedens hilaris apereas ostendens tales res, [177] Hominem vel Mulierem furtum sive aliqui de aliud ita puer isse possit cognoscere sine aliquo nocumento vel Impedimento per donum quod dedit nobis	capacity which they have, O God, in the land and water, in the air, fire, and sky, and in his seat, and by his most sacred resurrection, that you appear in the nail of the right thumb of this boy sitting in your seat, cheerfully showing such things,* [177] the man or woman theft, or anything else about it, such that the boy himself can recognise it, without any harm or hindrance, by the gift that has he gave to us.
* At bottom is another "res," seemingly indicating the first word of the following page?	

And if he fails to appear at first, read it a second and third time, and without doubt he will appear, provided the child is good. If not, it should be read, and when the blessed George has appeared, say "the boy desires that he may discover the identity of the thief, or other person who was able to harm him, without any defect," and he will tell you himself. Tested 1,000 times.

The figure of the mirror

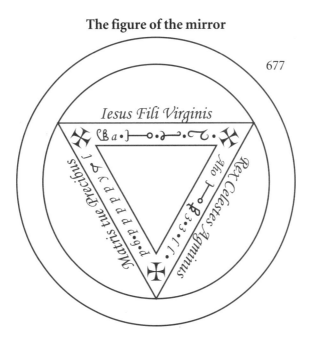

677

Iesus Fili Virginis

---

677. Words read: *Iesus fili virginis, Rex celestes Agminus, Matris tue precibus* ["Jesus, son of the Virgin, heavenly king Agminus, of your mother with prayers"]. *Agminus* could be a mistake for *agminum* ["of troops"].

Whoever **will carry these names on themselves will not be able to be arrested or detained by anyone.** • 2 • Ica are the highest names • 2 • Alma, Aloy, En plausmum Samuel, El + G + L + A + .[678]

[178]
Romulon [679] [+ Conjuration of the Spirit]

The most noble experiment is elegantly begun, whereby you call the spirit called Romulon, **which is in fact for stolen treasure, or all most true works, certifying that this is the infernal spirit** Romulon, **under the power of all small or great demons, and he is willing to satisfy the wishes of whoever prepared the circle by three conjurations.**

In the beginning, have two associates with you in the circle, and one holds that cross made from palm which will be blessed on the day of the palm branches, and the

---

678. "Ica" is pehaps a mistake for *ista* ["these"]. Also, ".2." is perhaps an abbreviation for "i.e."
679. In right marg.: "84."
680. Perhaps inspired by Boaistuau and Fenton, *Certaine secrete wonders of nature* (1569), 61.

master and associate kneel and say these Psalms: "Have mercy upon me, O God..."[681] and "Whoever will be saved...."[682] Repeat these with great devotion to each of the four parts of the circle. Then the master says this oration with good devotion:

Coniuro vos omnes demones magnos atque parvos, per omnias [*omnes] potentias domini nostri Iesu Christi ut vos faciatis illum spiritum Romulon festinare in pulcherima pulcra forma qua potestis et ipsum mittere nobis ut Narrat nobis veritatem de hac re N quam querimus per eius qui venturus est Iudicare vivos et mortuos et seculum per ignem Amen. Coniuro vos omnes demones maiores atque minores per deum vivum, per deum verum per deum sanctum.	I conjure all you demons great and small, by all the powers of our Lord Jesus Christ, that you make the spirit Romulon hasten to us in a pleasant or beautiful form, or send yourself to us, to tell us the truth in these things N., which we are seeking, by him who will come to judge the living and the dead and the world by fire. Amen. I conjure all you demons great and small, by the living God, by the true God, by the holy God.

Coniuro vos per totum corpus domino nostri Iesu Christi et per omnia verba dei.	I conjure you by the whole body of our Lord Jesus Christ, and by all the words of God.

Coniuro vos per omnia opera dei. Coniuro vos per omnia mirabillia dei.	I conjure you by all the works of God. I conjure you by all the wonders of God.

---

681. Psalm 50, 55, and 56 (KJV 51, 56, and 57) all start with these words.

682. The Athanasian Creed, given in full on Folger p. 28.

Coniuro vos per omnia nomina dei effabilia et Ineffabilia et per illa verba que non licet hominum loqui, et per omnia gaudia beate Marie virginis. Iterum Coniuro vos per quinque vulnera domini nostri Iesu Christi sanctam Trinitatem, per omnes virtutes et potestates quas deus dedit hominibus, herbis, verbis, et lapiddibus; Iterum Coniuro vos demones per ista sacratissima nomina dei + Sabaoth + On + Arphentex + Panton + Craton + Deminon + Eristimon + Gero + et per summum nomen dei + Tetragramaton + et per nomen + Athanatos + et per illum nomen excellentissimum dei + A + g + l + a + et per illum qui dixit fiant omnia et facta sunt omnia Iterum Coniuro per omnia predicta verba dei, ut faciatis illum spiritum Romulon militem festinare et nobis sine mora et narrare nobis veritatem cum viva voce quod possumus audire intelligere et audire sine aliqua falcitate et nocumento alicuius creature totius mundi et sine tempestate, tonitruo fulmine, pluvia, et vento, nive et grandine, et ab omnibus tempestatibus et respondere nobis Iam ad presens, per eum qui venturus est Iudicare vivos et mortuos et seculum per ignem.

Coniuro vos ad huc per virginitatem atque virtutem beate maria virgines, et per virginitatem atque virtutem beate Iuliane virginis, beate katherine virginis, et per virginitatem atque virtutem beate Margarete virginis, per virginitatem

I conjure you by all the speakable and unspeakable names of God, and by all those words which people are not permitted to speak, and by all the joys of the blessed Virgin Mary. Again I conjure you, by the five wounds of our Lord Jesus Christ, the holy Trinity, and by all the virtues and power which God has given to people, herbs, words, and stones. Again I conjure you demons, by these most holy names of God + Sabaoth + On + Arphentex + Panton + Craton + Deminon + Eristimon + Gero + and by the highest name of God + Tetragrammaton + and by the name + Athanatos + and by this most excellent name of God + A + G + L + A + and by Him who spoke "Let it be" and all things were. Again I conjure you by all the preceding words of God,[*] that you make the spirit soldier Romulon hasten to us without delay, and tell us the truth with a lively voice that we will be able to hear and understand, without any falsehood or harm to any living creatures throughout the world, and without storms, thunder, lightning, rain, wind, snow, or hail, and free from all storms to answer us now regarding the present, by him who will come to judge the living and the dead and the world by fire.

I conjure you here by the virginity and the virtues of the blessed Virgin Mary, and by the virginity and the virtues of blessed virgin Juliana, the blessed virgin Katherine, and by the virginity

---

[*] This suggests that this conjuration was adapted from one which contained a longer list of the words which God spoke at the creation, such as on Folger pp. 129 and 217.

atque virtutem beate Agathiae virginis, per virginitatem beate Cicilie, virginis.

Iterum Coniuro vos per virginitatem atque virtutem beate Eliene virginis, et per virginitatem atque virtutem omnium virginum et per virginitatem atque virtutem beate Iohannis Baptiste, et per virginitatem atque virtutem Sancti Iohannis Evangeliste.

Coniuro per virginitatem atque virtutem domini nostri Iesu Christi, et per omnes Martires et confessores dei, et per omnia verba et nomina dei, ut faciatis illum spiritum Romulon hue[ce] venire ad visum nostrum in forma [179] et specie pulcherime hominis et dicere nobis omnem veritatem sine aliqua falcitate et nocumento alicuius creature tocius mundi, et sine aliqua tempestate, per eum qui venturus est Iudicare vivos et mortuos et seculum per ignem. Amen.

and the virtues of the blessed virgin Margaret, and by the virginity and the virtues of the blessed virgin Agatha, and by the virginity and the virtues of the blessed virgin Cecilia.

Again I conjure you by the virginity and the virtues of the blessed virgin Eliene, and by the virginity and virtues of all the virgins, and by the virginity and the virtue of the blessed John the Baptist, and by the virginity and the virtues of St. John the Evangelist.

I conjure you by the virginity and the virtues of our Lord Jesus Christ, and by all the martyrs and confessors of God, and by all the words and names of God, that you make that spirit Romulon come here, visible to us in the form *[179]* and appearance of a most beautiful person, and to speak to us only the truth, without any falseness or harm to any living creatures anywhere in the world, and without any storms, by him who will come to judge the living and the dead and the world by fire. Amen.

Then the master humbly asks, saying:

Deus qui misisti Sanctum Tuum Spiritum super Apostolos tuos, mitte spiritum sanctum tuum super nos famulos, et super istum circulum ut illuminet et clarificet intellectum nostrum, ut in spiritum veritatis videre possumus et audire creaturas tuas ut nobis revelent omnem veritatem de rebus quas quesiti sumus qui vivis et regnas deus per omnia secula seculorum Amen.	O God, who has sent* your Holy Ghost over the Apostles, send your Holy Ghost over your servants, and over this circle, that it may illuminate and clear our understanding, that in the spirit of truth we may be able to see and hear your creatures, that they may reveal the whole truth concerning the things which we have been asking, by him who lives and reigns God through all the ages of the ages. Amen.
* Compare Sloane 3853, fol. 56v–57r.	

Then the master says: [683]

O spiritus miles Romulon, Coniuro te per fidem quam debes demone privato, Coniuro te spiritus romulon per purificationem dei. Coniuro te romulon per purificationem beate Marie virginis. Coniuro te romulon per Immundiciam Infernalem, Coniuro te romulon per idem maledictionem qua deus maledixit Caine, ut vos paratis illum venire huc festinanter, narare nobis veritatem Iuxta huc circulum. Coniuro te romulon et vos demones per spoliatorem Inferni Iesum Christum, et per prophetiam Sancti Iohannis Baptiste, per tabulas Moysy, per virtutem Sancte Michalis qui vos de celo expulcit et gloriosum Cyprianum Martirem qui vos suo nutu sub in~ ugauit [*subiugavit?], et per Salomon[em etiam] p[ruden]tissimum	O spirit soldier Romulon, I conjure you by the loyalty which you owe to (your) private demon.* I conjure you, O spirit Romulon, by the purification of God. I conjure you, O Romulon, by the purification of the blessed virgin Mary. I conjure you, O Romulon, by the infernal foulness. I conjure you, O Romulon, by the same curse by which God cursed Cain, that you prepare that one come here quickly next to this circle, to tell us the truth. I conjure you, O Romulon, and you demons, by Jesus Christ's plundering of hell, and by the prophesy of Saint John the Baptist, and by the tablets of Moses, and by the strength of Saint Michael whereby you were expelled from Heaven, and by the glorious martyr Cyprian, who subjugated you with

683. Compare parallel text for Mosacus on Folger p. 182 and Wellcome MS. 110, 71r. Compare Lansdowne MS. 795 as quoted in Elliot Stock, *The Bibliographer*, vol. 5 (New York: J. W. Bouton, 1884), 104. The British Library catalogue describes the Lansdowne MS. as "A collection of charms, conjurations, and exorcisms, in Latin; probably extracted from the Flagellum Dæmonum or some such work, by some person in the seventeenth or eighteenth century." In. right marg: "85."

qui vos suis fecit obedire mandatis, et per tremendum diem Iudicii, per vulnus lateris Iesu Christi, et per vulnera manum et pedum eius, per Anunciationem et praedicationem, per mortem et sepulturam, per resurrectiionem et ascentionem, et Spiritus Sancti missionem, per ipsum et eius patrem, et omnes sanctos ac gloriosus Apostolos et omnes virtutem celorum, et per septem dolores beate Marie virginis matris Christi, per suo filio, et quique eis gaudia, et per assumptionem et coronationem eiusdem gloriose virginis et instantissime vos etiam Coniuro te romulon per illud excellens nomen dei Ineffabile et infinite virtutis et tremendum + Tetragrammaton + quod in Anulo meo sculptum est, ut quid in isto ooptro Imperiali sculptum est, quatenus virtute omnium predictorum et specialiter istius venerandi nominis ad me celeriter accedas, et absque tonitruo, corustantibus vel horibilibus tonitruis, et sine horribili strepitu mihi apperere non tardabis et meo semper Imperio veniens cum obediens quatenus in te agnoscatur quante magnifficentie est nomen suum quod a quibuslibet adoretur tam celice terrenis et infernalibus, et per virtutem patris omnipotentis sui que benedicti filii ac paracliti qui unus deus et Trinus vivat et regnat in secula seculorum Amen.

his command, and also by the most wise Solomon, whose orders forced you to obey, and by the terrible Day of Judgement, and by the wound on the side of Jesus Christ, and by the wounds on his hands and feet, by the annunciation and proclaiming and death and burial, by the resurrection and ascension, and the mission of the Holy Ghost, by its self and his Father,[*] and all saints and glorious Apostles and all powers of Heaven, and by the seven sorrows of the blessed Virgin Mary, mother of Christ, and by her son, and each of her joys,[†] and by the assumption and coronation of the same glorious virgin, and I also conjure you most urgently, O Romulon,[‡] by that eminent name of God, ineffable, infinitely powerful and awe-inspiring + Tetragrammaton + which is carved on my ring, and on this imperial sceptre, inasmuch as by the power of all the preceding, and specifically of that venerable name, that you quickly come to me, and without thunder, flashing, or terrible thunder, and without terrible noise, that you always come without delay at my command, with obedience, insasmuch as you have recognized how vast is the greatness of that name of his, that it is so honoured by heavenly, earthly, and infernal beings, and by the power of his almighty Father, who lives and reigns with the blessed Son and the Paraclete, one God and Trinity, forever and ever. Amen.

---

* Compare *Verus Jesuitarum Libellus* ["The True Petition of the Jesuits"] included in vol. 2, p. 835 of Scheible's *Das Kloster* (1845).

† Prayers and meditations on the seven sorrows and joys of Mary were immensely popular in medieval times. See Eamon Duffy, *The Stripping of the Altars: Traditional Religion in England*, c. 1400– c. 1580 (New Haven, CT: Yale University Press, 1992), 257–259.

‡ In marg: "86."

Coniuro **te** romulon **et vos demones, per** Angelos **et** Archangelos, Tronos **et** dominationes, **per** principatus **et** potestates, **per virtutem celorum et omnia mirabilia** Iesu Christi, **et per eiectionem demonum de hominibus, et per flagellacionem eius, et per illum** Sanctissimum **cruorem defluentem a latere pedibus et manibus et omnibus eius corporis, partibus, et per omnia terrabilia in celo et in terra, et per** Angelos **bonos vestros dominos +** Analazabin **+** paripabazin **+** Collatizantin **vell, collizantu et ad huc coniuro et adiuro te** romulon **et requiro te in virtute crucifixi qui maior est omnium, et per eius nomen +** Tetragrammaton **+ quod est nomen honourabile et terribile ac etiam amabile, cuntis Christianis, et terribile demonibus, quatenus sine omni mora et dilacione mihi visibiliter apareas absque simulacionem et fraude et versucia qualicumque et mihi ad Interrogata fideliter respondeas, et meo Iussui omnium obedias, per virtutem** domini nostri **Iesu Christi** qui vivit et regnat **deus in secula seculorum Amen.**

I conjure you, O Romulon, and you demons, by the Angels and Archangels, by the Thrones and Dominations, by the Principalities and Powers, by the heavenly Virtues, and all the miracles of Jesus Christ, and by the expulsion of demons from men, and by his whipping, and by that most sacred blood flowing from his side, feet, hands, and all parts of his body, and by all terrible things which are in heaven and on earth, and by your masters the good angels + Analazabin + paripabazin + Collatizantin (or, collizantu),* and I conjure and adjure you here, O Romulon, and seek you in the power of the crucified one who is greatest of all, and by his name + Tetragrammaton + which confers honour and fear, but also inspires love in all Christians but fear in the demons. Therefore, appear to me visibly, without delay or postponement, and without pretence or fraud, or cunning of any kind, and faithfully respond to all that I ask, and obey all my orders,† by the power of our Lord Jesus Christ, who lives and reigns God forever and ever. Amen.

---

* Compare *Jesuitarum Libellus*, Cypriani citation angelorum: "Orphanim: Aralim: Hasmalim: Cherubim: Seraphim: et Malachim: per ternam dmonum damnationem: per hos angelos bonos: Malazim: Peripalabin et Calizantin." Also compare Wellcome MS. 110, 69v: "Citò imprecor, requiro atque exoro jam vos: o Almaziel, Ariel, Anathamia, Ezebul, Abiul, Ezea, Ahesin et Calizabin angelos Dei sanctissimos per omnes dominationes" and op. cit. 71v: "...Analazabin pephalsalin et colatizaltin."

† The words "omnibus pareatis et" should probably be supplied as in Wellcome MS. 110.

And if he come not within three hours, then curse him.

The bond of obedience [684]

Coniuro te spiritus et adiuro, per illud Infinitum verbum que cuncta creata sunt, cum dixit deus fiat et factum est. Requiro et adiuro te romulon Ibidem extra circulum vissibiliter apparens per bonitatem dei quam hominem ad Imaginem suam plasmavit et te per Iustitiam qua primos parentes nostros dampnavit, et per miserecordiam qua redemit, per virginitatem et humilitatem Marie virginis sacratissime matris domini nostri Iesu Christi, et per potestatem qua Infernum confregit et socios tuos spoliavit et cruciavit, ut mihi de quesitis a te per me fideliter dicas responsum ut numquam in eisdem fallaciam facias.

Coniuro te romulon sapientissime spiritus per obedientiam quam superioribus tuis adhibere debes, et per hoc sacratissimum nomen dei + Tetragramaton + quod in Summitate Sceptri huius et in Annulo meo cerius [*cernitis] veraciter obedientiam mihi virtute huius sacratissimi nominis in quantum permisses es celeriter facias, et si tu non possis Immediate incedens per aspersionem sanguinis Iesu Christi, aliam vel alios celeriter adducas qui potestatem habet et scientiam, mihi fideliter respondere de singulis rebus quas volueris et sine quacunque fraude simulacione et fallatia ad meum desiderium veraciter

* Adam and Eve.

I conjure and adjure you, O spirit, by that infinite word through which all things were created; when God spoke "let it be," and it was done. I demand of you and adjure you, O Romulon, into that place outside the circle, appearing visibly through the goodness of God, who made people after his own image, and you by the justice which has condemned our first parents,* and by the mercy which has redeemed us, by the virginity and humility of Mary the most holy virgin mother of our Lord Jesus Christ, and by the power which shattered the lower region and plundered and tormented your associates, that you provide reliable answers to my questions, and without any deceit.

I conjure you, O most wise spirit Romulon, by the obedience by which your superiors summon you, and through this most holy name of God + Tetragramaton + which you can perceive on the head of this scepter and on my ring, that you quickly make true obedience to me with the power of this most sacred name, as much as you are permitted, and if you are not able to come immediately, then by the sprinkling of the blood of Jesus Christ, quickly send another or others who have the power and knowledge to answer reliably to all of the things that I have wished, and without

---

684. Compare Wellcome MS. 110, 58r. In marg: "87."

adimplere ipso prestante cuius vera et sapientia [180] Salomon peritissimus te sibi obediencialiter subiugavit, et hac auctoritate Imperet qui sine fine vivit et regnat deus in secula seculorum Amen.	any sort of fraud or pretense or deceit, to appear in person to fulfill my desires truly, as you obediently subjugated yourself to the true and wise and most skilled *[180]* Solomon, and with God himself supreme, who lives and reigns without end, forever and ever. Amen.

Now when he is come, and standeth still, constrain him by this conjuration following

Coniuro te spiritus per obedientiam quam virtute huius benedicti nominis + Tetragrammaton + deo et mihi facias, et per ineffabilem eisdem nominis potenciam, et per Michalem Archangelum qui demones subiecerat Infernales in Infernum, et per Annunciacionem beate Mariae virginis Matris domini [+ nostri] Iesu Christi, et per eius Nativitatem, passionem et mortem, et Resurrectionem, et per Ascentionem, et per indefinentem fluxum lacrimas [*lacrimarum] beatissime Marie virginis, et (?) [in] sui filii passione et morte, [et per obumbracionem solis in sua morte, et per scissuram veli templi in eius morte] et per omnia que unquam fuerunt Scta [*facta] in celo, et in terra, vell Inferno, ut mihi Iam de omnibusque Interrogavero, et sine fraude sine terrore et mendacio qualicunque mihi fideliter respondeas ut certus de Inquisicionibus effectus ipso	I conjure you, O spirit, by the obedience you have shown to God and to me by the power of this blessed name + Tetragrammaton + and by the ineffable power of the same name, and by the Archangel Michael, who has subjugated the infernal demons into hell, and by the annunciation of the blessed Virgin Mary, mother of [+ our] * Lord Jesus Christ, and by his birth, passion, death, resurrection, and ascension, and by the unending flow of tears of the blessed Virgin Mary[†] at her son's suffering and death, and by the darkening of the Sun and the tearing of the veil in the Temple at the time of his death,[‡] and by all those which have been shed in Heaven, on Earth, or in Hell, that you reliably respond now to all that I will ask, without deceit or terror or fraud of any kind, that reliable inquiries are completed, with God the highest himself, Father, Son, and Holy

---

* Folger has a space, presumably for "nostri" in black ink.
† This section uses some different abbreviations (e.g., the -9 =-us has a tail here) and irregular t/c orthography (such as annunciaciõe), which probably partially imitates the older manuscript being copied.
‡ Matthew 27:51. This is evidently dislocated below, as evidenced by the reading in Sloane 3853, the actual timeline of the passion, and the stricken-through text.

summo deo patri filio et spiritu sancto deo et vivo et vero gratias referam te cui laudes refferam et graciarum acciones prestante in circumscriptibili Trinitate qui unus est et erit in eternum Amen.	Ghost, the living and true God I will bring gratitude, to whom I will bring praises and excellent acts of gratitude which can be written about, who is Trinity in Unity, and will be eternally. Amen.[*]

* Compare Sloane 3853, fol. 19r; Wellcome MS. 110, 58v-59r; D 388, 15.

Here follows the licence:[685]

Coniuro te romulon benigne spiritus per illud Indicibille templum et Salomonis preparavit summo deo et per omnia elementa, et per illud nomen excellentissimum et sculptum in summitat septri meo viz nomen + Tetragrammaton + quatenus quod nunc recedas pacifice requi esse, sine ? corusca pluvio et ventus, et quibuscunque tempestate, et alios cum te Invocavero vel sotios tuos citius quo poteris ad me sine mora veniatis nec turbare me valeatis nec laboretis ad perturbandum me nec socios meos per virginitatem domini nostri Iesu Christi filii dei vivi viventis in secula seculorum Amen.	I conjure you,[*] O kind spirit Romulon, by that unspeakable temple of Solomon, which he prepared to God on high, and by all the elements, and by that most excellent name which is carved on the top of my sceptre, which name is + Tetragrammaton + that you now retire peacefully, without lightning, rain, and wind, and any kind of storms, and the others whom I have invoked along with you, or your associates, but come quickly to me when called, without disturbance or trouble to me or my associates, by the virginity of our Lord Jesus Christ, son of the living God, living forever and ever. Amen.

Iterum Coniuro te romulon spiritum per omnia tremendum et horribilem in terra et in Inferno, et per tremendum diem Iudicii. Coniuro te romulon, coercio exoro et mando per sanguinis domini nostri Iesu Christi, et per virtutem omnium predictorum in isto Libro scriptos et consecratos, ut expectes donec licencia	Again I conjure you, O Romulon, by everything terrible and awful on Earth and in hell, and by the terrible Day of Judgment. I conjure you, O Romulon, I compel, persuade, and order you by the blood of our Lord Jesus Christ, and by the power of all the preceding that is written and consecrated in this book,

685. Compare Sloane 3850, 128v; Sloane 3853, fol. 21r–v; and Wellcome MS. 110, 59v. In marg: "88."

fueris ame et quando recederis recede in pace et quiete ad loca tua dibita summo Iudice sine corusca pluvio et tempestate et sine nocumento corporis mei et anime mee et socios meorum hic aliter existe, et sine Nocumento cuiuscunque creature dei cuiuscunque generis sine spe extiterit et terrore, et ad huc coniuro te romulon mando et ligo te per virginitatem omnium nominum predictorum quod in isto libro scriptum et consecratum est, ut no venias ad me temptare, necere me in diebus neque noctibus nec socios meos amodo, nequ alios socios tuorum vell spiritus pro te, et ad huc coniuro, exoro, premando, et ligo te per omnium nominum predictorum et per nominatum, et in isto libro scriptum et consecratum et spes [*specialiter] istius nominis venerandi + Tetraagrammaton +, et cum vocavero te statim Citisse festinatissime et celeriter mihi apereas in quo loco ego te Invocavero vell assignavero in pulchra forma humana, et sic expectabis in illo loco donec licencia fueris a me, et hoc facies absque pluvio et tempestate terrore, et si invenio te vell socios tuos rebelles vell contra coniurationem et voluntatem meam, condemno te et socios tuos in Inferni et maledico te per [+ Dei] vivi et veri vel omnia miraculorum Christi Iesu, et tunc omnes sentencias et male et quod in isto Libro scripti sunt descendat super te et socios tuos, et nichill hoc feceris.

that you wait until you are dismissed by me, and when you depart, depart peacefully and quietly to your rightful place, as appointed by the highest judge, without lightning, rain, or storm, and without harming my body or soul, or those of my companions, and without disturbing any creatures of God of any kind, without spectacle or terror, and still I conjure you, O Romulon, and I order and bind you, by the virginity of all those named previously, which are written and consecrated in this book, to not tempt me, or harm me by day or night, nor my companions henceforth, nor any of your companions or spirits on your behalf, and furthermore I conjure, exhort, and order you, and bind you by all the previous names, and by all the names which are written and consecrated in this book, and specifically* this venerable name + Tetragrammaton +, and come immediately whenever I will call you, and quickly appear to me in whatever place I will call you or assign you to, in a fair human form, and then wait in that place until I have dismissed you, and do this without rain or storms or terror, and if I discover that you or your associates rebel or resist my conjurations and will, I will condemn you and your associates to hell, and I will curse you by the living and true [+ God], and by all the miracles of Christ Jesus, and then all decrees and misfortune which are written in this book will descend upon you and your associates, and you will accomplish nothing thereby.

---

* Compare parallel passages, e.g., Folger p. 104.

Coniuro te ut nulla requiem habeas vel habere poteris a modo et usque in eternum, sed multipliciter pene tue Innumerabiliter graviores quam prius sicut stelle celi, et sic expectabis donec licentia fueris a me et sub coniurationem istius et omnium istorum prenominatorum vade in pace et pax domini nostri Iesu Christi sit inter me et te, et inter socios meos et socios tuos, et situ desideras vell socii tui desiderat aliquem spiritum per vobis habere thesaurum, maledictionem et omnes sentencie prenominate descendat super te et super socii tui Amen Amen. Amen.	I conjure you, that you may have no respite from now to eternity, but rather your punishments will increase innumerably as the stars in the sky, and so you will be waiting until dismissed by me, and under this same conjuration, and all those previously named: "go in peace, and may the peace of our Lord Jesus Christ be between me and you, and between your associates and my associates," and if you or your associate desires any spirit to have treasure from you,* the curse and all previously-named sentences will descend upon you and upon your associates. Amen. Amen. Amen.

* The Latin seems to be corrupt here, and JHP hasn't found any parallel texts to help clarify the intent.

Romulon his cir[c]le is the book which came out of Derbyshire fol. 55.[686]

[181]

Mosacus [+ Conjuration of the Spirit]

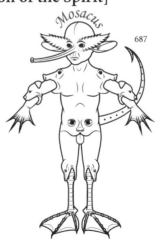

686. This is in brown ink. At the bottom of the page is a flourish in pencil, resembling a serpent, obviously inserted at a later date.

687. Figure seems to have been inspired by Boaistuau and Fenton, *Certaine secrete wonders of nature* (1569), 14, where it is described as follows: "This hideous monster… was born in base Pologne, in the noble city of Cracouie, in ye month of Februarie and yeare of grace, 1543, or as some write, 1547, and upon the even of the conversion of S. Paule… who after he had lived foure houres died, saying only: Watch, the Lorde commeth."

First make a circle upon the ground[688] with a palm[689] hallowed upon Palm Sunday, saying: *in nomine patris et filii et spiritus sancti* ["in the name of the Father, the Son, and the Holy Ghost"]. Amen. Then strew the ashes of palm so hallowed about the circle, saying as above. Then make a + on thy forehead with ashes, saying: *in nomine patris et filii, et spiritus sancti* ["in the name of the Father, the Son, and the Holy Ghost"] etc.

Then put thy right foot into the circle, saying: *in nomine patris* ["in the name of the Father"] etc. and there stand still, saying:

Benedicat me imperialis maiestas, protegat me divinitas, custodiat me sempiterna deitas, foveat me gloriosa unitas, defendat me Immensa Trinitas, dirigat me inestimabilis [*ineffabilis] bonitas, regat me potentia patris, vivi[fi]cet me sapientia filii, Illuminet me virtus spiritus sancti, [salvet me +] α et ω deus et homo sit mihi famulo tuo N vocatio ista saluus et protectio in eternum + Iesus transiens per medium illorum, Ibat in pace Amen.	May the imperial majesty bless me; may the Divinity protect me; may the eternal Deity guard me; may the glorious Unity favour me; may the infinite Trinity defend me; may the priceless [*ineffable] * Goodness direct me; may the mighty Father rule over me; may the wise Son vivify me; may the virtuous Holy Ghost enlighten me, [save me] † Alpha and Omega, God and Man. May I, your servant N., the same one who is calling, have health and protection forever. + But Jesus passing through their midst, went his way.‡ Amen. §

* Perhaps an error for "ineffabilis" as on Folger pp. 99 and 101, however Sloane 3849 also reads "inestimabilis."
† So Sloane 3849.
‡ Luke 4:30.
§ Compare Folger pp. 99 and 101.

688. Compare Sloane 3849, fol. 19r, with drawing of circle: "Here after ys shewed the cerkle and a commune exorzysynge for cercles owght to be hallowyd and sprynklyd with holly watter. / Make on the grond a cerkle with palm tre that ys holowyd on palme sonday sayng In nomine patris *altissimi* filii *sapientissimi* et spiritus sancti *paraclite* ["in the name of the *most high* Father, the *most wise* Son, and the Holy Ghost the Paraclete ('comforter')"] Amen. And with the asshes of the palme strewe abowt in the cerkle sayng in nomine patris *altissimi* filii *sapientissimi* et spiritus sancti *paracliti* Amen. *than cast in the cerkle holy watter sayng In nomine patris and filii et spiritus sancti Amen.* And then make a cross on thi forhede say In nomine patris &c. Then put thy Ryght fott in to the cerkle sayng *In nomine patris* ["in the name of the Father"] and Benedicat me + custodiat me sempiterna deitas + ..." Compare also Wellcome MS. 110, fol. 41r.

689. In reality, during the Middle Ages, the "palms" consecrated on Palm Sunday would typically have been yew, box, or willow. See Duffy, *The Stripping of the Altars*, 23. These objects were believed to have apotropaic qualities.

[690]This done, thou art safe and needest to fear nothing, for there may no spirit come within that circle, but I warn thee come not out of thy circle until thou have avoided the spirit, for if thou do, he will slay thee without the great mercy of God defend[ing] thee. Therefore I command thee in the name of God to keep thee within thy circle till thou have made an end.

Make thy circle seven foot from the midst to the brim, and stand[691] in the midst thereof thyself, and that with steadfast faith. Note thou art at liberty to stand or sit. Then make a circle 2 foot broad and seven foot from the other circle[692] and write the spirit's name therein and bid him appear in likeness of a child of three years of age with a red head, and he will heave from the ground about a shaftment,[693] but look not too much on him, for it is not wholesome, and if thou wilt, thou mayest have two fellows with thee.[694] And then thou mayest call any spirit thou wilt for what faculty thou wilt, and write in new vellum[695] thy intent, and cast it out of thy circle unto him, and bid him to fulfill thy will, and doubtless it shall be done shortly,[696] and he will tell thee how you may have your purpose, and by this invocation you may call any spirit that you will, for this invocation this spirit may not withstand, for it was the secrets of Solomon.

In Nomine patris pa[ra]cliti et filii et spiritus sancti Amen. Mosacus spiritus veni festinate.	In the name of the Father Paraclete ("advocate"), and the Son, and the Holy Ghost. Amen. O spirit Mosacus, come quickly.

Coniuro te spiritum nomine Mosacum per deum patrem omnipotentam, per deum vivum, per deum verum per deum sanctum, qui te de paradiso eiecit,	I conjure you, O spirit named Mosacus, through God the almighty Father, through the living God, through the true God, through the holy God, who cast you

---

690. Sloane 3849 adds "Then kneele downe in the cerkell apon thi knees sayng ther a *pater noster* and *ave* and a *crede,* then *confiteor* and *misereatur* and the absolucion then this psalme Iudica me deus [Ps42] with gloria patri deus in nomine tuo, deus misereatur nostri with thys sequence: Alma chorus domini And then thou art sayffe...."

691. Sloane 3849: "ther stand sytt or kneel."

692. Sloane 3849: "assynyth hiym in a cerkle of two foote broade in as fayre a colloure as he may..."

693. Shaftment: the length across the hand, measured from the end of the extended thumb.

694. Sloane 3849: "thou mayst have ii or iii felowes with thee in the cerkyll."

695. Sloane 3849: "wrytt hym in parchment or vellum...."

696. Sloane 3849: "he wyll fullfyll thyn Intent Anon that shall be don ffor he wyll do more in a howr then thow wyll do in vii yeare."

et per hec sacra sancta nomina + Messias + Sother +Emanuell + Sabaothe + Adonay + Otheos + Athanatos + hely + panton + Craton + Ysus + Eleyson + Alpha + et Omega + Iesus + Christus + Nazarenus + Rex Iudeorum + On + El +. Per hec sacra sancta nomina coniuro te Mosacus per nomen dei principalis + Tetragrammaton + homousion + Amorison +, et per hec nomina + Onas + oo + Man + Delabogramaton+ Sanctum + Altonat + Spirion + regon + On + Ongon + Agla + hely + heloy + lamazabatany + et per sanctam Mariam Matrem domini nostri Iesu Christi, et per omnes sanctos et sanctas dei, et eorum virtutes, et merita preciosa, [182] Et per quinque vulnera Iesu Christi, et per omnes Sanctos et Sanctas dei et eorum virtutes, et per merita preciosa, et per virginitatem beate Maria virginis ac Sancti Iohannis Baptiste et Evangeliste, et per hoc nomen + Maoth + et Mohosthe + Naoth + et Nohesthe + per quem Salomon te constringebat, ut ubicunque fueris statim et sine mora te in pu[l]chra forma pueri 7em Annorum mihi monstres habens colorem album et rubicum capitem [*capillum]. O Mosacus spiritus te Invoco per fidem quam debes demoni tuo privato, et per virtutem dei viui veri piissimi et potentissimi, et per omnes

out of Paradise, through these holy sacred names + Messias + Sother + Emanuel + Sabaoth + Adonay + Otheos + Athanatos + Hely + Panton + Craton + Ysus + Eleyson + Alpha and Omega + Jesus + Christ + of Nazareth + King of the Jews + On + El +. Through these sacred holy names I conjure you, Mosacus, through the principal name of God + Tetragrammaton + Homousion + Amorison +* and through these names + Onas + Oo + Man + Delabogramaton+ Sanctum + Altonat + Spirion + Regon + On + Ongon + Agla + Hely + Heloy + Lamazabatany + and through Mary the holy mother of our Lord Jesus Christ, and through all the saints of God, male and female, and their virtues and precious merits, *[182]* and through the five wounds of Jesus Christ, and through all the saints of God, male and female, and through the virginity of the blessed Virgin Mary, and through Saint John the Baptist and the Evangelist, and through these names + Maoth + and Mohosthe + Naoth + and Nohesthe +† by which Solomon constrained you, that wherever you might be to come at once and without delay, in the form of a handsome boy seven years old, showing yourself to me having white colour and red hair.‡§ O spirit Mosacus, I invoke you through

---

* Sloane 3849: "tetragramaton + the prynsypall [=principal]; name of god Ionas et me~nelaba gramaton homo usion...."
† Sloane 3849: "by this name [sic] mahot and nahot."
‡ Or perhaps *caput* ["head"].
§ Sloane 3849: "shewe thy sylfe to me In a fayre shappe of a man and that thow hast most whytysh coller."

Angelos Archangelos, Tronos, et dominationes, virtutes, principatos, et potestates, cherubine et seraphine, et per omnes reliquas sanctorum et sanctarum, que in universo mundo continentur neque in celo, et si hoc sit verum quod Maria fuit virgo ante partum in partu et post partum, et si hoc sit verum quod hostia Christi que de pane fit vertitur in corpus domini nostri Iesu Christi, sic fit verum ut visibiliter in circulo hic tibi assignato appereas, et per ista nomina que sunt maxime in Nicromancie Artis sillicet + Balsac + super Balsac, + Sarie + Sarapye [*Sararye?] + pomulion [*romulion?] + de sed sarporis in potestate + Aye + per quem aque restuunt et elementa concuciuntur vel gremitentur, et per ista nomina Iubeo te per charitatem dei et occulos eius, et per omnia membra eius, et per divinitatem, Maiestatem, et dietatem eius per potestatem et humilitatem eius, et per omnem bonum et malum que quatuor elementa sustinentur, ut ubicunque fueris statim in ictu occuli appereas et monstres mihi in forma pueri septem Annorum et Imples omnem desiderium meum in vero et debito modo secundum velle meum, et nullo modo Anime mee seu corpori meo vell Aliquibus membris meis offerre Aggravare seu nocere poteris, ne quicunque

the loyalty which you owe to your private demon, and through the virtue of God, living, true, and most holy and mighty, and through all Angels, Archangels, Thrones, Dominations, Virtues, Principalities, Powers, Cherubim, and Seraphim, and through all the relics of the saints—male and female—which are contained on the whole world and not in heaven, and if it is true that Mary was a virgin before giving birth, as well as after giving birth, and if it is true that the consecrated host of Christ is the bread which is turned into the body of our Lord Jesus Christ, then it will be true that you will appear visibly in the circle that has been assigned to you, and through these names which are powerful in the art of necromancy, namely + Balsac + over Balsac, +Sarie + Sarapye | Pomulion + but from their seat they grant (?) power + Aye +* by which the waters were held back and the elements are shook violently or consumed by fire, and by these names I order you by the love of God, and by his eyes, and by all his limbs, and by his divinity, the greatness, and deity, by his power and humility, and by all the good and evil which are sustained by the four elements, that now wherever you are in the blink of an eye appear and show yourself to me in

* Sloane 3849: "Balsake sarie super balsake panulon in power & help they do graunt to all noiat [=troubled?] thyngs from their sette...."

spiritus sub dei potestate poterit nec ali-cui Animali creature nec domi nec Campanile quibuscunque factis a deo vel ordinatis quovismodo nocere aggravare seu offendere poteris nec quicunque spiritus malignus sub dei potestate poterit, sed tu vell illi michi demonstres seu demonstrent et veraciter mihi respondeas aut unus vestrum mihi veraciter respondeat non sofisticaliter nec figmentaliter, sed sicut fuit, est, et erit, in facto de presentibus preteritis et futuris ad omnia que que exte Interrogabiuntur vell ex illis et sic fiat per ipsum deum cui est honor et gloria, virtus, Imperium, Iubilatio deitas humanitas, ac eterna potestas per infinita seculorum secula Amen.	the form of a boy seven years old, and satisfy all my desires truly and in due manner according to my will, and in no way cause aggravation or harm to my body or soul, or even to my limbs, not of any spirit under the power of God, nor any animal creature, neither house* nor belfry which is made [*consecrated]† or ordained before God, so that you are not able to cause harm, aggravation, or offense, anywhere, nor will any evil spirit under the power of God, but explain to me, or show and truly answer all things that you or they will be asked, without sophistry or fabrication,‡ but as things actually are in the present, past, and future, and thus let it be done by the same God to whom is honour and glory, virtue, authority, gladness, deity, human, and eternal power by the infinite world of worlds. Amen.

* So Sloane 3849 and from the context, but Folger has "doñi" in red, another example of the scribe's poor grasp of the Latin he is copying.
† So Sloane 3849.
‡ So Sloane 3849, 21r: "figuratively."

Then say this Psalm: "*Quicunque vult*" ["whoever will (be saved)"],[697] and before thou have done, he will be before thee in his circle, and will ask [call for] thee what thou wilt, and see thou be ready to speak to him, and dread nothing, saying:[698]

Coniuro te Mosacum spiritum in nomine patris peracliti et filii et spiritus sancti ["I conjure you, O spirit Mosacus, in the name of the Father Paraclete (Advocate) and the Son and the Holy Ghost"]. Amen. I charge thee in the name of God, and by all the words that hath been rehearsed to thee constraint, to abide still visibly in fair form, without any hurt doing or noying[699] to me or my fellows, or any other thing, till I give

697. Athanasian Creed.

698. In left marg: "wg" (?).

699. Noying: hurt or bother.

thee leave to depart and go, and that thou fulfill truly mine intent that I shall desire of thee.

This done, cast thy petition to him, and he anon[700] will do it, and give thee a ready answer, and when thou wilt avoid[701] him, say this.

Mosacus spiritus cum te iterum Invocavero esto mihi paratus et sis mihi benevolens ad omnia que tibi precipiam in his que pertinent ad officcium tuum, vade ad locum tuum predestinatum ubi deus te ordinavit quousque te alias invocavero, et tunc mihi presto sis et pronus in omnibus desideriis meis, pax sit inter me et te, et inter nos et vos. In nomine patris et filii et spiritus sancti Amen.	O spirit Mosacus, I again have invoked you to be friendly to me and prepared [to fulfill] all that is ordered you insofar as falls within your office; go quickly to your predestined place which God has ordained, until such time that I may call on you, and then may you be ready and inclined [to fulfill] all my desires. Peace be between you and me, and between all of us and all of you. In the name of the Father, Son, and Holy Ghost. Amen.

In nomine + Iesu + hoc signum T tau facio ["In the name of + Jesus + I make this sign T tau"]. And then say this Psalm, *"Quicunque vult"* ["Whoever will (be saved)"],[702] and as he came, he will go again, but if he rebel, say this.

O tu maligne spiritus princeps totius nequitie, recede + Effnnelion (?) + cum omni tuo excercitu in ictu occuli quia tibi pariunt demones ["O you evil spirit, prince of iniquity, + Effnnelion + depart from my sight, in the blink of an eye, along with all your army, because they are obedient to you"]. And straight way he will be out of sight and may no longer abide, then go whither thou wilt and break up thy circle, saying:

Gratia dei sit semper nobiscum et conservet nos nunc et Imperat per et[er]num (?) Amen qui est unus omnipotens cui est laus honor et gloria per Infinita secula seculorum ["May the grace of God be with us always, and preserve us now, and rule forever. Amen. Who is one almighty, to whom be praise, honour, and glory forever and ever"]. Amen.

---

700. Anon: immediately.

701. Avoid: archaic "to be rid of."

702. The Athanasian Creed.

[183]

Mosacus's circle[703]

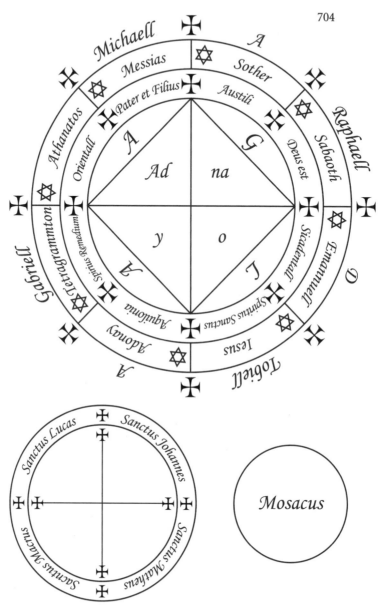

704

---

703. In bottom left marg.: "wg" (?).

704. Around outside of first: + a + *Raphaell* + *D* + *Tobiell* + a + *Gabriell* + + *Michaell*. Just inside outer circle: * *Sother* * *Sabaoth* * *Emanuell* * *Iesus* + * *Adonay* * *Tetragrammaton* * *Athanatos* * *Messias*. Sother: [Gk. "Saviour"]; Athanatos: [Gk. "Immortal"]; Messias: [Gk. "Messiah"]. Inside second circle: + *Austili [*austelli]* + *Deus est* + *Sicadentall [*Chelidonias?]* + *Spiritus Sanctus* + *Aquilon[i]a* + *spiritus remedium* + *Orientall* + *pater et filius* ["Southern + is God + Sicadental (*Western?) + Holy Ghost + Northern + spirit medicine + Eastern + Father and Son"]. Inside inner circle: *A G L A*; inside inner square: *ad – na / y – o* ; the letters of the name Adonay rearranged.

[184]

[+ Orobas][705]

Orobas[706] is a great prince. He cometh forth like a horse, but when he putteth on him a man's shape, he talketh of divine virtue. He giveth true answers of things present, past, and to come, and of the divinity, and of the creation. He deceiveth none nor suffereth none to be tempted. He giveth dignities and prelacies, and the favour of friends and foes, and hath rule over twelve legions.

---

705. In right marg: "89." Further down in left marg.: "wg" and in right marg.: "198."

706. Compare Weyer, *Pseudomonarchia Daemonum*, spirit #58.

[185]

Oberyon [+ Conjuration of the Spirit][707]

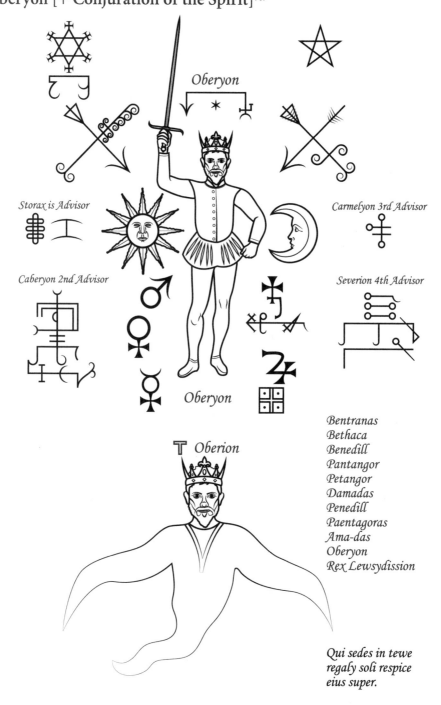

Oberyon

Storax is Advisor

Caberyon 2nd Advisor

Carmelyon 3rd Advisor

Severion 4th Advisor

Oberyon

Oberion

Bentranas
Bethaca
Benedill
Pantangor
Petangor
Damadas
Penedill
Paentagoras
Ama-das
Oberyon
Rex Lewsydission

Qui sedes in tewe
regaly soli respice
eius super.

707. Compare Folger p. 196. In right marg.: "205" and further down "69."

[186]

[+ Figures and Characters of Oberyon and His Followers][708]

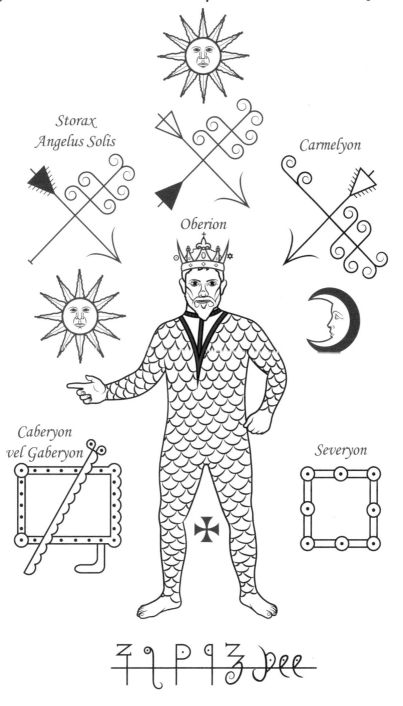

Storax
Angelus Solis

Carmelyon

Oberion

Caberyon
vel Gaberyon

Severyon

---

[187][709]

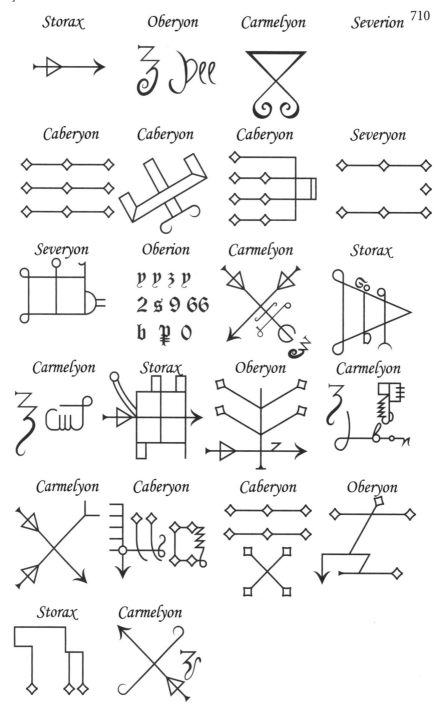

Storax   Oberyon   Carmelyon   Severion [710]

Caberyon   Caberyon   Caberyon   Severyon

Severyon   Oberion   Carmelyon   Storax

Carmelyon   Storax   Oberyon   Carmelyon

Carmelyon   Caberyon   Caberyon   Oberyon

Storax   Carmelyon

---

709. In left marg: "wg"; in right marg: "68."

710. Severion doesn't have a first figure supplied in Folger.

[188]

The Characters of King Aozol ~ 711

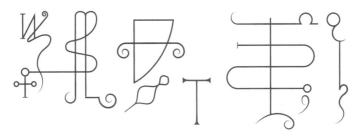

The Characters of King Restun ~ 717

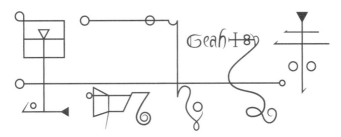

Two Characters of Ramalath ~

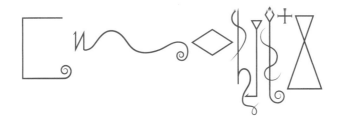

The Characters of Ramalath ~

---

711. In left marg: "[????] teri uner (?)/ [???]embrsone"; further down: "wg"; in right marg.: "206."

[189]

The Characters of King Zaseres ~

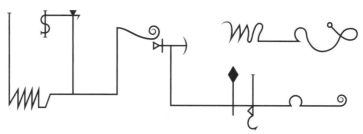

The Characters of King Castriel ~ [712]

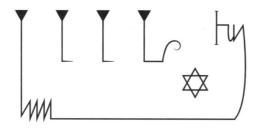

The Characters of King Saziel ~ [713]

The Characters of King Ydial ~

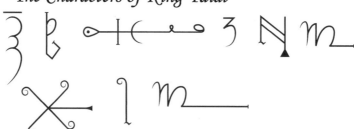

---

712. In right marg: "207."

713. In left marg: "wg."

[190]

Invocation of Oberion

In nomine patris et filii et spiritus sancti Amen. Exaudi nos quesumus domine clamantes ad te et te deprecantes sicut dignatus es (?) exaudire Ionam in ventre ceti, Moysen in monte Synay, danielem in lacu leonem Tres pueros in camino ignis, ut voluntatem et desiderium meum perficere digneris per dominum nostrum Iesum Christum etc.	In the name of the Father, Son, and Holy Ghost. Amen. O Lord, hear our cries to you, and deem us worthy, just as you saved Jonah from the whale's belly, Moses on Mount Sinai, Daniel from the Lion's den, the three children from the fiery furnace, that we may be worthy to completely accomplish our desires, through Jesus Christ our Lord, etc.

O N., thou noble, excellent, and spirit of great power, I bid and request thee, yea, and in the name of the Father, etc. I charge and command thee to stir and remove out of the place unto thee appointed wherein thou now art, and hearing me to invocate upon God's holy and most reverent names, and knowing that I will not cease nor leave off those my clamours and cries until the most high God hear me, grant my request, and thereby give me instand [instant(?)] good cause to laud and glorify his said most holy names. I admonish thee, O most noble spirit N., to prepare thyself in a readiness, and seek the ways and means possible, and that in the uttermost of thy power lieth to take unto thee, viz. a fair body, a comely body, and a human body, even a body like to a child of the age of three years old, and in the same body, O N., thou spirit of great power, I pray thee, as there may be friendship betwixt thee and me, come speedily unto me, and appear here before me without any long tarrying or delay, and that to the sight of me and my fellows now in this holy and consecrate circle at this instant present, looking and aspecting the same thy coming and appearance, wherefore, O N., worthy spirit, be willing as now to be made obedient to me and my fellows and that to our proper sight, and so that thou, O N., neither hurt me nor fear me, nor trouble me neither in my limbs, body, soul, ne members, neither in sight, hearing, nor speaking, nor any other creature of God's holy creation having in it the breath of life, but in the lovingest shape that may[714] appear, now to appear before me and us, and that with speed, so that I may be well contented therewith and not feared, nor have any farther cause to pronounce any farther conjuration or threats of God's wrathful indignation against thee, O N., noble and loving spirit as thou art a king and hast under thee ministers and subjects which do obey thee, I being the

---

714. This word added later in brown ink.

image of God [715] and servant of the same true and everliving God by the authority of my function, calling which thou knowest is honourable, O N., together with my humanity and baptism, do exorcise and charge thee make haste. Come and appear unto me, and enter into the circle and bound which I have provided for thee in this place and distant from this holy circle wherein I now stand and that thou have no power to hurt me nor my fellows nor any living creature inhabiting under the Moon globe and upon the face of the earth, with fire, lightning, thunder, nor water, nor by any other mean. Hereto I charge thee, by virtue of the blessing wherein my baptism at the font I was blessed in the name of the Father and of the Son etc. Amen. O N., by virtue of all gifts given to me by God from above, and by the omnipotent power of the Holy Trinity, I charge thee, that thou tarry not in thy place wheresoever it is in earth, in the air, in fire, in water, in stock, in stone, in frith, [716] in fen, nor in none other appointed place that ever God made or created, but that thou do straight way busk [717] and prepare thyself to come and appear quickly in all haste and with all speed unto me and us, and before me and us, and that perfectly to our sight, so that we may perfectly see thee, and make me a true answer of all such things as I or my fellows shall ask or demand of thee, and to do the uttermost of thy office to fulfill my request and desire in all things that I shall bid and command thee. O N., most gentle and worthy spirit which wast sometime an angel of light, I charge thee, for the love of thy God and by my authority and power, to perform this quickly in all haste wheresoever thou be, in air, in fire, in water, in earth, in stock, in stone, in frith, in fen, in wood, in tree, in mountain, in hill, in plain, in valley, in east, in west, in north, in south, or in any kind of appointed place that ever God made or created, and I charge thee, O N., thou kingly spirit, by this holy name of God + Tetragrammaton + I bind thee, O N., to obedience, in the name of the Father etc. Amen. Amen.

Now say this three (times).

Then say devoutly, sitting on thy knees, turning in to the east:

I conjure thee, O thou unbelieving spirit N., I conjure thee by all the hours of the day and night, that every planet doth reign in, that thou spirit never have no rest, night nor day, tide ne time, hours nor minutes, until thou come in all haste, fulfilling my commandments and requests in all points, unto the end as I shall command thee

---

715. In marg: "71."

716. Frith: a lightly wooded area, or the space between woods.

717. Busk: equip.

upon the pain of all other conjurations that shall be laid upon thee by me or any of my fellows.

Say this also three times, and if he come not, say as follows.

[191]

If he come not [+continue as] follows:

In nomine patris filii et spiritus sancti etc. ["In the name of the Father, Son, and Holy Ghost...."] O N., thou unbelieving spirit, I charge thee quickly to come, and appear before me, perfectly to my sight in the humblest estate of thy power, or else as heretofore I have assigned unto thee, so that I may be well-contented therewith and not feared, so that thou neither hurt me, fear me, nor trouble me, neither in soul nor body, mind, member nor sense, neither any other Christian or living creature of God's creation others than I shall assign unto thee, but in the lovingest shape and form aforesaid thou come and appear before me and us and that in all haste, so that I may be well-contented therewith, and nothing disturbed but without all fear make me a true answer of all such things as I shall demand of thee. I charge thee, in the name of the Father etc., that thou, O N., come and go into the bound and circle provided for thee, and that thou rest not in the east, west, north, nor in south, in fire, water, air, nor in earth, nor in no other appointed place whatever it be that God ever created or made: but that thou come, and quietly appear before me, and my fellows and perfectly[718] to our sight. O N., herein use haste, and make herein no delays. O thou unbelieving spirit N., I conjure thee by the high and reverent name of God + Tetragrammaton + and by all the great names of God known and unknown, both effable and ineffable. I conjure thee, O unbelieving spirit N., I charge thee by all the planets that ruleth day and night, be officers against thee, the Sun, Moon, stars, and all other things of God's holy creation, be witness against thee, till thou do appear to us, so that we may perfectly see thee. O N., I charge thee that thou come and presently in proper form as before is said, appear and show thyself to me, etc., even as thou intendest and believest to be saved at the latter day of judgment, even so I yet charge, O N., that thou come and appear before me, etc. in form, shape, and order as I before have said, and as in the citation was pronounced whereof thou art not ignorant. O N., if thou wilt not appear, no yet if thou be so thou canst not come, and will not send one of thy ministers that shall shew me the cause why thou canst not come, then I shall shortly take from thee thy power, deprive thee of thy office, take thee from thy dignity, and by the power and virtue of our Lord Jesus Christ, the all only saviour of

---

718. In marg: "72."

mankind, which is the everlasting and everliving God, throw and cast thee into the fire and pit of hell, where is weeping, wailing, and gnashing of teeth, woe unspeakable, darkness palpable, fire unquenchable, and worms whose gnawing is perdurable, and being there, thou shalt be never out of the eternal and intolerable pains thereof, nor never see the light, never possess thy former place, never enjoy the fruits of thy faith, nor never be partaker of Christ's death and passion, but the said death and blood of our Lord Jesus Christ, which in the same was shed, shall be unto thee for thy contumacy and disobedience everlasting condemnation. O N., all those things that I have now rehearsed be a witness against thee for thy contempt, now and at the last day, if thou do not come and appear with all speed and that perfectly to my sight without hurting or harming of me or my fellows or any other living creature of God's creation in form aforesaid. O N., come, come. In the name of the Father etc.

If he appear and will not go into his circle, thou must have a hazel wand of one year's growth which is a defensative,[719] whereupon must be written these names, and therewith he must by the master be enforced to go into his circle.

+ Tetragrammaton + Adonay + sacaman + Sadalay + Secamose + Sepitate + Ebreell + Ioell +

An Invocation [720]

O glorious God, thou that sittest upon cherubim and seraphim in light of lights, to the which the frailty and imbecility of human nature may not attain, O worthy God, to whom be praise forever, I most humbly pray and beseech thee, everlasting and divine Majesty, to give and grant me of thy grace, that I may urge and compel the spirit N. that he may forthwith, with all festination and speed possible, come and appear in fair and human form, etc., grant this good Lord through the power of thine unspeakable Name + Tetragrammaton + and of thy wonderful and marvelous name + Ieses + Amen. Amen. Fiat. Fiat.

[192]

I conjure, invoke, and call thee N., by the Father, the Son, and the Holy Ghost, and by him which said and it was done, he commanded and it stood fast and it was created, and by his son Jesus Christ, in whose name all heavenly, earthly, and hellish creatures do bend and obey, and by this unspeakable and great name + Tetragrammaton + O N., I charge thee wheresoever thou be that thou come and appear unto

---

719. Defensative: item that protects.
720. In marg: "73."

me, N. M., and that without hurting of me, my fellows, or any living creature of God's creation. O N., I adjure thee there unto by the head of thy prince, and by the obedience thou owest unto him, come, come, come, for thou art called by him that was, is, and is to come, who shall judge the world, both quick and dead, and that by fire. In the name of the Father and of the Son and of the Holy Ghost. Amen.

Invocation

I conjure thee, N., by God the Father omnipotent, and by him that is called the living God, the true God, and the holy God, which is the mighty God which cast all wicked and disobedient spirits out of paradise, and by these most holy names of God + Messias + Sother + Emanuell + Sabaoth + Adonay Otheos + Athanatos, Eloy, Panton, Craton, Iesus, Alpha and Omega, Christus Nazarenus, On, El, and by all these holy names of God, Anodab, Acon, Mandall, ao, grammaton, Atanall, and by the Virgin Mary, the mother of our Lord Jesus Christ, and by all the virgins, and by the five wounds of Jesus C[hrist], and by the virtue of Saint John the Baptist, and by the virginity of Saint John the Evangelist, and by these words, Nyoth, Naoth, that Solomon bound spirits in vessels of glass, O N., I charge thee that wheresoever thou be, thou do appear here before me, in the circle prepared for thee, and that quickly upon pain of everlasting fire, *fiat fiat fiat* Amen

I exhort thee, spirit N., by God the Father, Creator of heaven and earth, the sea, and all that therein is, and by the four elements, fire, air, earth, and water, and by the powers of heaven, and by the virtue of stones most precious, as well in heaven as in earth, by the virtue of the everliving God, the true God, and the holy God, and by the obedience that thou owest unto him, I bind thee that thou appear quickly as is before said through Jesus Christ our Lord, who shall come to judgment at the last day with majesty and great glory. Amen. Amen.

Invocation [721]

O omnipotent and everlasting God, which sittest most gloriously in thy seat of majesty and dost from thy throne behold and see all things done upon the earth, I humbly beseech thee of thy mercy and grace, O heavenly Father, whereas thou hast promised to hear the prayers of them which ask in thy son's name, so grant that I, thy humble and unworthy servant, may obtain so much of thine inestimable gifts of grace, and thy holy spirit of thine inestimable gifts of grace, may embolden and

---

721. In marg: "74." Compare this with the conjuration in Mathers, *Key of Solomon*, Book I, chap. VI.

strengthen me that I may call the spirit N. that he may be constrained to come unto me. Through the virtue of thy holy and thy mighty power, grant this, O most merciful Father for thy mercy's sake, and for thy dear son Jesus Christ's sake, my Lord and Saviour. Amen.

Hearken, O thou spirit N., I conjure thee with a conjuration of ineffable glory. I adjure thee with an adjuration of mighty honour. I bind thee with a bond most marvelous. I call thee with a call of nobility. I constrain thee with a constraint most terrible. I compel thee with a compulsion most dreadful. I command thee with a commandment of fame. I bid thee with a bidding that thou mayest not deny. I will thee with a will that thou canst not gainsay. I wish thee with a wishing of most high virtue. I charge thee with a charge of most great weight and importance, that N., come and appear quickly, and that thou do faithfully, truly, and to all intents without fraud, covine,[722] deceit, or guile, surrender unto me the help and succours that to thy office apperaineth as touching the achieving of my desire, will, and purpose. Even I, N., speak these words unto thee, O thou spirit N., most wicked, ungracious and rebellious, yea, I, N., the servant of the everlasting, true, and everliving God, to whom be all honour and praise now and forever, command thee, spirit N. [193] that thou quickly remove out of thy place where thou now art, and come and appear in manner and form as is before said. O N., I charge, conjure, bid, and command thee, wheresoever thou be in fire, air, earth, or water, in east, west, north, and south, that thou tarry not in any of these nor in the depths and bowels of the same, but that thou forthwith fly from fire to fire, from air to air <to air>, from water to water, and from earth to earth, from east to west, from north to south, and from all and all manner of depths, heights, lengths, and breadths, and abide not nor tarry within any of them nor any part nor parcel of them, but to come and appear as before I have said and commanded you, and coming nor going that thou have no power to hurt me nor none of my fellows, nor none other living creature of God's creation, ne to depart and go from hence without special licence of me, your commander. Larcken,[723] O thou spirit N., I, N., the servant of the true and everliving God, do conjure, adjure, constrain, compel, charge, and command thee, that thou do all and all manner of thing that I before have spoken, yea, I, the unworthy servant of the everlasting and most glorious God, a wretched sinner, a feeble and frail person, a miserable creature, a worm and no man. In the name of mine and thine God, who for thy pride and disobedience cast thee down from Heaven, deprived thee of thy glory, and hath appointed unto thee a place until the last terrible glooming and most fearful Day of Judgement, wherein he

---

722. Covine: intrigue, fraud, deceit.
723. Larcken: harken?

shall come with power and great glory, to judge thee and me and all mankind from the four winds, as well the quick as the dead, as those in grave lying, do adjure, conjure, constrain, compel, charge, and command thee, with an adjuration, conjuration, constraint, compulsion, charge, and commandment of honour, worthiness, fame, and nobility, might glory ineffable from above, that thou speedily depart from the place thou now art in and come and appear unto me and enter the circle appointed for thee, that is of thee, O wicked disobedient and contumate[724] spirit, be done. I adjure thee, N., by the man of many years whose garments be as white as snow, and the hairs of his head, like unto most pure wool, whose seat is of flaming fire, the wheels of his chariot glistering[725] beams of fiery brightness, a fiery flood doth proceed even before him, and 10 M times 10 M him do serve by these words and by these most holy, great, sacred, and worthy names of God + Agla + Tetragrammaton + Anabona + Adonay + Eloy + Eloin + On + Messias + Sother + Emanuell + Sabaoth + Almazamen + El + by all these names and by all other names of the ineffable and most gracious Lord God of Israel, which inhabiteth above all manner places local, and in the Eii (7?) heaven is his seat, and in the earth is his footstool, that thou, O spirit N., make no more delays nor tarry not, but come now, I charge thee, and that speedily come, I say, and do that to thy office appertaineth, that we may safely and without hurt, either of soul, mind, or body, have, possess, and enjoy that our will and intent is, grant this, O Lord God, with the Son and the Holy Spirit now at this present and ever, world without end. Amen.

O spirit N., I conjure[726] thee by all names marvelous, and I command thee by all power wonderful, and I bid thee by him that said and it was done, and by the mighty name + Agla + that Noah named and he was delivered from the deluge or universal flood wherein all flesh else was destroyed, and by the name + Tetragrammaton + and in the name + Tetragrammaton + that Enoch and Elijah did name[727] when they went out to fight with and against that leviathan, and they were brought to the land of permission, and by the name + Anabona + and in the wonderful might of the great name + Anabona + in the which God shall cast the whole vice of the earth upon the holy mountain, and by the name + Adonay + and in the name + Adonay + which God shall speak in the midst of the night, and at the same voice the good and the evil shall arise out of their graves even in the twinkling of an eye, and by the name + Eloy + and in the Name + Eloye + in the which God shall trouble the seas and floods and

---

724. Contumate: stubborn.

725. Glistering: brilliant, glittering.

726. In marg: "76."

727. Compare Sloane 3847, fol. 15v: ... *et per nomen Tetragrammaton quod Enoc et Helyas nominauerunt ad pugnandum contra Leviathan et terram permissionis reducti fuerunt...*

the fishes shall be vexed and fight one against another and they shall die in one day together with the third part of men dwelling upon earth, and by and in the name + Eloyn + with which God shall dry the seas and make them fall down into the depths, and by and in the name + On + by the which God shall restore again the seas and floods and all manner of waters, and by and in the name + Messias + by the which God shall make the beasts wild and tame to be furious and mad, and to fight one against another so that all they shall die in one day, and by and in the name + Arbitrell in which God shall destroy towers, houses, and all manner of buildings in one day, and there shall not remain one stone upon another that shall not be destroyed, and by and in the name + Sother + in which [194] God shall make the stones to fight one against another, and then shall the nations of the earth say, you mountains, come fall upon us, and you little hills cover us, and by and in the name + Emanuell + in which God shall make all flying fowls and birds of the air to fight one against another, and in one day to consume and vanish as though they had never been, and by and in the name + Almazameñ + in which God shall cast down all mountains and fill up the valleys and then all the earth shall be level and plain, and by and in the name + Pentatormion + in which God shall make the Sun and Moon and all stars of the firmament to fall and lose their light, and by and in the name + Sabaothe + in which God shall come with his orders of angels with great power and glory to judge quick and dead, you and me and all mankind, and then shall the ungodly with you disobedient spirits be stricken with lightnings and fire of which is spoken, the fire shall go even before him, and about him shall be a mighty strong tempest, and by and in the name + Athanatos + in which God after he hath finished his dreadful judgment shall cast the devil with all wicked spirits into a terrible prison, even a castle invincible of lightning and devouring fire, which never shall be quenched and whose worm shall never die nor leave gnawing, and then shall God with all his holy and elect people enter into joys of celestial paradise with all triumph and glory, and by and in the name + Alpha + and Omega + in which God once made the waters and floods to ascend up above all mountains, so shall make fire to arise up above the earth by fifteen cubits, and then shall heaven be folded up as it were a book, and it shall be gathered together even like to a tabernacle, his present state shall be innovated which is spoken of *Mutabis ea et mutabuntur* ["you will change them, and they will be changed" [728]], O thou spirit N., by all this great and mighty names of God effable and ineffable, to thee known and unknown, I charge and command, enforce and compel thee to appear, and not once to be so hardy as to rest or stay there where thou now art, or in any place east, west, north, and south, in air, fire, earth, or water, in skies or in hell, until thou come and

---

728. I.e., You will change them like a garment. Psalm 101:27 (KJV 102:26).

appear and enter into the circle here appointed for thee, made and prepared with thy name written therein, and coming that thou be not letting or hindering unto us, but that thou do that in thee lieth and that we may purchase, obtain, possess, and enjoy the uttermost of our will, and that to thy office appertaineth, in manner and form as before is said that this be done. N., I conjure thee by the power and virtue of these great and wonderful names of God + Adonay + Sabaoth + Eloy + Saday + Tetragrammaton + and by the power and virtue of wise Solomon, Cyprian, and Roger Bacon, who had power to command, bind, and enclose you and all spirits, etc.

+ *Nota Bene* ["Note well"] [729]

This king or spirit is between the Sun and the earth. Note: in the first Monday after the change,[730] and in the hour of the Moon, Mars, Mercury, or Saturn, make thy tables and this image or picture with the characters as is before set forth, saying over them,

O vos Angeli solis et Lune coniuro vos et exorsizo vos per virtutem filii domini + On + et Omega + et per hoc quod est mirabile, et per illum qui vos creavit, et per omnia signa dei et characteres firmamenti continens, faciatis spiritu Oberion in obedire et aperere in hac Anula Camera, vell tabella stannea, in forma humana, et me certe facere de omnibus rebus, sine dolo et fantasia vell fraude seu aliqua timore quicum[que respondens] ipsum Interrogavero,	O you angels of the Sun and Moon, I conjure and exorcise you by the virtue and power of the Son, the Lord + On [*Alpha] and Omega + and by the name that is marvellous ⌊+ *El +⌋, and by him that made you and formed you, and by all these signs of God, containing the firmament, that you make this spirit Oberion obey and appear in this ring, chamber, or plate of tin, in human form, and inform me of all things, without deceit, delusion, fraud, or any fear, [responding] in person to whatever I have asked.

O you angels of the Sun and of the Moon, I now conjure and pray you and exorcise you that by the virtue and power of the most high God + Alpha and Omega + and by the name that is marvelous + El + and by him that made you and formed you, and by these signs that be here so portrayed in these tables of wood or in this plate of

---

729. This heading is in faded brown ink and in a different hand. The *Oxford English Dictionary* places the first instance of the English usage circa 1721. In right marg.: "90."

730. The appearance of the new Moon.

brass, etc., and now in the might and virtue of your creator, and in the name of him the most shining God and by the virtue of the Holy Ghost, that now or whensoever that I shall call on Oberyon,[731] whose image is here pictured, made, or fashioned, and his name that is here written, and his signs here all drawn, graven, written, or made in this plate or tables, etc., that now you angels to make Oberyon or any other spirit here to obey me, and here to appear to me, openly in a fair form or child's likeness, or in the likeness of an angel of God, and that without hurt or fear of my body or soul, or the body or soul of any other Christian or living creature, and that you now without fraud, guile, or delays, here and in this place present, fulfill my request and desire, I beseech you, and that thou appear upon pain of everlasting damnation, to lighten and happen upon thee [195] Oberion and to thine associates, and thou, Oberyon, my desire fulfill as thou wilt have the reward of me for thee prepared, which I will give thee, Oberyon, and this finish the first day's work.

The next day, write or make the name of his first counselor, Caberyon, and that on the right side, with the sign and characters to it, etc., saying,

Exorsizo te spiritum caberion,* per omnia celestia terrestria et Infernalia, et per Salomonem regem qui te ligavit, et per omnia elementa quibus totus mundus per conditum serpentum exaltatum in heremo, quatinus et \<deus\> concillium domino tuo, velle meum in omni posse et sense perficiat.	I exorcise you, O spirit Caveryon, by all celestial, terrestrial, and infernal powers, and by King Solomon who bound you, and by all the elements in the whole world, by the hidden serpent, exalted in the wilderness, that you counsel to thy Lord (i.e., Oberyon) to fulfill my desire completely in all things.
* In right marg: "91."	

And yet now,[732] I exorcise thee, Caveryon, and that by the power of God, and by the virtue of all heavenly things, earthly things and infernal things, and by King Solomon, the which bound thee and made thee subject unto him, and by all his signs and seals, rings and sceptre, and by the [four][733] elements, by the which the world is sustained and nourished, and by the serpent, that was exalted in the wilderness,[734] that thou, Caberyon, [sic] now to help to give true counsel to thy Lord Oberyon, that he

---

731. Corrected from "Oberion."

732. The English text here expands upon the Latin above.

733. A space left in the manuscript, evidently to switch ink. The red text seems to have been inserted after the black text, based on this and other omissions.

734. John 3:14: "And as Moses lifted up the serpent in the wilderness, even so must the Son of man be lifted up."

do show here himself, to me, to answer me and to fulfill my desire even to the uttermost of his power, and that on the pain to thee and to you all, of endless death and damnation.

Note that this must be said three times a day and three times a night over the plate.

And the third day in the third hour, write and make the fourth counselor Severyon with his signs and characters, above the name, and do it on the left side, and say over it.

O tu Severyon coniuro te per omnes spirittum ut sine mora, vell prebeas concillium domino tuo ut ipsum impleat socialem qui~ exibeat, per virtutem omnium nominum dei + Tetragramaton + Agla + Nalea + Emanuell + quatenus sine mora des concillium domino tuo Oberyonem ut ostenderet seipsum mihi, et respondeat ad omnia Interrogatio quod ego interrogabo de eum, et quod faciat sine fallacia, et sine timore, et meum voluntatem proficiat coniuro vos per deum vivum per deum verum per deum sanctum et per omnia nomina quibus nemo debet nominare nisi in omnibus negotiis + Usyen + Usyon + Panton + Craton + ut concilliares illum Oberyonem in obedire et aperere in pulcra forma humana, nulla creature nocendi nec terrendi, per eum qui vivit et regnat deus cum patrem et spiritus sanctus in secula seculorum Amen.	O you Severyon, I conjure* you by all spirits that without delay you give counsel to your lord that he show himself because of his allegiance, by the power of all the names of God + Tetragramaton + Agla + Nalea + Emanuell + that now without delay you give counsel to your Lord Oberion that he show himself to me, and answer all questions that I will ask him, and that without deceit or fear, and assist in my wishes. I conjure you by the living God, by the true God, by the holy God, and by all the names which nobody must name but in great need + Usyen + Usyon + Panton + Craton + to counsel Oberyon to obey and appear in a pleasing human shape, and not frightening or harming any creatures, by him who lives and reigns God with the Father and the Holy Ghost forever and ever. Amen.
* In right marg: "92."	

And thou, Severion, I exorcize and command thee, by this name Elyron + that none should name, but in peril of death, or in great necessity, and by all spirits both high and low, and that now without any tarrying, and that thou, Severyon, now to give counsel to thy lord Oberyon that he to show himself to me here, and that without dread or fear, or any disturbance to me or to any of my fellows, and that all you, his four angels and great counselors, I conjure and adjure you, O Storax,[735] Carmelion, Caberyon, Severion, and now I call you all together and command you to go now, and that without delay, to Oberyon, whose speaking with I desire, and that by the power of God and by the virtue of these names + Yraky + Collpus + & Trypus + and by the very quick God the which formed all the world, and by all his angels and Archangels, and by all the saints in heaven and earth, that now you go to and cause Oberyon your lord to appear to me here, and that with this some of gold, of good and perfect gold to the value of one 100,000 pounds without fraud or guile.

This done, suffumigate your plate with saffron, aloes, mastic, olibanum, and orpinent (?). Note the fire to be of elder or thorns.

Note that thou must make thy circle in a garden or secret place, and as thou goest to it, look that the tables be open, and that on thy breast, and kneel down and look into the east, but look you have a + on thy forehead, and another on thy breast and three + + + on thy foot, and so go to the place and work, and cast into thy circle a faggot of elder or thorn, and burn it there and hold the tables in that smoke and say,

Betranhas, bethala, Bendyll Benedyb, Pentagoras, Pentengor, Danadas, Amadas, Oberyon T Oberyon rex lussydyssem, qui sedes in tuo regalye solio respice nos semper, per omnia in universis mundo I[n] nomine domini nostri Iesu Christi Nazareni, et per eius Nativitatem mortem resurrectionem assentionem spiritus sancti peracleti per Sanctam Trinitatem per virginitatem beatem Marie virginis, per gloriosum chorum Apostolorum et Martirum, per laudabilem mundum, per prophetarum et virginitatem, [196] et per 4or Rx firmamentum coniuro te Oberion sub pena ignis et sulphuris ut [+in] ignas [*ignes] dessendas [*descendas], ac infernas, morias, et expecta vera omnia et singula	Betranhas, bethala, Bendyll Benedyb, Pentagoras, Pentengor, Danadas, Amadas, Oberyon T Oberyon King Lussydyssem, who sits on your royal throne, look upon us always, by everything in the whole world, in the name of our Lord Jesus Christ of Nazareth, and by his birth, death, resurrection, and ascension, by the Holy Ghost Paraclete, by the holy Trinity, by the virginity of the blessed Virgin Mary, by the glorious choir of apostles and martyrs, by the praiseworthy world of the prophets and virgins, [196] and by the four kings of the firmament. I conjure you, Oberion, under penalty of fire and sulfur so that you descend into the fire, die, and faithfully await each and every order that I will

---

735. Raine, "Proceedings Connected with a Remarkable Charge of Sorcery," 71–81: "Item, he saith that he graved the figure of Oberion demonis in the lamyna, and iiij. Names, wherof Storax was oone, and the other iij. aftir the booke."

precepta que tibi precipio, et ut apereas mihi in pulcra forma pueri tres annos nati nemini Ledentem ne ffrementem nec furience nec me in ullum perturbes, sed ad omnem questionem ut desiderium assignam obedias, et meam voluntatem per impleas, per tante domini nostri Iesu Christi quem factus et benedictus regnance, per omnia seculam seculorum Amen.	give you, and that you appear to me in the beautiful form of a three-year-old boy, hurting nobody, neither raging nor roaring, not disturbing me or anyone else, but obeying all my desires and answering my questions, and fulfilling my will, by our Lord Jesus Christ, who is great, who reigns blessed forever and ever. Amen.

Then say into the east

Domine Iesu Christe[736] *cuius potentia omnia et singula mundo et in rebus fabrica apparient et obediunt, tu domine ad Iuvam in virtutem tue sa[n]ctem crucis* ["O Lord Jesus Christ, by whose power each and every thing fashioned in the world will appear and obey you,[737] O Lord help, by the power of your holy cross"].

And make a + and say,

Quatenus rescipiam fortunam et potestatem ligandi super spiritum Oberion ["inasmuch as I may receive the fortune and power to bind the spirit Oberion"] and not only power, O Lord, I beseech thee, give me through the virtue of thy name to call him, bu[t] (?) also command him I calling immediately to yield and obey and in no case to resist, but to come or send some one of his councilors etc. *et meam voluntatem et desiderium per implere, In virtute tui nominis, et per eius qui venturus est Iudicare vivos et mortuos et seculum per ignem* ["and to fulfill my will and desires in the power of your name, and by him who will come to judge the living and the dead and the world by fire"].

And say over the tables, looking into the east when thou suffumigatest,

O thou Oberyon, the most shining spirit, whose name and image is here pictured, made, and written. Now O thou Oberyon, turn thy shape and similitude, that now here it may be openly showed, to my image here present, and to me and to my fellows, and come thou, Oberyon, toward the east, for I call thee, O Oberyon, here art thou worthily called by thy proper name, wherefore come and make no delays, but coming that thou, Oberyon, fly not again, but here shew thyself diligent, favourable, and serviceable to me now calling, and that not fearfully but pleasantly, and that by the virtue and strength of

---

736. In right marg: "93."

737. This passage is corrupt and translation conjectural.

Ysus Odas Otheos Yskyros + Alpha + et Omega + and by these holy names rodthe yaye heteth + Adonay and by the great and terrible name of God + Tetragrammaton + and by the virtue and power of the holy, just and most high God, the which all the Arabics, Greeks and Chaldees, Hebrews, Jews, and Englishmen and all kindreds, nations, peoples, and living creatures, do reverence and worship, and by that king in whose Legion that thou, Oberyon, art either going or abiding, and by the prayer of these whose names be here written, and engraven in these tables, etc., and by their signs and names i.e., Storax, Carmelyon, Caberyon, and Severion, and by the virtue that God gave to man, when that he said to spirits and informalities, be ye subject to man, and that now and that without any delay that thou, Oberyon, come here to me, and appear openly in this place in a circle here assigned for thee with thy name, Oberyon, written therein and that in a fair form like a child of three years of age, without hurting, harming, or grieving of me or any of my fellows, or any living creature. And now I have this table in my right hand therefore come thou now, O noble spirit Oberyon, and that readily and that with all speed possible, to accomplish and fulfill my petition, demand, and desire, and that perfectly even to the uttermost of thy power, and that under and upon the pain of eternal and everlasting damnation, but and thou Oberyon shalt to me be obedient and not stubborn and rebellious, but come, and appear in form aforesaid and that without hurting of me or any others, etc. and fulfill my desire in all things to the uttermost of thy power, that then I will that thou, Oberyon, with thy four nobles and prudent counselors Storax, Carmelyon, Caberyon, and Severyon, be free from pain and at liberty to go as soon as you shall have done that I shall require to the place that [...] [738] hath appointed for you.

This done, make three crosses + + + upon the ground, and kneeling, kiss them, and then stand up and thou shalt see a little cloud come afar off, and when that it is near, thou shalt see him openly in the place that thou callest him to, and then demand of him a 100,000 pounds of true gold and silver, and to be laid in this place or circle or such a place, etc., naming it, and also name an hour.

Note: talk not too much with him, for he will report to thee incredible things, but let it pass, and be not given to listen thereunto, but charge him to fulfill thy desire for 100,000 pounds of gold and silver, and that in the name of the Father and of the Son and of the Holy Ghost, three persons and one God in Trinity, so be it. Amen. Amen. The end. An oft-proved experiment.

This do as oft as need requireth until he come, etc.

---

738. The manuscript has a blank space, no doubt intending to switch to red ink.

[197]

Note: When thou art very earnest in calling, thou must hold the spirit's name and picture in thy hand, etc.

[+ The Oath]

Note: At the spirit's first coming, demand nothing of him, but swear him to obedience, and that in this wise: "I, N., do promise and bind myself as I hope to be saved at the last day or general doom, to be at the bidding and commandment of thee, N. N., the son of N. N., who by the power of God's most holy and mighty names hath convinced and overcome me, and for confirmation hereof, I have given my name and character as a pledge for the ratifying of the same." Let him write his own name, and seal and deliver it unto you.

Another way to invoke Oberion [739]

Oberion under *luna* ["the Moon"] *dentalyonbeancks*.

First, ere ye begin to call, you must kneel down upon your knees towards the east, and devoutly say these Psalms: "*miserere mei deus*" ["Have mercy on me, O God"] 51, "*Deus misereatur*" ["May God have mercy"], Psalm 67, "*Deus in nomine tuo*" ["Save me, O God, by your name"], Psalm 54, and "*deus deus meus respice in me, etc.*" ["O God, my God, look upon me"], # 63 [*21?],[740] and if you will call him to the glass or stone, lay them before you, saying this prayer following and with blessing the said speculative.

Let us pray

Almighty God, which of thy justice didst destroy with the floods of water the universal world and that for sin, except eight persons, whom of thy mercy the same time thou didst save in the ark, and when thou drownedest in the Red Sea wicked King Pharaoh with all his army, yet at the same time thou didst lead thy people, the children of Israel, safely through the midst thereof, whereby thou didst prefigurate[741] the new washing or holy baptism, and by the baptism of thy well-beloved son, Jesus Christ, didst sanctify the flood Jordan and all other waters to the mystical washing

---

739. In right marg: "118."

740. Psalm 62 (KJV 63) actually starts with *Deus Deus meus ad te* ["O God, my God, to you"]. Psalm 21 (KJV 22) starts with *Deus, Deus meus, respice in me* ["O God my God, look upon me"].

741. Prefigurate: foreshadow.

away of sin and uncleanness, I beseech thee, O Lord God, for thy infinite mercy, grant whatsoever uncleanness be in this M. that thou, O Lord God, through thy miracles may make it clean and undefiled, and that it may be sanctified by the Holy Ghost, that through the virtue and power of thy holy names, this spirit N. may come into this M., whether he will or no, for thy son Jesus Christ's sake. Amen.

I conjure [742] thee and I command thee, N, by the might and power of almighty Jesus, and by the power of the Father, the Son, and the Holy Ghost, and by the virtue, might, and power of all angels, archangels, martyrs, confessors, and virgins, and by all the virtues and might of Heaven, that thou dost come with all celerity and speed into this M. and shew thyself therein unto me in a fair form and shape, and give me a true answer of all such things which I shall ask or demand of thee, without any illusions, shewing unto me, or without any advantage taking of any of my words, but truth and truly according to my meaning, speedily and unfeignedly to fulfill my request to the uttermost of thy power. I conjure thee, N., in the name of God almighty and by the virtue, might, and power of the great and high name of God + Tetragrammaton + that thou come into this M. and show yourself here in a fair form and shape, setting all delays apart, and give a true answer of all such things as I shall ask or demand of thee. I conjure thee, N., by the virtue of Christ's flesh and his blood, and by the virtue of the five loaves, and by the virtue of the blessing wherewith he blessed them, and by the bread he broke and gave to his disciples, and by the sacrament that Christ made in the form of bread. I conjure and command thee that thou come into this M. and show thyself therein unto me in fair form and shape, and give me a true answer of all such things as I shall ask or demand of thee, without any illusion, showing unto me or without any advantage taking of me or of my words, but true and truly, according unto my meaning, speedily and unfeignedly, to fulfill my request, will, and desire, and that to the uttermost of thy power. I conjure thee, N., by the virtue of the seven sacraments of holy church, and by the virtue of Christ's passion, that thou come into this M., and by the virtue of the blood and water that Christ sweat in his passion, that thou show thyself therein unto me in fair form and shape, and give me a true answer of all such things as I shall ask or demand of thee, without lie, craft, or deceit. I conjure thee, N., and I command thee by the might and virtue of all holy works that ever were wrought in heaven and earth, and by the might and virtue of these holy high and ineffable names of God + Tetragrammaton + Omorison + and by the virtue of Jesus Christ. I command thee that thou come into this M. and show thyself therein [198] unto me in a fair form and shape, setting all delays apart, and give a true answer to all such things, as I shall ask or demand of thee, without any advantage taking at

---

742. In right marg: "119."

any of my words but truth and truly, according unto my meaning, speedily and un-feignedly, to fulfill my request to the uttermost of thy power, I conjure thee, N., by the might of the Father, the Son, and the Holy Ghost, and by the might of his marvelous ascension, and by the mighty power and strength of the coming of the Holy Ghost, and by the great day of judgment. I command thee that thou come into this M. and shew thyself therein in fair form and shape, and give a true answer of all such things as I shall ask or demand of thee. I conjure thee, N., by the might, power, and strength of God, and by his most holy, and high name of God + Semyphoras + and by this holy and mighty name of God + Adonay + *quod deus media nocte clamabat [*clama-vit] ad quam vocem omnes mortui boni et male in ictu occuli resurgent* ["which God will proclaim in the middle of the night, which being called, all the dead —good and evil—will be raised up in the blink of an eye"], and by this name + Sother + I com-mand thee that thou comest into this M. and therein to shew thyself unto me in a fair form and shape, and give me a true answer of all things that I shall ask or demand of thee, without any deceit or delusions, shewing unto me, or without any advantage taking at any of my words, but truth and truly according to my meaning, speedily and unfeignedly, to fulfill my request unto the uttermost of thy power. I conjure thee, N., by the virtue of the blessed blood that Christ Jesus, the saviour of all mankind bled upon the cross on Good Friday, that thou obey to my commandments, and I charge thee and constrain thee, and I command thee in the name of the Father etc., and by the power, might, and strength of these holy names of God + Messias + Sother + Emanuell + Sabaoth + Adonay + Panton + Craton + Annephepheneton + Theos + Otheos + Yskiros + Athanatos + Ymas + Ely + Ely + Alpha + et Omega + Tetragram-maton + Iesus + Christus + fillius + dei +. Amen. *In nomine patris et filii + et spiritus sancti* + Amen. Amen.

[In marg.:] This done, say, *quicunque vult* ["whoever will (be saved)"],[743] and *In principio erat verbum* ["In the beginning was the Word"] etc.[744]

Now if they do not appear in the M., then say as follows:

I conjure[745] thee, N., by the virtue and might of almighty God, and by our blessed Lady Saint Mary, Mother of Jesus Christ, and by the same, our blessed Saviour Jesus Christ, that was and is our maker, and by the baptism of Christ, and by the manhood of Christ that he took through his meekness, and by the Blessed Virgin Mary, our Lady, Christ's Mother. I command thee, that thou comest into this M. and show thy-self therein unto me in fair form and shape, and give a true answer unto me of all

---

743. The Athanasian Creed.

744. John 1.

745. In right marg: "120."

such things as I shall ask or demand of thee. I conjure thee, N., by the glorious passion of Christ, and in especial that he suffered in the Mount of Calvary in his blessed hands and feet, and by the blood and water that he sweated, sitting in prayer to his Father, sitting on the mountain when he said, *Pater si fieri potest transeat a me calix iste* ["Father, if it is possible, let this chalice pass from me"],[746] and by the blessed words he said *pater dimitte illis, quia nessiunt [*nesciunt] quid faciunt* ["Forgive them Father, for they know not what they do"].[747] I conjure thee, N., and I command thee that thou comest into this M., and show thyself there unto me in fair form and shape, setting all delays apart, and to give a true answer of all such things as I shall demand of thee, without any delay or advantage taking at any of my words, but truth and truly according unto my meaning, speedily and unfeignedly to fulfill my requests to the uttermost of thy power. I conjure thee, N., by the blessed blood of Jesus Christ, and by the virtue, strength, and power of the living God, the true God, and the omnipotent God, and by the divine power of the blessed Trinity, that thou tarriest not in no case, but even now, without any tarriance, that thou come into this M. and shew thyself therein unto me in fair form and shape, and give a true answer to all such things as I shall ask or demand of thee, and that immediately without delays or advantage taking at any of my words, or saying but truth and truly, according to mine intent and meaning, speedily and unfeignedly, to fulfill my will, even to the uttermost and extreme limits and bands of thy conscience. *Fiat. Fiat.*

Then say the four Gospels i.e., of Saint John, "*In principio erat verbum, etc.*" ["In the beginning was the Word"], next of Saint Matthew, the next of Saint Mark, the next of Saint Luke. This repeat three times, both conjurations and Gospels, and he will most certainly come, but if he do not, then say as follows:

I conjure thee, I constrain thee, and I pinch thee, N., for thy contempt and disobedience, in that thou comest not at this my commandment into this M., and according as I have appointed thee, therefore and because thou art not obedient, the Immaculate Lamb of God condemn thee, and that because thou comest not into this M. willingly and gently, with all celerity and [199] festination wherefore now come, or else the four holy evangelists reprehend thee, Michael, Gabriel, and Raphael reprove thee, the three patriarchs Abraham, Isaac, and Jacob and all holy prophets reprove thee, all the Apostles of Christ reprove thee, and all the elects of God both of men and angels condemn thee except thou comest into this M. by and by and therein show thyself as I have commanded thee, or else thy crafts, furies, and strengths fail thee day and night, hour and minute, tide and time, years and months, even as the Moabites did

---

746. Matthew 26:39
747. Luke 23:34

decrease, except that thou dost come into this M., and that incontinently, and that without any further tarriance, let, or delay, and fulfill and accomplish my will and commandment in all things, that I have before commanded thee, or else our Saviour Jesus Christ doth reprove thee which was born of the Virgin Mary, except that thou comest in to this M. even incontinent at this, my calling, O N. If thou despise this to do, Jesus of Nazareth, King of the Jews, reprove thee whose name and names thou dost disobey, wherefore now the slower thou art of thy coming at this my invocation, so much the more thy pains and torments may be increased and multiplied upon thee, all the curses and maledictions of God condemn thee for this thy disobedience and long tarrying, all the torments of hell, all the dolours of the damned souls, all vexation of the world, and all the passions of vexed and troubled minds, be multiplied upon thee, even in number as the stars of the sky, sands of the sea, fishes in the floods, and grasses upon the face of the earth, and that from day to day, from hour to hour, from week to week, from month to month, from year to year, from minute to minute, and from tide to time, until it so be as thou dost come and appear here in this M. unto me, in a fair form and shape, and be obedient unto all such things that I have before commanded thee, and until such time as thou hast fulfilled this my will and precept have thou never rest, but be thou in continual pains with most increase of sorrow, pains, griefs, and dolour, *fiat fiat fiat*. Amen.

When he is come, say this, and that before thou requirest anything of him·

I charge thee,[748] N., and command thee by all things that I have before rehearsed and said, and by the holy and high name of God + Tetragrammaton + and by all the holy names of God, that any spirit may be constrained by, that thou show truly and openly unto me all things that I shall demand of thee.

Then demand of him what thou wilt.

Beank

Then having thy purpose, licence him to depart on this wise as follows:

Licence

By all things that I have said and commanded thee, N., and by all things that are under the power of Jesus Christ, and by his licence, I bind thee, N., that thou be unto me always obedient in all things to be demanded, so often, whensoever and wheresoever, and in what place, within or without, whether it be within the house or without

---

748. In right marg: "123."

the house, in field, wood, or water, or wheresoever I am, and where I shall call thee, N., without any impediment, so long as I will, in all things thou shalt fulfill my will, and my desire, without lie, craft, or deceit, and without fear and hurt of me or any other creature of God, as well of body as of soul, and always at the opening of this my book, or any part of this whensoever I calling for thee without tarriance, that thou comest from every part, wheresoever thou be, and shew thyself to the presence of me, and make thyself ready and familiar through the virtue, power, and might of these sacred and holy names of God constraining thee at all times as well of the day as of the night, + Adonay + Saba[o]th + Adonay + Cados + Adonay + Ancora + Sother + Emanuell + Tetragrammaton + Iesus + Occinomos + Ioth + Beth + Heloy + Alpha + and Omega + and that thou, N., obey my words, which, by the licence of God, are as a sharp sword towards thee at all times of the day and night, by the might and power of our Saviour Jesus Christ, and by all his holy words and works, so that thou upon this condition, that I have before said and rehearsed to thee, that thou dost fulfill, that I licence thee till I shall call thee another time, by the power of Jesus Christ and his holy names, go thy ways in peace, and peace be always between us and you. In the name of the Father and of the Son and of the Holy Ghost. Amen. Amen. Amen.

Licence

Then mark thee with the sign of the + and if ye be fearful, say, "*In principio erat verbum*" ["In the beginning was the word"], and, "*quicunque vult* ["Whoever will (be saved)"]."[749] *Finis.* An oft-proved experiment.

A malediction with a condition

Si volueris facere precepta mea et iussionibus meis obedire O N dissolve te ab officio tuo et potestate in abissum aquarum usque in diem Iuditii ipsius Auctoritate qui venturus est Iudicare vivos et mortuos et seculum per ignem Amen.	If you wish to accept my precepts, and obey my orders, O N., unbind yourself from your duty and power in the watery depths until the Day of Judgment itself, by the authority of him who will soon come to judge the living and the dead and the world by fire. Amen.

---

749. The Athanasian Creed.

Licentialis pro 10 ["Before Licencing 10 (?)"][750]

Vade N ad locum predestinatum ubi dominus deus tuus te ordinavit quousque alias te Invocavero, sub pena damnacionis perpetue et maledictione dei omnipotentis patris et filii et spiritussancti que malediction descendat super te et semper tecum maneat nisi citius descendas et rescedas ad locum tibi a domino constitutum, sine aliquo dampno mihi, vell nobis inferrendo vel faciendo, Ita et nisi cito cum te Invocavero, sine aliquo modo poteris sine mora festinantur copareas siue in domo, sive extradomo, in campis siue extra campos, ubicunque te Invocavero, benedictione tui principis possidendo, *fiat fiat fiat*.	Go, O N., to the predestined place where the Lord God has ordained for you until the time that I will call upon you again, under penalty of eternal damnation, and the curse of God almighty, the Father, Son, and Holy Ghost, which curse will descend upon you, and will remain with you always, unless you quickly descend and retreat to that place which the Lord has established for you, without causing any harm to me or to us. And so it will be unless you quickly come when I call, if you are at all able, hastening to appear without delay, whether in a house, or outside the house, in a field or outside the field, wherever I will call upon you, having obtained the blessing of your prince.* Fiat, fiat, fiat.

* So Sloane 3853.

[200]

Licentialis pro 20 ["Before Licencing 20 (?)"]

Unus quisque vestrum in pace revertatur in locum suum et pax sit inter nos et vos. In nomine patris et filii et spiritus sancti Amen.	May each and every one of you return in peace to your places, and let there be peace be between you and us. In the name of the Father, Son, and Holy Ghost. Amen.

The let the master say the first chapter of the Gospel of St. John ("In the beginning was the Word" etc.), the Creed ("I believe in God the Father" etc.)

Then they may emerge from the circle, one after another, and wash their faces with water and hyssop, and return by another path than that which they arrived by.

---

750. Perhaps 10 is a mistake for ^{1o} = primo ["first"]. Compare Sloane 3853, fol. 21v.

Licentialis	The licencing
Ecce crucem + domini nostri fugite partes adverse vincit Leo de tribu Iuda radix Iesse filius David, nunc ite ad locum predestinatum, sive ad locum vestrum, ac pace unde venistis, et sit pax inter nos et vos, In nomine patris et filii et spiritus sancti Amen. fiat	Behold the cross + of our Lord, Flee ye adversaries! The Lion from the Tribe of Juda, the Root of David, son of Jesse has conquered, go now in peace to your predestined place or places from which you have come, and peace be between us, in the name of the Father, Son, and Holy Ghost. Amen. So be it.

Here followeth a constriction

Ego N fillius N. quoniam tu spiritus N Infernalles rebelles es, et contumaci nec in aliquo obedire curas, verbis que dicuntur per me ad circo in nomine patris et filii et spiritus sancti condempno te N in Infernum et maledictio dei vivi et veri sit super te N. maledictio te per eundem maledictionem qua deus maledixit Chayn, et Ignis et sulphur descendat te N. sicut destendebat supra in habitantes Sodomae gomorhe, Zeboim, Adame, et Zegor nisi velis mihi citius obedire, et perficere omnem voluntatem meam maledico tibi N per omnes Angelos et Archangelos, dei, et per omnia terribilia in celo et in terra et inferno, et nulla Requies sit in te N neque in die neque in nocte, donec perficias omnem voluntatem et desiderium meum privamus et N	I N., Son of N.,* because you infernal spirits N. are rebellious and insolent, and won't obey in any way the words which I have spoken to the circle [*from the circle?] in the name of the Father, Son, and the Holy Ghost, I condemn you N., to hell, and the curse of the living and true God be upon you N. I curse you with the same curse whereby God cursed Cain, and may fire and brimstone descend on you N., as it descended upon the inhabitants of Sodom and Gomorrah, Admah and Zeboyim,† and Zoar, unless you are willing to quickly obey me and accomplish all my wishes. I curse you, O N., by all angels and archangels of God, and by all the frightful things in Heaven, Earth, and hell, and there will be no rest for you, N., either by day or
* In right marg: "22 4." The 4 is in a lighter ink (or pencil?) † So Sodom and Gomorrah, Admah and Zeboyim, see Deut. 29:23 and Genesis 19:24.	

ab omnibus dignitatibus et officciis tuis, et in stagnum sulpheris et Ignis precipio te N ubi et bestia, et pseudo propheta cruciabuntur in secula seculorum fiat fiat. In nomine patris et filii et spiritus sancti, nisi cito obedias quiete et humilliter dictis meis et adimpleas omnem desiderium meum ipso prestante, qui in altissimis sedit et regnat deus Trinus et unus Amen cito cito cito Amen.	night, until you fulfill all my wishes and desires, and we deprive you, N., of all your dignities and offices, and I order you, N., into a lake of fire and brimstone, "where both the beast, and the false prophet will be tormented"* forever and ever. Let it be so; let it be so. In the name of the Father, Son, and Holy Ghost, unless you quickly and quietly and humbly obey my words and fulfill all my desires, with himself supreme, who sits on high and reigns, God, threefold and one. Amen. Quickly, quickly, quickly. Amen.

* Revelations 20:9–10.

Oberion's Circle

I.e., the circle belonging to his work which must be made on the ground, and the master and his associates to stand therein.[751]

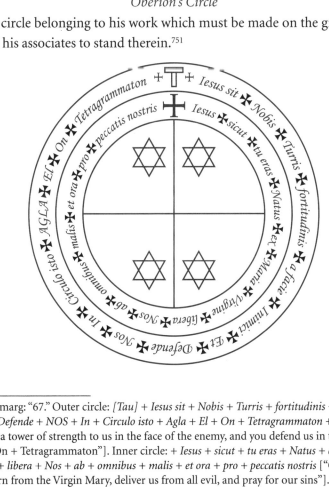

---

751. In right marg: "67." Outer circle: *[Tau] + Iesus sit + Nobis + Turris + fortitudinis + a facie + Inimici + ET + Defende + NOS + In + Circulo isto + Agla + El + On + Tetragrammaton +* ["[Tau] May Jesus be a tower of strength to us in the face of the enemy, and you defend us in this circle + Agla + El + On + Tetragrammaton"]. Inner circle: *+ Iesus + sicut + tu eras + Natus + ex + Maria + Virgine + libera + Nos + ab + omnibus + malis + et ora + pro + peccatis nostris* ["O Jesus, as you were born from the Virgin Mary, deliver us from all evil, and pray for our sins"].

[201]

This is the circle for the great work, i.e., to call the four kings and for all others that come with them or alone.

This circle must be made on the ground or on a table, or on boards.

Note: It must be made with oil, chalk, [??] ashes of palm sticks.[752]

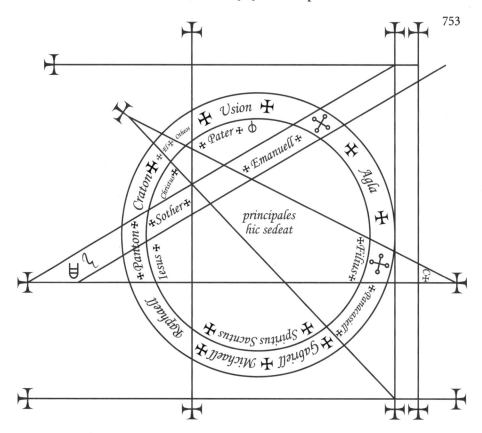

These be the seals of the angels which be full necessary to be made about every circle, for if you make all these about one circle, then shalt thou speed in thy work by the grace of God.[754]

---

752. In right marg: "67."

753. + Usion + + Agla + + Pancasiell + Gabriell + Michaell + Raphaell + Panton + Craton + + El + Otheos + Inside: Pater, filius, Sp[irit]us s[an]ctus ["Father, Son, Holy Ghost"] Iesus Christus, Sother, Emanuell. In very center: principales hic sedeat ["The chief sits (or settles) here"].

754. Sigillum Angelorum Primum ["The first seal of the angels"]; Sigillum Angelorum 2 ["Second seal of the angels"]; Sigillum Angelorum 3 ["Third seal of the angels"]; Sigillum Angelorum 4 ["Fourth seal of the angels"]. In right marg: "252."

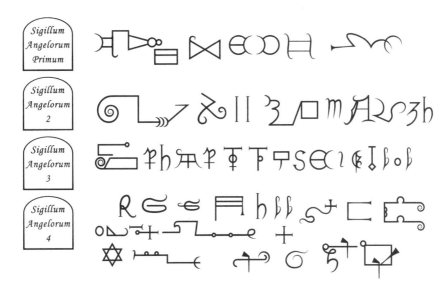

[202]
On the nigromantic doctrine for all useful experiments

The first chapter[755] teaches how to practice conjurations over the spirits, and thus depends the key to the whole art and all arts and all experiments and although all solemnities will have been observed, without this chapter nothing can be completed.[756]

First he who wishes to perform an operation or experiment should consider what kind of art or experiment he should perform, then he must write the whole thing out on paper or parchment as will be taught below, and then he must note carefully the hour and day to begin this art, and what things are necessary for preparing it, and what can be added or dispensed with, and he must note on which day and in which hour it should be done, and when it is so prepared, he must consider in what place he will do it, and so before he begins anything in this art, he must consider all necessary things convenient for this art, and when he has considered and noted it, the exorcist should enter his chamber or other secret place, so that none can see or hinder him, and he should disrobe,[757] and he should have a bath prepared with exorcised water, as will be taught later concerning water. Then let him take the water, and put it upon the top of his head, so that it may run down to his feet, while saying this prayer:

---

755. For this section, compare Mathers, *Clavicula liber* II cap. 1. In particular, Additional MS. 36674, 14r; Sloane 3847, 40v; Aubrey 24, 63v; Additional MS. 10862, 102v.

756. Compare Aubrey 24, 63v: *Ex isto enim capitulo, et ex ejus diligenti observatione pendet clavis omnium atrium, et experimentorum. Et sine isto quamvis omnes solemnitates adhibueris in nulla tamen Arte, aut Magico experimento ad finem perduces.*

757. Latin: *expoliare*. Compare *despoliare*.

Domine Iesu Christe qui formasti indignum de terra et miserabilem peccatorem ad simillitudinem tuam benedicere et sanctificare digneris hanc aquam ut sit michi mundificato et salvamentum mei corporis et anime ut nulla fallacia in me ullo modo possit aparare	O Lord Jesus Christ, who has made me, an unworthy and wretched sinner, after your own likeness; deign to bless and sanctify this water, that it may be a purifier and salvation of my body and soul, so that no deceit may be able to appear.
omnipotens et Ineffabiles pater sicut unigenitum filium tuum a Iohanem Baptista Baptizari confecisti licet Indignus et contemptus suum queso ut aqua ista sit baptismus meus ut mundatus sui ab omnibus peccatus presentibus preteritus et futurus per dominum nostrum Iesum Christum amen.	O almighty and ineffable Father, who permitted John the Baptist to baptize your only-begotten Son, grant I beseech you, that this water may be my baptism, although I am unworthy, and that I may be cleansed from all sins, past, present, and future, through our Lord Jesus Christ. Amen.

Then let him wash all his body, and put on a white linen cloth, and abstain at the least three days from all impurity and obscene language, as will be taught in the section on fasting, and each day recite this prayer, once in the morning, once around noon, around the sixth hour three times, again in the evening four times, and five times [+ when you go to bed],[758] and thus do three days space. And this is the prayer:

Prayer

Oracio Ebraxio Asa, Asaha, Naldrimibas siloe, Anabona, biza, bonilla, ladodoc Acacal vel Cicacal vel achatel cephice penci vel pam~ aru Atabanchata Adonay Eloy emagio Ebraaio acedith vel achedele brach vel barach spannel vel samanul melcadac Eray lyoia Amistra Ugana Machea danit dama yarael vel Rachiel helel homon segon gemas Iesus dominus deus concede mihi ut preservare possim qui facere Intendo ut per te piissime Adonay merear adimplere per dominum nostrum amen	Ebraxio Asa, Asaha,* Naldrimibas siloe, Anabona, biza, bonilla, ladodoc Acacal (or Cicacal or Achatel) cephice penci (or pam~) aru Atabanchata Adonay Eloy emagio Ebraaio acedith (or achedele) brach (or barach) spannel (or samanul) melcadac Eray lyoia Amistra Ugana Machea danit dama yarael (or Rachiel) helel homon segon gemas Jesus Lord God, grant to me that I may be preserved that I intend to accomplish, through O holy Adonay, may I be worthy to accomplish this through our Lord. Amen.
* Compare Mathers, *The Key of Solomon*, p. 85.	

758. So *Clavicula*, e.g., Mathers p. 85, and to complete the sense of the text.

These three days having passed, begin to prepare as described, the art or experiment intended. These three days the weather should be very clear and pleasant, before the day and the hour of the undertaking. After these three days you must begin to prepare, and await the appointed hour, and when that hour has begun, then work. Afterward you will be able to continue in subsequent hours if needed, and all those mentioned above, and thus the exorcist will be able to accomplish his wishes and art.

[+ Concerning the Baths]

This chapter teaches[759] how the baths are to be done. The bath is necessary for the arts, therefore, when you wish to perform any art, on the final day of preparation of your art, all things necessary being arranged, according to the day and hour, with good faith, you must go to a running fountain or a flowing stream, have warm water ready for a bath. Then remove all your clothes, and say these Psalms, "The Lord is my Light"; [760] "The fool has said"; [761] "I said: I will take heed"; [762] "Save me O Lord"; [763] "Let us sing"; [764] "Give glory"; [765] "Whoever will be saved." [766]

And when you are naked as you were born, enter the bath or water, and the exorcist should say:

Exorzizo te creature aqua per ipsum qui vatum [*in locum] constituit ut sine mora aliqua eicias omnem spiritum [im]mundum atque fantasma ut mihi nocere non valeat per dominum nostrum Iesum filium tuum defensorem nostrum qui vivit et regnat per Infinita secula seculorum Amen.	I exorcise you, O creature of water, by him who established you in your place, that without any delay expel all impure spirits and phantasms that would harm me, through our Lord Jesus, your son, our defense, who lives and reigns forever and ever. Amen.

---

759. Compare *Clavicula*, e.g., Mathers p. 85,: Aubrey 24, 23v; Additional MS. 10862, 111r; Additional MS. 36674, 15r; Sloane 3847, 44v.

760. Psalm 26 (KJV 27).

761. Psalm 13 or 52 (KJV 14 or 53).

762. Psalm 38 (KJV 39).

763. Psalm 11 or 68 (KJV 12 or 69).

764. Exodus 15.

765. Psalm 105 (KJV 106).

766. The Athanasian Creed.

In nomine patris et postea Incipiant se lavare sic dicendo Narbalia Misalia dalphalia Annamalia, racharilia gedocheria balohalaria, gemaria, gegeon faria Iesse faria gogay vel goiodits gomtay yayl dayl mysayl yoyl trachyl punli godep Sabaoth Adonay Agalon vel Tetragramaton celion vel cedyon Agenefeton Stimulator primeunaton,	In the name of the Father, (and then they may begin to wash themselves, saying thus:) Narbalia Misalia Dalphalia Annamalia, Racharilia Gedocheria Balohalaria, Gemaria, Gegeon Faria Iesse Faria Gogay or Goiodits Gomtay Yayl Dayl Mysayl Yoyl Trachyl Punli Godep Sabaoth Adonay Agalon or Tetragramaton Celion or Cedyon Agenefeton Stimulator Primeunaton.

And when you have been washed, emerge from the bath, making the sign of the cross, and saying "In the name of the Father" and you should sprinkle exorcized water on your face, saying, "Thou shalt purge me with hyssop, O Lord" etc. Then, put on your clothes while saying these Psalms: "O Lord, rebuke me not";[767] "Blessed are they";[768] "Hear my prayer, O Lord";[769] "Out of the depths";[770] "When I called upon him";[771] "I will give praise";[772] "O how I love";[773] "When Israel went out"; "When the Lord brought back"; "O Lord, you have tested me";[774] and this following oration:

Adonay sanctissime et potens per potentissimum et corroboratissimum nomen domini + El + forte et admirabile bellum magnum et terribile te adoro te laudo te glorifico te benedico te Invoco tibi gracias ago ut hec sit aqua salutus [*salutaris] ut Immunditia abluatur	O Adonay, most holy and powerful, by the most powerful and strengthening name of the Lord + El + strong and wonderful, beautiful, great, and frightful, I honour you, I praise you, I glorify you, I bless you, I invoke you, I give you thanks that this water may be beneficial

767. Psalm 6.

768. Psalm 31 (KJV 32).

769. Psalm 101 (KJV 102).

770. Psalm 129 (KJV 130).

771. Psalm 4.

772. Psalm 9.

773. Psalm 118.97 (KJV 119.97).

774. Psalm 113, 125, and 138 respectively (KJV 114, 126, 139).

| a me et desiderium mei cordis per sanctissime Adonay possim omnibus in horis ad Implere tribuas pater omnium creaturarum queso qui vivis deus per Infinita secula seculorum amen. | and wash away all impurity from me, and that I may be able to accomplish all my desires, through the most holy Adonay. Grant this, I beg, O Father of all creatures, who lives God, forever and ever. Amen. |

[203]

| Deus est vere Jehovahh qui dat uniuersis ut sint quod sunt, et solo verbo vocali per fillium de nichillo produxit omnia qui sunt, ut sint, is vocat omnes stellas, omnem melitiam celi nominibus suis. etc. | God is truly Jehovahh who gives to the whole world in order that they are what they are, and with only his spoken Word, through the Son, brought forth all things from nothingness, in order that they may exist. He calls all the stars, all the hosts of heaven by their names, etc.* |

* *Arbatel* Aph. 13. in translation by Peterson, *Arbatel* (2009).

| Raphaell attributus fuit Tobiae ut parentum sanaret ex periculis liberaret fillium, et ei uxorem suam adduceret. Ita Michael dei fortitudo, populum dei gubernat. Gabriell dei nuntius missus fuit danieli, Mariae, Zachariae, Iohannis Baptiste patri. | So Raphael was sent to Tobias, in order that he free his son from danger, and to persuade his dear little wife. So Michael, the "strength of God," governs the people of God. Gabriel the "messenger of God," was sent to Daniel, Mary, and Zachariah the father of John the Baptist.* |

* Ibid.

| Huius utaris ministerio cum metu et tremore creatoris tui, redemptoris tui et sanctificatoris tui viz, patris et filii et spiritus sancti. | Therefore you should use his help with fear and trembling of your creator, your redeemer, your sanctifier, namely the Father, Son, and Holy Ghost.* |

* Ibid.

Vivit anima **tua** in eternum per eum **qui in te creavit invoca igitur** dominum deum **tuum, et** [+ **illi**] **soli servias.**	Your soul lives for eternity through him who created you. Therefore, call upon the Lord your God, and may you serve him alone.[*]
Invoca me in die tribulationis tue, et exaudi te eripiam te, et glorificabis me. dicit dominus, omnis ante Ignorantiae **est tribulatio animi. Invoco ergo in igno-rantia tua** dominum, **et exaudiet te,** & *above all remember* **ut honorem tribuas** deo, **ac dicas cum psalmista, non nobis domine non nobis etc.**	"Call upon me in the day of trouble; I will deliver you, and you will honour me,"[†] the Lord says. All ignorance is but the tribulation of the mind, therefore call upon the Lord in your ignorance, and he will hear you clearly. *And above all remember* that you assign the honour to God, and say with the Psalmist: "Not to us, O Lord, not to us but to your name be the glory."[‡]
Nulla enim est virtus, vel in celo, vell in terra, vell inferno, qui non descendat a deo	Indeed there is no power whether in Heaven, or Earth, or in hell, which doesn't descend from God.[§]
I syed, **et illi soli servias #** deus a te **requiret animum ut honores filium filii verbum custodias in corde tuo. Hunc si honoraveris, iam fecisti voluntatem pa-tris qui in celis est.**	I said, "may you serve him alone." God requires from you a mind, in order to respect the Son, and keep the words of his Son in your heart. If you have respected him, then you have done the will of your Father who is in Heaven.[⁋]

[*] Ibid., Aph. 14, in translation by Peterson, *Arbatel* (2009), p. 25.
[†] Psalm 49:15 (KJV 50:15).
[‡] Psalm 113:9 (KJV 115:1). This paragraph is taken from Arbatel Aph. 7, in translation by Peterson, *Arbatel* (2009), p. 15.
[§] *Op. cit.* Aph. 8, p. 17.
[⁋] *Op. cit.* Aph. 14, p. 25.

To us, **if the love of our neighbour be joined, the whole law and the** prophets are **fulfilled. True divinity.**

Hammond [775]

---

775. "True deuinitye / hammond" is in brown ink, and in a different hand. In right marg: "239."

776

[204]

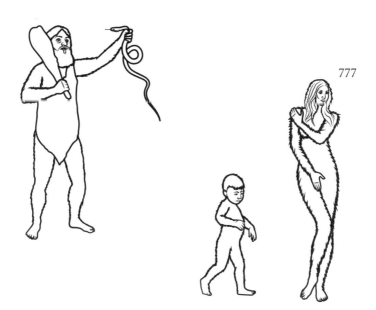

777

---

776. Seems to have been inspired by Boaistuau and Fenton, *Certaine secrete wonders of nature* (1569), 70, depicting a man instructing a dog to pull up a mandrake.

777. Perhaps inspired by Boaistuau and Fenton, *Certaine secrete wonders of nature* (1569), 12, which says: "there was brought to [Charles III] a maide, rough and covered with haire like a beare, the which the mother had brought forth in so hideous and deformed a shape, by having too much regarde to the picture of S. Iohn cloathed with a bears skinne … By the like meanes … a princesse … was delivered of a childe blacke lyke an Ethiopian … lyke unto a Moore, accustomably tied at hir bed."

[205]⁷⁷⁸

779

[+ Notes]⁷⁸⁰

---

778. To judge from original foliation jumping from 110 to 114, there appears to be six pages missing here, probably additional spirit portraits. In right marg.: "236."

779. The second drawing seems to have been inspired by Boaistuau and Fenton, *Certaine secrete wonders of nature* (1569), 49, supposedly showing a monstrous fish seen by over two hundred people in Paris, including doctors of the university.

780. The next eight pages are blank, save for material inserted at later times. This material includes a five-line attempt at an index, a poem by E. H. W. Meyerstein entitled "Fairy Lore," and the following note: "This magical MS, which should not be sold for under £100, contains the rite of Oberyon (i.e., Oberon) explicitly called (p. 80) 'Kinge of the fayries' together with pictures of him and other spirits. E.H.W.M."
    Below that the note: "R.C.S., who was responsible for colouring and mutilating (?) the initials, &c in this MS was R.C. Smith the Astrologer, and the charm against thieves on p. 51 is [????] (looks like "suffered") with the date here offered (?), in his 'Astrologer of the Nineteenth Century', 1825."

PART 2: KEY OF SOLOMON[781]

781. At the beginning, this section includes the following typed note:

Key of Solomon

Contained in this volume is an English, late sixteenth century manuscript fragment. Folio, thirty pages on fifteen leaves (9 inches x 13 inches). Written in black ink in a secretary hand, sixty lines to the page. Rubricated in places, the rubrication invariably faded and with fourteen magical diagrams in black and red, plus a number of marginal diagrams in black and one leaf containing eighteen (of twenty) sigils in black and red. This leaf is however defective having a lower corner torn off (some 2 ½ x 3 ½ inches) losing the whole of two sigils and part of the margin of another. All the leaves are frayed, some with marginal tears and one with a piece torn from the margin losing the last few letters of fourteen lines and a part of a marginal diagram. Some leaves have margins mounted. Repairs have been carried out as necessary.

Magical manuscripts in English of this date are of great rarity, even when—as in this instance— in incomplete state. The text consists of a substantial fragment of a version of the Clavicle, or KEY OF SOLOMON, written in English with some Latin invocations and showing interesting variations from the usual renderings of the text. The Hebrew letters are heavily and inaccurately drawn, the copyist being evidently ignorant of their proper form, while on the seals and diagrams the six-pointed Star of David is in almost every case replaced with a cross. In the body of the text are biblical quotations from the Prologue to St. John's Gospel, a variation not recorded in continental texts. The parts of the Clavicle on these leaves concern the elaborate preparations for invoking demons (with variations on their names: e.g. Reatonay, Elzeph, Terebinthus) and various spells of a largely protective or beneficial nature "To make theives stande." "To make one fair." The pages are numbered from 206 to 235, but in a much later hand, and as no known version of the Key of Solomon has anything remotely approaching another two hundred pages, this fragment may be presumed to have been disbound from a miscellaneous manuscript volume. The scribe and original owner cannot be identified with certainty, but it appears to have been copied from a similar manuscript belonging to "Thomas .... Clarke in Divinitie." Its later provenance is unknown.

[206]

[+ The Eye of Abraham, for proving persons guilty of theft, that they confess their guilt]

To this experiment[782] thou must take litharge[783] of silver, that is to say, the purifying of silver, that goldsmiths make [and green oxidized copper (?)][784] and bray[785] him [*them] small, and grind it upon a marble stone, and distemper[786] it with the white of an egg. And when it is tempered, make an eye on the wall or in parchment, and stick him on the wall. Then take a nail of latten[787] of the weight of a penny and hammer of ewe (?) the head and the steel of box, that is a mallet. And then make in the eye two circles and write in the first of the two, *Iesus Saluator* ["Jesus the Saviour"], and in the lesser circle write, *Iesus siens [*sciens] rerum occultarum & manifestarum verus purgator, ocuins nomine precioso* ["Jesus knowing [+ all] hidden and manifest things, the true purifier, O you whose name is precious"].[788]

Then say this charm:

I conjure all the lookers on this eye, and all them that in this thing be guilty of and is beholding of this eye; I conjure them by the virtue of the Father and of the Son and of the Holy Ghost, and by all the names of God, Alpha & Omega + and by all the apostles, and by all the evangelists and martyrs and confessors and by the holy elements, and by St. Mary, the mother of our Lord Jesus Christ, and by all their works, that all them that be guilty of such things which is gone, and all they that behold this eye so fast, strike it on his eye, by the virtue of the holy names of our lord Jesus Christ, before said, that it never cease till his eye be out, or give answer and for them be brought again, and God for his mickle[789] might, that right as I smite this nail on this place, that we may believ[e] that all virtue that is in these words aforesaid, may form to pain and to confusion.

And while thou smitest, say "*Rabat, vel Rabas, Selarinum Reatonay seliare Reatony facite apperere qui illam Rem, furatus sine de qua querimus*" ["Rabat (or Rabas), Se-

---

782. Sloane 3850: *Oculus Abraham: Ad probandum culpabiles personas de furto ut confiteantur Reatus suos. Accipe lethargirum. ...* Compare Eye of Abraham discussion in Klaassen, "Three Early Magic Rituals to Spoil Witches" *Opuscula.* Vol. 1, No. 1 (2011): 1–10. Compare also Sloane 3846, 41r and 83r.

783. Litharge (Latin: *lithargyrus*): lead oxide.

784. So Sloane 3850: *viride aeris ana.*

785. Bray: beat in a mortar. Latin: *tere* ["grind"].

786. Distemper: moisten or mingle.

787. Latten: a mixed yellowish metal resembling brass.

788. Sloane 3850, 33v: *IHS Saluator + IHS saluator seculi + / IHS sciens omnium rerum occultarum + / + IHS Sciens omnium rerum ocultarum / IHS saluator IHS saluator.*

789. Mickle: great.

larinum Reatonay seliare Reatony, make appear that thing stolen, or other thing which we seek"], and thou shalt see the right eye water, and if water not, smite the eye again with the hammer, and begin this so oft till thou hast tidings of the theft. And begin this charm on the first quarter of the Moon, or in the last quarter of the Moon, when thou wilt, &c. Now follows the form of the eye as it ought to be made.

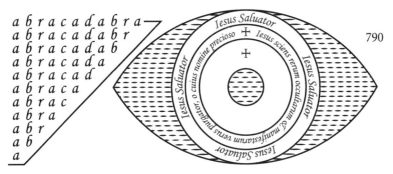

790

[+ For the toothache]

sicut deleo hanc literam de isto sanctissimo nomine de abracadabra ita per virtutem huius sacratissimi nominis deleatur morbus et dolor dentrum a I B, In nomine patris et filii et spiritus sancti deleat te morbum deus filius + deleat te morbum spiritus sanctus + deleant te morbum Amen.	As I erase this letter from this most sacred name Abracadabra, thus by the power of this most sacred name may this sickness and toothache be erased from I B., in the name of the Father, Son, and Holy Ghost; may you erase the sickness, God the Son + may you erase the sickness, God the Holy Ghost + may they delete the sickness. Amen.

For the toothache He . corbe . hor . horss . gaubell . X . peboxtem *probatum* ["proven"] [791]

bgbdñutc trthbehc vcb dn thc cyc [.]vcot ro wcnu [.]ro dbsnicou utceh [.]ro mrthco ro bnd [.]cscbvcv [792]

---

790. The eye has very faded lettering inside, evidently matching the directions in the text: Write in the first of the two, *Iesus Saluator* ["Jesus the Saviour"], and in the lesser circle write, *Iesus s[c]iens rerum occultarum & manifestarum verus purgator, o cuius nomine precioso* ["Jesus knowing [+ all] hidden and manifest things, the true purifier, O you whose name is precious"].

791. *Peboxtdm* is evidently a cipher for "probatum" ["proven"], which is written beside it in pencil.

792. Translation may be: Againste toothache sea in the eye sent ?or wenn or iaunders stech ?or other or any ?eveases.

This abovesaid,[793] must be written in a little piece of parchment, and at the scraping out of enenery lime, you must say, *ut pot[??]*, I think it were mought,[794] if only the eleven letters, abraca[da]bra, were written and scraped out, singulatar, you must en[??] begin at the furthest or lowest letter, and so ascend upwar[ds], saying as is above written &c.

Many hath healed diverse diseases this way, it were by little and little away (?) [207] to call any [????????????????] the earth, or water or fire, and to make any spirit of any d[?????????????????????] to appear and give answer to thee. In the second or fourth day of the Moon, thou shalt work this, or in the sixth, eighth, tenth, twelfth, or fourteenth, or else not. And when thou will call this art, read this conjuration, three times or nine times, and of warrants he shall appear to thee, having these characters that shall follow.

I conjure thee thou spirit, N., by the power and might of the Father the Son, and the Holy Ghost. Amen. *Benedisite dominus* ["Bless ye, O Lord"], O thou spirit, N., I conjure thee and charge thee, and bind thee, that thou come and appear, in this stone of crystal, in a fair form as visible as one man seeth another, by all power and strength of all spirits, by the Virgin Mary that bare our lord Jesus Christ, and by Michael, Raphael, and Gabriel. Also I conjure thee by the ten virgins, which waited with their lamps for the Lord. I conjure thee and bind thee, and adjure thee, thou spirit N., that thou dost come and appear as is before rehearsed, I charge thee, thou spirit N., by heaven, earth, and the sea, and hell, and by all things contained in them, and by Mary Magdalene and her fellowship, by the faith of the martyrs and twelve Apostles, by Matthew, Mark, Luke, and John by the praises and prayers that ye said to the honour of God. Also I conjure thee, N., that thou come to this stone, by and by, without any delay or tarrying, by all the host of angels and archangels, and by all the holy company of saints and good spirits. Also I bind thee, thou spirit N., by the virtue of all herbs and stones and grass and spices and glasses, and by these holy names of God, Sother + Emanuell + Panton + Craton + Eleyson + theamaton + agla + Alpha + & Omega + Tetragramaton + Sabaoth + vermes + Athanatos + Ely + Eloy + caramatos + Jesus + Also I conjure thee and bind thee, thou N., by all light and lights and stars and frost and cold, ice and snow, winter and summer, days and nights times, years and months, hours and minutes, degrees and by all the course of the air, that thou come and appear in this stone that I may see thee so well as one man seeth another, to do all this, and to tell me the truth of all things that I shall ask of thee. I conjure thee, N., by the virtues of Christ, by his agony and bloody sweat, by his cross and passion, by his death and burial,[795] by his glorious resurrection and ascension, and by the coming of the Holy Ghost our comforter, that thou, N., come and fulfill all my mind and intent as I have before rehearsed, to all these things that I would know.

---

793. I.e., "He . Corbe" etc.

794. Enenery line: error for "every line." Mought: permitted.

795. In left marg.: "w-" glyph.

Also, I conjure thee by the holy psalter of David and by all the holy prayers therein contained, and by the faith of the faithful. Also I conjure thee by the sacrament of the supper of the Lord, and by the altar of the testament, both new and old, and all the virtue in them contained. Also I bind thee, thou spirit N., by these three words + tetagramaton + anatemate + anatematereth + and by all that belongeth to these three words. Also I conjure, charge, adjure, and bind thee, N., that thou come and appear in this stone of crystal, and give me a true answer of all things that I shall ask thee of. I command thee by the help of God, and by the power and virtue of all that move upon the earth, or in the earth, or water of the sea, or in the fire. This I charge thee, N., by the high God omnipotent that suffered his death on Good Friday and rose again the third day to the redemption of all mankind, by his fasting and by his carrying to the steeple (?) and mountain and by the power with the which he answered the devil, when he said, "Lo, Jesus, command these that thee be made bread," and by God the Father, the Son, and the Holy Ghost, praised be the holy Trinity, three persons in unity. Amen.

[208]

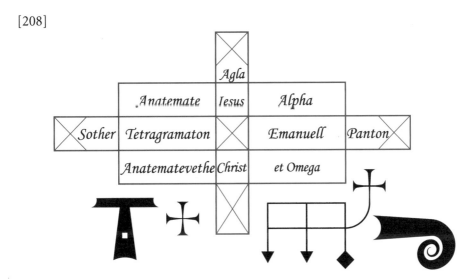

This experiment that followeth is to overcome any enemies [796]

and to get favour of all men. If thou wilt bear these characters with thee and say this every day before thou either eat or drink, and it is true and proved by Friar Bacon, who ever used this.

O Lord God, the devil goeth about like a roaring lion, seeking whom he may devour, the flesh lusteth against the spirit, the world persuadeth unto vanities, that I may forget thee my lord God, and so forever be damned. Thus am I miserably on every side besieged of cruel and unrestful enemies, and like at every moment to perish, if I be not defended with thy godly power, against their tyranny. I therefore,

---

796. In marg.: "w" glyph. Below it in marg.: "HP."

wretched sinner, despair of my own strengths which indeed are none. Most heartily I pray thee to indue[797] me with strength from above, that I may be able through thy help with strong faith, to resist Satan, with fervent prayer to mortify these raging lusts of the flesh, with continual meditation of thy holy laws, to avoid the fleshly vanities and transitory pleasures of this wicked world, that I through thy grace being set at liberty from the power of my enemies, may live and se[rve?] thee in holiness and righteousness all the days of my life. Amen.

This character following, belongeth to the prayer aforesaid and ought to be worn about thee, when thou hast many enemies and [by] the grace of God, thou shalt overcome them all be they never so strong.

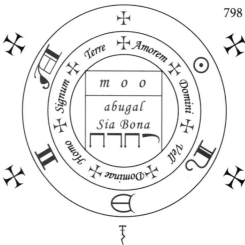

Depart in peace or spirit that have unto me, without damage, hurt, or any other creature. always ready and A[nd come] where you, in the name of the Son and of the The peace of God tween me and you.

798

from me, ye spirits or hath appeared any manne[r of] disquiet unto me or And be ye or you obedient unto me. soever I shall call the Father and of Holy Ghost. Amen. be alwa[ys] be Amen &c.

MILANT VAH VITALOT

fro bll mbnnco rf Hcbibehc ["For all manner of headache"][799]

Jesus • Jesus • Jesus • *filii dei propicius esto mihi peccatore* ["Son of God, be propitious to me, a sinner"] + marce heie [mark here (?)] gotheuwai • abose • abose • abose •

---

797. Indue: cover or clothe.

798. Outer circle has symbols. The second circle has the words *amorem + domini + vel + dominae + homo + signum + terre +* ["the love of a lord or a lady"]. Inner circle includes the words *m o o / abugal (?) / Sia bona* and in Hebrew letters: *YHVH.* Below the circle is another variant of the headache charm from Cardano, reading *Milant, Vah, Vitalot.* See Folger p. 52.

799. Above 'c' is written 'e'; above 'b' is written 'a'; above 'i' is written 'g'.

[209]

For to bind any ground or house or field that nothing shall be stole out, by no thief, be he man or be it woman, and this characters that shall be made hereafter must be laid in the field, yard, or house. And as long as they there lie, no thief can carry anything away and if this bond be read three times when the characters be laid. *Probatum* ["Proven"]:

They that trust unto the Lord are like the Mount Sion, which moveth not from his place but standeth fast forever. So I conjure all thieves that thee be unmoveable, as thee have or become, into this ground to fetch anything out as Jerusalem is closed round about with mountains, even so doth the Lord close about this ground on every side. Also I bind this ground and house with all that in them is, lest the tyrannous power of the ungodly, should press and fet[800] any thing out of it without the leave of the just. Also I beseech thee, Holy Ghost, here to set, all thieves to let, they do not any of these good away fet. I bind all thieves by all these true and godly sentences that none of them have power, to carry any of these goods, except they (?) lord sustaineth the house, they labour in vain to hold that up, and the city also except the Lord keep it, the watchmen wake in vain. Also you thieves that hither come, I bind you: that you carry nor drive nothing from hence. It is but vain after your rest to rise early and eat your bread, in sweet and in sorrow, you shall tarry here till I do give leave, by the virtue of the Father and of the Son and of the Holy Ghost, also I bind you, so fare and fast here, as ever was the fiend in the bottomless pit, heretofore, by the virtue of the holy names of God, + Elsca + abbadra + Alpha + and Omega + Leysce + oristion + Ieremon + hefan + Egerquerpone + Elzepha + Res + egerion + petha + hombonar + Stimulamaton + nathanathoy + Erio moymos + peb + theou + and by all these afore rehearsed and shall be here after I conjure you thieves, and bind you all by the living and true God, that did descend into the lower parts, and by Mary, the mother of him, and by St. John the Baptist, and by that same power that God gave to King Solomon, when he bound all spirits into a vial of glass. So I bind all thieves that hither come, any good away to fet, I beseech God he will them all let, this I trust and this I believe, that God will do his good works to preve.[801] Also true and also sound, as I do stand here on this ground, by the virtue of God's might, I bind you thieves by day and night, yet I adjure and charm all thieves, be they never so evil that ye stand here still, and have no power to move, more than a stone, by the virtue of persons three, God one, and truth and might most, let these thieves with all their boost.[802] Also I conjure

---

800. Fet: fetch.

801. Preve: prove.

802. Boost: casket or box. Perhaps an error for "boot," ie., stolen goods.

and bind all this ground with all the goods therein by the virtue of this holy prayer the which I shall say to the honour of God and for the safeguard of these goods against all thieves.

Lord, remember this good work with all my affections whom I have sworn and vowed unto the Lord God of Jacob, saying I will not enter into the tabernacle of my house, nether climb up into my bed, I will not sleep with mine eyes neither slumber with mine eyelids until I prepare a place for the Lord, even a tabernacle for the mighty God of Jacob, this place. Lo, we have heard of him in Ephrata where we have found it in the bushfield. Let me therefore enter into this tabernacle, let us all fall down before his footstool. Arise, Lord, unto thy mansion, thou and the ark of thy strength. Let the priests do on righteousness and thy faithful rejoice for thy servant David's sake, defer with the coming of thine anointed, for the Lord hath made a faithful oath unto David himself, which he will not change. Of the seed of thy belly shall I set on the seat royal, if thy children will keep my covenants and ordinances, which I shall teach them, then shall the sons of them sit in the seat royal from age to age, for the Lord hath chosen Sion, he hath chosen her for his habitation. This quiet place shall be my perpetual rest, here will I dwell for it delighteth me. I will among the yearly fruits, and satisfy the poor man with food. I noughte [=would?] God shall clothe this place with health, and the faithful shall rejoice in safety, here shall I set forth the flourishing [210] Empire of David, and prepare the lantern for the right possession of (?) these goods, his enemies shall I clothe with confusion, but upon him shall I set his flourishing crown,[803] glory be to the Father and to the Son and to the Holy Ghost, as it was in the beginning, is now, and ever shall be, world without end. Amen. Amen. Amen.

Also, I conjure and bind all thieves by all these holy prayers, and by all other good words that be able to be spoken or thought.

All this truly done, of warranties there shall nothing be carried off thy ground, nor out of thy house. And thou must have this pentacle written in parchment and lay it in the house upon the ground, and if there be no house divide into some tree where it may not consume with wet nor mustiness, and thou shalt see it will do the pleasure by the grace of God.

---

803. Psalm 132 (not from *The Great Bible*): "I haue ordened a lanterne for myne anoynted. As for hys enemies, I shall clothe them with shame, but upon hym selfe shall hys crowne floryshe."

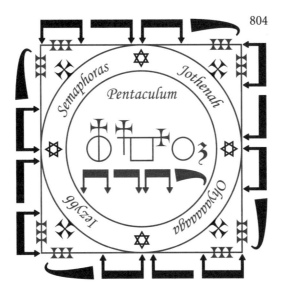

To find **treasure of the earth, make this figure following with the blood of a black whelp and hang it about a white cock's neck.** And go there as the treasure is suspected, and cast your cock out of your hand, and he shall go and stand right over it and crow. Dig there and take it out of the ground without any clerk, and your cock must have a cord or a lace of seven yards long about his leg to have him again when you will. *Probatum est* ["It is proven"].[805]

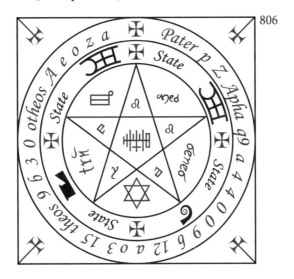

---

804. Includes words *Semaphoras * Jothenah * Ohyaaaaaga * Iezybb.*

805. In left marg: "HP."

806. Includes words *pater p Z Alpha q9 ...theos ... otheos A e o z a; state state state state* ["stop stop stop stop"].

[211]

[+ Ritual for hunting]

[??]⁸⁰⁷ in the which he enclosed all manner of beasts, and it must be made in linen cloth with the blood of such a beast as thou desirest, and look how many beasts so many seals, and put it upon an altar or under, the space of nine days the Moon waxing, the tenth day of July or else the fifth or seventh of August in the fourth hour. It must be written, and all this aforesaid observed. Put it under thy right arm, and go an hunting, and when thou seeth such a beast as is for thee, cast the seal against them, saying these words that hereafter followeth.

Christus Vincit Christus regnat Christus imperat, state, state state in virtu te istius sigillis imobiles quasi lapis o fere Coniuro vos per ista magnam nomina dei, Lemarii, agla thosauroste balgar enaloy tetragramaton, abrotanadoma vel anabrotam, nadoma Langime Lanaziryn (?) Lanagenagim, Lanaquiry, Lanagata, Lanarosy, Layfa Lafym, & per omnia terribilia [+ nomina] dei ut sato [*stes?] & sine mora stets & potestatem, non habeatis ab isto loco recedere, donec ego, N, filius N, de vobis voluntatem meam perfeci~ & hoc ego praencipio & impero ex vertute & in vertute, per vertutem que deus creatore nominem, dedit, ade & filius hominis, agios, agios, agios, fiat, fiat, fiat, amen, amen, amen.	Christ conquers, Christ rules, Christ commands; stop, stop, stop, by the power of this sigil, immovable as a stone; O wild beast, I conjure you by these great names of God: Lemarii, Agla Thosauroste Balgar Enaloy Tetragrammaton, Abrotanadoma (or Anabrotam), Nadoma Langime* Lanaziryn Lanagenagim, Lanaquiry, Lanagata, Lanarosy, Layfa Lafym, and by the terrible [+ names] of God, that you stop without delay or power, and may you not depart from this place, until I, N., child of N., have accomplished my will of you, and this I order and command from the strength and in the strength and by the strength which God the creator's name have given Adam and the Son of Man, agios, agios, agios, fiat, fiat, fiat. Amen. Amen. Amen.

* Compare Razielis: Lagumem Lanazirni, Lanagelagyn, ... in Peterson, *The Sixth and Seventh Books of Moses*, 268.

---

814. First line is missing.

Love experiment, true and proved of many

Take a frog that is using to dry land and put him into a pot, that is made full of holes and stop it fast. Then bury the pot in a cross highway in an anthill, with something, and let it be there nine days and look thou stop it fast, and that thou goest against the wind that it hear no noise, and at the nine days' end go and take out the pot, and thou shalt find two bones in it, take them and put them in a running water, and one of them will float against the stream. Mark it well but keep them both, and make thee a ring, and take part of that it swum against the stream, and set it in the ring, and when thou wilt have any woman and put it on her right hand, or else touch her therewith, and she shall never rest till she hath been with thee &c. If thou wilt no more of her, and will have her to go away, touch her with the other bone, and she will not tarry with thee. Proven.[808]

For Love

To send her away

finis ["end"]

For showtinge [=shooting] write these names,

and put them into the arrows' heads that thou wilt win with: suad, magas, lumbit imbro cramunth pullus, cralcrach, bith, Inflew, cabeanthew, and the pouc[h] of her pookke,[809] defellarwff, calphe, bath, bts Iuncts now~ ber Impemath, bts yngle Ingrye, ell, Ryborw, in canus, horre, haroront ne t°ra., nothing except but power in flight. Take these names and put them in thy arrows' heads, and that day that thou wilt shoot for any great wager, say "ago marownt" three times, and shoot now (?) that arrow, but when you will win and get the game, and then prick the second finger on the left hand and bet the head of the arrow in the blood, that same day that you will

---

808. This is the earliest known practitioner's account of the magical amulet called the toad bone. The element of the bone that floats against the current is hitherto unknown before the nineteenth century. See Chumbley, *The Leaper Between: An Historical Study of the Toad-bone Amulet; Its Forms, Functions and Praxis in Popular Magic* (Three Hands Press, 2012).

809. Pookke: possibly poke, a pocket, or a wallet.

shoot, and say in the loosing of your arrow, "power in flight," and that day if you shoot for a 1,000 pounds, you shall win it. Proven.

[212]

[????] a white (?) lofe (?) & [???] [+ Rite using bread loaf to find a thief]

Make two circles on the bottom, and within the circles, write *Matheus, Marcus, Lucas, Iohannes* ["Matthew, Mark, Luke, John"], and then make a double cross over the bottom, and then make on the over part a double circle, and within the circles write the names abovesaid and then make a double cross and within the four spaces write the words following,

> *hec munera* + *hec sancta sacafacta [?????]* + *illumina [???]* ["this money + this holy ...."] [810]

+ Then take a key with cross wards and write on the one side of the key, *Ieseus [*iustus] es dominum* ["You are just, O Lord"], and on the other side *& rectum iudicium tuum* ["and your judgment is right"].[811] Then let the key lie till it be dry, then take four knives with white hafts, all of one make, and write on the first knife Tetragramaton ☩ ☩☩, and on the second knife, Sabaoth ☩ ☐☩ and on the third knife Emanuel ☩ ☩☩, and on the fourth knife, Occinomos ☩ Ð. Then take your key that is written and thrust the wards in at the top of the loaf, thus saying,

Infigo te clauis in panem istum per patrem & filium, & spritum sanctum, & per quinque vulnera, domini nostri Iesu Christi & per virginitatem beatem marie virginis ut tu panis mihi demonstres veritatem & non falcitatem, de re qua dubitamus, in nomine patris & filii & spritus sancti, amen.	I fasten you nails to this bread through the Father, Son, and Holy Ghost, and by the five wounds of our Lord Jesus Christ, and by the virginity of the blessed Virgin Mary, in order that you, O bread, may disclose to me the truth and not the falsehood, regarding the thing which we debate, in the name of the Father, Son, and Holy Ghost. Amen.

Then take your first knife and put it in at the side of the loaf saying, *Infigo te cultelle in panem* ["I fasten you dagger to this bread"] &c. Say thus at the putting in of every of the other knives at the three quarters, then say thus,

---

810. The rest is illegible.

811. Psalm 118:137 (KJV 119:137).

I charge you, bread, key, and knives, by the virtue of the Father, the Son, and the Holy Ghost, and by the virtue of our blessed lady, and by the virtue of all those blessed words that be written within thee, or upon thee, or about thee, that if such a person have such a thing, that thou turnest about with the sun, and if not, thou turnest against the Sun, or else stand still.

Then take the key betwixt you and another, betwixt your fingers, thus saying:

Coniuro te pane per patrem et filii, & spiritum sanctum, & per deum qui fecit celum & terra, mare & omnia que in eis sunt, ego coniuro te panem per sanctum trinitatem et per Christi baptismalis puritatem, & flagillantem Christi & per alapas & clauos quibus crucifixus fuerit in crucem & per verum sanguinem, sanctum preciosum quo rede[??]* sumus ut tu panem mihi demonstres veritatem & not (!) falcitatem, de re qu[a] suspicionem habemus. Coniuro te panem per istud nomen quod est, Tetragramaton +, domini quod aaron tulitt in ffronte scriptum, & per maiestatem dei & per omnes angelos & archangelos tronos & dominaciones principatus & potestates, & per omnia miracula que deus fecit, Coniuro te panem per illud miraculum quod deus fecit in deserto, quando ex quinque panibus & duobus piscibus safiauit [*saturaverunt] quinque milia homini, & per illam cenam quam Christus cenauit cum discipulis suis quando	I conjure you, O bread, by the Father, Son, and Holy Ghost, and by the God who made Heaven and Earth, the sea, and everything that is in them; I conjure you, O bread, by the holy Trinity, and by the whipping of Christ, and by the beating, and by the nails which attached him to the Cross, and by the truth, the sacred precious blood, by which we have been redeemed, that you, O bread, reveal the truth to me concerning the matter that we have suspicions about. I conjure you, O bread, by this name which is Tetragrammaton +, which was written on Aaron's front, and by the greatness of God, and all the Angels and Archangels, Thrones and Dominations, Principalities and Powers, and by all the wonders which God has made. I conjure you, O bread, by the miracle which God performed in the desert, when he satisfied five thousand people with five loaves and two fish. And by that supper which Christ dined with his disciples, when he

* Reading *redditi*.

ben[e]dixit panem fregit & dedit, eis dicens, accipite, & manducate, hoc est enem corpus meum quod pr[o] vobis, tradetur, ut tu panus nobis demonstres veritatem, de, r[e] qua, modo, querimus.	blessed the bread, broke it, and gave it to them, saying, "take this and eat it—this is my body, which is given for you—it will be handed over."* That the bread will reveal the truth to you concerning the thing which we are now asking.
* Luke 22:19–20.	

812

---

812. Solomonic hexagram and pentagram, similar to that in *The Lesser Key of Solomon* book Goetia. Words include: "*Alpha et ω, sig-num* ["the sign"] *tav, Te-tra-gra-ma-ton, Iesus Christus,* and (in Hebrew characters) *IHVH*."

The second seal is labeled *pentaculum Solomonis* ["the pentacle of Solomon"], similar to that in Goetia, words include: *abdiato, ballarot, bell[on]y, hally, hulliza, Soluzen.* Later analogues can be found in Sloane 3824, 100v: *Abdia, Ballarot, Tulliza (?), Bollony (?), Halla (?)*; Sloane 3825: *Abdia, Ballator (!), Bellony, Hally, Halliza, Soluzen*; Wellcome MS. 3203, 41: *Abdis, Ballator, Bellony, Hally, Hallias, Soluzen.*

[213]

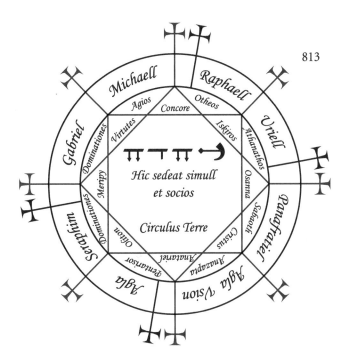

813

[+ Instructions to the Steward]

This Regal Regent made by me person Clarcke [clerk?] in divinity, Thomas Drowre, with other four or doctors and masters of the high science under God, two of the high schools of Orleans, and two of the universities within the realm of England, with the help and counsel of Friar Bacon. These six consenting in one that this experiment used after this manner following in all degrees is as sure as the gospel, and a eleven times by them proved having a carrier at their commandment to deliver or shew any manner of things that they demanded, either of treasures hidden, or any other things, Now this clarcke [clerk (?)] in divinity and master under God, Thomas

813. Compare with *de nigromancia*, e.g., Sloane 3853, 50v; Wellcome MS. 110, fol. 17r. Words and names include: *Raphaell, Uriell, Pan*ª*fratiel, agla vsion, agla, seraphim, Gabriel, Michaell, / otheos, athanathos, Sabaoth, anazapta, pentarisor, dominationes (?), agios / concore, iskiros, osanna, cristus, anatariel, oliton, merip~u, virtutes / hic sedeat simull, et socios* ["he may likewise sit here, and the associates"] / *Circulus terre* ["the circle of the earth"].
Leipzig, Cod. Mag. 16, 276: *Raphael, Uriel, Pancratyel, Usion, Agla, Serapin, Gabriel, Michael, / Agyos, O Theos, Athanatos, Sabaoth, Amalyesin, Pontarizin, Carisar, S. Dominationes / Concors, Yskyros, Osanna, Christus, Amatariel, Eliton, Merison, Virtutes.*
Sloane 3853, 50v: *Raphael, Uryel, [Pan]craciel, Amaliezim, Pantarizim, Seraphyn, Gabriel, Michael, / Agyos, Agyon, Otheos, Sabaoth, Usyon, Agla, Carizar, dominationes sancte / concore, iskyros, osanna, Christus, amaturiel, Olicon, Iesus, Virtutes / Magister et Socio* ["master and servant"].
Compare also Additional MS. 36674, 158r.

Drowre aforesaid, at God's calling of him before his departing of his life, out of this world, gave his full power and authority at the request and hearty desire of this steward, asked of charity, he gave fully all their powers to him in all causes to obtain as they had done, to that he used himself and his company, punishing themselves for the love of Jesus Christ in all degrees after this manner as hereafter followeth, the which this steward promised him faithfully, to see all things always before his working, by God's grace to be fulfilled, wherefore he made him very perfect in the science, wherefore thou parson or priest, ask ever counsel of thy steward.

This being done so the (?) steward so to deat (?) for (?) [for] (?) the love of thy (?) God [?????????????] [814]

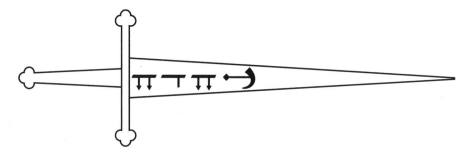

[214]

Nine days before thou begin this work, and nine days after, pena[nce] (?) straightly, I charge thee to take, fasting with bread and water. Five days before thou begin, and five days after thou hast sped, also secretly I command thee to fulfill thy pilgrimages, what time thou hast spe[d] (?) furthermore steward, I charge thee in any wise to be pure and clean and to come in with thine apparel very cleanly cleanly [*cleansed (?)] and to be contrite and sorry for thine offences done against God, and clearly forgive all the world as freely as Christ forgave his death and as thou wouldst be forgiven thyself of him, Also, steward, I charge thee in the pain of eternal damnation that thou be true in fulfilling this work, as thou wilt answer at the dreadful day of doom, both for them that be dead and for them that be alive, also I charge thee to wear next upon thy body a shirt of hair and very sharp of hair, also thou must privily punish thy body with a sharp rod of birch, once a day, nine days before thou begin thy work, and nine days after for thine offences done against our saviour Jesus Christ. Also I charge thee, steward, to do thy duty to hear mass of St. Cyprian, devoutly offering thereat, re (?).[815] Now I charge thee to fulfill all these things, steward, as thou wilt

---

814. Very faded.

815. Perhaps "etc."

obtain thy purpose, and these things doing, truly, without doubt thou shalt obtain. But I charge thee, look all thy garments that long [816] to this work be purely clean and sweet smelling & c.

This longeth to the priest to use after this manner following

Seven days before the proof of this experiment, this I charge thee, to be pure and clean, contrite and sorry, and purely meek in all causes, but specially live chaste, and use things, before said, in any wise three days before, then with good devotion say the Mass of St. Cyprian, and look thou have none upon thee but pure clothes, honest and clean smelling, of sweet odours and spices very sweetly. Look privily that thou have upon thee thy holy sacrament of an (?) element, and let it be so privily kept, that it be known to [no] person living but to the steward and to thyself, and with that holy oil thou shalt make a cross on the forehead of the sword bearer, what time thou and he enterest into the circle, saying the prayers that he shall thee shew turning you into the east, and let you have privily a stole to give the steward and look that you have holy water made as the book makes mention to cast upon you and the sword bearer, and in any wise look that no hastiness, nor no swearing be used, nor do nothing but ask counsel of the steward and in no wise fear nothing whatsoever thou hearest or seest. Speak not but keep thy mind on thy book, and sometime thou mayest cast up thine eye and look to the steward, and if thou see him smile thou mayest (?) be glad, but no wise smile not thou, for it may lose all the work that we go about and put us in danger. Moreover this longest to the steward and to the priest for any wise you must be purely clean, I[??] [sur- (?)]rounding of you and shaving and you must clean wash you in a bath made with leaves of laurel. And after confession, it behooveth thee to be arrayed, forsooth when ye in according time desirest to enter the circle, and beware you have no spot in your clothes, nor in your souls, for if there be any spot, within you or in your clothes, without doubt the spirit taketh disdain to come to you, as to persons unworthy. Also, three days before you work, keep you from any manner of communication with or of women and natural pollution, and in no wise but little drinking, and before you go to your work, take your rest in a clean bed and in clean clothes that thou mayest rest well. After that arise up and haste thee to work that thou wilt do, but before take, this little recreation of bread and water, and small fishes, for take not upon thee to eat flesh before thy working, nor yet thou with fasting stomach to go to thy work, at the least for dread of sights, to be overcome and for weariness of spirits, and keep you from lights of candles three hours before.

---

816. Long to: pertaining to.

[215]

Also if you work on the day, keep you from light of it three hours before, then the sword bearer must have the ring, wearing it always on the little finger, on the left hand fashioned as the steward hath one longing to this work. Now followeth the conjuration for this work: (&c.)

I conjure thee[817] by the virtue of this bond that thou keep thy appearance to the situation in pain that may fail me it. I conjure thee or you, N., In the name of God the Father, the Son, and the Holy Ghost, that you spirits that be within this ground beneath, or above, or about, that you go from this place a mli [million (?)] ells and there still to abide, till we have our purpose. I conjure thee wheresoever ye be, that ye away hence that we may fulfill our desire and will *per hoc deninum (*dominum?) dutum (*dictum?) miscuem (?) prolatum s (*scilicet?) verbum caro factum est, et per preciosum sanguinem innocentum domini nostri Iesu Christi quem ipsum effundit, abiunt (*abiicit?) in ara cruce pro nobis steleratis quem virgo viri nesia, igne santissime, illuminata, concepit peperite (?) quae semper immaculata, Coniuro vos etiam, N., I[n] nomini (?) Iesu Christi cui omne genu flectatur celestium terrestium & infernorum & omnis lingua confiteatur que [*quia] dominus noster Iesus Christus in gloria est dei patris & per hoc nomen sanctum carno [*carnem] & sanguinem ex maria virgine conseptum & notum [*natum] ace (?) per hoc universum genus humani red[e]merete in cruce humillitate immolatum fugite, fiat, fiat, fiat.* ["by this … (?) 'the word was made flesh,' and by the precious innocent blood of our Lord Jesus Christ which he poured out himself on the altar of the cross, debased as a criminal for us, which virgin, unknown by man, with the most holy fire, illuminated, … (?) she wedded while always immaculate, I conjure you also, O N., in the name of Jesus Christ, at which every knee should bow, in Heaven and on Earth and in hell, and every tongue confess that our Lord Jesus Christ is the glory of God the Father[818] and by this holy name, flesh and blood conceived of the Virgin Mary, and born … (?) by this you redeemed the whole human species sacrificed on the humble cross. Flee! Fiat, fiat, fiat."] Also I conjure you, N., devils, elves, or firedrakes hence, also you spirits that oweth this treasure, help us to it, and as I am a true priest, I shall do for thee to thy help, and in releasing of thy pains and increasing of thy great joy and bliss, wherefore I charge thee or you and conjure, bind, and constrain thee or you keepers of these goods, by the virtue of the glorious and high name of God, Tetragrammaton, that thou suffer it not to

be changed into any kind delineable (?) nor yet to be removed,

---

817. Very faded.

818. Philippians 2:10–11.

from our hands. I conjure you, N., out of this ground and also to avoid peaceable without wind or weather, without thunderings or lightnings, we having knowledge of your going away, without hurting or harming of me or any of my company, or any creature, or of any manner of thing that ever God created, I conjure you, N., and charge you by the blessed blood of our lord Jesus Christ, and by the power of the holy sacrament of the altar, the blessed body of God our saviour Jesus Christ, in form of bread, I conjure you, N., if you were a Christian man or woman or child, I charge thee by the baptism of Jesus Christ. I require thee by the sacrament that thou hast received and taken, and by the manhood of Jesus Christ, I require thee, N., by the virtue and power of the manhood, the which was dead and rose again openly from death to life on the third day through his own power, and so the Godhead and the manhood ascended into Heaven, both body and soul, on the Ascension Day, saying these words to his disciples.

Patrem meum et Patrem vestrum et Deum meum et Deum vestrum ["(I ascend to) my Father, and your Father; and to my God, and your God"],[819] so I charge you, N., for to help us, to this treasure that is in this circle, whereas we have made it through the miracle of the almighty God and by the might and power of almighty God, and by the might and power of all saints in Heaven. I conjure you, spirit N., by the might and power of the precious blood that was contained and childed [820] in a maid, pure and clean without any spot of sin also, Enoch and Hely [821] shall be dead in Jerusalem, and they shall rise again openly, through the might and power of Almighty God, and of his glorious deity. I conjure and require and charge thee or you by the curses of Almighty God that thou avoid by the words of whom thou oughtst to be obedient and all creatures heavenly, earthly, and helly,[822] and by the obedience that thou oweth to our lord God, three persons and one God, in trinity [????????] [823] thee or you and I conjure, charge, coarete [coarctate (?)], and constrain thee or you in the most mightiest and most highest name of God On,[824] (?) ell and oo Alpha and Omega, I constrain thee, I conjure thee and bind thee, and charge thee or you to help us unto this treasure not defrauding of me nor any of my fellows etc.

---

819. John 20:17.

820. Childed: (Mary) brought forth a child.

821. I.e., Enoch and Elijah, who were transported directly to Heaven because they were sinless.

822. Helly: "hellish" or "from hell."

823. Text is faded beyond recognition.

824. Compare "...names of god, On, & oo, alpha et [omega]" on next page.

[216]

[??] and drive thee out of this ground, we se[???] by the [???????] of God, *deus deorum* ["God of gods"], and by the great strength of God that made all heaven with all wise glorious and all dignities, worthiness, worships, and all suffrages, and by all the worthiness and dignities in Heaven, and by all the princes in Heaven under God and by all (?) angels and archangels under God, and by all holy evangelists and by the power of their offices, and by all the holy apostles, and by the power that God gave them and leve[825] them, and by all prophets and power, and faith, and by all holy martyrs and by their martyrdom and by all virgins and virginity, and by all holy saints and their livings to the pleasure of God, and by all the holy innocents and their joys and by all the holy seniors and their power and joys and by the holy altar of gold, and by all the glorious joys, merits, and dignities in the high lordship of God and by all the holy hallowed names of God, On, and oo, Alpha and Omega, Tetragrammaton, Emanuell, *Iesus Christus, deus et homo maiestas, de ita dignitas humanitas* ["Jesus Christ, God and sublime man, from thus mankind dignified"], and by all other the holy and mighty names of God. Amen.

Then say the Gospel, *In principio erat verbum* ["In the beginning was the word"][826] etc. *Deo gratias* ["Thanks be to God"]. *dirige domine deus meus actus meos In bene placito tuo* ["Direct my steps and my deeds, in your good pleasure"] and *viam Iniquitatus amove a me & <de> lege tua miserere mei* ["remove from me the way of iniquity, and out of your law have mercy on me"].[827] [+ Then:]

agla, sabaothe, adonay, In nomine patris omnipotentis qui celum verbo & cuncta creauit ex nichilo, hunc c[irculum] incipio in nomine filii unigeniti qui humanum genus, suo precioso, sanguine redement [*redemit] & hunc circulum, circumfero, In nomine spiritus sancti paraclit[us] qui carda [*corda] apostolorum, & prophetarum sua Invisibili puenetravit potentia & omnia nomina dei nota & ignota. O sancti angeli	AGLA, Sabaoth, Adonay. In the name of the almighty Father, who with the Word, created Heaven from nothing. This circle I begin in the name of the only-begotten Son, who redeemed mankind with his own precious blood, and this circle I move around. In the name of the Holy Ghost Paraclete, who entered the hearts of your apostles and prophets with invisible power, and all the names of God, known and unknown. O holy

---

825. Leve: grant.

826. John 1.

827. Psalm 118:29 (KJV 119:29). Folger reads "Inidlatus" for "Iniquitatis."

dei, Raphaell, gabriell, samuell, michaell, salamell, anaell, capciell, adiutate nos in omnibus operibus nostris,	angels of God, Raphael, Gabriel, Samuel, Michael, Salamel, Anael, Capciel, help us in all our works.

And he should read that decree written below. Then quickly sitting himself judicially, [+ read] as follows:

Ego Cito, & moneo te, N, ut veniatis ad hunc circulum fatum in honore sancte trinitate Semell, bis ter quatro per emptorie ut compares in pulchra forma hominis vel humana coram me & sociis meis, sedentibus vel sedendo in hoc circulo cito & moneo te, vel vos spiritus circum - stantes in ayre	I summon, and warn you, N., that you come to this circle spoken in the honour of the holy Trinity. Once, twice, three times, four times decisively, that you appear before me and my associates sitting in this circle, in a fair form of a man or human. I summon and warn you spirit or spirits, staying around in the air.

Summons to deter them.

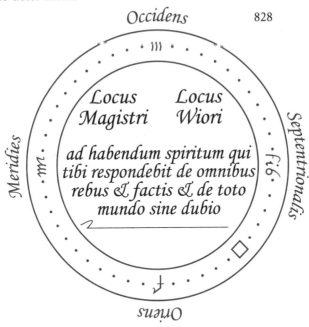

828

828. Circle includes *locus mag[ist]ri* ["master's place"]; *locus wiori* ["???'s place"]; *ad habendum spiritum qui tibi respondebit de omnibus rebus & factis & de toto mundo sine dubio* ["for having a spirit who will respond to you about all things and deeds and about the whole world without doubt"]. Around the outside are marked the cardinal directions: *Occidens, Septentrionalis, Oriens, Meridies* ["west, north, east, south"].

In nomine patris filii & spiritus sancti amen.	In the name of the Father, Son, and Holy Ghost. Amen.
& prima [?] cita[tion] [?] Semell bis ter quater, per quemlibet unum ut fitt legittimem citatus per auctoritatem domine nostri Iesu Christi per prima monicione tres horas ut pena sua duplicitur & per secunda monicione, iterum tres horas, & per tertia monicione totus tempus quem inter prima monicionem & ultimam & per sua inobediencia pena sua semper invalescat, &c.	& First summons (?). Once, twice, three times, four times, by which anyone of them may be lawfully summoned, through the authority of our Lord Jesus Christ, by the first admonition three hours in order that his penalty should double, and by the second admonition, again three hours, and by the third admonition the whole time which [is] between the first and the final admonitions, and through his disobedience, his penalty should always increase in strength, etc.[*]
Ex auctoritate mihi—commissa, vel admissa 1o 2o 3o clamando ad 4or partes circuli,—veni festina[n]ter	By the authority committed to me, or granted with the first, second, third proclaiming, towards the four parts of the circle, "come quickly,"
[*] This whole paragraph is unclear.	

And if he doesn't come, the master should sit and write the condemnation against him. Then he should sit judicially and read the condemnation thus:

O immunde spiritus N, per eo quia non obedisti mandatus domini nostri Iesu Christi dei tui nec precepta eius custodus, responde mihi quaere non excomunico te propter inobedienciam tuam & contumationem tuum, responde mihi ubicunque fueris in toto mundo qui precerto scio qui tu fuisti & es legittime sitatus premonitus, Semel bis ter quater, & propter tuam in obedienciam & contumacionem excomunico & anathematizo te, de hiis scriptus anathematizat dei & domini nostri Iesu Christi &	O unclean spirit N., whereas because you have not obeyed the commands of our Lord Jesus Christ your God, nor heeded his warnings to respond to me when questioned, I excommunicate you because of your disobedience, and your stubborn refusal to appear to respond to me, wherever you have been in the whole world, because I know for certain that you have been lawfully summoned and forewarned, Once, twice, three times, four times, and on account of your disobedience and refusal to appear,

omnem sanctorum e[ius] ut non tu qui estas quosque desiderium & voluntatem meam compleas ac multiplico penas tuas, in infinitum, [???]* spiritus exorzisate & coniurate & obedias mandatis domini dei tui amen.	I excommunicate and condemn you, according to these written documents God curses you, and our Lord Jesus Christ, and all his saints, unless you fulfill each of my desires and wishes, and I will multiply your punishment forever [???] O Spirit exorcized and conjured and may you obey the orders of the Lord your God. Amen.
* Lettering is faded beyond recognition.	

[217]

Veni, veni, veni, & post quam venerit spiritus respiciate magister uersus illam plagam & videbit spiritum & dicat ei, O tu spiritus N per omnia supradicta te coniuro ut dicas mihi talia, & fiat tunc peticiones deo gracias. [.... God ...... (faded)] I coniure thee by these words followlng, the whlch God said in the creation of the world, ffirst when he made light he said fiat lux & facta est lux, the, 2, word when he made the firmament he said fiat firmamentum in medio aquarum & deuidat aquas ab aquis the, 3, word when he made the firmament he gathered all the waters that were under Heaven, & then he said congregentur aque qui sub celo sunt in locum unum & appareat arida, the, 4 word, when he made to spring all trees & herbs, he said Germinet terra herbam virentem & faciunt semen & lignum pomiferum faciens fructum, Iuxta genus suum cuius semen in semet ipso sit super terram, the, 5,	Come, come, come, and after the spirit comes, the master should look around, and he will see the spirit and he should say to it, O you spirit N., by all the above-mentioned, I conjure you that you say such-and-such to me, and the petition will be done God willing. ... God ... [faded]. I conjure you by these words following, the which God said in the creation of the world, first, when he made light he said "let there be light, and there was light"; and by the virtue of the second word that he said when he made the firmament, "let there be a firmament in the midst of the waters, and let it divide the waters from the waters"; and by the third word when he made the firmament, he gathered all the waters that were under Heaven into one place, he said, "let the waters which are under the heavens be gathered together in one place, and let the dry land appear"; and by the virtue of the fourth word when he

word whan he made [the] Sun, Moon, & stars he said, fiant luminaria in firmamento celi & [*ut] diuidant diem [ac] noctem & fuit in signa & tempora & dies & annos, & [ut] luceant in firmamento celi & illuminent terra, the, 6, when he made fishes in waters & birds of the air he said producant aque reptile anime vivent[is] & volatile super terram sub firmamento celi, the, 7, when he blessed them & said Crescite & multiplicamini, & repleta [*-e] aquas mapauisque [*maris avesque] multiplicentur super terram, the, viii worde when he maid beasts & wormes & serpents he said Producat terram animam viuentem in genere sue [*suo] numenta [*iumenta] et reptillia & bestias terre secundum species suas, the, 9, word when he made man he said faciamus hominem ad ymaginem & simillitudinem nostram & precipit [*praesit] pissibus ma[ris] & volatillibus celi, & bestiis terre & universeque creature, omnique retileque [*reptili quod] moventur in terra, the, 10, word when he said Crescite & multiplicamini, & replete terram & subicite eam & dominamini pissibus maris & volatilibus celi, & universis animantibus qui moventur super terram.

made to spring trees and herbs, he said, "let the earth sprout forth green herbs, and those producing seeds, and trees bearing fruit in which is seed of its kind, over the earth"; and by the virtue of the fifth word when he made the Sun and the Moon and the stars, he said, "let there be lights in the firmament of heaven, and may they divide the day and the night, and may they be for signs and seasons, days, and years, to shine in the firmament of heaven, and light up the land"; and by the virtue of the sixth word, when he made fishes and birds, he said, "let the waters bring forth the creeping things with living souls, and those that fly over the earth under the firmament of heaven"; and by the virtue of the seventh word when he blessed them, he said, "go forth and multiply and fill up the waters of the sea, and let the birds be multiplied upon the earth"; and by the virtue of the eighth word when he made beasts, worms, and serpents, he said, "let the earth bring forth living creatures and beasts of burden and creeping things according to their own kinds"; and by the virtue of the ninth word, when he made man, he said, "let us make man in our own image and likeness, and let him preside over the

> fishes of the sea, and flying creatures of the heavens, and the beasts of the earth, and all creatures which move or crawl upon the earth"; and by the virtue of the tenth word, when he put Adam and Eve into paradise, he said, "increase and multiply and fill the earth, and subdue it, and be master of the fishes of the sea, and the flying things in the heavens, and the beasts of the earth, and all creatures which move upon the earth."

Thus endeth the speech that God spake in the creation of the world, and of all creatures.

And if there be any spirits he shall arise on warrantise, and if he appear, ask him in thy mother tongue what he doth there, and charge him to tell you, how ye shall have that goods, and by what means, and by what craft, and what time is best, or in what day or night, or in what time or hour ye shall dispose the goods, and then charge him that he be ready to you, when that you come again, and appear to you, and fulfill your commandments.

In nomine domini Iesu Christi [??] potenciam virtutes altissimi Signum sancte crucis +. super me facio ut spiritus non venient me ledere offendere agnare [*aggrauare] vel molestare non valeant Christus ad iuuante protegente & defendente, cui celestia terrestia & infernalia subiciuntur qui viuet & gloriatur solus per cuncta, secula seculorum amen.	In the name of the Lord Jesus Christ, the strength, the power of the most high. Make the Sign of the Cross + over me, so that the spirits will not come to me to hurt, annoy, or molest. May they not prevail. Christ will help, protect, and defend, to whom the heavenly, earthly, and infernal creatures are subject, who lives in glory forever and ever. Amen.
[Salua me (?)] domine & saluabor + salua me domine & salus ero + qm laus mea tu es, & omnibus diebus vite mee. agios + athanatos + Christus vincit Christus regnat + Christus imperat + Christus me benedicat & ad spe~ com	Save me, O Lord, and I will be saved. + Save me, O Lord, and I will be saved. Because you are my glory, and all the days of my life Agios + Athanatos + Christ conquers + Christ rules + Christ commands. + May Christ bless me and help me compel the spirits to be driven

* Compare Wellcome MS. 110, 86r.

pellendos ab istus thesaurum hic in ista terra absconditus amovere me ad iuuet amen.

Domine Iesu Christe filii dei viui te suppliciter deprecar & exoro ut conserues me, Indignum famulum tuum, N, hodie & quotidie in omnibus operibus meis, & deprecor te sanctum patrem creatorem mundi, & per filium dominum nostrum Iesum Christum redemtorem humani generis & per omnia ineffabilia nomina tua & per omnes sanctas virgines tuas quod sunt in celo & terra, & quatenus me famulum tuum ad omni impedimento conseruare digneris, hodie & semper in isto opere ut maligne spiritus non possit me deridere, ruit (?) decepit Domine Iesu Christe filii dei viui qui celum & terram fundasti, & omnia qui in eis sunt mandasti, ut fierent digneris domine die isto & aures tue pietatis inclinare & exaudi preces meis ut opere mea valea ducere in effectum secundum meum desiderium & voluntatem.

away from this treasure hidden in this earth. Amen.

O Lord Jesus Christ,* son of the living God, I humbly beg and implore you to preserve me, N., your unworthy servant, today and every day, in all my works, and pray to you by the holy Father, creator of the world, and by the Son, our Lord Jesus Christ, the redeemer of human kind, and by all your ineffable names, and by all your holy maidens who are in Heaven and on Earth, and that you deign to preserve me, your servant, from all hindrance, today and always in this work, so that the evil spirit is not able to mock, ruin, or cheat me. O Lord Jesus Christ, son of the living God, who created Heaven and Earth, and you have ordered all things therein to happen; deign to incline the ears of your goodness this day, and hear my prayers, that my work will be brought to its desired end, and I will accomplish my desire and will.

[218]

Custodi me in opere iste ut maligni spiritus non possunt irredere me sed ut ergo possim super eos habere [potestatem] constringendi eos sicut meam eius, & sic ego volo, & [tu pater sancte] tibi clamo clamore magni per suam [*tuam] sanctam benignitatem & [misericordiam et] pietatem quatenus in me digneris sancta sanctam gracia[m] et intele-[ctum] infundere ut possim facere venire omnis spiritus in figuris h[uius]

Guard me in this work, so that evil spirits will not be able to mock me, but that I may have [the power]* of constraining them, and have my will, and to you [O holy Father] I proclaim with a great proclamation, through your holy benevolence and [mercy and] piety, inasmuch as you have deemed me worthy to infuse the holy grace and [understanding], in order that I am able to make all spirits come into the figure of

* Damaged parts of this page can be reconstructed by comparing with Wellcome MS. 110.

impleant omnem voluntatem meam in omnibus que precipiam eis ad mea[m] voluntatem per nomine sanctum tuum ineffabilem, tu qui es trinus & unus deus patris & filius, & spiritus sanctus. qui	this [circle, and] they may fulfill all my will and all things which I order them, so that I can make the forms of all spirits appear at my will, though your ineffable name, who are three and one, God the Father, and the Son, and the Holy Ghost.
[Tu qui es trinum et unus deus pater et filius et spiritus sanctus, pater misericors pius et iustus,] adiuua sanum & incolumem cum omnibus sociis meis ab istis spiritibus malign[is] ut non valeantur, nec possit me offendere, nec ledere, nec der[idere] sed in omnibus, & per omnia mea desideria, adimpleant, vel adimple[re] faciant cum effectum amen.	[You who are three and one God, Father and Son and Holy Ghost, Father merciful and kind and just,] help me be healthy and unharmed with all my associates, from all these evil spirits, that they not prevail, nor be able to attack, nor hurt, nor mock us, but in all things to fulfill all my desires, and bring them to effect. Amen.
Explicit ....[faded]	**The end** ... [faded]

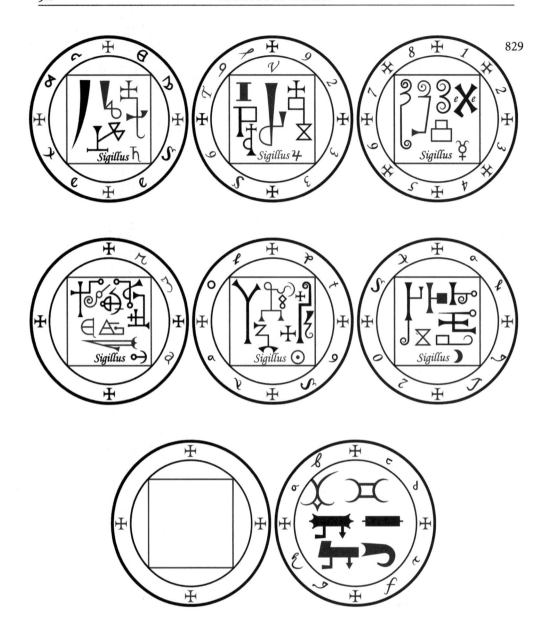

829

829. Part of the seventh seal (sigillum [sic] veneris) is damaged in the manuscript.

[219]

830

830. Eleven talismans, a twelfth is completely lost except for part of an edge. Second has the words *Richalivi arum + Risechardimare+ / santi eli malem + pettolomus +*. The fifth has *Puellus, Pantatar, tharcasser, Sabam (or Gabam (?))*.

[220]

[................]⁸³¹ **any spirit, or spirits, as hereafter followeth, first thou shalt**
tur[n] thyself with thy face into the east and say thus,

In the name of the Father and of the Son and of the Holy Ghost, all you spirits
that be here within this ground or water, fire or air, by the space of a hundred ells on
every side round about me, I conjure you and charge you every one that you depart
and go from this ground and treasure, and that you come no more here, till that I and
my fellows have done all that we will, and that you turn not the treasure to no other
place, or likeness, nor that you hurt not me, nor none of my company. And to all
things, I conjure, adjure, and charge, and bind all you spirits, by the might and leave
of God our Lord Jesus Christ, by his flesh and by his blood, by his temptation, fasting,
and agony, by his death and passion, and by his resurrection, and by that power and
might, that he shall have, when he shall come, to judge all the world. And yet I conjure you spirits all and every one of you, by all angels and archangels, martyrs and
confessors and virgins, and by all the holy company of heaven, that you do as is before rehearsed, to you. Also I conjure you by the power, might, and virtue of heaven,
earth, water, fire and hell, and all things contained in them, by Sun, Moon, and stars
and lights, and by all the torment of hell and all spirits. Also I conjure you, by all signs
and planets and by the angels of them all, so I conjure you by all these holy names of
God, + Sother + Panton + Craton + Alpha + & Omega + Agla + Ely + Eloy + Tetragrammaton + Emanuell + Sabaoth + Adonay + and yet I conjure you spirits by all the
things that ever God made, created, or ordained, that you avoid from this treasure,
and leave it here till I and my company have wrought all our minds, and that you hurt
not me nor none of my company. To this I conjure you and adjure you by all the
power, strength, and might of God the Father, the Son, and the Holy Ghost, by all airs,
earths, waters, fires, elements, planets, characters, stones, woods, grass, and herbs, and
relics, by all iron, steel, brass, copper, and tin, by all silver, gold, books, and all virtue
of all things that belongeth to man or beast, and yet I conjure you and adjure you in
God's name, and in the name of Matthew, Mark, Luke, and John, and by Mary, the
mother of God, our Lord Jesus Christ, that you go and depart from this ground by
the space of one hundred ells, on every side and that you never come here to this
place, here where I do make this cross   by the virtue of him that died on
the cross of wood for man's sake and   sin. I conjure you, spirits or spirit
that keeps this treasure here in the   ground, that you go your ways
and that incontinent, I charge you by   the dreadful Day of Doom in the
which day God shall judge me and   you, and all mankind in whose

---

831. There might be a first line, completely faded.

sight the wicked and disobedient spirits shall not be able to abide, but shall be cast down into hell, so be you plagued, and cast into torment and pain, if you do not depart and go from this ground, by and by, for I do believe that to what spirit or spirits so ever these bonds shall be read, that if they do not fly and go from the treasure and ground, even at my commandment, as I believe that they shall, I conjure you into the power of the fiend there to remain till the day of judgment. Also I do believe that you shall fly and go your way from this ground, by the space of an hundred ells on every side. Also I conjure you, by the power and belief of the three kings that offered to Christ Jesus our lord and saviour and by that which they offered and by the names, and by the sound of their names as these, Jaspar + Melchior + Balthazar + and by all good and faithful men and women and by all their beliefs that they have in God and his works. Also I conjure you and adjure you and b[ind (?)] you, by all the kings of the air, and of the earth and water and fire, and air of hell, that you go from this ground, and that you leave the treasure here where it stands, and that you, not none of you, nor no other spirit or spirits carry it not from us, nor turn it not into no other likeness or fash[ion]. Also I conjure and bind you all spirits and elves and men, beast and all dogs that none of you do away or let us, by God the maker and redeemer of all things both visible and unvisible, and by his wounds and hairs, sinews, and veins, I charge you by the blessed Trinity, three persons and one God omnipotent and celestial, without beginning and shall be God without end. [Amen.]

[221]

Also I bind and conjure you spirits and all other before rehearsed, by these holy names of God that I shall speak and have spoken, + Tetragramaton + Anatemate + Anatematevethe + Alpha + & Omega + Agla + Jesus +יהוה + by the holy service that we have and by our preachers of the Gospel, by our faith, hope, and belief that we have in God and his words. Also I conjure you spirits by the mystery of God and by the holy Cross on the which Jesus Christ suffered his passion and death, by his burial and rising again, and by his ascending into Heaven. Even by and by go your ways and leave all this ground and things therein, as I have commanded you, by God the Father, the Son, and the Holy Ghost to whom be glory, honour, and praise for ever and ever. Amen.

You must read this bond four times over, that is, towards every quarter of the world, once having these characters pinned on thy breast, and thou shalt speed on warranties,[832] for this did Bacon.

---

832. On warranties: certainly.

alph

r e m i o b a d

e r i a b o d u

fbe outing bf x [dbg] abggr xuure be sixkr thxt ediirth in thr wbbu ["For biting of a dog, adder, or snake that runneth in the wood"] [834]

+ pote + porrexero + zebita + zerox (?-) + zarapton + peraclitos, *in nomine patris et filii et spritus sancte* ["In the name of the Father and Son and Holy Ghost"]. Amen.

Say these three times over a cup of ale, beer, or wine, then write these words in a piece of paper and wash the letters out with the liquor, and let the party drink it.

Another for the same

+ Caro + Cara + redibit + Samim + Saboroth + Emanuell + paracletus + *pater noster* ["Our Father"]

---

833. Includes words: *magnam + nomen + domini + Quod + tulit + Aaron* . + ["Great name of the Lord which Aaron brought"].

834. The deciphered text is written above in a different hand.

[t]b cxdsr slrpr ["To cause sleep"]

In nomine patris et filii et spiritus sancte Amen + Beres + Reres + res + spes + In nomine domini + rares + res + spes ut iste quiescat Amen. ["In the name of the Father and the Son and the Holy Ghost. Amen. + Beres + Reres + res + spes + In the name of the Lord + *rares + res + spes* in order that this one rests. Amen."]

[222]

[In *sec. man.*:
The index
x r n b d
7 7 7 7 7
a e i o u
   r n b d]

Terebinthus

It stoppeth tenesmus,[836] made in a suffumigation upon the coals Terebinthus ounce ii often washed in fennel, and or fine water, then put into it the powder of new

---

835. Includes words: *emanuell messias eleyson zapnachad/ hafbefa ampheniton anatymateveth tetragramaton / ely eloy panton Sabaoth deus Craton mon gane~ ortha Christe archima theos hon anatymate agla Sother.*

836. Tenesmus: a condition of straining the bowels constantly without effect.

saffron, and Hiera simplex,[837] ana 3 (dram?) pound (?), and keep this in a box, and whoso feeleth grief within their guts or reins let them eat of this, dram two, every morning during four days [inset:]

     1   2   3

T955n49n9 7935549on t903e5490

     4   5 6 7

T9035n4 793en 7a35 7a3

  c be

x n r x n

7xc7p7 7m7gd

    et

x d r   n r

7l7m 7t scr7b7

  deroum (?)

d d dr d

7n7m 77rb7m

pro atum amen+1 give it seavn dayes for an ague written

b d d nr ndr n red xur b x x dr n r

pr7 7n7m d77m, G777 7t s777n d777s f7r 7n 7977 wr7tt7n

  d b rxdr x b r x r rxdr r

      7pp7n s7777n 7lm7nd7s 7nd th7 s7777nth7

      uppon seaven almondus and the seaventhe

      x b r ndr d b x b r

      7lm7nd7 g777 7nt7 7 d7gg7

      almonds give unto a dogge

alphabet

bcdrb / r

aeiou / s

---

837. Hiera simplex: also known as the Hiera of Galen, a general remedy consisting of aloes and other herbs and spices in a honey base.

Tr eb5uc ernecptdrn ["To cause conception"][838]

Write these letters either upon a thin plate of lead or tin:

v g b o f e o r e o n i a p v, d

And let the part wear them about her. And if it be possible, let her not know thereof, but especially no creature but the giver.

bn rthco fro thc vbmc p5oprvc bui vr tr [.]nc 5vci ["Another for the same purpose, and so to [b]e (?) used"]

$S + S + l{\sim}n + mx + ks + n + nn + P + xx + l + x + 6 + conn + xix + s + i + l + l + m + Ry + 8 + x + l{\sim}n + ur\ (?) + ij + l{\sim}i + 6 + , Porab5tm\ cvtc$

[223]

A special good for women in travail [839]

Write in a piece of paper these words following:

Elizabeth peperitt Iohannem Baptystem, Anna Mariam, et maryam peperitt dominum nostrum Iesum Christum sine sorde syne dolore, in Honore scante [*sancte] marye et sanctem Iohannes baptiste, exeas Infans ab utro matris tue sine periculo, vell, tue, vell matris tue, amen.	Elizabeth gave birth to John the Baptist, Ann to Mary, and Mary gave birth to our Lord Jesus Christ, without bodily pain, in honour of Saint Mary and Saint John the Baptist, may you emerge, O infant, from your mother's womb without danger, either to you or to your mother. Amen.

Being thus written, lay it secretly on the top of her belly and praise God. *prabstsm.*[840]

---

838. Deciphered in pencil by later hand. This charm dates back to the twelfth century, with examples from the Middle Ages appearing in England, Austria, and Norway. See Helm, "Mittelalterische Geburtsbenediktionen"; Hunt, *Popular Medicine in Thirteenth-Century England*, 90; Knirk, James E., Aslak Liesstøl, Magnus Olsen, and Kjeldeskrift-Institutt Norsk Historisk. *Norges Innskrifter Med de Yngre Runer*, 6.1, p. 51.

839. Women in Travail: women in labor. In marg.: "HP."

840. I.e., *probatum* ["proven"].

ffro thc bgsc ["For the ague"] [841]

1 Calendant 2 calendan 3 calenda 4 calend 5 calen 6 cale 7 call 8 ca, ebndv.

For one that is bewitched

First say the Gospel of St. John three times, then say,

In the name of the Father, the Son, and the Holy Ghost, that even as this water and urine doth now wast consume and burn, so may his or hers their witchcrafts enchantments sorcery or charms which did or hath bewitched this person, N., may presently by and by return and lighten upon themselves again, and to this I do charge you, by these names of God our lord Jesus Christ Tetragramaton, Alpha et Omega, Messias, Sother, Emanuell Adonay, Algramay, Diagramay, Agla, Joth, Tetragram, Saday, by these names and by all other names, and by all other names of our lord Jesus Christ, do I conjure you, that you do cause that even as this urine doth, etc.

842

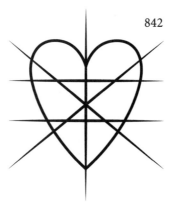

[In marg.: The Alphabet or letters

b c r d s 6 6

a e o i v w v]

Tbkc thc sodnc rf thc pbotdc thbt dn acsdethci bni ucthc dt dn b prtc elruc erscoci, then tbke a pdgcrn hbotr bni utdehc fdsc ncilcu dn dt, bni ucthc sdthc thc sodnc tdll thc sodnc ac ernusmci ubdngc bu du barsc sodttcn ["Take the urine of the party that in be-

---

841. In marg.: "ffor the ague." Ague is a fever accompanied by chills and shivering. Compare Sloane 3854, fol. 82 (in a sixteenth-century hand), on the word "Calendant." Also see Sloane 3851, 127, and Gauntlet, *Grimoire of Arthur Gauntlet*, 287. A very similar charm against ague that was popular, made similar use of the word "Abracadabra."

842. Pigeon heart: reminiscent of Three of Swords Tarot.

witched and sethe[843] it in a pot close covered, then take a pigeon heart and stitch five needles in it, and sethe with the urine till the urine be consumed saying as is above written"].[844]

In the beginning was that word, that word was with God, and that word was God. This same was in the beginning with God. All things was made by it, and without it was nothing that was made. In it was life, and that light was the life of man. And that light shineth in the darkness and the darkness comprehend it not. There was a man sent from God whose name was John, this same came for a witness to bear witness of that light, that all men through him might believe. He was not that light, but was sent to bear witness of that light. This was that true light which lighteneth every man that cometh into the world. He was in the world, and the world was made by him, and the world knew him not. He came unto his own, and his own received him not, but as many as received him, to them he gave prerogative to be the sons of God. Even to them that believe in his name, which are born not of blood nor of the will of the flesh, nor of the will of man, but of God. And that word was made flesh, and dwelt among us, and we saw the glory thereof, as the glory of the only begotten son of the Father, full of grace and truth.

- - - - -

The Lord was the first man that ever there (?) was prick upon.

[224]

To cause a spirit [to] appear in thy bed chamber

On Mercury day and hour, enter into thy bed chamber or in some chapel far from the barking of dogs with a burning candle of clear wax. Thou must have lignum aloes at thy head. And say these words following thrice:

---

843. Sethe: boil.

844. "Take the urine of the partie that in bewitched and sethe it in a pote close covered, then take a pigeon harte and stiche five nedles in it, and sethe withe the urine till the urine be consumed, sainge as is above written." A combination of the English witch-bottle with a charm depicted, among other places, in the *Dragon Noir* of Dumas, *Grimoires et rituels magiques*, pp. 314–316.

Sanctus 3 in dye mercurye dominus noster Iesus Christus fuytt prodytus syve tradytus + sanctus sanctus sanctus in dye Iovis domynus noster Iesus Christus fuytt captius tentus et flagelatus + sanctus sanctus sanctus in dye venery domynus noster Iesus Christus fuytt suspensus plagatus et sepulltus sanctus sanctus sanctus deus cum omnybus sanctis tuis mytte mychy ballanchum	Holy, holy, holy. On Wednesday our Lord Jesus Christ was handed over. + Holy, holy, holy. On Thursday our Lord Jesus Christ was imprisoned and flogged. + Holy, holy, holy. On Friday our Lord Jesus Christ was hung up, injured, and buried. Holy, holy, holy. O God, with all your saints send me Balanchus.

And upon the day of ☿, if thou wilt do this work, thou shouldst first confess thyself that day and say the aforesaid words three times and then go to bed and watch, and a bearded man will come unto thee. Then ask of him his name, his name is Balanchus. Then ask of him what thou wilt, and he shall tell it thee with all truth, and will answer thee without deceit. This hath been held a profitable experiment.

Magrano [+ Conjuration] [845]

Go under an elder tree at midday when the Sun is hottest, and under the shadow strew consecrated rushes and call thrice "Magrany *vel* ['or'] magrano," and there will appear before thee an herb shining like gold and behind it a fair woman, which will ask thee what thou wouldst have, and thou shalt have anything that thou wilt ask, then take up the herb, and thou shalt not want anything whilst thou keepest it.

An excommunication

I conjure thou or ye S[pirit] d (O?) N. by the powerful words before rehearsed *vel* ["or"] proceeding from my mouth, having been lawfully called, warned, and cited to appear before me, and for as much as you have not made your true appearance according to the tenor of my call or conjuration in yielding your due obedience thereunto as ye ought, ye have run into the great contempt of God that made both thee and me, and therefore by all the power and authority given me by our Lord God I pronounce ye excommunicate and accursed and forever to be deprived of all your ease, honour, and offices, to go into utter darkness and to burn in hellfire without re-

---

845. In left marg.: "HP", and further down "w". Compare Sloane 3851, 129, and Gauntlet, *Grimoire of Arthur Gauntlet*, 289.

demption and all ways and from time to time to be vexed, grieved, and tormented with infernal pains and tortures, until ye willingly and diligently appear unto me and yield your obedience unto me, and be ready and willing at all times and in all places to obey my invocation, by the virtues and powers given me from my Lord God which is the true eternal and ever-living God through Jesus Christ our Lord. Amen.

fiat   fiat   fiat   Amen.

[225]

For a crystal [846]

In the first place, make the sign of the holy cross before the woman, saying + "In the name of the Father, Son, and Holy Ghost. Amen."

Say three Our Fathers, three Hail Marys, and three Creeds. The same four Psalms 67, 54, 57, 150,[847] and then the following prayer:

Domine Iesu Christe Rex glorie dignere mittere nobis tres angelos bonos, viz, anchor, annachor annulos qui dicant et ostendant nobis veritatem sine falsitate vell fallacia, de omnibus rebus de quibus inter rogabo, domine Iesu Christe qui conseptus es de spiritu sancto natus ex maria virgine passus sub ponsio pilato, crucifixus, mortuus & sepultus descendisti ad inferes tertio die resurrexit a mortuis & sepultus ascendisti, ad celos sedes ad dextram dei patris omnipotentis, inde venturus es	O Lord Jesus Christ, King of Glory, deign to send to me the three good angels, namely Anchor, Annachor, Annulos,* who will tell us and show us the truth, without deceit, concerning all that I will ask. O Lord Jesus Christ,† who was conceived by the Holy Ghost, born of the virgin Mary, suffered under Pontius Pilate, was crucified, died, and was buried. He descended into hell, and on the third day he arose from the dead and from the tomb, and ascended into Heaven, where he sits at the right hand

* Note connection with *Key of Solomon*, and Dee/Kelley workings. See Dee, *John Dee's Five Books of Mystery*, 12, 26–29, 66–68. These three magic words or names, with many variations, are widely found in magic texts. For examples, see Mathers, *The Key of Solomon*, 93; Véronèse, *Ars Notoria*, 43; LIH, 81; Sloane 1727, fol. 42r; Additional MS. 36674, fol. 82v; Rawlinson D. 252, fol. 117v; Sloane 3846, fol. 23r; Sloane 3849, fol. 3v-4v; Wellcome MS. 110, fol. 106r.

† Compare creed on Folger p. 25.

846. Compare Sloane 3849, art. 1, and Mun. A.4.98, 103.

847. In marg. in *sec. man.*: "Thes be the fower psalms followinge: / psal. lxvii / psal. liiii / psal lvii / psal cl."

iudicare viuos et mortuos & seculum per ignem, & sicut tu es verus deus & homo, mitte huc nobis tres angelos bonos, palam comperituros, vell qui compareant statim, in isto cristallo, viz, anchor anachor & analos [sic] ad visum istius, N, per ista sanctissima nomina dei, eloy, tetragra<gra>mmaton sabaoth, alpha et omega, principium et finis, expediatus, & vos angeli & prophetis requiro vos rogo & contestor per sanctam mariam matrem dominum nostri Iesu Christi, et per novem ordines angelorum cherubin & seraphin, thrones, dominationes; principatus et potestates, & per virtutem archangelicam, michaelem, gabrielem, raphaelem, uriel, qui non sessant clamare ante thronum dei, semper nocte, dieque cantantes, sanctus sanctus sanctus dominus deus, sabaothe, qui est qui erit & qui venturus est, Iudicare mundum, & per omnes relequias que sunt in celo & in terra, per lac quod dominus noster Iesus Christus, de mamillis santem marie virginis exuxit cum vere puer erat ille in hoc mundo & per vestem, coccineam quia indutus est Iesus Christus, & per unguentum quo sanctam maria magdalena unxit pedes Iesu Christi, & torsitt eos capillis, capitis, sui, quod palam, & sine mora comparatis ad visum istius N, in isto cristallo,

of God the Father almighty, who will come to judge the living and the dead and the ages by fire, and thus you are true God and man. Send to us here the three good angels, that they appear openly, or who will appear immediately in this crystal, namely Anchor, Anachor, and Analos [sic], to the vision of this N., by these most holy names of God, Eloy, Tetragrammaton Sabaoth, Alpha and Omega, the Beginning and the End; may you arrange it, and you angels and prophets I ask you and appeal to you, by holy Mary, mother of our Lord Jesus Christ, and by the nine orders of angels: Cherubim and Seraphim, Thrones, Dominations, Principalities, Powers, Virtues, [+Angels,] and Archangels, by Michael, Gabriel, Raphael, and Uriel, who continually proclaim before the throne of God, by night and day, "holy, holy, holy, Lord God of hosts," who is and who shall be, who will come to judge the world, and by all those who dwell in Heaven and on Earth, by the milk which our Lord Jesus Christ sucked from the breasts of the holy Virgin Mary when he was a small child, that in this world and by the scarlet garment which had been placed on Jesus Christ, and by the oil which Saint Mary Magdalene used to anoint the feet of Jesus Christ, and dried them with the hairs on her head, that you openly and without delay appear in this crystal to the vision of this (skryer) N.

* Here it will appear like as it were a claw in the crystal and if it do not appear begin again, and if it do appear then speak to the first, and call for the second as you did for the first, beginning again and so proceed till you have all three, and to the first say thus.

To the first angel:[848]

| O angele dei bene venisti, In nomine patris et filii, & [spiritus] sanctus amen. & per illam intencionem quam habuit deus in mente, quem deposuit Luciferum de celo, ad, puntem (?) inferiorem inferni & elegit vos pro valentissimis angelis | O angel of God, welcome in the name of the Father, and the Son, and the Holy Ghost. Amen. And for that effort which God intended, as he has cast Lucifer out of Heaven into the stinking depths of hell, and chose you among the mightiest of angels. |

To the second angel:

| O angele dei bene venisti in nomine pa[tris...], amen, et per virginitatem beatem marie, virginis, matris dominum nostri Iesu Christi, & per virginitatem, sanctem Iohannis Baptisti & per caput eius. | O angel of God, welcome in the name of the Father, and the Son, and the Holy Ghost. Amen. And by the blessed Virgin Mary, virgin mother of our Lord Jesus Christ, and by the virginity of Saint John the Baptist, and by his head. |

To the third angel:

| O angele dei bene venisti in nomine pa[tris...], amen, & per reuerenciam passionis domini nostri Iesu Christi, et per reuerenciam sacramentum altarum quod deus noster Iesus Christus fecit in cena sua, & dedit, discipulis suis, quando dixit hoc enym est corpus meum hic cessat puer | O angel of God, welcome in the name of the Father, and the Son, and the Holy Ghost. Amen. And by the reverence for the suffering of our Lord Jesus Christ, and by the reverence for the sacramental offering which our Lord Jesus Christ made at his [last] supper, and gave his disciples, when he said "this is my body" this child rests. |

[In marg.: "and the master says 'O you' as follows:"]

---

848. In Mun. A.4.98, 105, the following greetings read "O Anacor thou art welcome... O Anchor thou art welcome ... O Analos thou art welcome."

[226]

Then say this exorcization over the cross [*crystal],[849] and make the sign of the cross.

O vos angeli, rogo vos precipio vobis et vos exorcizo per omnia [prin]cipalia nomina dei que non licet homini loqui nisi in articlo mortis & per virtutem spiritus sanctus, & per reuerenciam passionis dominum nostri Iesu Christi & per reuerenciam sacramenti altarem, quod deus noster Iesus Christus fecit in cena sua et dedit discipulis suis quando dixit, hoc est corpus meum, quod monstretis, mihi veritatem, sine falcitate vell fallacia petita vell requisita & petenda vell requirenda.	O you angels, I ask you, and I order you, and I exorcise you by all the principal names of God who must not be spoken except in mortal danger, and by the power of the Holy Ghost, and by the reverence for the suffering of our Lord Jesus Christ, and by the reverence for the sacramental offering which our Lord Jesus Christ made at his [last] supper, and gave his disciples, when he said "this is my body." Because you show me the truth, without falseness or deceit, sought or required, or to be sought, or to be desired.

Thus must you say at every time that they show not the very truth

If the spirit will not answer directly, or refuse to answer thee, use these words spoken out loud.

O vos angeli improbe maledicti produri cervicis, obstinati & profracti cordis quid moratis, cur non respondetis, plane & sine mora quid inquam statis, cur non obediatis sanctis nominibus dei, cur resistatis sanctissimo nominem Iesu, cui omnis potestas in celo & in terra & in inferno data est, cui omnes creatura, in celo, in terra, in inferno & in abisso, obediunt audiunt, & cui milla creatura resistere potest, ego vos o maledicti & obstinati in hoc nomine sanctissimo Iesu &	O you disloyal angels, cursed, cruel, stiff necked, and brokenhearted—why do you delay? Why have you not answered clearly and without delay? What, I say, detains you? Why are you not obedient to the holy names of God? Why do you resist the most holy name of Jesus, to whom all power in Heaven, on Earth, and in Hell has been given; to which all creatures in Heaven, on Earth, in hell, and in the abyss hear and obey, and whom no creature is able to resist? O

---

849. Per Sloane 3849, fol. 4v.

nomen anamatizo, & maledico, sicut ipse maledixit, ficui fructum, non ferentem & in stagnum ignis & sulpheris, vos religo usque in extremum diem Iudicii et vos privo ab omni virtute dignitate et officio, nisi statim plane, delucide sine mora fraude vell fallacia, respondeatis et ostendatis requisita, et requirenda, per eum qui venturus est Audicare, vivos et mortuos et seculum per ignem, fiat, fiat, fiat.	you cursed and stubborn creature, in the most holy name of Jesus, and by the most holy name of Jesus, I curse and invoke divine punishment upon you, just as he cursed the fig tree which bore no fruit, and I bind you firmly into the fire and brimstone, all the way until the final Day of Judgment, and I deprive you from all power, dignities, and offices, unless you immediately show yourself clearly, and answer without delay, fraud, or trickery, as required, through him who will come to judge the living and the dead and the world by fire. May it be so; may it be so; may it be so.

A conjuration, proven, regarding a theft

This can be done by the person himself, without any others, for all kinds of stolen or lost things, and all doubts, in a crystalline gemstone, without the assistance of a child. You will see the angels in the stone, and they will tell you the truth, without doubt or fraud, about all things in question, or about a theft or homicide or hidden treasure, the state of things, of the living, of the dead, and hidden things, or and concerning whatever things you wish.[850]

Take a crystal, clear, bright, and slightly large, and a strip of leather from a large deer, and the crystalline gemstone should be place in the middle, so that it shines through, and he should say as follows: *In nomine sancte deitatis* ["In the name of the holy Deity"].

This should be spoken while turning the whole which covers the gem, in your right hand, towards the hot Sun around midday, and you will see whatever you wish. And command him with the following conjuration, to appear with his associates, in a fair form, with a wreath or crown on his head, and other garments of dignity, and sometimes he will come alone, and other times with the others. Then you may speak with him, and ask him to show you the thief, or whatever you ask for, and he will go away and immediately return, and will point out the thief with his finger, along with

---

850. Compare Sloane 3846, 34r. Sloane 3853 adds: "But beware ye be clene from lecherye by the spase of vii dayes before."

the things stolen, and the place and way that they entered, and who his accomplices were, and their names, and will write them out if you wish, and if you wish they can tell you about other hidden things or buried treasure, and whether it is fitting to retrieve or not, and whose they were, and all their crimes, and whether they are still alive or dead, and you can verify it with their father and mother and others, and he will teach you everything.[851]

Coniuro te N, viteon, muron, qui habitatis in bosco, o vos coniuro e[t] socios vestres adiuro et adduco, & impero vos ut cito et sine mora comp[are] in hac gemma cristallina et pati situs ad omnia precepta mea obediend[o in] omnem voluntatem meam, complendo.	I conjure you, N., Viteon, Muron, who inhabit the woodlands. I conjure you and your associates, I adjure and compel and command you, and provoke you without delay, to become visible in this crystalline gemstone, and may you be ready to obey all my orders and fulfill all my wishes.
[227]	*[227]*
Coniuro te bostael et bosco & bollo, per pat. &c et per Alpha et Omega, et per tremendium diem Iudicii, et per virtutem die metitam et per omnia nomina dei in effabilia et fabilia quatenus cito et sine mora in gemma ista cristallina compereas in propria persona et pulchra forma indutus et sertu in capite tuo deferas, et aducas, tecum socies tuos, ut te, et illos videre possum per preseptum meum, mihi non terendo nec alicui creature nocendo, et per istam coniurationem, de, te, mihi, et omnibus hic stantibus et omnibus quibus ego missero et nisi hoc, facias, ego, te, per vertutem	I conjure you,* Bostael and Bosco and Bollo, by the Father, Son, and Holy Ghost, and by the Alpha and Omega, and by the terrible Day of Judgment, and by the power and merit of God, and by all the names of God, both those which cannot be spoken, and those which can be spoken, that you quickly and without delay appear in this crystalline gemstone in person and putting on a fair form, and wearing a wreath on your head, and lead your associates [+ to me], such that you and they will be visible to my sight and perception, without frightening me or harming any creature,

* Compare Sloane 3853, fol. 218r.

---

851. This whole paragraph is corrupted and confused in all versions, but this is the best JHP has been able to reconstruct it.

dei omnipotentis, et per virtutem omnem sanctorum nominum condemnabo in ignem eternum, usque in die Iudicii mitti, iubeam:	and by this conjuration do all that I order, and if you do not, by the power of almighty God, and by the power of all his holy names I will condemn you into the eternal fire until the Day of Judgment.

With this complete, you should tell him that he should return whenever called, and immediately appear in your gemstone or elsewhere, and briefly respond to everything asked. But if he has not appeared, condemn him thus:

Ego te condemna estatell et in ignem internalem [*infernalem] te mitte iubio, per virtutem dei viui et veri omnipotentus & per virtutem omnium sanctorum suorum, et per pietatem [*potestatem] quam habeant deus [*super vos] ut semper, sis in inferno ligatus catenis ignis, donec visibilem nobis appereas in hac gemma cristallina, et meam implemeris voluntatem	I condemn you, O Estatell,[340] and order you to be sent into the *infernal fire, by the power of God, living, true, and almighty, and by the power of all his saints, and by the power which they shall have over you as always, that you be bound in hell with chains of fire, until you show yourself visibly to us in this crystalline gemstone, and fulfilled my will.
* Estatell: Sloane 3853: Alkates; Wellcome MS. 110: Alkatel.	

But if he doesn't appear on the first day,[852] say the conjuration likewise on the second day, and if he doesn't appear, say again on the third, etc.[853]

Omnipotens et eterne deus conditor celi et terre, et eorum que in ea sunt qui es primus et novisimus, innitiam et finis, qui Adam ex limo terre creasti, ad imaginam tuam formasti et in paradiso locasti, O tu adonay, ip'm, adam, ob, prevericationem mandati tui iterum a paradiso expulisti et custodes cherubin	O almighty and eternal God, maker of Heaven and Earth, and of all things which are in them, who is the first and the last, the beginning and the end, who created Adam from the mud of the earth, and made him after his own image, and placed him in Paradise, O Adonay, you commanded that Adam

852. Wellcome MS. 110: *prima vice* ["on the first time"].

853. Wellcome MS. 110 concludes the operation here with the words, *et voca eum et tunc veraciter veniat, et ad interrogata respondebit etc.* ["and call him., and then he will certainly come, and respond to your questions."]

et seraphin posuisti eum gladiis, quasi igne vibrantibus ut terrerent eum ab introitu, O clementissime et miserecordissime deus, qui ex immensa misericordia, et inestimabili bonitate filium tuum unigenitum Iesus Christum dominum nostrum salvatorem et redemptorem mundi, in mundum mittere dignatus fuisti, ut humanam naturam assumeret, deitati uniret ut perfectus esset Christus quem angelo annunciante carnem ex maria virgine assumere et inde nasci voluisti, ut perfectum se ostenderet hominem quem tradi ligari, conspui alaphis cedi pro agonia guttas sanguinis sudari corona spinea capite suo imponi flagris cedi vestimentis denudari purpurea circundari et iterum vulneribus infixum vi avelli et crucem vastam humeris suis temerimis, imponi, et amlari ut pro pendere corpus tenerimam sustenere, tantum omnis non potens gemens, succumbere coactus fuit quem trahi velli et extendi in cruce, ut, hia~nt Iuncture, rumpunt nervi et vene in altum elevi et pro augustia, et dolore, clamare Lamathabathani felli, et aceto poturi spiritum emittes et mori postea latus eius sanctissimum, lancea perforari voluisti, unde fluxit flumen sanguinis et aque in redemtionem mundi, quem sepeliri et ad inferos discendere et captiuos inde reducere et paradisum aperire et iterum ad te assendere voluisti, unde venturus est iudicari vivos et mortuos et seculum per ignem.

himself be expelled from Paradise because of his deception, and you placed the cherubim and seraphin to guard it with swords like flashing fire to frighten him away from the entrance, O most gentle and merciful God, who from the immensity of your mercy and incalculable goodness of your only-begotten son Jesus Christ our Lord, saviour and redeemer of the world, you have been deemed worthy to be sent into the world in order that he might take human nature; he will unite with the Deity in order that he might be completed, Christ which the angel announcing him taking the flesh from the Virgin Mary and thence to be born, in order that he might show himself as a man, who would be handed over to be bound, to be spit upon, beaten bloody, a crown of thorns set on his head, allowed himself to be whipped, his own garments torn off and a purple robe put on, and again* inflicted with wounds and fastened onto the huge cross with his most tender arms … and stretched out on the cross … in pain you cried out "Lamazabathany," drank vinegar and gall, expelled your breath, and died. Then your most holy side was pierced with a spear, and blood and water flowed therefrom, for the redemption of the world; you were buried and descended into hell to free those imprisoned there, and again arose and ascended into Heaven, from there you will come to judge the living and the dead and the world by fire.

* The text is corrupt, but is obviously a simple recounting of the passion.

O sanctissima Adonay per crucem sanguinem et per passionem eius et sacratissimum nomen eius Iesum benedica & sanctifica hoc experimentum siue charaterem ut obteneat effectum ut ego ipsum prorgaue (?) favourem gratiam, et amorem omnium hominum habeam et teneam, ita ut quidcunque petiero rogavero seu postulavero ab alique homine impetrem et obteneam, nec habeant potestatem [228] Denegandi, sed statim voluntatem meam adimpleant, et quod omne spiritus et potestates aereas sine infernales, nec non enemici mei visibiles et invisibiles noceri mihi non queant sed a malitia disistentes voluntati mei obediant, et eam sine mora impleant, per eum qui venturus est Iudicari vivos et mortuos et seculum per ignem. Finis.	O most holy Adonay, by his cross, blood, and passion, and by his most holy name Jesus, bless and sanctify this experiment or character, so that it may obtain the effect which I asked to have and keep the favour, grace, and love of all people, just as whatever I have asked for from the other person I will obtain and keep, and may they not have the power *[228]* to refuse, may they immediately fulfill my wishes, and may all spirits, and aerial or infernal powers, and all my enemies visible or invisible, be unable to harm me through malice, or resist, but obey my will, and fulfill it without delay, through him who will come to judge the living and the dead and the world by fire. The End.

Experiment for having the spirit Sibilla in the light of a candle [854]

To have a true answer, whether regarding a theft or treasure, or concerning whatever you wish, first you must have a pure conscience, and then take a candle of new wax, and light it and hold it in your right hand, and say as follows:

Coniuro te sibilla per patrem filium & spiritum sanctum, per deum verum deum vivum per sanctum & per deum qui omnia ex nihilo condidit & creavit, & per virginitatem beate marie & per virginitatem beati Ioannis evangelisti, per virginitatem beate margarite & per omnes virtutes celorum, per omnia [+	I conjure you, Sibilla, through the Father, Son, and Holy Ghost, through the True God, through the living God, through the holy [God], who created and established all things from nothing, and through the blessed Virgin Mary, and the blessed virgin John the Evangelist, blessed Margarite, and all the powers of

---

854. Compare Rawlinson D. 252, 13r and 92r.

nomina] devina que sunt in celo & in terra, & per omnia nomina que sunt in hoc libro contenta, & per ista nomina agla, tau, tetragramaton, adonay, unigenitus via sapientia virtus que que tu sibilla mihi virtute verbore predictorum appereas hic in candela & te mihi in pulchra forma humana & decora in specie angeli & de qualibet de quam te interrogavero dicas veritatum, Ita que ego vocem & demonstrationem audiam et intelligam & ita venias ut mecum maneas et cum te licentianero recedas nec in aliquo me molestes per eum qui venturus est iudicare vivos et mortuos & seculum per ignem amen.

Heaven, and all the divine [+ names]* in Heaven and on Earth, and through all the names which are contained in this book,† and through these names: Agla, Tau, Tetragramaton, Adonay, Only-begotten, the Way, Wisdom, Virtue, that you, O Sibilla, appear to me through the power of the preceding words, here in the light of this candle, in a fair and beautiful human form, and angelic appearance, and truly answer whatever I ask, such that I can hear your voice clearly and understand, and thus remain with me, and when licenced to depart, do so without disturbing anyone, through Him who will come to judge the living and the dead and the world by fire.

* So Rawlinson D. 252.

† This ascribes a particular sacred nature to the book itself, a la *Liber Spirituum* in Donald Tyson, *The Fourth Book of Occult Philosophy* (Woodbury, MN: Llewellyn, 2009), 93.

Ad huc coniuro te Sibilla per deum vivum per deum verum per deum sanctum & per deum qui cuncta creavit ex nihillo, & per sanctam mariam matre domini nostri Iesu Christi & per Michaelem, Gabrielem, Raphaelem, Raquelem, et per omnes angelos, [+ archangelos,] thronos, & dominationes, principates, potestates, et per omnes virtutes celorum per celum et terram per solem et lunam per stellas celi & undas maris per sanctam Ioannem evangelistam, per sanctum Ioannem

I conjure you here, O Sibilla, by the loving God, by the true God, by the holy God, and by the God who created all things out of nothing, and by Saint Mary, mother of our Lord Jesus Christ, and by Michael, Gabriel, Raphael, and Raquel, and by all Angels, [+ Archangels,]* Thrones, Dominations, Principates, Powers, and by all the virtues of heaven, and by heaven and earth, by the Sun and Moon, by the stars of the sky and earth, by the Sun and Moon, by the

* So Rawlinson D. 252, and also to complete the influential list of angelic orders or choirs, according to Pseudo-Dionysius, Colm Luibhéid, and Paul Rorem, *Pseudo-Dionysius: The Complete Works* (New York: Paulist Press, 1987), 160 ff.

Baptista qui Christum in flumina Iurdanis baptizanie, per evangelistas, m, m, L, I, per mortem & passionem domini nostri Iesu Christi, per spiritum sanctum paracletum per tremendum diem Iudicii & per partum beatem marie virginis & per omnes sacerdotes dei qui coram deo sunt coronati & coram eo exorate & per Alpha, et Omega, initium & finem & per hoc nomine tetragramaton vinificabile & per alia sancta nomen dei agla, tau, anazapta, anapheneton, stimulaton * adonay * sabaoth * emanuell * & per omnia nomina sancta que dicta sunt vell dici possunt de deo vell nominari que ubiqumque fueris Sibilla huc accedat [*accedas] sine mora et molestia te viriliter coniuro & exorcizo per planetam modo regna[n]tem, ut in candela mod[o] mihi visibiliter appereas sine mora & de omnibus a te inter rogatis veraciter respondeas sine aliqua falatia vell dolo, vell falsitat[.] per eum qui venturus est Iudicare vivos et mortuos & seculum per ignem amen.

stars of the sky, waves in the sea, and by Saint John the Evangelist, and by Saint John the Baptist who baptized Christ in the river Jordan, and by the evangelists Matthew, Mark, Luke, and John, by the death and passion of our Lord Jesus Christ, by the Holy Ghost Paraclete ("Advocate"), by the terrible Day of Judgement, and by the birth of the blessed Virgin Mary, and by all priests of God who have been crowned in the presence of God, and who have made petitions in his presence, and by Alpha and Omega, the beginning and the end, and by this life-giving name Tetragrammaton, and by the other holy names of God, Agla, Tau, Anazapta, Anapheneton, Stimulaton, Adonay, Sabaoth, Emmanuel,* and by all the holy names which have been spoken, or which are able to be named or spoken about God, that wherever you are, O Sibilla, that you come here without delay or trouble. I powerfully conjure and exorcize you by means of the ruling planet, that you appear visibly to me here in this candle, without delay, and respond truthfully to all my questions, without any deceit, trickery, or falsehood, through Him who will come to judge the living and the dead and the world by fire. Amen.

* Rawlinson D. 252: *Agla, Thau, Anonizapta, Anapheneton, Stimulamiton, Adonay, Sabaoth, Emanuel.*

And when the spirit appears, say:

Coniuro te sibilla qui appereas in hec candela, in nomine patris &c amen. & per virtutem presiosi sanguinem Iesu Christi & per hec sancta nomina dei * Agla * Tau * Anazapta * Anaph[e]neton * Stimulaton * Sabaoth * Adonay * Emanuell * & per totam coniurationem predictam, tuum adventum constringentem ut non resedas ab hac candela, quosque veraciter mihi ad omnia mea, inter rogata, respondeas, & a me licentiata fueris amen.	I conjure you, O Sibilla, who appears in this candle, in the name of the Father etc. Amen. By the power of the precious blood of Jesus Christ, and by these sacred names of God: Agla, Tau, Anazapta, Anapheneton, Stimulaton, Sabaoth, Adonay, Emmanuel, and by the whole preceding conjuration, binding your arrival, that you do not withdraw from this candle, until you truthfully answer all my questions, and have been dismissed by me. Amen.

Then ask whatever you intend, and dismiss as follows:

Coniuro te Sibilla per patrem filium & s. s. & per hec quinque nomina dei * agla * tau * Ioth * tetragramaton * adonay * ut ad locum tibi adeo summo destinatum vadas, & que nulle creature noceas nec molestas, & [229] Honesto modo recedas & nulle creature nocueris, & quando cunque et ubicunque te invocauero, sis mihi parata & statim mihi incontenentis obedias, in nomine patre & filii & spiritus sanctus amen.	I conjure you, O Sibilla, by the Father, Son, and Holy Ghost, and by these five names of God: Agla, Tau, Ioth, Tetragrammaton, Adonay, that you go to that place destined you by God on high, and without harming or disturbing any creature, and [229] depart in an honest manner, harming no creature, and whenever and wherever be prepared to obey me as agreed, in the name of the Father, and the Son, and the Holy Ghost. Amen.

For to take fowls with your hands

Take the seed of henbane, and the seed of poppies, the seed of lettuce, and the seed of hemlock, and stamp them well and beat them all together in dregs of wine, and do wheat therein, and let it set well, and then strain it and take the wheat, and fiat.

For a maid's thought

Take a stone that men call agagats and lay it on her left breast [855] when she is asleep.

For love in the day and hour of Venus[856]

Write this figure in thy left hand and touch a maid or a woman the which thou wouldst have before the Sun rising on the Friday and in his hour, and she shall follow thee, and if thou canst not touch her, shew it her and she shall follow thee, with these words & R. & ye, asseraph, assmobias, Nil i eye asseraphe, assmobias. Characters (written) with the blood of a bat or dove.

Against thieves[857]

Carry with thee these characters written in virgin parchment,

Against thy enemies

Visible and invisible by God['s] grace, his almighty power as well, against evil pestilence and all ill famine, these letters written in a clean linen cloth, let them be borne oyson the angel did give them to King Karroll, & did command him to bear them of the part of God in peril

---

855. Folger: tethe.

856. In left marg.: "HP."

857. In marg.: "HP."

858

Write these, and always bear these characters with thee, and ye asserephe asmobias

Whosoever these letters or characters shall bear with him, his enemies shall have no power to hurt him, but rather to fear him.

Bgbenvtc wdeeobstc ["Against witchcraft"]

That thy enemies shall not overcome thee in thy cause, write on three laurel leaves and bear them with thee, **Michaell + Gabriell + Raphaell** + *hbngc thcm bbrstc yrso ncekc* ["hang them about your neck"].

For axis [859] or ague

Write this verse in an apple, that is to say, in three parts, and let the sick confess himself to God, and the first day to eat one part, that is + *In nomine patris* + *pater est vita vivens Alpha et Omega* ["+ in the name of the Father + the Father is the life of the living Alpha and Omega"] the second + *Et filii* + *filis est sapiencia patris geniti* + *Emanuell,* ["and the Son + the Son is the wisdom begotten of the Father + Emanuel"]

858. Cross has words *ardes nia sugit* / *my-cha-ell spiritus* ["you burn ... the spirit Michael"].

859. Axis: aches or pains; sometimes used as a synonym for ague.

the third + *Et spiritus sancte est amor* + *ab utroque precedens paraclitus* ["and the Holy Ghost is the love + from each proceeding the Paraclete"]. Amen.

For sorrow of the teeth

Write these three names in a hazel wand of one year's growth. And if he be a man, say "John, where is your pain," and if it be a woman, say "Joan, where is your pain." marga, dura, trazam, i pega ii tega iii Sega iiii dera and femmam.

[230]

A charm for *thndbr drrdm prbbxtdm* ["Thieves *issim* (?) proven"]

God that sitteth (?) in trinity, that is one God and persons three, as westly [??] I believe in, for thy grace and for thy might, save me good lord both d[ay and] night, from all my enemies and from all thieves, and from all that be [???] and by the virtue of thy right arm, save me good lord from all ha[rm] I conjure Him by the virtue of thee, that all thieves abide [???] wheresoever that I go or ride, make him lord me to abide, and d[??] to him what me list in field or in town, or wheresoever that [??] ne let no thieves go me fro, er[860] that I have my will done, me [???] him never further run, Father and Son and Holy Ghost, in thee is [???] and might and [???] must.[861] In thee is the beginning and ending, in thee is virt[ue (?)] of all things of wood and stone, grass, herb, and tree, and all these virtues lieth in thee, and by the virtue of all good prayers, t[hat] ever was said by faithful heirs, and if there come any thieves for to rob or to kill, that by thy power and might they do stand still. And that they stand as stiff as any stone, and have power away for to be gone, thieves, thieves, thieves still do you stand by the might and power of God's holy hand. And by the virtue of the holy Trinity, sweet Lord in persons three, as ye be holy in trinity, lord ye grant that it so be. Fiat fiat.

prbptrr fdrtb ["*propter furto* / in the event of theft"]

For St. Charity, fiat, fiat, fiat, then say this three times: "Lux amia moria, & c. Eye asserephe, assmubias vel assnobyas, Cospax."

---

860. Er: or.

861. Must: a duty or obligation.

prbptrr fdrbrrm prbbxtdm ["*propter fur[t]orum probatum* / in the event of thefts, proven"][862]

In Bethlehem God was borne between two beast to rest, he was laid in the stead, where was never thief ne man, but the Holy Ghost, the Trinity, that same God there was borne, defend [our (?)] bodies and our goods and our cattle from all thieves, and from harms, and from all manner of mischiefs, wheresoever [??] bin by land or by water, betide or betime, *in nomine patris et filii et spiritus sancti amen* ["in the name of the Father and Son and Holy Ghost. Amen"]. lux amia moria lux amia moria, lux amia moria Eye assarephe assmobias vel ["or"] assnobias, Cos[pax].

Erxprrrmrntr fbr thrnbdrs ["Experiment for thieves"]

I cbnndrr yld thrndrs ["I command you thieves"], by the virtue of the Father, the Son, the Holy Ghost, the holy Trinity, as westely[863] as I believe in thee through thy virtue and thy might, save me, good lord, both day [and] night, both within and without, in every place and all abou[t] from all mine enemies, and from all thieves, that no man ha[rm] us through our beliefs by the virtue of Heaven, earth, water and lands, and by all that ever was wrought by God's hands, and by the virtue of wood, herb, stone, grass, and by all the virtue that may be, and by the virtue of every sacrament, that ever was wrought by God's judgment, and all that ever God hath wrought, or ever did or ever th[???] And if [t]her[e] come to me any thieves, or anybody me to hurt or harm to rob or to slay (?), so some him or them to bind and to [??] taking robbing or to slay, that they may stand as still as stone, till I bid him or them be gone, And as westely me[??] him behindeth and walking out of their minds as the Jew[s] were blinding, when Jesus hid him in his Godhead in the temple, God grant that ye may be true, as westely t[??] God believe, then say, p, n, a, & the c,[864] *fiat*.

+ And if he may not go hence on God's name bid him go hence on the devil's name, and come no [more] there.

---

862. In pencil in marg.: *probatum / prapt firaoom / ho-aaxtam*; "propter fur[t]orum"?
863. This must mean something like "surely," but JHP can't find it in any dictionary.
864. I.c., Pater Noster, Ave [Maria], and the Creed.

ffbr t7ld m7k7xbr th777rdrs tb st7xnd7r ["For to make thieves to stand"]

In nomine patris filii et spritus sancti fiat ["In the name of the Father, Son, and Holy Ghost, let it be."]

N cbnndrr, ybd thdrdrs ["I conjure you thieves"], by the virtue of the Father and *N cbnndrr yld thrdrs* ["I conjure you thieves"], by the virtue of God['s] passion, and of his ascension and of his resurrection, *N cbnndrr yld thrdrs* ["I conjure you thieves"], the virtue of the rawmyge [k-?] that God was rawmye [k-?] with all the bawmynge[865] stone, *N cbnndrr ybd thrdrs* ["I conjure you thieves"], by the virtue [of] the baptism that God look in [blank space] sarden (?), *N, cbnn[drr]* [231] *ybd thrdrs* ["I conjure you thieves"] by the virtue of the wounds of God that bled one good fridaye *N cbnndrr ybd thrdrs* ["I conjure you thieves"], by the virtue of the sepulcher that God was buried in, still that you stand, and no further go, *in nomine patris filii et spritus sancti fia*t ["In the name of the Father, Son, and Holy Ghost, may it be so"].

Domine Iesu Christi Salvator huius mundi (?) et redemptione omni fideliter, tu alpha et, omega, messias, sother, Sabaothe, adynay salva me ab omnibus viciis [*viscatoriis] diabolicis et ab omnibus latronibus et si aliqui latrones veniunt hic exspectabunt, per virtute flori nomine dei ali qui actipere, agla [*Alpha] et, Omega, et, ola, ely, eloy, sabaothe, adonay, tetragramaton, fiat. ["O Lord Jesus Christ, saviour of this world, and redeemer of all the faithful, you are Alpha and Omega, Messias, Sother, Sabaoth, Adonay; save me from all snares of the devil, and from all robbers, and if any robbers come, they will wait here, by the power of the shining name of God, (unable) to take anything, Agla [*Alpha] and Omega, and Ola, Ely, Eloy, Sabaoth, Adonay, Tetragrammaton. May it be so!"]

Tb m7xkr bnr fxnrr ["To make one fair"]

You must take vine water one quarter, one M (?) of wild tansy, one M of Higramen, put them in a glass together until the water doth stink, and then strain it, and put it into the glass again then put in di (?) oz (?) of sugar candy small beate [bit?] then put a little camphor, then put as much white burras, then put three leaves of gold, then shake all these together, and set the glass in the Sun one fortnight, then strain it again. At night take a piece of scarlet and rub *ybdr f7xcr* ["your face"] overnight with it, then in the morning take a piece of clean white linen, and dip the same

---

865. Bawmynge = *bauminge* ["anointing"]? The stone of the anointing was the supposed place where Jesus's body was prepared for burial.

in the water, then when *yldr fxcr* ["your face"] is dry, within a quarter of an hour, rub *ybdr fxcr* ["your face"] with the scarlet again.

Take a lemon and pull out the carnels [kernels (?)] then put in a little sugar candy, and two leaves of gold, and put it in. Then take a thread and bind on the cover of the lemon again and set it on the embers and roast it like an egg, for the space of half an hour, then let it be cold, then rub *ybdr f7xr* ["your face"] with the scarlet, and then take a little out of the lemon on a piece of linen cloth and wipe *ybdr f7xr* ["your face"] with it.

For the toothache
Write these letters in a square piece of wood:

✠ *Te* ✠ *tra* ✠ *gra* ✠ *ma* ✠ *ton* ✠

annis buclo

866

and when you have done, clean the wood in the midst (?) and burn it x *f7r thr s7m7 s777ngr th7s7 w7rds 7s f7l7w7thr* ["for the same, saying these words as followeth"], Maria Emanuell ananizapta *s77the g77th* ["saithe goith"?] margery longe in the name of the Father & c.

Tb m7k7 [??] *7nd w7* [??] *t7 d7nnc* [?]*7 xs f7l7 th7* ["To make a maiden (?) to dance as followeth"]

First wr7ght in v7rg7n p7rch7m7nt7 7r w7x7 opvcns nepos castor popas cely puphas, lendula pendula, and say this 7 c7n7nry thy, per, or, w, by th7 n7m7s that are wr7t7n in th7, that whosoever c7m7 in h7r7 sh7ll7 d7nnc7 ["First write in virgin parchment as wa[??] opvcns nepos castor popas cely puphas, lendula pendula, and say this I conjure thee per pater (?) by the names that are written in thee, that whosoever came in here shall dance"].

---

866. Below is "annis buclo."

Tr m7b7 7n7 [??] f7l7w7 [?]7 ["To make one follow thee"]

Write th7s7 l7tt7rs 7n7 th7 w7dn7sd777/ d. n. ss g g h h, before the sunrise, and t7uch7 h7r in what place th7d7 w7lt7 and sh7 sh7ll f7l7w7 th7, and if thou wilt prove it, t77ch7 7 d7dg7 and h7 w7ll f7l7w7 th7 ["Write these letters on the Wednesday d n ss g g h h before the sunrise, and touch her in what place thou (?) wilt and she shall follow thee. And if thou wilt prove it, touch a dog and he will follow thee."]

Pr7 7m7r7 m7l77r7 ["***Pro amore muliere/*** For a woman's love"]

Write 7n7 7 7ppl7 th7s7 n7m7s f7l7w7ng7, guell, faste, nel, elsell, Ilysell, and g777 h7r t7 77t7 and 7t sh7lb7 ["Write on an apple these names following, 'guell, faste, nel, elsell, Ilysell,' and give her to eat and it shall be."]

If thou wilt know *?7 7s 7 m77d7 & ?7 7sn7t* ["[if] she is a maid and or (?) is not"]

When they sit in a bath together *c7st7 q77ck7 s7l77r th7r7n & th7 m77d7n shall st7rt7 7p* ["cast quicksilver therein and the maiden shall start up"], and the other shall stoure therein.

[232]

T7 m7?7 l777 betw7n7 m7n7 & w7f7m ["To make love between men and women"]

First take of the root of valerian, and give [it to] them to drink in powder *7nd th7y sh7ll l777* ["and they shall love"].

If any be *7ngr7 w7th th7 s777 7s f7l7w 7th7* ["angry with thee say as followeth"]

Inbarros, vitenis, ageos, salvator, adonai, alpha, et, omega. agla, aca[.] taw, tetragramaton, ananizapta, on, adeflos, sabaoth, vis, atque [???]

Also to make thieves to stand as well by night as by day

Thou shalt, at every corner of the house where the goods do stand, say this orison following:

Michell, Gabriell, Uriell, Canaphnell, parathyell, panteferon, anguell, Iobiell, I do swear you thieves by the living God, by the holy God, that none of you or any other have power to hurt me, nor my house to break in, nor to carry away my goods. *Omnipotens sempiterne deus que orductor [*orditur (?)] florem et diriges, Itener[??] Iustorum dirige sanctum angelum tuum Raphaelem assit nichill comitatus [*commeatus], Iocundus ut mulus [*nulus], surripiat vias meas nec res meas Inuicus [inimicus?], et timeas me esse dignetur propter stantis per tetragraton [sic] propolens Bartolemeus patina pathmazeus, In nomine patris &c. Iesu autem transiens per alla lux, a, amen."* ["Almighty eternal God, who who *ordained and directed the flower, direct the path of justice. May your holy angel Raphael be present, pleasant company, that my enemies may be unable to steal away my things... through Tetragra[ma]ton, thus on behalf of the dish of mighty Bartholomew ....[867] Jesus passed through their midst, and went his way. Amen."]

In nomine patris ["In the name of the Father"] &c.

I beseech thee, Holy Ghost, this place that here is set, the Father the Son thieves for to let, And if there come any thieves any goods away to fetch, the Holy Ghost be then before, and do him for to let and do make him abide till I again come, through the virtue of the Holy Ghost, the Father and the Son, betide what will betide, and if there come any thieves here they shall abide, through the virtue of Matthew, M[ark], L[uke], and J[ohn], the four evangelists according all in one, that ye bind the thieves so fast and do him noi~e (?), so as St. Bartholomew did bind the devil with his beard hair, so here thieves, thieves, thieves, stand ye thieves in the name of the Father and of the Son and of the Holy Ghost, and in the name of the Trinity, and for the passion of Christ, and for his death and his uprise, in the name of the Father the Son and of the Holy Ghost, three persons and one God, that ye still stand, till I bid you go on a God's name, or on the devils' name and come no more here.

An experiment for thieves

Whosoever be afraid of thieves, to be robbed by night or by day in his house, or else that he hath a pond of fish, or garden of fruit or a field of sheep, or a horse that is tied in the field, that he would have kept from all thieves and saved, let him say this charm next following like as it standeth written here hereafter. They shall have no

---

867. JHP would expect to see "as St. Bartholomew bound the devil by a hair of his beard" as in the following two experiments, but the text is corrupted.

power to bear away his goods nor to rob him, but they shall stand as still as mazed [868]
men, till they have leave to go of[f] from him that feareth the goods. And if it befall
that any such come there within the danger, when that thou cometh to him say to
him whatsoever you will to the uttermost peril. And when thou hast said what thou
list, then bid him go hence on God's name, and come no more here, and if he will not
go so, bid him go hence in the devil's name and come no more here.

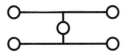

And be thou ware that thou bewray not his name from this day forth, for if thou
bewray him, peradventure it might be the cause of his undoing and death, and therefore keep thine own counsel.

In nomine patris et filii et spiriti sancti" ["In the name of the Father, Son, and Holy
Ghost"]. Amen.

The Holy Ghost *benedicitie* ["bless"] the Father the Son with us be.

In the name of the Father, the Son, and the Holy Ghost. Amen. Apostles, angels,
archangels, last I bequeath this place all about on and all my goods within and without on to the blessed Trinity that is one God and persons three, and to St. John the
Evangelist that died on earth with Jesus Christ [233] that no thieves away it takes but
keep it well John for Mary's sake. And that they mought [869] no foot hence flee but keep
them still the blessed Trinity through thy virtue of thy passion and manhead, [870] and
through the virtue of thy blessed body in form of bread, and through the virtue of
every prayer that ever was said by thy faithful heirs and by the virtue of wood, herbs,
grass, and stones, I charge you apostles, every choue (?)Mark, Matthew, Luke, and
John, the Sun, the Moon and the stars, and you elements clear, I charge you keep him
still here.

Saturnus, Jupiter, Mars, Sol, Venus, Mercurius, and Luna, Aries, Taurus, Gemini,
Cancer, Leo, Virgo, Libra, Scorpio, Sagittarius, Capricornus, Aquarius et Pis[c]es, I
charge you seven planets and twelve signs clear, I charge you keep him still here, and
that he press no foot away, till he have told every stone in the way, and every drop of
water in the sea.

I pray you all that it so be, by the virtue of the Trinity and that you bind him also
hard, as St. Bartholomew did the devil with the hair of his beard, thieves, thieves,
thieves, still stand ye, by the virtue of the blessed Trinity and in the virtue of the

---

868. Mazed: stupefied.

869. Mought: may.

870. Manhead: human nature

blessed Trinity, and in the virtue of the passion of Christ, and of his death and his uprise, till tomorrow I come here and speak to you on my manner. I charge you all that it so be, by the virtue of the Trinity that is the Lord of mightiest most, the Father, the Son, and the Holy Ghost. Amen. *fiat fiat.*

Then say the p n, the A, & the Cr,[871] with good devotion.

Lux amia moria, say three times, asseraphe, assmobias vel assnobias gaspax + yeboel + hebne + *O alltissime pater noster* ["O our highest Father"] + *fac mecum signum in bono ut videant Omnes quoniam tu domine adiuvisti me et consolatus es me*[872] *in nomine patris et filii et spiriti sancti amen Iesu nazasenus [*Nazarenus] Rex Iudeorum filii dei, viui miserere mei amen* ["make me a sign of what is good, that they may see all, for you have helped me and consoled me, in the name of the Father, and of the Son, and of the Holy Ghost. Amen. Jesus of Nazareth, the king of the Jews, the Son of the living God, have mercy on me. Amen"].

Slecov rs p obdi cv albiico & yboic ["ulcers or p raid es (?) bladder & yard"][873]

The milk of an ass or goat sod with the juice of plantain and drunk.

* * *

Pistus from the liver into the secrets descending by the vein of the back, through heat and cold, into the secrets, and in the end thereof between the two skins breaketh out like a scab, it being taken in time doth good rather than hurt, otherwise it corrupteth the whole body. He riseth hard and watering, with a thick skin like a sponge, it is a raw humour, mastic, quicksilver, alum burnt, *attramentum* ["ink"] dried.

fro focttdngc rf thc ...ycbod ro bnd rthco ?bot ["For fretting of the yard or any other part (?)"]

Alum burnt, boil in milk, the crud skinned (?), wash with the wate[r.]

---

871. I.e., the Pater Noster, Ave Maria, and Creed.

872. Compare Psalm 85:17 (KJV 86:17).

873. Yarde: penis.

[???] b ocsmcn ["... a reumen"]

+ Bras + capras + seduces + feceas *thdv msvtc ac wodttcn podscly dn vrmc thdngc bni gcsc hdm tr cbtc cdthco aocbic ro rhcvc* ["this must be written privily in something and give him to eat either bread or cheese"] etc. *Finis* ["end"].

[234]

hsdsv ldaod Gsdldclmsv Aobdsv porfcv~ro ["Huius libra Guilielmus Braius professor"][874]

First you must know that none of the spirits will obey thee or do reverence, or give thee any [ser]vice unless thou shalt observe those thing[s] following.[875]

First it is necessary that thou have a ring consecrated by art, ke[ep] (?) therefore clean and pure from all venery actions, at the least, for the sp[ace] of three days. Neither must thou eat or drink much, but sparingly. And th[e] ring must be of gold, or of pure copper well gilded. And it ought to [be] made in the day of Venus ♀ and in the twelfth hour afore dinner, so that it be made afore dinner or before noon, and if it cannot be made in that hour, then l[et] it alone in that state which it is in, until the next day of Venus, and then making [the] ring he shall recite devoutly these names of God very often, + Agla + the[os] (?). Then you shall burn it with white frankincense, cloves, balsamum, and saffron, and consecrate the ring with these speeches which follow, and thou shalt keep it rever[ently] in a clean place, which hath great in itself, of almighty God, so that it sh[all] bind all the spirits of the air, and also of hell. And this ring will keep thee from all the tumults and powers of the spirits, and when thou wilt consecr[ate] this ring, it is behooveful[876] that thou be clean, and well-confessed from all sins, [and] clothed with clean garments, and that thou have fire nigh unto thee, to put [into the] frankincense, and put the ring on the thumb on the right hand, and ho[ld it in] the smoke of the frankincense, and say, having good hope in God [and request] his aid.

How to call the king of the *pdg mcdcv* ["pigmies"]

By what means, and how you may call the *Kdnge rf thc pdgmcdcvc* ["king of the pigmies"] in what place so ever, and what hour so ev[er you] please, by the force and

---

874. Guilielmus Braius professor, i.e., Professor William Bray. Unknown.

875. In marg.: "w" glyph.

876. Behooveful: necessary.

virtue of a certain number, by whom [these] numbers were made and invented, first the number doth appea[r here]

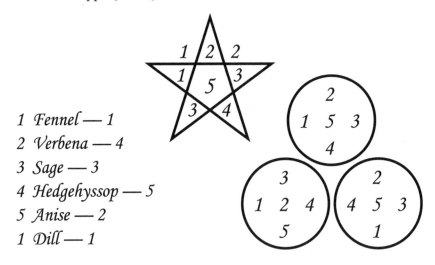

1 Fennel — 1
2 Verbena — 4
3 Sage — 3
4 Hedgehyssop — 5
5 Anise — 2
1 Dill — 1

Then thou shalt repeat five times the Lord's Prayer, and the salutations of the angels, and onc[e] the creed Simballes.[877] By putting the numbers according to the multiplication of those prayers, whether one will call them into a *codvtbll* ["crystal"], or any other fit place, doing all things secretly, but by requesting the *kdngc r[???] Qscnc* ["i.e., king or queen"] by the wounds of Christ and by the joy of the blessed [Virgin] Mary, and by the virtue of the multiplied number & c. you shall [request], and beseech him earnestly that he will offer himself to the eyes to be seen. [This] being done, anoint or paint thine eyes with dew that is in the field, [in the] compasse of thy circle in which thou art conversant, so thy matters [shall] end happily. *St porabtsm cvtc* ["*ut probatum est* / proven"].

Therefore by this reason, all will appear true.

---

877. I.e., the well-known Athanasian Creed (*Symbolum Athanasianum*).

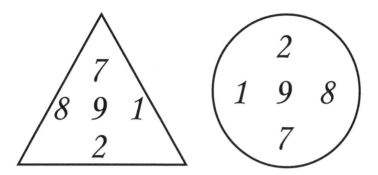

[In marg. in *sec. man.*:]

The Moon increasing *dic* ["say"] 3 p. n., three A & three C,[878] then these Psalms: *Domine exaudi orationem meam auribus* ["O Lord hear my prayer; incline you ear..."] etc. and the 52nd Psalm, and so do your effect, the Moon being in the fiery signs, as Aries, Leo, and Sagittarius.

I *erndsoc* ["conjure"] thee, O thou spirit of Tobyas, by God I bind thee Tobyas, by the mother of God I *bidsoc* ["adiure"] thee, Tobyas, by all the angels of God I conjure and charge thee, Tobyas, by the faith that thou owest unto thy pr[ivate] God, that thou come speedily unto me in this *eodvtbll* ["crystal"] without all d[elay] without hurting, without guile, and without fallacity, also without h[urt] of any other creature of God, and that thou give me a true answer [of] all things which I shall ask of thee, and that thou depart not from th[is] *eodvtbll* ["crystal"], until thou hast finished my will, so that I licence thee to [go] as thou wilt answer the lord thy God, at the last Day of Judgement and the world by fire. Amen. + In the name of the Father + and of the Son + and of the Holy Ghost, so be it + I bind thee by God + the Father + God the Son + and God the Holy Ghost. Amen.

Thou spirit of Tobyas, thou knowest that Christ liveth, Christ conquereth, Christ reigneth and ruleth in Heaven, in earth, in [the] water, in the sea, and in all deep places, wherefore if thou [wilt] not appear in perfect form and shape above named, I commit into the hands of these infernal spirits, that is to say, Luc[ifer], Sathan, Tatalion [Catalion?] and Pasill, there to be burnt with fire [and] brimstone until thou hast fulfilled my will.

[235]

When it appeareth, say thus:

---

878. Three Pater Nosters, three Ave Marias, and three Creeds.

Now the cross of God almighty + the Father + the Son + and the Holy Ghost come upon thee, Tobyas, and deprive thee from thy duty, unto the deepest pit of hell until the last Day of Judgment, and that thou never come again unto thy honour, except thou stand and appear, by form, and in a fair likeness of a man or woman, and not hurting me nor any other creature of God, answering to my request, and also to fulfill my desire, without delay, rest, or any other cavillation[879] or falsehood, writing or printing the same and showing to me or telling it [to] me by some manner of means, whereby I may receive the benefit of the charge,[880] under the pain aforesaid. And thus I bind thee by the blessed power of heaven and earth, and by the blessed blood of our saviour Jesus Christ, and by all his miracles that ever he wrought, and by the blessed passion of our saviour Jesus Christ, suffered for me and all mankind. Amen. * * *

When he shall depart, say thus:

Depart in peace unto the place prepared for thee, and the peace of God be between thee and me and all other creatures of God. And when I shall call thee again, I will call thee + In the name of the Father + & c. So rest in peace.

If any man work any work, or play at any game in the days that be contrary to his constellation, he shall not prosper. Therefore it is needful, saith Robarte Cane,[881] that every man do know his constellation, or else nothing will avail him. Whosoever is born from the middle of December unto the middle of January is days of good fortune.

[For the] Swallow [882]

First go to the place where the swallow hath her nest with four young ones. Bind one of them upon the nest by the space of four days and, on the fourth day, take him out of the nest. Cut him in the middle, and you shall find within the belly of it three stones of diverse colours, the one brown of colour, the second is red, the third is white. The virtue of the first is, if thou wilt give it to any woman that travaileth with child she shall be speedily delivered. /2/ The virtue of the red stone is, if thou wilt put

---

879. Cavillation: to make frivolous objections.

880. In left marg.: "w" glyph three times in a row.

881. Robarte Cane: Unknown

882. In left marg.: "HP."

it in thy mouth, thou shalt obtain any thing thou wilt demand. /3/ The virtue of the white stone is, if any man bear it with him, he shall not be athirst, as long as he hath the said stone with him.

[The] virtue of vervain

First go to the place where the herb groweth, the second day of May, after the setting of the Sun. Kneel down upon thy knees before the herb & say p. n., A, and a C.[883] Then dig it with an instrument that hath no iron about it, until the roots do appear. And then lay ☽ or ☉[884] about the roots, and let it alone until the morrow after. Then come before the rising of the ☉, unknown to any. Say these words:

Mobles, rardem, congrue tu mihi, per patrem et filium et spiritum sanctum &c per virginem mariam et per 24 seniores et per angellos et Archangelos, Apostolos et evangelistos, et per lac S Marie, et per matrimonium honestarum, et per passionem et multem vertutem terram, relinquas et Regnum intres.	O Mobles, Rardem, come meet with me, by the Father, Son, and Holy Ghost, by the Virgin Mary, and by the twenty-four Seniors, and by the angels and archangels, apostles and evangelists, and by the milk of Saint Mary, and by the honourable marriage, and by the passion and great power, the earth, may you leave behind and enter the kingdom.*

> * At the end of the page appears a note, "Friar Bacon Original Manuscript." The next page includes the following modern note: "At the bottom of sheet 212 verso are two diagrams which indicate a familiarity with the 'LEMEGETON.' 212) See: THE LESSER KEY OF SOLOMON. GOETIA THE BOOK OF EVIL SPIRITS. Ed. de Laurence. 1916. Also: Waite / Shah / etc. THE HEXAGRAM OF SOLOMON Fig: 155."

---

883. p.n....: Pater Noster (Our Father), A (Ave Maria) and a. C. (creed).

884. ☽ or ☉: silver or gold.

BIBLIOGRAPHY

Agrippa von Nettesheim (1) - *De occulta philosophia libri tres.*

Agrippa von Nettesheim, Heinrich Cornelius. *Opera I.* With an introduction by Richard H. Popkin. Hildesheim: G. Olms, 1970.

Agrippa von Nettesheim, Heinrich Cornelius, and Petrus de Abano. *Henrici Cornelii Agrippae liber qvartvs De occvlta philosophia, seu de cerimonijs magicis.* [Marburg?:] Impressum, 1565. Facsimile included in: Agrippa von Nettesheim, Heinrich Cornelius, and Karl Anton Nowotny. *De occulta philosophia.* Graz: Akademische Druck u. Verlagsanstalt, 1967.

Agrippa von Nettesheim, Heinrich Cornelius, Robert Turner, and Petrus de Abano. *Henry Cornelius Agrippa His Fourth Book of Occult Philosophy. Of Geomancy. Magical Elements of Peter de Abano. Astronomical Geomancy. The Nature of Spirits. Arbatel of Magick. Translated into English by Robert Turner, Philomathes.* London: Printed by J. C. for John Harrison, at the Lamb at the East-end of Pauls, 1655.

Agrippa von Nettesheim, Heinrich Cornelius, and V. Perrone Compagni. *De Occulta Philosophia Libri Tres.* Leiden; New York: E. J. Brill, 1992.

Albert. *Secrets merveilleux de la magie naturelle et cabalistique du Petit Albert.* A Lyon: Chez les Héritiers de Beringos Fratres, 1782.

Anonymous. "The Magic Scroll. Described by Bro. W. J. Hughan." *Ars Quatuor Coronatorum: Transactions of the Quatuor Coronati Lodge No. 2076 London* 16, no. 2 (1903): 132–156.

Aquinas, Thomas. *The De Malo of Thomas Aquinas: with Facing-page Translation by Richard Regan.* Oxford, England; New York: Oxford University Press, 2001.

Bacon, Rogerus, and Michael-Albion Macdonald. *De Nigromancia: Sloane Ms. 3885 & Additional Ms. 36674.* Gillette, NJ: Heptangle Books, 1988.

Bain, Frederika. "The Binding of the Fairies: Four Spells." *Preternature: Critical and Historical Studies on the Preternatural* 1, no. 2 (2012): 323–354.

Barbierato, Federico. "Writing, Reading, Writing: Scribal Culture and Magical Texts in Early Modern Venice." *Italian Studies* 66, no. 2 (2011): 263–276. doi:10.1179/17 4861811X13009843386710.

Barrett, Francis. *The Magus, or Celestial Intelligencer; Being a Complete System of Occult Philosophy,* 1801.

Bartholin, Thomas. *Thomæ Bartholini Acta Medica & Philosophica Hafniensia. vol. III. & IV.* Hafniæ: Haubold, 1677.

Bassnett, Susan. "Revising a Biography: A New Interpretation of the Life of Elizabeth Jane Weston (Westonia), Based on Her Autobiographical Poem on the Occasion of the Death of Her Mother." *Cahiers Élisabéthains* 37 (1990):1–8.

Bataille, Georges. *The Trial of Gilles de Rais.* Los Angeles: Amok, 1991.

Berners, John Bourchier, and Steele, Robert W. *Huon of Bordeaux: Done into English.* London: G. Allen, 1895.

Black, George F. "Notes on a Silver-Mounted Charm-Stone of Rock-Crystal from Inverleny, with Notices of Other Scottish Balls of Rock-Crystal and of Superstitions Connected Therewith." *Proceedings of the Society of Antiquaries of Scotland* 39 (May 1894): 439–448.

Boaistuau, Pierre and Edward Fenton. *Certaine Secrete Wonders of Nature Containing a Descriptio[n] of Sundry Strange Things, Seeming Monstrous in Our Eyes and Judgement, because We Are Not Privie to the Reasons of Them. Gathered out of Diuers Learned Authors as well Greeke as Latine, Sacred as Prophane.* London: Henry Bynneman, 1569.

Boudet, Jean-Patrice. *Entre Science et Nigromance: Astrologie, Divination et Magie Dans L'occident Médiéval, XIIe-XVe Siècle.* Paris: Publications de la Sorbonne, 2006.

———. "Les who's who démonologiques de la renaissance et leurs ancêtres médiévaux." *Médiévales* 44 (2003). Web, accessed June 10, 2014, http://medievales.revues.org/1019.

Braekman, Willy Louis. *Magische experimenten en toverpraktijken uit een middelnederlands handschrift: with an English Summary.* Gent (Belgie): Seminarie voor Volkskunde, 1966.

———. *Middeleeuwse witte en zwarte magie in het Nederlands taalgebied: Gecommentarieerd compendium van incantamenta tot einde 16de eeuw.* Gent: Koniklijke Academie voor Nederlandse Taal- en Letterkunde, 1997.

Briggs, K. M. *The Anatomy of Puck; an Examination of Fairy Beliefs Among Shakespeare's Contemporaries and Successors.* London: Routledge & Paul, 1959.

———. "Some Seventeenth-century Books of Magic." *Folklore* 64, no. 4 (1953): 445–462.

Brown, Carleton F., and Johann Georg Hohman. "The Long Hidden Friend," *The Journal of American Folklore* 17, no. 65 (1904): 89–152.

Campbell, Colin. *A Book of the Offices of Spirits, the Occult Virtue of Plants & Some Rare Magical Charms & Spells, Transcribed by Frederick Hockley from a Sixteenth Century Manuscript on Magic & Necromancy by John Porter.* York Beach, ME: The Teitan Press, 2011.

Cardano, Girolamo. *De subtilitate libri XXI*, 1663.

Catholic Church. *Breviarium Romanum ex Decreto Sacrosancti Concilii Tridentini Restitutum, Etc.* [Cambrai]: ex Ducali Campidonensi Typographeo, 1796.

———. *Officium B[eatae] Mariae Virginis, nuper reformatum, et Pii V. Pont[ificis] M[aximi] iussu editum.* Antverpiae [Antwerp]: Ex Officina Christophori Plantini, 1575.

———. *The Primer, or Office of the Blessed Virgin Mary with a New and Approved Version of the Church-Hymns. Translated from the Roman Breviary. To Which Is Added a Table, according to the New Regulations, of the Festivals of Obligation, Days of Devotion, Fasting, and Abstinence, as Observed by the Catholics in England.* London: J. P. Coghlan, 1780.

Catholic Church, Francis Procter, and Christopher Wordsworth. *Breviarium ad usum insignis Ecclesiae Sarum.* Cambridge: Cambridge University Press, 1879.

Catholic Church, Poenitentiaria Apostolica, and Ambrose St. John. *The Raccolta: Or Collection of Indulgenced Prayers.* London, 1880.

Catholic Church, Robert of Jumièges. *The Missal of Robert of Jumièges.* London: [Henry Bradshaw Society], 1896.

Cecchetelli, Michael. *Crossed Keys.* n. p.: Scarlet Imprint, 2011.

Chumbley, Andrew D. *The Leaper between: An Historical Study of the Toad-Bone Amulet; Its Forms, Functions and Praxis in Popular Magic.* n. p.: Three Hands Press, 2012.

Church of England, and William Keatinge Clay. *Liturgical Services Liturgies and Occasional Forms of Prayer Set Forth in the Reign of Queen Elizabeth.* Cambridge [England]: Printed at the University Press, 1847; Google eBook.

———. *Private Prayers, Put Forth by Authority during the Reign of Queen Elizabeth: The Primer of 1559, the Orarium of 1560, the Preces Privatae of 1564, the Book of Christian Prayers of 1578, with an Appendix, Containing The Litany of 1544.* Cambridge: Printed at the University Press, 1851.

Clucas, Stephen. *John Dee: Interdisciplinary Studies in English Renaissance Thought.* Dordrecht, The Netherlands: Springer, 2006.

Crowley, Aleister. *The Book of the Goetia of Solomon the King*. Boleskin, Foyers, Inverness: Society for the Propagation of Religious Truth, 1904.

de Laurence, L. W. ed. *The Lesser Key of Solomon: Goetia, The Book of Evil Spirits*. Chicago, IL: de Laurence, Scott & Co., 1916; Google eBook.

Dee, John. *John Dee's Five Books of Mystery: Original Sourcebook of Enochian Magic: from the Collected Works Known as Mysteriorum Libri Quinque*. Boston, MA: Weiser Books, 2003.

Dee, John and Meric Casaubon. *A True & Faithful Relation of What Passed for Many Yeers between Dr. John Dee … and Some Spirits: Tending (had It Succeeded) to a General Alteration of Most States and Kingdomes in the World: His Private Conferences with Rodolphe Emperor of Germany, Stephen K. of Poland, and Divers Other Princes about It: The Particulars of His Cause, as It Was Agitated in the Emperors Court, by the Pope's Intervention: His Banishment and Restoration in Part: As Also the Letters of Sundry Great Men and Princes (some Whereof Were Present at Some of These Conferences and Apparitions of Spirits) to the Said D. Dee: Out of the Original Copy, Written with Dr. Dees Own Hand, Kept in the Library of Sir Tho. Cotton …: With a Preface Confirming the Reality (as to the Point of Spirits) of This Relation, and Shewing the Several Good Uses That a Sober Christian May Make of All*. London: Printed by D. Maxwell for T. Garthwait…, 1659.

Delatte, Armand. *Anecdota Atheniensia*. Liège; Paris; [puis] Paris: H. Vaillant-Carmanne; E. Champion; Les Belles Lettres, 1927.

Douglas, James. *Nenia Britannica or, a Sepulchral History of Great Britain; from the Earliest Period to Its General Conversion to Christianity. By the Rev. James Douglas*. London: printed by John Nichols for George Nichol, 1793.

Duffy, Eamon. *The Stripping of the Altars: Traditional Religion in England, c. 1400–c. 1580*. New Haven, CT: Yale University Press, 1992.

Dumas, François Ribadeau. *Grimoires et rituels magiques*. Paris: P. Belfond, 1972.

Dunglison, Robley. *A Dictionary of Medical Science …* Philadelphia; New York: Lea Bros. & Co., 1903.

Edge, Joanne. "Licit magic or 'Pythagorean necromancy?' The 'Sphere of Life and Death' in late medieval England." *Historical Research* 87, no. 238 (2014).

Fanger, Claire. "Introduction: Theurgy, Magic, and Mysticism." In *Invoking Angels: Theurgic Ideas and Practices, Thirteenth to Sixteenth Centuries*. Magic in History series. University Park, PA: Pennsylvania State University Press, 2012.

Ferguson, John. *Clement of Alexandria*. New York: Twayne Publishers, 1974.

Forbes, Thomas Rogers. "Verbal Charms in British Folk Medicine." *Proceedings of the American Philosophical Society* 115, no. 4 (1971): 293–316.

Foxe, John, Thomas Cranmer, and John Gough Nichols. *Narratives of the Days of the Reformation: Chiefly from the Mss. of John Foxe the Martyrologist; with 2 Contemporary Biographies of Archbishop Cranmer.* London: Camden Society, 1859.

Gairdner, James, John Page, John Lydgate, and William Gregory. *The Historical Collections of a Citizen of London in the Fifteenth Century.* Westminster; New York: Printed for the Camden Society, Johnson Reprint Corp., 1965.

Gauntlet, Arthur, and David Rankine. *The Grimoire of Arthur Gauntlet: a 17th Century London Cunning-man's Book of Charms, Conjurations and Prayers: Includes Material from the Heptameron, the Arbatel, the Discouerie of Witchcraft; and the Writings of Cornelius Agrippa and William Bacon.* London: Avalonia, 2011.

Gerbert, Martin. *Monumenta Veteris Liturgiae Alemannicae.* S. Blas: Typis San-Blasianis, 1777.

Gibson, Marion. *Witchcraft and Society in England and America, 1550–1750.* Ithaca, NY: Cornell University Press, 2003.

Gilly, Carlos. "The First Book of White Magic in Germany." In *Magia, alchimia, scienza dal '400 al '700: L'influsso di Ermete Trismegisto = Magic, Alchemy and Science 15th–18th Centuries: the Influence of Hermes Trismegistus /ca Cura Di = Edited by Carlos Gilly, Cis van Heertum*, 1:209–16. Firenze: Centro Di, 2002.

Grasset, Gabriel. *Enchiridion Leonis Papae Serenissimo Imperatori Carolo Magno: in munus pretiosum datum, nupperrimè mendacis omnibus purgatum.* Anconae [i.e. Genève?]: [G. Grasset?], 1775.

Green, I. M. *Humanism and Protestantism in Early Modern English Education.* Farnham, England; Burlington, VT: Ashgate, 2009.

Greene, Robert, and Norman Sanders. *The Scottish History of James the Fourth.* London: Methuen, 1970.

Greenfield, Richard P. H. *Traditions of Belief in Late Byzantine Demonology.* Amsterdam: Adolf M. Hakkert, 1988.

Greg, W. W. *Marlowe's Doctor Faustus, 1604–1616: Parallel Texts.* Oxford: Clarendon Press, 1950.

Harford, George. *The Prayer Book Dictionary.* London: Sir I. Pitman, 1912.

Hearne, Thomas. *Remarks and Collections of Thomas Hearne, 3, May 25, 1710–December 14, 1712.* Oxford: Clarendon Press, 1889.

Helm, K. "Mittelalterische Geburtsbenediktionen." *Hessische Blätter Für Volkskunde* 9 (1910): 208–11.

Hockley, Frederick. *Experimentum Potens Magna in Occult Philosophy Arcanorum.* Edited by Harms, Daniel. Hinckley: Society for Esoteric Endeavour, 2012.

Hockley, Frederick, and Silens Manus. *Occult Spells: A Nineteenth Century Grimoire.* York Beach, ME: The Teitan Press, 2009.

Honorius, and Gösta Hedegård. *Liber Iuratus Honorii: a Critical Edition of the Latin Version of the Sworn Book of Honorius.* Stockholm, Sweden: Almqvist & Wiksell International, 2002.

Horae secundum ordinem sancti Benedicti. Barcelona: Johannes Luschner, [1498?].

Hoskins, Edgar. *Horae Beatae Mariae Virginis; or, Sarum and York Primers, with Kindred Books, and Primers of the Reformed Roman Use Together with an Introduction.* London: Longmans, Green, 1901.

Hunt, Tony. *Popular Medicine in Thirteenth-Century England: Introduction and Texts.* Cambridge; Wolfeboro, N.H., USA: D. S. Brewer, 1990.

Huray, Peter le. "The Chirk Castle Partbooks." *Early Music History* 2 (January 1, 1982): 17–42. doi:10.2307/853761.

Jacobus and William Caxton. *The Golden Legend; Or, Lives of the Saints.* London: J.M. Dent and Co., 1900.

Jones, Norman. "Defining Superstitions: Treasonous Catholics and the Act Against Witchcraft of 1563" in Charles Carlton, Robert L. Woods, Mary L. Robertson, and Joseph S. Block, eds., *State, Sovereigns & Society in Early Modern England: Essays in Honour of A. J. Slavin.* New York: St. Martin's Press, 1998.

Karr, Don. "Liber Lunae and Other Selections from British Library MS. Sloane 3826." *Esoterica* 3 (2001): 295–318.

Karr, Don, and Stephen Skinner. *Sepher Raziel, Also Known as Liber Salomonis: a 1564 English Grimoire from Sloane MS 3826.* Singapore: Golden Hoard Press, 2010.

Kieckhefer, Richard. *Forbidden Rites: a Necromancer's Manual of the Fifteenth Century.* University Park, PA: Pennsylvania State University Press, 1998.

Klaassen, Frank. "Medieval Ritual Magic in the Renaissance." *Aries* 3, no. 2, 2003.

———. "Religion, Science, and the Transformations of Magic: Manuscripts of Magic 1300–1600." PhD Thesis, University of Toronto, 1999.

———. "Ritual Invocation and Early Modern Science: The Skrying Experiments of Humphrey Gilbert." In *Invoking Angels: Theurgic Ideas and Practices, Thirteenth to Sixteenth Centuries,* edited by Claire Fanger, 341–366. Magic in History. University Park, PA: Pennsylvania State University Press, 2012.

———. "Three Early Modern Rituals to Spoil Witches." *Opuscula* 1, no. 1 (2011): 1–10.

Knirk, James E., Aslak Liesstøl, Magnus Olsen, and Kjeldeskrift-Institutt Norsk Historisk. *Norges Innskrifter Med de Yngre Runer. 6,1, Bryggen I Bergen.* Oslo: Dybwad, 1980.

Lancre, Pierre de. *L'incredulité et mescreance du sortilege plainement convaincue.* Paris, 1622.

LaVielle, C. "Erreurs et préjugés populaires concernant la médecine." *Bulletin de La Société de Borda* 20, no. 1 (1895): 115–133.

Le Forestier, René. *La Franc-maçonnerie occultiste au XVIIIe siècle: & L'ordre des Elus Coëns.* Paris: La table d'emeraude, 1987.

Lea, Henry Charles. *Materials Toward a History of Witchcraft.* New York; London: Thomas Yoseloff, 1957.

Lettenhove, le Baron Kervyn de. *Relations Politiques Des Pays-Bas et de l'Angleterre: Sous Le Règne de Philippe II, vol. 2, Régence de La Duchesse de Parme.* Bruxelles: F. Hayez, 1883.

Levack, Brian P. *The Literature of Witchcraft.* New York: Garland, 1992.

———. *The Witch-hunt in Early Modern Europe.* London; New York: Longman, 1987.

Marathakis, Ioannis. *The Magical Treatise of Solomon or Hygromanteia Also Called the Apotelesmatike Pragmateia, Epistle to Rehoboam, Solomonike.* Singapore: Golden Hoard Press, 2011.

Marshall, Peter, "The Guardian Angel in Protestant England." In *Conversations with Angels: Essays towards a History of Spiritual Communication, 1100–1700,* edited by Joad Raymond, 295–316. Houndmills, Basingstoke, Hampshire, UK; New York: Palgrave Macmillan, 2011.

Martin, Michael. "Officium Parvum de Septem Doloribus." *Thesaurus Precum Latinarum,* 2013. Accessed September 6, 2014, http://www.preces-latinae.org /thesaurus/BVM/OPSDMariae.html.

Mathers, S. L. MacGregor, ed. *The Key of Solomon the King (Clavicula Salomonis).* York Beach, ME: Samuel Weiser, 2000.

Mathiesen, Robert. "The Key of Solomon: Toward a Typology of Manuscripts." *Societas Magica Newsletter* no. 17 (2007): 1, 3–9.

Mesmer, Josef Anton. "Über den Mittelalterlichen Kunstausdruck Galiläa." *Mittheilungen der Kaiserlich-Königlichen Central-Commission zur Erforschung und Erhaltung der Baudenkmale* 6, no. 4 (n.d.): 104–5.

Meyerstein, Edward Harry William. *Of My Early Life, 1889-1918.* London: N. Spearman, 1957.

Millunzi, Gaetano, and Salvatore Salomone-Marino, eds. "Un processo di stregoneria nel 1623 in Sicilia." *Archivo storico siciliano* 25 (1900): 253–379.

Mowat, Barbara A. "Prospero's Book." *Shakespeare Quarterly* 52, no. 1 (2001): 1–33.

Nicholl, Charles. *The Reckoning: the Murder of Christopher Marlowe*. New York: Harcourt Brace, 1992.

Parry, G. J. R. *The Arch-conjuror of England: John Dee*. New Haven: Yale University Press, 2011.

Peterson, Joseph H. *Arbatel—Concerning the Magic of the Ancients: Original Sourcebook of Angel Magic*. Lake Worth, FL; Newburyport, MA: Ibis Press; Distributed Red Wheel/Weiser, 2009.

———. *Grimorium Verum*. Scotts Valley, CA: CreateSpace, 2007.

———. *The Lesser Key of Solomon: Lemegeton Clavicula Salomonis: Detailing the Ceremonial Art of Commanding Spirits Both Good and Evil*. York Beach, ME: Weiser Books, 2001.

———. *The Sixth and Seventh Books of Moses, or, Moses, Magical Spirits-Art: Known As the Wonderful Arts of the Old Wise Hebrews, Taken from the Mosaic Books of the Cabala and the Talmud, for the Good of Mankind*. Lake Worth, FL: Ibis Press, 2008.

Peuckert, Will-Erich. *Pansophie: Ein Versuch zur Geschichte der Weissen und Schwarzen Magie*. Berlin: E. Schmidt, 1976.

Pingree, David Edwin and Warburg Institute. *Picatrix : the Latin Version of the Ghiyat al-hakim*. London: Warburg Institute, 1986.

Porter, B. *The Refugee Question in Mid-Victorian Politics*. New York: Cambridge University Press, 2008; Google eBook, 2008.

Pseudo-Dionysius, Colm Luibhéid, and Paul Rorem. *Pseudo-Dionysius: The Complete Works*. New York: Paulist Press, 1987.

Raffel, Burton, trans. *Nibelungenlied: Song of the Nibelungs*. New Haven, CT: Yale University Press, 2006.

Raine, James. "Proceedings Connected with a Remarkable Charge of Sorcery, Brought Against James Richardson and Others, in the Diocese of York, A.D. 1510." *The Archaeological Journal* 16 (1859): 71–81.

Raleigh, Walter, William Oldys, and Thomas Birch. *The Works of Sir Walter Raleigh, Kt., Now First Collected: To Which Are Prefixed the Lives of the Author*. New York: Franklin, 1965.

Rankine, David and Paul Harry Barron, trans. *The Complete Grimoire of Pope Honorius*. London: Avalonia, 2013.

Raphael and Merlinus Anglicus. *The Astrologer of the Nineteenth Century*. London: Knight & Lacey, 1825.

Raziel, (pseud.). "Liber Salomonis: Cephar Raziel," 2006. Web. http://www.digital -brilliance.com/kab/karr/Solomon/LibSal.pdf.

Rohrbacher-Stickler, Claudia. "From Sense to Nonsense, from Incantation Prayer to Magic Spell." *Jewish Studies Quarterly* 3 (1996): 24–46.

Rolle, Richard. *Yorkshire Writers: Richard Rolle of Hampole, an English Father of the Church, and his Followers*. London; New York: S. Sonnenschein & Co.; Macmillan & Co., 1895.

Rolt, L. T. C. *The Aeronauts: a History of Ballooning, 1783–1903*. New York: Walker, 1966.

Schaff, P. *The Creeds of Christendom: The Evangelical Protestant Creeds, with Translations, Vol. 3*. New York: Harper, 1877; Google eBooks, 2006.

Scheible, J. *Das Kloster. Weltlich und Geistlich. Meist aus der Ältern Deutschen Volks-, Wunder-, Curiositäten-, und Vorzugsweise Komischen Literatur*. Stuttgart: J. Scheible; [etc.], 1845.

Scot, Reginald. *The Discouerie of Witchcraft: Wherein the Lewde Dealing of Witches and Witchmongers Is Notablie Detected, the Knauerie of Coniurors, the Impietie of Inchantors, the Follie of Soothsaiers, the Impudent Falshood of Cousenors, the Infidelitie of Atheists, the Pestilent Practices of Pythonists, the Curiositie of Figure Casters, the Vanitie of Dreamers, the Beggerlie Art of Alcumystrie, the Abhomination of Idolatrie, the Horrible Art of Poisoning, the Vertue and Power of Naturall Magike, and All the Conueiances of Legierdemaine and Iuggling Are Deciphered: And Many Other Things Opened, Which Have Long Lien Hidden, Howbeit Verie Necessarie to Be Knowne: Heerevnto Is Added a Treatise Vpon the Nature and Substance of Spirits and Diuels, & c.* London: William Brome, 1584.

Sibley, Ebenezer, Frederick Hockley, and Joseph H. Peterson. *The Clavis or Key to the Magic of Solomon*. Lake Worth, FL; Newburyport, MA: Ibis Press; Distributed by Red Wheel/Weiser, 2009.

Simpson, W. Sparrow. "On the Measure of the Wound in the Side of the Redeemer, Worn Anciently as a Charm; and on the Five Wounds as Represented in Art." *Journal of the British Archaeological Association* 30 (1874): 357–374.

Skemer, Don C. *Binding Words: Textual Amulets in the Middle Ages*. University Park, PA: Pennsylvania State University Press, 2006.

Skinner, Stephen, and David Rankine, eds. *A Collection of Magical Secrets Taken from Peter de Abano, Cornelius Agrippa, and from Other Famous Occult Philosophers, and a Treatise of Mixed Cabalah, Which Comprises the Angelic Art Taken from Hebrew Sages, Translated from Wellcome MS4669 by Paul Harry Barron from the Original French Manuscript Dated 1796.* London: Avalonia, 2009.

Spenser, Edmund, eds. Thomas P. Roche and C. Patrick O'Donnell. *The Faerie Queene.* New York: Penguin, 1978.

Stanley, George and Richard Cosway. *A Catalogue of the Very Curious, Extensive, and Valuable Library of Richard Cosway, Esq. R.A.: Consisting of a Numerous Collection of Early Works on Divinity, History, Poetry, Fine Arts, an Unusual Assemblage of Treatises on Magic, Necromancy, Apparitions, Vampires, &c. &c. a Variety of Literature and About 50 Lots of Most Excellent Manuscript Music.* London: s.n., 1821.

Stock, Elliot. *The Bibliographer.* New York: J. W. Bouton, 1884.

Tailliar, Eugène François Joseph. *Chroniques de Douai.* Douais: Dechristé, 1875.

Thomas, John Wesley. *Ortnit and Wolfdietrich: Two Medieval Romances.* Columbia, SC: Camden House, 1986.

Thomas, Keith. *Religion and the Decline of Magic.* Harmondsworth, Middlesex: Penguin, 1971.

Thompson, C. J. S. *The Mysteries and Secrets of Magic.* New York: Causeway Books, 1973.

Trithemius, Johannes. *Ioannis Tritemii Liber octo quaestionum ad Maximilianum Cesarem.* Oppenheym: impensis Joh. Hasselberger, 1515.

Turner, Dawson. "Brief Remarks, Accompanied with Documents, Illustrative of Trial by Jury, Treasure-trove, and the Invocation of Spirits for the Discovery of Hidden Treasure in the Sixteenth Century." *Norfolk Archaeology* 1 (1847): 55–64.

Tyson, Donald. *The Fourth Book of Occult Philosophy.* Woodbury, MN: Llewellyn, 2009.

University of Oxford and Foster, Joseph. *Alumni Oxonienses: The Members of the University of Oxford, 1500–1714: Their Parentage, Birthplace, and Year of Birth, with a Record of Their Degrees.* Vol. 4. Oxford and London: Parker and Co., 1891.

Venn, John. *Alumni Cantabrigienses; a Biographical List of All Known Students, Graduates and Holders of Office at the University of Cambridge, from the Earliest Times to 1900.* Cambridge: University Press, 1922–.

Véronèse, Julien. *L'Ars Notoria au Moyen Âge: Introduction et édition critique.* Firenze: SISMEL edizioni del Galluzzo, 2007.

Waegeman, Maryse, and Hermes. *Amulet and Alphabet: Magical Amulets in the First Book of Cyranides*. Amsterdam: J. C. Gieben, 1987.

Waite, Arthur Edward. *The Book of Ceremonial Magic*. Secaucus: Citadel, 1911.

Wallis, Faith. *Medieval Medicine: a Reader*. Toronto: University of Toronto Press, 2010.

Warrack, John. *Carl Maria von Weber*. Cambridge, England; New York: Cambridge University Press, 1976.

Warren, Frederick Edward. *The Liturgy and Ritual of the Celtic Church*. Oxford: Clarendon Press, 1881.

Weyer, Johann. *De praestigiis daemonum, & incantationibus ac veneficiis*. Oporinus, 1583; Google eBook.

———. *Opera Omnia. Editio nova et hactenus desiderata*. Amstelodami: Apud Petrum vanden Berge, 1660.

Wickersheimer, Ernest. *Les manuscrits latins de médecine du haut Moyen Age dans les bibliothèques de France*. Paris: Centre national de la recherche scientifique, 1966.

Wiener, Carol Z. "The Beleaguered Isle. A Study of Elizabethan and Early Jacobean Anti-Catholicism." *Past & Present* no. 51 (May, 1971), Published by Oxford University Press on behalf of The Past and Present Society. Web. http://www.jstor.org/stable/650402.

Williamson, George Charles. *Richard Cosway, R. A.* London. G. Bell and Sons, 1905.

Wilson, Stephen, *The Magical Universe: Everyday Ritual and Magic in Pre-Modern Europe*. London; New York: Hambledon and London, 2000.

Manuscripts

Bayerische Staatsbibliothek, MS. Clm 849.

Bodleian Library, Ashmole 1406; Aubrey 24; e. Mus. 173; Michael 273, 276; Rawlinson D. 252, 253.

British Library, Additional MS. 10862, 36674; Harley 181, 3420; Lansdowne 795; Sloane 1727, 3824, 3825, 3826, 3846, 3847, 3849, 3850, 3851, 3853, 3854, 3885.

Det Kongelige Bibliothek, Ms. GkS 1612.

Manchester, Chetham's Library, MS Mun. A.4.98

Universitätsbibliothek Leipzig, Cod. Mag. 12, 16, 96.

University of Wisconsin, Duveen collection, D 388

Wellcome Institute, MS. 110, 517, 4669.

INDEX